p.5 dist. btwn hum + schol.
p.1 J.J. Murphy Rhet. in M.A.
p.2 outline of development
p.3 Aristotle — my paper su[...]
p.5 divc. of modus by med
p.6 schol. vs human

Medieval
Literary Theory
and Criticism
c. 1100–c. 1375

Cut works on
[...]
comm. on classics

p.5-7 TERMS!!
p.8-9 more on hum + scholasticism
p.9 — ren. hum!!! bibliogr. (in f.n.)
p.38 — on rel btwn sacred + secular
literature (p.57!)

p.45 — fourfold   p.112 artistae —
p.54 — intentio auctoris
p.67 Hugh. + StV on author!!
p.69 Abelard on Genesis PL 178
transfer of type C prologue
p.70 order followed by Lombard
p.121 — alleg. of pagan lit.
see p.110 — cf. w/ Calvin of Q
p.165 — n.b. on indecorous images
p.203 — style crucial to med.
p.204 — a little on Jewish exeg.
p.118 — attitude to fiction
p.119 — pars philosophiae; also
signifying like allegory !!!
p.120 — "secular allegory"
p.122 — div. of sciences
p.168-73 — anagogic w accommod!!
p.316 — Nich of Trevet !!! (Kristeller)
317 — a benedictine !
p.319 — ** crosssen from Into pagan

al.
see Cambr. Hist. of Lit. Crit.
vol III The Renaiss.
Ovid Moralisé!!
PN 8726 C4

JON BAUSERMAN
ON PLANE TO SAN DIEGO
TO SBL
CONFERENCES
MOSTLY READ ON WAY / 7/07 ON WAY
29/7/07

- meeting w/ Hannah
Maleka
- carl toman
- phd   ms29
- James
- Inst applic
+ Italian girl

p. 320 — persona (see p. 23/-2)   the four
p. 321 — alleg. of Ovid?   p. 324 the four senses in poetry
                                  + scripture
p. 325 Trevet on Seneca
p. 326 - persona! ← p. 379 too
                              alleg. of the theolog.
p. 383-84 — alleg. of the poets —
p. 385 — see footnotes : primacy of literal sense !!
                        re: Dante !!

Medieval Literary Theory and Criticism

c. 1100–c. 1375

The Commentary-Tradition

Revised Edition

EDITED BY

A. J. MINNIS

AND

A. B. SCOTT

with the assistance of

DAVID WALLACE

CLARENDON PRESS · OXFORD

*This book has been printed digitally and produced in a standard specification
in order to ensure its continuing availability*

OXFORD
UNIVERSITY PRESS

Great Clarendon Street, Oxford OX2 6DP

Oxford University Press is a department of the University of Oxford.
It furthers the University's objective of excellence in research, scholarship,
and education by publishing worldwide in

Oxford New York

Auckland Bangkok Buenos Aires Cape Town Chennai
Dar es Salaam Delhi Hong Kong Istanbul Karachi Kolkata
Kuala Lumpur Madrid Melbourne Mexico City Mumbai Nairobi
São Paulo Shanghai Taipei Tokyo Toronto

Oxford is a registered trade mark of Oxford University Press
in the UK and in certain other countries

Published in the United States
by Oxford University Press Inc., New York

ISBN 0-19-811274-2

TO
THE MEMORY
OF
BERYL SMALLEY

PREFACE

IT would be impossible to cover adequately the whole range of medieval literary theory and criticism in a single anthology. That would require, at the very least, a substantial series. We have chosen to concentrate on one branch of the subject in one of the most significant periods of its development: the tradition of systematic commentary on authors both sacred and profane, Latin and vernacular, 'ancient' and 'modern', from around 1100 until around 1375.

The 'prescriptive' branches of medieval literary theory (for example, the *artes poeticae*, *artes praedicandi*, and *artes dictaminis*) are, therefore, not part of our brief. Besides, they have received the attention they deserve from modern scholars, and many of the major texts are available in translation. The commentary-tradition, indeed, is so rich and varied in itself that we cannot claim to be comprehensive even in dealing with it alone. But we have tried to be representative, illustrating the continuities and the new developments, the typical and the exceptional, the well-known and the relatively obscure. The following selections offer by turn insight, confusion, originality, conventionality, misunderstanding, and creative transformation, as the interpreters make and remake the deposit of the past in the image of their own culture and interests. The essays which introduce the selections have been so written that they may be read in a sequence. Our aim is to offer at once a 'reader' of medieval literary discourse, a 'sampler' which may encourage our readers to go back to the original documents themselves (and not just to the few which we have chosen—many important sources require editing and explanation), and a collection of essays towards the history of medieval literary theory and criticism. Our point of departure is *c.* 1100, the time in which the 'Introductions to the Authors' of the type represented in Ch. I were becoming established in medieval grammar-schools. Our *terminus ad quem* is *c.* 1375. That is the year of Boccaccio's death and of Benvenuto da Imola's Dante lectures at Bologna, Benvenuto being the last Dantist to be discussed in the introduction to the final chapter. The period thus demarcated is one of the most significant for the development of the commentary-tradition. It saw the 'Twelfth-century Renaissance', the establishment of scholasticism in that same century and its subsequent flowering, the rise of the universities (with an educational system in which commentary played a major part), the acceptance as a major authority of pseudo-Dionysius (perhaps the single most important source of medieval notions of imagery and symbolism), and the emergence, in the later thirteenth century, of Italian scholasticism and humanism as intellectual movements which fed and provoked each other. It was predominantly in Italy that the methods— and the prestige—of the Latin commentary-tradition were appropriated

for the description and justification of major vernacular texts, Dante
being the great innovator. In this development may be found the roots of
literary criticism as we know it today.

It remains to say something about our use of the terms 'theory' and
'criticism'. 'Literary theory' is, we trust, neutral enough to require no
defence, but 'literary criticism' has certain asociations which might, in the
eyes of some, make our use of it seem inappropriate and anachronistic. A
simple reply would be to point out that classicists have, for long, found
the term to be at once useful and apt as applied to certain kinds of literary
discourse, and so it should be available to medievalists as well. A fuller
reply could take the form of a consideration of what precisely we mean by
'criticism'. The *OED* defines the word as 'the art of estimating the qualities and character of literary or aesthetic work', and this does fit the
materials provided below, providing it be accepted that the Bible must be
included among literary and aesthetic works, in deference to medieval
sensibilities: as the Book of Books, the Bible was supposed to have made
superlative use of all the figures, colours, tropes, and stylistic registers
with which the classical authors had adorned their works.

All the commentaries and treatises excerpted below are, in a manner of
speaking, descriptive and evaluative (in contrast with the 'prescriptive'
traditions of literary theory already mentioned), and to that extent may be
called 'critical'. They engage in meticulous *explication de texte*, striving to
elicit the meaning of the work and the plan of its arrangement, and to
identify all its formal literary features. In the introductions or prologues
(sometimes called *accessūs*) to such textual exposition is found a more
theoretical framework (such as the standard twelfth-century *accessus*-
headings, or the Aristotelian 'four causes' as used later), in the course of
which the text is evaluated in so far as it has succeeded in reaching the
intended objective (termed the *finis* or *finalis causa*), this end and the
means thereto being determined by the branch of learning, the *pars philosophiae* or *scientiae*, under which the text was subsumed. Here, then, is
literary theory of a type which, far from distancing itself from the text,
rather provides an analytical programme in accordance with which each
and every important work can be analysed. Even when such theorizing
takes place outside the context of a commentary—as, for example, in the
theological treatises of Thomas Aquinas and Henry of Ghent, which are
represented below—the interests and assumptions are essentially hermeneutic.

That said, it must immediately be noted that there is much in
medieval literary theory and criticism which seems contrary to the spirit
of at least one of the major schools of criticism characteristic of our age,
namely 'New Criticism' (now designated, in some quarters, as the 'Old
New Criticism'). John Dryden, who has a certain claim to be regarded as
the founding father of that movement, speaks of criticism as 'a standard of

judging well; the chiefest part of which is, to observe those excellences which should delight a reasonable reader'. This emphasis on delighting a reasonable reader, with its overtones of the good taste and humanistic virtue of a group of initiates, is quite at variance with the priorities of medie-val literary theory, which is concerned with profit rather than with delight as such and assumes that reason is a God-given faculty which should operate to bring the individual into line with the great divine plan. Hence, all that is written is, in the final analysis, written for our doctrine (to echo Rom. 15: 4); more specifically, to make us better Christians. Seen in this light, medieval literary theory and criticism has far more in common with the ideologically based and philosophically patterned types of 'New New Criticism' which are currently in vogue; in particular, with formalism, structuralism, semiotics, and reception-theory, and especially with those approaches which have a sharply defined teleology, such as feminist criticism, and political criticism of whatever persuasion. Of more fundamental importance is the fact that nowadays it is being claimed, *pace* the 'Old New Critics', that *no* criticism is free of ideology, that every approach to a text reflects, and is ultimately dependent on, a particular world-view. In such an intellectual climate, medieval literary theory and criticism can hope to receive a fair hearing.

This volume is the result of an elaborate and full co-operation between Dr A. J. Minnis (University of York) and Dr A. B. Scott (Queen's University of Belfast), so much so that it would be impossible to specify who is responsible for what. However, lest some of the views expressed in the General Introduction and the chapter-introductions should prove to be controversial, it seems appropriate to record that they are, for the most part, those of A. J. Minnis.

Dr David Wallace (University of Minnesota) translated the extracts from Dante's *Convivo* (in Ch. IX) and Boccaccio's *Short Treatise in Praise of Dante* and *Expository Lectures on Dante's Comedy* (both in Ch. X), and provided most of the footnotes to those sections. In addition, he wrote the introduction to Ch. X and part of the introduction to Ch. VIII (on Giovanni del Virgilio), together with the relevant footnotes. Professor James McEvoy (Queen's University, Belfast) revised for inclusion in Ch. V extracts from his unpublished MA thesis 'Robert Grosseteste on the Celestial Hierarchy of Pseudo-Dionysius: An Edition and Translation of his Commentary, chapters 10–15'. We are also grateful to him for answering several queries which arose in the course of our translation of scholastic texts. David Wallace would like to thank James H. McGregor (University of Georgia) and Janet Levarie Smarr (University of Illinois, Urbana) for their prompt and expert assistance with problems in translations from Italian. He also wishes to acknowledge financial assistance received from the University of Texas Research Institute.

PREFACE

For advice on specific points we are indebted to Beverly Allen (Stanford), the late Judson B. Allen, Steven Botterill (Berkeley), J. A. Burrow (Bristol), John V. Fleming (Princeton), K. M. Fredborg (Virum, Denmark), Ralph Hanna III (Riverside, Calif.), Robert B. Hollander (Princeton), H. A. Kelly (Los Angeles), Jeffrey Schnapp (Stanford), John Stevens (Cambridge), David Thomson (Banbury, Oxon.), Wesley Trimpi Jr. (Stanford), and Winthrop Wetherbee (Cornell). A special word of thanks is due to Leofranc Holford-Strevens, our learned copy-editor at the Oxford University Press, who suggested several improvements and provided some additional information.

Specific acknowledgements to the publishers whose editions we used in preparing this anthology are made in the relevant footnotes.

We wish to dedicate this volume, with affection and admiration, to the memory of Beryl Smalley. Miss Smalley knew of this intention and professed herself to be touched by it, but remarked (frank and factual to the end): 'You may have to put it as "In Memory . . ."!' And so it must be. Thank you, Beryl, for your wit and wisdom.

* * *

For advice which we followed in preparing the revised edition we would like to thank Martin Irvine (Georgetown, Washington), Deborah Parker (Charlottesville, Virginia), James Simpson (Cambridge) and Siegfried Wenzel (Pennsylvania).

A.J.M.
A.B.S.

CONTENTS

Notes on Style and Presentation   xiii

Abbreviations   xv

General Introduction: The Significance of the Medieval Commentary-Tradition   1

I An Anthology of Literary Prefaces: Introductions to the
Authors   12

II A Critical Colloquy: Conrad of Hirsau   37

III Scriptural Allegory and Authority: Hugh of Saint-Victor,
Peter Abelard, and Peter Lombard   65

IV Poetic Fiction and Truth: William of Conches, 'Bernard
Silvester', Arnulf of Orléans, and Ralph of Longchamps   113

V The Dionysian Imagination: Thomas Gallus and Robert
Grosseteste   165

VI Scriptural Science and Signification: From *Alexander's Sum of
Theology* to Nicholas of Lyre   197

VII Placing the *Poetics*: Hermann the German; An Anonymous
Question on the Nature of Poetry   277

VIII Updated Approaches to the Classics: William of Aragon,
Nicholas Trevet, Giovanni del Virgilio, and Pierre Bersuire   314

IX The Transformation of Critical Tradition: Dante, Petrarch,
and Boccaccio   373

X Assessing the New Author: Commentary on Dante   439

Select Bibliography   520

Index   531

NOTES ON STYLE AND PRESENTATION

THIS anthology offers not only extended passages of literary discussion but also examples of the structured and detailed textual analysis which characterizes the commentary-tradition. The inclusion of the latter is not without its problems. By translating the important and/or obscure Latin terms and constructions in the quotations we are, in some cases, rendering redundant or infelicitous the following glosses—for we have removed the very difficulties which the medieval critic was addressing. Translation is interpretation, a kind of commentary, as medieval scholars knew full well. 'Translation is the exposition of meaning through another language', declared Hugutio of Pisa in the *Magnae derivationes* which he compiled between 1197 and 1201, a work which formed the basis of John of Genoa's *Catholicon* (1286, often printed in the Renaissance) and which has become known as 'Dante's dictionary'. We hope, however, that the experience of seeing a medieval mind at work grappling with an author's text will compensate for the occasional awkwardness which the reader may feel about our own *translatio et interpretatio*.

All scriptural references are to the divisions and numberings of the Latin Vulgate Bible, though we have used the normal English forms of biblical names and book titles. Our translations of scriptural quotations generally follow Challoner's revision of the Douay Bible, as being close to the Latin Vulgate, but where a quotation differs markedly from the accepted Vulgate text, we have followed the variant. Although the text of the *Glossa ordinaria* on the Bible published in J. P. Migne's Patrologia Latina is the most easily accessible, because it is incomplete (lacking the interlinear gloss) and often inaccurate, we have quoted the early printed version of the *Biblia sacra cum Glossa ordinaria* which was available to us, the Lyon edition of 1589.

Readers who are unfamiliar with the form of the medieval *quaestio* should turn to p. 212, where an explanation of its analytical procedure is provided.

Square brackets indicate our own additions or alterations to the text; angle-brackets indicate the additions and alterations of previous editors. Lemmata, i.e. the medieval commentators' citations of the text they are expounding, have been printed in small capitals. Medieval citation, it should be remembered, is often very free, with words being added or substituted, and the original syntax being altered or simplified, in order to clarify the meaning as the interpreter understood it.

ABBREVIATIONS

THE following abbreviations have been used in the Notes.

AFP	*Archivum Fratrum Praedicatorum*
AHDLMA	*Archives d'histoire doctrinale et littéraire du moyen âge*
ALKM	*Archiv für Litteratur- und Kirchengeschichte des Mittelalters*
Allen, *Ethical Poetic*	J. B. Allen, *The Ethical Poetic of the Later Middle Ages* (Toronto, 1982)
BEC	*Bibliothèque de l'École des Chartes*
BGDSL	*Beiträge zur Geschichte der deutschen Sprache und Literatur*
BGPTM	Beiträge zur Geschichte der Philosophie und Theologie des Mittelalters
Bibl. glos.	*Biblia glossata*, i.e. *Biblia sacra cum Glossa ordinaria et Postilla Nicolai Lyrani* (Lyon, 1589). References to numbered columns.
Boccaccio, *Opere*	*Tutte le opere di Giovanni Boccaccio*, ed. V. Branca (Milan, 1964–)
CCCM	Corpus christianorum, continuatio medievalis
CCSL	Corpus christianorum, series Latina
CIMAGL	*Cahiers de l'Institut du Moyen-Âge Grec et Latin*, University of Copenhagen
CP	*Classical Philology*
CSEL	Corpus scriptorum ecclesiasticorum Latinorum
Curtius	E. R. Curtius, *European Literature and the Latin Middle Ages*, tr. W. R. Trask (London, 1953)
de Lubac, *Exég. méd.*	H. de Lubac, *Exégèse médiévale* (Paris, 1959–64)
Dom. Stud.	*Dominican Studies*
ED	*Enciclopedia dantesca*, ed. Umberto Bosco (Rome, 1970–8)
EETS, ES	Early English Text Society, Extra Series
GCS	Die griechischen christlichen Schriftsteller der ersten drei Jahrhunderte (Leipzig, 1897–)
GL	*Grammatici Latini*, ed. H. Keil (Leipzig, 1857–80); vols. ii–iii (Priscian) were ed. by M. J. Hertz
Hardison, *The Enduring Monument*	A. B. Hardison, *The Enduring Monument: A Study of the Idea of Praise in Renaissance Literary Theory and Practice* (Chapel Hill, NC, 1962, repr. Westport, Conn. 1973)
HLF	*Histoire littéraire de la France*
HSNPL	*Harvard Studies and Notes in Philology and Literature*
Hunt, 'Introductions to the *Artes*'	R. W. Hunt, 'The Introductions to the *Artes* in the Twelfth Century', in *Studia medievalia in honorem R. M. Martin, O.P.* (Bruges, 1948), pp. 85–112; repr. in id., *The History of Grammar in the Middle Ages: Collected Papers*, ed. G. L. Bursill-Hall (Amsterdam Studies in

	the Theory and History of Linguistic Science, ser. iii, vol. 5, Amsterdam, 1980), pp. 117–44
Huygens, *Accessus ad auctores, etc.*	*Accessus ad auctores; Bernard d'Utrecht; Conrad d'Hirsau*, ed. R. B. C. Huygens (Leiden, 1970)
Isidore, *Ety.*	Isidore of Seville, *Etymologiae*, ed. W. M. Lindsay (Oxford, 1911)
JAOS	*Journal of the American Oriental Society*
JEGP	*Journal of English and Germanic Philology*
JWCI ·	*Journal of the Warburg and Courtauld Institutes*
Kristeller, *CTC*	*Catalogus translationum et commentariorum: Medieval and Renaissance Latin Translations and Commentaries*, ed. P. O. Kristeller *et al.* (Washington, 1960–)
Med. et hum.	*Medievalia et humanistica*
Med. Stud.	*Mediaeval Studies*
MGH, Scr. Mer.	Monumenta Germaniae historica, Scriptores rerum Merovingicarum
Minnis, *Authorship*	A. J. Minnis, *Medieval Theory of Authorship: Scholastic Literary Attitudes in the Later Middle Ages* (London, 1984)
MLQ	*Modern Language Quarterly*
NCE	*New Catholic Encyclopedia* (New York, 1967)
New Schol.	*The New Scholasticism*
ODCC	*The Oxford Dictionary of the Christian Church*, 2nd edn. by F. L. Cross and E. A. Livingstone (London, 1974)
OLD	*The Oxford Latin Dictionary*, ed. P. G. W. Glare (Oxford, 1968–82)
PG	Patrologia Graeca, ed. J.-P. Migne (Paris, 1857–66)
PL	Patrologia Latina, ed. J.-P. Migne (Paris, 1844–64)
RFN	*Rivista di filosofia neo-scolastica*
RP	*Romance Philology*
RSO	*Rivista di studi orientali*
RT	*Revue thomiste*
RTAM	*Recherches de théologie ancienne et médiévale*
Sandkühler, *Die frühen Dante-kommentare*	B. Sandkühler, *Die frühen Dantekommentare und ihr Verhältnis zur mittelalterlichen Kommentartradition* (Münchner romanistiche Arbeiten, xix, Munich, 1967)
SSCISAM	*Settimane di studio del Centro italiano di studi sull'alto medioevo*
Smalley, *Study of the Bible*	Beryl Smalley, *The Study of the Bible in the Middle Ages*, 2nd edn. (Oxford, 1952)
SP	*Studies in Philology*
TAPA	*Transactions of the American Philological Society*
Vincent of Beauvais, *Speculum quadruplex*	Vincent of Beauvais, *Speculum quadruplex* (Douai, 1624; repr. Graz, 1965), comprising the *Speculum historiale*, *Speculum doctrinale*, *Speculum naturale*, and (not by Vincent) the *Speculum morale*
Whitbread	L. G. Whitbread, *Fulgentius the Mythographer* (Colombus, Ohio, 1971)

General Introduction:
The Significance of the Medieval
Commentary-Tradition

THERE are many branches of medieval literary theory and criticism, only
one of which has received the attention it deserves, namely the 'arts' of
composition (*artes poeticae*, *artes praedicandi*, *artes dictaminis*).[1] This anthology concentrates on another branch, the most fundamental and
important of them all within the medieval educational system, and one
which has a lot to say about a far wider range of literary matters than those
which fall within the terms of reference of the pragmatic and prescriptive
'arts'. For the texts translated below comprise sophisticated discussions
of such topics as fiction and fable (in classical works *and* in the Bible); the
ethical effects and purpose of literature; authorship and authority; the
function of biography in interpreting a writer's work; stylistic and didactic modes; literary form and structure; allegory and 'literal' or historical
sense; symbolism; imagination and imagery; the semiotics of words and
things; the moralization of classical texts; the status of poetry within the
hierarchy of the human arts and sciences. Quite obviously, this rich array
of literary discussion and analysis falls within the sphere of 'literary
theory and criticism' as normally understood.

It is the medieval commentary-tradition which is the subject of this
book. Our translated extracts are either expositions of the 'set texts'
studied in medieval schools and universities (ranging from the poetry of
Ovid and Virgil to the Psalter, Peter Lombard's theological *Sentences*, and
the pseudo-Dionysian corpus) or what might loosely be termed 'off-
shoots' of such exposition. For example, the scholastic 'questions' on
literary matters found in the *summae* of Thomas Aquinas, Henry of
Ghent, and the one linked with the name of Alexander of Hales are
extended treatments of issues canvassed to some extent in every late
medieval commentary on an individual book of the Bible. Pierre Bersuire's exhaustive moralization of the pagan deities constitutes a comprehensive application of hermeneutic techniques and principles of a type
used in, for example, 'Bernard Silvester''s commentary on the *Aeneid* and
the expositions of Boethius' metres by William of Conches, William of
Aragon, and Nicholas Trevet, all of which are represented below.
Boccaccio's *Genealogy of the Gentile Gods* is also heavily indebted to this
tradition of what was dubbed by Dante 'the allegory of the poets'.
Petrarch's 'lives' of classical poets (for his letters to ancient authors may

---

[1] For outlines of these traditions, and relevant bibliography, see J. J. Murphy, *Rhetoric in the
Middle Ages* (Berkeley and Los Angeles, 1974).

be regarded as such), and even Boccaccio's *Short Treatise in Praise of Dante* have their roots in the moralistic *vitae auctorum* which formed part of the twelfth-century 'Introductions to the authors' or *accessūs ad auctores* and subsequently of the prologues to exegesis of scriptural texts. So, viewed synchronically, the edited materials have many interests, priorities, and strategies in common and exhibit a considerable degree of internal cohesion.

Viewed diachronically, these extracts, duly placed in historical sequence, tell a story. They trace the application of a literary-theoretical apparatus and critical idiom in the 'Twelfth-century Renaissance', which vocabulary is picked up and adapted by scholastic philosophers and theologians of the thirteenth century, and subsequently appears in the first commentaries on vernacular authors (Dante, Guido Cavalcanti, the anonymous writer of the Old French 'Chess of Love', etc.),[2] commentaries written in Latin and in several vernaculars, Italian offering the most sophisticated examples. In that final stage, wherein literary attitudes and hermeneutic techniques which had long been used in expounding ancient and revered Latin authorities (the *auctores*, for the term denotes not just writers but also authorities) were transferred to the exposition of 'modern' and inventive writers in the vernacular, may be detected the origins of modern literary criticism as we know it. This is a large claim, but the passages translated below are witnesses to its truth.

The main phases of this process may be identified as follows, as far as the theory is concerned (the techniques of actual textual analysis remaining fairly constant throughout the period). In the twelfth century a critical idiom became widely used in commentaries on all kinds of 'set text', whether sacred or secular, whether in schools of grammar or theology, which entailed analysis of authorial intention (*intentio auctoris*), book-title (*titulus*), stylistic and didactic mode of procedure (*modus agendi* or *modus tractandi*), the order in which the contents are arranged (*ordo*), the pedagogic and/or moral usefulness of the work (*utilitas*), its subject-matter (*materia*), and the branch of knowledge to which it belongs (*cui parti philosophiae supponitur*).[3] This idiom was considerably elaborated in the thirteenth century, when it was assimilated to a new series of technical terms which came into use as a result of the new methods of thinking and procedures of study which scholars derived from Aristotle. The 'Aristotelian

[2] On these commentaries see esp. Sandkühler, *Die frühen Dantekommentare, passim*; O. Bird, 'The *Canzone d'Amore* of Guido Cavalcanti according to the Commentary of Dino del Garbo', *Med. Stud.* ii (1940), 150–203, iii (1941), 117–60; J. E. Shaw, *Guido Cavalcanti's Theory of Love: The Canzone d'Amore and Other Related Problems* (Toronto, 1949), pp. 149–63; J. M. Jones, '"The Chess of Love": Translation of a Prose Commentary on *Echecs amoureux*' (unpub. Ph.D. diss., University of Nebraska, 1968); J. V. Fleming, *The Roman de la Rose: A Study in Medieval Iconography* (Princeton, 1969), pp. 62–5.

[3] For a discussion of this process, and bibliography, see Minnis, *Authorship*, pp. 9–39, 219–34.

prologue' which introduced commentaries on authors both sacred and profane was based on the four major causes which, according to 'the Philosopher', governed all activity and change in the universe. Hence, the author would be discussed as the 'efficient cause' or motivating agent of the text; his materials, as its 'material cause'; his literary style and structure, as twin aspects of the 'formal cause', the *forma tractandi* and the *forma tractatus* respectively; while his ultimate end or objective in writing would be considered as the 'final cause'. It was, therefore, the terms of reference of Aristotle's *Physics* and *Metaphysics*, rather than those of his *Poetics*, which defined the parameters of much scholastic literary theory. To be sure, a version of the *Poetics* did enjoy a certain amount of influence in the later Middle Ages, this being the version offered by the *Middle Commentary on the Poetics* of the great Arab scholar Averroes, which was made available to the Latin West by Hermann the German's translation of 1256. The extent of its influence is a matter of debate among modern scholars, but it seems clear that, for the most part, the work was used to the extent that it reinforced trends which were already well established and in which other sources, notably the pseudo-Dionysian discussions of imagery and symbolic language, figured far more largely.

To return to the Aristotelian interpretative system, which did command wide assent, the four causes, as applied in literary analysis, brought commentators considerably closer to their authors. The *auctor* remained an authority, someone to be believed and imitated, but his human qualities began to receive more attention. This crucial development is writ large in the prologues to commentaries on the Bible.[4] In twelfth-century exegesis, the dominance of allegorical interpretation had hindered the emergence of certain kinds of literary theory; for instance, God was believed to have inspired the human authors of Scripture in a way which defied literary description. Twelfth-century exegetes were interested in the author mainly as a source of authority. But in the thirteenth century, a new type of exegesis emerged, in which the focus had shifted from the divine author to the human author of Scripture. Particularly important here were the analytical strategies provided by the efficient cause and the formal cause respectively. Once God was identified as the primary efficient cause and the ultimate source of the authority of Scripture, the commentator could concentrate on its instrumental and inspired human authors. Although technically subservient, these writers were supposed to have acted personally and with a measure of independence; they had, for the most part, expressed themselves through the literal sense of Scripture, in a variety of literary styles and structures, thereby bringing—to put it in the scholastic idiom—the formal cause from potential into actuality.

In their accounts of the formal causes of literature, scholastic philosophers and theologians described two kinds or series of procedural mode:

4 Ibid., pp. 73-159.

the modes of human science (involving such logical methods as definition, division, argument-formation, and the application of examples
designed to aid the teaching of these methods) and the modes of sacred
science (involving such poetic and rhetorical methods as narrative, fiction
and parable, affective exhortation and warning, allegory, figure and metaphor, exemplification, etc.). The latter series, the *modi* of sacred science,
were found mainly in the Bible; the former, in books supposed to have
been produced by merely human agency (e.g. the textbooks of the trivium
and quadrivium). This distinction was motivated by the wish to establish
theology as the queen of the sciences (applying an Aristotelian conception of science) and to identify the ways in which it both differed from and
resembled the 'subordinate' sciences which were its handmaidens. Once
the suggestion had been made that theology might be basically affective
and in some deep sense 'poetic', no theologian could avoid considering
those aspects of poetics and rhetoric which Alexander of Hales and his
successors had deemed appropriate to the subject. Here, then, is the late
medieval version of 'the Bible as literature'.

In the thirteenth and fourteenth centuries it was the scholastic
philosophers and theologians who set the pace for speculation concerning many literary matters, and made significant advances in the techniques of textual exposition. They produced a critical vocabulary which
enabled the authors, materials, styles, structures, and effects of scriptural texts to be considered thoroughly, and which encouraged the emergence in the fourteenth century of a more liberal attitude to classical
poetry. For something of the new status which had been afforded to
scriptural poetry in particular and to the poetic and rhetorical modes
employed throughout Scripture in general, seems to have rubbed off on
secular poetry. Scriptural authors were being read literally, with close
attention being paid to those poetic methods believed to be part of the
literal sense; pagan poets, long acknowledged as masters of those same
methods, were being read allegorically or 'moralized'—and thus the
twain could meet.

This 'coming together' of sacred and secular texts within the scope of a
universal interpretative model made possible a rich harvest of critical
insights and techniques which may be seen at work in, for example, the
literary polemic of Petrarch and Boccaccio, the 'Aristotelian prologues'
and scholastic procedures of the first commentaries on Dante (here
represented by those of Guido da Pisa, Pietro Alighieri, and Boccaccio),
and, of course, in the innovative criticism of Dante himself. A good
example of an appropriation of an academic method of textual analysis is
provided by the elaborate *divisio textus* (meticulous division and subdivision of the text in order to elicit its full meaning) practised by Dante in
both the *Vita nuova* and the *Convivio*, a method which had been refined in
generations of commentaries on the works of Aristotle and other philoso-

phical authorities, and on the Bible.[5] A good example of an appropriation of academic vocabulary occurs in a work once believed to be by Dante (but now the attribution is hotly disputed), the *Epistle to Can Grande della Scala*. There the *modi* employed in the *Divine Comedy* are listed as follows: 'The form or mode of treatment is poetic, fictive, descriptive, digressive, and figurative; and further, it is definitive, analytical, probative, refutative, and exemplificative.'[6] This constitutes a claim that Dante's poem combines two kinds of mode, the 'definitive, divisive, and collective' mode of human science and those literary *modi* which were the stock-in-trade of poets both sacred and profane. Behind this passage lies a rich tradition of discussion of *modi agendi* by medieval schoolmen.

The same process of literary assimilation also created the intellectual environment in which a major development in the history of literary theory and criticism could take place: scholars felt free to resort to scriptural exegesis for much of their vocabulary and many of their interpretative methods. In the *Convivio* Dante showed the way by invoking, with (in our opinion) full awareness of the momentous nature of what he was doing, the 'fourfold' system of interpreting the Bible in expounding his own 'modern' fictions—a point to which we shall return (see below, pp. 382–7).

These facts are sufficient to give the lie to the claim that the later Middle Ages produced little if any literary theory and criticism worthy of the name. All too many general histories of the subject have ignored or glossed over the medieval period, moving from 'Longinus' to Sir Philip Sidney. Representative of the assumptions which make this leap possible is the following statement from Wimsatt and Brooks' *Short History of Criticism*:

Let us say, in summation, that the Middle Ages . . . were not in fact ages of literary theory or criticism . . . In short, it was an age of theological thinking in a theologically oriented and theocratic society. Such a society does not characteristically promote the essentially humanistic activity of literary criticism . . .[7]

Behind this lies an anachronistic and highly misleading notion which, in our opinion, has greatly hindered a proper understanding of the medieval contribution, namely the distinction between 'humanism' and 'scholasticism'; specifically, on the one hand, the contrast between twelfth-century humanism and thirteenth-century scholasticism, and on the other the contrast between late-medieval scholasticism and early Renaissance humanism. These may now be examined in turn.

[5] Cf. our introduction to Ch. IX.
[6] *Dantis Alaghierii epistolae*, ed. P. Toynbee, 2nd edn. C. G. Hardie (Oxford, 1966), pp. 175, 200.
[7] W. K. Wimsatt and C. Brooks, *Literary Criticism: A Short History* (London, 1975), p. 154. A similar position is adopted by O. B. Hardison, 'Towards a History of Medieval Literary Criticism', *Med. et hum.* vii (1976), 1–12.

According to the old clichés, by the end of the twelfth century grammar had been roundly defeated by logic, a situation dramatized in the satiric poem *La Bataille des VII ars* which Henri d'Andeli wrote probably in the second quarter of the thirteenth century. Rhetoric and poetic gave way to logic and dialectic; humanism retreated before scholasticism.[8] Orléans, where the songs of the Muses had once been zealously guarded, became a law-school; in the schools the pagan *Fasti* (by Ovid) was replaced by a blatantly Christian one, the *Ecclesiale* of Alexander of Villa Dei. Hence, the study of grammar and rhetoric—and therefore of 'literature'—was generally impoverished. In such unfavourable conditions, literary theory and criticism died or at least went underground. This view is untenable, as the evidence presented below will attest. It is impossible to square with, for instance, the sophisticated literary discussions of texts—particularly scriptural texts—produced by commentators of the thirteenth and fourteenth centuries. At a time when the study of grammar had developed, in one of its main branches, into speculative analysis of the theoretical structures of language itself,[9] theologians and Bible-scholars were devising a comprehensive and flexible interpretative programme for examining the various *modi* supposed to be employed in the literal sense of Scripture, and the diverse roles and functions, both literary and moral, believed to be performed by the human authors of the Bible.

Moreover, several recent writers have countered the facile distinction between twelfth-century humanism and thirteenth-century scholasticism by emphasizing the ways in which thirteenth-century scholasticism actually grew out of twelfth-century scholasticism, a scholasticism which governed most of the scholarly activities once hailed as evidence of humanism. Sir Richard Southern can speak of a 'process of accumulation and increasingly refined analysis of the deposit of the past' which continued from the twelfth century into the thirteenth;[10] the work of R. H. and M. A. Rouse offers a similar conclusion.[11] This 'process of accumulation and increasingly refined analysis' determined, among other things, the development of scholastic literary theory and practice. In the twelfth century, certain scholars—notably Peter Abelard and Gilbert of Poitiers—

---

[8] For a convenient statement of this position, see L. J. Paetow (ed.), *Two Medieval Satires on the University of Paris: La Bataille des VII Ars of Henri d'Andeli and the* Morale Scolarium *of John of Garland* (Memoirs of the University of California IV, Berkeley, 1927), pp. 13–30.

[9] On medieval 'speculative grammar' see esp. J. Pinborg, *Die Entwicklung der Sprachtheorie im Mittelalter* (BGPTM XLII, 1967), and the publications of the series 'Grammatica Speculativa' (Stuttgart and Bad Cannstatt), ed. J. Pinborg and H. Kohlenberger.

[10] *Platonism, Scholastic Method, and the School of Chartres* (The 1978 Stenton Lecture, University of Reading, 1979), p. 36; cf. the general tenor of Franco Giusberti, *Materials for a Study on Twelfth-century Scholasticism* (History of Logic II, Naples, 1983).

[11] See esp. R. H. and M. A. Rouse, *Preachers, Florilegia and Sermons: Studies on the* Manipulus florum *of Thomas of Ireland* (Studies and Texts XLVII, Toronto, 1979); R. H. Rouse, 'Florilegia and Latin Classical Authors in Twelfth- and Thirteenth-century Orléans', *Viator*, x (1979), 131–60.

had in their Bible-commentaries applied to sacred literature the conventions and categories of secular literary theory and criticism;[12] thirteenth-century theologians built on this by, for example, elaborating a comprehensive system (as summarized above) of describing the diverse literary styles and structures which they were finding in Holy Writ. It would seem, then, that there is another way of interpreting the historical facts. Instead of regarding scholasticism as a malevolent tide which caused the submergence of literary awareness, it can be argued that it actually channelled such awareness into areas of study where it was enabled to enjoy a new prestige. In their philosophical and theological commentaries and treatises, some of the best minds of the later Middle Ages brought their considerable intelligence to bear on matters figurative, fictive, affective, and imaginative.

Indeed, it is perfectly possible to turn the tables on those who disparage scholastic literary theory on the grounds that it is not 'humanistic' by claiming that in reality this theory is one of the products of what should be identified as humanism of a high order. Southern has argued that 'the period from about 1100 to about 1320' was 'one of the greatest ages of humanism in the history of Europe: perhaps the greatest of all':

... far from the humanism of the twelfth century running into the sand after about 1150 to re-emerge two centuries later, it had its fulfilment in the thirteenth and early fourteenth centuries—in the period which the humanists of the Renaissance most despised.[13]

For Southern a period in which the 'elements of dignity, order, reason and intelligibility are prominent in human experience' may reasonably be regarded as humanistic. This principle, the true starting-point of inquiry into the subject,

has been confused by the tendency to start with the humanism of the Renaissance. This has given the love of ancient authors an exaggerated importance in judging medieval humanism. If we start with the concepts of natural nobility and of reason and intelligible order in the universe, the whole subject takes on a different appearance.[14]

The literary theory produced in the period indubitably partakes of that different appearance, for what could be more indicative of confident belief in 'the concept of natural nobility and of reason and intelligible order in the universe' than the thirteenth-century hierarchies of the sciences, with theology clearly visible at the top of the tall yet accessible mountain of human knowledge rather than residing in some far and distant land which few travellers could reach? Within these schemes there was ample room for a literary sensibility which may, in Southern's

[12] See Minnis, *Authorship*, pp. 44, 50–4, 59–62.
[13] 'Medieval Humanism', in id., *Medieval Humanism and Other Studies* (Oxford, 1970), p. 31.
[14] Ibid., p. 32.

terms, be described as humanistic, since the human authors of Scripture were supposed to have employed styles and literary devices which were also the tools of the classical poets' trade. Scholastic literary theory was, therefore, at the very centre, and not on the fringes, of academic endeavour and achievement.

Having established that 'the love of ancient authors' should not be allowed an exaggerated importance in our inquiry, it may now be asked precisely what happened to the classics, since fewer commentaries on them were produced in the thirteenth and early fourteenth centuries than had appeared in the twelfth. The basic answer is that, far from being made redundant, they were redeployed. Twelfth-century scholars had produced collections of extracts, or 'flowers', from the classics: later compilers incorporated this material into their more sophisticated compilations. For example, the *Florilegium Gallicum*, an anthology of secular *auctoritates* produced at Orléans, was almost entirely absorbed by Vincent of Beauvais, the extracts being disposed throughout his *Speculum historiale*.[15] Another Orléans collection, the *Florilegium angelicum*, seems to have furnished material for various thirteenth- and fourteenth-century manuals written for the use of preachers.[16] It may be added that information derived from the 'lives of the authors' as provided in twelfth-century *accessūs* found its way into such later reference-books as Vincent's *Speculum historiale*, the *Communiloquium* and *Compendiloquium* of John of Wales, and Walter Burley's *De vita ac moribus philosophorum*.[17] Moreover, scholars of secular literature working in the thirteenth and fourteenth centuries substantially developed and modified twelfth-century theories of poetic fiction. The moralization process became more systematic and exhaustive, producing such works as the Old French *Ovide moralisé*, John Ridevall's *Fulgentius metaforalis*, and the 'Ovid Moralized' which constitutes the fifteenth book of Pierre Bersuire's *Moral Reduction* (this last text, being the most elaborate of its kind, has been chosen for partial translation below).[18] Apparently, this story is not one of decadence but rather of development and adaptation; the legacy of the twelfth century was refined and related to later academic interests within an intellectual system which

[15] Rouse, 'Florilegia', pp. 157–8.
[16] Ibid., pp. 156–7.
[17] On the late-medieval genre of *compilatio* see A. J. Minnis, 'Late-medieval Discussions of *Compilatio* and the Role of the *Compilator*', *BGDSL* ci (1979), 385–421; M. B. Parkes, 'The Influence of the Concepts of *Ordinatio* and *Compilatio* on the Development of the Book', in J. J. G. Alexander and M. T. Gibson (eds.), *Medieval Learning and Literature: Essays presented to R. W. Hunt* (Oxford, 1976), pp. 115–41.
[18] On such works see esp. P. Demats, *Fabula: Trois Études de mythographie antique et médiévale* (Publications romanes et françaises CXXII, Geneva, 1983), pp. 61–105; J. B. Allen, 'Commentary as Criticism: The Text, Influence and Literary Theory of the "Fulgentius Metaphored" of John Ridewall', in *Acta Conventus Neo-Latini Amstelodamensis: Proceedings of the Second International Congress of Neo-Latin Studies, Amsterdam 19–24 August 1973*, ed. P. Tuynman, G. C. Kuiper, and E. Kessler (Munich, 1979), pp. 25–47.

we can call scholasticism or high-order humanism, depending on our taste. The label matters little if the facts themselves are clear. Turning now to the alleged gulf between late medieval scholasticism and early Renaissance humanism (particularly Italian humanism), it may be argued that, here again, the process of transition and change has been oversimplified and distorted. What is striking about the commentaries on Dante (cf. the extracts from those of Guido da Pisa, Pietro Alighieri and Boccaccio printed below) are their similarities to, rather than their differences from, the commentaries which medieval teachers produced on their textbooks—as is demonstrated by Bruno Sandkühler's book *Die frühen Dantekommentare und ihr Verhältnis zur mittelalterlichen Kommentartradition*. Even the most 'original' literary theory produced in fourteenth- and fifteenth-century Italy takes its points of departure and many of its categories and basic ideas from scholastic literary theory: witness the way in which scholars like Albertino Mussato, Francesco da Fiano, and Leonardo Bruni set about discussing the usefulness (*utilitas*) of poetry, its place within the hierarchy of the sciences, its spiritual and moral senses, the ancient poet-theologians (or 'myth-lovers'), the styles common to both classical and scriptural writers, and so forth.[19] Of course, there are new beginnings, which are being made by way of reaction against traditional notions: in these cases, knowledge of the old is crucial for understanding of what is new and why it is new. Alexander of Hales and his successors discussed theology as poetry; Albertino Mussato discussed poetry as theology; Pico della Mirandola evolved a poetic theology. We cannot fully comprehend the significance of any one of these intellectual positions without some awareness of the others.

To put it another way, in Italy both the humanists who aggrandized poetry and the latter-day scholastics who classified it as the lowest branch of logic owe a considerable debt to the schoolmen—particularly the Parisian schoolmen—of the thirteenth and early fourteenth centuries. These facts have been fully recognized by C. C. Greenfield, who has, as it were, reached them from the other end, by means of her work on the early Italian Renaissance period. Building upon the important scholarship of P. O. Kristeller, which emphasizes the extent to which the Aristotelian tradition of learning continued long into the Renaissance, and the fact that in Italy scholasticism developed simultaneously with humanism,[20] she states that

[19] For statements of the positions of these Italian authors, and relevant bibliography, see C. C. Greenfield, *Humanist and Scholastic Poetics, 1250–1500* (London and Toronto, 1981); also the chapter on 'From *Theologia Poetica* to *Theologia Platonica*' in C. Trinkaus, *In Our Image and Likeness: Humanism and Divinity in Italian Humanist Thought* (London and Chicago, 1970), pp. 683–721. See further the relevant references below, in Ch. IX.

[20] It is incorrect, therefore, to say that in Italy scholasticism as an old philosophy was superseded by the new philosophy of humanism: see P. O. Kristeller, *Renaissance Thought: The Classical, Scholastic and Humanistic Strains* (New York, 1961), p. 52; cf. id., *Renaissance Thought and its Sources*, ed. M. Mooney (New York, 1979), pp. 40–2, 85–105. Similarly, Walter Ullmann has emphasized that Renaissance humanism cannot adequately be understood

... one can no longer consider Humanism a new movement superseding the old medieval scholastic philosophy. Humanist and scholastic poetics, and thus Humanism and Scholasticism, were not replaced the one by the other. They were revived about the same time and grew side by side until the Renaissance. Their relationship was dialectical, so that rather than simply opposing each other, they stimulated persistently each other's revival and growth. Practically every scholastic statement on poetics is countered by a belligerent humanist answer and vice versa. This investigation of humanist poetics in relation to scholastic poetics casts a new light on many humanist beliefs, and it changes a number of notions traditionally held by scholars who have examined humanist poetics as an isolated growth.[21]

Unfortunately, Greenfield's generally helpful investigation, *Humanist and Scholastic Poetics, 1250–1550*, is marred by its cursory and sometimes misleading consideration of earlier scholastic poetics. Thus, the scholastic philosophers and theologians are depicted as striving to cut off poetry from philosophy and theology; in particular Thomas Aquinas is regarded as one who, having dismissed poetry in his earlier days, subsequently conceded that it had a humble part to play as the lowest branch of logic.[22] But the truth of the situation is far more complex and various than that. For a start, it should be recognized that when schoolmen classified poetry as the lowest part of logic they certainly did not think of themselves as having condemned it (cf. below, Ch. VII). That is made abundantly clear by the anonymous Parisian question on the nature of poetry which we have translated, wherein poetry, as discourse which employs the imaginative syllogism, is afforded the strategy of appealing to the individual's imagination and faculty of desire, which is important because everyone is especially fond of 'his own instinctive estimations and relies particularly on his own imaginings'. And commentators on classical literature had no qualms about applying logical categories in introducing their authors. For instance, Giovanni del Virgilio, a friend of Dante's who is often described as a proto-humanist, described the general mode of proceeding in Ovid's *Metamorphoses* as offering definitions and being discursive and inferential; we have already noted similar vocabulary in the *Epistle to Can Grande della Scala*. One wonders what Henri d'Andeli would have made of that.

More specifically, one of the most unfortunate coincidences of cultural history (at least as far as the modern appreciation of medieval literary theory is concerned) is the fact that the schoolman who is best known and most widely read today had little time for matters imaginative without taking into account the various forces which had shaped the age (i.e. the later Middle Ages) out of which it was to grow: *Medieval Foundations of Renaissance Humanism* (London, 1977), p. 196. Cf. the general tenor of A. B. Collins, *The Secular is Sacred: Platonism and Thomism in Marsilio Ficino's Platonic Theology* (The Hague, 1974).

[21] Greenfield, *Humanist and Scholastic Poetics*, pp. 11–12.
[22] Ibid., pp. 49–50, 52–3; cf. pp. 314–15.

— poetry as ethics [handwritten annotation]

and poetic.[23] It was Aquinas' views on the relative inferiority of such resources which were taken up and amplified by conservatives like Giovannino of Mantua and Gerolamo Savonarola in the debates between Italian scholastics and humanists on the nature of poetry.[24] But in his own time Aquinas was by no means typical in this respect, as the exegesis of such thinkers as Bonaventure, Giles of Rome, and Henry of Ghent makes abundantly clear. Moreover, when Aquinas does concentrate his mind on such issues, his comments are so concise and economical that their significance can scarcely be understood unless they are placed within the wider context of the early thirteenth-century debates on the nature of theology and the functions of the styles and genres found in Holy Scripture. Poetry both sacred and profane was frequently described as pertaining to a major branch of philosophy, namely ethics, and many scholastic philosophers and theologians believed that theology was in some sense poetic. How much higher could a schoolman go in terms of respect for style and divine eloquence?

Certainly, a thorough reappraisal of the debt of Renaissance literary theory and criticism to its late medieval antecedents and shaping influences is long overdue. Closer examination of the works of the Italian humanists who felt obliged to define and defend their own intellectual positions by berating the schoolmen will reveal the considerable extent to which they were biting the hand that had so lavishly fed them.

All this makes it abundantly clear that J. W. H. Atkins's opinion, as expressed in his *English Literary Criticism: The Medieval Phase*, that it is 'unavailing and fruitless' to look in the Middle Ages for 'original and lasting contributions to literary theory, or for illuminating appreciations of literary works themselves',[25] is simply incorrect; the assumptions on which that opinion rests have been eroded away by recent scholarship. Medieval literary theory and criticism stands as a valid subject-area in its own right, and one which must be investigated within the framework of the history of literary theory and criticism.

[23] As is admitted even by such an admirer of Aquinas as M.-D. Chenu, *Towards Understanding St. Thomas*, tr. A.-M. Landry and D. Hughes (Chicago, 1964), pp. 169–70, 228. The problems involved in deriving an aesthetic from Aquinas' thought are well brought out by Umberto Eco, *Il problema estetico in Tommaso d'Aquino* (Idee nuove LIII, Milan, 1970). Humanist reservations concerning Aquinas are vividly conveyed by Lorenzo Valla's sermon 'In Praise of St. Thomas Aquinas', tr. M. E. Hanley in L. A. Kennedy (ed.), *Renaissance Philosophy* (The Hague and Paris, 1973), pp. 13–27.

[24] Cf. Greenfield, *Humanist and Scholastic Poetics*, p. 50. On the adoption of Aquinas' thought by the Dominican Order and its subsequent influence, see M. Burbach, 'Early Dominican and Franciscan Legislation regarding St. Thomas', *Med. Stud.* iv (1942), 139–58; P. O. Kristeller, *Medieval Aspects of Renaissance Learning* (Duke Monographs in Medieval and Renaissance Studies I, Durham, NC, 1974), pp. 29–91. On the specific issue of Aquinas' *auctoritas* see further M.-D. Chenu, 'Maître Thomas est-il une "autorité"?', *RT* xxx (1925), 187–94.

[25] J. W. H. Atkins, *English Literary Criticism: The Medieval Phase* (Cambridge, 1943), p. v.

I
An Anthology of Literary Prefaces: Introductions to the Authors

GRAMMAR is not simply a matter of learning how to write and speak well, declared Thierry of Chartres (who became chancellor of Chartres in 1141), echoing a long-established definition: it also has as its proper task the explication and the study of all the authors.[1] The principles which governed that task are revealed in the introductory lectures to the grammarians' commentaries on their authors, which are sometimes called *accessūs*. There, each and every schoolbook was analysed in a systematic way, in terms of its author, the style and structure of its material, and the educational ends which it served.

The precise number of headings under which the various aspects of the text are discussed vary somewhat from *accessus* to *accessus*; in our selection the most comprehensive set is offered by the introduction to the *Paschale Carmen* of Sedulius: the life of the poet (*vita poetae*), the title of the work (*titulus operis*), the nature of the verse (*qualitas carminis*), the intention of the writer (*intentio scribentis*), the number of the books (*numerus librorum*), the order of the books (*ordo librorum*), and the textual exposition (*explanatio*). This paradigm, the 'type B' introduction as described in R. W. Hunt's pioneering study of academic prologues, was associated with the fourth-century grammarian Servius because it is found at the beginning of manuscript copies of his commentary on Virgil's *Aeneid*.[2] It was applied to the *Paschale Carmen* because Sedulius was regarded as a Christian Virgil—or rather as a poet whose achievement had transcended that of Virgil. Whereas Virgil had recounted the ancient deeds of kings and princes, Sedulius had as his subject the miracles of the King of Kings. This instance of the application to a Christian work of an apparatus which originally prefaced a pagan text, coming as it does at the beginning of the present collection of medieval literary discussions, will serve to emphasize the interrelation between the secular and the sacred which is one of its chief concerns.

However, the Servian or 'type B' introduction was not the form of academic prologue which dominated in the twelfth century (as the *accessūs* translated below amply illustrate). Writing between 1076 and 1099, Bernard of Utrecht described it as an ancient schema which had fallen out of favour with the 'moderns'.[3] The 'modern' paradigm is well represented in the following *accessūs*; it comprises analyses of a given text's title (*titulus*), subject-matter (*materia*), intention (*intentio*), method of stylistic and/or didactic treatment

---

[1] E. Jeauneau, 'Le *Prologus in Eptatheucon* de Thierry de Chartres', *Med. Stud.* xvi (1954), 174. Cf. Ph. Delhaye, 'L'enseignement de la philosophie morale au XII⁰ siècle', *Med. Stud.* xi (1949), 80–1.

[2] Hunt, 'Introductions to the *Artes*', p. 94 (repr. p. 126); *Serviani in Vergilii Carmina commentarii*, Harvard edition (Cambridge, Mass., 1946), ii. 1–5; cf. Minnis, *Authorship*, pp. 15–16.

[3] *Accessus ad auctores, etc.*, ed. Huygens, p. 59.

(*modus*), utility (*utilitas*), and the part of philosophy to which it pertains (*cui parti philosophiae supponitur*). The last of these headings gives us a clue concerning the origins of this paradigm. In the first version of his commentary on Porphyry's *Isagoge*, Boethius listed six Latin headings which must be considered at the beginning of every book of philosophy, and gave their Greek equivalents.[4] E. A. Quain has traced these back to late-antique Greek commentaries on works by Aristotle.[5] Much work remains to be done on the development and dissemination of such vocabulary. However, there is no doubt of the wide popularity of its medieval version—designated as the 'type C' prologue by Hunt—in the twelfth century. Not only did it win against the Servian or 'type B' model as described above; it also replaced the 'type A' paradigm based on the rhetorical circumstances (*circumstantiae*), a prologue-form which had been used extensively by Remigius of Auxerre (*c.* 841–*c.* 908).[6]

However, it should be noted that headings from the 'type A' or 'type B' paradigms could find their way into 'type C' prologues. For instance, in the third *accessus* to Ovid's *Epistles* translated below, the *vita poetae*—a 'type B' or Servian term—is included as one of the six things which must be enquired into at the start of this book. On many occasions, even when the term *vita poetae* does not actually appear, some biographical details concerning the author are supplied. More rarely, a commentator who is using the 'type C' paradigm may mention the 'place' in which the book under discussion was written or its 'time' of composition, obvious survivals from the form of prologue which was based on the series of *circumstantiae*.

The success of the 'type C' prologue was probably due in large measure to the fact that it enhanced the prestige of secular literature—mainly the work of pagan philosophers and poets—within the standard frameworks of knowledge as defined in the twelfth century. The statement that 'almost all' the grammatical authors 'direct themselves towards ethics' is found in many *accessus*,[7] and in the examples translated below text after text is declared to 'pertain to ethics' (*ethice supponitur*). The other two paradigms we have been discussing were concerned with more exclusively literary matters; the 'type C' paradigm, having originated in introduction to philosophical works, was naturally geared to displaying the philosophical credentials of any poem to which it was applied. To be sure, such application was not made without controversy (see below, p. 122), but most arts scholars, or *artistae*, were happy to accept that

---

[4] *In Isagogen Porphyrii commentaria*, ed. S. Brandt (CSEL xlviii. 4–5).

[5] E. A. Quain, 'The Medieval *Accessus ad auctores*', *Traditio*, iii (1945), 228–42.

[6] On this type see Minnis, *Authorship*, pp. 16–17. The *circumstantiae* formed a series of questions (who? what? why? in what manner? where? when? and whence? or by what means?) which grew out of ancient rhetoricians' attempts to summarize everything which could form the subject of a dispute or discussion. This theory can be traced back to Hermagoras, *Fragmenta*, ed. D. Matthes (Leipzig, 1962), pp. 13 ff. For further bibliography see Minnis, *Authorship*, p. 224 n. 53.

[7] *Accessus* to Ovid's *Metamorphoses* in Munich, Bayerische Staatsbibliothek, Clm 4610, cit. F. Ghisalberti, 'Medieval Biographies of Ovid', *JWCI* ix (1946), 17 n. 5. For other examples see G. Przychocki, '*Accessus Ovidiani*', *Rozprawy Akademii Umiejętności*, wydział filologiczny, 3rd ser. iv (1911), 89; K. Young, 'Chaucer's Appeal to the Platonic Deity', *Speculum*, xix (1944), 5, 6.

they were practitioners in moral science, a branch of practical philosophy (the others being economics and politics, within an *ordo scientiarum* that goes back to Aristotle).[8] Grammar, then, was an art of living as well as an art of language, and the single method of instruction was the explication of the poets (*enarratio poetarum*).[9]

The 'type C' prologue, to some extent modified and amplified by critical vocabulary and concepts from other types of introduction, flourished throughout the later Middle Ages and continued to be used well into the Renaissance period.[10] It soon appeared in commentaries on the books of the Bible (see below, pp. 69–71). In particular, the biography of the writer, the *vita auctoris*, which had been assimilated to its plan, exercised a major influence. The collections of the lives of the poets and philosophers which appear in late-medieval encyclopaedias and reference-books like the *Speculum maius* of Vincent of Beauvais (*c.* 1190–1264) and the *Compendiloquium* of John of Wales (regent master at Oxford *c.* 1260) draw heavily on *accessus*-material.[11] Moreover, convincing parallels have recently been adduced between the *vitae poetarum* and the Old Provençal *vidas* or lives of the troubadours, the earliest of which date from the middle to the late thirteenth century.[12] Both types of biography draw supposed historical 'facts' about the writer's life from his writings; both speak of his origins and describe his social position, literary, and other achievements, and perhaps even his travels; both describe the literary text which they preface, and there are stylistic and thematic similarities as well. Finally, it should be noted that the *vita auctoris*, having undergone important changes at the hands of commentators on biblical authors, served as a model for the first lives of the 'new poet' and 'new author', Dante Alighieri (see below, p. 377). The changes of style and substance which occurred within the late-medieval and Renaissance tradition of composing lives of

---

[8] On this *ordo* see J. A. Weisheipl, 'Classification of the Sciences in Medieval Thought', *Med. Stud.* xxvii (1965), 65–6; D. E. Sharp, 'The *De ortu scientiarum* of Robert Kilwardby', *New Schol.* viii (1934), 16–18; Hardison, *The Enduring Monument*, pp. 3–5 and the relevant nn. on pp. 199–208.

[9] The relationship of grammar with ethics is well brought out in the articles by Ph. Delhaye, 'La Place de l'éthique parmi les disciplines scientifiques au xiiᵉ siècle', *Miscellanea moralia in honorem A. Janssen* (Gembloux, 1948), pp. 29–44; 'L'enseignement de la philosophie morale', 77–99; '"Grammatica" et "Ethica" au xiiᵉ siècle', *RTAM* xxv (1958), 59–110. See further Allen, *Ethical Poetic, passim*.

[10] E. M. Sanford, 'The Manuscripts of Lucan: Accessus and Marginalia', *Speculum*, ix (1934), 278; also the prologues to humanistic commentaries on Juvenal and Persius in Kristeller, *CTC* i. 205–6, 211, 212–23; iii. 248, 249, 258; cf. Roberto Weiss, *Humanism in England during the Fifteenth Century*, 2nd edn. (Oxford, 1957), pp. 10, 31 n. The Servian or 'type B' prologue enjoyed something of a revival in humanistic commentaries on poets: for examples see Kristeller, *CTC* i. 208; iii. 250, 251, 272, 288–9, 306; cf. Bernard Weinberg, *A History of Literary Criticism in the Italian Renaissance* (Chicago, 1961), pp. 47–9.

[11] See e.g. *Speculum historiale*, vi. lx–lxiii, lxvii–lxx, cviii–cxxii, on Virgil, Horace, and Ovid; *Speculum doctrinale*, iii. cix–cxxv, esp. the material on Aesop (*Speculum quadruplex*, iv. 193–4, 195–9, 210–18; ii. 287–96); also John of Wales, *Compendiloquium*, ed. L. Wadding (Rome, 1655), *passim*.

[12] *The Vidas of the Troubadours*, tr. M. Egan (Garland Library of Medieval Literature, ser. B, 6, New York and London, 1984), pp. xxv–xxvi; cf. her conclusions in 'Commentary, *Vitae poetae* and *Vida*: Latin and Old Provençal "Lives of Poets"', *RP* xxxvii (1983/4), 36–48.

authors both old and new mark the transition from scholastic to humanistic methods of literary biography.[13]

The following translation follows the revised edition by R. B. C. Huygens of the *accessūs* which are found in full in Munich, Clm 19475 (XII s., Tegernsee) and in part in two other manuscripts, both dating from the end of the twelfth or the beginning of the thirteenth century. Generally, Huygens follows the order in which the *accessūs* appear in his base manuscript, although he tidily groups together all the introductions to Ovid's works, which gives the collection the appearance of being better-structured than is warranted by the manuscript evidence. Huygens's chart of the contents of his three manuscripts reveals quite clearly that there was no fixed order for the *accessūs* (although two of the manuscripts do agree closely at some points in their sequences),[14] and therefore it is best to think of each *accessus* as an individual unit which may appear in the company of different *accessūs* in different manuscripts, the exact number of such items varying from manuscript to manuscript. Collections of this kind—the work of many scholars whose names have been lost—grew haphazardly and without any advance planning in respect of arrangement. Yet they offer us a golden opportunity for comprehensive study of the principles of literary theory behind the *explication de texte* to which they normally served as prefaces.

INTRODUCTIONS TO THE AUTHORS[15]

Introduction to Cato[16]

There were two Catos at Rome, Cato the censor and Cato of Utica.[17] Cato the censor is so called because he was a good judge, and gave good and just judgements on all matters. Cato of Utica is so called because he conquered Utica, a region in the Roman empire. When Cato the censor saw that young men and girls were living very wicked lives he wrote this book to his son, showing him the proper way to live, and through him teaching all men to live just and moral lives. Others say that this book got its name, not from its author, but from the subject matter. For *catus* means 'wise'.[18] It is said that the father directed it to his son, so that he [i.e. Cato] may be

---

[13] Cf. the central argument of Ghisalberti, 'Medieval Biographies of Ovid', *passim*.

[14] *Accessus ad auctores, etc.*, ed. Huygens, p. 5.

[15] Tr. from *Accessus ad auctores, etc.*, ed. Huygens, pp. 21–2, 25–38, 44–5, 48–53, with the permission of E. J. Brill Ltd. From the beginning of the *Accessus ad auctores* we have omitted two *accessūs* to Prudentius.

[16] i.e. to the *Disticha Catonis*; ed. M. Boas and H. J. Botschuyver (Amsterdam, 1952); tr. W. J. Chase, *The Distichs of Cato: A Famous Medieval Textbook* (University of Wisconsin Studies in the Social Sciences and History VII, Madison, Wis., 1922). On Cato in the Middle Ages see especially R. Hazelton, 'The Christianization of Cato', *Med. Stud.* xix (1957), 157–73.

[17] This *accessus* is apparently influenced by Remigius of Auxerre's commentary on the *Disticha*: see the passages cit. Huygens, *Accessus ad auctores, etc.*, p. 21 n.

[18] Cf. Servius on *Aeneid*, i. 423; Isidore, *Ety.* XII. ii. 39.

seen to have collected more useful precepts than did the latter [i.e. his son]. Precepts for living a good and moral life form the subject matter of this book. Its intention is to show us by what way we may reach true salvation, and that we should seek after it and zealously search for it, not just for a time but with perseverance. The usefulness of this book is that those who read it should learn to order their lives wisely. It pertains to ethics, for its aim is to make a useful contribution to men's morals. And so the writer prefaces his work with a prologue in which his aim is to make us attentive, receptive to his teaching, and well disposed.[19] For when he says SERIOUSLY[20] he makes us attentive; when he tells us where he has detected that error, namely IN THE PATH OF BEHAVIOUR, in bringing morals under his scrutiny he makes us receptive to his teaching; and when he calls us sons, saying MY DEAREST SON, he makes us well disposed.

Introduction to Avianus

The title of this book is *Avianus*. He was a Roman citizen who was asked by Theodosius, a Roman noble, to write him fables (*fabulae*) in which he might take pleasure. Avianus complied with this request, and wrote some fables for him. Not only was he able to enjoy these, but also to observe an allegorical sense (*allegoricus sensus*) in each, for each fable has its own intention and its own moral (*moralitas*). The fables, then, are either Libystic or Aesopic.[21] They are Libystic when conversation between men talking to beasts, or beasts talking to men, is feigned. They are Aesopic when animals (or else inanimate objects, such as trees and the like) are feigned talking among themselves. The stories themselves and the common profit conveyed by the allegory form the subject-matter. His intention is to amuse us in the fables and to profit us by correcting our morals.[22] Their usefulness is the pleasure given by the verse and the correction of behaviour. It pertains to ethics because it deals with the correction of behaviour....[23]

Introduction to Homer[24]

Homer wrote two books in Greek, the *Odyssey* and the *Iliad*. Virgil imitates both these books of Homer. In the first six books [of the *Aeneid*]

[19] Cf. *Rhetorica ad Herennium*, I. iv. 6; Isidore, *Ety.* ii. vii. 2.
[20] *Disticha*, ed. Boas-Botschuyver, p. 4.
[21] This distinction and the following definitions are from Isidore, *Ety.* I. xl. 2.
[22] For the pairing of profit and delight see Horace, *Ars poetica*, 333.
[23] We omit a summary of the allegorical points made by the fables, and also the *accessus* to Maximianus which follows.
[24] i.e. the *Ilias Latina*, a condensation of the *Iliad* in 1,070 hexameters, ed. Ae. (= E.) Baehrens, *Poetae Latini minores*, iii (Leipzig, 1881), pp. 7–59; normally dated to the 1st c. AD, but see D. Armstrong, *Philologus*, cxxx (1986), 114.

he imitates the *Odyssey*—this is a laudatory poem, for *ode* means 'praise'. For just as Homer showed Ulysses overcoming the dangers of the sea in his book, so Virgil showed Aeneas doing likewise in his. Virgil imitates the *Iliad* in his last six books. The *Iliad* is the tale (*fabula*) of the destruction of Troy. Here again Virgil imitates Homer in writing about the war between Turnus and Aeneas. But because Virgil did not describe all the action fully, a certain Latin Homer imitates the Greek Homer in that part, and his [i.e. the Latin Homer's] intention is either to imitate this Greek Homer or to describe the Trojan War. His [i.e. the Latin Homer's] subject-matter is Troy or Greece; the usefulness of his work is to give us a knowledge of the Trojan War. Or, alternatively, his subject-matter is drawn from those who, as a result of an illicit union, caused the war. His intention, then, is to dissuade anyone from such an illicit union, as a result of which he may incur the wrath of the gods, as did Paris, Helen, and the more courageous among their relatives who perished along with Troy in that war. The usefulness is that, having witnessed the destruction of the guilty, we may be afraid to offend the majesty of the gods by any offence, be it slight or serious. It pertains to ethics. He divides the poem into three parts: the statement of his purpose (*propositio*), the invocation (*invocatio*), and the narrative (*narratio*). He combines the statement of his purpose and the invocation. He begins the narrative where he says FOR HE MADE [6].

Introduction to the *Physiologus*[25]

This book is entitled *Phisiologus*. *Phisis* in Greek is *natura* ('nature') in Latin, *logos* in Greek is *sermo* ('discourse') in Latin. Hence *Phisiologus* is a discourse about nature. The animals which are introduced into it form its subject-matter. Its intention is to provide amusement in the form of the animals and to edify in its use of figures.[26] Its usefulness is that we should learn of the natures of animals and their figurative properties. It pertains to physical science because it deals with the natures of animals.

Introduction to Theodolus[27]

Theodolus, the son of parents of quite noble stock, who were Christians, was brought up as a boy in Italy and studied in Greece as a young man.[28]

[25] *Physiologus Latinus, versio B*, ed. F. J. Carmody (Paris, 1939); *versio Y*, ed. Carmody (University of California Publications in Classical Philology XII/7, Berkeley and Los Angeles, 1941).

[26] Cf. Horace, *Ars poetica*, 333.

[27] *Sic* for Theodulus, here and below. See the edition of the *Ecloga Theoduli* by J. Osternacher (Urfahr, 1902); also R. P. H. Green, 'The Genesis of a Medieval Textbook: the Models and Sources of the *Ecloga Theoduli*', *Viator*, xiii (1982), 49–106; G. L. Hamilton, "Theodulus: A Medieval Textbook', *MP* vii (1909/10), 169–86.

[28] This follows the most ancient *vita* of Theodulus, which appears for the first time in Bernard of Utrecht's *Commentum in Theodulum*: see *Accessus ad auctores, etc.*, ed. Huygens, pp. 59–60.

So, being well versed in both languages, while he was at Athens he heard pagans debating with Christians. He gathered up their arguments and on his return to Italy put them all into an allegorical eclogue. This poem he did not revise, as his work was cut short by his death, and so you will find a few verses in this work which have false quantities, like: *Dic et Troianum lauderis scire secretum*, which has shortened the *se* incorrectly.[29] He was a man distinguished by his high moral qualities and his knowledge, and when he died was living under the clerical rule. The word *Egloga* was derived from goats, for *egle* in Greek is *capra* ('goat') in Latin, while *logos* is *sermo* ('discourse'), hence the word *egloga* means 'a discourse relating to goats'.

His subject-matter is a comparison of profound sayings (*sententiae*) drawn from ecclesiastical and from pagan writings, and the characters (*personae*) who debate in these. His intention is to show the strength of truth and the inadequacy of falsehood, and that traditional Catholic teaching excels the pagan religion as truth excels falsehood. The usefulness is that, when we have seen falsehood vanquished, we may abandon it and follow the light of truth. It pertains to ethics. Its title is *Here begins the Egloga of Theodolus*. Two characters (*personae*) are introduced here, Pseustis and Alithia. Their names are very appropriate. For Pseustis takes her stand on falsehood, and Alithia is interpreted as the divine truth. *Ali* in Hebrew means 'truth', *thia* 'God'.[30] The author is not called Theodolus without good reason, for he is treating of truth and falsehood. *Theos* in Greek is *deus* ('God') in Latin, *dolus* is 'deceit', which is shown up in the subject-matter and by the characters (*personae*) introduced into the poem. Or, according to some, Theodolus means 'the servant of God', because it behoves every servant of God to separate truth from falsehood. So the title breaks down to give the following meaning: *Incipit Egloga Theodoli*, that is, 'a discourse concerning goats held among shepherds and put together (*compositus*) by Theodolus'.

Introduction to Arator[31]

This Arator was a pagan and a Roman citizen, for at that time Christians and pagans lived together at Rome. In the time of Pope Vigilius Rome was besieged by Theodoric, king of the Goths. With God's help Vigilius freed the Romans from actual physical death and by converting some saved their souls also. Now, when Arator saw that the god of Vigilius, by whose help he had been saved, was such a powerful god, he decided to accept

---

[29] The commentator is correctly pointing out that the *se* in *secretum* has been irregularly shortened in the scansion here. Cf. D. S. Raven, *Latin Metre: An Introduction* (London, 1965), p. 25.

[30] Not Hebrew, but highly fractured Greek.

[31] *Aratoris subdiaconi de actibus Apostolorum*, ed. A. P. McKinlay (CSEL lxxii).

the Christian faith and was baptized by Pope Vigilius. After he had accepted the faith he learned to read and progressed so far on the path of virtue that he was made a subdeacon in the church at Rome. He attained to such a degree of knowledge that he composed this book. The subject-matter of this book is an account of the acts of the apostles in historical and allegorical terms. Its intention is to encourage us in the direction of the Christian virtues by setting before us the good deeds of certain men whose authority stands high in the Church, namely, the apostles. Its usefulness is that we should follow their footsteps with simple hearts, lest by imitating them in the wrong way we incur the same condemnation as Ananias and Sapphira. It pertains to ethics, that is, to moral science, because it deals with behaviour. Arator composes two letters, which he uses as a prologue. One is to Abbot Florian, so that his work may be all the more acceptable when such an important man reads it. The other he writes to Pope Vigilius, thanking him because he has saved him from death of the body, and even more for having saved him from death of the soul. And he exhorts each and every one of us to give thanks for the benefits conferred upon him. . . .[32]

Introduction to Sedulius[33]

At the start of this book we must enquire into seven things: the life of the poet, the title of the work, the nature of the verse, the intention of the writer, the number of the books, ⟨the order of the books,⟩ and the explanation.[34] The poet's life is said to have been as follows.[35] He was a layman and a pagan, but he studied philosophy in Italy in the time of the consuls Theodosius and Valentinus. Then he was converted and baptized by a Macedonian priest, and came to Achaia, where he composed this book to demolish the erroneous teaching of the pagans. According to Servius the term *titulus* ('title') comes from Titan, that is, the sun, either by a process of diminishing (*diminutio*) or by comparison.[36] It is said to come through diminution because the light of that work is small in relation to the whole sun; by comparison ⟨because⟩, just as the rising sun gives light to the whole world, so the title illuminates the work that follows. The title of

---

[32] *Accessus* to Prosper omitted.

[33] *Sedulii opera omnia: Accedunt excerpta ex Remigii expositione in Sedulii Paschale carmen*, ed. I. Huemer (CSEL x. 14–146). The *Carmen Paschale* has been translated by George Sigerson, *The Easter Song, by Sedulius* (Dublin and London, 1922).

[34] This is the 'type B' prologue, as found at the beginning of Servius's commentary on the *Aeneid*. Cf. our introduction to this chapter.

[35] Cf. the brief *vita* in Remigius of Auxerre's *Expositio in Paschale carmen*, ed. by Huemer in the appendix to his edition of Sedulius (CSEL x. 316).

[36] For this etymology cf. Remigius, *In Artem Donati minorem commentum*, ed. W. Fox (Leipzig, 1892), p. 1; also Bernard of Utrecht, *Commentum in Theodulum*, ed. Huygens, *Accessus ad auctores, etc.*, p. 61. The Servius reference is to his gloss on the *Aeneid*, vi. 580, where, however, the explicit equation of Titan with the sun is not made; that is found in Isidore, *Ety.* viii. xi. 53.

that work is: *Incipit Paschale Carmen* ('Here begins the Easter Song'). We can see what the subject-matter is by the title, for this book treats of the miracles of the paschal lamb, that is, Christ. The nature of the verse can be discerned in this, that it is said to have been composed in heroic verse, for the deeds of kings and princes were recounted in heroic verse in olden times.[37] In this verse he has written of the miracles of the King of Kings. Its intention is to destroy the pagan religion and to reveal the path of the true faith. The number of books is this: he divides this work up into four books. Their order is as follows. In the first book he treats of those miracles which God the Father (together with the Son and the Holy Spirit) performed in the Old Testament. Then in the following three books he treats of those miracles which the Son performed, together with the Father and the Holy Spirit, under the new dispensation. Next comes the explanation. This entails setting out the contents of the whole book. For, like other poets, he reveals his purpose, invokes and narrates.[38] He reveals his purpose when he says EASTER SACRIFICE [i. 1], he invokes when he says ALMIGHTY [i. 60], he begins his narration when he says FIRST OF ALL [i. 103].

Introduction to Ovid's *Epistles* [= the *Heroides*] ⟨I⟩

The intention of this work is to castigate men and women who are held fast in the grip of foolish and unlawful love. Heroes and married women form its subject-matter. It pertains to ethics, which inculcates good morality and eradicates evil behaviour. In the first epistle Penelope[39] is commended because she held fast to her lawful love and, contrariwise, those who act differently are castigated. Ulysses was one of the Greeks who had come to destroy Troy. Because he had offended the gods in many, ways there, he spent seven years wandering, though his intention had been to return home. But though his wife Penelope was being courted by many suitors, her love of her husband made her scorn them all. Since she did not know where he was, she sent him this letter which, if he could be found, might be brought to him.

Introduction to Ovid's *Epistles* [= the *Heroides*] ⟨II⟩

It must be understood that Ovid was the first to have written letters at Rome, not in imitation of any Roman—for no Roman poet had written letters up to that time—but of a Greek whose letters he had seen. *Epistola* ('letter') means 'sent aloft', because it sends words aloft.[40] The senders

[37] Cf. Isidore, *Ety.* i. xxxix. 9.
[38] Cf. Remigius, *Expositio in Pas. carm.* (CSEL x. 323).
[39] Here, and often in the following introductions to Ovid's *Epistles*, the form 'Penelope' is used.
[40] Cf. the similar statements concerning Horace's *Epistles* made in the Introduction to the *Art of Poetry* (and other works by Horace), translated below.

and recipients of letters are Ovid's subject-matter in this work. His intention is to commend lawful marriage and love, and, in keeping with this end, he deals with love in three forms: lawful love, unlawful love, and foolish love. He uses the example of Penelope to discuss lawful love, the example of Canace to discuss unlawful love, and the example of Phyllis to discuss foolish love. He includes two of the forms, foolish and unlawful love, not for their own sake, but in order to commend the third. Thus, in commending lawful love he criticizes foolish and unlawful love.[41] The work pertains to ethics, because he is teaching good morality and eradicating evil behaviour. The ultimate end (*finalis causa*) of the work is this, that, having seen the advantage (*utilitas*) gained from lawful love, and the misfortunes which arise from foolish and unlawful love, we may shun both of these and may adhere to chaste love.

So, the intention in this first letter is that of the sender Penelope, namely, to remove the grounds for any accusations which Ulysses may make against her and to persuade him to hasten his return, and she informs him of the many hardships caused at home by his long delay. Ulysses had offended the gods in many ways during the siege of Troy. After the destruction of Troy, when he wished to return home, he wandered seven years at sea. His wife Penelope kept her marriage-vow inviolate. She rejected many who were frequently her suitors because of her beauty. Not knowing where Ulysses was she wrote him this letter which would be given to him if found somewhere. Ovid, speaking in the character (*persona*) of Penelope, says: ULYSSES, PENELOPE SENDS YOU THIS GREETING, OR RATHER THIS LETTER. I WHO AM CONSTANT IN MY LOVE OF YOU, AM ADDRESSING YOU WHO ARE SO SLOW IN RETURNING [cf. *Her.* i. 1–2].

⟨Introduction⟩ to Ovid's *Epistles* [= the *Heroides*] ⟨III⟩

At the start of this book we must enquire into six things: the life of the poet, the title of the work, the intention of the writer, the subject-matter, the usefulness of the book, and to what part of philosophy it pertains.

The life of this poet is as follows. He is said to have been a native of Sulmona, a fact to which he himself bears witness: 'Sulmona is my native soil.'[42]

---

[41] For discussion of the commentators' attempts to defend the use of contrary *exempla* within an overall moral framework, with special reference to expositions of Ovid's *Heroides* and of the Psalter, see Minnis, *Authorship*, pp. 54–6.

[42] *Tristia*, IV. x. 3. On the other *vitae* of Ovid see the bibliography in Quain, 'Medieval *Accessus ad auctores*', p. 222 n. 13; also F. Munari, *Ovid im Mittelalter* (Zurich, 1960), and Ghisalberti, 'Medieval Biographies of Ovid', *passim*. Cf. the *vita* in the prologue to Giovanni del Virgilio's *Metamorphoses* commentary, tr. below, Ch. VIII. On Ovid as a scientific *auctor* and teacher of ethics see S. Viarre, *La Survie d'Ovide dans la littérature scientifique des XIII* et XIII* siècles* (Poitiers, 1966), and Demats, *Fabula*, pp. 107–77. For the view that John Gower's *Confessio amantis* was influenced by *Ovidius ethicus* see A. J. Minnis, '"Moral Gower" and Medieval Literary Theory', in id. (ed.) *Gower's* Confessio amantis: *Responses and Reassessments* (Cambridge, 1983), pp. 55–9.

He was born in the region of the Paeligni; his father was called Publius
and his mother Pelagia. His brother Lucius joined the ranks of the rhetoricians, but Ovid studied poetry. It must be understood that before Ovid's
time no one wrote letters at Rome, but Ovid, in his time, was the first to
compose letters, in imitation of a certain Greek author.

The title of a literary work is derived from its subject-matter, as is the
case with letters.[43] It is also derived from a place and a character (*persona*),
as is the case with the *Phormio* and *Eunuchus*, or from the actions performed by the characters, as in the *Auctontumerumenos*,[44] that is, 'The Self-
Tormentor', and in *Sic faciunt astra* ('This the stars do'),[45] or from its
subject-matter as with Cicero, *On Friendship*. This title too is derived
from the subject-matter, for it is entitled by some, 'Ovid, [*Book of*] *Letters*',
the reason being that there are various letters in this volume, which could
have been sent, or were sent, to Greeks who were at the siege of Troy, or
on their way to or from there, in each case the letters being sent by their
wife. *Epi* in Greek is *supra* ('aloft') in Latin; *stola* is *missa* ('sent'). Letters
are sent for some necessary reason and are received by the persons who
form the subject-matter of the letter. So, some give the book the title,
'*Ovid, Heroum*', that is, '[book of] married women', or *librum Heroidos*
(*heros, herois* is a Greek masculine word and signifies 'noble Greek
women' [*sic.*]). It gets its title for this very reason, that it was written in the
persons of those noble Greek women whose husbands were still detained
at the siege of Troy, and because *heroides* were the more noble matrons in
Greece, and it was by them, and for the most part to their loved ones, that
these letters were sent.

So much for the title. Now let us consider the intention. His intention
is to write about the three kinds of love: foolish love, unchaste love, and
demented love. For his example of foolish love he takes Phyllis, who
allowed Demophon to return home to settle his affairs, and, being unable
to await his return, hanged herself out of an excess of love. For his
example of unchaste love he takes Helen, who was snatched from her lawful husband Menelaus and married Paris. His example of demented love
is Canace, who loved her own brother Machareus. Another interpretation
is that the intention of this book is to commend chaste love as it appears in
certain *heroides*, that is, noble Greek women, one of whom is Penelope,
wife of Ulysses; or to attack unchaste love as it appears in unchaste
married women, one of whom was Phaedra. Another interpretation is that
the intention is to praise some of those who write the letters for their

[43] This begins a list of the ways in which a literary work may be titled. Letters are named
after their subject-matter, the *Phormio* and *Eunuchus* are named after a place and a character
respectively, and so forth.

[44] *Sic* for the *Heautontimorumenos*, a play by Terence, as are the *Phormio* and *Eunuchus*.

[45] Apparently taken from Macrobius, *In somnium Scipionis*, i. xix. 27; tr. W. H. Stahl,
Macrobius: Commentary on the Dream of Scipio (New York and London, 1952), p. 168. But
Macrobius has 'si faciunt astra', not 'sic faciunt'.

chastity, and to blame some for their unchaste love. According to another interpretation, Ovid's intention is that since, in his manual on the art of love, he does not explain how someone might be courted by letter, he completes this part of his teaching here. According to another interpretation his intention in this book is to encourage the pursuit of virtue and to reject vice. He was himself accused before Caesar of having in his writing taught Roman married women how to conduct unchaste love-affairs. So he wrote this book for them, setting it forth in an exemplifying manner, so that they might know which women they should or should not imitate in their love. It must be understood also that although throughout the whole book he has this intention, and those mentioned above, there are two further intentions in this book, one general and one particular. The general intention is to give pleasure and to give profitable advice to all his readers. But he has a particular intention in individual letters, either praising chaste love as in THIS LETTER YOUR PENELOPE [i. 1], or attacking unchaste love, as in UNLESS YOU GIVE THIS [iv. 1].[46] And different letters have different intentions, because he had different purposes in mind in setting out ⟨to commend⟩ some for their chastity and blame others for their unchaste love.

The subject-matter consists of the letters themselves, or the married women who write them. The usefulness or ultimate end (*finalis causa*) of the book differs according to the various intentions, depending on whether the intention is the recognition of unchaste or foolish forms of love, or else to show how some women may be courted by letter, or how the results of living chastely may benefit us. Alternatively, the ultimate end of the book is that by commending those who engage in chaste love, he may encourage us to chaste love. Or else, having seen the advantages (*utilitas*) of lawful love and the disasters or disadvantages which result from unlawful and foolish love, we may reject and shun foolish love and adhere to lawful love. It pertains to ethics, since it teaches us about lawful love.

There are three methods of reciting, the exegematic, the dramatic (where characters are introduced), and the *misticon* or *cinamicticon* (where [both the poet and the introduced characters speak]).[47] Ovid uses the dramatic method, because he has no invocation, nor does he set out what his subject is to be. If he were to do that he would be using the exegematic method.

In this first letter [is seen] the steadfastness of the chastity of Penelope, wife of Ulysses, whom the poet has introduced as an example of chastity.

[46] i.e. the greeting (*salus*) of Phaedra to Hippolytus, with a play on the alternative meaning of *salus*, 'life': the letter gives him new life and hope.

[47] A commonplace distinction, so the lacuna in the text may confidently be filled with the information we have supplied within square brackets. It goes back to Servius' prologue to his commentary on Virgil's *Bucolics*: *In Vergilii carmina commentarii*, ed. G. Thilo and H. Hagen (Leipzig, 1881), iii. 1–2, and is found in Isidore, *Ety.* viii. vii. 11. Cf. Minnis, *Authorship*, pp. 22, 57–8.

His purpose is to praise Penelope, not only for her chastity but also for the way in which she kept faith with her husband Ulysses all the time he remained at the siege of Troy. For, while other wives did not wait for their husbands even for two or three years, she waited for hers for nineteen, and remained most chaste, though many nobles and wealthier men than Ulysses wished to take her to wife. Ulysses of Ithaca was one of the Greek leaders who had banded together and come to destroy Troy. At first he had feigned madness and did not go to the war with the other leaders, but ploughed with two quite different animals yoked together and sowed salt. Palimedes, putting his own son Antilochus in the furrow, recalled Ulysses and forced him to go to Troy. After the destruction of Troy, though he was intending to return home, he wandered for ten years because he had offended the gods in many ways. Some say that he stayed at the war for seven years, some for twelve, and some for ten. While his wife Penelope was being courted by other men she sent him this letter, so that if he could be found it might be brought to him, for, scorning all the suitors, she was fired with longing only for her husband. But because she surpassed all other women in chastity, the author gives her first place [i.e. in the collection of letters] and, because she was faithful to her husband, she is commended in this letter, and by contrast those who do not do likewise are castigated. So, with the intention of drawing him back to her she sends him these chaste words of greeting THIS LETTER YOUR PENELOPE [i. 1] that is, she who continues in her love for you SENDS THIS namely the letter or greeting. . . .

⟨Introduction⟩ to Ovid, *On the Art of Love*

His purpose in this work is to instruct young men in the art of love, and how they should behave towards girls when having a love-affair. The young men and girls, and the advice in love which it is his intention to give the young men, form his subject-matter. The way he proceeds (*modus*) in this work is to show how a girl may be picked up,[48] how when picked up she may be won over, and, once won over, how her love may be retained. His ultimate objective (*finalis causa*) is that, when the book with the instructions he gives in it has been read thoroughly, the course they should follow in a love-affair should be made clear to young men. It pertains to ethics, because it speaks of the behaviour of young girls, that is, the sort of morals they should have, and how they may be kept faithful.[49] One should also observe that Ovid follows the custom of correct writers. He puts forward his case, he makes an appeal, and he narrates. He puts forward his case when he says IF ANYONE IN THIS [i. 1], he makes an appeal when he says BE PRESENT, MOTHER [i. 30], he narrates when he says FIRST OF ALL [TRY TO FIND] SOMETHING TO LOVE [i. 35].

48 Lat. 'ostendere quo modo puella possit inveniri'.
49 Or, how these may be retained. Lat. 'quibus modis retineri valeant'.

Introduction to Ovid, *On the Remedy for Love*

This author, Ovid, wrote a manual of love in which he taught young men where to acquire mistresses, and how to treat them well when they had acquired them, and he had given girls the same instructions. But some young men indulged their passion to excess and were not in the least reluctant to have affairs with virgins, and even married women and female relatives, while the young women submitted themselves to married just as much as to unmarried men. The result was that Ovid became very unpopular with his friends and with others. Afterwards he regretted what he had done, and, being anxious to be reconciled with those he had offended, he saw that the best way of achieving this was to discover the antidote for the love he had proffered to them. So he set out to write this book in which he advises both young men and girls trapped in the snares of love as to how they may arm themselves against unlawful love. He prescribes just like a doctor. For a good doctor gives medicine to the sick to heal them, and to the healthy so that they may escape illness.

At the beginning of certain works some points will occur which need to be investigated so that, once they have been carefully gone into and understood with discernment, they may make it easy for the readers (*auditores*) to understand that work. Just so, at the beginning of this book we ought to investigate certain points so that through a thorough and intelligent investigation of them the whole work that follows may be made clearer to us. Let us then consider how many things are examined in this book and what they are. There are four in all: first of all the subject-matter, secondly the intention, then the reason for the intention (*causa intentionis*), and finally to what division of philosophy it pertains. Young men and girls caught in the grip of unlawful love form the subject-matter of this book. Its intention is to give certain precepts whereby it may remove unlawful love.[50] The reason [for the intention] is that those who are held captive by unlawful love may be set free, and those who are not as yet captives may know how to avoid being made captive. So he begins his book with a question which someone might pose to him, saying: IN YOUR EARLIER BOOK, THE *ART OF LOVE*, YOU TAUGHT YOUNG MEN HOW TO MAKE LOVE. BUT NOW YOU ARE WRITING A *REMEDY FOR LOVE* FOR THEM. YOU APPEAR TO BE CONTRADICTING YOURSELF. Ovid's reply is: YOU MUST NOT CAST THIS UP AT ME, FOR LOVE HIMSELF HAS ALREADY DONE SO, AND I GAVE HIM MY ANSWER: AND LOVE BLITHELY WENT HIS WAY AND TOLD ME TO COMPLETE MY WORK [cf. 39–40].

Introduction to Ovid, *From Pontus*

In this book, as in all the others, the usual questions are asked: the author's intention, the subject-matter, its usefulness, to what division of

[50] i.e. eradicate it from the heart of the lover.

philosophy it pertains. His intention is to persuade each and every one of us to help a true friend in his hour of need. The author's friends, to whom he writes, are its subject-matter—he sends each of them a different letter—or else the words he uses to plead with them. Its usefulness is very great, if he can obtain mercy from Octavian Caesar through the intercession of his friends to whom he sends the letters. It pertains to ethics, that is, to moral science, for in each letter he discusses behaviour.

This book is said to have been composed in Pontus, an island in Scythia, where Ovid had been exiled by Octavian Caesar because of the book he had written about love, which had been the means of corrupting Roman matrons. Or, some people think that it was because Octavian had discovered that Ovid had had an affair with his wife or son [sic]. It was while he was suffering many hardships there in Pontus that he sent individual letters to each of his friends asking them to help him. These he collected and sent to the keeper of the treasury, Brutus, asking him to store them in a chest along with his other books. He writes this first epistle, beginning as follows: NASO, IN THE LAND OF TOMI [I. i. 1]. Ovid's other name was 'Naso'. It is a surname[51] bestowed on him from the circumstances of his having a large nose. He writes THE LAND OF TOMI because it was there that Medea tore her brother limb by limb to delay her father, who was pursuing her when she was fleeing with Jason. For *thomos* means 'a dividing', whence comes *Thomitanae*, that is, 'division'. He continues NOT A NEW SETTLER because he had languished there for a long time.

⟨Introduction⟩ to Ovid's *Tristia*

In this book of Ovid's we must look into six things: the title of the work, its subject-matter, the intention, the reason for that intention, its usefulness, and the division of philosophy to which it pertains. This work gets its title from the reason why it was written (*causa*), because its author was enduring a life of sadness (*tristitia*). Its subject-matter is a description of the dangers facing Ovid, or else it is the friends, to each of whom he sends letters. His intention is to urge each of them, through his writings, to intercede for him with Caesar. The reason for that intention is that, because he had been sent into exile, yet with some hope of return, they should assuage Caesar's anger by their entreaties and obtain permission for him to return. The usefulness is that the work might cause Caesar's

---

[51] An *agnomen*, an additional name denoting a characteristic; a nickname or appellation (*OLD*). In the Roman system of naming, a citizen had three names: the personal name (*praenomen*), the family or clan name (*nomen*), and the *cognomen*, an extra name, usually derived from a characteristic, but not necessarily one which that particular person possessed (i.e. it could have been common in one's family as a distinguishing name for several generations). For this reason grammarians of the late classical period use *agnomen* to denote an extra nickname appropriate to one person, as distinct from the *cognomen*, which was a nickname that had been handed down within a family.

fierce anger to subside, and allow Ovid to regain his beloved native land. It pertains to ethics because it treats of behaviour. The question of why he was sent into exile is asked. Three opinions are given. The first is that he had an affair with Livia, Caesar's wife.[52] The second is that, being on close terms with Caesar, and chancing to pass through his portico, he saw Caesar cohabiting with his favourite male lover, and so Caesar, fearing that he might be betrayed by him, sent him into exile. The third reason is that he had written a book, *On the Art of Love*, in which he had taught young men how to deceive and attract married women. This gave offence to the Romans, and it was for this reason that he is alleged to have been sent into exile.

There are said to have been four kinds of exile among the Romans: proscription, proclamation, relegation, and exile. The man whose goods were made public property, while he himself was sent into exile without any hope of return, was said to be 'proscribed'. The man whose goods equally became public property but who was kept under arrest at home among his friends was said to be 'proclaimed'. The man whose goods did not become public property, while he was sent into exile with some hope of return, was said to be 'relegated', while the man whose goods became public property while he was sent into exile with some hope of return was referred to as 'an exile'.

⟨Introduction⟩ to Ovid's *Book without a Title* [= the *Amores*] ⟨I⟩

Various reasons are given as to why this book is entitled *without a title*. One is that he [i.e. Ovid] feared those enemies who habitually criticized his writings lest, having read the title, they would denigrate the work. Another is that he feared Augustus Caesar who he knew had taken offence at the *Art of Love*, because in that book Ovid had fictitiously placed the Roman matrons in the setting of a brothel. He knew that he would be even more offended if he read this title. For here too some of the subject-matter relates to love. The third reason was that Augustus had ordered him to write of his war against Antony and Cleopatra; so Ovid had intended to compose five books [on this subject] but was deflected by Cupid, and thus composed these three books, in which he takes his mistress, or love, as his subject. His intention is to give pleasure. The book pertains to ethics. Ovid is said to have begun a book about the war between the giants at Octavian's command, but Cupid removed him from this task. Having finished the first book, he prefaces the second by a prologue in which he reveals the true name of the author, and gives a sketch of the subject-matter of the following, and of the preceding book. Having completed two books, he prefaces the third with a prologue in which he reveals that he had been compelled by Elegy to write the third

[52] i.e. the wife of Caesar Augustus.

book about love. By writing about love he achieved very great fame, but also incurred very deep disgrace. While he was hesitating as to what subject he should take as the starting-point of his work, Tragedy suddenly came to him and urged him to write about her. But Elegy came and contradicted Tragedy and forced Ovid to make her the subject of his third book, as described above. At the beginning of the prologue he describes the beauty of the place where those great goddesses forgathered. It should be understood that Tragedy is the goddess of poetry about the deeds of nobles and kings, while Elegy is said to be the goddess of sorrow—and in love various misuses and adversities befall men. Elegy is written in an unequal metre,[53] and in hexameters.

⟨Introduction⟩ to Ovid's *Book without a Title* [= the *Amores*] ⟨II⟩

This book of Ovid's is said to be about love. Its subject-matter is his mistress Corinna. The end he has in view (*finalis causa*), that is, the usefulness of the book, is that we should recognize in it verbal embellishments (*ornatus verborum*) and an attractive word-order (*pulchras positiones*). One should appreciate the difference between Ovid's *Amores*[54] and his *On the Art of Love*. In his *On the Art of Love* Ovid gives certain precepts to lovers to put them on their guard. But here, in the *Amores*, he puts these precepts into practise in his own case. The reason why this book [i.e. the *Amores*] has no title must be understood as follows. Before he wrote it, he had written *On the Art of Love* and had made adulteresses of almost all the married women and maidens. This had made the Romans hostile towards him, and so, in case this book should incur even greater disfavour, he did not give it a title, and we readers call it Ovid's *Book without a Title*. His original purpose had been to describe the battle between gods and giants in the Phlegraean valley, in five books, but to avoid boring his readers (*lectores*) he removed two of these five; and he speaks of his purpose (*propositum*) in writing in the light of this. Here he has a prosopopoeia, that is, the books talking as if they were rational beings, inanimate objects talking as if they were alive.[55]

⟨Introduction⟩ to Ovid's *Fasti*

They say that certain books existed at Rome from time immemorial which got their title from the function they performed, for they were called *Fasti*. It should be understood that that noun was derived from *fas* ('right', 'what is lawful'), for *fastus* means 'what is permitted'. So certain days were called *fasti*, meaning so to speak 'permitted days'. It was the custom for

---

[53] i.e. the pentameter.
[54] i.e. the 'Book without a title' which the commentator is here introducing.
[55] With this definition cf. Isidore, *Ety.* II. xiii, II. xxi. 45.

the Romans of old to have any day on which they suffered adversity or disaster marked off in the *Fasti*, so that by thus marking them off they should bequeath to posterity an example of upright living, and in this way encourage them to the pursuit of eternal renown. It should be understood also that the Roman poets wrote about the history of their state, sometimes at such length, and sometimes in such brief compass, that, out of ignorance of which days are lawful (*fasti*) and which unlawful (*nefasti*), they were almost all so far out in their calculations, that they turned upside-down the whole usage of sacrifice, so much so that they did not sacrifice on lawful days and sacrificed to the gods on unlawful days.

Ovid knew that just then he was unpopular with the Romans because of his poem *On the Art of Love*, for many were being led astray by that guide to love. So he undertook to set in order that material [that is, the garbled knowledge of lawful and unlawful days] and compressed lengthy volumes into a compact treatise, for two reasons: to unravel the usage of sacrifice, and to pacify the Romans whom he had offended. The title of this book is: *Here begins Ovid's Fasti*. At this point this objection is made. Why, when that book treats of both days which were lawful and days which were unlawful to the Romans, should it have the title 'lawful' (*fasti*) rather than 'unlawful' (*nefasti*) days? The answer to this is that the book received its name from its more impressive part. We see this happening in many cases. For example, in the case of Horace his work is entitled *The Book of Lyrics and Odes*, and yet laudatory poems do not make up the entire contents, but it draws its name from its more impressive element. Likewise in the case of Terence, the plays get their title from the characters (*personae*) who have the biggest role in the comedy, as for instance *Andria* from the island of Andros, and *Eunuchus* from the character of the eunuch.

One should also be aware of the excessive subtlety of some of those who write about lawful and unlawful days, for they interpret them in quite the wrong way. We said above that 'lawful days' were favourable days, on which it was lawful to administer the laws and make sacrifices, but 'unlawful days' were days on which the Roman senate decreed that none of these activities should take place. But some are of the opinion that 'lawful days' were so called from the business of the city, and that on those days men ought to be at leisure, and it was not permitted to administer the laws of the Romans or to sacrifice any victims to the gods. And they call 'unlawful' those days on which it had been laid down that men should not abstain from taking part in the aforesaid activities. Ovid's testimony will help you to recognize the errors of these and similar writers, for he says: THAT DAY WILL BE UNLAWFUL DURING WHICH THREE WORDS ARE NOT SPOKEN; THAT WILL BE LAWFUL, DURING WHICH LEGAL BUSINESS CAN BE DONE [i. 47–8].[56] ·

[56] The three words were *do*, *dico*, *addico*, used formally by the *praetor*, the highest law officer of the Roman state. When he gave leave to bring a suit into court under the procedure of the Twelve Tables, he said *do* 'I grant [leave]'; when he laid down the law on a particular

There is also some doubt as to when he composed this book. Some say that he composed it when he was in exile, others that it was written before he was exiled, so that by writing it he might mollify Caesar.

Now, since we have explained about the stumbling-blocks which are to be found right at the beginning of the work, let us proceed to discuss his subject-matter and intention. In this work his subject-matter is lawful and unlawful days, his intention is to compress lengthy volumes and similarly tedious material into a compact treatise. The reason for his intention is that he should be able to teach the usage of official sacrifices and how sacrifices ought to be presented on solemn feast days.

The question arises as to why he interpolates into his treatise a discussion of the rising and setting of the stars. The answer is that he has interpolated this material about the heavenly bodies so that he may show (by the setting or rising of some constellation) that day is at hand. One should pay careful attention to the question of what part of philosophy it pertains to, but it must be recognized that for the most part it falls within the sphere of ethics. However, as regards the part we have just mentioned, where he interpolates material about the heavenly bodies, it clearly pertains to physical science. . . .[57]

Introduction to Tully [i.e. Cicero][58]

Cato, a master of the Latin language, migrated to Greece. Since it was his intention to pursue studies there, he joined the Stoic school and became perfectly versed in their teachings. Subsequently, he came to Rome and promulgated many judgements (*sententiae*) in the senate which he subsequently made effective, but did not collect into a book. So, after his death, his enemies used all their efforts to try to nullify everything that they saw he had enforced during his lifetime. Brutus, a relative of the aforesaid Cato, realized this, and asked his friend Cicero, whom he knew to be very well versed in logic, to confirm Cato's judgements and completely overthrow the machinations of his enemies. Wishing to meet this request he has made Cato's judgements the subject-matter in this little book, but he has [two] different intentions. His main intention is to confirm Cato's judgements and refute those of his enemies. The usefulness of this work is the confirmation of these judgements. But another intention is to profit his readers and give pleasure.[59] Here the usefulness is the attaining of

point he said *dico ius* 'I state the law', and when he decreed that property rightfully belonged to one or other of two claimants he was said *addicere bona*, 'to assign the property'. Cf. J. G. Frazer's note to *Fasti*, i. 47 in his edition of this text (London, 1929), ii. 63. Thus, on a *dies nefastus* the praetor would not receive suits under this procedure.

[57] *accessus* to Lucan omitted.
[58] Apparently an introduction to Cicero's *Paradoxa*.
[59] Cf. once again Horace, *Ars poetica*, 333; note the use of this tag in the *Accessūs* to Avianus and the *Physiologus*, tr. above.

perfection. By reason of the ethical element in it, it pertains to theoretical philosophy (*theorica*); because of its confirming of judgements by the use of argument it pertains to logic. . . .[60]

⟨Introduction⟩ to Priscian

Though there are [two] separate volumes, 'The Greater Priscian' which is concerned with the eight parts of speech and 'The Lesser Priscian' which deals with constructions, yet they are regarded as one book.[61] In the same way, the Book of Psalms is regarded as a single book, even though the individual psalms may (according to some sacred [i.e. Christian] writers) be regarded as separate entities.[62] In the same way, among the [classical] authors for example Ovid's *Metamorphoses* and Lucan [i.e. the *Bellum civile*] are each regarded as one book, though being made up of several books.

This is also the case with Priscian, a conclusion we can draw from the fact that this book [i.e. 'The Lesser Priscian'] is continuous with the one mentioned above [i.e. 'The Greater Priscian']. For Priscian himself asserts at the beginning of his work that he is going to treat of the construction or ordering of words in his eighteenth book.[63] He makes the work continuous with the aforementioned when he begins SINCE.[64] All this makes it clear that this work [i.e. 'The Lesser Priscian'] is continuous with the aforementioned, and so we do not need to ask what its subject-matter or particular intention is. But because this [i.e. 'The Lesser Priscian'] is the crowning achievement of his work, and because his argument is more subtle here, and also because all praise must be bestowed at the end of a task, for all these reasons it is not out of place to ask at this point what his subject-matter and intention are. The subject-matter in this work is the construction which is perfect in sound and meaning, as for example *Socrates legit* ('Socrates chose'). His intention is that we should make constructions out of words which fit together properly when linked up, and pronounce these in a reasonable way, so as to make our meaning clear or make the construction

[60] A second *accessus* to Cicero's *Paradoxa*, and an *accessus* to Boethius' *Consolation of Philosophy*, are here omitted.

[61] Priscian's *Institutiones* were written in eighteen books as one unit, with 16 chapters on 'syntax' (what we should call morphology) followed by a treatment of the levels of discourse, and two chapters on 'constructions' (what we should call 'syntax'). The first sixteen books comprised 'The Greater Priscian', and books xvii–xviii, 'The Lesser Priscian', the latter offering the more advanced teaching. This *accessus* is essentially to 'The Lesser Priscian', but, since it follows on from 'The Greater Priscian', that earlier work or part must be included in the discussion.

[62] Cf. Peter Lombard's prologue to his Psalter commentary, and the relevant discussion and notes, below, Ch. III.

[63] Cf. *Inst.*, 'Prisciani ad Iulianum ep.' (*GL* ii. 4).

[64] i.e. the beginning of the seventeenth book; *Inst.* xvii. 1 (*GL* iii. 107).

complete.[65] I mention both suitable pronunciation (*apta pronuntiatio*) and the proper fitting together of words (*congrua copulatio*), because in grammar faulty pronunciation is just as serious a fault as faulty linking of words. For instance, if one were to say *domine venit* one would make as serious a mistake in pronunciation as if one were to say *dominum venit*, because the vocative requires the second person but the nominative requires the third.

Priscian's mode of procedure (*modus*) is as follows. He shows us whom he has imitated in the preceding work [i.e. 'The Greater Priscian'] and whom he is going to imitate in the subsequent one [i.e. 'The Lesser Priscian']. In the preceding work he treats of words taken on their own out of constructions, while in the subsequent work he treats of words joined together meaningfully in constructions. His order of treating his material (*ordo tractandi*) is as follows.[66] Though his intention had been to treat of the subject-matter as outlined at the start, that is, the construction made up of noun and verb, he prefaces his treatment with endless comparisons.[67] Then, lest it should be asked why the noun is put before the verb without any reason being given for this in 'The Greater Priscian', before he discusses the construction of noun and verb he first of all gives a reasoned explanation of why the noun is put before the verb, and does the same for the other questions, and thus concludes the first book. Subsequently, in the second book he begins to treat of his subject-matter, that is, the construction of noun and verb, and thus concludes his treatise.

In the latter book [i.e. book xviii] he deals with the intrinsic art (*intrinseca ars*), and in the first book [i.e. book xvii] with the extrinsic art (*extrinseca ars*). We call the extrinsic art those rules which have been laid down following the agreed usage (*placitum*) of authors. Grammar is called the knowledge of letters, that is, a body of received knowledge (*scientia*) relating to letters. That is a very useful science (*ars*), and no other branch of learning can be known without it, and it is more necessary than dialectic, just as water is more necessary than balsam.

Introduction to *The Art of Poetry* [and other works by Horace]

Horatius Flaccus, the son of a freedman, was born in Apulia and migrated with his father to the Sabine country.[68] His father sent him to Rome to

[65] On *pronuntiatio* see William of Conches's *accessus* to Priscian, tr. below, Ch. IV. It should be realized that a syntactic error, as we should term it, could be a fault in 'pronunciation'.

[66] i.e. this describes how the material in books xvii and xviii (comprising 'The Lesser Priscian') is organized.

[67] Priscian does not actually say that he is going to talk about the construction of the noun and verb (though in practice he does give them prominence): the commentator's statement here reflects his own idea of what grammar is about. Priscian's 'endless comparisons' are in fact a quite sophisticated demonstration of linguistic phenomena such as iteration which operate across linguistic levels, and are used to prove that if the idea of *ordinatio* be conceded at one linguistic level (e.g. in the alphabet) then it must be conceded at the others.

[68] With this first paragraph cf. *Pseudoacronis scholia in Horatium vetustiora*, ed. O. Keller (Leipzig, 1902), i. 2–3.

receive education,[69] on a very tight allowance, but he overcame his father's straitened circumstances by his ability (*ingenium*), and as a young man cultivated the friendship of Brutus. He served as military tribune under him in the war and was taken prisoner by Caesar Augustus. But after a long period spent in captivity, thanks to the kindness of Maecenas he was not only rescued but actually admitted to his [i.e. Caesar's] friendship.[70] Consequently, in all his writings he always rises to give Maecenas and Augustus a respectful greeting. He wrote four books of lyrics, a book of epodes, the *Carmen saeculare*, one book *On the Art of Poetry*, two books of satires, and two books of epistles. Porphyrion, Modestus, and Helenus all wrote commentaries on his works, but Acron is the best commentator.

Here begins the Book of Poesy or *Poetry*, or *The Art of Poetry*, that is, the skill which poets employ in writing. That is the title. His intention in this book is to give certain precepts to aid the art of writing poetry, so that each poet may know what he is to follow and what he is to avoid. He addresses this book to Piso and his two sons, and particularly the elder of the two, who was a writer of comedies. Lest their writings be rejected on publication, as had happened in the case of some other writers, their father asked Horace to give some precepts for writing comedies in particular. For this reason Horace took the subject back to basic principles, and so he begins by discussing the writing of poetry in general. So his function is to put right, in so far as he addressed himself to his own contemporaries, but it is to introduce the subject, in so far as he writes for later generations. You can gather what the usefulness of this work is from the author's intention, which is that the poet should be instructed in all the precepts given in this book. It pertains to ethics, since it shows what behaviour is appropriate for a poet,[71] or rather to logic, because it guides us to a knowledge of correct and elegant style and to habitual reading of authors who may serve as models. So, while he gives advice relating to every sort of writing, he keeps to the proper order, first of all removing what a writer should avoid, then teaching him what he should do.[72]

His *Art of Poetry* is in four parts. In the first part he removes three faults which are most detrimental to writers, namely inconsistency within a single character (*persona*) or subject and tasteless alteration; pointless digression, for example, where he says TO WEIGHTY BEGINNINGS [14]; and unsuitable variation of style, for example, where he says THE GREATER PART

---

[69] Lat. 'in ludum litterarium', which in classical Latin would mean 'to an elementary school'.

[70] Lat. 'set etiam in amiciciam est receptus', which is ambiguous: it could mean the friendship of Caesar and Maecenas, or Maecenas' friendship, or Caesar's friendship. We favour the last of these options.

[71] Here the standard *ethice supponitur* analysis is being narrowed to specify the behaviour of a poet. Cf. below, p. 279.

[72] The 'quid sequendum et quid fugiendum' formula is here made to designate specifically poetic 'virtues' and 'vices'.

[24]. In the second part he shows us what sort of subject-matter each writer should choose, namely one that is well matched to his abilities, for example, where he says CHOOSE A SUBJECT [38]. In the third part he shows us what rhetorical colours may be used in polishing and embellishing the chosen subject matter, for example, where he says YOU [LISTEN] TO WHAT [153]. In the fourth part he indicates the judges and critics to whom he would entrust the work for correction, for example, where he says YOU [WILL SAY OR DO] NOTHING WORTHWHILE, [IF MINERVA IS] AGAINST YOU [385].

Note that Horace himself in this work is called a maker of verse (*poetrides*), while his work is called *Poetria*, that is, 'the poet's rule-book' (*lex*). For anyone who follows out the precepts laid down by Horace here is called a poet, that is, one who creates or shapes verse (*fictor vel formator*); the work of one poet is a poem (*poema*), that is, the result of feigning (*fictio*), while the writings of all poets collectively are called poetry (*poesis*).[73] Note also that we call poets (*poetae*) those who speak in such a way as to suggest that that which does not really exist is true, so that, if their subject-matter did exist in reality it could not be spoken of more accurately than they have done. Examples are Virgil, Ovid, and Terence. But because he [i.e. Horace] does not do this, but speaks rather of something which does actually exist, he is not called a poet (*poeta*) but rather a maker of verse (*poetrides*).[74]

Here begins the Book of Discourses (Sermons). That is the title. Note that a title has to be prefaced in this way so that an author's intention may be briefly indicated—but this does not happen here. For his intention in this work is to reprehend the various vices of the Romans, which are not revealed in the title. But we can observe the method he employs in his reprehension. For one can reprehend in various ways, sometimes using a lowly style (*humilis oratio*), as in this case, and sometimes using other modes. This is shown by the actual definition of *sermo*. *Sermo* ('discourse') is style that is loosely organized—this with an eye to setting out the subject clearly—and is very close to everyday speech, a feature which has to do with the subject-matter. The author humbles himself because he tells us that he is writing a lowly style. The discourse (*sermo*) is so called because it is distributed between the writer and at least two other persons, and is tailored to suit the character speaking. For this reason too, the preaching of bishops is rightly called 'a sermon' (*sermo*). Note this, that although he is criticizing here, which is one of the characteristics of satire, yet it is not called satire, for it is a property of satire to reprehend someone by name, something which does not happen here. Likewise, notice that he reprehends the vices for the purpose of persuading men to give them up and urging them on to the opposite, that is, to the virtues. Note moreover that, although in all his discourses he reprehends the vices, yet,

[73] Cf. Isidore, *Ety.* I. xxxix. 21.
[74] Cf. Isidore, *Ety.* VII. vii. I.

because he reprehends different vices, his particular intention in each discourse should be set out separately. His intention in the first discourse is to reprehend avarice. So, he writes this first discourse to Maecenas reprehending the inconsistency and changeableness of men, whose opinions are often mutually inconsistent, and who are displeased with their allotted place in life. Then he accuses Maecenas himself of excessive avarice, not in order to stigmatize him in particular but others through him. When he begins to speak about inconsistency he addresses Maecenas thus: HOW—that is, in what way—IS IT . . . [I. i. I].

The Book of Epistles was Horace's last work. In these he is not a scoffer (derisor) as in the Odes, not a reprehender as in the Discourses, not giving an introduction to a subject as in The Art of Poetry. Rather his purpose is to deal seriously and fearlessly with the engrafting of virtues and the improvement of behaviour. From this one can conclude that his principal intention is to deck men out with [good] morals, and to make them distinguished by their virtues, and that his subsidiary intention is to remove vices. His principal subject-matter is virtues and good morals, his subordinate subject-matter the vices which he reprehends. The work pertains to ethics because it is concerned with education in morality. Epistola means 'sent above'. So this book is entitled The Book of Epistles either because it surpasses the other works of Horace, or else because the letters are sent over and above the words of the emissary who is sent with them. The Book of Discourses and this book appear to be similar in that here, as in that book, the tone is of reprehension. But there is a considerable difference between them, for in the Discourses he addresses those who are present, here those who are absent. In this case his principal motive is instruction, and reprehension plays a secondary role. But in the Discourses it is quite the reverse. There is also this difference, that here he employs fine, dignified words to encourage us to pursue the virtues, but there he hacks away at the vices using unadorned, unambiguous language.

Throughout the whole book he has the intention we have spoken of, but in each individual letter he has a particular intention. For instance, in the first letter his purpose is to educate us in virtue and in shunning the vices. He indicates that shunning the vices means virtue when he says: VIRTUE IS TO SHUN VICE AND THE FIRST ELEMENT OF WISDOM IS TO RID ONESELF OF FOLLY [I. i. 41–2].

Each of the letters is divided into four parts. The first part of the first letter takes the form of a kind of prologue; for the writer is seeking to attract Maecenas' goodwill right at the start, then he excuses himself for not writing lyrics. He gives five reasons: because he is not well versed in this genre (genus scribendi); because it is not seemly for one of his years, and even if it were he would not enjoy writing in it; he wishes to avoid suffering the same fate as the gladiator Veianus; and also to give full heed to his friends' advice. Next he gives a brief foretaste of the work that is to follow, as when he says: I PONDER, AND ASK, WHAT IS TRUE AND FITTING [I. i. II]. Subsequently he commends his work to the reader, where he draws a comparison from a lover and a hired servant and an orphan. He has thus included everything appropriate to a prologue, for he defends his work; gives a sketch of it, and commends its virtues [to the reader]. The second, third, and fourth part are indicated in [the commentary on] the book itself.

II

A Critical Colloquy: Conrad of Hirsau

CONRAD of Hirsau (*c.* 1070–*c.* 1150?) is supposed to have been a school-master in the Benedictine abbey of SS Peter and Paul at Hirsau, in the Black Forest of Germany. In addition to his *Dialogue on the Authors*, from which selections are translated below, he has been credited with several other works, including *Dialogus de mundi contemptu vel amore* and a *Speculum virginum*.[1] The *Dialogue on the Authors* has resisted efforts at exact dating. Its editor, R. B. C. Huygens, regards it as having been produced late in Conrad's life, mainly because the surviving manuscripts have a number of errors and gaps which, in his judgement, indicate a penultimate draft; it might even be his final work, left slightly incomplete at the time of his death.[2] But, as L. G. Whitbread has pointed out, 'faults in later copies may well be due to circumstances other than the author's age or demise'.[3] The single incontrovertible fact about the work's genesis seems to be that it often makes use of Bernard of Utrecht's commentary on Theodulus, which was written between 1076 and 1099. Three parallels with Hugh of Saint-Victor's *Didascalicon* (*c.* 1127) are inconclusive and may simply reflect a common training in the *artes*. In sum, as Whitbread concludes, 'a very provisional dating within the period *c.* 1100–50 is all that the evidence seems to warrant'.

The surviving text of the *Dialogue* is certainly far from perfect. Some of its errors and omissions are of a kind which are difficult to explain by reference to the vagaries of manuscript transmission. There are several passages of misunderstood or garbled information which would have annoyed a more careful grammarian (to view the matter in the light of medieval standards of competence). But Conrad's overall plan is quite clear and rather impressive. The work falls into three sections, beginning with the 'necessary prelimi-naries to reading the authors', that is, basic definitions of literary terms (like book, prose, *rhythmus*, metre, and so forth). Here Conrad follows Bernard of Utrecht, who had drawn on Isidore of Seville's *Etymologiae* either directly or through some medieval intermediary. The second section comprises a series of introductions to the prescribed grammar school texts. Conrad has gathered together a series of *accessūs*,[4] arranging them in such a way as to proceed from the minor to the major authors. The twenty-one authors formally discussed are not in chronological order but arranged in an ascend-ing scale of the difficulties they present to the student. The first four—Donatus, Cato, Aesop, and Avianus—are classified as beginners' reading.

[1] L. G. Whitbread, 'Conrad of Hirsau as Literary Critic', *Speculum*, xlvii (1972), 234.
[2] Huygens, *Accessus ad auctores, etc.*, pp. 13–15.
[3] Whitbread, 'Conrad of Hirsau', p. 237.
[4] Conrad's *accessūs* have been discussed, with reference to German vernacular prologues, by E. C. Lutz, *Rhetorica divina: Mittelhochdeutsche Prologgebete und die rhetorische Kultur des Mittel-alters* (Berlin and New York, 1984), esp. pp. 50–4.

The Christian poets Juvencus, Prosper, Theodulus, Arator, and Prudentius then appear. Clearly Conrad was anxious that his pupils had a grounding in wholesome Christian poetry before proceeding to its pagan counterpart. But first three prose writers were to be studied, namely Cicero, Sallust, and Boethius. Finally, we come to the following sequence of pagan poets: Lucan, Horace, Ovid, Juvenal, Homer, Persius, Statius, and, topping them all, Virgil, the master of the three styles and of all the liberal disciplines.[5] The third and last part of the *Dialogue* consists of an analysis of the various branches of learning, wherein the study of grammar is given its proper position within the hierarchy of knowledge.

We should pause for a moment over this notion of hierarchy, since it is of fundamental importance for an understanding of Conrad's attitude to pagan literature. Like so many of his contemporaries, Conrad could say scathing things about the lies of the poets when contrasting them with the certainties of Holy Scripture. Why should the young recruit in Christ's army be forced to read Ovid? He is being asked to look for gold in the midst of dung, yet that dung could taint his impressionable mind (see below p. 56). Remarks of that kind should not be misread as blanket condemnations of classical literature and learning. Rather they are tacit statements of the subordination of such knowledge to Christian doctrine, a principle well conveyed by, for example, the commonplace metaphor of 'despoliation of the Egyptians', here cited in St Augustine's formulation:

... what they [i.e. the pagans] have said should be taken from them as from unjust possessors and converted to our use. For, just as the Egyptians had not only idols and heavy burdens for the people of Israel to abominate and eschew, but also vessels and ornaments of gold and silver and clothing for that people, departing from Egypt, secretly to rescue for itself, as if to put them to a better use, not on its own authority but at God's command, while the Egyptians unwittingly supplied them with things which they themselves did not use well, so all the doctrines of the pagans contain not only simulated and superstitious imaginings and grave burdens of unnecessary labour, which each one of us leaving the society of pagans under the leadership of Christ ought to abominate and avoid, but also liberal disciplines more suited to the uses of truth, and some most useful precepts concerning morals.[6]

If used in the proper manner, therefore, the deposit of the past was invaluable to the Christian teacher. In particular, the reading of classical texts, which fell within the province of grammar, was regarded as an essential preparation for the study of the infinitely more complex 'sacred page' of theology. Christ's army soldiered on, gathering their rich plunder in the conviction that they would put it to better use, taking their chances with the pagan dirt. Anyway, to

---

[5] On the medieval grammar-school canon according to Conrad and other writers see Curtius, pp. 48–9, 260–4, 466–7. The *Dialogue on the Authors* is a major source of Hugh of Trimberg's *Registrum multorum auctorum*, which has been edited by K. Langosch (Berlin, 1942).

[6] *De doct. Christ.* II. xl. 60 (CCSL xxxii. 73–4); our tr., after D. W. Robertson, *St. Augustine: On Christian Doctrine* (Indianapolis, 1958; repr. 1980), p. 75. On the concept of despoliation see Quain, 'Medieval *Accessus ad auctores*', pp. 223–4; cf. J. de Ghellinck, *Le Mouvement théologique du XIIe siècle*, 2nd edn. (Bruges, 1948), pp. 10–16; J. Leclercq, *The Love of Learning and the Desire for God*, tr. C. Misrahi (Fordham, 1961), pp. 55–6.

the pure all things were pure. The true Christian, declares Conrad, will not be harmed by the liberal arts; on the contrary, they 'liberate' him from what is worldly and false. Hence Conrad and his fellow monks sought to serve the King of Heaven by pursuing ethical studies.

The basic form of the *Dialogue on the Authors* is that of the colloquy, or set conversation-piece between master and pupil or pupils, a genre often used for teaching Latin grammar and vocabulary. But the doctrine which Conrad conveys through it is more sophisticated than what is often encountered. Moreover, the 'Pupil' figure is no man of straw who simply requests and meekly receives the erudite answers of the 'Master'. He 'knows the Bible well, has heard of the Donatist heresy, cites Horace and Prudentius, is aware of the theory of universals, and reveals prior knowledge of a number of the classical authors to whom he is being introduced'.[7] There are, therefore, several instances of real dialogue between the speakers. Certainly, occasional awkwardnesses do exist, as when an author is abruptly brought into the discussion without having been mentioned by the Pupil. But in general the form works well. Conrad deserves credit for the ambitious conception, if not for the imperfect execution, of his critical colloquy.

CONRAD OF HIRSAU

Dialogue on the Authors: Extracts[8]

Pupil. Since I see that for a long time now you have been sunk in silent inactivity which does nothing to lessen my ignorance, having found an opportune time I am now at last rousing you to fulfil the promise you have made.[9] I am not so much jealous of your reputation, which you have won by imparting sound teaching, as eager for my own advantage, being anxious to perfect my eloquence or my talent. But the style of this long-awaited discourse must be carefully controlled so that the debtor discharges his debt more fully than is demanded of him.[10] For thus, on the one hand, the teacher is better able to exercise his goodwill, while on the other, the slower partner, that is the learner, who is in dire need, is helped.[11]

Teacher. Though I have held many discussions with you, even far beyond my ability, I cannot recall what promise I am now being forced to make good by resuming my studies. Indeed my previous efforts were so maliciously attacked by my envious detractors, Bavius and Maevius,[12]

---

[7] Whitbread, 'Conrad of Hirsau', p. 238.

[8] Tr. from Huygens, *Accessus ad auctores, etc.*, with the permission of E. J. Brill Ltd.

[9] Huygens points out that here, as elsewhere in the *Dialogue*, Conrad appears to be imitating Augustine's *De quantitate animae*; with this opening sentence cf. *PL* xxxii. 1035.

[10] A reference to the doctrine of supererogation.

[11] What Conrad seems to mean is: if you, as the teacher, do more than your strict due (*debitum*), (1) you will have greater influence over me, the pupil, and (2) I shall learn more readily.

[12] Cf. Virgil, *Bucolics*, iii. 90–1.

that I am deterred from holding any studious discussions with you on a private basis. What a lamentable and miserable condition, to be unwilling to learn or teach, and yet jealously to criticize both activities in others!

Pupil. It is perfectly clear that nothing is more loathsome and darker than the eye of the envious, whose way to advancement is another man's error. If houses had no smoke the loathsome soot would not be seen by those who love handsome buildings.

Teacher. For that very reason silent inactivity is better than having someone else take offence at the results of my studies.

Pupil. You must not fear anything of this sort. I shall lay such an equitable burden on your powers that you will not win much praise if you stand up under it, nor incur any great disgrace if you collapse.

Teacher. On this firm condition I take on the burden you have laid upon me. Whatever way I advance, I hope I may not deviate from it out of a desire for vain glory, but if I should, may I have your pardon. So ask what you wish at this crossroads where each flank can be protected between the love and hate of friend or enemy.

Pupil. You formerly promised to teach me the rudiments of worldly learning, in keeping with my slow understanding, whereby I might begin with minor authors and work my way through these to the more important ones, and the rungs provided by the less important authors might provide me with my opportunity to learn the teachings of the major ones.[13] When my attention strayed from the more insignificant teaching of the minor authors, and I spent all my spare time on the major ones, you used to joke, and rally me to the effect that I was holding my course straight through the thickets of the woods,[14] but was straying shamefully from it in the flat open plain. In other words, I was creeping along somehow or other among the weighty thoughts of the noble authors and yet was falling short as far as the less important were concerned. So you used to say that failure in studying the most unimportant authors is unpardonable, even though the student may be well-versed in the major ones, and whatever knowledge was gained from a study of the major authors would be rendered obscure by neglect of the minor ones.

Teacher. What, then, am I to say, when faced by these puzzling problems? What is your question, and what is the subject of your enquiry?

Pupil. I want you to explain briefly and in summary form what we must look for in each of the school authors who are used in training the blossoming minds of beginners, namely, who the author is, what he has written, the scale of his work, when he has written it, and how, that is whether it is in prose or verse, with what subject-matter or intention each

[13] Cf. Jerome, *Epist.* lxx. 2 (CSEL liv. 550).
[14] Cf. Hugh of Saint-Victor, *Didascalicon*, v. v, ed. C. H. Buttimer (Washington, DC, 1939), p. 103; tr. J. Taylor, *The* Didascalicon *of Hugh of St. Victor* (New York and London, 1961), p. 126.

has begun his work, what end the composition has in view.[15] I also want to find out about the introductory page:[16] what is the difference between a title, a preface, a proem, and a prologue; between a poet, a writer of history, and a writer of discourses, between poesy and poetry; between explanation and exposition and detailed study[17] and transference of meaning (*translatio*); between allegory, tropology, and anagogy. I wish to have the meaning of 'book' defined, and to find out the nature of prose, verse, fable, the figures which are called tropes, and any other question that must be asked concerning ecclesiastical or pagan authors. A brief answer to all these questions seems to me to constitute a way in to the understanding of authors important and unimportant alike.

Teacher. In making these requests you seem to me to have painted the picture of an expert on the authors[18] who, having a first-rate knowledge of the secular disciplines, is wont to use the key of knowledge to open the door to those who knock; a man whose lively memory never lets the most insignificant fact elude it, when he has to sort out great truths in terms of place, time and person.[19] But all these powers are quite foreign to my intelligence. For I have no 'faculties trained by practice' to give solid food, but only a little milk to nourish the very young.[20] Besides, when you lay upon me the task of expounding secular literature you forget the words of the prophet.

Pupil. What did he say?

Teacher. 'The Lord has destroyed the tongue of the sea of Egypt' [Isa. 11: 15].

Pupil. What does this mean?

Teacher. The tongue of the sea of Egypt represents the teachings of worldly knowledge, which is hardly ever, or perhaps not at all, without the obscurity which derives from sin or worldly vanity. The Word made flesh has destroyed this because, once the mysteries of the Scriptures had been opened up by the key of the divine wisdom, the vanity of worldly knowledge fell silent. Why, therefore, do you seek from me knowledge which may be pardoned in the pupil, but earns censure as a blemish in the character of the teacher?

Pupil. To want to help no one is wicked and abominable. Whatever is done under compulsion is excused by the zeal of the will which resists that compulsion. Anyway, I am not asking you for much. I do not ask you

---

[15] With this version of the *circumstantiae*, cf. Conrad's list of the 'seven questions' asked by the ancients, below, p. 46. Cf. also Ch. I, n. 6.

[16] A common expression of Conrad's, following St Augustine, *Epist.* xl. 2 (CSEL xxxiv. 71).

[17] Literally 'the result of work done through the night', hence concentrated, close study.

[18] Lat. *auctorista*. Cf. Hugh of Trimberg, *Registrum multorum auctorum*, ll. 3, 45, ed. Langosch, pp. 160-1.

[19] A reference to the *circumstantiae*. For discussion and relevant bibliography see Minnis, *Authorship*, pp. 16-17. Cf. above, n. 15 and Ch. I, n. 6.

[20] Cf. Heb. 5: 13-14.

to examine the furniture of the whole house you have thrown open to me, but simply to insert the keys in the closed doors. I am not seeking a commentary on or exposition of the authors, but simply the chance to form an impression of the contents of the central and final parts of their work from their beginnings, that is their subject-matter or their intention.

Teacher. Your insistence has defeated me, and I will meet your request and share with you the knowledge I have received from others. If I should fall into error I am only too happy to be put right, just as I have corrected others in the past. I cannot give you precise information on all the questions you asked above, concerning the amount each author has written, or when he wrote, especially since most of them wrote a great deal which has not been transmitted to our times or to our part of the world. But it will not be difficult for me to rely on the paths others have blazed and bring you to the elements of those authors whom you seek to know, as it were to the threshold of a door.

Pupil. Begin, then.

Teacher. I will follow the order of your questions and, when I have cleared these up to the best of my ability, we may then talk about the initial aspects of each author's work. First of all you enquired about the introductory page, in other words the title and suchlike things. But because it is in books that you always find these, let us first consider the nature of the book.[21]

Pupil. As you wish.

Teacher. The word 'book' (*liber*) has two meanings.[22] For a book is the name given to parchment with marks on it. This name originated from the bark of a tree on which men used to write before the use of animal skin. 'Book' is also the name given to a collection of speeches, histories, or commentaries or the like brought together to form one body of work. 'Book' (*liber*) is so called from the verb 'to free' (*liberare*), because the man who spends his time reading often releases his mind from the anxieties and chains of the world. A book is made up of prose, *rhythmus*, or metre.

Pupil. Explain these three terms.

Teacher. Prose is a discourse not constrained by the law of metre. it is so called from *proson*, which means 'drawn out' or 'diffuse'. Indeed, Greek words are most often slightly altered to fit the Latin pattern of declension, and so *proson* becomes *prosa*, *prologos* becomes *prologus*, etc. *Rhythmus* is when only the number of syllables matters, for *rithmus* means 'number'.[23] Metre is that which is measured by precisely fixed feet, that is by long and short feet. For *metron* means 'measurement'. There are several kinds of

---

[21] This series of definitions, which ends with the discussion of *glossa* and *lingua*, is heavily dependent on Bernard of Utrecht's *Commentum in Theodulum*; cf. Huygens, *Accessus ad auctores, etc.*, pp. 7, 9. Bernard, in his turn, was heavily dependent on Isidore of Seville's *Etymologiae*. The most significant uses of Isidore are noted below.

[22] Cf. Isidore, *Ety.* VI. xiii.

[23] On *rhythmus* see Murphy, *Rhetoric in the Middle Ages*, pp. 77–8, 157–61, 208–10.

metres. They get their name from the feet, like the dactylic from the dactyl, or from their inventors, like the sapphic from Sappho, or from those writers who habitually used them, like the asclepiad from Asclepiades, or else from the number of feet, like the hexameter and pentameter, or from the subject-matter like the heroic metre which, because of its name, has the chief place among the other metres. In all metres the length of the final syllable is indeterminate. The book entitled *Centimetrum* appears to discuss these matters more fully.[24]

As to your question about the introductory page, namely the difference in meaning between title, proem, preface, and prologue, you may make the following distinctions. The title (*titulus*) is derived from a certain Titan and is so called for reasons of similarity.[25] It is a brief indication of the work to follow. The proem is the preface to the work. The prologue is a preliminary statement before a discourse. The difference between a prologue and a title is that the title briefly indicates the author and his subject-matter but the prologue makes the reader or listener readily taught, attentive, and well disposed.[26] Every prologue is either apologetic or else commendatory. For the writer either excuses himself, or tries to commend himself [to his readers]. Finally, the title prefaces all books, while the prologue prefaces comic and prose-writers and explains what each work is, why or how it has been written, or how it should be read.

Pupil. Tell me also, what is the difference between an author, a poet, a writer of history, a commentator, a bard, an expositor of texts, and a writer of discourses.

Teacher. Well, listen then. The author (*auctor*) is so called from the verb 'increasing' (*augendo*), because by his pen he amplifies the deeds or sayings or thoughts of men of former times.[27] History is something seen, an event, for Greek *historin* is *visio* ('sight') in Latin.[28] Hence the writer of history is said to write of the event he has witnessed. Moreover, the poet (*poeta*) is called a maker, or one who gives shape to things, because he says what is false instead of the truth, or else sometimes intermingles truth with falsehood.[29] The bard (*vates*) gets his name from his mental power.[30] For it argues great mental powers to bypass the present and show future events as if they were right before one's eyes. Commentators are those who can work out many ideas, beginning with just a few facts and illuminate the obscure sayings of others. Expositors are those who unravel the

[24] Here Conrad simply follows Bernard of Utrecht's reference (cf. Huygens, *Accessus ad auctores, etc.*, pp. 58–9) to the *Centimeter* of Servius (GL iv. 456–67).

[25] Cf. the *accessus* to Sedulius translated in Ch. I, and ibid., n. 36.

[26] Cf. Cicero, *De inventione*, I. xv. 20; *Ad Herenn.*, I. iv. 6; Isidore, *Ety.* II. vii. 2.

[27] For discussion of this etymology, and references, see Minnis, *Authorship*, p. 10.

[28] Cf. Isidore, *Ety.* I. xli. 1.

[29] Ibid. VIII. vii. 2; cf. *Anonymi Historia Troyana Daretis Frigii*, ed. J. Stohlmann (Ratingen, 1968), p. 267. See further the introduction to Ch. IV.

[30] Cf. Isidore, *Ety.* VIII. vii. 3, and the way in which Boccaccio appropriated this etymology for his own polemic in the *Genealogy*, XIV. viii; discussed below, p. 392.

mystical sayings of Holy Scripture. Writers of discourses are those who compose discourses on various subjects containing exhortation for the edification of their audience. A poem (*poema*) is the work of the poet and that alone, while poesy (*poesis*) is a work consisting of many books. *Poetria* or *poetrida* is a woman who studies verse. A fable (*fabula*) is something which neither happened nor could happen.[31]

Pupil. You still have to give some additional information about the different kinds of verse. For there are great differences between them.

Teacher. The nature of the verse depends on the author's inclination. There is bucolic, that is pastoral verse; comic, that is 'village verse', for *comos* means 'village'; tragic verse, in which public events and the wicked deeds of potentates are described, for *tragos* in Greek is *hircus* ('goat') in Latin—a goat was given as a prize to the person who recited the verse. There is also satiric verse, which criticizes all vices. It gets its name from the naked, mocking satyrs, because in this poem depraved morals are stripped of their clothing and mocked. Or else the name is derived from *satyra*, that is a great dish full of different fruits or other kinds of food offered to the gods. The kind of work in which there are laudatory songs or odes (*odae*), or strong abuse of the wicked, is also called *satyra*. The verse-form in which drinking-parties with their accompanying amusements are described is lyric. It gets its name from *apo to lirin*, that is from variation, hence *delirus* ('crazy') is he who alters from what he was. There is apologetic verse, that is verse defending the writer; there is also panegyric, that is wholly laudatory verse; *epithalamium*, that is verse written concerning the wedding couch; epitaph, that is verse written on a tomb; there is chronicling verse, that is a description of various historical periods; there is elegiac verse, that is mournful verse, so called from the Greek word *elegos*, that is, misery.

Pupil. What should be understand by the word 'argument' (*argumentum*)?

Teacher. Argument 'makes credible something which is in doubt', as Tully says.[32] This is referred to in three ways, as either argument from the whole or from its sides or from reputation.[33]

Pupil. Please explain these three ways.

Teacher. Argument from the whole occurs when the definition looks towards the question asked, as Paul says: 'Faith is that which gives substance to our hopes, the proof of things we cannot see' [Heb. 2: 1]. Argument from one side occurs when the man who is defending himself either denies the action, or bases his defence on the justice of the action. Thus

---

[31] Cf. Cicero, *De invent.* I. xix. 27, *Ad Herenn.* I. viii. 13, and Isidore, *Ety.* I. xliv. 5, where *fabula* is defined in contrast with *historia* and *argumentum* (i.e. fictitious but verisimilar narrative).

[32] Cicero, *Topica*, ii. 8.

[33] With the following discussion of these three types of argument cf. Isidore, *Ety.* II. xxx. 1–4.

St Paul, when unjustly accused by raging enemies on the grounds that he was leading the people astray from God's law, cleared himself of the charges levelled at him and supported by outstanding reasoning his just action in teaching.[34] Argument from reputation happens when there is mention of an author's own name, as the Church says: 'I sought for the man my heart loved, I sought for him and did not find him', etc. [S. of S. 3: 1–2].

Pupil. I should like to know how one sets up an argument.

Teacher. In various ways, but I have no time to show you these. They are created from grammatically related words, when one moves from a verb to a noun or vice versa; from class, from kind, from likeness and from difference, from contrary ideas, and ideas that follow on from what precedes, from prior circumstances, from facts that argue against a case, from causes, effects, and comparison.[35] It is not difficult for an intelligent reader to spot all these things if he possesses [i.e. has mastered] a valid authority (*auctor*) through hearing lectures.

The order at the beginning of books is also something one looks into, to see whether it is natural or artificial.[36]

Pupil. I do not quite see what the difference is.

Teacher. You will recognize a natural order when the beginning of the book follows the natural sequence of the matter narrated, and an artificial order when the order of events appropriate to the beginnings of books is not observed. An example is Virgil in his *Aeneid*, where he puts the narrative of events, namely the fall of Troy, in the second book rather than in the first.

In books a fourfold explanation (*explanatio*) is allowed: the literal explanation, the explanation in terms of the meaning (*sensus*), and the allegorical, and moral explanations.[37]

Pupil. Explain these four kinds.

Teacher. The literal explanation is when one is told how the unadorned text (*nuda litera*) is to be understood; the explanation in terms of meaning is ⟨when one is told⟩ what the author's words really mean; the allegorical explanation arises when one thing is signified and something else is understood;[38] the moral explanation is when what is said is adapted to encourage and cherish good moral qualities. Tropology is the spiritual

---

[34] Cf. Acts 25: 6ff.　　　　　　　　　　　　　[35] Cf. Isidore, *Ety.* II. xxx. 5–13.

[36] 'Natural order' was discussed by Donatus in his life of Virgil, ed. J. Brummer, *Vitae Vergilianae* (Leipzig, 1912), p. 18; the distinction between the two kinds of order was elaborated in the *Scholia Vindobonensia ad Horatii Artem poeticam*, ed. J. Zechmeister (Vienna, 1877), pp. 4–5 (on *Ars poetica*, 42–5). Cf. Bernard of Utrecht, *Commentum in Theodulum*, in Huygens, *Accessus ad auctores, etc.*, p. 64, and 'Bernard Silvester''s prologue to his commentary on the *Aeneid*, tr. below, Ch. IV.

[37] Cf. Bernard of Utrecht, *Commentum in Theodulum*, ed. Huygens, p. 64. But see also Conrad's later statement (below, p. 50), that only divinely inspired Scripture has any deep significance.

[38] Cf. Isidore's definition of *allegoria* as *alieniloquium*, in *Ety.* I. xxxvii. 22.

explanation or the understanding of a text in moral terms; anagogy is understanding that text on a higher level.

There are three styles of writing, the lowly, the middle, and the lofty, and the author adapts the tone (*ordo*) of his style to the nature of his subject-matter.[39] In a word, a great many poets have followed their predecessors in the way they write verse. For instance, Terence followed Menander, Horace followed Lucilius, Sallust followed Livy, Boethius in his *Consolation* followed Martianus [Capella], Statius followed Virgil's *Aeneid*, while Theodolus followed the same author's *Eclogues*.[40] Likewise, many church authors have followed others.

You must also be aware that in interpreting books the ancients asked seven questions: who the author was, the title of the work, the nature (*qualitas*) of the verse, the intention of the writer, the order and number of books, and the actual exposition [of the text]. But modern writers have laid down four questions that have to be asked: the subject-matter, the intention of the writer, the final cause of the writing, and to what part of philosophy that which is written pertains.[41]

Pupil. Tell me then, what is subject-matter, intention, and final cause?

Teacher. Matter (*materia*) is that from which everything is made up, hence it gets its name, as it were 'the mother of substance' (*mater rei*). Matter has two meanings: in a building there are pieces of wood and stones; so too in the realm of words there are kinds and classes and other means which achieve the task the author sets out to do. The intention (*intentio*) is what the author intends to do, what, how much, and about what he proposes to write. The final cause (*finalis causa*) is the profit derived by the reader. I will teach you about the parts of philosophy, to which every author's work pertains, later on in the book, when we shall set out the names of the liberal disciplines rather than their effect. Philosophy is the knowledge of matters human and divine in so far as this is humanly possible.[42]

When we indicate the basic meaning of one word with another single word that is called *glosa* in Greek and *lingua* in Latin.[43]

Pupil. That's enough of these necessary preliminaries to reading the authors. Now, as you promised, you must begin with the lesser authors and so proceed to the major ones, give milk to little babies and solid food to those who have been weaned. . . .[44]

[39] On the 'three styles' in medieval criticism see F. Quadlbauer, *Die antike Theorie der genera dicendi im lateinischen Mittelalter* (Vienna, 1962).
[40] Cf. Bernard of Utrecht, *Commentum in Theodulum*, ed. Huygens, p. 65.
[41] On these two types of introduction or prologue to an author see the introduction to Ch. I. Here Conrad is once again following Bernard of Utrecht, *Commentum in Theodulum*, ed. Huygens, pp. 59, 66–7.
[42] Cf. Isidore, *Ety.* viii. vi.
[43] Cf. ibid. i. xxx.
[44] Conrad's introductions to Donatus and Cato are here omitted.

ON AESOP

Teacher. This Aesop flourished in Phrygia, a man who had a considerable grasp of secular learning. And because the role of poets is either to be useful or to give pleasure,[45] this author, from his observation of human nature, wove together the false fictions of his fables, inventing nonsensical or at any rate illogical stories, intertwining the childish and the serious, and making it all serve as a comparison with human life. For fable (*fabula*) is fiction, not fact, hence it gets its name from *fando* ('speaking').[46] We know that fables were invented so that by introducing the fictitious conversation of dumb animals or insensible objects, certain similarities in human morals and behaviour might be criticized. 'Fable' really means two different things. For there are 'Aesopic' fables, so called from their originator, where animals which do not possess the power of reasoning, or even other objects which have no powers of sensation at all like mountains, cities, and rivers, are imagined discussing some particular point among themselves. There are also 'Libystic' fables, where an exchange of words or actions is imagined between beings that have the power of reason and those that do not.

In that they are made to relate to a moral end, and have been invented to give pleasure, Aesop's fables differ from the lying fictions of Terence, Plautus, and other similar poets. For their invented stories about human events and characters correspond with the truth, even though only in a certain sense, but the material Aesop invented never happened, nor could it have happened.

You should know also that there is another sort of fable written and slanted to fit in with the facts of natural history. Thus Vulcan is imagined as lame because fire never rises straight up, and Neptune's hair is dripping with water. Or else it is adapted to fit in with human nature. Thus the same Aesop invents the story about the wolf and the lamb standing by a stream of flowing water. The lamb was downstream, and the wolf upstream, but the wolf unjustly accused the lamb and strangled him without any reason.

Pupil. Since fables of this sort seem to be applied to a creature who possesses the power of reason and has, morally speaking, gone astray, explain at least this one about the wolf and the lamb.

Teacher. There is a great distance between their natures: the one rages with horrible ferocity, while the other is possessed of a kind of natural simplicity.

Pupil. What sort of people are they like?

Teacher. You may call thieves, robbers, and heretics ravening wolves,

[45] Cf. Horace, *Ars poetica*, 333, and the *accessus* to Avianus tr. in Ch. I.
[46] With this entire discussion of fables cf. Isidore, *Ety.* 1. xl. 1–7. Cf. Boccaccio's unusual use of the *fari* etymology, *Geneal. deor. gentil.* xiv. ix, tr. below, Ch. IX.

who prey upon the lives of the innocent, the lambs so to speak, though not for any reason, or because of any fault on the part of the innocent, but because the stronger, by their wickedness or power, can prevail over the weaker.[47] For when power is added to evil, then what remedy is there left for the defence of the innocent?

Pupil. For the poor man every encounter he has with the rich is dangerous, even though both belong to the same kind and breed. But what is your opinion as to his [i.e. Aesop's] subject-matter or intention?

Teacher. I should say that the subject-matter, that is the story of the fables, is drawn from his observation of human habits or behaviour. For he has drawn the subject-matter of his work from human nature, which we know to be open to corruption, changeability, and suffering to such an extent that it 'never remains in the same position' [Job 14: 1] and, impelled by a wide range of vices, transgresses beyond the proper bounds of its own [human] nature through malice, wiliness, folly, and madness, and may quite properly be compared with wild beasts, domestic animals, stones and pieces of wood. Surely you have something like this in Holy Writ [Judg. 9: 7–15], where Jotham, the only one to be saved when his brothers were killed by Abimelech, ascended Mount Gerizim and cursed the men of Shechem and the king chosen by them? For he said that the trees of the wood, the vine and the olive and the fig, had come together and sought to create a kingship over them from among their own number, but all to no avail, so that in the end they got the bramble as their king.[48]

Pupil. Well, just so. But it is clear from the above, and the consequential arguments [that follow from it] how insensible objects are at one with intellects which are capable of reason in being able to be understood in a way that conveys an added significance.

Teacher. Hear what Our Lord himself says: 'Foxes have holes, and birds of the air nests' [Matt. 8: 20; Luke 9: 58] and again: 'Say to that fox' [Luke 13: 32], that is to Herod, comparing his wiliness to that of a wild beast. You will find many things of this sort in Holy Scripture where insensible objects are moulded to fit good or bad human qualities, so that a comparison with the lower creature may show whether the God-given grace of the superior being has been increased or lost.

Pupil. Add a few words about the author's intention.

Teacher. The author's intention is clearly seen from his choice of subject-matter. For through this work, assembled as it is from various invented stories, he wanted to delight and also to recall irrational human nature to its true self by a comparison with brute beasts. The final cause is the profit (*fructus*) to be derived from reading the book.

[47] Cf. Ezek. 22: 27.
[48] For later uses of this scriptural passage in defences of secular fables, see Pierre Bersuire's prologue to his *Ovid Moralized*, and Boccaccio, op. cit., xv. viii, translated in Chs. VIII and IX below.

Pupil. I wonder when Faunus, that well-known pagan god, came forth from the woods.[49]

ON AVIANUS

Teacher. Avianus is the next stage in the ascent of the young [to knowledge]. He comes at the stage when they are not yet weaned, still cannot take solid food or give their attentions to the sterner discipline of more important authors.

Pupil. Please answer a few questions about him and tell me who preceded whom; did Aesop come first, then Avianus, or is it the other way round?

Teacher. Neither was the inventor of fables. Alcimon of Croton is said to have been the first to have spent his labour in putting together fables.[50] For everyone who speaks an untruth expends labour.[51] Aesop followed him, and Avianus followed Aesop, but was superior to both, for he was a Catholic and was a skilful composer in prose and verse. Avianus, seeing that in his times the ways of men were more inconstant and arrogant than in the previous generation, unfolded this work.[52] First of all he countered their presumption by making a comparison, beginning from a woman's treachery, because all the misery suffered by the human race originates with the woman [i.e. Eve]. Next, mocking the vain madness of the human heart, he put in the story about the snail[53] who, growing tired of his over slow nature, on being given a reward sought the lofty heights but soon repented of his wish because the reward for his presumption was ruin.

What else does this comparison show but the presumptuous ways of men, who are not in the least content with their own nature, but trespass outside its proper limits by going beyond their capacity, and always want to do more than they can? Surely it is about these men that the Apostle says: 'Dangerous times will be at hand in the last days', etc. [2 Tim. 3: 1].

You must understand that the subject-matter of Avianus is the actual fables. These he put in order and narrated in verse of ⟨unequal⟩ length, ⟨that is⟩ hexameter and pentameter, wishing to be of some service in both fields of boyish endeavour.[54] His purpose is to describe the ignorance and stupidity of those who err, and thus to summon the straying conscience

[49] This inconsequential remark, which does not seem to fit the context, is one of several cases which Huygens takes as evidence of the unrevised and unfinished state of Conrad's text. See Huygens, *Accessus ad auctores, etc.*, p. 14.
[50] Isidore, *Ety.* I. xl. 1. Isidore writes 'Alcm(a)eoni'.
[51] Cf. Jer. 9: 5.
[52] i.e. opened it up like a scroll for all to see.
[53] In Avianus, this story is actually told of a tortoise: see *Fabulae Aviani*, no. ii, ed. F. Gaide (Paris, 1980), pp. 79–80.
[54] Presumably these two fields are, the teaching of boys how to read, and the training of their characters.

back to a state of goodness by these comparisons. Do you wish to know the profit eventually gained from reading him?

Pupil. I'm listening.

Teacher. Do not put much trust in oaths given by women, particularly when it concerns the loss of the fruit of their womb. Be content with your own nature lest, if you overreach yourself, presumption may strip you of the gifts nature bestowed on you at birth. Follow out your own advice or teaching by first acting on it yourself. Use skill rather than strength. Do not seek to usurp honour which belongs to another, and which you do not deserve. Do not readily promise to give someone something of which you know nothing, and have no power to give. Do not make the mistake of thinking that what is imposed on you as a punishment is an honour.[55] You can guess how each of the other fables is related to a moral purpose on these lines, for in them the author wished to show the meaning (*sensus*) and profit of his writings. Finally, he briefly indicated what his purpose was in the fable either after the conclusion or before the beginning of each.

Pupil. Is it at all clear who he was, or when he lived?

Teacher. It is clear that Avianus lived in the time of Theodosius, for he wrote to him thus in his prologue: WHO COULD TALK WITH YOU ABOUT ORA-TORY, OR POETRY? FOR IN BOTH KINDS OF LITERATURE YOU SURPASS THE ATHENIANS IN GREEK LEARNING AND THE ROMANS IN LATIN LEARNING.[56] He tells us that Aesop was the model of his work, not in that he treated the same fables, but because his technique of poetic feigning was the same. For fable is something feigned, not an actual event, which delights the mind of the reader and commends the message of the fable to him through the comparison drawn from the events that occur in it.[57] But leaving aside the monsters in fable, let us focus our attention on the divinely inspired oracles. Just as there are two meanings in these [i.e. the divinely inspired oracles], so too reading them is profitable in two ways, in terms of the literal truth and the spiritual interpretation. For you have in divine writings [i.e. Holy Writ] the power of the significative word, but in a fabulous poem, only the sound of the word, which has no significative function.[58]

---

[55] Here Conrad has given the morals of the first seven fables.
[56] 'Ad Theodosium', in Avianus, *Fabulae*, ed. Galde, p. 76.
[57] Cf. the etymology of *fabula* in Conrad's introduction to Aesop, and the references in n. 31.
[58] Here Conrad seems to be saying that, when faced with the words of Scripture, which have deep spiritual meaning, the fables of the pagans seem to be empty sounds (cf. the derivation of *fabula* from *fando*, 'speaking'). A more sophisticated version of this distinction is that pagan literature has only one type of signification, i.e. the obvious meaning of the words, whereas sacred Scripture has many senses: see the relevant material below, Ch. VI.

ON SEDULIUS

Teacher. Let us add Sedulius to the authors mentioned above. In his work, new and old teachings are set out to educate young beginners in the divine law of Christ.

Pupil. Pray stay your pen for a little. I am unable to make any headway here because, if you will excuse my saying so, it is clear that you are at odds with yourself in your argument.

Teacher. One or other of two things must be true. Either I have been mistaken in what I said, or you have not understood what I said.

Pupil. Just so.

Teacher. Tell me, therefore, at what point you are troubled, so that we can see if any solution of this worrying problem is possible.

Pupil. If the fabulous figments of the poets, which you were discussing, are related to a moral purpose, then no doubt they have some significance. For the poets would never make their fables relate to men's morals unless they signified something by them.

Teacher. I think you have not quite understood this, to make you troubled over such a trivial question. For poems, and among them common proverbs which have no weight, are one and the same thing, for they are transient, like a slight sound that is heard, but God-inspired sayings, which are founded in and made eternal by their spiritual meaning, are quite different. Words, or rather simple unadorned letters, are outward indications of a hidden meaning (*sensus*), but are quite different from the eternal, unchanging Word. Do you think that when 'heaven and earth shall pass away' [Mark 13: 31] the fables of Aesop will endure? But 'the words of the Lord will not pass away' [Luke 21: 22]. Letters written in any language belong to the same family, whether they speak to confirm the truth or are uttered in a tissue of falsehoods. But they are differentiated by a distinction of a particular kind which arises out of their inequality of signification.

Pupil. For instance?

Teacher. I will tell you. There are said to be innumerable pagan gods. Bel, the god of the Babylonians, Dagon, the god of the Philistines, the god Accaron,[59] and in brief there were as many gods worshipped as there were regions in the world. But there is one true God, the king of heaven. 'The true God' (*Deus verus*) and 'the false god' (*deus falsus*) are each words of two syllables, but in terms of signification they belong to different groups. 'The god Accaron' signifies something, 'the God of Heaven' does not lack this quality in its signification also. But consider the difference between them and you will see the real weight of each.

Pupil. I think you will not deny that poets have sometimes added to their tissue of vain imaginings some truth, albeit not justified by historical fact.

[59] Cf. Daniel 14; 1 Kgs. 5. 'The god Accaron' misreads 1 Kgs. 5: 10 Vulg., omitting 'in'.

Teacher. Whatever truth can be found in man (treacherous and wicked though he is) is the work of Him who created man and gave to man what man did not have in himself. There are, therefore, in secular literature certain words which have a signification, but bear no relation to spiritual understanding and do not contribute to the formulation of the truth.

Let us then consider Sedulius, 'active' indeed (*sedulus*) in writing about the gospel, a skilled scholar at the height of his powers (*vernans*), who shared the fruits of this knowledge with the Church. He saw that, in his time, the puerile nonsense of pagan writers was commonly used in teaching in the schools, while ecclesiastical literature was completely neglected by students. So he made his pen serve the common good and turned the Gospels into verse, so instructing the first formative years of children that, having imbibed the draughts of truth, henceforth they would not revel in the poison of falsehood.[60] For the young take a tight grip on whatever knowledge they have imbibed in their earliest years, to their great advantage in later life.

Pupil. Our friend Flaccus [i.e. Horace] is of the same opinion: 'The jar will retain for years the smell with which it was tinged when newly made.'[61] But say something briefly about Sedulius' intention or his subject-matter.

Teacher. His subject-matter consists of certain great deeds performed by God taken from the Old or New Testaments and narrated to restrain and correct human wickedness. For every divinely inspired miraculous event is designed to elevate rational created beings by the signs it gives them. Sedulius' intention is to dissuade idolaters from their error by means of a divinely inspired exhortation in metre, as he writes: WHY, SONS OF THESEUS, DO YOU STRAY IN THE MAZE-LIKE CAVE? [*Pas. carm.* i. 43],[62] and so on, and also to steer students away from fabulous figments, and by stimulating them with the teachings of the Gospel to make them cultivate the Christian virtues.

Another interpretation is that Sedulius' intention in this book is to show that all things in heaven, earth, or hell are subject to the divine will. This he does by exhorting the good to do good and by instilling fear into the evil so that they may refrain from sin. The reason behind his intention (*causa intentionis*) is that he sees that some men go astray in worshipping not the Creator, but the things He has created.[63] His subject-matter comprises certain miracles of the Old and New Testaments, as I have stated, and that is what he treats of in this work. This author also wrote an alphabetical hymn in praise of God, beginning with the birth of Our Lord, and ending with His resurrection and ascension. He also wrote a hymn in

[60] Lucretius, *De rerum natura*, i. 936–8, cit. Jerome, *Epist.* cxxxiii. 3 (CSEL lvi. 246).
[61] *Epist.* i. 2, 69–70, cit. Augustine, *De civ. Dei*, i. iii.
[62] i.e. the cave of error. (CSEL x. 18).
[63] Cf. Rom. 1: 25.

hexameters and *reciproci*,[64] beginning with the creation of the world and
the fall of Adam, and going as far as the second coming of Our Lord.
Sedulius began by studying philosophy as a layman in Italy. Afterwards
he taught heroic and other forms of verse, with the encouragement of the
priest Macedonius.[65] He wrote his books in Achaea in the time of Valentinian and Theodosius.

ON JUVENCUS[66]

Pupil. You must give Juvencus a place next to Sedulius. He turned the
literal text of the Gospel into verse,[67] and began his work with Herod, in
whose reign Christ was born.

⟨*Teacher*⟩. He is an excellent writer of verse, for he is praised even by
Jerome. When Jerome in one of his works was dealing with the mystical
gifts of the three magi and their mystical meanings, he said: 'The priest
Juvencus briefly summarized this when he wrote: "incense, gold, and
myrrh, for the king, the man, and the God respectively".'[68]

Pupil. I wonder that such an able writer followed the bare, literal narrative of the Gospel in metre, without appearing to reveal any mystical
meaning therein.

Teacher. If he had added to his literal account the mystical meanings
that arise from it, his work would have been unending. Like Sedulius, his
purpose was to suckle with milk those who were as yet infants in the
Church, and who would subsequently need educating in the more subtle
discipline of allegory, when their innate wisdom had been supplemented
by study. For he who has first thoroughly implanted in his mind the words
of any divine author, be it the prophets or the Old Law or the gospels, will
later on have no difficulty in seeing the fruits of allegory, either learning of
them from his teacher, or even on his own, if his spirit has been stirred.

Pupil. That is absolutely clear. For who could understand the allegorical meaning (*misteria*) of a text if he does not know its literal meaning?[69]
But add something about the subject-matter and the intention of Juvencus to what you have just said about him. For both figure prominently
among the things you promised to deal with.

Teacher. The subject-matter of this author is the Gospel according to
Luke, or rather the four Gospels, put into metrical form, and following
the sequence of the historical events. His intention is to impart the

[64] Hymn I, ed. I. Huemer (CSEL x. 155–62). In the *versūs reciproci* as used by Sedulius the
first part of the hexameter in each distich is repeated in the second half of the pentameter.
[65] This follows the *vita* printed by Huemer, pp. viii–ix n. 1.
[66] i.e. on the *Evangeliorum libri IV* of Juvencus, ed. I. Huemer (CSEL xxiv).
[67] Literally 'he turned it, altered it, in the direction of metre'. There may be a hint here
concerning the imperfect and irregular metre used by Juvencus.
[68] *Comm. in evang. Matth.* (PL xxvi. 26C–D). Cf. Juvencus, i. 250.
[69] Cf. Hugh of Saint-Victor, *Didascalicon*, iv. iv, viii, both translated in Ch. III.

primary meaning of the text of the Gospels in the course of giving a literary education to the sons of the Church, and thus to wean their minds away from the frivolities and inventions of the poets. The end (*fructus finalis*) he hopes to achieve in this work is the growth of faith and hope in the minds of his readers, so that what they have learned through faith they may follow through hope, avoiding the judgement that awaits the wicked and imitating the merit of the good, so that they may also obtain the reward.

This author lived in the time of the Emperor Constantine. He was a Spaniard of noble family, and he turned [the four Gospels] into hexameters, almost word for word. He also wrote some verse in the same metre on the subject òf the order of the sacraments.[70]

Pupil. The young in the Church can benefit from a simple, literal reading of Sedulius and Juvencus. But more advanced students can exercise their minds rigorously in a more profound study of these authors. . . .[71]

ON HORACE

Pupil. Please do not withhold what you know of Horace—they say he was a lyric poet and a very pungent ⟨satirist⟩—so that if there is any advantage (*utilitas*) to be gained from reading him I may profit from it.

Teacher. I will bow to your persistence and tell you what I can, considering the way in which the nourishing milk you draw from the poets may provide you with an opportunity for taking solid food in the form of more serious reading. Indeed, seekers after wisdom should regard secular knowledge in such a light that, if they find in it, in its words and ideas, any steps on the ladder of their common progress from which the higher wisdom may be grasped more firmly, these should not be altogether scorned, but the mind exercised on them for just as long as it takes to find what one seeks through the medium of secular knowledge. For just as dill is thrown out when food has been seasoned with it and eaten, so worldly knowledge should be separated out from sacred studies once it has done its work in students, lest it get in the way of the sacred knowledge.[72]

Horace, then, was a writer of great talent, and clearly so successful that he surpassed many poets of his own time in the nobility of his verse. Also, by his writings and the precepts he laid down for writing, he showed many writers the correct way to write. This was very necessary. For many who claimed a knowledge of the art of poetry, and who did know how to write, were disfiguring the matter of their work because the order was confused.

---

[70] Cf. Jerome, *De viris inlustribus*, lxxxiv, ed. E. C. Richardson (Leipzig, 1896), p. 44.

[71] Introductions to Prosper, Theodulus, Arator, Prudentius, Cicero, Sallust, Boethius, and Lucan here omitted.

[72] Cf. Conrad of Hirsau's *Altercatio synagogae et ecclesiae*, cit. R. Bultot, 'L'auteur de l'*Altercatio synagogae et ecclesiae*: Conrad d'Hirsau?', *RTAM* xxxii (1965), 269.

For they separated the connected sequence of middle and end from the beginning so that the whole body of the work was dominated by confusion rather than a proper order. So Horace was urged by his friend Piso, a philosopher, and Piso's sons, to set down new rules for writing correctly, using a new method, for he employed precepts based on the various genres. At the very beginning of his work, by comparing them with a monstrous creature irrationally conceived,[73] he exposed faulty poems and condemned any work lacking a proper order, in which the sequence of ideas (*sententiae*) did not match up to the splendour of the subject-matter, as conceived by the author; just as if the limbs of a human being were not jointed together in the usual concatenation, but had adopted various features drawn from various animals. He appears to have adapted the illusory images seen in dreams by the man who is ill to create this composite figure. For he, being deranged, misled by the distorted forms of corporeal things, believes illusions to be truth. By making this comparison Horace condemns the mind which is completely devoid of solidly based knowledge or poetic skill, and which yet assumes a knowledge of something of which it is totally ignorant.

Pupil. Why did he give his book the distinctive title 'Poetry' (*Poetria*)? What is poetry?

Teacher. Poetria or *poetrida* is a woman whose aim is [the writing of] verse.[74] The poet is thought to have chosen this title because he displays the beginning of his work as a woman of superlative beauty. He wishes her to be understood as representing the subject-matter, in which are found or from which arise those ideas (*sententiae*) which, when combined with the apt ordering of the arguments, perfect the whole work.

Pupil. What then is the subject-matter (*materia*) of this work?

Teacher. Horace appears to take as his grounds for writing on this subject (*occasio materiae*) the suggestion or request of friends or at any rate those who were writing books without a properly ordered argument. The subject of this book is the method of writing well, and instruction in it, and also reasoned precepts for beginning each poem correctly and concluding it in the same correct order. His intention in this work is to criticize the arrogance of certain poets, who, wrongfully claiming to be writers, produced a work of indeterminate style, giving their work neither the correct method (*modus*) or a proper order. Having proved them guilty of culpable temerity or ineptitude he taught what method, general principles, and order are to be employed, what course is to be followed in the way digressions develop, and what style is to be used and kept to in describing events, places, times, and seasons or persons.[75] He gave instructions as to how the limbs should be jointed to the head, that is the

---

[73] i.e. the *Ars poetica*. With Conrad's discussion cf. ll. 1–13 of that work.
[74] Cf. the Introduction to the *Art of Poetry* [and other works by Horace], tr. in Ch. I.
[75] The *circumstantiae*, on which see the references in Ch. I n. 6, and cf. above, nn. 15 and 19.

different ideas to the single subject, using many different comparisons, and showing up the virtues or defects of authors. Furthermore the ultimate end (*finalis causa*) he has in view in writing is very useful to those readers who pay particular attention to the guidelines laid down for writing. For whatever you write, be it long or short, in your writing the material in later parts must always fit in with the material used at the start. Be quite clear about this, that even in composing a brief letter you incur the risk of making that fable of the monstrous shape described on Horace's first page a reality, if you do not regulate your pen by a reasoned method of writing.

Pupil. I should surely be right in believing that a poet who was able by his writings to correct other poets who had gone astray could not himself make similar errors in his own verse.

Teacher. Indeed this same Horace wrote other books, the *Satires, Odes*, and so on. Someone who is beginning his studies may derive great profit from these. Yet in certain parts reading Horace is unprofitable for the religious, because [his subject-matter] is concerned with vice (*vitiosa*). But when what Horace has to say concerns vice, in this matter it is rather the case that individual examples of vice are recorded rather than that the author himself is subject to those vices. This same Horace died at Rome in his fifty-seventh year.[76]

Pupil. When we have so many works available which, if we read them properly, add an edge to our own ability and encourage us on the road to various virtues, why should we seek out writings tainted with vice whose meaning taints minds that should be trained by what they study? Why should the young recruit in Christ's army subject his impressionable mind to the writing of Ovid,[77] in which even though gold can be found among the dung,[78] yet the foulness that clings to the gold defiles the seeker, even though it is the gold he is after?

Teacher. Your aversion to the error of falsehood is grounded in good sense. Even though some of the writing of that same author Ovid might have been tolerated up to a point, namely the *Fasti, The Letters from Pontus, The Nut*, and some others; who in his right mind would endure him croaking about love, and his base deviations in different letters? Should I not name him as the inventor of a large part of idol-worship in his *Metamorphoses*, that is the transformation of substances? There the faculty of reason in man, whereby he is made in the image and likeness of God,[79] is obscured; a man is turned into a stone, an animal or a bird, when Ovid

---

[76] Following the dating in Jerome's version of the chronicle of Eusebius, *Eusebii Pamphili chronici canones*, ed. R. Helm, GCS xlvii. 167.

[77] Cf. the beginning of Conrad's discussion of Sedulius.

[78] Cf. Cassiodorus, *Institutiones*, 1. i. 8, ed. R. A. B. Mynors (Oxford, rpr. 1963), p. 14. This is what Virgil was supposed to have found among the writings of Ennius: see the life of Virgil known as Donatus auctus, ed. E. Diehl, *Die Vitae Vergilianae und ihre antiken Quellen* (Bonn, 1911), p. 35.   [79] Cf. Gen. 1: 26.

describes the gods' transformation of a rational being, part of creation, into different animals?

For the Apostle says [Rom. 1: 18–23]: 'For the wrath of God is revealed from heaven against all the impiety and wretchedness of those men who imprison God's truth in their injustice.' Explaining why this is so, he continues: 'Because what is known about God is plainly known among them. For God has shown it to them. For from the creation of the world His invisible nature seen by means of those things which He has created, is known to them, also His everlasting power and divinity. And so they have no excuse, for although they knew God they did not honour Him as God or give thanks to Him, but their thinking was futile and their heart darkened and lacking in wisdom. For even while they claimed to be wise they became foolish and exchanged the glorious concept of an incorruptible God for images resembling mortal men and birds and animals and serpents.'

Who then would reject the knowledge he has gained from the divinely inspired Scriptures and fling himself into the abyss of the deceitful pagans? Do you think that that same Ovid whom we are discussing here did not know that there is one Creator of all things, whom he seems to refer to hesitantly when he appears to be speaking of the creation in the words: 'Whoever that god was'—just as the Athenians set up an altar to 'the unknown god' [Acts 17: 23].[80] By that very ambiguity he seems to rule out any chance that he may have been ignorant of the true God, even though, confused by his own blindness, or held back by [fear of] human authority, he was unwilling to show due reverence to the almighty God, whom he recognized as the creator of the universe.

Pupil. It is not so much the hardness of heart of ungrateful men, I mean the wise of this world, that I marvel at as the way the Apostle in the above passage[81] speaks of divine revelation. He says: 'For God has shown it to them.' If God has given them a revelation in order that He should become known to them, why has He not helped them in order that He might be worshipped?

Teacher. 'O man, who are you to answer back to God? [Rom. 9: 20]'. Since the beginning of the world there have been two ways whereby God has been revealed to the human heart, partly through human reason and partly by divine revelation. For when the Apostle says 'what was known about God' [Rom. 1: 19], that is, knowable about God, in other words what can be known about God, he teaches us that neither is everything hidden nor is everything revealed. For when he says 'it is plainly known among them' and not 'plain to them' he wants to indicate that their Creator was known to them not only through divine revelation, which they had been given by way of their most sensitive inborn intelligence

---

[80] Cf. *Metamorphoses*, i. 32.
[81] i.e. Rom. 1: 18–23, cit. earlier in Conrad's text.

(*ingenium*), but also by the human power of reasoning which was a part of them. For the human mind is too frail and inadequate to view higher mysteries unless divine revelation has been added to the human condition of 'knowing the truth'. So if any of the ancient philosophers had a right idea of God, in so far as he [that is, a human being] was able to, if full knowledge of Him had been granted him, the grace which gave that knowledge would have been denied, while if all knowledge of Him were taken from him, so that he should have no knowledge of Him at all, then man would have been given a chance to excuse his ignorance.

Pupil. Very true, for they would not have been, as the Apostle says, totally inexcusable[82] if they had not gained that perception which could help them advance to an understanding of the nature of things incorporeal from one or the other quarter, that is, either from the human reason or divine revelation. But what opinion do you think we should have about the other authors on whom worldly learning expends its toil, namely Terence, Juvenal, the greater and lesser works of Statius, Persius, Homer, or Virgil? For the foolish young seek and find in these authors sanction for their own vanity to be wise for a season.

Teacher. In the case of all the [pagan] authors you have listed, it is for those Christian writers who, we know, inserted many of their ideas (*sententiae*) in writings which are in conformity with Christian teaching, to judge how much profit is to be gained by students from their words or weighty sayings (*sententiae*).

Pupil. If it turns out that you can prove your argument, no matter in what way, my doubts regarding this issue will be removed. But I shall not have been wrong in believing that the shining splendour, nay rather the whole face of sacred writing, can be defiled by the citations of pagan authors, if a writer boldly inserts them without good reason.

Teacher. Are the books of Moses and the prophets to be rejected just because they have sometimes used the words or ideas (*sententiae*) of pagan writers? If so, what meaning has our statement above that whatever truth and right thinking has ever been found in anyone has come from Him who created man?

Pupil. Up to now I have not been quite clear whether such statements can be found inserted in Holy Scripture.

Teacher. Why so, unless you have been deceived by two things? For either you have not entered the library of Greek authors, where of all pagan writings philosophical teachings are to be found in the greatest profusion; or else you have not considered the quite different mode of translation used in the Holy Scriptures. For notions found in the poets, written under the constraints of metre, could not be translated word for word into prose. That is why the very fact that you had committed some phrase in a [pagan] poet to memory has caused you to miss it once it had

[82] i.e. Rom. 1: 20, cit. above.

been translated in the Bible. Where did St Paul borrow the words 'Bad companions ruin good morals' [1 Cor. 15: 33] from, if not from that most ancient of poets, Menander? From what source did he take his famous testimony to his disciple Titus, 'The Cretans are always liars, evil beasts, more slothful bellies' [Tit. 1: 12], if not from the pagan poet Epimenides?[83] How often does Paul display his mastery of dialectic by putting forward a proposition, making a deduction, proving his point, and concluding his argument?[84] It would take too long to go through individual instances in order to undo the knot by which you are bound, for even in your *Rule* 'that there should be nothing in excess' has been taken from Terence,[85] a phrase which was greeted with universal applause when it was declaimed in the theatre by Calliopius.[86] What of the fact that the principal commentators on the Holy Scriptures, Augustine, Jerome, and others, use citations from pagan authors in their writings, but only when they are forced to give an account of the true meaning of the words, so that the quotation may be to the profit rather than the detriment of readers? I pass over the fierce attack made by St Augustine against the error of superstitious beliefs in the twelve [*sic* for twenty-two] books of *The City of God*, where he hurls against them the weapons of their own sect, taken from their own books. Let it suffice to mention two passages which he takes from Virgil and Horace and inserts in his own books. When, in his *On the Holy Trinity*, he was discussing the fact that even memory was concerned with the present in time, he inserted the citation about 'secular literature where the correctness of the words was a greater preoccupation than the truth of the subject-matter' and said: 'Ulysses did not allow this, nor did he forget himself though faced with such a perilous situation.'[87] Again, to show that eternity is sometimes substituted for the temporal he backs up his statement with a quotation from Horace, 'He will be for ever in bondage to his possessions because he does not know how to use them.'[88] Likewise, writing about the perfect man perfectly made in the likeness of a solid figure, he quotes 'strong and completely smooth and rounded out', and thus infinite in that sense.[89] Furthermore, I do not think I need to mention Jerome, who was all the more ready to insert quotations from secular literature in his own writings inasmuch as he was more renowned for his knowledge of that literature than many teachers of the Church.

[83] As Huygens points out, this passage, down to the reference to Epimenides, follows Jerome, *Epist.* lxx. 2, 3 (CSEL liv. 701, 704).

[84] Cf. Isidore, *Ety.* ii. ix. 3.

[85] *Benedicti regula*, lxiv. 12, ed. R. Hanslik (CSEL lxxv. 150); cf. Terence, *Andria* 61 1. Cf. also Jerome, *Epist.* lx. 7 (CSEL liv. 556), and *Epist.* cxxx. 11 (CSEL lvi. 191).

[86] Calliopius is mentioned in the *Scholia Terentiana*, ed. F. Schlee (Leipzig, 1893), pp. 79, 94, cf. p. 9.

[87] Augustine, *De Trinitate*, xiv. xi. 14 (CCSL lA. 441–2), cf. Virgil, *Aeneid*, iii. 628–9.

[88] Augustine, *Quaest. in Hept.* i. xxxi (CCSL xxxiii. 13); cf. Horace, *Epist.* i. x. 41.

[89] Augustine, *De quant. animae*, i. xvi. 27 (PL xxxii. 1051); cf. Horace, *Serm.* ii. vii. 86.

[ON JUVENAL]

Juvenal, that excellent satirist, sometimes routs the vices of the Romans by foul abuse and shows that one's health is to be preferred to all the riches of kings. He says: 'If the head, lungs, or feet are in good shape what more can a king's riches add?' Likewise, in pointing out that it is the deaths of poets rather than their lives that makes their works revered, he says: 'Nothing is sacred except that which Libitina [i.e. the goddess of undertakers] has consecrated.'[90]

[ON HOMER]

Homer, a Greek poet, composed his book about the fall of Troy and its ten-year siege, and this was his principal subject-matter. Furthermore, his intention is entirely centred on the praise of the Greeks and the confusion of the Trojans. He also composed a smaller book, entitled *The Smaller Homer*, where he particularly displays the lineage and prowess of Achilles. Pindar, a very highly esteemed philosopher, translated Homer from Greek into Latin. Jerome recalls this poet in his book *On the Best Kind of Interpretation*: 'If someone should take the trouble to translate the Greek poet Homer literally (*ad verbum*), breaking up the pattern of the metre, he will see that that most eloquent of men has hardly anything to say at all.'[91] Horace also speaks of him: 'Sometimes even good Homer nods off to sleep',[92] a drowsiness which he [i.e. Horace] excuses by the lengthy nature of his [i.e. Homer's] work. Virgil was Homer's apprentice, and recounted the actual history of the Trojan war in twelve books. This same Homer flourished in the time of . . .'[93]

[ON PERSIUS]

What shall I say about Persius, a most excellent and renowned Roman poet, as was Juvenal, a satirist who without restraint castigated the vices of the Romans and branded and exposed with a witty pen all who were subject to those vices?

Pupil. I am not sure what you mean by 'satirist'.

Teacher. Among the ancients *satyra* was a very large dish on which the people placed all sorts of different morsels of food.[94] Then the priest of

---

[90] As Huygens points out, these verses come not from Juvenal but from Horace, *Epist.* I. xii. 5–6 and II. i. 49.

[91] Jerome, *Eusebii chron.*, GCS xlvii. 4.

[92] *Ars poetica*, 359.

[93] Here a lacuna exists in both the MSS used by Huygens, who argues that this and other features (cf. above, nn. 49 and 90) support the hypothesis that Conrad left his text slightly incomplete at the time of his death.

[94] With this discussion cf. the earlier attempts at defining *satyra*, above, p. 44.

the gods used to take freely from the portions placed in the dish whatever he pleased, and no one could say him nay. In the same way satiric poets boldly criticized in their writings anyone who indulged in vice, and they always found sufficient material for their criticism just like the dish (*satyra*) which held lots of pieces of food. So they freely castigated the vices of the depraved because they relied on their own clear conscience and did not fear any criticism of their writings.

Pupil. Let me hear that again, but put differently.

Teacher. That I will do. Satyrs and fauns are monstrous creatures of the forest which are always quite shamelessly naked. So, just as satyrs expose themselves totally naked[95] to the gaze of strangers without the least embarrassment, so satiric poets are not prevented by embarrassment, in the presence of their readers, from continuing to use a style which is itself faulty (*viciosa*), providing they are seen to make the depraved suffer under the naked outspokenness of their words. Accordingly, Persius' subject-matter was the chaotic life of the vicious Romans. His intention was, by his reprehension, to rescue the erring from their vices and to transform them and lead them to a better way of life.

Pupil. Add to the names of the other poets [you have mentioned] that of Statius who wrote the *Thebaid* and the Statius who wrote the *Achilleid*, and tell me whether the two books were in fact written by the same person.

[ON STATIUS]

Teacher. Statius indeed composed both books, but the subject-matter of each is different. The subject of the first named was the war between Thebes and king . . .[96] and the destruction of that city; and of the second the birth of Achilles and his upbringing at the court of Diomedes. Writing to Domitian he has this to say concerning it: LITTLE ACHILLES WILL PLAY FOR YOUR AMUSEMENT.[97] Moreover, the Thebans or men of Thebes were always most unfortunate according to the historians . . . and the Athenians had advanced so far in the literary skills that their achievements, even though slight, were celebrated as though they were of great consequence.[98] Statius, who wrote on the subject of the misfortunes of the Thebans, took the subject-matter of his work from the beginning or from the end of the actual war. The aforesaid Statius lived in the time of Titus and Vespasian and in his writings offered them this subject of the Theban war as an example of the various virtues. For in it Adrastus, the king of the

---

[95] Literally 'without caring about coverings (*tegumenta*)'; likewise, satiric poets do not employ the coverings of *integumenta* of myth but rather employ language which is naturally outspoken (cf. our discussion of the Juvenal commentary partially tr. in Ch. IV).

[96] Another lacuna in the text; cf. above, n. 93.

[97] Cf. *Achilleid*, i. 19: 'magnusque tibi praeludit Achilles'.

[98] Cf. Sallust, *Catilina*, viii. 2–3.

Greeks, after the fighting had gone now one way and now another, eventually conquered Thebes and destroyed it.

ON VIRGIL

Teacher. Virgil, according to Augustine, looms very large among Latin writers,[99] and by the amazing effectiveness of his writings has persuaded many noble minds to study his work. He produced three works, employing the threefold range of styles, that is the lowly, middle, and grandiloquent,[100] in the *Bucolics*, *Georgics*, and *Aeneid* respectively. In the weighty thought expressed in these works, and the text (*litera*) presented to him in a manner that is most appropriate, the penetrating reader will be able to observe that this great poet has acquired a full grasp of all the liberal disciplines, and seems to be inferior to no other author in his use of metre, set apart by a unique possession of his own individual style.

In his *Bucolics* he adopts the manner of the eclogue, that is, a shepherd's song, which gets its name from its principal constituent, for in this work are related the conversations, arguments, and songs not only of cowherds but also of shepherds and goatherds. There are those who think that these *Bucolics* should be read or understood other than literally, since one should seek out what subtler meaning the author is conveying by the plain words of the text. This may indeed be so in certain places, so that the hidden inner meaning of the text may lead the reader to understand something quite different. This often happens in common proverbs, so that we say one thing and mean something quite different from what the words seem to signify. But I think I should cite one example from the actual *Bucolics*, where the poet appears to be attacking his rivals Bavius and Maevius in a distich, and in a very few words clearly succeeds in confounding utterly their life and writings. He says: 'May he who does not detest Bavius enjoy your poems, Maevius, and may he yoke up a pair of foxes and milk he-goats.'[101] You can see the double meaning in these verses, that a man's punishment for not detesting Bavius should be to be forced to like the poems of Maevius, and in consequence be driven insane to the point of thinking that foxes can be yoked up like pairs of oxen and he-goats milked like she-goats, something which nature does not permit. Or else by employing unspoken mockery the poem includes within the scope of his attack, under the guise of foxes and he-goats, the slyness and deceit of his enemies, and the foulness of their verse.

In this work the author has as his intention to describe the way of life and characters of shepherds, their serious occupations and amuse-

---

[99] Literally 'forms a great part of Latin literature'. Cf. Augustine, *Epist. ad Romanos inchoata expositio*, 3 (CSEL lxxxiv. 147); *De civ. Dei*, I. iii.
[100] Cf. Conrad's earlier definition of the three styles of writing, above, p. 46.
[101] See above, n. 12.

ments, the difference between the secluded countryside and the city, his own affection towards Caesar [Augustus], and to praise Caesar's protection of him, and thus to exercise the able minds of his readers with hidden significations. Furthermore the subject-matter caters for this intention from every quarter, for he has composed that eclogue in the manner (*modus*), and with the setting, period, and characters of those whose task it is to tend flocks. The profit for the reader is to understand the precise meaning of the Latin to the fullest possible extent.

In the *Georgics* Virgil describes the method, nature, and the correct timing of farming operations relating to the sowing of seed, the husbandry of cattle and management of flocks, and the method, timing, and treatment employed in planting vines. He also describes the farmer's vigilance, the great intricacy of nature displayed, and the skill required, in bee-keeping: what position should be chosen for the hive, cut off from the rude assault of the winds; what food is beneficial, and what harmful, in bee-keeping. He shows the orderly way in which they keep and maintain the cells, swollen with nectar,[102] and each of them maintain their separate functions [in the hive]. He shows the difference between the two groups enclosed within the hives, the struggle between the two and the victory of one side, and the marvellous devotion of the bees to their leader. All this he shows us, employing a very subtle middle style. In short, you must understand that the subject-matter of this work is the cultivation of the land. If the poet had not had a perfect understanding of the skills involved in farming, he would not have been able to write anything about agriculture. His intention is to instruct mortals in how to live the simple life, that is, a life devoted to tilling the land, so that being thus employed they may learn their own [real] nature and divert their thoughts from empty idleness and preoccupations that are positively harmful.

Pupil. Add his third work, the *Aeneid*, to your account of the first two.

Teacher. The history of the destruction of Troy is known to all, how on account of Helen Troy endured a siege lasting ten years and was captured by the Greeks. Aeneas became a fugitive from them, sailed to Italy, founded a city, conquered Turnus, and personally furnished the Romans with their ancestry and their inherited valour. Thus he performed great deeds in Italy, cruelly assailing all its inhabitants. Finally he was killed by a thunderbolt sent from heaven. Virgil has taken both his subject-matter and his intention from this history. There has never been a ⟨greater⟩ author in terms of style and metre, and no one, when he ought to have told the truth,[103] nevertheless lied in a more polished and civil fashion.

This author ended his life at Brindisi.[104] His corpse was removed to

---

[102] Cf. *Georgics*, iv. 164.   [103] Literally 'when forced to give way to truth'.

[104] Following Jerome, *Eusebii chron.*, GCS xlvii. 165–6; cf. *Vitae Vergilianae antiquae*, ed. C. G. Hardie, 2nd edn. (Oxford, 1966), pp. 14, 37; H. R. Upson, 'Mediaeval Lives of Virgil', *CP* xxxviii (1943), 105.

Naples and buried there. His tomb is distinguished by a distich dictated by himself which goes something as follows: 'Mantua gave me birth, the Calabrians snatched me from life, now Naples possesses me; I sang of pastures, farms, and leaders.' On his death Varrus [*sic* for Varius] and Tucca, friends of Virgil and Horace, took on the task of editing the *Aeneid* for Augustus, with the stipulation that they should erase what was superfluous but should add nothing of their own.

Teacher. Pay attention![105] The soul has no greater pleasure in this world than to feed on God's word and, because it hopes and believes that it will enjoy rest after its labours, while it is still on the path of pilgrimage it hides the word of God as a pledge of its hope and is [thus] already coming into its heavenly patrimony. So we must always devote our efforts to the study of the teachings of philosophy, that is, those which consist not just in words but in the recounting of deeds, which urge us to despise the things of this world and inculcate love of those things which are eternal, which teach us 'to walk in the spirit' and 'to deny the rights of the flesh' [Gal. 5: 16]. Their net result is to inculcate love of God, the cultivation of things invisible, and hatred of the world, and to produce a state of mind that holds strongly to the truth, and a detestation of all that is false. 'We have been called forth to receive freedom' [Gal. 5: 13]. Let us then serve our king by pursuing liberal studies.[106]

Pupil. Shall we, then, devote ourselves to learning dialectic and the other arts, since Christ, 'the power and wisdom of God', has turned 'the wisdom of this world into folly', and Paul, who 'speaks of wisdom among those made perfect', knew nothing save 'Christ and Him crucified'? [1 Cor. 1: 20, 24; 2: 6, 2.]

Teacher. He who learns his philosophy in Christ[107] always finds the liberal arts instructive and, triumphing over the vices, passes 'to the freedom of the sons' [i.e. of God; Rom. 8: 21]. Otherwise any progress beyond other men in the liberal arts is useless if you still cultivate the vices and have submitted yourself to the lowest form of slavery.

Pupil. If one follows through your train of reasoning it seems to me that he who prostitutes his life is a slave to the vices, while he who loves the virtues is free....[108]

---

[105] No comment from the Pupil has intervened here—further evidence that this text is a penultimate draft rather than the final draft? Cf. above, nn. 93 and 96.

[106] i.e. the liberal arts.

[107] i.e. as a Christian with Christ at the centre of all things.

[108] Conrad proceeds to discuss the order and nature of the liberal arts, which serve divine science.

Quite a bit on rel. of sacred to sec. literature + why the KL would want to learn the latter.

III

Scriptural Allegory and Authority: Hugh of Saint-Victor, Peter Abelard, and Peter Lombard

'THE idea that the sacred Scriptures have (aside from their literal value) a symbolic value is ancient and not irrational',[1] declares Jorge Luis Borges, offering this insight into the motivation of those who sought to plumb the depths of divinely-inspired writing:

> They thought that a work dictated by the Holy Spirit was an absolute text: in other words, a text in which the collaboration of chance was calculable as zero. This portentous premise of a book impenetrable to contingency, of a book which is a mechanism of infinite purposes, moved them to permute the scriptural words, add up the numerical value of the letters, consider their form, observe the small letters and capitals, seek acrostics and anagrams and perform other exegetical rigours which it is not difficult to ridicule. Their excuse is that nothing can be contingent in the work of an infinite mind.[2]

To some extent this is true of twelfth-century biblical exegesis. The present section has as its subject the way in which three outstanding scholars of that period, Hugh of Saint-Victor (*c.* 1096–1141), Peter Abelard (1079–1142 or 1144), and Peter Lombard (*c.* 1100–60), approached their 'absolute text', striving to trace the blueprint of its 'mechanism of infinite purposes' in a way which illustrated and confirmed its supreme authority in the world of books.

About 1118 Hugh entered Saint-Victor, the house of Augustinian canons recently founded in Paris by William of Champeaux (who had once instructed Abelard in the arts and subsequently became his bitter rival). After studying under William, Hugh remained at Saint-Victor to teach the elements of the liberal arts and scriptural commentary.[3] His teaching methods and priorities are clearly described in the *Didascalicon* (*c.* 1127), a work in which, as Jerome Taylor has put it, Hugh seeks 'to select and define all the areas of knowledge important to man and to demonstrate not only that these areas are essentially integrated among themselves, but that in their integrity they are necessary to man for the attainment of his human perfection and his divine destiny'.[4] More specifically, the first three books of the *Didascalicon* instruct the reader of the arts while the second three instruct the reader of Holy Writ. The basic rules for reading any text, whether secular or sacred, are said to be three in number: 'first, each man should know what he ought to read; second, in what order he

---

[1] 'The Mirror of Enigmas', in id. *Labyrinths* (repr. Harmondsworth, 1981), p. 244.
[2] Ibid., pp. 246–7.
[3] On Hugh's life and works see esp. Smalley, *Study of the Bible*, pp. 83–106; J. Ehlers, *Hugo von St. Viktor* (Frankfurter historische Abhandlungen VII, Wiesbaden, 1973), esp. pp. 5–50. For an excellent introduction to Hugh's thought see Roger Baron, *Science et sagesse chez Hughes de Saint-Victor* (Paris, 1957).
[4] *The* Didascalicon *of Hugh of St. Victor*, tr. Taylor, p. 3.

ought to read, that is, what first and what afterwards; and third, in what manner he ought to read'.[5] Throughout the work Hugh's obsession with orderly process is evident: the order in which study should proceed, the order of the arts in relation to each other, the order and number of the books of the Bible, the order in which the budding exegete should be taught (beginning with the study of history and graduating to consume the solid food of allegory), and the order of expounding the Bible itself, always starting with the secure foundation of the 'letter', then moving to the 'sense', and finally seeking the *sententia* or deeper meaning.

For Hugh, as for St Augustine before him, the special power of biblical language lay in its unusual method of signification. In *On Christian Doctrine* Augustine had adumbrated a distinction between two kinds of signs: words, whose very *raison d'être* consists in their function of signifying, and things, which on special occasions can signify something else, as when the wood which Moses cast into bitter waters to make them sweet (Exod. 15: 25) signifies the cross of Christ.[6] Elsewhere in the same work he declares that signs are either literal or figurative. They are literal when they are used in accordance with their normal signification, as when the word 'ox' refers to an animal in a herd because linguistic convention decrees that this be so. Figurative signs, he continues, 'occur when that thing which we designate by a literal sign is used to signify something else; thus we say "ox" and by that syllable understand the animal which is ordinarily designated by that word, but again by that animal we understand an evangelist, as is signified in the Scripture, according to the interpretation of the Apostle, when it says, "Thou shalt not muzzle the ox that treadeth out the corn"' (Deut. 25. 4; cf. the Apostolic interpretation as given in 1 Cor. 9: 9 and 1 Tim. 5: 18).[7] Hugh's version of this doctrine is that in merely human and philosophical writings we have only significant words, whereas in the Bible things can have a meaning too, as when the lion mentioned in 1 Pet. 5: 8 stands for the Devil.[8] Such meaning which exists beyond 'the bare surface of the letter' sets the Bible apart from other books and makes allegorical interpretation necessary.

But Hugh was highly discriminating in his approach to allegory. In the *Didascalicon* VI. iv (translated below) he remarks tartly that we must not make the text 'the letter killeth' an excuse for preferring our own ideas to the divine authors.[9] 'All things in the divine utterance must not be wrenched to an interpretation such that each of them is held to contain history, allegory, and tropology all at once' (v. ii). Not every passage of Scripture has a *sententia*; sometimes only the letter and the sense exist; sometimes the letter is all there is, clearly signifying what is meant (cf. VI. viii). Reacting against the Gregorian allegorizing tradition with its 'sublime disregard for the letter of Scripture' (as Beryl Smalley describes it),[10] Hugh makes a remarkable plea: when choosing

[5] *Didascalicon*, pr. (ed. Buttimer, p. 2; tr. Taylor, p. 44).
[6] *De doct. Christ.* 1. ii. 2 (tr. Robertson, p. 8).
[7] *De doct. Christ.* 11. x. 15.
[8] *Didascalicon*, v. iii (ed. Buttimer, p. 97; tr. below). Cf. Gillian R. Evans, *The Language and Logic of the Bible: The Earlier Middle Ages* (Cambridge, 1984), pp. 52–6.
[9] Cf. Smalley, *Study of the Bible*, p. 94.   [10] Ibid., p. 95.

from among the great number of patristic explanations, let us select that which appears to have certainly been intended by the author of the biblical passage in question (VI. xi).[11] This appeal to authorial intention was to be echoed over and over again by the theologians of the thirteenth and fourteenth centuries (see below, Ch. VI).

Generally, however, Hugh's achievement was that of the conservatively erudite and methodical teacher rather than of the technical innovator whose thinking was far ahead of his time. For him the arts were the humble and submissive handmaidens of theology.[12] But for Peter Abelard, a man with a far more aggressive and combative mind, they offered the exegete techniques which could transform the way in which theology was approached and understood.[13] The spirit of twelfth-century grammar, rhetoric, and dialectic animates the *Sic et non*, a work which Abelard seems to have revised no fewer than five times, to judge from the eleven extant manuscripts. The first three versions have been dated between 1122 and 1127; the subsequent ones between 1132 and 1142 (or 1144).[14] In its fullest form the work contains 158 questions or problems, in each case the relevant views of the biblical authors and the Church Fathers being brought together in such a way as to reveal their apparent divergence and even contradictoriness. Difficulties are raised but not resolved; that is the challenge offered to the student, who has to apply the general rules set down in the Prologue.

The Prologue states that the obscurity and apparent contradictions in theological writings can be explained on many grounds, and can be examined without impugning the authors' good faith and insight.[15] Many problems may be considered as matters of signification. A writer may use different words to mean the same thing; indeed, different writers may use different words in discussing the same topic. Sometimes common and vague words are employed in order that the common people may understand. Sometimes rhetorical and poetic language may be used, which is often obscure and vague. Moreover, there are passages in which an author may be speaking to exhort

---

[11] Here Hugh is following Augustine, *De Genesi ad litteram*, I. xxi (CSEL xxviii. 31).

[12] 'It is clear that all the natural arts serve divine science, and that the lower wisdom, rightly ordered, leads to the higher', *De sacramentis*, prol. vi (PL clxxvi. 185), tr. R. J. Deferrari, *Hugh of St. Victor on the Sacraments of the Christian Faith* (Mediaeval Academy of America LVIII, Cambridge, Mass., 1951), p. 5. Cf. Evans, *Language and Logic*, pp. 30, 32–3; also ead., *Old Arts and New Theology: The Beginnings of Theology as an Academic Discipline* (Oxford, 1980), pp. 60–2.

[13] Cf. Evans, *Old Arts and New Theology*, pp. 79–90, and esp. J. Jolivet's admirably thorough study, *Arts du langage et théologie chez Abélard* (Études de philosophique médiévale LVII, Paris, 1969).

[14] On Abelard's life and the different versions of the *Sic et non* see *Petri Abaelardi opera theologica*, i, ed. E. M. Buytaert (CCCM xi, pp. ix–xii, xiv–xvi, xxiii–xxv); *Peter Abailard: Sic et non. A Critical Edition*, fasci. i, ed. B. Boyer and R. McKeon (Chicago and London, 1976), pp. 1–80.

[15] Abelard's techniques and methods have been interpreted as a development of techniques used by canon lawyers in their reconciliation of discordant canons: see M. Grabmann, *Die Geschichte der scholastichen Methode* (Freiburg, 1901–11), i. 234–46; cf. R. McKeon, 'Rhetoric in the Middle Ages', repr. in R. S. Crane (ed.), *Critics and Criticism: Ancient and Modern* (Chicago, 1952), pp. 283–4. On the precedents for the application of such techniques in theology see E. Bertola, 'I precedenti storici del metodo del *Sic et non* di Abelardo', *RFN* liii (1961), 255–80.

rather than give information; sometimes advice and precepts are given, which may either have general relevance or may apply only to special cases. Many of these principles reveal Abelard's interest in the historical contexts of authoritative statements and the personal purposes of their authors: once these facts are known, a scholar may well be able to reconcile his discordant *auctoritates* and get at the truth.[16] Other principles turn on the issue of authenticity: apocryphal works are often attributed to the saints; authors may on occasion merely reiterate the opinions of other men, including erroneous opinions.

Most striking of all are Abelard's applications of the principle that not all writings are of equal authority. All the patristic writings are to be read with full freedom to criticize, and with no obligation to accept anything without question. By contrast, the Holy Scriptures are of far greater authority and therefore must be treated with reverence and respect: when anything therein strikes us as absurd, we may not say that the writer erred, but that the scribe made a blunder in copying, or we must make some similar excuse. Yet at one point Abelard dares to ask if even the apostles and prophets were sometimes in error, then hastily points out that to be in error is not the same thing as to lie. And, if it be conceded that even those great authors 'were not altogether strangers to error', and on occasion did not show themselves to be inspired, one need not wonder that the Church Fathers could sometimes be mistaken. Abelard cites the example of St Augustine, who found himself mistaken in some cases and did not hesitate to compose a book of retractions.[17] Augustine himself warned his admirers not to look upon his writings as they would upon the Scriptures, but to accept only those things which, on examination, they found to be true. Here Abelard is managing—with typical casuistry—to call in question the consistency of the Fathers' authority, by appealing to the authority of the greatest of them.

By suggesting that Holy Scripture might contain error, Abelard departed, as Gillian Evans has pointed out, 'from the assumption that the divine inspiration of Scripture extends to the minutest detail of the choice of words',[18] an assumption which permeates the exegesis of Hugh of Saint-Victor. But this bold statement was not supported by his own biblical exegesis, wherein he seems as eager as any medieval theologian to accept and justify every detail of the 'absolute text'. In his *Commentary on St Paul's Epistle to the Romans* we find Abelard's version of the commonplace that the Bible was produced 'as though the finger of God had written it, that is, as though it were composed and written at the dictation of the Holy Spirit'. 'The authority of Scripture which God Himself gave' is pronounced to be 'unalterable'.[19] Abelard's successors, however, were to return again and again to consider the awful possibility that Holy Scripture might contain error or even downright falsehood, as Ch. VI will illustrate.

---

[16] The *auctoritates* were not persons but extracts from the works of *auctores*, i.e. the authoritative writers. For discussion and bibliography see Minnis, *Authorship*, pp. 10–11.

[17] On the significance of the *Retractions* for later views of Augustine's authority see ibid., pp. 154, 158.

[18] Evans, *Language and Logic*, p. 138.

[19] *Comm. in Rom.* III. vii. 15, II. iv. 11 (CCCM xi. 205, 132); cit. Evans, *Language and Logic*, p. 138.

Many of the principles outlined in the *Sic et non* prologue can be seen in operation in Abelard's Bible commentaries.[20] In the prologue to his *Commentary on St Paul's Epistle to the Romans* he cleverly reconciles those received opinions which appear to contradict each other on the issue of who first preached to the Romans. Abelard's interest in St Paul's historical situation is obvious; one wonders if he was influenced by the *vitae auctorum* which he would have encountered in the course of his training in grammar. Certainly, the first section of the prologue to this commentary follows the pattern of the 'type C' schema as used in the *accessus ad auctores* (see above, pp. 12–13), focusing on the text's intention (*intentio*), subject-matter (*materia*), and mode of treatment (*modus tractandi*). One may compare the sophisticated discussion of *materia* and *intentio* at the beginning of his commentary on the six days of creation in Genesis.[21] Moreover, Abelard's training in rhetoric comes out when he discusses St Paul's style in terms of the art of letter-writing (*ars dictaminis*).[22] The arts have made great inroads into theology.

But was Abelard the first person to transfer the 'type C' prologue from the arts to theology? Beryl Smalley thought that this might have been the case,[23] but the theory, whilst attractive, is impossible to prove. All we can say with assurance is that the paradigm was coming into use in scriptural exegesis in the first quarter of the twelfth century, and that Abelard and Gilbert of Poitiers (*c.* 1080–1154), both pupils of Anselm of Laon (one of the originators of the *Glossa ordinaria* or standard Bible commentary, who died in 1117), were among the first to use it.[24]

The trend soon became established, and Peter Lombard introduced his Psalter glosses in this way as a matter of course. This commentary, read in the schools shortly before the Lombard's election as Bishop of Paris in 1159, was a highly influential work which replaced the *Glossa ordinaria* on the Psalter—largely the work of Anselm of Laon—as the most popular exposition of that text in use among students. Together with Peter's commentary on the Pauline Epistles (written between 1148 and 1159) it was known as the *Magna* or *Maior glosatura*. Even more successful—indeed, the most successful of all medieval theological textbooks—was his *Libri sententiarum*, compiled between 1155 and 1158.[25] In the next century, at some time within the period 1223–7, the Franciscan Alexander of Hales substituted the *Sentences* for the Bible in his lectures in the Parisian faculty of theology.[26] A flood of commentaries followed; the

---

[20] Cf. Minnis, *Authorship*, pp. 59–63.

[21] *Expositio in Hexaemeron* (PL clxxviii. 731–3); cit. Evans, *Language and Logic*, p. 31.

[22] On the tradition of *ars dictaminis* see Murphy, *Rhetoric in the Middle Ages*, pp. 194–268.

[23] Beryl Smalley, 'Peter Comestor on the Gospels and his Sources', *RTAM* xlvi (1979), 110–11; cf. N. Häring, 'The Lectures of Thierry of Chartres on Boethius, *De trinitate*', *AHDLMA* xxv (1959), 120–1.

[24] Cf. Minnis, *Authorship*, p. 41, for full discussion and bibliography.

[25] These datings are by I. Brady in the prolegomena to *Petri Lombardi sententiae in iv libros distinctae*, i, pars I (Spicilegium Bonaventurianum IV, Grottaferrata, 1971). See further Smalley, *Study of the Bible*, pp. 64–5.

[26] See I. Brady in *Magistri Alexandri de Hales, Glossa in quattuor libros sententiarum Petri Lombardi* (Bibliotheca franciscana scholastica medii aevi XII–XV, Grottaferrata, 1951–7), i. 102–3.

'Master of the Sentences' was still being glossed as late as the seventeenth century.

The Prologue begins with a statement of David's great eminence and authority among the prophets and an affirmation of the Psalter's unique excellence, this being explained with reference to its names, its structure and numerological significance, and its liturgical use. Then the Lombard proceeds to a discussion of the text's title (*titulus*), subject-matter (*materia*), intention (*intentio*) and mode of treatment (*modus tractandi*); a brief comment on its arrangement (*ordo*) is appended. The discussion of the Psalter's full title, 'Here begins the book of hymns or soliloquies of the prophet concerning Christ', is by far the longest, since each of its elements is discussed in turn. The final part of this discussion, of the lemma 'concerning Christ', leads quite naturally into an analysis of subject-matter, since Christ is the *materia* of the Psalter; the *intentio* is then declared to be the remaking of man in Christ's image. The mode of stylistic and didactic treatment is varied, according to which aspect of Christ is to the fore.

Peter then says that this framework of interpretation, which he has just applied to the Psalter in its entirety, must also be applied to its individual components, to each and every psalm. He illustrates this by discussing the first psalm's title (or rather its lack thereof), subject-matter, intention, and mode of treatment. Similarly, Abelard had first described the general intention of all the Pauline epistles, and then proceeded to investigate the particular intention, subject-matter, and mode of treatment of each of them. One is reminded of the way in which commentators on Ovid's *Heroides* used to explain the general intention of the work as a whole and the particular intentions of the individual epistles (cf. above, pp. 22–3); similar vocabulary is to be found in twelfth-century *accessūs* to the Roman satirists.[27]

Here we have two types of literature—the sacred and the profane—divided by a common language of evaluation. The significance of the Psalter is believed to consist in its Christological level of meaning; that of the *Heroides* and the satires in their contribution to a system of ethics which, while non-Christian in historical terms, was not held to be incompatible with Christian morality. The ethical significance of a work like the *Heroides* was not immediately evident: Ovid's *intentio* had to be 'piously interpreted' for its Christian audience. By contrast, the Psalter's significance was indubitable, having been guaranteed by the one true God who had inspired its human authors. Therefore, a technique of analysis which in grammarians' *accessūs* had formed part and parcel of the defence of a work's purpose and worth became, in the hands of twelfth-century theologians, a means whereby the literary features of a work which needed no apology could be adequately characterized.[28]

In this new context the 'type C' headings altered in meaning. As described by Peter Lombard and other twelfth-century exegetes, the *materia* of the Psalter is not—as is usually the case with the *materia* of a secular work—the subject matter understood literally, but rather its central allegorical referent,

[27] See Kristeller, *CTC* i. 188, 195–6; iii. 224–5, 227.
[28] Cf. Minnis, *Authorship*, pp. 54–7.

So Minnis is with / *to see some alteration w/in a type proof,*

the whole Christ. Similarly, the heading *intentio* introduces a statement about allegorical rather than literal sense. This approach renders superfluous any consideration of the work's usefulness (*utilitas*). In place of the arts scholar's identification of the subdivision of philosophy (*pars philosophiae*) relevant to the text is a statement of the subdivision of prophecy (*genus prophetiae*) under which David's prophecies may be classified.

Concomitant with this is a tendency to emphasize the divine rather than the human authorship of the Psalter. By contrast with Abelard's interest in at least certain aspects of the life of St Paul, the Lombard regarded David's human characteristics as relatively unimportant—what did matter was that he was a 'trumpet of the Holy Spirit'. Consistently, he declares that the names mentioned in the psalm titles[29] do not refer to individual psalmists, but are there to direct the reader to the allegorical mysteries hidden behind the letter. All problems regarding the composite authorship and the apparent disunity and lack of cohesion of the psalms are cleverly allegorized away.[30] The contributions, even the identities, of the human (though inspired) *auctores* must pale into insignificance in face of the divine *auctoritas* of the 'absolute text'.

The nexus between allegory and authority was called in question, however, during the thirteenth century, which saw a new emphasis on the 'literal sense' of Scripture. Then new solutions were sought to the problems of description presented by the unusual methods of signification characteristic of biblical language. But discussion of such matters must be reserved for Ch. VI.

HUGH OF SAINT-VICTOR

Didascalicon: Extracts from Books V and VI[31]

FROM BOOK V

Chapter ii: Concerning the Threefold Understanding[32]

First of all, it ought to be known that sacred Scripture has three ways of conveying meaning—namely history, allegory, and tropology. To be sure, all things in the divine utterance must not be wrenched to an interpretation such that each of them is held to contain history, allegory, and tropology all at once. Even if a triple meaning can appropriately be

---

[29] On the *tituli psalmorum* in medieval manuscripts of the Psalter see P. Salmon, *Les 'Tituli psalmorum' des manuscrits latins* (Collectanea biblica latina XII, Rome, 1959).

[30] Cf. Minnis, *Authorship*, pp. 47–8.

[31] Repr. from *The* Didascalicon *of Hugh of St. Victor*, tr. Taylor, pp. 120–2, 135–50, with the permission of Columbia University Press and Professor Jerome Taylor. The following notes often draw on Professor Taylor's.

[32] Cf. *Didascalicon*, VI. iii, where the threefold scheme of historical, typical, and moral interpretation is quoted, with slight adaptations, from Gregory the Great's *Moralia in Job*: see below, n. 47.

assigned in many passages, nevertheless it is either difficult or impossible to see it everywhere. 'On the zither and musical instruments of this type not all the parts which are handled ring out with musical sounds; only the strings do this. All the other things on the whole body of the zither are made as a frame to which may be attached, and across which may be stretched, those parts which the artist plays to produce sweetness of song.'[33] Similarly, in the divine utterances are placed certain things which are intended to be understood spiritually only, certain things that emphasize the importance of moral conduct, and certain things said according to the simple sense of history. And yet, there are some things which can suitably be expounded not only historically but allegorically and tropologically as well. Thus is it that, in a wonderful manner, the whole of sacred Scripture is so suitably adjusted and arranged in all its parts through the Wisdom of God that whatever is contained in it either resounds with the sweetness of spiritual understanding in the manner of strings; or, containing utterances of mysteries set here and there in the course of a historical narrative or in the substance of a literal context, and, as it were, connecting these up into one object, it binds them together all at once as the wood does which curves under the taut strings; and receiving their sound into itself, it reflects it more sweetly to our ears—a sound which the string alone has not yielded, but which the wood too has formed by the shape of its body. Thus also is honey more pleasing because enclosed in the comb, and whatever is sought with greater effort is also found with greater desire.[34] It is necessary, therefore, so to handle the sacred Scripture that we do not try to find history everywhere, nor allegory everywhere, nor tropology everywhere but rather that we assign individual things fittingly in their own places, as reason demands. Often, however, in one and the same literal context, all may be found together, as when a truth of history both hints at some mystical meaning by way of allegory, and equally shows by way of tropology how we ought to behave.

Chapter iii: That Things, too, have a Meaning in Holy Scripture

It ought also to be known that in the divine utterance not only words but even things have a meaning[35]—a way of communicating not usually found to such an extent in other writings. The philosopher knows only the significance of words, but the significance of things is far more excellent than that of words, because the latter was established by usage, but

[33] As Taylor points out, this is quoted verbatim from Isidore of Seville's *Quaestiones in Vetus Testamentum*, pr. iv (PL lxxxii. 208). Cf. Augustine, *Contra Faustum Manichaeum*, xxii. 94 (CSEL xxv. 701).

[34] Cf. Augustine, *De doct. Christ.* ii. vi. 8.

[35] Cf. Hugh, *De sacramentis*, pr. v (PL clxxvi. 185), tr. Deferrari, p. 5: 'in other writings words alone are found to have meaning, but in it [Holy Scripture] not only words but also things are significant'. See further the similar statements by later theologians, discussed and quoted below, Ch. VI.

Nature dictated the former.[36] The latter is the voice of men, the former the voice of God speaking to men. The latter, once uttered, perishes; the former, once created, subsists. The unsubstantial word is the sign of man's perceptions; the thing is a resemblance of the divine idea. What, therefore, the sound of the mouth, which all in the same moment begins to subsist and fades away, is to the idea in the mind, that the whole extent of time is to eternity. The idea in the mind is the internal word, which is shown forth by the sound of the voice, that is, by the external word. And the divine Wisdom, which the Father has uttered out of His heart, invisible in Itself, is recognized through creatures and in them.[37] From this is most surely gathered how profound is the understanding to be sought in the sacred writings, in which we come through the word to a concept, through the concept to a thing, through the thing to its idea, and through its idea arrive at truth. Because certain less well instructed persons do not take acount of this, they suppose that there is nothing subtle in these matters on which to exercise their mental abilities, and they turn their attention to the writings of philosophers precisely because, not knowing the power of truth, they do not understand that in Scripture there is anything beyond the bare surface of the letter.

That the sacred utterances employ the meaning of things, moreover, we shall demonstrate by a particular short and clear example. The Scripture says: 'Watch, because your adversary the Devil goeth about as a roaring lion' [1 Pet. 5: 8]. Here, if we should say that the lion stands for the Devil, we should mean by 'lion' not the word but the thing. For if the two words 'Devil' and 'lion' mean one and the same thing, the likeness of that same thing to itself is not adequate. It remains, therefore, that the word 'lion' signifies the animal, but that the animal in turn designates the Devil. And all other things are to be taken after their fashion, as when we say that worm, calf, stone, serpent, and other things of this sort signify Christ.

FROM BOOK VI

Chapter i: How the Sacred Scripture should be Read by Those who seek Knowledge in it.

Two things I propose to you, my student—namely, order and method— and if you pay careful attention to them, the pathway of study will easily open up before you. In my consideration of these, however, I shall neither leave all things to your own natural ability nor promise that from my own

---

[36] As Taylor points out, Nature here means the divine Wisdom, the second person of the Trinity. Cf. *Didascalicon* 1. x (ed. Buttimer, p. 96; tr. Taylor, p. 57).

[37] These are Augustinian ideas; cf. *In Iohannis evangel.* xiv. 7 (CCSL xxxvi. 145–6); *De Genesi ad litteram*, v. 19 (CSEL xxviii. 161–3); *De civ. Dei*, xvi. vi.

diligence you will get everything you need. Instead, by way of foretaste for you, I shall briefly run over certain matters in such a way that you may find some things set forth to provide instruction and some things skipped over to allow scope for your own effort.

I have mentioned that order in study is a fourfold matter: one thing in the disciplines, another in books, another in narrative, and another in exposition.[38] How these are to be applied in the divine Scripture I have not yet shown.

Chapter ii: Concerning the Order which exists in the Disciplines

First of all, the student of sacred Scripture ought to look among history, allegory, and tropology for that order sought in the disciplines—that is, he should ask which of these three precedes the others in the order of study.[39]

In this question it is not without value to call to mind what we see happen in the construction of buildings, where first the foundation is laid, then the structure is raised upon it, and finally, when the work is all finished, the house is decorated by the laying on of colour.[40]

Chapter iii: Concerning History

So too, in fact, must it be in your instruction. First you learn history and diligently commit to memory the truth of the deeds that have been performed, reviewing from beginning to end what has been done, when it has been done, where it has been done, and by whom it has been done. For these are the four things which are especially to be sought for in history—the person, the business done, the time, and the place.[41] Nor do I think that you will be able to become perfectly sensitive to allegory unless you have first been grounded in history.[42] Do not look down upon these least things. The man who looks down on such smallest things slips little by little. If, in the beginning, you had looked down on learning the alphabet, now you would not even find your names listed with those of the

[38] See *Didascalicon*, iii. viii, 'Concerning order in expounding a text' (ed. Buttimer, p. 58; tr. Taylor, pp. 91–2).

[39] As Taylor emphasizes, Hugh conceives of these three categories not simply as senses of Scripture but as separate studies as well, studies to be pursued in succession. Cf. *De sacramentis* i, pr. (PL clxxvi. 183); tr. Deferrari, p. 3).

[40] Cf. Gregory the Great, *Moralium libri*, 'Ad Leandrum', iii (CCSL cxliii. 4).

[41] A version of the *circumstantiae*, on which see Ch. I, n. 6, and cf. Ch. II, nn. 15, 19, and 75. See further Hugh's extensive treatment of the 'circumstances' in history in his *De tribus maximis circumstantiis gestorum*, ed. W. M. Green, *Speculum*, xviii (1943), 484–93. On the 'circumstances' pertinent to allegorical interpretation see Hugh's *De scripturis et scriptoribus sacris praenotatiunculae*, xivff. (PL clxxv. 20ff.); cf. his *Adnot. elucid. in Pent.* (PL clxxv. 74B-C, 87–8), and *In Salom. Ecclesiasten hom.* xix (ibid. 115).

[42] On Hugh's attitude to history and its cultural context see especially M.-D. Chenu, 'Theology and the New Awareness of History', in id., *Nature, Man and Society in the Twelfth Century*, tr. Jerome Taylor and L. K. Little (Chicago, 1968), pp. 162–201; Ehlers, *Hugo von St. Viktor*, pp. 156–77; de Lubac, *Exég. méd.* i. 425–87.

grammar students. I know that there are certain fellows who want to play the philosopher right away. They say that stories should be left to pseudo-apostles. The knowledge of these fellows is like that of an ass. Do not imitate persons of this kind.

'Once grounded in things small, you may safely strive for all.'[43] I dare to affirm before you that I myself never looked down on anything which had to do with education, but that I often learned many things which seemed to others to be a sort of joke or just nonsense. I recall that when I was still a schoolboy I worked hard to know the names of all things that my eyes fell upon or that came into my use, frankly concluding that a man cannot come to know the natures of things if he is still ignorant of their names. How many times each day would I make myself pay out the debt of my little bits of wisdom, which, thanks to their shortness, I had noted down in one or two words on a page, so that I might keep a mindful hold on the solutions, and even the number, of practically all the thoughts, questions, and objections which I had learned. Often I proposed cases and, when the opposing contentions were lined up against one another, I diligently distinguished what would be the business of the rhetorician, what of the orator, what of the sophist. I laid out pebbles for numbers, and I marked the pavement with black coals and, by a model placed right before my eyes, I plainly showed what difference there is between an obtuse-angled, a right-angled, and an acute-angled triangle. Whether or not an equilateral parallelogram would yield the same area as a square when two of its sides were multiplied together, I learned by walking both figures and measuring them with my feet. Often I kept watch outdoors through the winter nights like one of the fixed stars (*horoscopus*)[44] by which we measure time. Often I used to bring out my strings, stretched to their number on the wooden frame, both that I might note with my ear the difference among the tones and that I might at the same time delight my soul with the sweetness of the sound. These were boyish pursuits, to be sure, yet not without their utility for me, nor does my present knowledge of them lie heavy upon my stomach. But I do not reveal these things to you 'in order to parade my knowledge, which is either nothing at all or very little, but in order to show you that the man who moves along step by step is the one who moves along best, not like some who fall head over heels when they wish to make a great leap ahead.

As in the virtues, so in the sciences, there are certain steps. But, you say, 'I find many things in the histories which seem to be of no utility: why should I be kept busy with this sort of thing?' Well said. There are indeed many things in the Scriptures which, considered in themselves, seem to

[43] Taylor points out that this is quoted from Marbodus, *De ornamentis verborum*, pr. (PL clxxi. 1687).

[44] On *horoscopus* as one of the fixed stars see the Latin *Asclepius*, v. xix, ed. A. D. Nock, tr. A.-J. Festugière, *Hermès Trismégiste: Corpus Hermeticum* (Paris, 1945-54), ii. 319.

have nothing worth looking for, but if you look at them in the light of the other things to which they are joined, and if you begin to weigh them in their whole context, you will see that they are as necessary as they are fitting. Some things are to be known for their own sakes, but others, although for their own sakes they do not seem worthy of our labour, nevertheless, because without them the former class of things cannot be known with complete clarity, must by no means be carelessly skipped. Learn everything; you will see afterwards that nothing is superfluous. A skimpy knowledge is not a pleasing thing.

But if you ask if I have any opinion about the books which are useful for this study. I think the ones to be studied most are: Genesis, Exodus, Joshua, the Book of Judges, and that of Kings, and Chronicles; of the New Testament, first the four Gospels, then the Acts of the Apostles. These eleven seem to me to have more to do with history than do the others—with the exception of those which we properly called historiographical.

But if we take the meaning of the word more broadly, it is not unfitting that we call by the name 'history' not only the recounting of actual deeds but also the first meaning of any narrative which uses words according to their proper nature.[45] And in this sense of the word, I think that all the books of either Testament, in the order in which they were listed earlier, belong to this study in their literal meaning.

Possibly, if it did not seem childish, I should interject in this place a few instructions on the manner of construing sentences, because I know that the divine Scripture, more than all other books, is compressed in its text: but these matters I wish to refrain from, lest I protract the task before me by excessive digression. There are certain places in the divine page which cannot be read literally and which it is necessary that we construe with great judgement, so that we may not either overlook some things through negligence or, through misplaced diligence, violently twist them into something they were not written to say.

This, then, my student, is what we propose to you. This field of your labour, well cultivated by your plough, will bear you a manifold harvest. All things were brought forth in order: move along in order yourself. Following the shadow, one comes to the body: learn the figure, and you will come to the truth. I am not now saying that you should first struggle to unfold the figures of the Old Testament and penetrate its mystical sayings before you come to the Gospel streams you must drink from. But just as you see that every building lacking a foundation cannot stand firm, so also is it in learning. The foundation and principle of sacred learning, however, is history, from which, like honey from the honeycomb, the truth of allegory is extracted.[46] As you are about to build, therefore, 'lay first the

---

[45] i.e. words according to their 'proper' or standard meaning in normal usage, their literal signification.

[46] Cf. Jerome, *Epist.* cxxix. 6 (CSEL lvi. 173).

foundation of history; next, by pursuing the "typical" meaning, build up a structure in your mind to be a fortress of faith. Last of all, however, through the loveliness of morality, paint the structure over as with the most beautiful colours.'[47]

You have in history the means through which to admire God's deeds, in allegory the means through which to believe His mysteries, in morality the means through which to imitate His perfection. Read, therefore, and learn that 'in the beginning God created heaven and earth' [Gen. 1: 1]. Read that in the beginning He planted 'a paradise of pleasure wherein He placed man whom He had formed' [Gen. 2: 8]. Him sinning God expelled and thrust out into the trials of this life. Read how the entire offspring of the human race descended from one man; how, subsequently, flood destroyed sinners; how, in the midst of the waters, the divine mercy preserved the just man Noah with his sons; next, how Abraham received the mark of the faith, but afterwards Israël went down into Egypt; how God thereafter led the sons of Israël out of Egypt by the hand of Moses and Aaron, brought them through the Red Sea and through the desert, gave them the Law, and settled them in the land of promise; how often He delivered them as sinners into the hands of their enemies and afterwards freed them again when they were penitent; how first through judges, then through kings, He rules his people: 'He took His servant David from following the ewes great with young' [Ps. 77: 70]. Solomon he enlightened with wisdom. For the weeping Ezekiel [*sic* for Hezekiah] He added on fifteen years [4 Kgs. 20: 5–6]. Thereafter He sent the straying people captive into Babylon by the hand of Nebuchadnezzar. After seventy years He brought them back, through Cyrus. At last, however, when that time was already declining, He sent His Son into our flesh, and He, having sent His apostles into all the world, promised eternal life to those who were repentant. He foretold that He would come at the end of the ages to judge us, to make a return to each man according to his deeds—namely, eternal fire for sinners, but for the just, eternal life and the kingdom of which there shall be no end. See how, from the time when the world began until the end of the ages, the mercies of God do not slacken.

Chapter iv: Concerning Allegory

After the reading of history, it remains for you to investigate the mysteries of allegories, in which I do not think there is any need of exhortation from me, since this matter itself appears worthy enough in its own right. Yet I wish you to know, good student, that this pursuit demands not slow and dull perceptions but matured mental abilities which, in the course of their searching, may so restrain their subtlety as not to lose good judgement in what they discern. Such food is solid stuff, and, unless it be well chewed,

---

[47] Quoted, with slight modifications, from Gregory, *Moral. lib.*, 'Ad Leand.' iii (CCSL cxliii. 4–5).

it cannot be swallowed. You must therefore employ such restraint that, while you are subtle in your seeking, you may not be found rash in what you presume; remembering that the Psalmist says: 'He hath bent His bow and made it ready. And in it He hath prepared the instruments of death' [Ps. 7: 13–14].

You remember, I suppose, that I said above that divine Scripture is like a building, in which, after the foundation has first been laid, the structure itself is raised up; it is altogether like a building, for it too has its structure.[48] For this reason, let it not irk us if we follow out this similitude a little more carefully.

Take a look at what the mason does. When the foundation has been laid, he stretches out his string in a straight line, he drops his perpendicular, and then, one by one, he lays the diligently polished stones in a row. Then he asks for other stones, and still others, and if by chance he finds some that do not fit with the fixed course he has laid, he takes his file, smooths off the protruding parts, files down the rough spots, and the places that do not fit, reduces to form, and so at last joins them to the rest of the stones set into the row. But if he finds some to be such that they cannot either be made smaller or be fitly shaped, he does not use these lest perhaps while he labours to grind down the stone he should break his file.

Pay attention now! I have proposed to you something contemptible to gapers but worthy of imitation to those who understand. The foundation is in the earth, and it does not always have smoothly fitted stones. The superstructure rises above the earth, and it demands a smoothly proportioned construction. Even so the divine page, in its literal sense, contains many things which seem both to be opposed to each other and, sometimes, to impart something which smacks of the absurd or the impossible. But the spiritual meaning admits no opposition; in it, many things can be different from one another, but none can be opposed. The fact, also, that the first course of stones to be laid upon the foundation is placed flush with a taut cord—and these are the stones upon which the entire weight of the others rests and to which they are fitted—is not without its meaning. For this is like a sort of second foundation and is the basis of the entire superstructure. This foundation both carries what is placed upon it and is itself carried by the first foundation. All things rest upon the first foundation but are not fitted to it in every way. As to the latter foundation, everything else both rests upon it and is fitted to it. The first one carries the superstructure and underlies the superstructure. The second one carries the superstructure and is not only under the superstructure but part of it. The foundation which is under the earth we have said stands for history, and the superstructure which is built upon it we have said suggests allegory. Therefore, that basis of this superstructure ought also to relate

[48] Cf. *Didascalicon*, VI. ii, tr. above, and n. 40.

to allegory. The superstructure rises in many courses of stones, and each course has its basis. Even so, many mysteries are contained in the divine page and they each have their bases from which they spring. Do you wish to know what these courses are? The first course is the mystery of the Trinity, because this, too, Scripture contains, since God, Three and One, existed before every creature. He, from nothing, made every creature—visible, namely, and invisible. Behold in these the second course. To the rational creature He gave free judgement, and He prepared grace for it that it might be able to merit eternal beatitude. Then, when men fell on their own will He punished them, and when they continued to fall He strengthened them that they might not fall further. What the origin of sin, what sin, and what the punishment for sin may be: these constitute the third course. What mysteries He first instituted for man's restoration under the natural law: these are the fourth course. What things were written under the Law: these, the fifth course. The mystery of the incarnation of the Lord: this, the sixth course. The mysteries of the New Testament: these, the seventh course. Finally, the mysteries of man's own resurrection: these, the eighth course.[49]

Here is the whole of divinity, this is that spiritual structure which is raised on high, built, as it were, with as many courses of stones as it contains mysteries. You wish also to know the very bases themselves. The bases of the courses are the principles of the mysteries. See now, you have come to your study, you are about to construct the spiritual building. Already the foundations of history have been laid in you: it remains now that you found the bases of the superstructure. You stretch out your cord, you line it up precisely, you place the square stones into the course, and, moving around the course, you lay the track, so to say, of the future walls. The taut cord shows the path of the true faith. The very bases of your spiritual structure are certain principles of the faith—principles which form your starting point. Truly, the judicious student ought to be sure that, before he makes his way through extensive volumes, he is so instructed in the particulars which bear upon his task and upon his profession of the true faith, that he may safely be able to build on to his structure whatever he afterwards finds. For in such a great sea of books and in the manifold intricacies of opinions which often confound the mind of the student both by their number and their obscurity, the man who does not know briefly in advance, in every category so to say, some definite principle which is supported by firm faith and to which all may be referred will scarcely be able to conclude any single thing.

Do you wish that I should teach you how such bases ought to be laid? Look back at those things which I listed for you a moment ago. There is

[49] These eight 'courses' determine the structure of Hugh's *De sacramentis*; see esp. pr. i–iii (PL clxxvi. 183–4); tr. Deferrari, pp. 3–5; also the discussion in G. Paré, A. Brunet, and P. Tremblay, *La Renaissance du XIIe siècle* (Paris, 1933), pp. 263–4.

the mystery of the Trinity. Many books have already been composed on this mystery, many opinions given which are difficult to understand and complicated to resolve. It would be too long and too burdensome for you to work through absolutely all of them and possibly you would find many by which you were more muddled than edified. Do not insist on doing this: you will never have done. First learn briefly and clearly what is to be believed about the Trinity, what you ought unquestionably to profess and truthfully to believe. Afterwards, however, when you have begun to read books and have found many things obscurely, many things clearly, and many things doubtfully written, take those things which you find clear and, if it should be that they conform, add them to their proper base. The doubtful things interpret in such a way that they may not be out of harmony. But those things that are obscure, elucidate if you can. But if you cannot penetrate to an understanding of them, pass over them so that you may not run into the danger of error by presuming to attempt what you are not equal to doing. Do not be contemptuous of such things, but rather be reverent toward them, for you have heard that it is written: 'He made darkness His hiding-place' [Ps. 17: 22]. But even if you find that something contrary to what you have already learnt should be held with the firmest faith, still it is not well for you to change your opinion daily, unless first you have sought the advice of men more learned than yourself and, especially, unless you have learnt what the universal faith, which can never be false, orders to be believed about it. Thus should you do concerning the mystery of the altar, thus concerning the mystery of baptism, that of confirmation, that of marriage, and all those things which were enumerated for you above. You see that many who read the Scriptures, because they have not a foundation of truth, fall into various errors and change their views almost as often as they sit down to read. But you see others who, in accordance with that knowledge of the truth upon which, interiorly, they are solidly based, know how to bend all scriptural passages whatever into fitting interpretations and to judge both what is out of keeping with sound faith and what is consonant with it. In Ezekiel you read that the wheels follow the living creatures, not the living creatures the wheels; it says: 'When the living creatures went, the wheels also went together by them: and when the living creatures were lifted up from the earth, the wheels also were lifted up with them' [Ezek. 1: 19]. So it is with the minds of holy men: the more they advance in virtues or in knowledge, the more they see that the hidden places of the Scriptures are profound, so that those places which to simple minds and minds still tied to earth seem worthless, to minds which have been raised aloft seem sublime. For the text continues: 'Whithersoever the spirit went, thither as the spirit went the wheels also were lifted up withal, and followed it: for the spirit of life was in the wheels' [Ezek. 1: 20]. You see that these wheels follow the living creatures and follow the spirit.

Still elsewhere it is said: 'The letter killeth, but the spirit quickeneth' [2 Cor. 3: 6], because it is certainly necessary that the student of the Scripture adhere staunchly to the truth of the spiritual meaning and that the high points of the literal meaning, which itself can sometimes be wrongly understood too, should not lead him away from the central concern in any way whatever. Why was that former people who received the Law of life reproved, except that they followed the death-dealing letter in such a way that they did not have the life-giving Spirit? But I do not say these things in order to offer anyone the chance to interpret the Scriptures according to his own will, but in order to show the man who follows the letter alone that he cannot long continue without error. For this reason it is necessary both that we follow the letter in such a way as not to prefer our own sense to the divine authors, and that we do not follow it in such a way as to deny that the entire pronouncement of truth is rendered in it. Not the man devoted to the letter 'but the spiritual man judgeth all things' [1 Cor. 2: 15].

In order, therefore, that you may be able to interpret the letter safely, it is necessary that you not presume upon your own opinion, but that first you be educated and informed, and that you lay, so to speak, a certain foundation of unshaken truth upon which the entire superstructure may rest; and you should not presume to teach yourself, lest perhaps when you think you are introducing you are rather seducing yourself. This introduction must be sought from learned teachers and men who have wisdom, who are able to produce and unfold the matter to you both through the authorities of the holy Fathers and the evidences of the Scriptures, as is needful; and, once you have already had this introduction, to confirm the particulars they have taught you by reading from the evidences of the Scriptures.

So the matter appears to me. Whoever is pleased to follow me in this, I accept with pleasure. Whoever thinks things ought not to be done in this way, let him do what he pleases: I shall not argue with him. For I know that a number of people do not follow this pattern in learning. But how certain of these advance, this too I am not unaware of.

If you ask what books are best for this study, I think the beginning of Genesis on the works of the six days; the three last books of Moses on the mysteries of the Law; Isaiah; the beginning and end of Ezekiel; Job; the Psalter; the Song of Songs; two Gospels in particular, namely those of Matthew and John; the Epistles of Paul; the Canonical Epistles; and Revelation; but especially the Epistles of Paul, which even by their very number show that they contain the perfection of the two Testaments.[50]

---

[50] As Taylor points out, 'The Pauline Epistles are fourteen in number; the number fourteen is twice seven, the perfect number.'

Chapter v: Concerning Tropology, that is, Morality

Concerning tropology I shall not at present say anything more than what was said above, except that it is more the meaning of things than the meaning of words which seems to pertain to it. For in the meaning of things lies natural justice, out of which the discipline of our own morals, that is, positive justice, arises. By contemplating what God has made we realize what we ourselves ought to do. Every nature tells of God; every nature teaches man;[51] every nature reproduces its essential form, and nothing in the universe is infecund.[52]

Chapter vi: Concerning the Order of Books

The same order of books is not to be kept in historical and allegorical study. History follows the order of time; to allegory belongs more the order of knowledge, because, as was said above, learning ought to take its beginnings not from obscure but from clear things, and from things which are better known. The consequence of this is that the New Testament, in which the evident truth is preached, is, in this study, placed before the Old, in which the same truth is announced in a hidden manner, shrouded in figures. It is the same truth in both places, but hidden there, open here, promised there, shown here. You have heard, in the reading from Revelation [5: 5], that the book was sealed and no one could be found who should loose its seals save only the Lion of the tribe of Judah. The Law was sealed, sealed were the prophecies, because the times of the redemption to come were announced in a hidden manner. Does it not seem to you that that book had been sealed which said: 'Behold a virgin shall conceive and bear a son: and his name shall be called Emmanuel'? [Isa. 7: 14]. And another book which says: 'Thou, Bethlehem Ephrata, art a little one among the thousands of Judah: out of thee shall he come forth unto me that is to be the ruler in Israël: and his going forth is from the beginning, from the days of eternity' [Micah 5: 2]. And the Psalmist: 'Shall not Zion say: This man and that man is born in her? and the Highest himself hath founded her' [Ps. 86: 5]. And again: 'And of the Lord, of the Lord are the issues of death' [Ps. 67: 21]. And yet again he says: 'The Lord said to my Lord: Sit thou at my right hand' [Ps. 109: 1]. And a little later in the same place: 'With thee is the principality in the day of thy strength, in the brightness of the saints; from the womb before the day-star I begot thee' [Ps. 109: 3]. And Daniel [7: 13–14] says: 'I beheld therefore in the vision of the night, and lo, one like the son of man came with the clouds of heaven, and he came even to the Ancient of days . . . And he gave him

---

[51] Cf. Rom. 1: 19–20.
[52] Cf. the Latin *Asclepius*, I. iv, III. xiv, and esp. VI. xxi ed. Nock, tr. A.-J. Festugière, ii. 299–300, 313–14, 321–3.

power, and glory, and a kingdom: and all peoples, tribes, and tongues shall serve him: his power is an everlasting power that shall not be taken away.'

Who do you think could understand these things before they were fulfilled? They were sealed, and none could loose their seals but the Lion of the tribe of Judah. There came, therefore, the Son of God, and He put on our nature, was born of the Virgin, was crucified, buried; He rose again, ascended to the skies, and by fulfilling the things which had been promised, He opened up what lay hidden. I read in the Gospel that the angel Gabriel is sent to the Virgin Mary and announces the coming birth [Luke 1: 26–31]: I remember the prophecy which says: 'Behold, a virgin shall conceive' [Isa. 7: 14]. I read that when Joseph was in Bethlehem with Mary, his pregnant wife, the time for her to give birth arrived 'and she brought forth her first-born son' [Luke 2: 4–7], who the angel had foretold would reign on the throne of David his father: I remember the prophecy, 'Thou, Bethlehem Ephrata, art a little one among the thousands of Judah: out of thee shall he come forth to me that is to be the ruler of Israel' [Micah 5: 2]. Again I read: 'In the beginning was the Word; and the Word was with God: and the Word was God' [John 1: 1]: I remember the prophecy which says: 'His going forth is from the beginning, from the days of eternity' [Micah 5: 2]. I read: 'The Word was made flesh and dwelt among us' [John 1: 14]: I remember the prophecy which says: 'You shall call His name Emmanuel, that is, God with us' [Isa. 7: 14; cf. Matt. 1: 23]. And in order not to risk making this tedious to you by following through each item: unless you know beforehand the nativity of Christ, His teaching, His suffering, His resurrection and ascension, and all the other things which He did in the flesh and through the flesh, you will not be able to penetrate the mysteries of the old figures.

Chapter vii: Concerning Order of Narration

Concerning order of narration it ought especially to be remarked in this place that the text of the divine page keeps neither to a natural nor to a continuous order of speech, both because it often places later things before early ones—for instance, after it has listed a number of items, suddenly the line of discourse turns back to previous ones, as if narrating subsequent ones; and because it often connects even things which are separated from each other by an interval of time, as if one followed right on the heels of the other, so that it seems as if no lapse of time stood between those events which are set apart by no pause in the discourse.

Chapter viii: Concerning the Order of Exposition

Exposition includes three things: the letter, the sense, and the deeper meaning (sententia).[53] The letter is found in every discourse, for the very

[53] Similarly, William of Conches distinguished between syntactical structure (continuatio), exposition of 'the letter' (expositio litterae), and profound meaning (sententia): Glosae super

sounds are letters; but sense and a deeper meaning are not found together in every discourse. Some discourses contain only the letter and sense, some only the letter and a deeper meaning, some all these three together. But every discourse ought to contain at least two. That discourse in which something is so clearly signified by the mere telling that nothing else is left to be supplied for its understanding contains only letter and sense. But that discourse in which the hearer can conceive nothing from the mere telling unless an exposition is added thereto contains only the letter and a deeper meaning in which, on the one hand, something is plainly signified and, on the other, something else is left which must be supplied for its understanding and which is made clear by exposition.

Chapter ix: Concerning the Letter

Sometimes the letter is perfect, when, in order to signify what is said, nothing more than what has been set down needs to be added or taken away—as 'All wisdom is from the Lord God' [Ecclus. 1: 1]; sometimes it is compressed, when something is left which must be supplied—as, 'The Ancient to the lady Elect' [2 John 1: 1]; sometimes it is in excess, when, either in order to inculcate an idea or because of a long parenthetical remark, the same thought is repeated or another and unnecessary one is added, as Paul, at the end of his Epistle to the Romans, says: 'Now to him . . .' and then, after many parenthetical remarks, concludes, 'to whom is honour and glory' [Rom. 16: 25–7]. The other part of this passage seems to be in excess. I say 'in excess', that is, not necessary for making the particular statement. Sometimes the literal text is such that unless it is stated in another form it seems to mèan nothing or not to fit, as in the following: 'The Lord, in heaven the throne of Him' [Ps. 10: 15], that is, 'the throne of the Lord of heaven'; 'the sons of men, the teeth of those are weapons and arrows' [Ps. 56: 5], that is, 'the teeth of the sons of men'; and 'man, like grass the days of him' [Ps. 102: 15], that is, 'man's days': in these examples the nominative case of the noun and the genitive case of the pronoun are put for a single genitive of the noun; and there are many other things which are similar. To the letter belong construction and continuity.

Chapter x: Concerning the Sense

Some sense is fitting, other unfitting. Of unfitting sense, some is incredible, some impossible, some absurd, some false. You find many things of

Platonem, ed. E. Jeauneau (Textes philosophiques du moyen âge XIII, Paris, 1965), p. 67; also his commentaries on Priscian and Macrobius, cit. E. Jeauneau, 'Deux rédactions des gloses de Guillaume de Conches sur Priscien', *RTAM* xxvii (1960), 234–6; repr. in id., *Lectio philosophorum: Recherches sur l'école de Chartres* (Amsterdam, 1973), pp. 346–7. Hugutio of Pisa incorporated William's definitions into his highly popular dictionary, the *Magnae derivationes*: see G. Robert, *La Renaissance du XIIᵉ siècle: les écoles et l'enseignement* (Paris and Ottawa, 1933), p. 55 n. 2. These were reiterated by Giovanni de' Balbi, *Catholicon*, s.v. *commentum* and *glosa* (Venice, 1495), fos. 101ʳ, 153ᵛ.

this kind in the Scriptures, like the following: 'They have devoured Jacob' [Ps. 78: 7]. And the following: 'Under whom they stoop that bear up the world' [Job 9: 13]. And the following: 'My soul hath chosen hanging' [Job 7: 15].[54] And there are many others.

There are certain places in divine Scripture in which, although there is a clear meaning to the words, there nevertheless seems to be no sense, either because of an unaccustomed manner of expression or because of some circumstance which impedes the understanding of the reader, as is the case, for example, in that passage in which Isaiah says: 'In that day seven women shall take hold of one man, saying: We will eat our own bread, and wear our own apparel: only let us be called by thy name. Take away our reproach' [Isa. 4: 1]. The words are plain and open. You understand well enough 'Seven women shall take hold of one man.' You understand 'We will eat our own bread.' You understand 'We will wear our own apparel.' You understand 'Only let us be called by thy name.' You understand 'Take away our reproach.' But possibly you cannot understand what the sense of the whole thing together is. You do not know what the prophet wanted to say, whether he promised good or threatened evil. For this reason it comes about that you think the passage, whose literal sense you do not see, has to be understood spiritually only. Therefore, you say that the seven women are the seven gifts of the Holy Spirit, and that these take hold of one man, that is, Christ, in whom it pleased all fullness of grace to dwell because He alone received these gifts without measure; and that He alone takes away their reproach so that they may find someone with whom to rest, because no one else alive asked for the gifts of the Holy Spirit.[55]

See now, you have given a spiritual interpretation, and what the passage may mean to say literally you do not understand. But the prophet could also mean something literal by these words. For since he had spoken above about the slaughter of the transgressing people, he now adds that so great would be the destruction of that same people and to such an extent were their men to be wiped out that seven women will hardly find one husband, for only one woman usually has one man; and, while now women are usually sought after by men, then, in contrary fashion, women will seek after men; and, so that one man may not hesitate to marry seven women at the same time, since he might not have the wherewithal to feed and clothe them, they say to him: 'We will eat our own bread, and wear our own apparel.' It will not be necessary for you to be concerned about our well-being, 'only let us be called by thy name', so

---

[54] As Taylor points out, this and the previous example are cited by St Gregory the Great to show the impossibility of understanding all things in Scripture literally: *Moral. lib.*, 'Ad Leand.' iii (CCSL cxliii. 4).

[55] Taken from Origen; see Jerome's *Translatio homiliarum Origenis in visiones Isaiae*, hom. iii (PL xxiv. 910–12). Cf. Jerome's own *Comment. in Is. prophet.* ii. iv (PL xxiv. 73 A–B).

that you may be called our husband and *be* our husband so that we may
not be heralded as rejected women, and die sterile, without children—
which at the time was a great disgrace. And that is why they say, 'Take
away our reproach.'[56]

You find many things of this sort in the Scriptures, and especially in the
Old Testament—things said according to the idiom of that language and
which, although they are clear in that tongue, seem to mean nothing in
our own.

Chapter xi: Concerning the Deeper Meaning

The divine deeper meaning can never be absurd, never false. Although
in the sense, as has been said, many things are found to disagree, the
deeper meaning admits no contradiction, is always harmonious, always
true. Sometimes there is a single deeper meaning for a single expression; sometimes there are several deeper meanings for a single expression; sometimes there is a single deeper meaning for several
expressions; sometimes there are several deeper meanings for several
expressions. 'When, therefore, we read the divine books, in such a great
multitude of true concepts elicited from a few words and fortified by the
sound rule of the Catholic faith, let us prefer above all what it seems
certain that the man we are reading thought. But if this is not evident,
let us certainly prefer what the circumstances of the writing do not dis-
allow and what is consonant with sound faith. But if even the circumstances of the writing cannot be explored and examined, let us at least
prefer only what sound faith prescribes. For it is one thing not to see
what the writer himself thought, another to stray from the rule of piety.
If both these things are avoided, the harvest of the reader is a perfect
one. But if both cannot be avoided, then, even though the will of the
writer may be doubtful, it is not useless to have elicited a deeper
meaning consonant with sound faith.'[57] 'So too, if, regarding matters
which are obscure and furthest removed from our comprehension, we
read some of the divine writings and find them susceptible, in sound
faith, to many different meanings, let us not plunge ourselves into headlong assertion of any one of these meanings, so that if the truth is perhaps more carefully opened up and destroys that meaning, we are
overthrown; for so we should be battling not for the thought of the
divine Scriptures but for our own thought, and this in such a way that
we wished the thought of the Scriptures to be identical with our own,
whereas we wought rather to wish our thought identical with that of the
Scriptures.'[58]

[56] Cf. Jerome's exposition *ad litteram*, ibid. (PL xxiv. 72 B-D).
[57] See above, n. 11.
[58] Augustine, *De Gen. ad litt.* I. xviii (CSEL xxviii. 27).

PETER ABELARD

Prologue to the *Yes and No*[59]

In the vast amount of writings which exist, some statements, even those of the holy Fathers, appear not only to differ from each other, but even to be contradictory. Consequently, one should not make a rash judgement on those by whom the world itself is to be judged, according as it is written: 'the saints shall judge nations' [Wisd. 3: 8], and again: 'You shall sit judging' [Matt. 19: 28]. We must not presume to accuse of lying, or despise as erroneous, those to whom our Lord said: 'He that heareth you, heareth me, and he who despiseth you despiseth me' [Luke 10: 16]. So we must have regard to our own inadequacy, and believe that it is we who lack God's grace to understand, rather than they who lacked it in their writings. For the Truth Himself said to them: 'It is not you who speak, but the spirit of our Father that speaks in you' [Matt. 10: 20]. So it is little wonder that if we lack that Spirit, by whose agency these writings were written and dictated, and communicated directly by it [i.e. that Spirit] to the writers, we may fail to understand their actual writings.

The greatest barrier to our understanding is the unusual style (*locutionis modus*) and the fact that very often the same words have different meanings, when one and the same word (*vox*) has been used to express now one meaning (*significatio*), now another. For each writer has an abundant supply of words, just as he has of thoughts.[60] According to Tully: 'In all things uniformity is the mother of satiety', that is, begets loathing.[61] So the writer should vary the words used in describing one and the same subject, and should not reveal all his thoughts in words which are ordinary and in common usage. For, as blessed Augustine says, these thoughts are concealed lest they become commonplace, and are all the more attractive in proportion to the effort spent in searching them out and the difficulty in grasping them.[62] Moreover, we often have to vary our language according to the different conditions of those to whom we are speaking. For it often happens that the correct meaning of words is unknown to some of them, or little used by them. If we wish to speak with a view to teaching them, as is right we should, we must aim at imitating their usage rather than achieving a correct style (*proprietas sermonis*), as indeed that prince of grammar and instructor in the various styles, Priscian, teaches.[63] That most zealous teacher of the Church, St Augustine, realized this. When, in the fourth book of his *On Christian Doctrine*, he instructs the teacher in the

---

[59] Tr. from *Peter Abailard: Sic et non*, fasc. i, ed. B. Boyer and R. McKeon, pp. 89–104, with the permission of the University of Chicago Press.
[60] Lat. 'in sensu . . . in verbis'.
[61] Cicero, *De invent.* i. xli. 76.
[62] Cf. Augustine, *Enarr. in ps.* ciii (CCSL xl. 1490); *De doct. Christ.* ii. vii. 8.
[63] Cf. Priscian, *Inst.* vii. 28 (*GL* ii. 310).

church, he warns him to omit everything which prevents his hearers from understanding, and to have scant regard for literary ornament and correctness of style, if he can succeed more readily in making his audience understand without them. 'For', he remarks, 'the teacher does not care how eloquently he teaches, but rather how clearly. Sometimes passionate enthusiasm for the subject is indifferent to the elegant choice of words. Hence a certain writer, when treating of this kind of style, asserted that there was inherent in it a studied carelessness.'[64] Again he says: 'Good teachers should give teaching such a high priority that a word which cannot be good Latin without being obscure or ambiguous, but is used in its colloquial form to avoid ambiguity and obscurity, should not be spoken in the form used by the educated, but rather that habitually used by the unlearned. For if our translators are not ashamed to say *de sanguinibus* ('of blood-offerings' [Ps. 15: 4]), since they realized that it was relevant to the subject that this word which in Latin is also found in the singular should there be put in a plural form, why should the teacher of holiness, when speaking to the uneducated, be ashamed to say *ossum* rather than *os*, lest that syllable [i.e. the monosyllable *os*] should be thought to belong not to the word [meaning 'bone'] which gives *ossa* in the plural, but that [meaning 'mouth' or 'face'] which gives *ora*. For what is the use of correct diction (*locutio*) which does not result in understanding on the part of the hearer? For there is absolutely no point in speaking if those to assist whose understanding we are speaking do not understand what we say. So the teacher will avoid all words which do not teach.'[65] And again: 'It is the mark of a brilliant mind to love the truth enshrined in words rather than the words themselves. For what use is a golden key if it cannot open what we want? Or what harm is a wooden key if it can do so, when we seek only that that which has been closed should be open?'[66]

Surely everyone must realize how rash it is to make any judgement about someone else's mind and capacity for understanding (*sensus et intelligentia*), since men's hearts and thoughts are open to God alone. God, dissuading us from this arrogant attitude, says: 'Judge not, and you will not be judged' [Luke 6: 37]. And the Apostle says: 'Judge not before the right time, before He comes who will illuminate the things now hidden by darkness and will reveal the purposes of men's hearts' [1 Cor. 4: 5]. This is as if he were to say openly: 'Commit to His care judgement in such matters, who alone knows all things and sees into the very thoughts of men.' In keeping with this, we read the following words on the subject of the Passover lamb, referring to God's hidden mysteries, presented in typological guise: 'If there shall be anything left, you shall burn it with fire' [Exod. 12: 10]. In other words, if there is any part of the divine

[64] Augustine, *De doct. Christ.* IV. ix–x; cf. Cicero, *Orator*, xxiii. 78.
[65] *De doct. Christ.* IV. ix–x.
[66] Ibid. IV. xi.

mysteries which we cannot understand, we must reserve these to be taught by that Spirit through whose inspiration they were written, rather than rashly attempt to define them.

We must also be very careful not to be deceived by a false attribution of authorship or by a corrupt text, when our attention is drawn to seemingly contradictory or untrue statements among the words of Christian writers.[67] For many apocryphal works have taken their title from the names of Christian writers so as to have authority, and even in the writings of the God-inspired Testaments there are some corrupt passages due to scribal error. Jerome, that most reliable writer and most faithful translator, has given us forewarning of this. Writing to Laeta, *On the Instruction of her Daughter*, he says: 'Let her beware all apocryphal books, and if she ever wishes to read them, not with an eye to the truth of their teachings but out of respect for the wonders they relate, let her understand that they are not written by those whose names are in the titles, and one needs to be very skilful to seek gold in mud.'[68] Again, commenting on the seventy-seventh psalm, he writes about its title, which takes the form: *Understanding for Asaph*. This is what he says: 'It has been written in the gospel according to Matthew: "when the Lord had spoken in parables and they did not understand, etc." [Matt. 13: 34]. All this was done "to fulfil what was written by Isaiah the prophet: 'I will open my mouth in parables.'" The Gospels to this day have these words in this form. Yet it is not Isaiah who says this, but Asaph.'[69] Again, Jerome says: 'Let us state candidly that it is written in both Matthew and John that our Lord was crucified at the sixth hour, but in Mark that it was at the third hour, that this is due to scribal error, and that "the sixth hour" was originally in the text of Mark also. But many have mistaken the *episemon* for the Greek *gamma*,[70] and in exactly the same way there was an error on the part of the scribes which caused them to write "Isaiah" instead of "Asaph". For we know that the greater part of the Church was recruited from among gentiles who had no knowledge of Scripture. So, when they read in the Gospel "so that that which was written in the prophet Asaph might be fulfilled" [cf. Matt. 13: 35], the first scribe to write out the Gospel began to say: "Who is this prophet Asaph? He was not known among the people." And what did he do? He made a new error in his efforts to emend an error. We must mention a similar instance in another text of St Matthew's Gospel [Matt. 27: 9]. It says: "he took back the thirty pieces of silver, the price of him who was prized, as was written in the prophet Jeremiah." We have not been able to find this at all in Jeremiah. In fact, it is in Zechariah

---

[67] Literally 'holy writers'.

[68] *Epist.* cvii. 12 (CSEL lv. 303).

[69] Jerome, *Tractatus sive homil. in ps.* lxxvii (CCSL lxxviii. 65–6). Jerome is making the point that St Matthew's gospel has attributed these words wrongly to Isaiah. But since it is Holy Writ, the false attribution has been allowed to stand out of respect.

[70] *Episemon*, the symbol for 6 (originally the letter wau or digamma).

[11: 13]. So you see there was error here, just as in the previous example.[71] So it is no wonder, if there are some corrupt passages even in the Gospels owing to the ignorance of scribes, that this should sometimes happen also in the writings of the Fathers who wrote at a later period, who have far less authority. So if any statement in the writings of the Fathers should appear to be at odds with the truth, it is not irreverent, is consistent with humility, and is in fact a duty we owe to charity—which 'believes all things, hopes all things, and bears all things' [1 Cor. 13: 7] and so finds it difficult to credit faults in those things which it embraces in its love— that we should believe that that part of the text has either not been correctly interpreted or is corrupt, or else that we should admit that we do not understand it.

We must also give equal consideration to the possibility that such statements may be among those made by the Fathers, but which have either been retracted by them elsewhere, when they have subsequently come to know the truth, as St Augustine did in many instances, or alternatively they may have reported the opinions of others rather than stating their own conclusions. For instance, in many places the writer of Ecclesiastes introduces contradictory views of differing origin; hence his name is interpreted as meaning 'one who causes debates' (*tumultuator*) according to St Gregory in the fourth book of *Dialogues*.[72] Or else they have left a question-mark hanging over the problems into which they were enquiring, rather than settling them conclusively. St Augustine, that highly respected teacher, whom I mentioned above, tells us that he has done exactly that when writing his *On the Text of Genesis*. For in the first book of his *Retractions* he has this to say about that work: 'In this work more questions were asked than answers found, and few of those answers were firmly resolved, while the rest were expounded in such a way as to need further research into them.'[73] We know on the authority of St Jerome, also, that it was customary for Catholic teachers in their commentaries to insert some of even the very worst opinions of heretics among their own conclusions, while in their search for perfection they took a deliberate delight in omitting none of the teachings of ancient writers. Thus, replying to St Augustine when he was being attacked by him for his exposition of a certain passage of the Epistle of St Paul to the Galatians, he said: 'You ask why in my commentary on Galatians I asserted that Paul had not been able to blame Peter for doing what he had done himself. And you assert that this was not carefully assumed[74] pretence on the part of the Apostle, but was true, and that I should not teach a falsehood. My reply is that

---

[71] Jerome, *Tract. in ps.* lxxvii (CCSL lxxviii. 66–7).

[72] Gregory the Great, *Dialogi*, iv. 4 (PL lxxvii. 324A). Gregory's term is *contionator*; his meaning is that the various opinions of many people are brought into harmony by the reasoning of the preacher. Cf. the use made of the term by Bonaventure and Giles of Rome, in Ch. VI.

[73] Augustine, *Retractationes*, II. xxiv. 1 (CSEL xxxvi. 159–60).

[74] Here *dispensatoriam* seems to mean 'careful, providential; the act of a wise steward'.

someone as wise as you are should have remembered the short preface to my expositions, since, being fully conscious of the inadequacy of my own powers I followed the commentary of Origen. For he wrote weighty tomes (*volumina*) on Paul's Epistle to the Galatians. I pass over Didymus, who saw my commentary, and Apollinaris of Laodicea, who has lately left the Church, and Alexander, that heretic of long standing. They also left some commentaries on this matter. I read all this material, and, having stored up a great many opinions in my mind, I summoned a secretary (*notarius*) and dictated opinions which were indifferently my own or other men's.'[75] Likewise, he says: 'It behoved someone of your deep scholarship to ask whether the views I have expressed in writing were held among the Greeks so that, if they had not expressed them, you could then condemn my opinion on its own merits; and all the more so because I freely confessed in my preface that I had followed the commentary of Origen and had dictated views which were indifferently my own or other men's, so that I might leave it to the reader's discretion (*lectoris arbitrio*) whether they should be approved or rejected.'[76] Likewise, I am in no doubt that St Hilary and a number of other holy Fathers [of the Church] in making their judgements inserted much from the writings of Origen himself, or of others who were in error, setting out for our benefit the opinions of others, rather than proffering their own; a fact which has become known to us not so much through the writers themselves as through others who wrote subsequently. This is what prompted the aforesaid teacher of the Church, Jerome, when he was excusing himself to the priest Vigilantius for either citing or transferring into his own work statements by Origen, to say: 'If this is a crime, then the confessor Hilary must be accused. For he lifted his interpretation of the psalms and his homilies on Job from Origen's books.'[77] Indeed, in his writings, when we chance to find statements at variance with the truth, or contradicting the writings of other Fathers, these are to be ascribed to Origen rather than to Hilary, even though Hilary himself may not make this distinction. Such, for instance, is that attempt, right at the beginning, to show that the first psalm must not be understood as relating to one individual, but in general terms to any just man.[78] Jerome himself has inserted this view, again following in Origen's footsteps,[79] in an exposition of certain psalms. There is perhaps no doubt that even Origen himself, on his own admission, uttered much that was entangled in great errors, when following the opinions of others. So Jerome, writing to the priest Avitus, gathered together the many errors which Origen inserted in his books *Peri Archon*, and said this about him:

---

[75] Jerome, *Epist.* cxii. 4 (CSEL lv. 370–1).
[76] Ibid. (pp. 371–2).
[77] Jerome, *Epist.* lxi. 2 (CSEL liv. 577).
[78] Cf. Hilary, *Tract. super ps.* i. 2–4 (CSEL xxii. 20–2).
[79] i.e. Jerome does this just as much as Hilary did.

'After such a disgraceful argument with which he has assailed the mind of the reader, he [i.e. Origen] says: "These teachings do not accord with my opinion, but have only been sought out and thrust before the reader lest they should seem to have been left completely untouched."[80] So too Jerome himself, in the passage cited above, said that he often dictated indifferently his own views or those of other men, so that he might leave it to the reader's discretion as to whether they should be approved or rejected.

In the course of correcting and retracting much from his own works, St Augustine admits that he included in them much that came from the opinion of others rather than from his own. For even in the gospel some things seem to be said which agree with the opinion of men rather than with the true state of things. For instance, when Joseph is called Christ's father by Our Lord's mother herself, in this following common belief and custom, when she says: 'Thy father and I sought thee sorrowing' [Luke 2: 48]. The Apostle also, imitating the words of his critics on many occasions, is not afraid to speak about himself in terms quite different from his real feelings, as for example in the words: 'We are fools for Christ's sake, but you are wise in Christ' [1 Cor. 4: 10]. That same Apostle speaks of Melchizedek as being 'without father, without mother, without genealogy', having 'neither beginning of days, nor end' [Heb. 7: 3], no doubt because we cannot know that which Scripture does not tell us, not because this was the real truth of the matter. Moreover, Samuel is said to have appeared to the wise woman in the form of an apparition, not in reality, but having an appearance which resembled the true reality, and so engendered a false belief in those who saw it.[81] For as St Augustine recalls, that apparition was called Samuel because it had the likeness of Samuel, in the same way as someone says that in dreams he saw Rome, because he conceived the likeness of Rome in his mind.[82]

Poets and philosophers also, in their writings, make many statements in which they are similarly quoting another man's opinion as if they were based on solid truth, and yet it is clear that they are completely at odds with the truth; hence Ovid says: 'The crop in other men's fields is always more productive, and your neighbour's herd has heavier udders!'[83] When Boethius, in the third book of his *Topics*, said that accident and substance were the two main classes of things, he had his eye fixed upon opinion rather than truth.[84] Tully, in the second book of his *On Duties*, clearly admits that philosophers enunciated much that was based on the opinion

---

[80] Jerome, *Epist.* cxxiv. i. 4 (CSEL lvi. 100–1). For Origen's (Greek) work see PG xi. 180D n. 44.
[81] Cf. 1 Kgs. 18: 7–12, the 'wise woman' being the witch of Endor.
[82] Cf. Augustine, *De diver. quaest.* ii. iii. 2 (PL xl. 142–3).
[83] Ovid, *Ars amatoria*, i. 349–50.
[84] Boethius, *De differentiis topicis*, iii (PL lxiv. 1197C); tr. E. Stump (Ithaca, NY and London, 1978), p. 66.

of others rather than their own judgement, when he says: 'Whereas justice without wisdom has sufficient authority, wisdom without justice has not the strength to command confidence, for the more shrewd and cunning a man is, so is he all the more hated and suspect once he has lost his reputation for probity. So justice coupled with wisdom will have as much power as it wishes to command confidence. Justice without wisdom will have much power, but wisdom without justice none at all. But lest anyone should wonder why, when it is generally agreed among philosophers, and I have myself often maintained, that he who possesses one virtue possesses all, I should now make a distinction of this sort, supposing that one could be just who is not at the same time wise: one state of affairs holds good when the very truth is being carefully refined in philosophical debate, and another when discourse is being adapted to the generally accepted opinions. So here we speak in popular terms, and call some men strong, others good, yet others wise. For when we speak [in public] we must employ words from the language of ordinary people, and ordinary usage.'[85]

Finally, it is a part of the usage of everyday speech that many things are spoken of as they are judged by the bodily senses, and are referred to in terms other than they really are. For, whereas in all the world there is no place that is completely empty, and not filled with air or else some solid body, yet we say that a chest in which, with our faculty of sight, we see nothing, is completely empty. Forming our judgement on the evidence of our sight, we say that sometimes the sky is full of stars, and sometimes not; sometimes the sun is warm, sometimes not in the least warm; or that the moon is shining more or less brightly, or at times is not shining at all. Yet in fact all these continue to have a constant force, although they do not always appear equally constant to us.

It is no wonder, then, that judgements have sometimes been expressed or even written by the holy Fathers which are grounded upon opinion rather than on truth. When different views are expressed about the same thing, one should also carefully consider what the author is aiming at in the way of enforcing [God's] precept, granting pardon, or exhorting his readers to perfection, so that we may seek a solution for that incompatibility in the difference between the intentions of the authors. If the statement is laying down a precept, we must ask whether it is of general or particular application, that is, directed to all generally or to certain individuals in particular. One should also make a distinction between times and reasons for dispensations [i.e. for relaxations of rules], because often that which is allowed at one time is found to be forbidden at another, and that which is prescribed to be rigorously enforced is often tempered as a result of a dispensation. It is particularly essential that these distinctions should be made in drafting the decrees or laws of the Church. An easy

[85] Cicero, *De officiis*, II. ix. 34–x. 35.

solution to controversies will often be found if we are able to put up the plea that the same words have been used by different authors with different meanings.

The careful reader will attempt to resolve controversial points in the writings of the holy Fathers in all the ways I have mentioned. But if the dispute is so obvious that it cannot be resolved by having recourse to reasoning [i.e. rational argument], then authorities must be compared, and that authority retained which has more value as evidence and greater weight. Hence the words of Isidore, writing to Bishop Massius: 'I thought that this ought to be added at the end of the letter, so that whenever contradictory opinions are found in the *acta* of councils, one should retain the opinion which is based on the older or better authority.'[86]

It is clear also that the prophets themselves sometimes lacked God's gift of prophecy and, by dint of their sheer practice in their craft, produced false prophecies, emanating from their own spirit, while all the time believing that they possessed the spirit of prophecy. This was permitted to preserve their humility, so that in this way they might the better perceive the differences between prophecies which originated in the divine Spirit and those which originated in their own, and might realize that, when they had that which knows not how to lie or deceive, they had it as a gift. When a man has this spirit it does not confer all its gifts upon one person, and likewise it does not illumine the mind of the person whom it possesses on all matters, but reveals now one thing and now another, and when it reveals one thing it covers up another. Blessed Gregory, in his first homily on Ezekiel, shows this, giving clear examples.[87] The very prince of the apostles [i.e. St Peter], who was distinguished by possessing so many gifts of God's grace, and performing so many miracles, even after the special outpouring of the Holy Spirit which Our Lord promised would come to teach His disciples the truth in its entirety, fell into error, in no uncertain fashion, on the question of the continued observance of circumcision and certain other ancient rites. But when he had received severe and salutary correction in public from his fellow apostle Paul, he was not too proud to abandon his pernicious hypocrisy.

So when it is agreed that the very prophets and apostles were not altogether strangers to error, it is no wonder if, in such a vast amount of writings by the Church Fathers, some doctrines appear to have been   . uttered or written in error for the reason mentioned above. But we must not accuse holy men of being liars if, holding opinions on some matters which were at variance with the truth, they speak, not out of a desire to deceive, but through ignorance. No statement which is prompted by charity, and aims at some sort of edification [of the hearer], should be put

---

[86] Isidore, *Epist.* iv. 13 (PL lxxxiii. 901 D–2A).
[87] Cf. Gregory, *Hom. in Ezech. prophet.* I. i, II. vi. 9–11 (PL lxxvi. 785A–95A, 1002B–4A).

down to arrogance or sinfulness. For it is clear that in God's sight all actions are judged in terms of their intention, as was written: 'If thy eye be single, thy whole body shall be full of light' [Matt. 6: 22]. Hence the words of St Augustine, when treating *Of Discipline in the Church*: 'Have charity, and [if you have that] do what you will.'[88] The same author, writing on the Epistle of St John, says: 'Those who do not have charity are not from God. Have whatever you want. But if you have not charity, then nothing else is of any avail to you. If you have not other things, have charity, and you have fulfilled the law.'[89] Again he says: 'Once for all, then, you are given a brief commandment: love, and do what you will.'[90] Again, in *On Christian Doctrine*, in book i, he says: 'Whoever thinks that he has understood the Holy Scriptures or any part of them, but is not helped by that understanding to build up the twofold love of God and of his neighbour, has not understood them. But the man who delivers an opinion (*sententia*) based on Scripture, of such a sort that it helps to increase charity, even if he has not succeeded in expressing what the writer of that text clearly intended, is not hopelessly deceived, nor is he completely a liar. For the liar has inherent in him the desire to say what is false.'[91] Again, in his *Against Lying*: 'Lying is giving a word a false meaning with intent to deceive.'[92] Again, in his *Enchiridion*, ch. 23, he says: 'No one is to be considered a liar who says something which is false, but which he believes to be true because, as far as he himself is concerned, he does not deceive, but is the victim of deception. So the man who, without exercising sufficient caution, trusts false statements and regards them as true, should not be accused of lying, but sometimes of rashness. Rather, the opposite is true, and the man who says something which is true, but which he believes to be false, is a liar. For as far as his intention is concerned, because he does not say what he really thinks, he does not speak the truth, even though what he says may be found to be true. Likewise, the man who unwittingly utters the truth is in no way free from the charge of lying, but rather, though he knows the truth, in his intention he is a liar.'[93] Again, he says: 'Everyone who utters a lie contrary to what he inwardly believes speaks with intent to deceive.'[94] Again, writing *On the Gospels*, in book ii he says: 'If you carefully consider what Jacob did at his mother's instigation, so that he appeared to be deceiving his father, that is not a lie but a mystery.[95] For a statement, whose meaning expresses the truth, can in no way rightly

---

[88] Cf. the similar quotation in Ivo of Chartres, *Decretum*, prol. (PL clxi. 48B), also attributed to Augustine, and the parallel in pseudo-Augustine, *Sermo* cvii. 4 (PL xxxix. 1958).
[89] Augustine, *In epist. Ioan. ad Parthos*, tract. v. 7 (PL xxxv. 2016).
[90] Ibid., tract. vii. 8 (PL xxxv. 2033).
[91] *De doct. Christ.* i. xxxvi. 40.
[92] Id., *Contra mendacium*, xii. 26 (CSEL xli. 507).
[93] Id., *Enchiridion*, 18 (CCSL xlvi. 58).
[94] Ibid. 22 (CCSL xlvi. 62).
[95] i.e. a statement with allegorical meaning.

be called a lie.'⁹⁶ For the spiritual teacher does not accept that a lie occurs in this situation unless he accepts that a sin occurs also. For God, who is 'a prover of heart and loins' [Jer. 20: 12], weighs up the action, paying more attention to the intention of the speaker than the nature of what is said, and having regard not so much to the acts themselves as to the intent which causes those acts. Whoever speaks sincerely and without deceit or duplicity what is in his mind is truly free from His wrath. As is written: 'he that walks sincerely, walks confidently' [Prov. 10: 9]. Otherwise we should have had to accuse the Apostle Paul of lying. For he is following his own judgement rather than the truth, when he says in his Epistle to the Romans [15: 28]: 'When therefore I have accomplished this and consigned to them this fruit, I will set out for Spain, visiting you on the way.' For it is one thing to lie, but quite another to speak in error and to deviate from the truth in words because of a simple mistake, and not through malice.

If, as we have said, God permits the very saints to fall into error, admittedly in those matters which do not damage correct belief, this experience is not without some benefit to those for whom all things work together for their good. The teachers of the Church themselves shrewdly perceived this, and believed that there were some statements in their own works which would need correcting, and so they gave those who came after them full licence to emend their teachings, or to refuse to follow them, if for some reason they themselves were not given the opportunity to retract or correct them. This is why the aforementioned teacher St Augustine, in the first book of his *Retractions*, says: 'It is written: "In the multitude of words you shall not escape sin"' [Prov. 10: 19],⁹⁷ and again: 'The apostle James says: "Let every man be swift to hear, but slow to speak"' [Jas. 1: 19],⁹⁸ and again: '"For we all offend in many things. If any man offend not in word, the same is a perfect man' [Jas. 3: 2]. I lay no claim to this perfection now as an old man, how much less so when I began to write, in my young days.'⁹⁹ Augustine also says in the prologue to the third book of *On the Trinity*:¹⁰⁰ 'Do not slavishly follow my writings as if they were canonical Scripture. When you find something there [i.e. in Scripture] which you had not already believed, believe in it unhesitatingly. But when you find something in my writings of which you were formerly unsure, unless you have understood it with certainty, do not hold it as a firm principle of faith.'¹⁰¹ Again, writing to Vincentius Victor, in book ii, he says: 'I cannot deny, nor should I wish to deny, that just as in my morals so too among all my many works there are many things which can be criticized justly, and

⁹⁶ Actually *Contra mendacium*, x. 24 (CSEL xli. 499–501).
⁹⁷ *Retract.*, pr. 2 (CSEL xxxvi. 8).
⁹⁸ Ibid.   ⁹⁹ Ibid. (CSEL xxxvi. 8).
¹⁰⁰ Abelard's text of the passage from *De Trinitate* differs slightly from the one printed in the CSEL edition, but the sense is the same.
¹⁰¹ Augustine, *De Trin.* iii, pr. 2 (CCSL l. 128).

without the critic incurring the charge of rashness.'[102] Again, in his epistle to Vincentius, he says: 'My brother, do not try to gather up from the writings of bishops, whether our writings or those of Hilary or Cyprian or Agrippinus, false statements opposed to such clear, God-inspired testimonies [i.e. of the Scriptures]. For writings of this sort must be distinguished from the authority of the sacred canon. For they are not to be read in order to provide testimony which cannot be contradicted, if at some point they give a different interpretation to that demanded by the truth.'[103] Again, writing to Fortunatianus, he says: 'We ought not to regard the arguments of any writers, even though they may be orthodox and highly regarded, in the same light as we could canonical Scriptures. The result of doing that would be that we should not be permitted, having due regard to the respect such critics deserve, to attack and reject anything in their writings, if we should find that they have come to a conclusion which is at variance with the truth. In reading the writings of others I adopt the same attitude as I hope to find in those who read my work.'[104] Again, in the eleventh chapter of the first book *Against Faustus*, he says: 'We must not say that Paul ever made a mistake and changed his opinion in the course of his progress [towards understanding]. For it can be said of these books [of Scripture] that they have a nature essentially different from those which we write, not with the authority of one teaching but as an exercise by one who still has to make progress towards understanding.'[105] Again, Augustine says: 'We are those to whom the same Apostle says: "And if any of you be otherwise minded, this also God will reveal to you"' [Phil. 3: 15]. In reading works of this sort there must be freedom to form one's own judgement, not compulsion to believe. But lest scope for making that judgement be removed, and posterity be deprived of that most beneficial exercise of tongue and pen in treating and discussing difficult questions, the pre-eminently authoritative position of the canonical books of the Old and New Testaments has been separated out from that of subsequent writings. In the case of Scripture, if the writer raises an absurdity, one cannot say that the author of this book strayed from the truth at this point, but either the manuscript is corrupt or the interpreter has made a mistake, or you are failing to understand it. But in the case of the works of subsequent writers, contained in vast numbers of books, even if they are thought to be erring from the truth because their meaning is not being properly understood, the reader or hearer has in this case free choice to approve what he has found pleasing, or attack what has offended him. So in the case of statements of this kind, unless protected by cast-iron arguments or by the aforementioned scriptural authority, so that it is

---

[102] Id., *De anima et eius origine*, iv. 1 (CSEL lx. 380).
[103] Id., *Epist.* xciii. x. 35 (CSEL xxxiv/ii. 480).
[104] Id., *Epist.* cxlviii. iv. 15 (CSEL xliv. 344–5).
[105] *Contra Faustum*, xi. iv–v (CSEL xxv. i. 320).

clearly shown that the matter under dispute or the matter related there, either is so, or could have been so, anyone who finds them repugnant, or refuses to believe them, is not therefore blameworthy.'[106]

So he calls the canonical Scriptures of the Old and New Testaments 'instruments' (*instrumenta*).[107] To dissent in any way from the truth as found in them is to utter heresy. Indeed, Augustine, in his fourth letter to Jerome, has this to say about them: 'In expounding the Epistle of St Paul to the Galatians we have found something which is causing us a lot of trouble. For if deliberate[108] lies have been admitted into the Holy Scriptures, what shred of authority will they retain? In short, what judgement can be based on passages of Scripture of which the dishonest message will be rendered null and void by the contentious burden of its own falsity?'[109] Again, writing to the same person about these same Scriptures, he says: 'It is to my mind a very harmful belief to consider that there is any falsehood in Scripture, that is, that those men through whom Scripture has been mediated to us and written down should have written any lies in their books. For once the possibility of deliberate deceit in a work of such pre-eminent authority has been admitted, each and every part of those books which the individual reader finds difficult in terms of moral teaching or hard to believe in terms of faith will (by the application of that most pernicious reasoning) be put down to the intention (*consilium*) and purpose (*officium*) in the author's mind.'[110]

Likewise, St Jerome gave some teachers of the Church precedence over others. But he counselled us that in reading them we should view them critically rather than follow them slavishly. Hence his advice to Laeta, on the instruction of her daughter: 'Let her always have in her hand the works of Cyprian; let her run without hindrance among the works of Athanasius and in Hilary's book. Let her delight be in the treatises and talented works of those writers in whose books belief, scrupulously held, does not waver. Let her read the rest, but let her judge them critically rather than follow them.'[111] Writing on Ps. 86 he virtually removes all authority from all these writers, saying: '"The Lord shall tell in his writings of peoples and princes, of those who have been in her [i.e. Sion]" [v. 6]. He did not say "who are in her", but "who have been in her". It is not enough that [the psalmist] should say "of peoples", but he also says "of princes". And of what princes? "Those who have been." Consider therefore how Holy Scripture is full of mystical meanings (*sacramenta*). We read the Apostle's words: "Do you seek a proof of Christ who speaks

---

[106] *Contra Faustum*, XI. v (CSEL xxv/i. 320–1).
[107] In the sense of 'documents', 'records'.
[108] Lat. 'officiosus', meaning 'serving the writer's purpose', 'deliberate'.
[109] i.e. by the fact that its false doctrine is open to dispute. Augustine, *Epist.* xl. iii. 3 (CSEL xxxiv/ii. 71–2).
[110] Augustine, *Epist.* xxviii. iii. 3 (CSEL xxxiv/i. 107–8).
[111] Jerome, *Epist.* cvii. 12 (CSEL lv. 303).

in me?" [2 Cor. 13: 3]. What Paul says, Christ says—"for whosoever receives you, receives me also" [Matt. 10: 14]—in "the writings of princes and in the writing of peoples", which is the Scripture written for all peoples. Note that he says "who have been", not "who are". So, apart from the words of the apostles, whatever else may be said subsequently is cut out and has no authority from henceforth. So, however saintly and eloquent may be anyone who lived subsequent to the apostles, he would not have authority.'[112] Again, writing to Vigilantius, Jerome says: 'Whoever has occasion to read many treatises must be like an experienced money-changer (*nummularius*), so that if any coin is adulterated and does not have the emperor's image, and is not stamped by the state mint, it must be rejected. But the coin which displays the image of Christ, shining brightly, should be laid up in the pouch of the heart. For we should not give weight to the opinion we have previously formed of the teacher, but rather the arguments employed in his teaching, as is written: "Prove all things: hold fast to that which is good" [1 Thess. 5: 21].'[113] But this referred to commentators, not to the canonical Scriptures, to which one must give unhesitating credence. Likewise, writing to Paulinus concerning teachers of the Church, on the text 'A good man out of the good treasure of his heart' [Luke 6: 45], Jerome says: 'I say nothing of those others, dead or still alive, on whom others after us will pass favourable or unfavourable judgement.'[114]

This having been said by way of preliminary, it is my purpose, according to my original intention, to gather together various sayings of the holy Fathers which have occurred to me as being surrounded by some degree of uncertainty because of their seeming incompatibility. These may encourage inexperienced readers to engage in that most important exercise, enquiry into truth, and as a result of that enquiry give an edge to their critical faculty. For consistent or frequent questioning is defined as the first key to wisdom. Aristotle, the most clear-sighted of all philosophers, urges us to grasp this wholeheartedly. For he exhorts the studious in the prologue *Ad aliquid*, in the words: 'Perhaps it is difficult to make a confident pronouncement on matters of this sort unless they have been thoroughly gone over many times. Likewise, it will not be amiss to have doubts about individual points.'[115] For by doubting we come to enquiry, and by enquiry we perceive the truth. As the Truth Himself says: 'Seek and you shall find, knock and it shall be opened to you' [Matt. 7: 7]. Christ gave us spiritual instruction by his own example when, at the age of about twelve, he sat and asked questions, and wanted to be found in the midst of the teachers, showing us the example of a pupil, by his asking

---

[112] Id., *Tract. in ps.* lxxxvi (CCSL lxxviii. 115–16).
[113] Id., *Epist.* cxxix. 11 (CSEL lv. 467–8).
[114] Ibid. lviii. 1, 10 (CSEL liv. 527, 539).
[115] Boethius, *In categorias Aristotelis*, ii (PL lxiv. 238 D).

questions, before he showed us that of a teacher by his preaching, even though God's wisdom is full and perfect.

When writings are quoted they arouse and encourage the reader to enquire into truth all the more, in proportion to the level of regard in which a given piece of writing is held. That is why I decided to prefix to this work of mine, which I have compiled from the statements of the holy Fathers gathered into one volume, the well-known decree of Pope Gelasius on the subject of authentic books.[116] In this way it may be clearly understood that I have not introduced anything from the apocryphal writings. I have also added excerpts from the *Retractions* of St Augustine, from which it may be clearly seen that none of the views which he later retracted has been inserted here.

Commentary on St Paul's Epistle to the Romans: Prologue and Beginning of Commentary[117]

The intention of all Holy Scripture is to teach or move men in the same way as a speech does in the sphere of rhetoric.[118] It teaches when it advises what we should do or avoid. It moves us when, by dissuading us with divine admonitions, it makes our will draw back from evil; and by persuasion it brings us to the good, with the result that we want to do what we have learnt we ought to do, or avoid whatever is opposed to that. The threefold teaching of the Old and New Testaments is in accordance with this purpose. For in the Old Testament, the Law, which is contained in the five books of Moses, teaches the precepts given by the Lord first of all. Then the prophetical or historical books, together with the other Scriptures, exhort us to act upon the precepts which have been given and stir men's affections (*affectus*) to obey those precepts. When the prophets or the holy Fathers felt that the people were failing to obey God's precepts, they brought to bear admonitions, so that they might constrain them to obedience by the use of promises or threats. Examples drawn from the historical books had to be added, in which the reward of the obedient and

---

[116] Abelard's prologue is followed by a section *Ex decretis Gelasii Papae de libris autenticis* (ed. Boyer–McKeon, pp. 105–11). Cf. the text ed. E. von Dobschütz, *Das Decretum Gelasianum* (Leipzig, 1912), pp. 36–60.

[117] Tr. from *Petri Abaelardi opera theologica, i: Commentaria in Epistolam Pauli ad Romanos, etc.*, ed. E. M. Buytaert (CCCM xi. 41–7), with the permission of Les Usines Brepols SA, Turnhout, Belgium.

[118] Cf. *Ad Herenn.* 1. ii. 2; tr. H. Caplan (London and Cambridge, Mass., 1954), p. 5: 'The task of the public speaker (*oratoris officium*) is to discuss capably those matters which law and custom have fixed for the uses of citizenship, and to secure as far as possible the agreement of his hearers.' Deliberative rhetoric is then defined as the type which involves persuasion and dissuasion. See further the development of this doctrine by a disciple of Abelard's who amplified his master's commentary on St Paul: *Commentarius Cantabrigiensis in epistolas Pauli*, ed. A. Landgraf (Notre Dame, Ind., 1937–45), i. 1–2; also the succinct discussion by McKeon, 'Rhetoric in the Middle Ages', pp. 282–3.

the punishment of transgressors should be set before them. These are the old rags which were tied around Jeremiah to draw him out of the vat with cords [Jer. 38: 11], in other words the examples of the ancient patriarchs, which might be employed with their divine admonitions to drag the sinner from the abyss of his sins.

The teaching of the New Testament is also threefold. There the Gospel takes the place of the Law and teaches the pattern (*forma*) of true and perfect justice. Then the Epistles and Apocalypse take the place of the prophets. They exhort us to obey the Gospel. The Acts of the Apostles and the various narrative accounts in the Gospel contain episodes of sacred history. Since it is the intention of the Gospel to teach, the intention of the Epistles or the Acts of the Apostles is to move us towards obedience to the Gospel, or to strengthen our belief in those things which the Gospel teaches us.

So no one should criticize the Epistles as being superfluous, coming as they do after the Gospel which contains the complete body of Christian teaching, when we recall that the Epistles were written to admonish rather than to teach, though they may contain some salutary examples or wise counsels which are not in the Gospel. Thus Paul, writing to the Corinthians, says: 'For to the rest it is I who speak, not the Lord. If any brother has a wife who is an unbeliever, etc.' [1 Cor. 7: 12]. Also he teaches us that circumcision or the other fleshly observances of the Law must now lose their force, something which had not as yet been revealed in the Gospel.[119] Again, writing to Timothy he teaches us a great deal about the position of a bishop, priest, or deacon which the Gospel had not mentioned.[120] But we affirm that the teaching of the Gospel was handed down in a form sufficiently perfect to serve as a model of true justice and for the salvation of souls, not as an embellishment of the Church or to increase its prosperity. For some of the possessions of a city pertain to its safety, but others to its aggrandisement, as Tully recalls at the end of the second book of the *Rhetoric*.[121] The possessions which relate to its safety are those without which the city cannot continue to exist in safety and intact, for instance a rampart, woods, and other things of this sort which are very necessary for a city. Other possessions are not so necessary, but lend distinction; that is, when the city possesses certain things over and above the bare essentials, which give it a greater status than other cities or make it safer. Examples are fine buildings, large amounts of wealth, dominion over many peoples, and other similar things.

The teaching of the Gospel concerning faith, hope, and charity, or the sacraments, might well have been sufficient for salvation even without the addition of the teachings of the apostles, or the rules or dispensations laid

[119] Cf. especially St Paul's epistles to the Romans and Galatians.
[120] e.g. 1 Tim. 3: 1–15; 5: 1; 17–25.
[121] Cf. Cicero, *De invent.* 11. lvi. 168–9.

down by the holy Fathers of the Church in the form of laws, decrees, monastic rules, and the large number of writings of holy men, all full of divine admonitions. If these had all been ignored, and no teaching had been based on them, no one could have incurred any blame. But the Lord wanted certain precepts or dispensations to be added by the apostles and the Church Fathers, so that these might embellish or enlarge the Church, which is God's city, or guard more securely the safety of its inhabitants. This can be clearly seen [as His motive] in individual cases. So He kept some things in reserve to be taught and to be determined by His disciples or those who came after them. This He did in order that He might hold in reserve some authority in the matter of teaching for those whom He permitted to work greater miracles than He had allowed Himself to perform. In this way He might add to their stature and make them all the more acceptable to His Church the more it recognized that it needed them.

So, as we have said, the intention of the Gospels is to teach us those things which are necessary for our salvation. The Epistles retain this intention with the aim of moving us to obey the teaching of the Gospel, or even of passing on more additional teachings to increase the extent of our salvation or to protect it more securely. This is the general intention of all the Epistles. But in the case of each individual epistle we must ask what the particular intention is there, or else enquire into the subject-matter of each, or the various methods of treating the subject (*modi tractandi*); and we must do this here in this letter. The intention here is to restore to true humility and brotherly concord the Roman converts from Judaism and paganism, who were pushing themselves forward in an arrogant rivalry against each other. The writer does this in two ways, by enlarging upon the gifts of God's grace and by diminishing the merits of our works, so that no one may any longer presume to glory in his own merit, but may ascribe everything in which he prospers to the divine grace, from which he recognizes that he has received whatever good quality he has. The subject-matter is completely taken up with those two subjects, our works and the divine grace.

The way in which the writer treats the subject (*modus tractandi*) is to diminish our works, as we have said, and enlarge upon God's grace, so that no one may presume to glory in his own works, but 'he who glories let him glory in the Lord' [1 Cor. 1: 31]. But the former Gentiles [i.e. among the Roman Christians] gloried in the fact that they were so quick to obey the teachings of the Gospel, as is written: 'A people which I knew not has served me: at the hearing of the ear they have obeyed me' [Ps. 47: 45]. Besides, as they thought, they would not have committed sin in anything which they had done prior to this, for at that stage they had not come to know God through the medium of any law. The Jews, on the other hand, were extremely arrogant because of their observance of the physical aspects of the Law. So, to crush the arrogance of both groups by inveighing against them alternately, he attacks now one group, now another, and sometimes both. His purpose is to show that the Gentiles had no excuse for sinning, for even if they had not received a written law, they had a natural law whereby they could come to know God and discern the difference between good and evil. On the other hand, the Jews were not justified by performing the works enjoined by the Law, as they think they are. But both have won that forgiveness, which alone can justify them, solely through the grace of God who calls them to Him.

The question arises who had first converted those Romans to whom this epistle is dedicated, by preaching to them. The *Ecclesiastical History* and Jerome, or Gregory of Tours, say that they had already been converted by the Apostle Peter. But Haymo disagrees, for he tells us that they had received their first instruction in the faith not from Peter or any of the twelve apostles, but from certain other Jewish believers who had come to Rome from Jerusalem. The *Ecclesiastical History* says, in book ii, ch. 14: 'In the time of Claudius, God in His merciful providence brought Peter to Rome. On his arrival he was the first in Rome to open the door of the heavenly kingdom with the key of his proclamation of the Gospel. So when the clear light of the word of God had arisen to illuminate the city of Rome, the darkness of Simon's teaching was quenched along with the source of that darkness.'[122] Jerome, in his commentary on this epistle, on the passage 'that I may impart to you some grace of the Spirit' [Rom. 1: 11], says: 'Paul is saying that he wishes to strengthen the faith of the Romans who held that faith as a result of Peter's preaching, not that they had received it in an imperfect form from Peter, but that their faith might be strengthened by the joint testimony of two apostles and teachers.'[123] Gregory of Tours also says in ch. 25 of the first book of his history: 'The Apostle Peter came to Rome in the reign of Claudius and, as he preached there, demonstrated in the clearest possible way, by the many miracles he performed, that Christ was the son of God. For from that time onwards there began to be a Christian community at Rome.'[124] But Haymo, in the preface to his commentary on this Epistle, says: 'The Apostle wrote this Epistle to the Romans from Corinth. They received their first instruction in the faith, not from Peter in person, nor indeed from any of the twelve disciples, but from some of the Jewish converts who, coming from Jerusalem to the city where dwelt the ruler of the world, whose subjects they were, preached to the Romans the faith which they had imbibed in Jerusalem.'[125]

But it should be noted that, if careful attention is paid to all that has

---

[122] Eusebius, *Hist. Eccl.* II. xiv. 6–xv. 1, in Rufinus' free tr. (GCS ix/i. 139–41).

[123] Actually John the Deacon, *Comment. in Epistolas S. Pauli*, i (PL xxx. 648c).

[124] Gregory of Tours, *Historia Francorum*, i. 24, in *Gregorii ... libri Historiarum X*, ed. B. Krusch and W. Levison (MGH, Scr. Mer. i/1², Hanover, 1951), p. 19.

[125] Haymo, *In Epist. ad Rom.*, argum. (PL cxvii. 361c).

been said, the above doctors and Haymo do not contradict each other. For if we examine the abovementioned chapter of the *Ecclesiastical History* in every detail we will find that Peter was the first apostle, not the first teacher, to have preached to the Romans. Besides, Jerome's statement that the Romans had accepted the faith or held it from Peter as a result of his preaching raises no obstacle, since that could have come about through disciples of Peter who had come from Jerusalem, not through Peter himself. But what Haymo is denying is that Peter himself was responsible for that happening. Consequently, when he mentions Peter by name, he adds 'himself'. Besides, Haymo does not say that Peter did not instruct them but that 'he was not the first to give them instruction'. As for the statement of Gregory of Tours that Peter preached at Rome in the reign of Claudius, he did not add that he was the first to preach, but that he clearly demonstrated that Christ was the son of God by the many powerful miracles he performed. His adding that there began to be a Christian community at Rome from that time can be understood to mean that Christians who could possibly have been secret believers before that time now became open believers as a result of Peter's efforts.

Although this epistle is not thought to have been written first, it has been placed first by the holy Fathers because it is directed against that vice which is the first, and the root of all others, namely pride. For, as the Scripture says, 'Pride is the beginning of all sin' [Ecclus. 10: 15]. Or else it is placed first because it is addressed to the Church of the first city of the empire. Haymo also refers to this, in the words: 'In the corpus of letters that epistle is not in the order in which it was written, but was given first place because of the pre-eminence of the Romans who at that time ruled the world. However this was not done by the Apostle, but by the person who was responsible for gathering Paul's letters together into one corpus.'[126] Again, he says: 'The name "Romans" is interpreted "proud", or "those who thunder forth",. because at the time when the Apostle sent them this epistle they ruled over all peoples, and thundered out their commands.'[127]

The Apostle is believed to have sent the present letter from Corinth to Rome by the hand of Phoebe, the servant of the church at Cenchreae, which is 'a place near Corinth, or rather the port of Corinth', as Origen remarks, commenting on this epistle.[128] The Apostle himself speaks of this Phoebe in the following terms at the end of the epistle: 'I commend to you our sister Phoebe, etc.' [Rom. 16: 1]. When Jerome is expounding this passage he says: 'Here the Apostle shows that no distinction should be made as between man and woman, when he sends this letter to the Romans, as is said here, by the hands of a woman, etc.'

PAUL After the manner of letter-writers he prefaces the epistle with the salutation which exhorts them to strive after true salvation.[129] This saluta-

---

[126] Haymo, *In Epist. ad Rom.*, argum. (PL cxvii. 363 A–B).   [127] Ibid. (PL cxvii. 364 C).
[128] Origen, *Comment. in Epist. S. Pauli ad Rom.*, pr. (PG xiv. 835 B).
[129] With this paragraph cf. Rom. 1: 1–7.

tion, along with some other matter which he adds to it, is prefixed to the epistle, taking the place of a preface (*proemium*), his intention being to make his readers attentive quickly, ready to be taught, or well disposed towards himself.[130] He makes them attentive, basing his appeal on his own person, and that of Christ who sends him, and also on his subject, namely the teachings of the Gospels which he is exhorting them to follow. He bases his appeal on his own person when he commends it as set apart for the apostolate and called by God to preach the Gospel. He commends the person of our lord Jesus Christ, whom he calls the son of God. He asserts that Christ is He who had been promised to the patriarchs as the redeemer of the human race, and who was conceived by the Holy Spirit and has triumphed in his raising of the dead. But he does not omit to commend the Gospel too, when he says that He was the son of God promised in the holy writings of the prophets. Readiness to be taught is indicated in this statement because, by saying that the duty of preaching the Gospel has been laid upon him, he informs us that he is going to write about those things which relate to the teaching of the Gospel. Moreover, when he confesses that he is a servant of Christ and that he is also their servant, he makes his readers well disposed towards him, because of his humility and their love for Christ, and also because of what he adds about his love towards them, when he gives fervent thanks to God for their conversion, and expresses the wish to come to them so that he may instruct them more fully or strengthen them in the faith. Now let us study the text.

PETER LOMBARD

Commentary on the Psalter: Prologue[131]

It is generally accepted that, while all the prophets spoke by the revelation of the Holy Spirit, David stands out from the others in that he prophesied on a more exalted and distinguished level than they did, acting, so to speak, as the trumpet of the Holy Spirit. For other prophets gave their prophecies through the medium of images and words with a veiled meaning (*verborum integumenta*), but David uttered his prophecies by the direct inspiration of the Holy Spirit, without any external aid.[132]

---

[130] Cf. *Ad Herenn.* I. iv. 6; Isidore, *Ety.* II. vii. 2. This formula often appears in the *accessūs ad auctores*; cf. above, Ch. I.

[131] Tr. from *Petri Lombardi in psalmos Davidicos commentarii praefatio* (PL cxci. 55–62). This preface blends together many authoritative statements on the Psalter in a way which often makes source-identification difficult; cf. the Psalter prologue in the *Glossa ordinaria* (PL cxiii. 841–4), and the discussion in Minnis, *Authorship*, pp. 43–8, 52–4. The Lombard's ultimate sources include Jerome's *Tractatus sive homiliae in psalmos* and the preface to his *Hebraica*, Augustine's *Enarrationes in psalmos*, Cassiodorus' prologue to his *Expositio psalmorum*, and pseudo-Remigius of Auxerre's prologue to his *Enarrationes in psalmos*.

[132] Cf. Cassiodorus, *Expositio psalmorum*, pr. i (CCSL xcvii. 7).

Hence, that book of psalms is fittingly called 'the book of soliloquies'. It is also called 'the Psalter', taking its name from a musical instrument which is called *nablus* in Hebrew and in Greek *psalterium*, from the Greek ψάλλειν, which means 'to touch'. In Latin it [i.e. the instrument] is called *organum*.[133] It has ten strings, and gives forth a sound when touched by the hand from above. According to the literal sense, the book gets its name from that instrument because David sang the psalms to its accompaniment before the ark of the covenant in the tabernacle of the Lord. Just as the individual notes of that instrument were called 'psalms', so too are the individual sections or parts of that book. According to the allegorical sense also, the book aptly derives its name from that instrument, for, just as the instrument has ten strings, so the book teaches the observance of the Ten Commandments.[134] And just as the instrument gives back a note when touched from above by the hand, so the book teaches us to work effectively, not for earthly ends but for heavenly things, which are above.

This book is made up of one hundred and fifty psalms. This too is not without a deeper significance, since this number is coupled with the most illustrious mysteries. For it is made up of eight added to seventy. 'Eighty' means the same as 'a group of eight' (*octonarius*), and 'seventy' the same as 'a group of seven' (*septenarius*). 'The group of eight' signifies the octave of the resurrection, for, while men go through six stages in their lives and the seventh stage is death, the eighth will be that of the resurrection, which begins when souls begin to repose in Christ's passion. By 'the group of seven' is signified the duration of this life, which is lived in a recurring cycle of seven days. It was appropriate, then, that this book should have been made up of psalms to that number. Its sections thus denote the aforesaid mysteries, for it teaches us to act and work in the sevenfold sequence of this life, so that in the octave of the resurrection we may not be clothed with the cloak of confusion, but with the robe of twofold glorification.

Alternatively, the book is made up of this number of psalms because, as we have said, this number is itself compounded of eighty and seventy, which signifies the same as 'a group of eight' and 'a group of seven'. The 'group of eight' then represents the New Testament, for the Fathers of the New Testament zealously observe the ogdoad, that is, 'the group of eight'. For they observe the eighth day of Christ's resurrection (that is, Sunday) and the octaves of the Saints, and they look for the octave of the resurrection. By 'the group of seven' is signified the Old Testament, because the fathers of the Old Testament observed the hebdomad, that is, 'the group of seven'. For they observed the seventh day, the seventh week, the seventh month, and the seventh year; also the seventh year of the seventh decade, which is called the jubilee. Hence, Solomon says: 'Give a portion to seven and also to eight' (Eccles. 11[: 2]), and Micah: 'We shall

---

[133] Cf. pseudo-Remigius, *Enarr. in ps.*, pr. (PL cxxxi. 147c).
[134] Cf. ibid. (PL cxxxi. 147D).

stir up against them seven shepherds and eight principal men' (Micah
5[: 5]). It is fitting, then, that this book should contain psalms to that
number, of which its parts represent the teaching of both Testaments, so
that thereby it may be shown that the teachings of both Old and New Testaments are contained in this book.

This book is divided up into three groups of fifty, by which are signified
the three conditions (*status*) of the Christian religion. The first is the condition of penitence; the second, that of justice; the third, that of praise of
eternal life. So, the first [group of] fifty psalms ends on a note of penitence, that is HAVE MERCY UPON ME, GOD, ACCORDING TO etc. (Ps. 50[: 1]); the
second [group of] fifty, on a note of justice, MERCY AND JUDGEMENT I WILL
SING TO THEE, O LORD (Ps. 100[: 1]); while the third [group of] fifty ends on a
note of praise of eternal life, that is, LET EVERY LIVING SPIRIT PRAISE THE LORD
(Ps. 150[: 6]). Because David is teaching all these things in this book,
there is threefold division of the psalms.

One should note also that this part of Scripture finds a place more frequently than others in the offices of the Church, for the whole of theology
is summed up in this book. For here we find described the rewards
received by the good, the punishment of evildoers, the elements necessary for the teaching of beginners, the stages by which men make progress
[in the Christian life], the perfection they attain to when they arrive at
their goal, the activities of those engaged in the active life, and the manner
of contemplation of those engaged in the contemplative life. Here also is
taught what sin takes away from a man, what repentance restores to him,
what a penitent who is conscious of his sin says, namely O LORD, REBUKE
NOT ME IN THY INDIGNATION (Ps. 6[: 1]) and elsewhere: HAVE MERCY ON ME, O
GOD, ACCORDING TO THY GREAT MERCY (Ps. 50[: 1]); and he also adds what a
man may achieve through penitence: I WILL TEACH THE UNJUST THY WAYS, AND
THE WICKED SHALL BE CONVERTED TO THEE [Ps. 50: 15]. This text shows that
no one, however serious his sin may be, should despair of being granted
God's mercy and pardon, once he has taken upon himself the humility of
penance. For when we see that by repentance David, a murderer and
adulterer, became a teacher and a prophet, no one can any longer doubt
the effectiveness of doing penance. Likewise, the account of Saul's conversion, and his being advanced to the ranks of the apostles, gives us full
assurance of God's mercy. So, the Church in its offices makes more use of
his epistles than those of other apostles, just as it makes more use of
David's prophecies than those of other prophets. Another reason why
David's prophecies are more frequently used is that they surpass others in
clarity of expression. For David, the most excellent among the prophets,
has so clearly revealed to us the facts about Christ's passion and resurrection, His begetting by the Eternal Being, and other mysteries, facts which
other prophets referred to obscurely and through enigmas, that he seems
to be playing the role of an evangelist rather than a prophet.

Having looked at these matters, we shall have to consider what is the title (*titulus*), and also the subject-matter (*materia*) and the intention of the author (*intentio*), and the mode in which the subject is treated (*modus tractandi*). The title, then, is as follows: HERE BEGINS THE BOOK OF HYMNS OR SOLILOQUIES OF THE PROPHET CONCERNING CHRIST. He says 'book', not 'books', thus contradicting those who used to say that there were several books because of the five divisions (*distinctiones*) made between the psalms by the words 'so be it, so be it' (*fiat, fiat*). Even Jerome took this view, but the arguments in favour of it are not strong.[135] For, even though there may be five divisions, that should not be a reason for our saying that there are five books. For there are many divisions in the Epistles of St Paul, but only one book. This is clear from David's own words. Speaking in the person of Christ he says: IT HAS BEEN WRITTEN ABOUT ME AT THE HEAD OF THE BOOK [Ps. 39: 8]. He says 'of the book', not 'of the books', thus showing that there is one book, not several. Again, in the Acts of the Apostles it is said: 'as is written in the book of psalms' (Acts 1[: 20]). The writer did not say 'the books'. So, there is one book, even though Jerome may assert that there are five because of the five divisions.

OF HYMNS OR SOLILOQUIES A hymn is praise of God accompanied by a canticle. A canticle is the exultation which the mind conceives concerning things eternal breaking forth and finding voice. So that book is quite properly called a book of hymns, because it teaches us to praise God with exultation for things eternal. This it does, not only with the heart, but also with the voice, so that he who hears it may say: 'Come, and let curtain draw forth curtain', and 'let our fountains be drawn off abroad' [cf. Rev. 22: 17]. These are hymns, written in metre among the Jews, but the metre could not be retained in translation.

OR OF SOLILOQUIES Here we should consider the nature of prophecy, how it arises, and the times to which it relates. Prophecy, then, is divine inspiration or revelation which proclaims the future outcome of events with immutable truth. Hence, a prophecy is called 'a vision' (*visio*) and the prophet 'a seer' (*videns*). Prophecy happens in four ways: through actual events or words, and through that which only seems to be said or to happen, that is, through dreams (*somnia*) and visions (*visiones*). Prophecy occurs through events, as for example through Noah's ark [Gen. 6: 14–16], which signified the Church; likewise through the iron pan placed between the prophet Ezekiel and the city [Ezek. 4: 3]. It occurs through words; for example, the words of the angel to Abraham and subsequently to other believers, words such as 'And in thy seed shall all the nations of the earth be blessed' (Gen. 22[: 18]), and similar utterances of this sort. It

---

[135] *Praef. S. Hier. in lib. ps. iuxta Hebraic. verit.* (PL xxviii. 1123–4); also *S. Hieronymi commentarioli in ps.* xl, ed. G. Morin (Anecdota Maredsolana III/I, Maredsous, 1895), p. 46, and his *Tractatus sive homiliae in psalmos, series altera*, lxxxxix (CCSL lxxviii. 414). Cf. also the discussion in Cassiodorus, *Exp. ps.*, pr. xii (CCSL xcvii. 15).

occurs through visions, as in the case of Jeremiah, who saw a boiling cauldron from the direction of the north [Jer. 1: 13], and Moses, who saw the bush burning without being consumed [Exod. 3: 2], while Ezekiel saw a wheel in the middle of a wheel [Ezek. 1: 16]. It occurs through dreams, as for instance the dream of Nebuchadnezzar, who saw a stone cut from the mountain without human hands [Dan. 2: 34]. For what was to the king simply a dream was to Daniel a prophecy. Or again, through the dream of Pharaoh, who saw seven oxen and seven ears of corn [Gen. 41: 2–7]. To Joseph, who understood the spiritual significance, this was a prophecy.

There is yet another kind of prophecy over and above these, which has a more honourable status than they have. This happens when prophecy takes place as a result of the pure, unaided inspiration of the Holy Spirit, without any outside help in the form of an event, words, vision, or dream. This was how David prophesied, solely through the inspiration of the Holy Spirit; hence his words: I WILL HEAR WHAT THE LORD GOD WILL SPEAK IN ME (Ps. 84[: 9]). This is why the book is called a soliloquy, as being the utterance of the Holy Spirit alone. For, although in the titles [i.e. the *tituli psalmorum*][136] and in certain psalms David referred to various historical events, he did not learn anything from them, but realized that that which he already knew through the Holy Spirit is represented figuratively in them. Alternatively, the book is called 'Soliloquies' since its discourse is solely about Christ. For others have prophesied about Christ obscurely and through riddles. But because David spoke in the clearest terms about Christ's incarnation, passion, begetting by the Eternal Being, and resurrection, the book is entitled 'The Book of Soliloquies'.

Just as prophecy occurred in various ways so it relates to various times. Some prophecy concerns the present, some the past, and some the future. There is prophecy concerning the present, as when Elizabeth said: 'Whence is this to me, that the mother of my Lord should come to me?' (Luke 1[: 43]); concerning the past, as when Moses says: 'In the beginning God created heaven and earth' (Gen. 1[: 1]); and concerning the future, for example: 'Behold a virgin shall conceive' (Isa. 7[: 14]). The instruments of prophecy may be good men, for example, Isaiah, Jeremiah, and others, and also evil men like Balaam, Caiaphas, and others. Likewise, some prophecies are made out of foreknowledge granted by God, and these are destined to be fulfilled in every detail, even in terms of the precise literal meaning of the words; for example: 'a virgin shall conceive'. Others take the form of a threat; for example: 'Yet forty days, and Nineveh shall be destroyed' (Jonah 3[: 4]). This is not fulfilled according to the outward meaning of the words, but in terms of the hidden, inner significance.

Because of the special excellence of this prophet, when we say 'Prophet' without adding a proper name, we mean David, just as when we

[136] On the *tituli psalmorum* see the study by Salmon (cit. above, n. 29).

say 'the Apostle' we mean Paul, and when we say 'the City' we mean Rome. This argues against some writers who have said that the psalms were the work of several writers or authors because their names are found in the titles;[137] for instance, Asaph, Heman, Ethan, and Jeduthun. We shall show that this was done in that book for the sake of the mysterious [i.e. allegorical] significance which is obtained from the interpretations of the names. So, they were not authors of psalms, but the presence of their names there serves a mysterious purpose.

CONCERNING CHRIST Note that the soliloquies deal with the whole Christ, that is, both the head and the body. So, the subject-matter (*materia*) of this book is the whole Christ, that is, the betrothed and His spouse. Its intention (*intentio*) is to remake men, whose image had become distorted in the person of Adam, in the image of Christ, the new man. The mode of treating the subject (*modus tractandi*) is as follows. Sometimes he treats of Christ in terms of the head, sometimes in terms of the body, and sometimes concerning both. He treats of Christ in terms of the head in three ways. Sometimes he treats of His divine aspect, as in the words WITH THEE IS THE PRINCIPALITY (Ps. 109[: 3]); sometimes of His human aspect, as when he says I HAVE SLEPT AND TAKEN MY SLEEP (Ps. 3[: 6]); sometimes he uses substitution (*transumptio*), as when he assumes the voice of the limbs, for example: FAR FROM MY SALVATION, etc. (Ps. 21[: 2]), and O GOD THOU KNOWEST MY FOOLISHNESS (Ps. 68[: 6]). Likewise, he deals with the Church in three ways: sometimes he treats of those who have been made perfect, sometimes with those who are imperfect, and sometimes with the wicked who are in the Church in body but not in mind, in name but not in spirit.[138]

As regards the order of those psalms which are out of line with the historical sequence of events, the question is often asked why they are not in the order in which they were composed. It is quite clear that this is the case, for the events which form the historical background (*historia*) to HAVE MERCY ON ME, O GOD (Ps. 1[: 3]) preceded in time those which form the historical background to WHY, O LORD, ARE THEY MULTIPLIED (Ps. 3[: 2]), while BLESSED BE THE LORD MY GOD WHO TEACHES MY HANDS, etc. (Ps. 17[: 35]) was written before both the above. The answer is that if in some cases

---

[137] In his *Homiliae in psalmos*, Jerome reported two points of view: some said that David composed all the psalms, which were performed by the choirmasters (Asaph, Jeduthun, the sons of Korah, and others) whose names are found in the titles of individual psalms; others believed that these titles refer to actual authors, and that David was one psalmist among many. See Jerome's *Tract. in ps.* (CCSL lxxviii. 48, 64–5, 78, 95–6). Elsewhere Jerome affirmed his own belief in the multiple authorship of the Psalter: see *Epist.* cxl (PL xxii. 1169); cf. the *Hebraica* preface (PL xxviii. 1123). Ambrose, Augustine, and Cassiodorus thought that David was the sole author of the psalms: for Ambrose see PL xiv. 922B, 923C, 966D, 1039, 1087B–C; Augustine, *De doct. Christ.* II. viii. 13 (CCSL xxxix. 39–40), *De civ. Dei*, XVII. xiv; Cassiodorus, *Exp. ps.*, pr. ii (CCSL xcvii. 10). Cf. Nicholas of Lyre's discussion in Ch. VI.

[138] Here Peter Lombard is adopting the 'type C' prologue headings as applied to the Psalter in the *Glossa ordinaria*; cf. PL cxiii. 844B–C.

a reason for the order can be given, this is not so with all the psalms—yet even in those [seemingly anomalous] cases they have not been given that order without some reason. For the prophet Ezra, who, by the inspiration of the Holy Spirit, recreated the Psalter and the whole Bible after it had been burnt by the Babylonians, gave the psalms this order through the same inspiration of the Holy Spirit, and added titles (*tituli*) which are, so to speak, keys to the psalms. For, just as one enters a house with a key, so, through apt explanations of the titles, one is given a clear understanding of the psalms which follow that title.

These are all points which have to be considered as applying to the book as a whole. There are, in addition, some particular points which have to be considered in the case of individual psalms.

Let us, then, look at the first psalm. Here we have to consider why it has no title prefixed to it, as the others have, what is its subject-matter (*materia*), what is the author's intention (*intentio*) and the mode of treatment (*modus tractandi*). No title is prefixed to the first psalm because that psalm is the beginning and preface, and 'the head of the book', as the following text puts it: IN THE HEAD OF THE BOOK IT IS WRITTEN OF ME [Ps. 39: 8]. It treats of Him who is the beginning of all things, that is, Christ, who has no beginning. So, it has no title, lest any title prefixed to it might seem to be the 'head' and beginning of the book. Or else it is because the psalm is, so to speak, [in itself] the title and the prologue of the work which follows. For it contains in itself the sum of the subject-matter of the entire book. The subject-matter of this psalm is that of the book in its entirety, namely, the whole Christ. Likewise, the intention.[139]

The mode of treatment (*modus tractandi*) is as follows. The psalm is in two parts. First, he treats of the man who is blessed, using that blessedness to entice us [to follow God]. Secondly, he treats of the various punishments of the wicked, terrifying us by the adversities they suffer, where he says NOT SO THE WICKED, NOT SO [4]. He treats of the man who is blessed as follows. In the first verse he shows that he is free from all evil; in the second, that he is in himself replete with every good thing, and hence is useful to others, and this brings him up to the division in the psalm. To show that he is free from every evil he compares him with the old man, that is, Adam, showing us that Adam is replete with every sort of evil. For there is no better way of pointing up the excellence of anything than to make a point of mentioning the worthlessness and complete suppression or degradation of its opposite.

So, he shows us that the old Adam sinned in three ways: in thought; in will and deed; and in the teaching of the word, or habit.[140] Taken in its widest sense, [sinful] thought comprises three things, namely the first

---

[139] Cf. Cassiodorus, *Exp. ps.* (CCSL xcvii. 27–8); Jerome, *Tract. in ps.* i (CCSL lxxviii. 3–4).

[140] This tripartite analysis of Adam's sin is indebted to Jerome, *Tract. in ps.* i (CCSL lxxviii. 4–6).

impulse of the soul, which is venial sin, and pleasure and consent, which are mortal sins. He who sins by consent sins also in thought, but he who does not sin in thought does not sin by consent or pleasure. Here the psalmist denotes the three kinds of sin by the three words HAS DEPARTED FROM, HAS STOOD, HAS SAT [1]. By HAS DEPARTED FROM he denotes the sins of the will; by HAS STOOD, the sin of the act committed; by HAS SAT, the sin of the word or of habit. Adam, then, departed from God, not in a geographical sense, but through being unlike Him, since he departed from God when he gave in to the persuasions of the Devil and of Eve. He stood, when he ate the forbidden fruit and took pleasure in his sin. He sat when, by excusing himself and laying the blame on his Creator, he was confirmed in his arrogance, saying: 'the woman whom thou gavest me has seduced me' [cf. Gen. 3: 12]. For he cannot return unless freed by the One who labours under none of these vices.

In saying this a comparison is drawn with exiles, who are recalled more easily when they are still journeying into exile. When they are standing [i.e. in a state of exile] this is more difficult. Finally, it is most difficult of all [to recall them] when they have become teachers and lords in that place [of exile]. So, the man who sins only through his will returns more easily. He who sins by his action, with greater difficulty. But it is most difficult of all to recall the man who sins through force of habit, or in the teaching of the word. These are the three people raised by our Lord from the dead, in the house, at the gate, and in the tomb: that is the period of three days within which Moses wished to lead the people of God from Egypt.[141] Note also the plagues carried by impious sinners. For the impious man is he who sins against God, who sins against himself, and who passes on the plague to his neighbour.

Adam sinned against God, against himself and against his neighbour. It is as if [the psalmist] were to say: 'The first man [i.e. Adam] was wretched and wicked "who walked in the counsel of the impious", that is, of the serpent and Eve, meaning that he sinned by letting his will consent. He "stood in the way of sinners", that is, he sinned by his action. He "sat in the chair of pestilence", giving others a precedent for sinning, that is, he sinned by teaching or through habit.' For the chair (cathedra) is the special seat of teachers, just as the throne is [the special seat] of kings, and the tribunal, of judges. The psalmist shows that the first man [i.e. Adam] sinned in three ways, for sin is committed by thought, by action, and by words and teaching. Now, these ought to be removed by the second man [i.e. Christ] in the same order in which they grew up in the first. It is as if [the psalmist] were to say: 'The first man was wretched in his walking, standing and sitting, but the second is blessed [in these three things].'

141 Cf. Augustine, *De sermone Domini in monte*, I. xii. 35 (PL xxxiv. 1247); *Sermones*, xc. 7 (PL xxxviii. 563-4).

IV
Poetic Fiction and Truth:
William of Conches, 'Bernard Silvester',
Arnulf of Orléans, and Ralph of Longchamps

ACCORDING to the literary theory which twelfth-century scholars derived from such authorities as Cicero, Macrobius, and Isidore of Seville, there was a clear distinction between history and fable. *Historia* was the literally true record of actual happenings (*gestae res, res factae*) which were removed in time from the recollection of our age, whereas *fabula* comprised untrue events, fictitious things (*res fictae*) which neither happened nor could have happened.[1] But it was also believed that certain authors had chosen to convey truths of morality, physics, and even metaphysics under a fictitious veil or covering (*integumentum, involucrum*):[2] Macrobius had gone so far as to claim that 'a conception of holy truths can be expressed under a seemly veil of fictions, conveyed by honourable matter honourably arranged'.[3] The present chapter has as its main theme the different kinds of truth, both literal and 'integumental' or allegorical, which were sought by five representative *artistae* of the twelfth century. They are: William of Conches (*c.*1080–*c.*1154), often hailed as one of the main embodiments of 'the spirit of Chartres', together with an anonymous disciple; a commentator on the *Aeneid* who has sometimes been identified as Bernard Silvester (*fl.* 1156) but who may in fact have been an English 'Chartrain' thinker;[4] Arnulf of Orléans (*fl.* 1156), a leading light of a famous grammar-school where 'the songs of the muses were zealously

---

[1] Cicero, *De invent.* I. xix. 27; *Ad Herennium*, I. viii. 13; Isidore, *Ety.* I. xliv. 5.

[2] On these terms see esp. E. Jeauneau, 'L'usage de la notion d'*integumentum* à travers les gloses de Guillaume de Conches', *AHDLMA* xxiv (1957), 35–100; repr. in id., *Lectio philosophorum*, pp. 127–92; M.-D. Chenu, 'Involucrum: Le mythe selon les théologiens médiévaux', *AHDLMA* xxii (1956), 75–9.

[3] *In Somn. Scip.* I. ii. 11 (ed. Willis, p. 6; tr. Stahl, p. 85).

[4] On the life and works of William and Bernard Silvester, and the recent controversy concerning the importance, or otherwise, of the cathedral school at Chartres, see Southern, 'Humanism and the School of Chartres', in id., *Medieval Humanism and Other Studies*, pp. 61–85; J. O. Ward, 'The Date of the Commentary on Cicero's *De inventione* by Thierry of Chartres (*c.* 1095–*c.* 1160?) and the Cornifician Attack on the Liberal Arts', *Viator* iii (1972), 219–73; N. Häring, 'Chartres and Paris Revisited', in J. R. O'Donnell (ed.), *Essays in Honour of A. C. Pegis* (Toronto, 1974), pp. 268–329; Southern, *Platonism, Scholastic Method and The School of Chartres*; id., 'The Schools of Paris and the School of Chartres', in R. L. Benson and G. Constable with C. D. Lanham (eds.), *Renaissance and Renewal in the Twelfth Century* (Oxford, 1982), pp. 113–37. See further the recent (controversial) article by P. E. Dutton, 'The Uncovering of the *Glosae super Platonem* of Bernard of Chartres', *Med. Stud.* xlvi (1984), 192–221. For the argument that the *Aeneid* commentary sometimes attributed to Bernard Silvester, and the Martianus commentary which is manifestly associated with it, were of English origin, see C. Baswell, 'The Medieval Allegorization of the *Aeneid*: MS Cambridge, Peterhouse 158', *Med. Stud.* xli (1985), 181–237; cf. below, n. 150.

114   IV. POETIC FICTION AND TRUTH

guarded';[5] and Ralph of Longchamps, a relatively humble scholar who flourished in the second half of the twelfth century and the first two decades of the thirteenth, whose claim on our attention is the commentary he produced on the main moral fiction produced by a poet-academic of outstanding calibre, the *Anticlaudianus* of Alan of Lille (*c.*1116–1202/3).[6]

Fiction and Historical–Moral Truth

> Oon seyde that Omer made lyes,
> Feynynge in hys poetries,
> And was to Grekes favorable;
> Therfor held he hyt but fable
>
> (Chaucer, *The House of Fame*, 1477–80)

Not just 'one' but many medieval writers attacked Homer for having mingled historical truths with poetical fictions of various kinds, ranging from the idealizing of the Greek cause to the introduction of impossible tales about the pagan gods. The remarks found at the beginning of Joseph of Exeter's *De Bello Trojano* or *Iliad* (*c.*1188), a work heavily influenced by Lucan's *Bellum civile*,[7] are typical: 'should I admire Homer, that old man of Maeonia, or the Phrygian master, Dares, who was there and to whom his eyes, a more reliable guide, revealed the truth which fiction (*fabula*) does not know?' Joseph opts for the eyewitness historian Dares and dismisses the 'poet who plays with fictions'.[8] Similarly, in his *Historia Destructionis Troiae* (completed 1287) Guido delle Colonne accused Homer of having 'turned the pure and simple truth of his story (*ystorie veritas*) into deceiving paths, inventing many things which did not happen and altering those which did happen'. Hence he maintained that the gods worshipped by the ancient pagans fought against the Trojans and were defeated with them just like mortal men. But Homer, Guido declares, was not the only author of falsehoods: Ovid and even the 'highest of poets' Virgil followed his example by

[5] According to Alexander Nequam, *De Naturis rerum*, 'De laudibus divinae sapientiae', 607–10, ed. T. Wright (Rolls Series, XXXIV, London, 1893), p. 454. On Arnulf's life, works, disputes, and influence see *Arnulfi Aurelianensis glosule super Lucanum*, ed. B. Martì (Papers and Monographs of the American Academy in Rome, Rome, 1958), pp. xv–xxix; also her articles 'Arnulfus and the *Faits des Romains*', *MLQ* ii (1941), 3–23, and 'Hugh Primas and Arnulf of Orléans', *Speculum*, xxx (1955), 233–8; J. Holzworth, 'Hugutio's *Derivationes* and Arnulf's Commentary on Ovid's *Fasti*', *TAPA* lxxiii (1942), 259–76; Bruno Roy, 'Arnulf of Orléans and the Latin "Comedy"', *Speculum*, xlix (1974), 258–66. For the attacks on Arnulf by Alexander of Villa Dei and Geoffrey of Vinsauf see *The Ecclesiale of Alexander of Villa Dei*, ed. L. R. Lind (Lawrence, Kans., 1958), pp. 2–3, 10–11; E. Faral, *Les Arts poétiques du XIIe et du XIIIe siècle* (Paris, 1924), pp. 109–10, 189, 190; cf. Matthew of Vendôme, *Ars versificatoria*, tr. R. P. Parr (Milwaukee, Wis., 1981), pp. 8–13, 17–18, 102, 104.

[6] For these datings see M.-T. d'Alverny, *Alain de Lille: Textes inédits, avec une introduction sur la vie et ses œuvres* (Paris, 1965), pp. 11–29; *Radulphus de Longo Campo, In Anticlaudianum Alani commentum*, ed. J. Sulowski (Wrocław, etc., 1972), pp. v, vi–ix.

[7] Cf. E. M. Sanford, 'Lucan and his Roman Critics', *CP* xxvi (1931), 233–57.

[8] *Yliados libri sex*, i. 24–6, ed. L. Gompf, *Joseph Iscanus; Werke und Briefe* (Leiden and Cologne, 1970), p. 78; tr. Gildas Roberts, *Joseph of Exeter: The Iliad of Dares Phrygius* (Cape Town, 1970), p. 3.

writing 'many misleading things in their books'.[9] Two of the passages translated below reveal how 'Bernard Silvester' and Arnulf of Orléans faced this problem of poetic history.

The great innovation of Lucan in the *Bellum civile* (or *Pharsalia*, to give it its medieval title) was to disregard all that supernatural machinery which Virgil had taken over from Homer, concentrating instead on the affairs of men. Indeed, Servius had claimed that 'Lucan did not deserve to be reckoned among the poets, for he seems to have written a history, not a poem'.[10] In his commentary on the *Bellum civile* Arnulf did not go that far: for him Lucan is 'not simply a poet but a poet and historiographer combined (*poeta et historiographus*)'. He follows the sequence of his *historia* without feigning anything, Arnulf declares; when anything fictional is introduced Lucan makes it quite clear that he is only repeating what others have related, said, or remembered—here the term *aliquid ficticii* refers not to intervening pagan deities or untruths motivated by political bias but rather to mythological allusions which the poet obviously recognized as such. In his commentary Arnulf carefully identifies the *fabulae* as they appear in Lucan's text, sometimes making statements like 'He does not affirm it to be true like a historiographer but merely mentions it like a poet.'[11] In certain passages Lucan is supposed to have written like a philosopher, but Arnulf emphasizes that as a poet he is not obliged to follow the philosopher's procedure in every respect, as in this comment on an astrological crux: 'in the manner of the philosopher he puts forward three opinions, but in the manner of the poet he neither resolves nor affirms any of them'.[12]

The greater part of Arnulf's prologue consists of a résumé of the true historical events on which the invented element (*figmentum*) of the *Bellum civile* is based. But for the historians of the Middle Ages (and beyond) their subject was at its best not a mere record of facts but a repository of illustrative stories (or *exempla*) which showed the reader what actions should be done and what should be shunned; not objectivity but a deliberate moral bias was what was valued. And so Arnulf, in applying the 'type C' prologue headings to his text, can present Lucan's moral *intentio* as valid both for his own time and for all time: he deterred the Romans from civil war, and the grisly fate of Pompey and Caesar will encourage us to steer well clear of such a war. Moreover, certain virtues are well illustrated by the activities of Cato and others, who show us admirable ethical behaviour in politics.[13]

[9] *Historia destructionis Troiae*, pr., ed. N. E. Griffin (Mediaeval Academy of America XXXVI, Cambridge, Mass., 1936), p. 4; tr. M. E. Meek (Bloomington, Ind., and London, 1974), pp. 1–2. On Virgil as the 'highest of poets' see the Epilogue, ed. Griffin, p. 276, tr. Meek, p. 265.

[10] Servius on *Aeneid*, i. 382; repeated by Isidore, *Ety.* VIII. vii. 10. This issue remained a matter of controversy in the 16th–18th cc.: see H.-D. Leidig, *Das Historiengedicht in der englischen Literaturtheorie: Die Rezeption von Lucans Pharsalia von der Renaissance bis zum Ausgang des achtzehnten Jahrhunderts* (Europäische Hochschulschriften XIV/26, Frankfurt, 1975).

[11] *Glosule super Lucanum*, ii. 410 (ed. Marti, p. 128).

[12] Ibid., i. 412 (ed. Marti, p. 55).

[13] It is interesting to note that Arnulf's moral concerns are shared to some extent by the modern critic F. M. Ahl, who argues that Lucan *had* to expel the Olympians from the poem

But narratives did not have to be historically true in order to offer true morality—a fact already witnessed by the wide range of texts classified as pertaining to ethics in the *accessūs ad auctores*, including the moral fables of Aesop and Avianus (cf. above, pp. 13, 16, 47–50). It was this fact which enabled 'Bernard Silvester' to defend Homer's imitator Virgil as poet (his justification of Virgil as philosopher will be discussed later). There is a frank declaration that Virgil did not write the true version of historical events (*historie veritas*), as Dares Phrygius did; rather he extols the deeds of Aeneas using poetic figments. Historians wrote both to please and to profit, and indeed so did Virgil, for the rhetorical and narrative qualities of the *Aeneid* are pleasing while the stimulus of its examples are profitable. Thus, the labours of Aeneas teach us patience while his immoderate love for Dido deters us from desiring unlawful things, and so forth.

Historical accuracy and exemplification may be regarded as two kinds of literal truth; another is afforded by the outspoken, unveiled reprehension of actual vices which was regarded as the prerogative of the Roman satirists.

The Naked Truth of Satire. Whereas other pagan poets had used *integumenta* to clothe their valuable doctrines, Horace, Juvenal, and Persius had—according to their medieval readers—torn aside falsehoods and disguise to reveal facts about society which were unadulterated by poetic invention. As a twelfth-century commentator on Juvenal asserted, 'satire is naked . . . because it censures the vices of the Romans nakedly, and openly, and clearly, and without circumlocution and periphrasis, and without an *integumentum*.[14] We have already seen how Conrad of Hirsau, in comparing the satyrs with the satiric poets, stated that while the former are not embarrassed to expose themselves publicly without care for clothing (*nichil tractantes de tegumentis*), the latter are not restrained from their objective of making 'the depraved suffer under the naked outspokenness of their words' (p. 61). Similarly, in the Juvenal commentary represented below, which has some connection with William of Conches, those writers 'who cover up (*velant*) their reprehension' are contrasted with the satirists who engaged in 'naked and open reprehension'. As Paul Miller has said, 'It was unnecessary to analyse the works of the satirists *per integumenta* because Roman satire conveyed its morality at the

in order to 'bring the moral issues into the foreground': *Lucan: An Introduction* (Ithaca, NY, and London, 1976), p. 69.

[14] Cited from Oxford, Bodleian Library, MS Auct. F. 6. 9, by P. S. Miller, 'The Mediaeval Literary Theory of Satire and its Relevance to the Works of Gower, Langland and Chaucer' (unpub. Ph.D. thesis, The Queen's University of Belfast, 1982), p. 27. The Juvenal commentary edited by R. J. Barnett, Jr., 'An Anonymous Medieval Commentary on Juvenal' (unpub. Ph.D. thesis, The University of North Carolina at Chapel Hill, 1964), makes the same basic point by declaring that satire is naked because, although it represents through the concealment (*tegendo*) of certain ambiguities, it manifestly lays bare (*retegens*) all things (pp. 1–2). On medieval theory of satire in general see further P. S. Miller, 'John Gower, Satiric Poet', in A. J. Minnis (ed.), *Gower's Confessio amantis*, pp. 79–105, and U. Kindermann, *Satyra: Die Theorie der Satire in Mittellateinischen: Vorstudie zu einer Gattungsgeschichte* (Nuremberg, 1978).

first, *literal* level of meaning.'[15] Medieval commentators on Roman satire saw themselves as simply describing the aggressive and blatant didacticism of texts which, as it were, contained their own moral commentary. This is well illustrated by the approach which our anonymous scholar takes to Juvenal's fourth satire.

Juvenal, unlike Horace, did not write his satires according to a carefully thought out plan, passing skilfully from one theme to the next and dovetailing each into the other. The two themes of Satire IV are treated at very unequal length. First we get a picture of Crispinus, one of the emperor Domitian's favourites who, as a foreign upstart, was a natural target for the xenophobic satirist. But this occupies only ll. 1–27, while the rest of the satire, ll. 28–154, is taken up with a masterly account of an alleged meeting of Domitian's semi-official privy council of *amici* ('friends') of Caesar, to discuss the footling business of what is to be done with a huge fish which has been presented to the emperor. The link with the first section is the tenuous one that Crispinus occurs again among the councillors of state summoned to discuss this 'weighty' matter.

The first section is fairly standard satire of Crispinus on grounds of low birth, sexual perversions, and foreign origins. Viewed in this light, our commentator's emphasis on his gluttony and riotous living are seen to be too selective and over-specific, these being but minor matters here. But this emphasis is dictated by what has been taken as the main unifying factor of the whole poem, the supposed similarities in the vices practised by the favourite and his master, here (incorrectly but interestingly) identified as Nero, an emperor whose gluttony and riotous living were well known to, and much berated by, medieval scholars. When Juvenal sets the scene for the ridiculous 'cabinet meeting' by saying 'When the last Flavian was torturing a world already half dead, and Rome was slave to a bald Nero' (38), he is brilliantly deploying his talents as a satirist by making several points in a very few words. Domitian was the last and worst Flavian emperor, as Nero was the last and worst Julio-Claudian emperor. Domitian was as much a tyrant as Nero, and in addition was vulnerable to caricature because of his baldness. So, the 'bald Nero' to whom Juvenal refers is Domitian. The anonymous commentator does not grasp this and thinks that the emperor referred to throughout is Nero, and so sets the entire events of the satire in Nero's court (i.e. before AD 69) rather than in Domitian's (before 96). There is, of course, the further complication

---

[15] Miller, 'Mediaeval Literary Theory of Satire', p. 27. Our Juvenal commentator could find only one *integumentum* in his text: Juvenal dared not reprehend Nero directly, so at one point he concealed the emperor's identity under a veil by calling him Marius: *Guillaume de Conches: Glosae in Iuvenalem*, ed. Bradford Wilson (Textes philosophiques du moyen âge XVIII, Paris, 1980), p. 108; cf. Jeauneau, '*Integumentum*', in *Lectio philosophorum*, p. 148. Here the term refers to a specific and purely local use of a rhetorical trope. 'It has no bearing on the moral or spiritual interpretation of the text as a whole', declares Miller, op. cit., p. 343 n. 67; this serves to support his general contention that one of the essential defining characteristics of the satiric genre was believed to be its direct expression of the naked truth about vices. Wilson's attempt (op. cit., pp. 54 ff.) to view the 'William of Conches' Juvenal commentary in the perspective of integumental analysis would, on this argument, appear to be misleading.

that, as Juvenal himself says (136), some of the cronies of Domitian were survivors from the last years of Nero. Naturally, the medieval scholar does not pick up this point.

In the second and main part of the satire Juvenal's main purpose was certainly not to satirize gluttony and riotous living. He is painting a realistic picture of the council of top advisers of an absolute ruler, each suspicious of the other, and hating the tyrant on whom they pour exaggerated flattery, which he, like most men who have held untrammelled power for too long, eagerly accepts. Regarded more narrowly, Juvenal's purpose is to show that the senatorial order, embodied by its most eminent members here depicted, has been degraded by being forced to stoop to discussion of trivialities. In short, Juvenal is not really reprehending the Romans in general, but rather commenting on the degradation of the governing class and the viciousness of Domitian's regime. Here too, gluttony and riotous living are subsidiary targets, hinted at once or twice. But such insight is rendered possible by information about the historical background which the medieval commentator did not possess. He was obliged to make sense of the text in terms of the knowledge which was available to him, and so presents us with a vision of Nero's court and the Romans in general acting in ways which reflect and reproduce the characteristic vices of their unruly ruler.

A substantial portion of the commentary consists of very detailed exposition of individual points. Because of its fragmented quality we strongly advise the reader to use it alongside a modern translation of Juvenal's fourth satire (the Loeb 'parallel text' edition being ideal for this purpose). Only in this way will it be possible to appreciate fully the way in which the classical text has been remade in a medieval image.

Veiled Truth: Philosophy covered with Fiction. At the beginning of the prologue to his commentary on the *Aeneid* 'Bernard' claims the authority of Macrobius for his view of Virgil as a poet-philosopher who combined poetic fiction with the truth of philosophy; at its end he defines *integumentum* in terms which echo Macrobius' seminal description of the fabulous narrative (*narratio fabulosa*), wherein a decent and dignified conception of holy truths, with respectable events and characters, is presented beneath a modest veil of allegory.[16] This, Macrobius had declared, is the only type of fable with which philosophers should be concerned. But there 'Bernard', like William of Conches, refused to follow him. While they found Macrobius' high claim for fabulous narrative a considerable improvement on the narrow Ciceronian distinction between true history and fictitious fable, his hierarchical classification of the different types of fable was at once over-elaborate and over-exclusive for their purposes. Their attitude to fiction was more comprehensive and more liberal, as may be illustrated by some of William's comments on Macrobius' classification.[17]

[16] *In Somn. Scip.* i. ii. 11 (ed. Willis, p. 6; tr. Stahl, p. 85).
[17] William's commentary on Macrobius is as yet unedited; the following paragraphs are based on the account and quotations in Peter Dronke, *Fabula* (Leiden and Cologne, 1974), pp. 25 ff. The MSS are described by E. Jeauneau, 'Gloses de Guillaume de Conches sur Macrobe: Note sur les manuscrits', *AHDLMA* xxvii (1960), 17–28; repr. in id., *Lectio philo-*

All those fables which merely please without profiting were rejected out of hand by Macrobius, who relegated them to children's nurseries. But William understands by these nurseries the schools of poets, in which young minds proceed from the easier to the harder authors (rather in the manner recommended by Conrad of Hirsau: see above, pp. 37–8, 46). Moving on to a superior type of fable, Macrobius had praised Aesop's exquisite imagination (*elegantia fictionis*) but concluded that his fables, in which both the argument and the manner of narration were fictitious, were also inappropriate to philosophical treatises. William chooses to omit Macrobius' negative remark and to emphasize his statement that Aesop's fables encourage us to good works. Although 'they signify nothing true', by them 'we are brought to some insight into behaviour'.[18] Obviously William has been influenced by the common grammarian's practice of identifying the *pars philosophiae* to which Aesop's work pertains as being ethics, the science of behaviour, a branch of practical philosophy (cf. above, pp. 47–9). Even more crucially, William refuses to accept Macrobius' blanket dismissal of those fables which contain certain base and unworthy elements, as when they tell immoral things of the gods. 'Consider Jupiter cutting off his father's testicles and throwing them in the sea so that Venus is born,' requests William. 'This is nothing but that the testicles signify the fruits of the earth, through which, in the course of time, the seed from the bowels of the earth is diffused more and more. . . . The fruits are cast into the sea, that is, into the hollow maw of the human belly, and thus Venus—that is, sensual delight—is born.'[19] Similarly, Jupiter's adultery with Semele is supposed to signify the influence of the ether on the earth, and Mars' adultery with Venus is given an astrological explanation.[20] In these cases, even though the words may be base, something honourable and beautiful may be meant by them. (This view seems to have something in common with the pseudo-Dionysian defence of base and low imagery concerning God,[21] one of the subjects treated below in Ch. V). The only type of fable which Macrobius had decreed worthy of the philosopher's attention, the *narratio fabulosa*, which functions by expressing honourable and true matter through words which are fictional but honourable, is of course approved of by William, his main contribution having consisted in eroding the distinctions between it and the more dubious kinds of fable. Many different kinds of fable, according to William of Conches and his 'Chartrain' colleagues, offer philosophy veiled with the covering of fiction.

---

sophorum, pp. 267–300. Cf. Dronke, *Fabula*, p. 76. On the general importance of Macrobius for 'Chartrain' philosophy see E. Jeauneau, 'Macrobe, source du platonisme chartrain', *Studi medievali*, 3rd ser. i/1 (1960), 3–24; repr. *Lectio philosophorum*, pp. 279–300.

[18] Tr. Dronke, *Fabula*, p. 18.

[19] Cit. ibid., p. 26. With this interpretation cf. Fulgentius, *Mitologiae*, i. 2, ed. R. Helm, *Fabii Planciadis Fulgentii opera* (Leipzig, 1898), p. 18; tr. Whitbread, pp. 49–50; also *The Commentary on the First Six Books of the Aeneid of Vergil commonly attributed to Bernardus Silvestris*, ed. J. W. Jones and E. F. Jones (Lincoln and London, 1977), pp. 10–11.

[20] Dronke, *Fabula*, pp. 28–9.

[21] As is pointed out by Dronke, *Fabula*, p. 31, cf. pp. 43 ff.

A System of Secular Allegory. In the hands of scholars like William and 'Bernard', the literary theory of *fabula* derived from Cicero, Macrobius, and Isidore was integrated and vastly extended to become an all-embracing system of 'secular allegory' which comprised historical, philosophical, physical/astrological, and moral interpretations of pagan myth and metaphor.[22] In this context, therefore, *historia* does not only mean literally true history as opposed to allegorically true fable; it can also designate one method of interpreting an *integumentum*. Both senses of the term are found in William's exposition of *The Consolation of Philosophy*, IV, met. vii. Boethius' intention in this metre, William says, is to encourage us to fight bravely against fortune, and we are encouraged to do so in three ways and in this sequence: by history, by *integumentum*, and by being shown the rewards which are to come (the last of these referring to the eventual stellification of Hercules).[23] First, Boethius provides the *historia* of how Agamemnon had to sacrifice his daughter in order to obtain a propitious wind for the Greek fleet which was sailing to attack Troy. Then, William continues, Boethius proceeds to exhort by means of two *integumenta*, the tales of Ulysses and Polyphemus and of the twelve labours of Hercules. But within the second of these integuments there is some historical truth—as, for example, in the account of the Centaurs. When the ignorant saw Ixion's cavalry they thought they were looking at monsters who combined certain qualities of men and horses. This euhemeristic reading, in which the *rei historia* underlying the fiction is brought out, is followed by an integumental reading of the fable of Ixion's unsuccessful attempt to copulate with Juno. Because a cloud intervened Ixion's seed fell on the earth, whence the centaurs were born. This is said to be an allegory of how greatness (*dignitas*), when attempting to join itself to action (Juno being the active life), is hindered by a cloud, that is, by the obfuscation of reason by ambition, and thus expends its whole effort on earthly things.

The same twofold approach is found in William's commentary on IV, met. iii, as translated below. In euhemeristic, historical terms Circe was a prostitute who seduced men, but the wise Ulysses was able to resist her charms. William then proceeds to a 'more subtle' explanation, this being a moral allegory which takes its point of departure from etymologies of the names 'Ulysses' and 'Circe'. Here, then, are further examples of how *fabulae*, even those with certain base or dishonourable elements, can serve the cause of truth, and so be of interest to the philosopher.

Indeed, William can be positively scathing about those who are unable or

---

[22] On the traces of the historical and euhemeristic, physical, and moral methods of secular allegory in Servius' commentary on the *Aeneid* see J. W. Jones, 'Allegorical Interpretation in Servius', *Classical Journal*, lvi (1961), 218–22; on Fulgentius' similar methods see Whitbread, *Fulgentius the Mythographer*, pp. 17–18, 22; see further J. R. O'Donnell, 'The Sources and Meaning of Bernard Silvester's Commentary on the *Aeneid*', *Med. Stud.* xxiv (1962), 234–7. On euhemerism see esp. J. D. Cooke, 'Euhemerism: A Medieval Interpretation of Classical Paganism', *Speculum*, ii (1927), 396–410.

[23] Cit. Jeauneau, '*Integumentum*', in id., *Lectio philosophorum*, p. 129. The following account is based on our own transcription of the text in London, British Library, MS Royal 15. B. III, fos. 120ʳ–122ᵛ, and Dijon, Bibl. mun., MS 254, fo. 121ᵛ–123ᵛ.

unwilling to recognize that philosophical truths are veiled in poetic fictions. Certain wise men, he declares, wished to understand the integument of the fable of Orpheus, 'not believing that so perfect a philosopher, namely Boethius, would have placed anything superfluous or of no account in such a perfect work. But today's whippersnappers (*gartiones*), intent on their own chattering and knowing nothing of philosophy, and therefore ashamed to say "I do not know" and, seeking solace in their own awkwardness, said that to expound [this fable] were a vain deceit.' 'We are not like them', declares William, and offers his own interpretation. 'Orpheus descended to the underworld in order to bring back his wife, just as the wise man (*sapiens*) must descend to a knowledge of earthly things in order to see that there is nothing of value in them before he can free himself from concupiscence.'[24] A similar outburst occurs in William's commentary on the *Consolation*, III, met. xi, where he seeks to refute the suggestion that his main philosophical authority Plato believed something which we now know in fact he did believe, namely the doctrine that knowledge is acquired through recollection of truths learned in a previous existence. William attacks those ignorant people 'who often unfairly condemn his [i.e. Plato's] words when at times he speaks about philosophy under his integuments', and then proceeds to expound the text of Boethius in a way which is compatible with Christianity.[25] A spectacular case of this sort of 'reverent interpretation' of Plato occurs in William's commentary on the most controversial part of the *Consolation*, the metre *O qui perpetua* (III, met. ix). There the world-soul (*anima mundi*) as described in the *Timaeus* is allegorized as that natural vigour which operates on all levels, causing plants and trees to grow, animals to have feelings, and men to have the power of discernment; it is to be identified with the Holy Spirit, that is, with divine and benign concord, the power by which everything grows and flourishes.[26]

Philosophy and poetry have come together within a single and common method of integumental interpretations. Plato's use of poetic imagery gave his 'Chartrain' readers powerful backing for their belief that 'the truest poetry' can be 'the most feigning', to adapt Touchstone's wisecrack.[27] Thus

[24] Latin text cit. J. B. Friedman, *Orpheus in the Middle Ages* (Cambridge, Mass., 1971), p. 106, and by Jeauneau, 'Integumentum', in *Lectio philosophorum*, pp. 137–8. On the 12th-c. *gartiones* or 'Cornifician' detractors of the *artes* see Ward, 'The Commentary on Cicero's *De inventione* by Thierry of Chartres', pp. 219–37.

[25] MS Royal 15. B. III, fol. 83ʳ.

[26] See the text from the 'first recension' of William's commentary (in Troyes, Bibl. mun., MS 1381) transcribed by Charles Jourdain, 'Des commentaires inédits de Guillaume de Conches et de Nicolas Triveth sur la *Consolation de la philosophie* de Boèce, *Notices et extraits des manuscrits de la Bibliothèque Impériale*, xx/2 (1862), 75–6. For a major difference between this account and that found in the 'second recension' of William's Boethius commentary see P. Dronke, 'L'Amor che move il sole e l'altre stelle', in id., *The Medieval Poet and His World* (Storia e letteratura, Studi e testi CLXIV, Rome, 1984), pp. 463–5. On William's theory of the world-soul see esp. Jeauneau, '*Integumentum*', in *Lectio philosophorum*, pp. 157–72, and Tullio Gregory, *Anima Mundi: La filosofia di Guglielmo di Conches e la Scuola di Chartres* (Florence, 1955).

[27] Or, to be more exact, 'Poets provide false stories; philosophers often turn these falsehoods into truth', to quote Theodulf of Orléans, *Carmina*, iv. 1 (PL cv. 331–2), cit. J. Seznec, *The Survival of the Pagan Gods*, tr. B. F. Sessions (New York, 1953; repr. Princeton, NJ, 1972), p. 90.

encouraged, William, 'Bernard', and their kindred spirits found philosophy in poetry and poetry in philosophy. Their thirteenth-century successors were to find poetry in theology—a subject which will be discussed in Ch. VI.

Problems of Classification. Not all twelfth-century scholars thought about philosophy and poetry in the manner of William of Conches and 'Bernard Silvester'. The 'songs of the poets' and the writings of 'the philosophers' were classed by Hugh of Saint-Victor as being mere 'appendages of the arts' and hence 'only tangential to philosophy'. 'Occasionally,' he admits, 'it is true, they touch in a scattered and confused fashion upon some topics lifted out of the arts, or, if their narrative presentation is simple, they prepare the way for philosophy.' But that is faint praise. Anyone who 'willingly deserts truth in order to entangle himself in these mere by-products of the arts' will find 'exceedingly great pains and meagre fruit.'[28] There is, moreover, something double-edged about John of Salisbury's famous description of poetry as 'the cradle of philosophy': grown men with mature minds cannot remain in their cradle.[29] Even that arch-defender of the Muses, Arnulf of Orléans, will not go so far as to say that Lucan actually gives moral instruction; rather he is supposed to encourage us to virtue after a fashion, 'in a certain way' (*quodam modo*). Master Bernard of Chartres, on the evidence of the Juvenal *accessus* translated below, seems to have been unhappy with the application of the *cui parti philosophiae supponitur* question (one of the 'type C' prologue headings) to literary texts—a question not to be asked, he thought. But William of Conches, the *accessus* continues, used to assert that in respect of their subject-matter such authors do in fact pertain to philosophy, the *pars philosophiae* being determined by the precise nature of the subject-matter. The fact that the songs of the poets were not, strictly speaking, 'parts of the arts' (i.e. did not teach the arts directly and explicitly) did not, in William's view, make them mere 'appendages of the arts', as in Hugh of Saint-Victor's theory: they afforded much matter which, under his integumental analysis, proved itself to be highly relevant to philosophy.

Such controversial issues are absent from the formal classification of grammar which is found in William's prologue to Priscian, as translated below; there it is the linguistic foundations of the subject which are at the centre of attention rather than the philosophical implications of the subject-matter of certain texts which fell within its province. A twofold classification is offered, perfectly in keeping with William's several discussions of the *ordo scientiarum*: grammar may be considered as either a branch of eloquence or a branch of logic.[30]

What is especially important about this introduction, however, is the fact

---

[28] *Didascalicon*, III. iv (ed. Buttimer, pp. 54–5; tr. Taylor, p. 88). By contrast, Scripture is 'the peak of philosophy and the perfection of truth': *Expositio in Hierarchiam Coelestem*, I. i (PL clxxv. 927A), cit. Taylor, p. 35.

[29] *Metalogicon*, I. xxii (ed. C. C. J. Webb (Oxford, 1929), tr. D. D. McGarry (Berkeley and Los Angeles, 1955), p. 63).

[30] On medieval divisions of the sciences, with special reference to poetry, see Hardison, *The Enduring Monument*, pp. 3–23. Cf. the relevant material below, Ch. VII.

that it is an early instance of an 'extrinsic' prologue. Since Priscian concentrated on the 'intrinsic' aspects of the art of grammar, William explains, he has felt obliged to discuss its 'extrinsic' aspects under the following headings: *quid sit ars ipsa*, *quod nomen ipsius*, *que causa nominis*, *quod genus*, *quod officium*, *quis finis*, *que materia*, *que partes*, *quod instrumentum*, *quis artifex*, *quis doctor*, *que auctoris intentio*.[31] This series (a variant of the 'type D' prologue paradigm identified by R. W. Hunt) apparently originated in Cicero's *De inventione* and was amplified by Boethius in his *De differentiis topicis*.[32] The terms *extrinsecus* and *intrinsecus* also had their origin in the rhetorical tradition,[33] and William's use of them was probably due to the example of his older colleague Thierry of Chartres (who became chancellor of Chartres in 1141). In the innovative prologue to his commentary on the *De inventione*, Thierry, amplifying a distinction made by the fourth-century rhetorician Victorinus,[34] stated that the 'extrinsic' art consisted of that which it is necessary to know in advance before commencing to practise an art, while the 'intrinsic' art comprised the rules and precepts which we must know in order to practise the art itself.[35] Thierry also distinguished between those things it is necessary to know concerning the art (*circa artem*) and concerning the book under discussion (*circa librum*) respectively. Concerning the art of rhetoric ten things must be considered, he continues, and provides a 'type D' series of headings which has much in common with the list by William of Conches quoted above.[36] Concerning the particular book, one must consider the *intentio auctoris* and the *utilitas*—terms which are part of the 'type C' prologue paradigm. Thierry's successors replaced his terms *circa artem* and *circa librum* with the terms *extrinsecus* and *intrinsecus* respectively. The 'extrinsic' prologue, or the extrinsic element of a prologue, provided a discussion of the art or science in question, while in the 'intrinsic' prologue or prologue-element various 'type C' headings provided the plan for an analysis of a specific text which

---

[31] This analysis was taken over by Peter Helias in the prologue to his *Summa super Priscianum*: see K. M. Fredborg, 'The Dependence of Petrus Helias' *Summa super Priscianum* on William of Conches' *Glosule super Priscianum*', *CIMAGL* xi (1973), 1–57. For Peter's prologue see L. A. Reilly, 'Petrus Helias' *Summa super Priscianum*: An Edition and Study' (unpub. Ph.D. thesis, University of Toronto, 1975), pp. 1–4.

[32] *De invent.* i. iv. 5; *De diff. topicis*, iv (PL lxiv. 1207A–B, cf. 1211B); tr. Stump, pp. 80–1; cf. Hunt, 'Introductions to the *Artes*', pp. 87, 97 (repr. pp. 119, 129); also McKeon, 'Rhetoric in the Middle Ages', p. 271.

[33] See Minnis, *Authorship*, p. 30.

[34] Comment. in *De Invent.* i. iv, in *Rhetores Latini minores*, ed. C. Halm (Leipzig, 1863), p. 170; cf. Hunt, 'Introductions to the *Artes*', p. 98 (repr. p. 130).

[35] See the edition of the prologue by N. M. Häring, 'Thierry of Chartres and Dominicus Gundissalinus', *Med. Stud.* xxvi (1964), 281–6. For the debate on the dating of this commentary see Ward, 'The Commentary on Cicero's *De inventione* by Thierry of Chartres', pp. 219–73.

[36] See Häring, op. cit., pp. 273–86. This schematic discussion of the act of rhetoric is more or less identical with the whole section on rhetoric in Gundissalinus, *De Divisione philosophiae*, ed. L. Baur (Münster, 1903), pp. 62–9. R. W. Hunt believed that Thierry was the source of Gundissalinus, 'Introductions to the *Artes*', pp. 91–3, 98 (repr. pp. 123–5, 130). N. M. Häring, op. cit., pp. 275–80, came to the opposite conclusion. Hunt's conclusion has been supported by Ward, op. cit., pp. 245–64, and K. M. Fredborg, 'The Commentary of Thierry of Chartres on Cicero's *De inventione*', *CIMAGL* vii (1971), 6–12.

pertained to that art.[37] This basic structure of an extrinsic prologue followed by an intrinsic one was to remain constant throughout the later Middle Ages, even though the style and vocabulary of each type of prologue changed considerably (see below, pp. 198–200, 319–20, 321, 377).

Poetry serving Theology. The *extrinsecus/intrinsecus* and *circa artem/circa librum* distinctions appear in Alan of Lille's commentary on the *Rhetorica ad Herennium*,[38] but here we are concerned with his *Anticlaudianus*, written between 1181 and 1184.[39] Alan's prose preface to his poem places it at the point of intersection between the lower and the higher disciplines:

> Let those not dare to show disdain for this work who are still wailing in the cradles of the nurses and are being suckled at the breasts of the lower arts. Let those not try to detract from the work who are just giving promise of a service in the higher arts. Let those not presume to undo this work who are beating the doors of heaven with their philosophic heads.

Each of these three groups of readers will find something of value in the *Anticlaudianus*:

> For in this work the sweetness of the literal sense will soothe the ears of boys, the moral instruction will inspire the mind on the road to perfection, the sharper subtlety of the allegory will whet the advanced intellect.[40]

The sequence presupposed here echoes Boethius' description of Dame Philosophy's garments, on which are woven steps by which one might climb from the embroidered letter *P* (practical philosophy) to the higher letter *Th* (theoretical philosophy, culminating in theology).[41] Alan's poem dramatizes the struggle of natural knowledge to reach out beyond the human and make contact with the science of the divine.[42] It is in many respects a Christian version of the late fifth-century *Marriage of Philology and Mercury*, in which the pagan Martianus Capella had described how the seven liberal arts can elevate the soul to be fit for heaven.[43] Hence, Ralph of Longchamps can claim that the book is not tied to any *pars philosophiae* in particular, but ranges over all its branches, ultimately climbing to the lofty heights of theology. Like Hugh of

[37] See Hunt, 'Introductions to the *Artes*', pp. 100–5 (repr. pp. 132–7); Minnis, *Authorship*, pp. 31–2.

[38] See d'Alverny, *Alain de Lille*, pp. 52–5; K. M. Fredborg, 'Petrus Helias on Rhetoric', *CIMAGL* xiii (1974), 31–3.

[39] For this dating see M. Hutchings, 'L'*Anticlaudianus* d'Alain de Lille, Étude de chronologie', *Romania*, l (1924), 1–13; d'Alverny, op. cit., pp. 33–4.

[40] Alan of Lille, *Anticlaudianus, or The Good and Perfect Man*, tr. J. J. Sheridan (Toronto, 1973), pp. 40–1.

[41] *De cons. phil.* i, pr. i, 18–22, ed. and tr. S. J. Tester together with Boethius' *Theological Tractates*, ed. and tr. H. F. Stewart, E. K. Rand, and S. J. Tester (Cambridge, Mass., and London, 1973), pp. 132, 134.

[42] This process is well described by J. M. Trout, *The Voyage of Prudence: The World View of Alan of Lille* (Washington, DC, 1979), pp. 40–150. On Alan's conception of theology see esp. M.-T. d'Alverny, 'Alain de Lille et la "Theologia"', in *L'Homme devant Dieu: Mélanges offerts au Père Henri de Lubac* (Paris, 1963–4), ii. 111–28.

[43] Tr. W. H. Stahl, Richard Johnson, and E. L. Burge, *Martianus Capella and the Seven Liberal Arts*, vol. ii (New York, 1971–7).

Saint-Victor, Alan regarded the arts as the handmaidens of theology, but he had a far higher conception of the services they could perform. As Gillian Evans puts it, 'He showed, as perhaps no other writer of the age was able to do, in exactly what way poetry and the *artes* could be made to serve the purposes of the theologian'.[44] And in the *Anticlaudianus* his chosen vehicle was poetic fiction.

As cleverly mythologized academica the *Anticlaudianus* at once reflected and stimulated the interests of twelfth-century *artistae*, and was warmly accepted by that literary establishment, who judged and explicated it according to the standards and learning of those same academica. Hence the thriving commentary-tradition on the poem, of which the exposition by Alan's pupil and friend Ralph of Longchamps was one of the earliest and certainly the most elaborate.[45] Its dedicatory epistle, addressed to Arnaud Amaury, Archbishop of Narbonne, has been dated 1212/13.[46]

Ralph's commentary is divided into nine *distinctiones*, reflecting the nine-book structure of the poem; however, the *capitula* or section-headings into which each distinction is divided cut across the sequence of the text, functioning as finding-devices for the learning which Ralph is unloading. Each distinction was to be followed by a *recursus* or *recapitulatio*, this being a close textual gloss. But the recapitulations following distinctions 5–8 are very short, and after distinction 9 Ralph felt he had done enough. The main aspect presented by the work, therefore, is that of an encyclopaedia of the liberal arts rather than a commentary proper. But such treatment may be said to follow the spirit if not the letter of Alan's donnish work. Ralph drew on many of the very sources which his beloved master had used[47]—and on other works penned by the *doctor universalis* himself. For instance, Ralph's exposition of Alan's prose preface, as translated below, is heavily indebted to Alan's *Expositio prosae de angelis*,[48] a work which, like the *Anticlaudianus* itself, evinces Alan's knowledge of *The Celestial Hierarchy* of Pseudo-Dionysius the Areopagite and its great commentator John Scotus Erigena (*c*.810–*c*.877).

The climax of the *Anticlaudianus* is clearly influenced by Dionysian negative theology. Prudence journeys upwards via the liberal arts, but then reaches the point at which Reason must be left behind as she is conducted by Dame Theology to the ultimate objective of 'a view of the celestial theophany', i.e. the triune God showing Himself. On entering the realm of joy the light dazzles prudence; her mind is benumbed and she faints.[49] Faith restores

---

[44] *Alan of Lille: The Frontiers of Theology in the Later Twelfth Century* (Cambridge, 1983), p. iv.

[45] On this commentary-tradition see R. Bossuat's edition of the *Anticlaudianus* (Paris, 1955), pp. 43–6, and M. T. Gibson and Nigel F. Palmer, 'Manuscripts of Alan of Lille, *Anticlaudianus*, in the British Isles', *Studi medievali*, 3rd ser., ii (1987), 927–37.

[46] *In Anticlaud. Alani comment.*, ed. Sulowski, p. viii.

[47] See Sulowski's introduction, pp. xlviii–liii. However, work in progress by K. M. Fredborg is demonstrating Ralph's debt to Thierry of Chartres.

[48] Cf. d'Alverny, *Alain de Lille*, pp. 105–6.

[49] For an interesting comparison of this incident with the lethargy and rapture of the Dante-*persona*'s mind in *Paradiso*, xxxiii. 94–9, see Peter Dronke, 'Boethius, Alanus and Dante', in id., *The Medieval Poet and his World*, pp. 431–8. On Alan's conception of *extasis* see

her to consciousness but, realizing that what is to come would be too much for
her feeble human capacities, supplies her with a mirror in which she may view
celestial beings and finally God Himself, all suitably dulled by means of
reflection.

Here a wedge has been placed between reason and faith, between philosophy
and theology. It was to be driven in hard by the later scholastics, who elaborated
on the differences between the human arts and sciences and the science of
theology (see below, Ch. VI). Prudence's faint symbolizes all the rules of the
seven liberal arts breaking down as they are confronted with something they are
not equipped to deal with, yet—nice paradox!—without their help Prudence
would have lacked the chariot which took her to heaven. The arts of language
are indispensable because human language is the only medium by which men
can convey to one another something, however inadequately, of what is essentially inexpressible. Moreover, figures, fictions, and other poetic devices of the
type used in the *Anticlaudianus*—and, indeed, in Holy Scripture itself—are particularly valuable by reason of their very non-referentiality in empirical terms.
Indeed, the more fictional and inappropriate they are the better, for then no one
can fall into error like that of those anthropomorphic worshippers who (to cite
Ralph citing Alan) 'believed that God was distinguished with all the features of a
human body, and was surrounded by angels as by a kind of army'. The truest
poetry is the most obviously feigning. The implications of that startling idea
were worked out by thirteenth-century students of *The Celestial Hierarchy*,
including Thomas Gallus and Robert Grosseteste, whose interpretations are
excerpted in our following section.

WILLIAM OF CONCHES

Commentary on Boethius, *The Consolation of Philosophy*
(Second Redaction): Exposition of Book IV, metre iii[50]

THE SAILS OF THE NERITIAN, etc. Construe thus: *Eurus* [i.e. the East wind, 3]
that is, natural poverty, which is aptly designated by the East wind, which
begins where the sun rises and blows towards the setting sun. Similarly,
need or poverty arises at birth and continues right up to the end of life.

his *Quoniam homines*, ed. P. Glorieux, 'La somme "Quoniam Homines" d'Alain de Lille',
AHDLMA xx (1953), 121. Cf. Evans, *Alan of Lille*, pp. 48–9.

[50] The following translation is based on London, British Library, MS Royal 15. B. III,
fos. 100ᵛ–101ʳ and Dijon, Bibl. mun., MS 254, fo. 104ʳ⁻ᵛ; we also consulted the texts offered in
Paris, Bibliothèque nationale, MSS Lat. 6406 and 16094. The text in these four MSS has been
regarded as a second redaction of William's commentary. For discussion see A. J. Minnis,
'Aspects of the Medieval French and English Traditions of the *De Consolatione Philosophiae*',
in M. T. Gibson (ed.), *Boethius: His Life, Thought and Influence* (Oxford, 1981), pp. 313–14 and
352 nn. The fullest discussion of the textual tradition to date is by S. Lenormand, 'Guillaume de
Conches et le commentaire sur le *De Consolatione philosophiae* de Boèce', *École nationale des
Chartes: positions des thèses . . . 1979* (Paris, 1979), pp. 69–74. [Subsequent work on this commentary by myself and Lodi Nauta have convinced us that the 'second redaction' is in fact a
thirteenth-century expansion and updating of William of Conches' commentary. A.J.M.]

DROVE HIM TO that is, brought his ship in to, THE ISLAND that is, land, as has been explained [below]. And [the East wind] brought to that land there THE SAILS OF THE NERITIAN [1] that is, the reason and understanding of Hercules,[51] that is, of the wise man (*sapiens*), AND BROUGHT IN HIS SHIPS WHICH HAD WANDERED OVER THE SEA [2–3] that is, his thoughts which had wandered through the world, which is called the sea or the ocean because of the saltiness and bitterness which are in it, as they are in the sea; ON WHICH [4] that is, island or land, Circe, that is, abundance of worldly possessions, THE GODDESS because foolish men regard her [i.e. that abundance] as a goddess and as the supreme good, BORN OF THE STOCK OF THE SUN [5] because all abundance of worldly possessions is begotten by the heat of the sun; MIXED POTIONS [6–7] that is, pleasures of various sorts, FOR HER NEWLY ARRIVED GUESTS because abundance of worldly possessions corrupts those who come to it as newcomers by use and experience of it; WHOM that is, the guests, WHEN HER HAND, SKILLED IN THE USE OF HERBS, TURNED INTO VARIOUS SHAPES [8–9]. The rest of the text will be made clear below.

THE SAILS OF THE NERITIAN. This metre is glyconic, consisting of a spondee and a choriamb and a pyrrhic. But sometimes one foot is substituted for another.

Lest anyone should think that this transformation was not something to be feared (because he had said that the men were changed into beasts in respect of their different characters, not of their physical appearance),[52] he proves in these verses that it is something to be greatly feared, because it is more far-reaching than mere physical change. First of all, one must note that there are three sorts of metamorphosis, that is, transformation. One is natural, and this is the transformation of elements. Another is

---

[51] That this is a genuine misunderstanding rather than a mere scribal error is made clear by an interlinear gloss which declares that Hercules was called *dux Neritius* after the river or island where he was born. In fact, Boethius was referring to Ulysses, who appears later in this commentary. Hercules and Ulysses had in common at least the fact of being interpreted as exemplars of virtue in ancient and medieval thought. See G. K. Galinsky, *The Herakles Theme: The Adaptations of the Hero in Literature from Homer to the Twentieth Century* (Oxford, 1972), pp. 101–25, 189–98, 200–3; cf. Fulgentius, *Mit.* ii. 2–4 (ed. Helm, pp. 41–3; tr. Whitbread, pp. 67–70), and see also below, n. 55, on Ulysses. In his exposition of *De Cons. phil.* iv, pr. vii, William expounds the labours of Hercules through the system of secular allegory described in our introduction to this section. Similarly, Coluccio Salutati interpreted Hercules as the epitome of man 'rich with all the endowments of the virtues and able to overcome all the assaults of vice': see R. G. Witt, *Hercules at the Crossroads: The Life, Works, and Thought of Coluccio Salutati* (Duke Monographs in Medieval and Renaissance Studies VI, Durham, NC, 1983), p. 216.

[52] Lat. 'in bestias morum qualitate non corporis specie'. On the face of it, this statement sits rather awkwardly with the subsequent statement that Circe could change men physically but not their minds. If, however, the 'he' in 'because he had said that the men ...' is taken as designating the impersonal 'one', while the 'he' in 'he proves in these verses ...' is taken as referring to Boethius, the matter may be resolved. But still one may feel that the literal and integumental senses of the text have not been described and distinguished with sufficient clarity.

magical transformation, when something seems to be what it is not. Another is moral transformation, as when a man takes to himself the character of an animal. But moral transformation is more far-reaching than natural transformation because, as the soul is more exalted than the body, so any change in its condition is more far-reaching than mere physical change.[53] This is proved here by Circe, who although she could change men physically, could not change their minds (*animae*). We will then look at the account (*narratio*) of this episode.

We read that Ulysses, on his return from Troy, was for a long time tossed about on the high seas, but eventually came to an island ruled by Circe, daughter of the sun. She fell in love with him, but when she could not keep him with her by force, entreaty, or bribe, realizing that he could not return home alone, she turned her attention to Ulysses' companions and, [offering them] cups treated with magic potions, turned them into various [animal] shapes. But they retained their human mind (*anima*), and knew that they had been men. On Mercury's advice the aforesaid Ulysses refused Circe's offer [of a drink], and so remained unchanged.

There are two explanations of this [story]. One is brief, and is as follows. Circe, who by her spells is said to have transformed the companions of Ulysses, but was unable to transform him because Mercury had freed him from her spells, has the following meaning.[54] In reality, Circe was a prostitute who by her charms seduced men from the virtues to the vices by making them heavy and lustful, and so sunk below the level of brute beasts by reason of the change which their minds had undergone. As for the fact that Ulysses was not transformed into an animal, and was set free by Mercury, this simply means that by reason of his wisdom he could not be attracted away from the virtues to the vices.

There is another and more subtle explanation. Ulysses is *olon senos*, that is, the sensation of all things, or wise in all things.[55] HIS SHIP that is, his

---

[53] This distinction between the various kinds of transformation is regularly found in commentaries on Ovid's *Metamorphoses*; see esp. Arnulf of Orléans' *accessus* to that work, printed by F. Ghisalberti, 'Arnolfo d'Orléans, un cultore di Ovidio nel sec. XII', *Memorie dell'Istituto Lombardo*, xxiv (1932), 178, 180–1; cf. the discussion and material in id., 'Medieval Biographies of Ovid', 18, 20, 21, 22, 42, 52, 53. See further J. B. Allen and T. A. Moritz, *A Distinction of Stories: The Medieval Unity of Chaucer's Fair Chain of Narratives for Canterbury* (Columbus, Ohio, 1981), pp. 18–20, and of course John of Garland, *Integumenta Ovidii*, i. 11–18, ed. F. Ghisalberti (Messina and Milan, 1933), pp. 35–6.

[54] Literally 'means none other than the following'.

[55] A garbled version of Fulgentius? 'For Ulysses in Greek is *olonxenos*, that is, stranger to all; and because wisdom is a stranger to all things of this world, so Ulysses is called crafty (*astutior*)', *Mit.* ii. 8 (ed. Helm, p. 48; tr. Whitbread, p. 73). On this kind of grammatical allegory see O'Donnell, 'Bernard Silvester's Commentary on the *Aeneid*', p. 236. For ancient views of Ulysses as a figure of intelligence, of virtue and strength, and of Platonic wisdom, see Félix Buffière, *Les Mythes d'Homère et la pensée grecque* (Paris, 1956), pp. 364–91; this study demonstrates how early Homer was subjected to allegorical interpretation. Cf. W. B. Stanford, *The Ulysses Theme: A Study in the Adaptability of a Traditional Hero*, 2nd edn. (Oxford, 1963), pp. 118–27. Among the Church Fathers Ulysses figured as an example of prudence,

will, he PUT IN that is, tied it up to an ISLAND that is, a land set in the middle of the sea, for the seas washed the shores of that land on every side. For an island is the name for land placed in the salt sea. In this island Circe ruled, that is, wealth of earthly possessions, of which Circe is the figure. For Circe is *cyron cyse*, that is, a judgement of the hands.[56] For *cyros* is 'hand' while *cyse* is 'judgement'. Hence Circe is as it were 'the judgement of the hands', which is a figure for abundance or wealth of earthly possessions, which comes from judgement, that is, the work of one's hands. Circe, that is, abundance, is rightly called the daughter of the sun because all prosperity in worldly things originates with the sun. She offers potions concocted from herbs, that is, desires which derive from the good things of this world, and by these the companions of Ulysses are turned into animals. Thanks to the advice of Hercules [*sic* for Mercury] she does not succeed in transforming Ulysses. By Ulysses you must understand the wise man (*sapiens*) whom Circe, that is, abundance of earthly possessions, does not succeed in transforming, thanks to the advice of Hercules, that is, his own wisdom. But she did transform the companions of Ulysses. And who are these companions of Ulysses? Assuredly, the companions of Ulysses are those who can distinguish between good and bad but, being led astray by lack of self-restraint, they desert the good and cling to the bad. They are companions of Ulysses in that they discern the good, but in that they cling to evil and desert the good they are changed into animals in the [evil] quality of their behaviour, as has been said.[57] These Circe, that is, abundance of worldly possessions, transforms into different kinds of animals, bestowing on one the appearance of a boar, on another that of a lion, and so on. But still she does not change their minds, because although they may have been corrupted by worldly things, yet they know that they have sinned.

Note that Mercury is said to be the god of eloquence; hence his name is interpreted as lord of merchants, that is, the god of merchants. Eloquence is the dominant element in merchants. And he is called Arcadian, who is worshipped on the Cyllenian mountain, which is in Arcadia. He is called 'winged' because his head and feet are winged. He is indeed depicted as winged because of his quickness in speaking, for he is said to be the god of

patience, and fortitude (ibid., p. 156). For the extent to which Dante's famous treatment of Ulysses was influenced by the standard interpretations see ibid., pp. 178–82; also D. Thompson, 'Dante's Ulysses and the Allegorical Journey', *Dante Studies*, lxxxv (1967), 35–58, and G. Mazzotta, *Dante, Poet of the Desert* (Princeton, NJ, 1979), pp. 74 ff.

[56] Cf. Fulgentius, *Mit.* ii. 9 (ed. Helm, p. 49; tr. Whitbread, p. 74): 'Circe . . . is named for *cironcrine*, judgment of the hand or working skill.'

[57] Here the text in the Royal and Dijon MSS reads: 'mutantur in beluas morum qualitate nichil est dcu' (—'dictum'?). Paris, Bibl. Nat. MS Lat. 16094, fo. 138ᵛ reads: 'in bestias morum qualitates ut dictum est'. We translate in accordance with the tentative emendation 'morum qualitate, ut dictum est'. This may be referring back to the discussion of the moral type of transformation, whereby a man takes to himself the character of an animal.

eloquence. He is said to carry a wand with which he parts the serpents, because he has the power of rebuking with which to crush the quarrelsome and those who pour out poisonous words.[58]

Commentary on Priscian's *Institutions* (Second Redaction): Prologue and Beginning of Commentary[59]

Since we know on the authority of Priscian that in all things devised by man there can be nothing that is completely perfect,[60] it is not inappropriate if in our old age we revise something we wrote in our youth, but which is incomplete. For 'knowledge flourishes among the aged, and wisdom among old men' [Job 12: 12]. So, we have undertaken the task of correcting in our old age our glosses on orthography, which we wrote in an incomplete form in our youth. The reader must not look for the composition of a new work here, but rather the correction of an old one in terms of the addition of things omitted and the cutting-out of superfluous material.

But orthography belongs to the field of grammar, which no one doubts is one of the arts, and every art is either extrinsic (*extrinsecus*) or intrinsic (*intrinsecus*). Priscian's exposition of the intrinsic aspect of the art of grammar is such that he does not discuss the extrinsic one. So let us say something about the extrinsic aspect of the art before we begin our exposition. In considering the extrinsic features of the art it is relevant to consider what the art is, its name, the reason for its name, the category within which it falls, what is its office or function, its end, subject-matter, parts or divisions, what instrument it uses [to achieve its ends], who is its practitioner, who is its teacher, and what is the intention of the author.

The art of grammar, then, is a collection of precepts by which we are instructed in writing correctly and in pronouncing correctly that which is written. It is called an art because its precepts constrain[61] the hands and tongues of men in a certain way so that they cannot either write or pronounce in any other way.[62] It differs from knowledge (*scientia*). For knowledge is that mental attribute which makes the person in whom it resides a grammarian. There are as many forms of that knowledge as there are grammarians and each of these forms is called grammar. But among us, and among Latin writers, there is only one art.

---

[58] Lat. 'habet increpationem qua rixantes et venena verborum effundentes fecerunt'. The last word seems to have been corrupted. 'fecerunt' may be a corruption of 'fecerit' or more indirectly of 'fregerit'. If we read 'fecerit', the passage could be translated: 'he has the power of rebuking, with which to make men quarrelsome and make them pour out poisonous words'. But this is awkward since the sense of 'chiding' in *increpatio* requires a verb of punishing. We therefore read 'fregerit' and translate accordingly.

[59] Tr. from Jeauneau, 'Deux rédactions des gloses de Guillaume de Conches sur Priscien', 243-7, with the permission of the editor and Abdij Keizersberg, Leuven.

[60] Priscian, *Institutiones*, 'Prisciani ad Iulianum ep.' 3 (*GL* ii. 2)..

[61] A play on words. Latin *arto*, *artare* means 'to constrain'.

[62] Cf. Isidore, *Ety.* 1. i. 12.

The name (*nomen*) of this art is the art 'of grammar', which is translated 'of letters', for *gramma* is a letter. The Latins call this art the art 'of letters' or 'pertaining to letters' (*ars litteratoria sive litteralis*), but the Greeks call it the art 'of grammar'. But because the Greeks have precedence over the Latins it is more frequently called the art of grammar than the art of letters. But since the object of its investigation is not only letters but also syllables and words, the question is asked, why is it called the art of grammar, that is, of letters, rather than the art of syllables or words or sentences? Some respond to this question as follows: 'Only letters are dealt with in that art.' For they say that letters are considered in four ways. For sometimes they are considered in their simple form, that is, without the addition of any other letters, and when this is the case they are called letters. Sometimes they are considered conjointly, but without sharing in the meaning of a syntactic structure (*consignificatio*),[63] and then they are called syllables. Sometimes they are considered as signifying a simple matter (*res*), that is, an expression of quality or quantity, and then they are called words (*dictiones*). And sometimes as signifying something which has full meaning and a fully expressed thought. Then they are called sentences. Thus, there are sentences, words, letters, and syllables, although they are all considered sometimes in one light and sometimes in another. Since, therefore, all those things with which one is concerned in this art are letters, but not all of them are syllables or words, quite rightly the art is called 'grammar', that is, the art 'of letters' and not the art 'of syllables' or 'of phrases'.

Others say that it is called [the art of] grammar not from the letters but from the words (*voces*) expressed by the letters, because it excludes words not expressed by letters and deals only with words so expressed. The difference between a word expressed in letters and a word not so expressed will be explained subsequently.

Others say that it was the habit of writers of antiquity to give their works titles from the subjects treated at the beginning of the book. For instance, the book of Genesis is so called not because the whole book deals with genesis, that is, the creation, but because it deals with it at the beginning. Likewise, they call one book Leviticus, so to speak 'the book of sacrifices', from the levites who in olden times used to perform these sacrifices, not because the book deals with sacrifices throughout, but because it does so in its first section. And in another instance Moses calls

---

[63] On William's theory of signification see L. M. de Rijk, *Logica modernorum* (Assen, 1962–7), ii/1, 221–8. On pp. 226–7 de Rijk cites a passage from later in William's Priscian commentary which gives the three meanings of *consignificatio*; the third, in which a *dictum* is said to consignify when it signifies something not by itself but with another *dictum*, is relevant here. Cf. J. Pinborg, *Logik und Semantik im Mittelalter. Ein Überblick* (Stuttgart and Bad Cannstatt, 1972), pp. 58–61; id., 'Semantic Representation in Medieval Logic', repr. in S. Ebbesen (ed.), *Medieval Semantics. Selected Studies on Medieval Logic and Grammar* (London, 1984), viii. 256–7.

a book the book of Deuteronomy, so to speak 'concerning the second law' (for *deuter* is 'second'; *nomen* is 'law'), because that book deals in its first section with the second law. So that art is called 'grammar', that is, 'of letters', because in its initial part it deals with letters.

The category (*genus*) within which this art falls is that of eloquence. Three things are necessary for someone to be perfectly eloquent. [The first is] to know how to write correctly for the enlightenment of those who are not present and to make men's recollection [of the subject] more enduring, and to know how to pronounce correctly that which has been written, in order to enlighten those present. This grammar teaches. The second skill is to know how to define, divide up, and argue. This logic teaches. The third is to know how to persuade and dissuade. This rhetoric teaches. There are, then, three divisions of eloquence: grammar, dialectic, rhetoric. But some say that grammar is not a division of eloquence, because a knowledge of eloquence is not dependent upon grammar. For [they say] it is not true that grammar is eloquence, because, if grammar were a kind of eloquence someone could be called eloquent because of his knowledge of that science. But if someone knew grammar without rhetoric and dialectic he would never seem eloquent. But I, on the contrary, assert that, if someone were a grammarian without being a logician or an orator, he would be eloquent and yet would not seem eloquent. For, following common usage, we do not grant this attribute [i.e. of eloquence] except to the man who has facility in finding words and shines in the way he puts them together. Likewise, although arithmetic is a division of wisdom, if someone knew the nature of numbers without knowing anything else he would not be considered wise. So grammar is eloquence, though it is not perfectly eloquence, and the grammarian is eloquent, though not perfectly so.

Alternatively, to remove all dispute, the category to which grammar belongs may be called logic applied through the medium of words (*logica sermocinalis*). One form of logic is that which works through reason, the other that which works through words. So this name 'logic' is applied equally to the two, a name which, in line with the use of *logos* among the Greeks, applies equally to speech (*sermo*) and to reasoning. Logic which works through words contains within its scope the *trivium*. But logic which works through reason embraces dialectic, rhetoric, and sophistic (*sophistica*), not grammar.

The function (*officium*) of this art is to write correctly, and to pronounce correctly what has been written. Its end (*finis*) is to know these things. Because we frequently speak of 'writing correctly' and 'pronouncing correctly what has been written', let us see what this means. To write is to represent, by means of visible symbols, something which is expressible (*pronunciabile*). So, to write correctly is to arrange these visible symbols according to the precepts of this art. Correct pronunciation is speaking without the fault of barbarism and solecism. Barbarism is every fault which occurs in the parts of a word (*dictio*). This happens sometimes in the substance of the word, when without any reason we remove a letter or syllable which has been in that word from the time when it was first thought of, or when we add things which ought not to be there. Sometimes the barbarism occurs in its incidental properties (*accidentes*), namely in its order, quantity, aspiration, accentuation, or writing.[64] It happens in its order when we put at the end a letter which ought to be put first, or vice versa. It happens in the quantity when that which is normally long is cut short or that which is short is lengthened. It happens in the aspiration when the rough is smoothed out and the smooth is pronounced roughly. It happens in terms of accent when he accent which ought to be acute[65] is turned into a grave or circumflex and vice versa. It happens in writing, for instance if the noun *quae* is written without the diphthong or the conjunction *que* with a diphthong. Every such fault is called a barbarism, that is, the usage of barbarians. For barbarians, since they lack the rules of the art of grammar, err in many respects. Solecism is every fault which occurs in the putting together of words. It gets its name 'solecism' from the city Soloe, of which the speech was corrupt because it lay on the border with barbarian lands. But the faults which are called barbarisms are called *metaplasmi* if they occur with reason [i.e. deliberately]. If solecisms occur with reason they are called *sc[h]emata* by the Greeks and 'figures' by the Latins. Thus, Isidore says: 'A figure is a fault which occurs with reason.'[66]

The subject-matter (*materia*) of this art is threefold: the letter, the syllable, and the word. Some add the sentence as a fourth, for they assert that Priscian deals with it in his book of constructions. But this seems to us not to be so for the following reason. When he shows what a letter is and what its properties are, and what letters may be put in front of which to constitute a syllable, the discussion is about the letter, not about the syllable. Again, when he shows what a syllable is, and what its properties are, and what syllables can be put in front of which to construct a word (*dictio*), the discussion is about the syllable, not the word. Likewise, when he shows what a word is, what its properties are, and which words may be put in front of which to construct a sentence, the discussion must be said to be about the word, not about the sentence. Again, if he were dealing with the sentence, he would define it, as he defines his other subjects, and would divide it into its various kinds, and would explain what difficulties there were concerning it. But even if he defines it to clarify the nature of words, in the course of defining which he had mentioned the sentence, nevertheless he never divides it up, nor does he explain what difficulties

---

[64] Lat. 'in ordine, tempore, spiritu, accentu, scriptura'.

[65] Lat. 'In tenore fit quando quod cui debet gravatur vel circumflectitur et e converso'. On David Thomson's suggestion we read 'acui' for 'cui'.

[66] Isidore, *Ety.* I. xxxv. 7. Reading 'ratione' for 'oratione' (see Lindsay's apparatus).

there are concerning it. Again, it is the task of a grammarian to lead his pupil towards the construction of a sentence. But it is the task of a logician to define and divide a sentence. So, the subject matter of this art is threefold: the letter, the syllable, and the word.

Grammar has two parts (*partes*): orthography, that is, correct writing (for *ort*[*h*]*os* is 'correct'; *graphia* is 'writing'), and correct pronunciation. This art has no separate subdivisions within itself. For we do not agree with those who say that Latin grammar and Greek grammar are separate divisions of this art. For one would have to make a similar concession in the case of the other arts, and [in that case] the arts would not be the same with us as with the Greeks.

The practitioner (*artifex*) of this art is the grammarian. A grammarian is he who knows how to write correctly and to pronounce correctly what has been written.

The author (*auctor*) is Priscian of Caesarea.

The author's intention (*intentio auctoris*) is to give the emperor Julian definite rules about the third declension of nouns and the past tenses of verbs, and to correct all the faults of the Latin grammarians, and to add what they have omitted.

SINCE [I FIND THAT THE TEACHING OF] ALL ELOQUENCE.[67] Since many had written about the art of grammar before Priscian, he prefaces his work with a prologue in which he sets out the various reasons for his having written after others had written, lest this work, coming after the work of others, should appear superfluous. In this prologue he makes the reader receptive to teaching, well disposed, and attentive. He makes him receptive to teaching by setting out the starting-point of his discussion; he makes him well disposed by setting out how he is going to conduct that discussion, and attentive by setting out his motives for engaging in it.

The first reason he alleges here is necessity. For that art had been imperfectly written about by all who had written about it, and had not been put right by any Latin author. So it was necessary that it should be put right by him.

Now let us expound the letter [of the text] . . .

SCHOOL OF WILLIAM OF CONCHES

Commentary on Juvenal[68]

PROLOGUE, BY AN ANONYMOUS GRAMMARIAN

We must first of all consider the author's starting-point (*unde*), and how (*qualiter*), and with what useful end in view (*qua utilitate*), and for what

[67] Priscian, *Inst.* 'Ad Iul. ep.' 1 (*GL* ii. 1).
[68] Tr. from *Guillaume de Conches: Glosae in Iuvenalem*, ed. Wilson, pp. 89–91, 180–5, with the

reason (causa), he treats of the subject, and to what, if any, division of philosophy the work pertains, and what the title is. He treats of the vices of the Romans, and this clearly forms his subject-matter, because an author's starting-point is his subject-matter. His mode of proceeding is to reprehend the actual vices, his purpose being to draw his reader from the clutches of the vices. The reason for his having written this work is as follows. This Juvenal, a native of the town of Aquinas,[69] came to Rome in Nero's time. Observing that the mimic actor Paris was on such close terms with the emperor that Nero never did anything except with his approval, he burst out into the following verses, moved by a sense of outrage: 'That which men of rank do not give, an actor will give. Do you still bother about the Camerini and the Bareae,[70] do you still bother with the waiting-rooms of influential nobles?'[71] Eventually, in order that he might reprehend them more adequately, he turned to writing satire, and not only against Nero and Paris, but his reprehension spilt over to include others who were leading wicked lives. When Nero learned of Juvenal's attack on himself, he did not dare to condemn him to exile openly, but sent him to Egypt as commander of an army, and moreover ordered the army to return but without Juvenal. So he died in exile in Egypt.

Some think that in his case and in that of other authors (auctores) we must enquire to what part of philosophy they pertain. Master Bernard,[72]

permission of the editor and Librairie philosophique J. Vrin, Paris. Is this commentary the work of William of Conches? Professor Wilson believes that William's glosses on Juvenal's satires i–vii have been preserved in Paris, Bibliothèque nationale, MS Lat. 2904 (= P), produced in Northern France in the second half of the 12th c., which also preserves this unique accessus, placed, according to Wilson's hypothesis, by some pupil of William's at the beginning of his master's work. In another late-12th-c. MS, Baltimore, Walters Art Gallery, MS 20 (= W), a scribe added to the text of Juvenal's first satire, and a second scribe added to the text of the second satire, glosses apparently related to, though certainly not identical with, the corresponding glosses in P. Wilson's conclusion is that P was the 'published' edition, as approved by William himself, whereas the glosses in W comprise a version of the notes that some student took down from William's lectures. A third MS, Oxford, Bodleian Library, MS Auct. F. 6. 9, is said to preserve Juvenal glosses 'not by William but including excerpts of much of the material from the P tradition'; this 'composite' work 'attests to the diffusion of the P version'. These theories of MS relationships seem to ignore the fact that, in a pre-copyright age, glosses on the auctores were common property, and that it was part and parcel of the educational method for a pupil to incorporate the work of his master into his own commentary, where it would be conflated with doctrine from other sources and some of the pupil's own ideas. We fully endorse the view of H. J. Westra, Mittellateinisches Jahrbuch, xviii (1983), 368–9, that Wilson's method is far too 'positivistic'. 'Indeed', Westra adds, 'the evidence is so slight and ambiguous that P . . . may well be the work of one of William's students, as the accessus would suggest.' All that can be held with confidence is that P, W, and B reflect a common tradition of teaching on Juvenal, a tradition to which William certainly contributed, but—given the nature of the evidence—the extent and nature of that contribution cannot be ascertained.

[69] Sic for Aquinum.
[70] These being two noble families.
[71] Juvenal, Sat. vii. 90–1.
[72] Presumably Bernard of Chartres, magister scholae at Chartres in the second decade of the 12th c., and chancellor there by 1124.

however, used to say that this question should not be asked in the case of writers (*actores*), since their works are not parts of philosophy, neither do they discuss philosophy. Master William of Conches, on the other hand, asserts that, even though they are not a part of philosophy, nor treat of philosophy itself, all authors (*auctores*)[73] pertain to philosophy because of the subject-matter of which they treat, and all pertain to that part of philosophy of which their subject-matter treats. Each of these judgements, then, is true. Authors (*auctores*) do pertain to philosophy, that is, on account of the fact that they treat of ethics, which is a part of philosophy, in that they provide moral instruction; and writers (*actores*) do not pertain to philosophy, that is, they are not a part of philosophy.[74]

Having pursued these questions to a conclusion, let us consider the title. The title is as follows: *Here begins the Book of Satires of Decius Junius Sillanus Iuvenalis*. He is called Decius [*sic* for Decimus] either because he was born in the tenth month or because he was the tenth in his family; Junior[75] because he was younger than his brother; Sillanus because he was of the family of Silla,[76] or as being a native of the woods, because he was the son of someone who lived close to woods. Iuvenalis is his own personal name.

Let us consider the nature of satire and the origin of its name. Satire is reprehension (*reprehensio*) composed in metre, and there is a difference between satire and invective (*invectio*), for satire is reprehension written in metre, while invective is reprehension written in prose. Palinode is a recantation of reprehension, as if you were first of all to reprehend someone, and then praise him, but it pertains to reprehension. According to some,[77] satire is so called from the satyrs, who were woodland gods, because the two are perfectly matched in all their characteristics. For satyrs are naked and have an unbridled tongue, advance with a leaping motion, imitate human movements, and have goats' feet.

However, the truth of the matter is that there are no such gods, but there are certain animals dwelling in woods which the ancients in their folly revered as gods because they advance with a leaping motion and are seen in a place, but immediately disappear. Satire, then, has the characteristic of the satyrs. They are naked and it is naked. For there are

---

[73] *Pace* Wilson, here *P* clearly reads 'auctores', not 'actores'.

[74] For the general sense of this difficult passage see above, p. 122. According to Miller, 'Mediaeval Theory of Satire', p. 20, a distinction is being made here between mere writers (*actores*) and authorities (*auctores*). *Actores* have nothing to do with philosophy, but *auctores* come under the heading of philosophy because they deal in moral instruction and, although they do not actually *discuss* philosophy, their subject-matter is relevant to ethics, which is a part of philosophy.

[75] *Sic* for Junius, correctly given in the title.

[76] Not only is Silanus misinterpreted in succession as Sullanus and Silvanus, being misspelt as Sillanus, but it is not even Juvenal's name, being imported from the noble house of the Iunii Silani.

[77] Wilson cites as one such Diomedes, *De arte grammatica*, iii (*GL* i. 485–6).

some writers who cover up (*velant*) their reprehension, as when Lucan, speaking of Nero's obesity, says: 'the axle will feel the weight' and then '[Nero will gaze on] Rome with oblique ray'.[78] True satire consists of naked and open reprehension.[79] Satyrs have an unbridled tongue; satire passes over no person in silence, and spares no one. Satyrs advance with a leaping motion, while satire [touches on one person] one moment and immediately jumps from there to deal with another. Both imitate the movements (*gestus*) of human beings. For satire in its base reprehension exactly matches the base lives of men. The goat is a smelly animal, and so satire, by reason of the stench of vices, is like the goat-footed satyrs.

Some think that satire gets its name from a dish which was kept in the temples of the gods.[80] It was customary in antiquity that when a sacrifice was being offered to the gods no left-overs of the sacrifices should remain in the temple. Moreover, they considered it unlawful to touch with their hands any remains of the sacrifices. So they had prepared a particular kind of vessel which they placed at the entrance of the temple when they were offering a sacrifice. And they arranged things so that the remains of the sacrifices flowed down into that vessel. This vessel was made in the shape of a helmet, but if a vessel of this sort were not propped up it would quickly fall on its side. So, while the sacrifice was going on they supported the vessel, once it had been placed in position, until all the remains of the sacrifice had flowed down into it. After that they stopped supporting it, the vessel soon fell on its side, and in this way the left-overs were poured outside the temple. Because of the pouring-out (*effusio*) of the liquid that vessel is called a pitcher (*futis*). Also from that vessel effusive babblers (*futiles*) get their name, for they can keep nothing to themselves, but blurt out whatever they know. Another name for this vessel was *satira*, so called from the abundance (*saturitas*) of the left-overs.[81] Satire (*satira*) derives its name from this, the *u* turning into an *i*, for in a certain sense satire is full of the vices which it reprehends. It shares another similarity with the aforesaid pitcher in that, like it, it pours out everything and passes over nothing in silence.

It is also possible that satire gets its name from *satiri*, that is, country folk. For we read in the *Saturnalia* of Macrobius that when the crops had been taken in, and again when they had been entrusted to the earth, the country folk of each district came together to do honour to Ceres and Bacchus.[82] When the victim had been prepared, the priests then went dragging it round the field-boundaries followed by the people, who

---

[78] Lucan, *Bell. civ.* i. 55, 57.

[79] Cf. Isidore, *Ety.* vii. 7; cf. above, pp. 116–17.

[80] Wilson cites Diomedes (op. cit., p. 486), and Varro, *De lingua Latina*, v. 119; cf. Isidore, *Ety.* v. xvi, viii. vii. 8.

[81] Cf. Isidore, *Ety.* v. xvi.

[82] With this account cf. Livy, *Ab urbe condita*, vii. 2; Virgil, *Georgics*, ii. 385–9; Horace, *Epist.* ii. i. 139–55; Macrobius, *Saturnalia*, iii. v. 7; Servius on Virgil, *Bucolics*, iii. 77.

invoked the blessing of Ceres and Bacchus. They called this sort of rite *arvambalia*,[83] from *arva* ('fields') and *ambio* ('I go around'). After the prayers had ended, they all shared out [the flesh of] the victim. Then they spent a great part of the day in self-indulgence, feasting, and drinking. Finally, the peasants of one estate or village (*villa*) used to rise up against the peasants of another, and they used to heap discordant abuse on each other, of the sort of which the mentality of peasants is capable. The aforesaid satires consist of abuse of this kind, that is, the cleverer among the peasants turned them into an art form and began to reprehend in metre. Reprehension of this kind, in metrical form, still retains the old name, and it is for this reason that the term is found written as *satira* [i.e. with *i* rather than *y*], according to various authors.

EXPOSITION OF THE FOURTH SATIRE OF JUVENAL

BEHOLD CRISPINUS AGAIN. In this satire he reprehends the Romans for several vices, but particularly Crispinus and Nero, and he criticizes them particularly for gluttony and riotous living. At the beginning he attacks Crispinus for committing incest, saying BEHOLD CRISPINUS AGAIN. This passage (*litera*) is found in several books;[84] AGAIN because he had reprehended him in earlier satires;[85] BEHOLD, comes to mind. Because of his various moral lapses he is found in several books [of the satires], and BEHOLD CRISPINUS should in that case be understood as meaning 'Here *is* Crispinus', for according to Priscian a demonstrative adverb without a verb could be understood as meaning 'is'.[86] TO BE CALLED, that is, deserving to be called, because he is unnatural, TO PLAY HIS PART [2] that is, to play his role in the composition of the satires of the book; A MONSTER, truly he must be called this, because he is not just vicious but vice incarnate, REDEEMED BY NO VIRTUE. Just one virtue could redeem a man from vice, but Crispinus, since he is in the grip of all the vices, is not redeemed from them by any virtue. SCARCELY [3] that is, that which is good. ALONE does not exclude avarice but rather its opposite, namely virtue.[87] WANTON, UNATTACHED

[83] Cf. Macrobius, *Saturnalia*, III. v. 7.
[84] The similar phrase 'Behold Crispinus offering me long odds' is found in Horace, *Satires*, I. iv. 13–14, and this is probably what the commentator means when he refers to the *litera* as occurring in 'other books'. (Horace was referring to a different Crispinus, but we need not expect the commentator to have known that). In Latin *ecce* 'behold' is not a verb but an adverb.
[85] Cf. Juvenal, *Sat.* i. 26.
[86] Priscian, *Institutiones*, xv. i (*GL* iii. 60).
[87] Lat. 'solaque', in the phrase 'aegrae solaque libidine fortes deliciae', which describes Crispinus as 'a feeble voluptuary powerful in his lust alone'. So the commentator is correct in his interpretation that, although the phrase initially sounds like a compliment to Crispinus' virtues ('fortes'), the fact that he is strong only in lust converts this from a compliment into a searing criticism. It should be added, though, that the commentator has misread the 'aegrae'—spelt 'egre' in the 12th-c. form—as an adverb, and also seems to take 'libido' as meaning 'greed, avarice'.

GIRLS [4] [88] He commits every crime, except that of having sex with unattached girls, as if they [i.e. the Romans?] found them too wicked; WANTON, UNATTACHED GIRLS that is, a wanton and unattached girl. WHAT MATTERS IT THEN? [5] since he is so prone to vice; WHAT avails him his wealth? THE EXTENT OF HIS PORTICOES, for he had extended his portico from his house all the way to the Capitoline hill. BEASTS horses. OF THE GROVES [6] the parklands along the river banks, which are compared to groves because of their great extent. [CLOSE] TO THE FORUM [7] where the land costs more. NO ONE [8] An evil man truly makes no headway because he is unhappy, and in truth he is unhappy because he is evil, and every evil man is unhappy, a fact we have stated in this phrase, consisting of two equally interchangeable parts, 'no evil man is happy'.[89] So, one who corrupts others is unhappy (arguing from the general to the particular). There are the following types[90] of corruptor: the adulterer, the fornicator, the man guilty of incest. Properly speaking, that man is guilty of incest who will beget offspring with a woman dedicated to religion or one of his own kin. He is called 'unchaste' from cestus, the girdle of Venus which a wife puts on in lawful wedlock. WEARING THE VITTA [9] crowned. DESTINED TO BE BURIED [10]. The law was that if any dedicated virgin had been caught in the act of incest she should be buried alive, for it was not lawful for someone, once a priest,[91] to be killed by the sword or by fire.[92]

BUT NOT [11][93] as if to say, 'I have accused him of this sort of crime, but these [i.e. the matters described subsequently in this satire] are more trivial crimes'. [IF] ANOTHER HAD DONE THE SAME [HE WOULD HAVE COME] UNDER A JUDGE, that is, he would have been condemned. For he who is found out by a court comes under a judge. FOR THAT WHICH [13] as if he were to say 'is he so wicked?' FOR THAT WHICH means 'at any rate';[94] TITUS

[88] Here the commentator misreads the Lat. 'deliciae, viduas . . .' as 'delicias viduas'. The 'deliciae' (plural used with singular meaning), meaning 'voluptuous man, libertine', is Crispinus.

[89] The phrase 'omnis malus infelix' consists of two subjects in apposition with each other and joined by the verb 'to be' to be understood by the reader; it can mean either 'every evil man is unhappy' or 'every unhappy man is evil'. This is what the commentator means by the meaning being 'interchangeable'. But Juvenal wrote 'nemo malus felix'.

[90] P here reads 'species' but Wilson has 'semper'.

[91] Sic; in this case a priestess.

[92] Vestal virgins guilty of adultery were, if the strict letter of the law was enforced, buried alive. Some time before 94 AD, probably in 90, Cornelia, the senior Vestal, was convicted, and Domitian had her immured alive, and all her lovers except one killed. For the date of this immolation see A. N. Sherwin-White's commentary on Pliny, Epist. IV. xi. 7 (Oxford, 1966), p. 283. It seems likely that Juvenal is referring to this recent and notorious case.

[93] The commentator appears to have had before him the Latin text 'sed nec de factis levioribus', a text difficult to translate but which might mean, 'But I have made no mention of his less serious offences'. However, the commentator interprets this as if he were commenting on the text we have in modern editions: 'sed nunc de factis levioribus', 'but now I will accuse him of less serious offences'. An alternative explanation is that the latter passage was indeed the text he saw before him, but the 'nunc' has been corrupted into 'nec' in this lemma.

[94] Juvenal: 'that which was disgraceful in the good Titus and Seius was quite all right for

AND SEIUS those good men, WHAT CAN YOU DO? that is, what can you say?, no doubt referring to what follows, because Crispinus is extravagant and gluttonous. MONSTROUS, by reason of the gluttony condemned here. THAN [ANY] CRIME [15] that is, full of guilt.[95] MULLET Here he censures Crispinus for extravagance; MULLET is the name of a fish. CRISPINUS.[96] The wisdom OF THE SMOOTH OPERATOR [18] that is, Crispinus, who bought the fish so that by giving such a lavish present he might win a legacy from some rich, childless man. 'If' is wanting.[97] HAS SNATCHED AWAY [19] has drawn into his clutches in turn,[98] THE WAX TABLET the will, because, before the use of parchment had been discovered, one wrote on wax tablets. PARAMOUNT that is, principal [legatee].[99] THERE IS A MOTIVE [20] This is as if he were to say, 'the motive for legacy-hunting is a laudable one', but this is ULTERIOR that is, an unworthy motive. Si ('if') is put for quia ('because'); GREAT rich. IN THE CAVERNOUS RECESS . . .[100] PIECES OF MICA [21] window-panes. NOTHING OF THE SORT [22] as if he were to say, 'don't expect anything of the sort, even though you hear similar stories about other people'. MANY many things besides the fish. APICIUS [23] Apicius was someone who went through his whole fortune by living extravagantly, and then turned his attention to the kitchen, and in that sphere wrote about condiments;[101] WRETCHED because he went through his fortune; FRUGAL, born to be useful and profitable compared with Crispinus. DID YOU DO THIS? The author

Crispinus'. Titus and Seius are simply representative names, used in legal documents and texts. Quite clearly, the commentator does not realize this.

[95] Juvenal: 'what can you do when the person [of Crispinus] is monstrous, and fouler than any crime?'

[96] 'Crispinum', which appears as a lemma in the commentary, is not in the text of Juvenal at this point. Perhaps 'Crispinus' was a gloss on the words 'mullum sex milibus emit' (l. 15; 'he bought a mullet for six thousand sesterces'), telling the reader who the subject of 'emit' was, and has become integrated into the continuous commentary and corrupted to 'Crispinum'.

[97] Juvenal's Latin (ll. 18-19) reads: 'consilium laudo artificis, si munere tanto praecipuam in tabulis ceram senis abstulit orbi', tr. 'I praise the wisdom of the smooth operator if, by making a great gift, he bore off as a prize the first mention in the will of such a rich, childless, and unmarried man'. Apparently in the text in front of our commentator the 'si' was missing; according to W. V. Clausen's edition (Oxford, 1959) the word is 'in' rather than 'si' in many manuscripts.

[98] Reading 'adinvicem' for the editor's 'admite'.

[99] Lat. 'precipuam id est capacem'. Here the adjective 'capax' has the legal sense of 'that has a right to an inheritance'. Roman wills were written on wax tablets, and the principal legatees were to be found in the first tablet (praecipua cera).

[100] A very small piece of the commentary is lost here, at the margin of the manuscript. It appears to have contained only the gloss on the one word 'antro' (l. 21), 'cavernous recess'. But the commentator obviously does not realize that here Juvenal is referring to a lady being carried in a 'cavernous' litter with the fitted luxury of mica windows, though he does comment on 'specularibus', 'pieces of mica'.

[101] M. Gavius Apicius, a well-known Roman gourmet of the first century AD. The only surviving Roman cookery-book goes under his name, though he is certainly not the author. There is a translation by B. Flower and E. Rosenbaum, The Roman Cookery Book: A Critical Translation of the Art of Cooking by Apicius (London, 1958; repr. 1961).

attacks Crispinus savagely, when he makes this charge against him, saying, DID YOU DO THIS? He understands the 'did you do?';[102] SECRETLY because he is a fisherman.[103] WITH PAPYRUS 'I conquer'. NATIVE LAND Egypt, as if he were to say, 'when you were a fisherman you used to sell fish at this [high] price, but . . .'.[104] SCALES [25] that is, a fish.[105] [THE FISHERMAN] COULD HAVE PERHAPS Truly you did not sell fish for a high price, because you yourself were of low degree. Or, perhaps, it is madness to buy a fish for such a high price, for you could have bought the fisherman for less.[106] A PROVINCE [26] is a region. BUT LARGER estates. SELLS at a lower price. WHAT SORT OF, THEN? [28] Crispinus bought a fish for such a high price, what must we imagine in the case of the emperor? INDUPERATOR [29] is used for *imperator* ('emperor'): that is epenthesis, the opposite of syncope. WHEN A BUFFOON [31] Crispinus clad in purple OF THE EXALTED PALATINE WAS BELCH-ING after a surfeit of food, SO MANY SESTERCES that is, a fish bought for so many sesterces, no doubt A PART not a large part, but A [SMALL] PART TAKEN FROM THE OUTER FRINGE [OF DINNER] that is, the end when the lesser dishes are set before the guests; OF DINNER when less is eaten, not lunch, and EVEN MODESTLY, HE WHO WAS NOW AN IMPORTANT MAN. This is the fisherman, for Nero made him ruler (*princeps*) of Arabia. SHENT FISH [33] these were a cheap sort of fish. FELLOW CITIZENS from whom they took gifts.[107] FROM A BROKEN-UP CONSIGNMENT because he did not get his asking price for them.

[102] The Latin text is in the form of a question addressed to Crispinus by Juvenal: 'hoc tu?' The verb in this phrase, which has to be supplied by the reader, is 'fecisti', 'did you do?'

[103] Lat. '*furtim* quod est piscator'. 'Furtim' does not occur in the text of l. 24, which is being expounded here. Perhaps it is a gloss on 'succinctus', explaining (incorrectly) that it means 'wrapped up' in the sense of 'concealed'.

[104] The commentator has completely misunderstood the sense here by taking 'papyro' as the first person singular of a verb meaning 'I conquer', 'surpass'. Juvenal's text might be correctly translated: 'Did you do this, Crispinus, you who were formerly swathed in your native papyrus?' The sense is: 'Did you, a former Egyptian slave, dare to do this?' Egyptians, even more than other Easterners, were detested by the Juvenal-*persona*.

[105] The plural 'squamae' is used to designate the fish, to which the scales belonged. Juvenal's text may be translated: 'do scales come at this price?', meaning, 'do scales (i.e. the fish) cost so much?'.

[106] Juvenal's text may be translated: 'Perhaps the fishermen could have been bought for less than the fish'. Thus, of the commentator's two explanations the second is closer to the real meaning of the Latin.

[107] Juvenal's text may be translated: 'What sort of dishes are we to assume the emperor himself guzzled, when the purple-clad clown ('scurra') of the mighty Palatine belched out food worth so many sesterces, that being but a small part, and taken from the very edge, of a modest dinner' ('partem exiguam et modicae sumptam de margine cenae': ll. 28–31), i.e. modest by the usual standard of dinners enjoyed by the emperor's ménage. The commentator saw the 'modicae' written as 'modice' in his Juvenal manuscript, and took it as an adverb. He also misinterprets the 'et' as 'even'. Juvenal's 'scurra' or clown of the Palatine is Crispinus, who, as the author goes on to say, once sold 'shent fish' (*silures*) from his native Egypt (l. 33). The text of Juvenal is quite clear on this point. Crispinus sold fish, he is not a fisherman. The 'fellow citizens' (*municipes*) is applied to the *silures* to suggest that Crispinus, like the fish, is of Egyptian origin. Our commentator does not realize that here *municipes* is an adjective, but thinks of it in its normal role as a noun, 'fellow citizens'. Hence his muddled gloss about the 'gifts'.

BEGIN, CALLIOPE [34] thus says the author, intending to reprehend the vices of Nero which were immense and unbelievable. Since it is no easy matter to relate them he calls on his muse (in the words of Horace, 'let no god stand in the way'),[108] saying HERE YOU MAY SIT DOWN that is, you may spend some time dwelling on the vice here set forth. YOU NEED NOT SING as if the subject were an invented one (*res ficta*).[109]

WHEN A HALF-DEAD [WORLD: 37] he begins; HALF-DEAD weakened by the tyrannical rule of Nero, WAS TEARING APART: this is well put, for he who ought to rule [well] was tearing apart [his kingdom]. FLAVIUS that is, not bald;[110] LAST because, as Suetonius tells us, Caesar's line died out with Nero.[111] For he was so wicked that no one of his family was raised to the imperial throne after him. WHICH SHOULD SERVE [38] which ought to serve as belonging to a lord.[112] FELL DOWN INTO [39][113] that is, fell into the net, A HUGE EXPANSE of immense size, OF A TURBOT a fish; ADRIATIC, not because it had been caught in the Adriatic sea but because it was comparable in size with fish caught in the Adriatic. ANCONA [40] describes the place where it was caught, BEFORE THE TEMPLE [OF VENUS WHICH] DORIC [ANCONA SUPPORTS] Dorica is a city in Italy which the Dorians built; AND IT FILLED [41] by reason of its huge size THE FOLDS of the net. [Juvenal] does right to say FOR NEITHER, for neither had any such fish filled a net. FOR NEITHER HAD [ANY] CLUNG to the net; THOSE fish; MAREOTIC [42] Mareotis is a marsh in Scythia where very large fish feed under the ice.[114] MADE FAT by the cold OF THE FAST-FLOWING BLACK SEA CURRENT [43]. As the scientists tell us, cold makes fish fat but heat makes them thin; DESTINES THIS MONSTROUS CREATURE [45] that is, the turbot; THE LINEN TRAWL the net; FOR THE PONTIFF [46] Nero. The emperors were called pontiffs; FOR WHO if indeed he destined it for NERO,

[108] Horace says that a god should not appear in a play (sc. *ex machina*) unless there is a problem therein that it takes a god to solve (*Ars poetica*, 171-2). The commentator seems to imply that Juvenal needs help in tackling the vices of 'Nero' as a subject, but, since Horace has decreed that no god should be called in to intervene directly, the Muses will have to stand in as his helpers. Hence 'it is no easy matter to relate them', i.e. those vices.

[109] Because this is a true account (*res vera*), not a fiction (*res ficta*), it requires a prosaic rather than a lyric treatment. Hence Juvenal tells his Muse that she need not sing.

[110] It is part of the commentator's basic error that, in thinking that Nero rather than Domitian is the subject of this satire, he does not realize that Flavius is the gentile name of the later Flavian emperor, Titus Flavius Domitianus. He assumes that the word here has the sense of 'flavus' ('yellow-haired') and therefore, as he says, 'not bald'. But how can this be squared with Juvenal's text in the next line, which refers to a 'bald Nero'?

[111] Suetonius, *De vita Caesarum*, vii. 1.

[112] Juvenal's word 'serviret' ('which should serve') and its gloss ('que ut domini servire deberet') have been dislocated in *P*; we have restored it to its rightful postion in the textual sequence. The commentator's 'que' seems (correctly) to refer to Rome, but why does he use the genitive 'domini' (according to Wilson)? If 'domino' is read here, there is no problem: 'for she (Rome) had to serve him as lord', the 'him' being Nero mistakenly for Domitian.

[113] The commentator's text of Juvenal read 'decidit'; the correct reading is 'incidit'.

[114] The commentator misunderstands the *sinus Maeoticus* (the sea of Azov) as Mareotica, a lake in the Nile delta, though the reference to Scythia shows a vague awareness that Juvenal is referring to the Black Sea region.

because he did not dare to sell it; TO OFFER for sale; WITH A DELATOR accuser; FORTHWITH that is, 'would offer the turbot'; SEAWEED the debris of the sea, and it is put here to represent the sea itself; SEAWEED the cause in dispute;[115] WITH THE OARSMAN the boatman [49]; NAKED, either girded up with rushes or naked; truly it would be false; CAESAR'S FISHPONDS [51]. These were by the sea, so that when the tide came in fish would easily swim in. IF AT ALL [53] Palfurius and Armillatus were flatterers,[116] as if he were to say: 'not only do they say that this fish belongs to Nero, but also, if at all we believe his [Nero's] servants, everything on land and in the sea belongs to Nero. This is what IF AT ALL means. FISCUS The *fiscus* is, properly speaking, the private purse of the monarch. But sometimes by an extension of its use it can refer to any bag. THEREFORE because he faces accusation if he offers it for sale; WILL BE GIVEN the fish will be given to the emperor, LEST HE PERISH, [he being] the fisherman.[117]

WHEN THE DEADLY [AUTUMN] WAS YIELDING [56] He defines the time of year when the fish was caught: the end of autumn and beginning of winter, when it could be preserved; DEADLY bringing death; HOPING [57] fearing, and he twists the meaning of the word here, for hope is usually used of something good—HOPING, fearing a longer duration.[118] WAS WHISTLING [58] with the blasts of its [i.e. winter's] winds; DISFIGURED [i.e. winter being disfigured] from the effects of the winds; BOOTY the fish; FRESH incorrupt; BUT YET even though the fish could be kept unspoilt YET HE the fisherman [hurried]. The south wind is so hot that it is said to cause fish to decay even in the sea. So the south wind bids us 'Cook this meat [quickly]'; [AS IF THE SOUTH WIND] WERE URGING HIM ON [59], compelling him to carry it [i.e. the fish] off lest it go bad. And AS (UT) that is, as if THE PONDS WERE AT HAND [60] that is, 'as if it were at hand', as if he were to say 'he hastens with such speed into the water, as if he were obeying some command given by the water'. Alternatively, the fisherman hastens ALTHOUGH (UT) that is, although the ponds were under his feet, that is, under the ice, being frozen. As if he were to say: 'although the time of year was right for keeping the fish fresh, even so he hurries'. Or alternatively, he was hastening to the water, even though he was obeying the command of the

---

[115] i.e. the object of the inspector's investigation.

[116] Juvenal's Latin may be translated: 'If we can at all believe Palfurius and Armillatus, every rare and beautiful thing in the wide ocean . . . belongs to the imperial treasury' (ll. 53–5).

[117] i.e. had the fisherman not offered the large fish to 'Nero' but tried to sell it, Nero would have heard of this and executed him. This is no doubt the underlying insinuation made by Juvenal. But the ostensible meaning of the Latin is 'so that the fish may not go for nothing', here taking 'pereat' in the sense of 'go to waste', 'be lost'. J. Ferguson, in his edition, *Juvenal: The Satires* (London, 1979), p. 163, rightly emphasizes the deliberate ambiguity in l. 55.

[118] The commentator misses Juvenal's sardonic humour: patients who have all summer being suffering from tertian fever (a fever every third day reckoned inclusively, i.e. every other day) are hoping for a quartan, a fever which recurs every fourth (i.e. third) day; perhaps all the more because it is never fatal. He thinks that Juvenal is saying the 'fevered patients were fearing a longer duration [of their disease]'.

water. This is giving *ut* the meaning of *quamvis* ('although').[119] WHERE
ALTHOUGH (*UBI QUAMQUAM*) [60] he indicates where the fish was offered to
Nero; RUINED he makes a historical allusion. When Alba had been overthrown by the Romans under Tullus Hostilius, and the Romans wanted
to seize the embers of the hearth, the perpetual flame which Aeneas had
brought [from Troy], a shower of hail fell with such violence that they
could scarcely endure it, and so they left the embers intact. LESSER [VESTA:
61] because there was a larger temple to her [i.e. Vesta] at Rome. A
WONDERING CROWD BLOCKED HIS [i.e. the fisherman's] WAY [62] because they
marvelled [at the fish] rather than from a desire to keep him out; GAVE WAY
[63] that is, subsequently [they] made room.[120] THEY WAIT (*EXPECTANT*) so
that they may be received and may see, or GAZE ON (*SPECTANT*) [64] admire
THE FARE, thus he names the fish. By 'fare' we mean a modest portion of
food taken in moderation among honest folk, and it is called *obsonium* as
being taken to counter dreams (*somnium*). He is castigating the gluttony of
Nero when he calls such a huge fish 'fare'. THE SON OF ATREUS [65] Nero [is
called this] either because he was of peasant stock on his mother's side, or
because he was similar [to Atreus] in his cruelty. PISCENS[121] the fisherman,
and that is his name, or he is called *piscens* from a town [named] Piscens;
[a fish] TOO GREAT FOR PRIVATE [HOUSEHOLDS: 66] for when we live privately
we live modestly. [LET THIS BE A DAY] DEDICATED TO YOUR GENIUS [66–7] He
who looks after himself well cultivates his [time of] generation (*genius*):
note that in antiquity men celebrated their birthday with very great
pomp.[122] TO DISTEND [YOUR STOMACH] BY CRAMMING in order to receive the
stuffed fish, or else TO DISTEND to fill.[123] THE FISH ITSELF WANTED TO BE
CAUGHT [69] he [i.e. the fisherman] flatters Nero, as if he were to say 'it
came into the net of its own accord'. WHAT COULD BE MORE BARE-FACED?

[119] The commentator is very uncertain of the meaning of 'ut' in l. 60, 'utque lacus
suberant', and gives two interpretations, both of them wrong. A correct translation might
read: 'When the lake, where Alba, though a ruin, guards the Trojan flame and worships
Vesta, was near at hand . . .'. 'Ut' here simply introduces a time-clause ('When . . .') but the
commentator takes it first as comparative, meaning 'as if', and then as concessive, meaning
'although'. Thus, both his conjectures are very inaccurate. There is no question of the Alban
lakes being under ice in late autumn.
[120] The meaning being that the crowds made room for the fisherman.
[121] *Sic* for 'Picens', a man from Picenum.
[122] Our commentator does not know the basic and original meaning of *genius* – 'guardian
spirit'. He does, however, sense the connection which the Romans made between the genius
and the person's birthday: the genius was supposed to look after the person from the day of
his birth. And he also defines very well the phrase 'genium colere', 'to look after oneself'.
[123] Juvenal's phrase (l. 67) is: 'propera stomachum laxare sagina', tr. 'hasten to distend your
stomach by cramming'. Our commentator's first interpretation goes wrong over 'sagina',
there being nothing in the Latin text to indicate that the fish is, or will be, stuffed. What the
fisherman may be inviting the emperor to do is to go on a sort of training course by eating a
lot, and thereby loosening up and distending his stomach so that it can subsequently cope
with this fish. 'Sagina' is simply a noun ('cramming'), and it is not stated what with. On the
other hand, our commentator's second interpretation, of 'laxare' as 'to fill', may be right, and
so it is the fish in question which will distend the emperor's stomach.

These are the poet's words, meaning that nothing is more bare-faced than this flattery; THEY [i.e. Nero's wattles (*cristae*)] [124] WERE RAISED UP [70] as if he were to say they became erect, since he [i.e. Nero] gloried in this flattery; and again because THERE IS NOTHING THAT the imperial power [will not believe]. BUT THERE IS LACKING [72] as if he were to say 'the fish has been offered BUT THE SIZE OF THE DISH [WAS INADEQUATE], that is, the vessel in which it should be cooked whole'. 'Dish' (*patina*) gets its name from 'being open' (*pateo*). THE PALLOR [75] Fear arises out of their [i.e. the councillors'] friendship with Nero. The consequence of that fear [i.e. paleness] is used to represent the fear that normally precedes it. MISERABLE [FRIENDSHIP: 74] for Nero's chief men who were killed; [FRIENDSHIP] because he [i.e. Nero] pretended to be a friend so that he could kill the man more freely. [125] WITH HIS LIBURNIAN SLAVE [SHOUTING: 75] that is, a crier, for the Liburnians are a nimble people. A CLOAK (*ABOLLA*) [76] an article of clothing worn by philosophers; SNATCHED grabbed hastily; BAILIFF [77]; STARTLED by Nero's cruelty; [WERE PREFECTS] ANY-THING ELSE [78] understand 'was there any other office to which they might be called?' The words are those of Pegasus. THEN following that, come the PREFECTS, chief men. INTERPRETER [79] expounder; UNARMED [JUSTICE: 80-1] Note that justice is always armed, for unarmed justice is no justice. [126] There is a contradiction in the adjective [127] used to describe CRISPUS [81], the counsellor of Nero, WHOSE CHARACTER MATCHED HIS ELOQUENCE [82] because he fulfilled what he preached, and because he was just the sort of man to be THE COMPANION [84] to an emperor—he understands the word 'emperor' by the phrase HE WHO RULES THE SEAS [83]; TO BRING [85] for 'to bring to bear'; IF THAT DISASTER the disaster of Nero's rule; AND PLAGUE [84] words are crammed one on another here; ON WHOM [87] that is, with Nero; TALK OF SHOWERS [87-8]. Note that if some-one close to Nero made any prediction about the future, as for instance that there would be showers and the like, and this did not happen, he was immediately killed. [128] SO HE [89] [i.e. Crispus], for he did not dare

---

[124] Juvenal says 'Yet his [i.e. the emperor's] wattles rose'. The cock's comb is indicative of pride and vanity.

[125] Our commentator cannot have known that *amicitia* ('friendship') as used by Juvenal here expresses a formal, quasi-political, and constitutional link. The *amici Caesaris* are Caesar's privy council. The Latin word *magnus* (in l. 74: 'miserae magnaeque') here has the sense of 'influential', 'friendship with the great'. The commentator simply assumes that it means 'close', and, seeing from the text that Juvenal regards this 'friendship' with the emperor as something to be feared, tries to imagine why this may be so. His answer is that 'Nero' cultivated friendships with men the better to destroy them.

[126] The commentator's rather general comment 'justice is always armed' seems to show that he did not fully understand the implication of Juvenal's words. Juvenal is describing Pegasus, an excellent interpreter of the laws, except in one respect: 'he thought that, even in those dreadful times, justice should always operate unarmed', i.e. proceed by legal process, without any recourse to physical force.

[127] i.e. the oxymoron 'iucunda senectus' ('pleasant old age', l. 80); the point being made by the commentator is that *iucunda* and *senectus* do not normally go together.

[See p. 146 for n. 128]

to cross Nero; CURRENT [90] the metaphor is drawn from someone sailing a boat who, if he struggles against the current, labours in vain. So Crispus did not strike out against the current, for he did not cross Nero in any matter, and no wonder, for THERE WAS NOT A SINGLE [sic] CITIZEN that is, anyone FREE; he speaks freely who is not afraid to say what he has in his heart; WHAT IS TRUE, the truth, IN THIS WAY because he [i.e. Crispus] was silent; EIGHTY SOLSTICES [90–3]; note that the solstice occurs twice in the year but [Juvenal] has prefaced this with FOR MANY WINTERS [92], and so he goes from the general to the particular meaning, namely the summer solstice; ARMED THUS [93] that is, with silence.

Not on the [same] footing[129] WITH THE YOUNG LAD [95] that is, with his [Acilius'] son Dormitius; WAS AWAITING because this [i.e. death] was in fact awaiting him, because he was so upright he [i.e. Nero] had him killed.[130] BUT LONG SINCE [96] These men who came were both elderly and noble, but it is a wonder that they reached old age because LONG SINCE that is, long ago, OLD AGE AMONG THE NOBILITY [97] that is, a noble of advanced years, IS A PORTENTOUS FREAK. For Nero so hated the nobles that if any noble enjoyed a long life it was considered a portent. SO THE RESULT IS THAT [98] since the nobles perish thus, I prefer to be a commoner and enjoy a long life than to be a noble and die young, hence THE RESULT IS THAT. Now he has to have recourse to a fable (fabula). After the giants had been killed by the gods, earth bore Antaeus. The gods sent Hercules to kill him and Antaeus perished. Earth, grieving that he had died because of his courage, bore a swarthy female to spite the gods, who is called the little sister of the giants. But Priscian read 'little brother', that is, Antaeus' big brother, the diminutive being a witticism.[131] WOUNDED NUMIDIAN BEARS [99–100] Bears were brought to Rome so that young men might test their strength there. FOR WHO [101] Without a break [Juvenal] goes on.[132] He [i.e. Dormitius] was upright, but it availed him nothing, for probity was so cheapened that everyone thought they [themselves] were upright. This is the point [Juvenal] is putting in the form of a question. THE PATRICIAN ARTS [101–2] that is, the arts of the nobles. O BRUTUS [103] a historical allusion. Tarquinus Superbus, a citizen of Rome, expelled from the city all those

---

[128] In fact Juvenal means that the courtiers dare not speak of anything but the weather, and even so fear to give offence.

[129] The edition's 'non ideo cum iuvene' makes no sense; we read 'non idem cum iuvene'.

[130] Juvenal's text (ll. 94–6) may be translated: 'Next Acilius hurried up, a man of the same age, with his lad, who [i.e. the lad] did not deserve the cruel death in store for him, a death hastened on by the swords of the tyrant'. M'. Acilius Aviola was consul in AD 54 and M'. Acilius Glabrio in AD 91; but the two may not have been father and son. See P. Gallivan, Historia, xxvii (1978), 621–5. The 'Dormitius' in the commentator's gloss must be a mistake for the Latin nomen Domitius; Nero was born a Domitius Ahenobarbus.

[131] Juvenal's point is that he would rather be a nobody, terraefilius, hence the little brother of Earth's brood the Giants.

[132] The commentator is saying, in an abbreviated way, that the first two words of a new sentence at l. 101 take up and elaborate on what has been said in the preceding sentence.

whom he knew were wise men in case they should resist his tyranny. But he left Brutus alone because he pretended to be stupid, and he it was who subsequently drove Tarquinus from the city and brought the citizens back to power in Rome. No one now marvels at that, for it is EASY for each, that is, it seems easy TO IMPOSE ON A BEARDED KING that is, to deceive a bearded king.[133] *Impono, -is*, as St Jerome says, is given as an added [alternative] to *decipere*, of which the supine forms are *impositum, imposita*, and the participle *impositus*.

AND NO BETTER [IN COLOUR: 104] that is, pale, ALTHOUGH OF UNDIS-TINGUISHED STOCK that is, even though, being of lowly birth, he [i.e. Rubrius] had nothing to fear; [GUILTY] OF AN OFFENCE LONG AGO because he had had intercourse with Messalina the wife of Nero, and THOUGH HE WAS MORE SHAMELESS [106] that is, having become more shameless THAN A COMIC WRITER[134] WRITING SATIRE that is, although a comic writer might write a satire taking him as a subject, or because a comic writer had written a satire about him, and he was now all the more shameless, or was more shameless than any comic writer. MONTANUS, THAT GREAT BELLY [107] Montanus is someone with a big belly, [SLOW] BY REASON OF HIS PAUNCH that is, slowed down by obesity. [BY PERFUME] APPLIED IN THE MORNING [108] either because he [i.e. Crispinus] anointed himself in the morning or because it was brought from the east;[135] [STRONGER THAN THE FRAGRANCE OF] TWO FUNERALS [109] formerly they anointed corpses with myrrh. MORE CRUEL more effective; IN OPENING [110] laying open [throats], WITH A QUIET MURMUR that is, unspoken flattery.[136] FUSCUS WHO DREAMED OF BATTLES [AND WHO WAS SAVING HIS GUTS FOR] DACIAN [VULTURES: 111–12], who was killed there [i.e. in Dacia] and so he says 'who was saving his guts' ironically. WITH DEADLY [113] accusation. A GIRL WHOM HE HAD NEVER SEEN [114] because he [i.e. Catullus] was blind; I say A HUGE MONSTER OF A MAN [115] that is, big and monstrous, [EVEN] IN OUR [TIME] in which there are many monsters. A HANGER-ON OFFICIATING AT THE BRIDGE [116] It is a well-known fact that he [i.e. Catullus] used to beg on bridges.[137] Nero transferred him thence to

---

[133] The bearded king is, in Juvenal, a reference to Tarquin. But the beard was also a sign of a simpler, less sophisticated age. According to popular tradition, from about 300 BC the Romans began to be clean-shaven, except for aspiring philosophers. In Juvenal's lifetime beards were beginning to become fashionable again.

[134] Juvenal's text (l. 106) is: 'et tamen improbior saturam scribente cinaedo' ('and yet he is more shameless than a passive homosexual writing satire'). Our commentator may have seen 'cinaedo' ('passive homosexual') in his Juvenal manuscript (if the lemma is anything to go by), but translated it as if it were the very similar 'comoedo', written 'comedo' in medieval manuscripts, which he takes to mean 'comic writer' (in classical Latin 'comic actor', a comic writer being *comicus*).

[135] This (incorrect) interpretation would produce as a translation of l. 108 'Crispinus anointed by some eastern perfume', the east being associated with the rising sun.

[136] The commentator is wrong in interpreting 'tenui susurro' ('a quiet murmur') as 'unspoken flattery'. It seems to be Juvenal's very realistic picture of a sinister *éminence grise* in an authoritarian state, who will simply whisper to the ruler a few words which will result in the death or disappearance of someone to whom he has taken a dislike.

[See p. 148 for n. 137]

the court and there he filled the role of hanger-on and flatterer. ARICIAN [117] [carriage wheels] travelling to the town of Aricia; THROW bestow [kisses]; as it [i.e. the carriage] WENT DOWNHILL [118], for he himself went downhill.[138] NO ONE [119] as if he were to say 'even though he was blind'; NO ONE MARVELLED MORE, this concerns his praise of the fish; TOWARDS THE LEFT [120] on the left side.[139] [THE FIGHTS] OF A CILICIAN [121] the Cilicians are said to have been pirates from Cilicia; here he puts 'of a Cilician' for 'of a gladiator'. STRUCTURE (PEGMA) [122] a kind of game unknown to us; BOYS SNATCHED AWAY In theatres there were curtained areas where boys were taken for shameful purposes after the end of the games.[140]

[VEGENTO] HELD HIS OWN [123] in flattery [LIKE] A RELIGIOUS FANATIC fanatics are priests of Faunus who when stirred by a demonic spirit used to prophesy; THE SPIRIT OF FRENZY (OESTRO), an *oestrum* is a kind of gad-fly used to rouse oxen. ARVIRAGUS [127] the name of a king of Britain; FROM THE CHARIOT [126] from the battle line. THE STAKES [128] the spines. THIS [ONLY] WAS LACKING as if he were to say 'Fabricius in response said exactly the same as Vegento', BUT THIS ONE THING WAS LACKING because he said nothing about the age and provenance [of the fish], or else Fabricius and Vegento are names of one and the same person.[141]

WHAT THEN [DO YOU THINK?: 139] these are the words of Nero, as if he were to say 'because you have spoken so well about the fish what is your opinion about the method of cooking it?' CONETI[142] for 'it will be cut up'.

---

[137] The heads of the various departments of the emperor's household at Rome had titles such as *ab epistolis* ('secretary'), *a rationibus* ('accountant'), *a libellis* ('supervisor of petitions'), and the like. Juvenal's phrase 'a ponte satelles' is obviously a parody of such titles; moreover, beggars were to be found on bridges. Our commentator is under the misapprehension that Juvenal is saying that Catullus had actually been a beggar: what he is in fact saying is that his relationship to Domitian is that of a beggar to a potential patron, also implying that his character would have fitted him to be an actual beggar at Aricia. Aricia was on the Via Appia, and had a steep hill which slowed down the coaches; thus it was a good pitch for beggars.

[138] Juvenal's line (l. 118) is: 'blandaque devexae iactaret basia raedae' ('and throw obsequious kisses at the carriage as it went downhill'). The beggar, having importuned the occupants of the carriage successfully as it was going up the hill at Aricia, would blow kisses at it as it departed down the other side. Alternatively, the sense could be that the carriage brakes hard coming down, so that the beggars can make their pitch, and then express their thanks. Our commentator's remark, however, shows that he has wholly misunderstood—hardly surprising, given the general lack of knowledge of the topographical background to Latin literature.

[139] Juvenal at this point makes the (to our minds) cruel jibe that the blind Catullus, 'a blind flatterer' (l. 116), passed many favourable comments on the fish, turning towards the left, whereas the object of his admiration was behind him on his right. The commentator does not seem to have grasped this.

[140] The *pegma* was actually a piece of wooden machinery in the theatre, with which the players were suddenly raised aloft. The commentator's ingenious misunderstanding doubtless arose from medieval awareness of Nero's homosexual exploits.

[141] As indeed they are: A. Didius Gallus Fabricius Veiento. 'Vegento' is a medieval corruption of 'Veiento'.

[142] An impossible form, maybe the result of a faulty Juvenal text used by the commentator. The correct word is 'conciditur'.

MAY THIS [DISGRACEFUL END] BE FAR FROM IT this is said by Montanus; DIS-GRACEFUL END [131] that it should be cut up; CASSEROLE an earthenware vessel; [LARGE ENOUGH] TO CONTAIN [132] encompass THE SPRAWLING ·CREATURE the fish WITHIN ITS [i.e. the casserole's] FRAGILE WALL He criticizes Nero's gluttony, for if the wall had been a thick one, it would have been harder to cook the fish.[143] PROMETHEUS [133] the potter's proper name stands for any potter; MIGHTY skilled; SWIFT quick and expeditious. RUSH IN POTTER'S CLAY AND A WHEEL [134] the kind of equipment with which a pot is made; BUT [FROM] THIS TIME FORTH as if he [Montanus] were to say: 'up to now you [i.e. Nero] have indeed had potters, but now order[144] them to follow you'.[145] [HIS OPINION] CARRIED THE DAY this pleased Nero. What he [i.e. Montanus] said was well calculated to please Nero, for HE HAD KNOWN THE EXTRAVAGANT WAY OF LIFE [136-7] that is, the gluttony OF THE IMPERIAL COURT, of the emperor, OF OLD habitual; AT MIDNIGHT [138] for he [i.e. Nero?] used to feast, beginning at midnight; THE SECOND [HUNGER][146] NO ONE HAD [139] could be interpreted, 'was there anyone so gluttonous?' The reply given is, 'no one'. TIMES [140] life-time, and ⟨Montanus⟩ was glut-tonous, for HE KNEW HOW TO TELL that is, he had expert knowledge WHETHER AN OYSTER—it is a kind of fish—[WAS BRED] IN CIRCEII that is a place in the sea, so-called from Circe [OR] BY THE LUCRINE ROCK [141] that is the Lucrine lake [OR] AT THE RUTUPIAN OYSTER-FARM Rutupi is a city[147] where oysters are cultivated; SHORE the native habitat SEA-URCHIN the name of a fish.

THE MEETING RISES [144] after what is to be done with the fish is proclaimed; [THE COUNCILLORS] SENT AWAY that is, dismissed; THE MIGHTY [LEADER: 145] ironically; AS IF [CONCERNING] THE CHATTI [147] these are peoples of Mauritania;[148] WITH WINGED FLIGHT [149] that is, a swift messenger; and he [i.e. Nero] called them together over a trivial matter.

DISTINGUISHED etc. [150-1] famed; ILLUSTRIOUS [152] noble; WITH IMPUN-ITY unpunished; but HE [i.e. Nero] PERISHED [158]. In the time of Nero the Roman army was sent to Spain where, because it detested Nero, it made

[143] Presumably the commentator's meaning is that a casserole with thicker walls would have taken longer to cook the fish, but since the gluttonous Nero wanted it done quickly a dish with a thin-sided ('fragile', Lat. 'tenui' in l. 132) wall was used. Hence, Nero's gluttony is implicitly being criticized. In fact, Juvenal may have intended to indicate fine workmanship by 'tenui'.

[144] Reading 'iube' for the impossible 'iubet'.

[145] At this point (l. 135) Juvenal has Montanus make two suggestions: one to deal with the immediate problem, the other to prevent the problem rising again. 'Rush up potters and a wheel [i.e. make a vessel large enough for this monstrous fish], but from now on, Caesar, let potters follow your camp' (i.e. in the event of such a fish being caught in the future the potters would be on hand to make a dish suitable for it to be cooked in).

[146] Wilson reads the Latin text as 'aliam aserentiam', which appears to conflate the lemma from Juvenal's text and a corruption of the paraphrase. Perhaps the commentator wrote 'aliam famem aliam appetentiam', 'ANOTHER HUNGER another appetite'.

[147] Actually Rutupiae, Richborough in Kent.

[148] Sic for Germany.

Galba (who was subsequently emperor at Rome) its commander. When Nero heard this he was grief-stricken, sent messengers to say that he was on his way,[149] and took two exceedingly sharp daggers which he held close to his side, as if he were going to kill himself. Then, when he heard that Galba was not close by, he drew back his hand. Eventually, when he heard that he [i.e. Galba] was entering the city, he killed himself. COBBLERS [153] shoemakers. [HIS HANDS DRIPPING WITH THE SLAUGHTER] OF THE LAMIAE [145] This was a most noble family at Rome, receiving its name from Lamius.

'BERNARD SILVESTER'

Commentary on the *Aeneid*, Books I–VI[150]

PROLOGUE

It is our view that in the *Aeneid* Virgil observed a twofold system of teaching. For, as Macrobius says, 'He taught philosophical truth and he did not omit poetic fiction (*ficmentum poeticum*).'[151] Consequently, whoever

---

[149] Lat. 'qui adventum praedicerent' ('to say that he was on his way'). Nero sent messengers to the approaching Galba to say that he, Nero, was coming to meet him, this being a ploy to enable him to have time to commit suicide and thus avoid falling into Galba's hands.

[150] Tr. from *The Commentary on the First Six Books of the* Aeneid *of Virgil commonly attributed to Bernardus Silvestris*, ed. J. W. and E. F. Jones (Lincoln, Neb., and London, 1977), pp. 1–3, 9–10, with the permission of the University of Nebraska Press. On this commentary see especially W. Wetherbee, *Platonism and Poetry in the Twelfth Century: The Influence of the School of Chartres* (Princeton, NJ, 1972), pp. 105–11; O'Donnell, 'Bernard Silvester's Commentary on the *Aeneid*' (cit. above, n. 22). A complete translation has been made, with helpful apparatus (to which on occasion we have been indebted), by E. G. Schreiber and T. E. Maresca, *The Commentary on the First Six Books of Virgil's* Aeneid *by Bernardus Silvestris* (Lincoln, Neb., and London, 1979). There have been some doubts concerning the attribution of this commentary to Bernard—see especially Baswell, 'The Medieval Allegorization of the *Aeneid*' (cit. above, n. 4)—but P. Dronke, in his recent edition of Bernard's *Cosmographia* (Textus minores liii, Leiden, 1978), pp. 3–5, and E. Jeauneau, reviewing this edition in *Medium Aevum*, xlix (1980), 112–13, can see no reason to deny it. The *Cosmographia* has been translated by W. Wetherbee, *The Cosmographia of Bernardus Silvestris* (New York, 1973). An edition of what some regard as Bernard's commentary on Martianus Capella (in Cambridge, University Library, MS Mm. I. 18) has recently been published by H. J. Westra, *The Commentary on Martianus Capella's De nuptiis Philologiae et Mercurii attributed to Bernardus Silvestris* (Studies and Texts, lxxx, Leiden, 1986); but see the objections to this attribution in Baswell, op. cit., and B. Stock, *Myth and Science in the Twelfth Century: A Study of Bernard Silvester* (Princeton, NY, 1972), pp. 36–7, n. 42.

[151] Macrobius, *In somn. Scip.* I. ix. 8, refers to Virgil's twofold training, 'the poet's imagination (*figmentum*) and the philosopher's accuracy (*veritatem*)' (tr. Stahl, p. 126). Cf. ibid., II. x. 11 (ed. Willis, p. 126; tr. Stahl, p. 218). Throughout the *Aeneid* commentary 'Bernard' draws freely on Macrobius and the Virgil commentary of Fulgentius (*fl.* late 5th and early 6th cc.; tr. Whitbread, pp. 119–35). On Macrobius' view of Virgil, see S. T. Collins, *The Interpretation of Vergil, with special reference to Macrobius* (Oxford, 1909). The debt of 'Bernard' to Macrobius and Servius is discussed by O'Donnell, art. cit.; the basis for a fuller comparison of Servius and

wishes to read the *Aeneid* as that book is intended to be read must first show what the author's intention is (*unde agat*), and how and why he writes,[152] and in revealing these matters he must not fail to consider that twofold system.

So, since in this work Virgil is said to be both poet and philosopher, let us first of all state briefly the intention of the poet, and his mode and reason for writing (*modus agendi et cur agat*). His intention is to recount the experiences of Aeneas and the sufferings of the other Trojans in their wanderings. He does this without following closely the true historical sequence of events (*historie veritas*)—Dares Phrygius does that—but throughout magnifies the flight of Aeneas and his deeds in fictional terms, with a view to winning the approbation of Caesar Augustus. Virgil is the greatest of Latin poets, and he writes in imitation of Homer, the greatest of Greek poets. For just as Homer in his *Iliad* described the destruction of Troy, and in his *Odyssey* the exile of Ulysses, so Virgil in his second book recounts the overthrow of Troy, and in the others the hardships undergone by Aeneas.

It should be noted that in this book the narrative has a twofold order, the natural and the artificial.[153] The natural order of the narrative occurs when the work is set out in accordance with the sequence of events and the times when they occurred. This happens as long as the events are narrated in the order in which they really occurred, and a distinction is made between that which happened first, that which happened next, and that which happened last of all. This is the order followed by Lucan. An artificial order occurs when we begin the narrative artificially right in the middle, and subsequently return to the beginning. Terence, and Virgil in this work, employ this kind of order. For the natural order would be to describe the fall of Troy first, and then take the Trojans to Crete, from there to Sicily, and from there to Libya. Virgil first of all has the Trojans meeting Dido, and introduces Aeneas recounting the overthrow of Troy and his other sufferings. Up until now we have explained Virgil's intention (*unde agat*), and how he proceeds. Next let us consider why he writes.

'Bernard' has been provided by J. W. Jones's article 'Allegorical Interpretation in Servius' (cit. above, n. 22).

[152] A version of the *circumstantiae*, on which see the references in Ch. I, n. 6, and Ch. III, n. 41.

[153] On the distinction between natural order and artificial order see the references in Ch. II, n. 36. As Schreiber–Maresca point out in their note (op. cit., p. 109 n. 2), 'Bernard', like Fulgentius, follows the artificial order actually employed in the *Aeneid*, whereas the humanist Cristoforo Landino (1424–1504) follows what 'Bernard' describes as natural order, beginning his allegorical exposition with Aeneas' origins in Troy. This last work has been edited and translated by T. H. Stahel, 'Cristoforo Landino's Allegorization of the *Aeneid*: Books iii and iv of the *Camaldolese Disputations*' (Ph.D. thesis, Johns Hopkins University, Baltimore, Md., 1986). On Renaissance allegorizing of Virgil see D. C. Allen, 'Undermeanings in Virgil's *Aeneid*', in id., *Mysteriously Meant: The Rediscovery of Pagan Symbolism and Allegorical Interpretation in the Renaissance* (Baltimore, Md., 1970), pp. 135–62.

Some poets write with a useful purpose in view, like the satirists, while others, such as the writers of comedies, write to give pleasure, and yet others, for example the historians, write to a useful end and to give pleasure. Hence, in the words of Horace, 'The aim of poets is either to profit or to give pleasure, or to say something which, at one and the same time gives pleasure and is helpful to men's lives.'[154] In this work a certain pleasure is derived from the verbal ornament and the beauty (*figura*) of the style and from the account of the various events and the actions of men. Whoever strives to imitate all these features attains to the highest skill in writing. The most impressive examples and precepts (*excogitationes*) for adhering more closely to what is honourable and shunning that which is unlawful are provided by the deeds narrated. So the reader derives a twofold benefit from this work. The first is skill in writing acquired by imitation. The second is the knowledge of how to act properly, acquired from the exhortation imparted to us by the examples. For instance, the trials of Aeneas give us an example of endurance; the love he showed towards Anchises and Ascanias an example of steadfast loyalty (*pietas*); the reverence he displayed towards the gods, his seeking out of oracles, the sacrifices he offered, and the prayers and vows he poured out attract us in a certain way towards religious observance. The excessive love of Aeneas for Dido restrains us from the desire for what is unlawful.

The purpose of a prologue consists entirely in gaining the goodwill of the reader or listener, and in making him willing to learn and attentive.[155] So, leaving aside the seven questions which most writers of prologues to books ask, let it suffice for us to consider these three points: the intention of the author (*unde agat*), this being to make the reader disposed to learn; his manner of writing, this being to make the reader well disposed; and his reason for writing, this being to make him attentive.[156] Let us now consider these same questions in terms of philosophical truth. In so far as Virgil is a philosopher he describes the nature of human life. His mode of proceeding is as follows. In the integument (*integumentum*) he describes what the human spirit, placed for a period of time in the human body, does or suffers. In describing this he uses the natural order, and so makes use of both kinds of order in his narration—as a poet he uses the artificial order, and as a philosopher, the natural order.

The integument is a kind of teaching which wraps up the true meaning inside a fictitious narrative (*fabulosa narratio*), and so it is also called 'a veil' (*involucrum*).[157] Man derives benefit (*utilitas*) from this work, the

---

[154] Horace, *Ars poetica*, 333–4.

[155] Cf. Cicero, *De invent.* I. xv. 20.

[156] Cf. the similar passage in William of Conches's prologue to his commentary on Priscian's *Institutiones*, tr. above, p. 134.

[157] Cf. the fuller account in the Martianus commentary which some would attribute to Bernard, quoted and discussed by Stock, *Myth and Science*, pp. 33–49; cf. Wetherbee, *Platon-*

benefit being self-knowledge. For, as Macrobius says, it is of great advantage to a man to know himself; hence his words: 'The motto "know thyself" descended from the sky.'[158]

Up to this point we have considered the intention of the writer, his manner of writing, and his reason for writing, all in the light of his twofold teaching. Next our plan is to expound the integument of each of the twelve books in due order.[159]

EXPOSITION OF BOOK I: EXTRACT

Aeneas is said to be the son of Anchises and Venus. For the name 'Anchises' means 'He who dwells in the lofty heavens',[160] whom we understand to be the Father of all, who presides over all things. We read that there are two Venuses, the lawful goddess and the goddess of lust. We read that the lawful Venus is the harmony of the universe, that is, the equally balanced proportion of all the parts of the universe, which others call Astraea, that is, natural justice. This proportion is found in the elements, the constellations, the seasons, and in living creatures. We say that the unchaste Venus, the goddess of lust, is carnal desire, which is the mother of all acts of fornication.

At this point we should note that, just as in other mystical writings, so

ism and Poetry, p. 267, and E. Jeauneau, 'Note sur l'école de Chartres', in *Lectio philosophorum*, pp. 28–31, 40–1.

[158] Macrobius, *In Somn. Scip.* i. ix. 2 (ed. Willis, p. 40, tr. Stahl, p. 124). The quotation is from Juvenal, *Sat.* xi. 27. Cf. the use made of it by Ralph of Longchamps, tr. below, p. 159, and Hugh of Saint-Victor, *Didascalicon*, i. i (ed. Buttimer, p. 4; tr. Taylor, p. 46); also the comprehensive study by P. Courcelle, '"Nosce teipsum" du Bas-Empire au haut moyen-âge', *SSCISAM* ix (1962), 265–95.

[159] The subsequent commentary, which covers only the first six books of the *Aeneid*, interprets the poems in terms of the ages of man. Book i refers to infancy, book ii, boyhood and the acquisition of speech; book iii, adolescence; book iv, young manhood; book v, manhood; book vi (incomplete, covering only about two-thirds of the text) begins with an account of the various ways in which one may be said to descend into the underworld (by nature, virtue, vice, and artifice) and proceeds to an allegory of the wise man's descent to a consideration of earthly matters, in order that 'he may recognize their fragility, reject them, and turn more completely to invisible things and so that he may come to know more clearly his creator through a knowledge of his creations, especially through a sort of philosophical study of man' (*Commentary on the Aeneid*, ed. Jones-Jones, p. xiv). The commentary breaks off before Virgil's account of Aeneas's entry into Elysium. This method of interpreting the poem was established by the *Expositio Virgilianae continentiae* of Fulgentius (n. 151): see J. A. Burrow, *The Ages of Man: A Study in Medieval Writing and Thought* (Oxford, 1986), pp. 118–19. For Pietro Alighieri's use of a similar scheme of ways of descending *ad inferos* see below, pp. 481–3. On Dante's indebtedness to the *Aeneid* as it was transformed by both the allegorical commentaries and the mythographies see Burrow, *Ages of Man*, pp. 118ff.; H. T. Silverstein, 'Dante and Vergil the Mystic', *HSNPL* xiv (1932), 51–82. Building on Silverstein's argument, D. Thomson, 'Dante and Bernard Silvestris', *Viator*, i (1970), 203, argues that, as allegorized by 'Bernard Silvester', the *Aeneid* 'represented a literary precedent for Dante's spiritual itinerary, the journey of the soul to God'.

[160] Cf. Fulgentius, *Expositio Virgilianae continentiae* (ed. Helm, p. 102; tr. Whitbread, p. 132).

too in this book there are 'alternative meanings' (*equivocationes*), and 'plurality of names' (*multivocationes*), and that the integuments relate to different things.[161] For instance,[162] in the book by Martianus [Capella], by Jupiter you understand at one point the superior [i.e. celestial] fire, at another point a star, at another the Creator. Saturn you understand sometimes as a star, and again, immediately after, as representing time. Likewise, Mercury you understand sometimes as representing eloquence, and at other times as a star. The possibility of the integuments relating to different things, and of multiple signification in all mystical material, must be taken into account if the truth cannot stand supported on one interpretation. So, in this work we find the same principle, that one and the same name designates different things, and conversely different names designate the same thing.

The same name designates different things, as for instance Apollo sometimes designates the sun, sometimes divine wisdom, sometimes human wisdom. Jupiter sometimes designates fire, sometimes the supreme God. As we said above, Venus sometimes designates carnal desire, sometimes the harmony of the universe. Different names designate the same thing, and this is 'plurality of names' (*multivocatio*). For instance, both Jupiter and Anchises designate the Creator. So, when you find Venus described as the wife of Vulcan and mother of Jocus and Cupid (pleasure and desire), you must understand that she represents fleshly desire, which is closely related to the property of heat in nature, and produces pleasure and intercourse. But when you read that Venus and Anchises had a son, Aeneas, understand Venus as representing the harmony of the universe, and Aeneas the human spirit. For the name 'Aeneas' is *ennos demas*, that is, 'dweller in the body', *ennos* in Greek being in Latin *habitator* ('dweller'). This is why Juvenal calls Neptune 'Ennosigeum', that is, 'the dweller in Sygeum'.[163] *Demas*, that is, 'a chain', means 'the body', because it is the prison of the soul. Aeneas is the son of Anchises and Venus because the human spirit comes from God and begins its life in the body as a result of harmony. We have said all this about Anchises, Venus and Aeneas because we see that a knowledge of them is essential at many points in this book.

---

[161] With this discussion cf. the prologue to the Martianus commentary sometimes attributed to Bernard, in Jeauneau, *Lectio philosophorum*, p. 41.

[162] The following are all examples of *equivocatio*. Examples of *multivocatio* are offered in the next paragraph.

[163] Juvenal, *Sat.* x. 182.

ARNULF OF ORLÉANS

Gloss on Lucan's *Pharsalia* [= the *Bellum civile*]: Prologue[164]

When we are dealing with any author we must ask who he was before we ask what he has done. Lucan, then, was born in Cordova, a city of Spain, hence the words 'Cordova gave me birth'. He was of not ignoble descent, and gifted with discerning wisdom. He was a nephew of the great Seneca whom he imitated not only in nobility of character but also in his manner of speaking, and in writing verse. When Cordoba was captured by Nero he was led to Rome among the other captives. Hence the words, 'Nero snatched him away'. So in Rome, when his boundless wisdom became known, he won very great popularity with the Roman people and senate. He took thought as to what he might write to advance that popularity. So he chose the wars of Julius [Caesar] and Pompey, and composed this book about them, hence the words 'I wrote of wars waged by two equals, a father-in-law on one side, a son-in-law on the other.'[165]

Lucan's subject-matter (*materia*) in this work is completely devoted to Caesar and equally completely to Pompey—completely devoted to Caesar, that is, Caesar himself and his associates, and to Pompey, that is, Pompey himself and those who aided him. His intention (*intencio*) is to deal with this historical episode (*historia*) both to please the Roman people and senate and to deter others from a similar war. The [work's] usefulness (*utilitas*) is great because, when it is seen what happened to each of the protagonists as a result of the civil war, that is, that Pompey had his head cut off and Caesar was transfixed by twenty-four wounds on the Capitol, we may steer clear of any similar war. It pertains to ethics (*ethice supponitur*) not because he gives moral instruction (*precepta morum*) but because in a certain way he encourages us to practice the four virtues, courage, wisdom, self-control, and justice, by means of appropriate characters (*per convenientes personas*), showing us good morality as in the case of Cato and other citizens who strive after those virtues in the state which pertain to ethics.

The title (*titulus*) is as follows: *Here begins the first book of Marcus Agneus Lucanus. Marcus* is a forename, and is put there to differentiate. *Agneos* in Greek is 'a bee' in Latin for, as Vac[c]a says,[166] when Lucan was born a swarm of bees settled on his head, and so he was called *Agneus* from that occurrence. *Lucanus* may be his own proper name, or else Lucanus is

---

[164] Tr. from *Arnulfi Aurelianensis Glosule super Lucanum*, ed. B. Marti, pp. 3–5, with the permission of the American Academy in Rome.

[165] *Epitaphium Lucani*, in *Anthologia Latina*, ed. F. Buecheler and A. Riese (Leipzig, 1895–7), I. ii. 139, no. 668; *M. Annaei Lucani de Bello civili*, ed. C. Hosius (Leipzig, 1892), p. 338.

[166] Cf. the *Vita Lucani* by the 6th-c. grammarian Vacca, printed in Lucan, *De bello civili*, ed. C. E. Haskins (London, 1887), p. xiv; ed. Hosius, p. 335.

a fictitious name, as being one who composes verse lucidly, because he excluded from his work all hyperbaton, that is to say, all lengthy, drawn-out constructions.

Juvenal is purely a writer of satire, Terence a purely comic writer, Horace in his odes a purely lyric writer. But, unlike them, Lucan is not simply a poet but rather a poet and historiographer combined (*poeta et historiographus*). For he works out his historical theme (*historia*) without inventing anything. So he is not referred to as a poet pure and simple, but a poet and a writer of history. For if he introduces anything which is invented (*aliquid ficticii*) he does so, not speaking on his own behalf but on that of other people. For he adds phrases such as 'as they relate', 'as they say', or 'as they recall'. He prefaces his narrative with four topics: his aim in writing, where he says [I SING OF] WARS [WAGED] ACROSS THE EMATHIAN [PLAINS i. 1]; attack, where he says WHAT MADNESS, CITIZENS? [i. 8]; invocation, where he says BUT TO ME YOU ARE ALREADY DIVINE [i. 63], and the causes of the war, where he says MY MIND MOVES ME [TO SET OUT THE] CAUSES [i. 67]. He begins his narrative where he says NOW CAESAR [HAD SWIFTLY CROSSED] THE COLD [ALPS i. 183]. For I do not agree with the statement that those first verses have been added by Seneca, because Lucan had begun WHAT MADNESS? [i. 8] but this was too abrupt. It seems to me absurd to say that a man of such literary authority (*auctoritas*) should have left anything uncorrected (*inemendatum*).

A résumé of the historical events (*historia*) on which the invented element (*figmentum*) of this work rests may be set out as follows. Since among the high offices at Rome that of dictator was of longer duration and greater eminence, it pleased the Romans in their collective wisdom that three dictators should be elected at one and the same time, the idea being that any dissension which arose among any two might be settled by the third acting as mediator. Now it so happened that the three most powerful and formidable men of that time, Marcus Crassus, Magnus Pompeius,[167] and Julius Caesar, were elected dictators. But it was decided that those who were more powerful should be sent on expeditions, while the wisest of the three should remain in the city. So Pompey remained, but Crassus was despatched to Parthia and killed by the Parthians, while Caesar was sent to Gaul and subdued it over a period of five years. But so that he might subdue the whole of the west he stayed for another five years, and vanquished not only the Gauls but also the Britons. At the end of that second period of five years he sent emissaries to Rome to obtain a triumph for himself, but, with the connivance of Pompey, not only was he denied a triumph but was accused of treason.

---

[167] 'Magnus Pompeius' for Cr. Pompeius Magnus follows a fashion for inverting *nomen* and *cognomen* that set in during the 1st c. BC and is common in imperial literature. See R. Syme, *Roman Papers*, i (Oxford, 1979), pp. 361, 363; J. P. V. D. Balsdon, *Romans and Aliens* (London, 1979), p. 156. For this instance, cf. Valerius Maximus, *Facta et dicta memorabilia*, v. iii. 5.

When Caesar heard this he gathered his forces and quickly advanced to punish Pompey and the senate. Pompey, fearing his approach, fled with part of the senate to Capua, and from there to Brindisi. Besieged there by Caesar, he only just managed to elude him with the help of darkness and made for Greece. Caesar retired to Rome, divided the state treasury among his supporters and himself assumed all offices. Subsequently he entered Spain by way of Marseilles and there defeated in battle Pompey's associates Petreius and Afranius. He returned from there to Brindisi by way of Rome, and hastened over to Greece in pursuit of Pompey. Sometimes one side got the upper hand, sometimes the other; they were alternately victorious and defeated. Eventually both sides advanced into Thessaly. After Pompey had been defeated there he fled to Egypt and was beheaded. In the course of his pursuit of Pompey, Caesar spent two years with Cleopatra and pursued the remaining survivors of the battle in Thessaly into Libya. After Cato, Juba, and Scipio had been killed there, Caesar forced the sons of Pompey to flee all the way to Spain.

When he had killed Gneius[168] Pompeius along with countless others there, Sextus fled to Sicily and lived the life of a pirate. Long afterwards Agrippa, Augustus' sister's son,[169] vanquished him under the shadow of Mount Etna. After the end of the fighting at Munda, Caesar returned to Rome, and in the second year after this, with the complicity of the senate, was stabbed with twenty-four wounds by Brutus and Cassius on the Capitol. But Mark Antony, who had been the commander of the army under Julius, spared no effort in pursuit of the aforesaid murderers to avenge his master. But because, as we have already said, it was the senate who had done this [i.e. murdered Caesar], the two consuls, Hirtius and Pansa, and also Augustus, the nephew of Julius,[170] were given the task of helping the murderers. But after the consuls had been killed in battle, through the good offices of Dorabella [sic for Dolabella], the commander of Antony's troops, Augustus made a treaty with the aforesaid Antony. They then returned to Rome, entered the city with great slaughter, and divided the Roman empire between them. Antony obtained the lands across the sea, Augustus those on this side of the sea. Then Lucius Antonius, Mark Antony's brother, began to disturb by armed aggression the portion assigned to Augustus, in order to extract some share in government for himself, but since he could not resist the force of Augustus he was besieged at Modena. Retreating from there to Perugia he was driven by famine to surrender. When Mark Antony heard this, out of hatred for Augustus he made a treaty with Brutus and Cassius. Then they all met [in battle] in Thessaly; Brutus and Cassius were killed and Antony fled to Cleopatra in Egypt and gave up Augustus' sister, whom he

[168] A common misspelling of Gnaeus.
[169] Actually son-in-law.
[170] Actually great-nephew.

had married, to his brother. Relying on Cleopatra's military resources he invaded the Roman empire in alliance with the Egyptians and fought a naval battle with Augustus beneath the promontaries of Leucas and Actium. Antony himself was killed, and on his death Cleopatra ended her life by attaching asps to her breasts.

Now the letter (*littera*) must be expounded, and it begins from the [statement of the author's] purpose.

RALPH OF LONGCHAMPS

Commentary on Alan of Lille's *Anticlaudianus*: Exposition of the Prologue[171]

At the beginning of this book, as at the beginning of other authors, we must first consider what is its subject-matter, intention, and usefulness, and whether it pertains to any part of philosophy, the reason (*causa*) for undertaking the work, the title of the book, and the order in which it proceeds.

1. ON THE FOUR MAKERS (*ARTIFICES*): GOD, NATURE, FORTUNE, AND SIN

The four makers, and the works of those four makers, form the subject-matter of this book.[172] For God, Nature, Fortune, and Sin are all makers. God is said to be particularly the maker of those things which he creates from nothing, for example, spirits and souls. Hence, God is rightly said to create, and His handiwork is called the Creation. Nature is rightly said to be the maker of those things which are made up of the pre-existing raw material. For Nature is a force naturally implanted into the lower order of things or causes, bringing forth like from like, such as a man from a man or an ox from an ox. So it is said 'to beget', as it were 'to create from afar' (*procul creare*), that is, to create from something outside itself, namely from the pre-existing raw material.

Fortune or chance—for they are here accepted as being identical—is the maker of those things which come about fortuitously; for instance, if a peasant digging up a field should find treasure.[173] Fortune or chance is an

---

[171] Tr. from *Radulphus de Longo Campo: In Anticlaudianum Alani Commentum*, ed. J. Sulowski, pp. 19–24, with the permission of the editor.

[172] Cf. Hugh of Saint-Victor's description of the 'three works—the work of God, the work of nature, and the work of the artificer, who imitates nature'. *Didascalicon*, I. ix (ed. Buttimer, pp. 16–17; tr. Taylor, p. 55).

[173] With this discussion cf. Boethius, *De consolatione philosophiae*, v, pr. i, 39 ff. (ed. Tester, pp. 386–9); *Timaeus, a Calcidio translatus commentarioque instructus* (Plato Latinus IV), ed. J. H. Waszink, 2nd edn. (London and Leiden, 1975), pp. 192–3. Cf. Boethius, *In lib. Aristotelis de interpretatione*, ed. secunda, iii (PL lxiv. 491).

unexpected event arising from the conjunction of several causes. This is clear from the example given above, for the finding of the treasure is an unexpected event. The conjoint causes are the factors which converge to cause this event, namely, the approach of the peasant to the treasure, the digging of the earth, and the like. The effects of this creative force are freedom, slavery, wealth, adversity, prosperity.

The role of sin as a maker is an evil one. Its effects are various kinds of vices.

The authors interpreted these four makers and their various effects as being the four sons of Saturn: Jupiter, Juno, Neptune, Pluto. By Jupiter one understands God and His works. For Jupiter means 'helping father' (*iuvans pater*), or 'universal father' (*ya-pater*), Greek *ya* being translated as 'universal' in Latin. For all things happen by God's authority. By Juno one understands Nature, for Juno is interpreted as 'the solitary one who helps' (*iuvans monos*). For everything which is produced, and which is in its essence new, comes into being through the medium of Nature. By Neptune, whose name is interpreted as 'thundering from the cloud' (*nube tonans*), and who is called the god of the sea, we understand the creative force of fortune and its effects. For Fortune flatters and befriends a man in prosperity, but is hostile and inimical in adversity. Pluto gets his name from *polis*, which means 'large numbers'. So, by Pluto, meaning 'large numbers', is understood the creative power of sin and its works. For, as Boethius says, 'all evil is infinite, but good is finite; and the vices are infinite and various, but all virtues share a common identity'.[174]

These four categories of works originate from Saturn, in other words almighty God, the first by Creation, the second by [His] generation, the third by [His] direction, and the fourth by [His] permission.[175]

The intention of the author is to deal with these four makers and their works. The usefulness or final cause is that heaven-inspired proverb *nothis elittos*, that is, 'know yourself'.[176] For a knowledge of one's origin is most important and useful. The reader obtains this useful knowledge in this work, so that he knows what within him comes from God, what he draws from Nature, what he receives from Fortune, and in what respect sin diminishes him.

This book is not tied to any area of philosophy (*pars philosophiae*) in particular, but ranges over all the branches of philosophy. For sometimes it touches on ethics, when it treats of morals and ways of educating in good behaviour; sometimes natural history or physics, when it deals with natural things; sometimes it is concerned with the complexities of mathematics, or again it climbs the lofty heights of

---

[174] Boethius, *Liber de persona et duabus naturis*, iv (PL lxiv. 1346c).
[175] i.e. God permits evil to happen.
[176] Cf. the use made of this proverb by 'Bernard Silvester', tr. p. 153, and above, n. 158.

theology. Therefore it is evident that it partakes of and considers all the parts of philosophy.[177]

The reason for undertaking the work is twofold: one reason concerns the common good, the other is a personal one. There is a reason relating to the common good because in this book the author writes in the interest of the common pool of understanding and the benefit of his readers as he treats of all the sciences, and touches upon matters terrestial and heavenly. The personal reason [for writing the book] is that the author may exercise his abilities (*ingenium*), lest they become rusty through lack of use.[178]

The title is as follows: *Here begins the Anticlaudianus of Alan, concerning the Antirufinus*. Three things are denoted in this title: the author of the work, what the author has done in the work, and the subject-matter of the work. The nature of the work is indicated by the fact that it is called *Anticlaudianus*. The author is indicated by the fact that it is called *of Alan*. The subject matter is indicated by the words *concerning the Antirufinus*. For the book is called *Anticlaudianus* antithetically, that is, to express opposition. For just as Claudian at the beginning of his book [i.e. the *Antirufinus*] introduces vices to deface the image of Rufinus,[179] so this author at the beginning of his book introduces the Virtues to fashion Antirufinus. So, this man, who is the subject of this book [i.e. Alan's *Anticlaudianus*], is called 'Antirufinus', as it were 'the opposite to Rufinus'. For as Rufinus was the worst of men so Antirufinus is a man supremely blessed.

The mode and order of proceeding is as follows. After the end of the preface and invocation, Nature is introduced, lamenting with her sisters, and grieving over the imperfection of all her works. She maintains that there is only one possible line of action and remedy open to her: a single being must be created, on which she lavishes all her gifts so that, having bestowed these gifts, she will be seen by all to be successful in ensuring that the goodness of this one creature cancels out the wickedness of the many. But subsequently Prudence seems to speak somewhat against this. For she says that in matters such as these the Virtues in themselves are

---

[177] Cf. Alan's prose preface: 'For in this work the sweetness of the literal sense will soothe the ears of boys, the moral instruction will inspire the mind on the road to perfection, the sharper subtlety of the allegory will whet the advanced intellect. . . . Since there emerge in this work the rules of grammatical syntax, the maxims of dialectical discourse, the accepted ideas of oratorical rhetoric, the wonders of mathematical lore, the melody of music, the principles of geometry, theories about writing, the excellence of the dignity of astronomy, a view of the celestial theophany, let not men without taste thrust their own interpretations on this work . . .' (tr. Sheridan, pp. 40–2).

[178] Cf. Alan's prose preface: 'It was no congestion of inward pride trying to belch its way out to the public that drove me to compose this work, nor was it the desire for the favour of popular applause that summoned me to unwanted toil, but a desire to prevent my discourses from growing rusty from the long intervals between my treatment of them and to save myself from overexerting myself in labour and study for the benefit of others' (tr. Sheridan, p. 42).

[179] Claudian, *In Rufinum*, i. 27–44.

not sufficient, because the birth of the soul requires other creative forces, and the soul is essential to the composition of a human being. After this assertion Reason rises, and commends the opinions expressed by Nature and Prudence, but adds that, since the Virtues are not sufficient in themselves to make a man, God should be asked to provide the soul which is a proper component of this sort of construction. She urges and advises that Prudence be entrusted with this mission. The sisters applaud this, and only Prudence herself is less than enthusiastic, and professes to be unequal to the arduous enterprise. While the Virtues are thus hesitating, Concord comes forward among them. She uses many arguments to urge Prudence not to oppose the wish and request of her sisters. So, Prudence gives in to her sisters' wishes, and to Concord's urging, and undertakes the arduous journey and mission.

Then her seven handmaids are introduced, the Seven Liberal Arts, who make the chariot by which Prudence ascends [to heaven]. Grammar fashions the wain, Dialectic the axis, Rhetoric paints both. Music makes a bronze wheel, Geometry one of lead, Arithmetic one of marble, Astronomy one of gold. We will explain in the appropriate parts [of the commentary] why these kinds of arts are introduced and why they work in these ways. In the clothing worn by each art is depicted the precepts of that art, while in the work of each art is depicted the authorities (*auctores*) of that art.

When the chariot has been made, and horses harnessed to it, Prudence climbs into the chariot, with Reason as her charioteer. She soars aloft into the infinite atmosphere, and there she sees the demons who lie in wait to trap any examples of perfection among human beings. While climbing aloft, she ponders the reason behind disturbances of the atmosphere, that is, where wind comes from, and what its nature is; what thunder and lightning are; what the rainbow is; and likewise about other phenomena. She also considers the nature of the planets.

But since the horses, who represent the five senses, were unable to reach such a height, Reason remained behind with four horses, while Prudence on one horse, namely the horse of hearing, climbed higher with Theology as her guide. When she had almost reached the heaven of the Trinity, she fell into a trance, but was restored to consciousness after Faith had intervened and helped her. She now saw, reflected in a mirror, the Father, Son, and Holy Spirit, and asked for the soul [i.e. the soul for Antirufinus]. This she was given, and descended with it carefully, avoiding the vicinity of any planet from which the soul might pick up infection.

Prudence then returned, and was joyfully welcomed by the Virtues. Thus was completed that perfect man, to whom each Virtue gave a gift. Generosity gave generosity, and so on with all the others. Then the Vices from the infernal regions were unleashed, and rose against Antirufinus, but were opposed by each of the opposite Virtues in turn, and thwarted. Thanks be to God.

WHEN THE POWERFUL THUNDERBOLT SCORNS TO UNFOLD ITS POWERS UPON THE TWIG [Prologue, 1]. In this prologue, of which the literal meaning is clear enough, the author says that in this work the emblem (*emblema*) of the celestial theophany resounds.[180] 'Emblem', properly speaking, means a piece of gold. Here the emblem denotes the golden rule of theology, so-called from its exalted position.

II. WHAT IS THEOPHANY?

Here [in the *Anticlaudianus*] theophany is called theology.[181] But John Scotus [Erigena] defines theophany as follows: 'Theophany arises from consequential signs (*signa*) and not from substantive natures; it is vouch-safed to minds that are cleansed of images; it is the pure and reciprocal manifestation of the origin which is above essence and has the power of delimiting'.[182]

But lest we should seem to be explaining the unknown by means of something even more mysterious, we must consider how this definition ought to be understood. For theophany means 'vision of God', *theos* in Greek being 'God' in Latin, and *phanes*, 'vision'.[183] The various terms used in defining this word seem to restrict it to the vision of God which the angels have.

So, we must note that sometimes information about the effect of something may be obtained from its cause, while sometimes a knowledge of the effect provides us with information about the cause. We know about an eclipse of the sun, because the moon comes between us and the sun. Likewise, we know that the moon has been interposed between us and the sun because we see that the sun is in eclipse. Similarly, in medicine the salient feature of a man's disposition is shown to be rooted in his physical temperament, or else his physical temperament is determined by the most prominent feature of his disposition (*ingenium*). When the effect is known by means of the cause, that is, when we have knowledge of things through their substantial natures, then the manifestation of that thing is effected through substantive kinds.[184] Philosophy, which discusses things, has this

---

[180] *Alain de Lille: Anticlaudianus*, ed. R. Bossuat, p. 56.

[181] An inference; cf. the *summarium* (ed. Bossuat, p. 201).

[182] The rest of Ralph's prologue consists of an explication of this statement, which is not to be found in the extant works of John Scotus Erigena. Alan of Lille himself uses the passage in his *Quoniam homines*, ed. Gloricux, p. 282, his *Expositio prosae de angelis*, ed. d'Alverny, *Textes inédits*, p. 205, and again in the *Hierarchia Alani*, ibid., p. 208 (here not attributed to Erigena). The same passage appears ſin Simon of Tournai's *Sententiae*, ibid., p. 307. For the rendering of 'ex substantificis geniis' as 'from substantial natures' cf. Alan's own gloss to that effect in his *Quoniam homines*, p. 282; cf. d'Alverny, p. 205 n. 36. In the *Hierarchia Alani*, *genius* is explained as 'nature, or the God of nature' (ed. d'Alverny, p. 228).

[183] Cf. *Quoniam homines*, p. 282.

[See opposite page for n. 184]

sort of manifestation. But when the cause is made known by means of the effect, as it were through the outward signs which are consequent on it, then that is manifestation through consequential signs. Theophany has this manifestation. So, at the very beginning of [John Scotus'] description of theophany we read: 'arising from consequential signs and not substantive natures'. Here, therefore, is a clear difference between philosophy and theophany.[185]

They differ in this respect also. Philosophy descends from the intellect to sensation, for it begins with the intellect and descends to sensory experience of things. So the expert in physics first of all knows in his mind whether or not pepper is hot, and only later proves through the senses that this is so. But theophany begins from sensation and moves towards the intellect. For when we see the beauty, immensity and order of the universe we come to know God, not fully but in part. Intellect finds its highest expression among the angels.[186] There follows: 'minds cleansed from images', that is, from products of the imagination. For, as Boethius says in his book *On the Trinity*, when we contemplate God, we must not be side-tracked to images as the anthropomorphic worshippers were, who believed that God was distinguished with all the features of a human body, and was surrounded by angels as by a kind of army.[187]

After that follows: 'of the origin which is above essence and has the power of delimiting'. For God is called 'the origin', because from Him all things are assigned their individual natures. That origin 'has the power of delimiting' because through God each thing is delimited within a class of things according to its substantial attributes. 'Above essence', because the divine superior being (*hyperousia*) surpasses all substance, without sharing its changeable nature. There follows: 'the pure (*simplex*) and reciprocal manifestation'.[188]

III. HOW MANY WAYS ARE THERE OF SEEING GOD?

Here it should be noted that there are many ways of seeing God.[189] For sometimes we grasp the [overall] moving cause of the universe by means of things unseen. Such a theophany, that is, a vision of God, is a

[184] Reading 'genera', as in Sulowski's edition, p. 23. But note that in the corresponding passage in Alan's *Expositio prosae de angelis* the word is 'genia'.

[185] With this whole passage cf. *Expositio*, ed. cit., p. 205; with the passage on the sun in eclipse cf. *Quoniam homines*, ed. cit., p. 282.   [186] Cf. *Expositio*, p. 205.

[187] Cf. Boethius, *De Trinitate*, iv, in *Theological Tractates*, ed. Stewart–Rand–Tester, pp. 16–24. Cf. also *Expositio*, pp. 205–6; *Quoniam homines*, p. 283; also Alan's *Theologicae regulae*, xxxv (PL ccx. 638A), and the important discussion by d'Alverny, p. 206 n. 40.

[188] Cf. *Expositio*, p. 206; *Quoniam homines*, pp. 282–3.

[189] The following discussion is a gloss on Erigena's phrase 'the pure and reciprocal manifestation'. Here, as elsewhere, Ralph's *distinctio* disrupts the sequence of the commentary. Ralph's gloss on the *modus videndi Deum* largely follows Alan's *Expositio*, pp. 203–4; cf. also *Quoniam homines*, p. 283.

composite one because it originates in that [overall] cause, which is composite. For example, a vision of a corporeal object is in a sense a composite one. For when the beam of sight is directed so as to see a corporeal object, it is diffused over the various parts of the body which it strikes.

There is another composite kind of vision by which we may behold God, that of reason. For when we are guided to an understanding of God by our reason we gaze upon the natures of God's creatures in so far as those natures are inherent in their subjects, and our reason concerns itself with the composite formed by their form and substance. Here again this theophany is in some sense a composite one, because it is the [overall] compounding cause which provides it [i.e. this kind of theophany] with its origin.

But the angels do not see God by means of such theophanies as these, but through a pure, uncompounded (*simplex*) theophany. For God is in every respect a simple being, and far removed from anything that is composite. Since the vision of God enjoyed by the angels is understood to be explicit (*expressiva*) and face to face,[190] the word 'reciprocal' is added. For that which is presented directly to the vision is said to be seen in a reciprocal way. But when we comprehend one thing through the medium of another, that is called a vision obtained through images (*immaginaria visio*);[191] for instance, if we can form an impression of a mother's beauty from looking at her son, and when we see the invisible qualities of God by means of those things which have been created and are visible.

[190] Cf. 1 Cor. 13: 12: 'We see now through a glass in a dark manner: but then face to face. Now I know in part: but then I shall know even as I am known' (Douay Bible).
[191] On later notions concerning 'imaginary vision' see the discussion and references in A. J. Minnis, 'Langland's Ymaginatif and Late-Medieval Theories of Imagination', *Comparative Criticism*, iii (1981), 92–5, 102–3.

V

The Dionysian Imagination:
Thomas Gallus and Robert Grosseteste

IN a single passage in his novel *The Name of The Rose*, Umberto Eco manages to allude to a great many of the thought-patterns and problems which medieval scholars found in the works of Pseudo-Dionysius, a Neoplatonic Monophysite of *c.*500, who successfully passed himself off as the 'Dionysius the Areopagite' whose conversion by St Paul is recorded in Acts 17: 34. Eco's character William of Baskerville has remarked that 'in sermons, to touch the imagination of devout throngs it is necessary to introduce exempla, not infrequently jocular';[1] this argument also serves to justify the monstrous images sometimes produced by manuscript illuminators. He proceeds to cite the testimony of Pseudo-Dionysius and his great twelfth-century commentator Hugh of Saint Victor:

'But as the Areopagite teaches', William said humbly, 'God can be named only through the most distorted things. And Hugh of St Victor reminded us that the more the simile becomes dissimilar, the more the truth is revealed to us under the guise of horrible and indecorous figures, the less the imagination is sated in carnal enjoyment, and is thus obliged to perceive the mysteries hidden under the turpitude of the images . . .'[2]

The opposing viewpoint is put forcibly by 'Jorge of Burgos',[3] who will turn out to be the villain of the piece, the narrow-minded monk who is attempting to suppress the second book of Aristotle's *Poetics*, a treatise on comedy (now lost, if it ever existed):[4] 'the man who depicts monsters and portents of nature to reveal the things of God per speculum et in aenigmate', he argues, 'comes to enjoy the very nature of the monstrosities he creates and to delight in them', thus warping his conception of God and creation alike.[5] There in a nutshell is the very essence of the challenge presented by Pseudo-Dionysius. The present chapter will illustrate how two of his most avid thirteenth-century readers, Thomas Gallus (Abbot of St Andrew's, Vercelli, 1219–46) and Robert Grosseteste (Bishop of Lincoln, 1235–53), warmly supported the ideas which Eco put in the mouth of William of Baskerville, while taking some note of the objections of the Jorges of their world.

In the twelfth century, Hugh of Saint-Victor had commented (twice) on *The Celestial* (or *Angelic*) *Hierarchy*, and Dionysian ideas appear in the writings of such figures as Richard of Saint-Victor, Alan of Lille, and Simon of

---

[1] Umberto Eco, *The Name of the Rose*, tr. W. Weaver (London, 1983), p. 79.

[2] Ibid., p. 80.

[3] In his *Reflections on 'The Name of the Rose'*, tr. W. Weaver (London, 1985), Eco assures us that the obvious pun on the name Jorge Borges was not meant to imply any criticism of the Argentinian writer.

[4] An attempt to recover Aristotle's views on comedy has recently been made by R. Janko, *Aristotle on Comedy: Towards a Reconstruction of Poetics II* (London, 1984).

[5] *The Name of the Rose*, p. 80.

Tournai; in the thirteenth century the Dionysian corpus was studied at the emergent University of Paris alongside the recently recovered works of Aristotle. Albert the Great and Thomas Aquinas wrote commentaries on the Pseudo-Areopagite and frequently quoted him, and he exercised a strong influence on thinkers like Alexander of Hales, Bonaventure, Ulrich of Strasburg, and Henry of Ghent, to name but a few (see Ch. VI).[6] But Gallus and Grosseteste were the greatest scholars of Dionysius of their day (the 1230s and 1240s).[7] Their similarities of approach and interpretation are remarkable, even though there is no clear evidence of direct literary influence of the one on the other. They seem, at least, to have encouraged each other to greater efforts in this sphere. A letter to Gallus by Grosseteste's friend Adam Marsh has been taken by D. A. Callus as evidence of an exchange of commentaries: Marsh sent Gallus a copy of Grosseteste's expositions of *The Celestial Hierarchy*, among other things, and requested on Grosseteste's behalf a copy of Gallus' *Extractio* on *The Mystical Theology*.[8] Indeed, Callus has tentatively suggested that the two scholars' acquaintance may have begun during the period *c.* 1209– *c.* 1218 when Gallus—then a Canon of Saint-Victor—was lecturing on theology in Paris at Sainte-Geneviève.[9] And Gallus' interest in Dionysius went back to those years, as he tells us himself.[10]

Gallus, who continued and developed many of the intellectual traditions of

[6] The scholarship is vast; see esp. H. F. Dondaine, *Le Corpus dionysien de l'Université de Paris au XIIIe siècle* (Rome, 1953); H. Weisweiler, 'Die Ps.-Dionysiuskommentare *In coelestem hierarchiam* des Skotus Eriugena und Hugos von St. Viktor', *RTAM* xix (1952), 26–47; Chenu, *Toward Understanding St Thomas*, pp. 226–30, 232; J. B. Bougerol, 'Saint Bonaventure et le pseudo-Denys l'Aréopagite', *Études franciscaines: Actes du colloque Saint Bonaventure, 9—12 Sept. 1968, Orsay*, xviii, supplément annuel (1968), 33–123. For extensive bibliography and summaries of modern scholarship see B. Faes de Mottoni, *Il 'Corpus Dionysianum' nel Medioevo: Rassegna di studi 1900–1972* (Pubblicazioni del Centro di studio per la storia della storiografia filosofica III, Bologna, 1977).

[7] On Thomas Gallus' life and works see the series of articles by G. Théry in *Divus Thomas*, xi (1934), 264–77, 365–85, 469–96; *Vie spirituelle*, supplements to vols. xxxi (1932), 147–67, xxxii (1932), 22–43, and xxiii (1932), 129–54; *AHDLMA* xii (1939), 141–208; also D. A. Callus, 'An Unknown Commentary on the Pseudo-Dionysian Letters', *Dom. Stud.* i (1949), 58–67. The most comprehensive study of his thought is J. Walsh, '*Sapientia Christianorum*: The Doctrine of Thomas Gallus, Abbot of Vercelli, on Contemplation' (unpub. D.Theol. thesis, Pontificia Universitas Gregoriana, Rome, 1957); cf. the summary provided by Rosemary A. Lees, *The Negative Language of the Dionysian School of Mystical Theology: An Approach to The Cloud of Unknowing* (Analecta Cartusiana CVII, Salzburg, 1983). See further R. Javelet, 'Thomas Gallus et Richard de Saint-Victor mystiques', *RTAM* xxix (1962), 206–33, xxx (1963), 88–121, and the introduction to *Thomas Gallus: Commentaires du Cantique des cantiques*, ed. Jeanne Barbet (Textes philosophiques du moyen âge XIV, Paris, 1967). On Grosseteste's Dionysian scholarship see especially U. Gamba, 'Roberto Grossatesta traduttore e commentatore del *De mystica theologia* dello pseudo-Dionigi Areopagita', *Aevum* xviii (1944), 100–32; F. Ruello, 'La *Divinorum nominorum reseratio* selon Robert Grosseteste et Albert le Grand', *AHDLMA* xxxiv (1959), 99–197; J. McEvoy, *The Philosophy of Robert Grosseteste* (Oxford, 1982), pp. 69–123.

[8] 'The Date of Grosseteste's Translations and Commentaries on Pseudo-Dionysius and the Nicomachean Ethics' *RTAM* xiv (1947), 186–210.

[9] Ibid., pp. 199–200.

[10] In the prologue to his *Extractio* in *Dionysiaca: Recueil donnant l'ensemble des traductions latines des ouvrages attribués au Denys l'Aréopagite*, ed. P. Chevallier (Paris, 1937), i, p. cix; cf. Callus, 'The Date of Grosseteste's Translations', pp. 190–1, 200.

the twelfth-century school of Saint-Victor,[11] carried out his major work on Dionysius between 1232 and 1244. First came a cursory exposition (the *Glossa*) of *The Celestial Hierarchy* and *The Mystical Theology*; next he wrote an *Extractio*, or paraphrase, of *The Celestial Hierarchy*, *The Ecclesiastical Hierarchy*, *The Divine Names*, *The Mystical Theology*, and two of the letters; then an *Explanatio*, or full commentary, on the four main Dionysian works. The text he used was the translation which John the Saracen had made around 1167. By contrast, Grosseteste made new translations as well as commentaries, and his standards were exceptionally high. He worked from a Greek text, duly corrected with the aid of 'helpers', and conducted a comparative study of the three already existing translations, those of Hilduin, John Scotus Erigena, and the Saracen. Within the period 1239–43 *The Celestial Hierarchy* came first, next *The Ecclesiastical Hierarchy*, then *The Divine Names*, and finally *The Mystical Theology*. He also translated the so-called *Scholia of St Maximus*.[12] In the prologue to his commentary on *The Celestial Hierarchy* Grosseteste announces his intention to preserve 'the intention of the author and the beauty of his style';[13] James McEvoy has praised his 'effort at total recovery of the alien medium': 'the reader is never allowed to forget that he is studying a text emanating from a foreign language, with all its irreducible specificity of syntax and semantics; he may not relax as though he were in his native culture'.[14] But the standard Parisian collection of *Dionysiaca* long maintained its dominant position. Grosseteste's scholarship was far too extensive and subtle for many readers, and thirteenth-century theologians, 'being more intent upon what they felt to be of eternal value in their authorities than upon investigating the history of doctrines, preferred the easier and more westernized body of comment' which depended upon the Saracen translation,[15] including the work of Gallus. It was 'Vercellensis' who influenced those masterpieces of affective piety, Hugh of Balma's *Viae Sion lugent* and Bonaventure's *Itinerarium mentis in Deum*, and Middle English works by the author of *The Cloud of Unknowing*, including the *Cloud* itself.[16]

[11] See especially Endre von Ivánka, 'Zur Überwindung des neuplatonischen Intellektualismus in der Deutung der Mystik: *Intelligentia* oder *Principalis Affectio*', in *Platonismus in der Philosophie des Mittelalters* (Darmstadt, 1969), pp. 147–60, and Javelet, op. cit.

[12] J. S. McQuade, 'Robert Grosseteste's Commentary on the "Celestial Hierarchy" of Pseudo-Dionysius the Areopagite: An Edition, Translation, and Introduction to his Text and Commentary' (unpub. Ph.D. thesis, The Queen's University of Belfast, 1961), p. 9; McEvoy, *Philosophy of Grosseteste*, pp. 69–70, 75.

[13] Cit. D. A. Callus, 'Robert Grosseteste as Scholar', in id. (ed.), *Robert Grosseteste: Scholar and Bishop* (Oxford, 1955), p. 58.

[14] McEvoy, *Philosophy of Grosseteste*, pp. 84–5.

[15] Ibid., p. 89. Neither St Bonaventure nor St Thomas Aquinas ever made use of it, nor (apparently) did Gerard d'Abbeville or Henry of Ghent. In Oxford, 'it made its way slowly': Richard Rufus of Cornwall and John Pecham used John the Saracen's version or Gallus' *Extractio*. However, Thomas of York knew it, as did early 14th-c. Franciscans in whose library Grosseteste's writings were preserved, and John Wyclif valued it. See Callus, 'Grosseteste as Scholar', pp. 60–1; McEvoy, *Philosophy of Grosseteste*, p. 89 n. 62.

[16] See von Ivánka, '*Intellectus* oder *Principalis affectio*', pp. 147–8, 150; Walther Völker, *Kontemplation und Ekstase bei Pseudo-Dionysius Areopagita* (Wiesbaden, 1958), pp. 231–7; F. Ruello, 'Statut et rôle de l'*intellectus* et de l'*affectus* dans la *Théologie mystique* de Hughes de Balma', in

Since 'the Blessed Dionysius uses an obscure style in all his books', to quote Thomas Aquinas,[17] we offer the following breakdown of several major Dionysian ideas as received by his medieval readers.

1. *'Reductive' and 'Anagogic' Imagery.* The function of the sacred imagery found in Holy Scripture is to manifest the heavenly orders to us in figures (*figurae*), formations (*formationes*), forms (*formae*), images (*imagines*), notes (*notae*), significations (*significationes*), signs (*signa*), symbols (*symbola*) and veils (*velamina*), to cite some of the vocabulary used by Gallus and Grosseteste.[18] The human mind cannot think without the images or phantasms which the imagination produces (as Aristotle said),[19] and hence scriptural symbolism is a mark of God's infinite condescension and goodness to His creatures. For our benefit the divine ray is enveloped in veils and figures, visible beauties being made to reflect the invisible beauties of heaven, sweet sensory odours being used as emblems of the intelligible teaching, and material lights serving as a likeness of the gift of immaterial enlightenment (see *The Celestial Hierarchy*, ch. i).[20] Richard of Saint-Victor describes this 'analogical' signification (i.e. a manner of expression proportionate to human understanding) very well in a passage in his *Benjamin minor* in which he praises the way in which the Holy Scriptures make use of an imaginative style:

For they describe unseen things by the forms of visible things and impress them upon our memories by the beauty of desirable forms. Thus they promise a land flowing with milk and honey; sometimes they name flowers or odours and describe the harmony of celestial joys either by human song or by the harmony of bird-song. Read John's Apocalypse and you will find that the heavenly Jerusalem is often described as being adorned with gold and silver, pearls, and other precious gems. Yet we know that none of these things are in that place from which no good thing is absent. . . . And we can immediately imagine these things as we like. The imagination can never be more useful to the reason than when she ministers to it in this way.[21]

Kartäusermystik und -mystiker, i (Analecta Cartusiana LV, Salzburg, 1981), pp. 1–46; A. J. Minnis, 'The Sources of *The Cloud of Unknowing*: A Reconsideration', in M. Glasscoe (ed.), *The Medieval Mystical Tradition in England: Papers read at Dartington Hall, July 1982* (Exeter, 1982), pp. 63–75; 'Affection and Imagination in *The Cloud of Unknowing* and Hilton's *Scale of Perfection*', Traditio xxxix (1983), 324–50.

[17] *In De div. nom.*, pr. ii, in *S. Thomae Aquinatis in Librum B. Dionysii de divinis nominibus expositio*, ed. C. Pera (Turin and Rome, 1950), p. 1.

[18] On Grosseteste's vocabulary, cf. McEvoy, *Philosophy of Grosseteste*, pp. 362, 365, and the helpful 'Glossary of Some Important Terms' compiled by McQuade in the introduction to his thesis, pp. 125–33.

[19] Aristotle, *De anima*, iii. 7 (431ᵃ16–17); see William of Moerbeke's version as tr. K. Foster and S. Humphries, *Aristotle's De anima in the Version of William of Moerbeke and The Commentary of St Thomas Aquinas* (London, 1951), p. 442. Cf. Thomas Aquinas, *Summa theologiae* Ia qu. lxxxiv, art. 7, *sed contra*, and the important discussion by McEvoy, *Philosophy of Grosseteste*, pp. 354 ff.

[20] Cf. R. Roques, *L'Univers Dionysien: Structure hiérarchique du monde selon le Pseudo-Denys* (Paris, 1983), pp. 200–9. Several modern translations of *The Celestial Hierarchies* are available, notably *The Works of Dionysius the Areopagite*, tr. J. Parker (London, 1897–9), i. 1–66; *The Mystical Theology and The Celestial Hierarchies of Dionysius the Areopagite*, tr. from the Greek by the Editors of the Shrine of Wisdom (Fintry, Surrey, n.d.), pp. 21–68, and the excellent Greek/French parallel text edn. by R. Roques, G. Heil, and M. de Gandillac, *Denys l'Aréopagite, La Hiérarchie céleste* (Sources chrétiennes, lviii, 2nd edn., Paris, 1970).

[21] *Benjamin minor*, xv (PL cxcvi. 10D–11B), tr. C. Kirchberger, *Richard of St Victor: Selected*

Scriptural authors, then, frequently employed imaginations, which stimulate the imaginations of their readers.[22]

But the limits of *imagines* must be fully recognized: we should not remain at the level of symbols derived from the material world, or confuse them with the spiritual realities which they symbolize, since those realities are in themselves without distinct figure or form. To fail to make this transition is to run the risk of thinking, as the uneducated do, that the heavenly intellects actually have many feet and faces, or are formed with the brutishness of oxen, or the savageness of lions, the curved beaks of eagles, and so forth (a detailed explanation of such imagery is provided in ch. xv of *The Celestial Hierarchy*). The fact that all images must ultimately be left behind does not, however, render them worthless: on the contrary, they usefully work in an 'anagogic' and 'reductive' way (i.e. an elevating and transcending manner) to raise up the mind towards things which are simple (because uncompounded) and pure. 'Without material forms and figures, and without phantasms, we shall [eventually] contemplate the divine and intellectual beings,' comments Grosseteste, 'yet we shall not be able to attain to this contemplation unless we first use both the uplifting forms and material figures.'[23] In sum, the reason and the imagination, working together as mistress and handmaiden, are to be respected in the early stages in the soul's journey to God but rejected in the higher reaches of contemplation.

It was the suprarational nature of the very highest type of contemplation which most interested Gallus. He firmly placed the will above the intellect, and affection or love above reasoning of however elevated a kind.[24] In the prologue to his *Explanatio* on *The Mystical Theology*, Vercellensis explains that most of our knowledge, including our knowledge of God, is based on cognition of visible things and intellectual apprehension. This manner of thinking, and hence of writing, is used in most of the works of Dionysius himself, but in *The Mystical Theology* and some of his letters he propounded a more profound way of knowing God, a superintellectual method which was unknown to pagan philosophers. The pagans thought that the intellect was the highest cognitive power, but there is a power which exceeds the intellect, namely the 'principal affection', by which unique means the tip of the mind (*apex mentis*) may be united with God.[25] By *principalis affectio* is meant the purest and most sublime activity of the affection, rising to its utmost limits with the aid of divine grace, leaving far behind all corporeal involvement and earthly emotion. Similarly, Grosseteste identified the superior function of the mind as

Writings on Contemplation (London, 1957), pp. 92–3; cf. the discussion by Minnis, 'Affection and Imagination', pp. 343–5.

[22] The literary implications of such ideas are intimated, with reference to John Scotus Erigena's Dionysian scholarship, by P. Dronke, '*Theologia veluti quaedam poetria*: Quelques observations sur la function des images poétiques chez Jean Scot', in id., *The Medieval Poet and his World*, pp. 39–53.

[23] Commentary, ed. McQuade, p. 20.

[24] For discussion and references see Minnis, 'Affection and Imagination', pp. 329–31.

[25] *Explanatio mysticae theologiae*, pr., in London, British Library, MS Royal 8. 6. IV, fos. 42ʳ–43ʳ.

love (*amor*).[26] By contrast, in his commentary on *The Mystical Theology* (1255) Albert the Great expressed his belief in the essential superiority of the intellect in unitive experience,[27] while in the second part of his *Sum of Theology* (1269–72) Thomas Aquinas attempted to synthesize the functions of the *intellectus* and the *affectus* in a comprehensive theory of contemplation.[28] These differences of opinion clearly reflect the great thirteenth-century debate on whether theology was essentially intellectual or affective in nature, a subject treated in our Ch. VI.

The importance which the author of *The Cloud of Unknowing* afforded to love and affection places him firmly beside Gallus, whose glosses he had used in translating *The Mystical Theology*. Moreover, the Dionysian doctrine of 'anagogic' imagery provides the key to an understanding of the central paradox of the *Cloud*, the fact that it can at one and the same time attack the imagination as a faculty which ties down the mind to the mundane and also offer a rich abundance of imaginative language, the most splendid image being that of the cloud of unknowing itself.[29] Such is the way of the Dionysian imagination.

2. *Affirmation and Negation: Like and Unlike Symbols.* This brings us back to William of Baskerville's Dionysian defence of horrible and indecorous images, as quoted above. In ch. ii of *The Celestial Hierarchy* Dionysius made a distinction between two kinds of image, likeness, or similitude as employed by the authors of Scripture, namely, the 'like' or similar and the 'unlike' or dissimilar. In the first case, God is described in terms of, for instance, light and life.[30] Since these are immaterial qualities it seems right and fitting to refer to Him in this way; in the process we are affirming that God does possess such qualities, albeit in superlative degree. On the face of it, this would seem to be the best policy, for if heavenly things are designated by lowly figures, 'the angelic names may become objects of general derision', to quote Gallus. Dionysius' response is that like and similar imagery can be misleading, because we may lose sight of the great distance between each and every created thing, however noble and admirable, and its Creator. 'God's divinity far surpasses all substance and life', as Gallus' version of the argument puts it, 'so that no light can worthily represent it.' It is, therefore, much more appropriate to describe God in terms which signify not what He is but rather what He is not, as when He is called *in*visible, *in*definable, and *in*comprehensible. The negative way is better than the positive way, denial better than affirmation,

[26] See J. McEvoy, 'Robert Grosseteste's Theory of Human Nature, with the Text of his Conference *Ecclesia sancta celebrat*', *RTAM* xlvii (1980), 153. In this regard, McEvoy sees an 'identity of thought' between Gallus and Grosseteste.

[27] *S. Alberti Magni opera omnia*, ed. A. Borgnet (Paris, 1890–9), xiv. 832, 834, 837; cf. Volker, *Kontemplation und Ekstase*, pp. 241–45.

[28] *Summa theologiae*, IIa IIae, qu. clvii. 2.

[29] On this paradox see Minnis, 'Affection and Imagination', pp. 337–50, and J. A. Burrow, 'Fantasy and Language in *The Cloud of Unknowing*', in id. *Essays on Medieval Literature* (Oxford, 1984), pp. 132–47.

[30] For an interesting attempt to relate scholastic light-metaphysics to Dante see J. A. Mazzeo, *Medieval Cultural Tradition in Dante's Comedy* (Ithaca, NY, 1960), pp. 56–132; cf. id., *Structure and Thought in the Paradiso* (Ithaca, NY, 1958), pp. 141–66.

and unlike images better than like ones. When God is referred to as an ointment, a stone, a wild beast, or indeed a worm, the mind is not allowed to rest
there, but stimulated to remove all material qualities from its thinking about
God, since the corporeal analogies used in these symbols are so obviously dissimilar to and remote from God. Even those who can easily believe that 'the
heavenly beings have the glitter of of gold, or shine with the splendour of the
fire and sun', will baulk at the notion that 'other celestial beings are like horses
or cattle or lions or some other such creatures',[31] Grosseteste explains. 'By the
evidence of their materiality and corruptibility [they] most manifestly cry out
that they are not the divine beings, but very far removed from them and very
unlike them.'[32] Such imagery may surprise by its ugliness but it will not
deceive.

Images like light and life are the highest and most similar kind used in the
Bible, while those like the stone and the worm are classed as 'the lowest of
forms'; 'middle' or intermediate images include fire and water. To these
categories Grosseteste adds that of imagery which has no basis in nature, such
as the traditional symbols of the Four Evangelists:

But not only are the teachers of the sacred Scriptures accustomed to signify the intelligible beings by corporeal forms which exist simply in the natural world, but they do so
in compositions such as do not exist in nature. For there is no animal in nature which
has four faces, nor an ox, or a man or a lion, with wings, and so on with such things as
are frequently ⟨found⟩ in Scripture.[33]

But it was Dionysius' clear preference for dissimilar imagery which his medieval readers found hardest to accept. Deferring to his great *auctoritas* they
allowed him his view, but tended to intrude the Pauline–Augustinian emphasis on the positive connections between creatures and Creator. 'For the
invisible things of Him, from the creation of the world, are clearly seen, being
understood by the things that are made: his eternal power also and divinity'
(Rom. 1: 20).[34] Or, as Alan of Lille puts it so memorably, 'Every creature in the
world is like a book and a picture to us, and a mirror; a faithful representation
of our life, our death, our condition, our end.'[35] Dionysius had justified his
attitude to unlike symbols with the declaration of Gen. 1 that everything God
created was good. Grosseteste extends this with the Augustinian notion of
vestigia, the imprints which God has left in His creation:

So that which participates in the Good, to the extent that it does so is, *per se*, a certain
imprint and a very distant imitation of the Good. And therefore every lower creature, in
so far as it is good and bears an imprint of the first goodness, proximate to it, suitably
figures that which is *per se* good, namely God . . .[36]

But, according to this same theory, the higher the creature the more clearly it
will display its divine mark. Here Grosseteste is, as McEvoy has pointed out,

[31] Commentary, ed. McQuade, pp. 70–1.
[32] Ibid., p. 65.   [33] Ibid., p. 21.
[34] The significance of this passage for medieval discussions of imagination and imagery is
discussed by Minnis, 'Langland's Ymaginatif', pp. 88 ff.
[35] PL ccx. 579 B; cf. Evans, *Alan of Lille*, p. 151.
[36] Commentary, ed. McQuade, p. 72.

making provision for a blend of *via positiva* and *via negativa* which seeks the
best of both worlds: the relative nobility of like symbols may be enjoyed, even
though these comparisons must subsequently be denied in respect of the
unknown God, who is inaccessible through even the most precious things
which creation has to offer.[37] And in modification of this kind we may detect
the spirit of Jorge.[38]

3. *Concealing yet Manifesting Veils.* There was a second Dionysian defence of
scriptural imagery, particularly that derived from ugly and base things. Not
only is figurative writing proportionate to human capacities, 'it is most befitting to the mystic Scriptures to conceal by means of hidden and sacred enigmas and to keep inaccessible to the many the sacred and secret truth of the
supermundane intellects, for not everyone is holy, nor, as the Scriptures say,
does knowledge belong to all' (Grosseteste).[39] 'The unworthy, who despise
descriptions couched in such lowly terms, . . . do not follow them up', declares
Gallus, whereas in the case of the worthy few such imagery agitates the mind
to struggle towards an understanding of heavenly things. The figures and veils
in Holy Scripture, therefore, at once conceal and manifest, depending on the
disposition and proficiency of the reader.[40] Grosseteste elucidates this point
most pleasingly with the metaphor of a book which the illiterate layman perceives only as a series of strokes, whereas the educated reader perceives letters
which represent elements of sound:

. . . the altogether ignorant layman not knowing what a book is or what sort of thing it is
or the nature and purpose of letters, on finding a book and looking in it, sees only the
various strokes of the letters, not imagining or understanding through these series anything other than the strokes themselves. Hence the series of letters are the manifestation
of nothing else to him, but rather his looking at them is only a hiding of the other things
from him. But one who knows that the strokes which he sees are letters, knows that they
signify something else, understanding by the letter the proper figure of each one, and of
what simple sound it is the sign; through the visible figure the audible element is
imagined and the visible figure is the manifestation to him of the audible element. Thus
every sign, considered as a sign, leads the mind of the one who considers it to the appre-
hending of some other thing through it, but the thing considered, in so far as it is a thing
on its own and not a sign, does not lead the mind of the one considering it to the apprehension of anything else, but rather hides the other things from his apprehension for a
time. There is nothing, then, to stop the same thing being a manifestation of something
to one and the concealment of the same thing to another.[41]

To the initiated Dionysius offers, in ch. xv of *The Celestial Hierarchy*, a
masterly 'decoding' of the symbolism used of angels in the Bible. It is carefully
explained why they are described in terms of fire, winds, and cloud, as

[37] McEvoy, *Philosophy of Grosseteste*, pp. 96–8, 365–6.
[38] Cf. the discussion of how, in scholastic notions of analogy, Dionysian and Aristotelian
elements are reconciled, in Mazzeo, *Medieval Cultural Tradition*, pp. 13–55.
[39] From Grosseteste's translation of *The Celestial Hierarchy*, ch. ii, ed. McQuade, p. 46. Cf.
1 Cor. 8: 7.
[40] As Grosseteste puts it, 'somehow the sacred veils, to some, are manifestations of the
thing veiled under them, but to others they are concealments' (Commentary, ed. McQuade,
p. 50).
[41] Ibid., pp. 50–1. Cf. the discussion by McEvoy, *Philosophy of Grosseteste*, pp. 360 ff.

possessing human form, emotions, and senses, as being unshod, clothed, and bathed in light, and carrying weapons and material instruments, and being associated with rivers, wheels, and chariots. Whatever the status of these images may be, whether they are low, intermediate, or high, not one of them is used without good reason. Never has the human imagination, that mental faculty which the author of *The Celestial Hierarchy* was so concerned to transcend, received more elaborate and efficient rationalization.

If, in the later Middle Ages, Aristotle established the importance of imagination in psychology and epistemology, it was Dionysius who, more than any other single authority, assured its position in theology.[42]

THOMAS GALLUS

Extraction of *The Celestial Hierarchy*: Chapters i, ii, and xv[43]

CHAPTER i

Every benefit given to us in the form of natural things, and every gift which perfects nature, is from on high, coming into being from the eternal Father who begets that light which is most simple in its nature, and yet supremely manifold in the way in which it operates. The universal light, which comes from the Father, not only admits the heavenly intelligences to a share and participation in knowledge of itself, but also comes to us through the distribution of its bounty, and again so fills us with itself, like some unifying power, that it separates us out from the lowest [part of nature], raises us from it to a longing for and knowledge of itself and, removing everything that distracts the mind, points us towards the unity of the eternal Father who gathers together the dispersed ones of Israel, and towards the simplicity which to some extent makes us like that God who is supremely simple.

So, since we must be made perfect by this light, which has but one name, let us with most chaste prayers call upon Jesus, who is the light from the Father which exists in truth, and is the true light 'which illumines every human being who comes into this world' [John 1: 9], 'through whom we have access to the Father' [Rom. 5: 2], the creator of all light. Thus, being first of all illuminated inwardly by our Lord Jesus Christ Himself, we may then view, in so far as this is possible to us, the anagogical illuminations of the Holy Scriptures handed down to us by the holy

---

[42] And it should be noted that Dionysian ideas continued to be influential long after the end of the Middle Ages. See especially E. H. Gombrich's discussion of their importance in Renaissance Art Theory in *Symbolic Images: Studies in the Art of the Renaissance* (London, 1972; repr. 1975), pp. 150ff.

[43] Tr. from *Dionysiaca*, ed. Chevallier, ii. 1043–7, 1062–6, with the permission of Desclée de Brouwer et Cie.

Fathers, and afterwards may contemplate (as far as we are able) the angelic hierarchies made manifest to us by those illuminations through anagogical symbols (*signa*).

Thus, having taken in with perceptive powers which are pure and strengthened by exercise the pre-eminent (or rather supremely pre-eminent) gift of God the father of light, which reveals to us the most blessed hierarchies of angels through the figurative symbols (*formalia signa*) of the Scriptures, may we finally, as a result of sharing in that light, be elevated to the undivided contemplation of that simple ray of light of the Father, that is, the Word of wisdom which shines eternally from the Father Himself.

That ray, though it pours itself in various ways into many people, is nevertheless never deprived of its own, single [i.e. undivided] unity. It communicates itself in many ways to achieve the raising and unifying oneness [with God] of the elect (according as befits its own bounty). Yet it remains fixed singularly within itself, its own identity remaining unchanged, and stretches down to those who have turned towards it, and are striving towards it according as they are able, according to the capacity of each, and unifies them with itself through its own simplified imitation of other things.[44]

For the divine, supreme ray cannot shine down upon us in this life unless it has been veiled with various veils consisting of sensible forms, as is fit and expedient to our being raised up, and by God's providence has been made like those things which are known to us by virtue of our nature and familiarity to us. So God's holy ordinance, which is the beginning of perfection, has deemed it right to make our most hallowed hierarchy an imitator, in heavenly terms, of the hierarchies of angels, and has described the actual angelic hierarchies, which have in themselves no material form, in Holy Scripture, using various material figures and figurative compositions, so that we, so far as each of us is able, through these hallowed signs, consisting in sensible forms, may be led back to the contemplation of the supernal virtues, which are simple, and which cannot be given any shape, and always remain the same.

For it is not possible for our mind to be uplifted to that immaterial imitation and contemplation of the heavenly hierarchies, unless that same mind, in line with its present blindness, employs the guidance of material figures. It then realizes, through a kind of inner realization, that beauties which are accessible through the senses are images of invisible beauty,[45] and that fragrances that please the senses are expressions of the distribution of fragrance which cannot be sensed,[46] and that material lights are

---

[44] In Parker's translation from the Greek, ii. 2: '[the divine ray of light] raises, according to their capacity, those who lawfully aspire to it, and makes them one, after the example of its own unifying oneness'.

[45] Cf. e.g. Ps. 18.   [46] Cf. Num. 15: 3.

images of a light visible to the intellect,[47] and that an understanding of Holy Scripture achieved through the mind is an image of that all-embracing contemplation which sates men's minds. As [the psalmist] says: 'I shall be satisfied when Thy glory appears' [Ps. 16: 15]. It also realizes that the various arrangements of categories (*congregationes*) which are accessible to the senses, when set out in order, are the images of the arrangements and conditions which exist in the orders of heavenly beings, which are structured in imitation of God; and that partaking of the divine Eucharist[48] while on our [earthly] journey is an image of the full sharing in Christ, which is achieved to perfection in our [heavenly] homeland. It makes a similar consideration of certain other things, which in terms of the world above us correspond to heavenly substances, but are imparted to us in the Scriptures under the guise of forms accessible to the senses.

Therefore, in order that we may attain to this likeness (*assimilatio*) to God, according to the various capacities of mortals, the benevolent prince of all perfection, making manifest to us the heavenly hierarchies, and making our hierarchy (in so far as this lies within our capacity) work with them through a process of assimilation to God whereby they are made like God, has described the celestial intellects by using images accessible to the senses, in the figurative inventions of Holy Scripture. His purpose in so doing is to lead us through material images to a knowledge of intelligible things, and from signs or symbols described in common terms (*catholice*) to the contemplation and imitation of the supreme celestial hierarchies.

CHAPTER ii

So, before we treat of hierarchies in specific terms, we must first describe in generic terms what a hierarchy is—this will be done in the third chapter—and what advantage a hierarchy confers on whatsoever persons are within it and serve it. Then we must praise, in specific terms, the celestial hierarchies according to the testimony of Scripture appropriate to them. This will be done in the fourth and tenth chapters, which are to follow. Last of all, we must, in the fifteenth and final chapter, describe by what sensible forms and figures the celestial intelligences are designated in the Scriptures, and what is the nature of that simple truth to which we must be led back through those forms and symbols. This is in order that we do not, as do many others, foolishly think that those celestial intellects, made in God's image, have many feet, just because it is said in Ezekiel [1: 7]: 'their feet are straight', or that some have many faces, because it is said, again in Ezekiel [1: 6]: 'each one has four faces'; or that they take the forms of oxen or lions or eagles, according to the words of the same

[47] Cf. Luke 2: 9.   [48] Cf. 1 Cor. 10: 16–17.

prophet [1: 10]: 'And as for the likeness of their faces: there was the face of a man, and the face of a lion on the right side of all the four, and the face of an ox on the left side of all the four, and the face of an eagle over all the four', and likewise the words of Revelation [4: 6]: 'and in the midst of the throne, and round about the throne, were four living creatures full of eyes before and behind'; or that they have three sets of wings, as we read in Isaiah [6: 2]: 'the one had six wings and the other had six wings'; or imagine fiery wheels up in the sky, just because Daniel [7: 9] says: 'the wheels of it are like a burning fire'; and actual physical thrones, as being necessary for Almighty God to recline upon, because it also says in Daniel [7: 9]: 'thrones were placed and the Ancient of Days sat', and multicoloured horses, according to the prophetic revelation of Zechariah [6: 2 ff.], where he says: 'I saw by night, and behold a man riding upon a red horse . . . and behind him were horses, red, dappled, and white'; and 'princes of princes' wielding soldiers' lances,[49] because Ezekiel [23: 22, 23] says: 'Behold I will raise up . . . the prince of princes and their renowned horsemen.' That added phrase 'carrying lances' is not found in that passage of Scripture, but we read of such a lance in Job [16: 14]: 'He has compassed me about with his lances: he has wounded my loins: he has not spared', and in the Book of Wisdom [5: 21]: 'He will sharpen his severe wrath for a spear, and the whole world shall fight with him against the unwise.'

The same can be said of all the other things which are handed down to us in Holy Scripture through sensible forms, according to the various kinds of symbols (*signa*) which reveal the condition of the heavenly intellects. For theology [i.e. Scripture] skilfully (*artificiose*) uses forms that have been adapted to signify intellects which cannot be expressed in visual terms (as has been said), having consideration for the infirmity of our mind, and providing for itself [i.e. theology] a way of elevating that mind which is familiar to it and shares the same nature (as has been stated above), throwing upon our mind the reflection of the holy anagogical Scriptures.

It may occur to someone that it is indeed apt that heavenly things should be designated in Holy Scripture by sensible figures, since these heavenly things are, in their own essence, unknown to us, and cannot be contemplated by us, but on the other hand that it is inappropriate that they should be designated by figures of such a lowly sort, and that as a result of this the angelic names may become objects of general derision. Moreover, he may believe that theologians [i.e. scriptural authors] should designate these heavenly beings by the most precious kinds of creatures or bodies accessible to the senses, since these are closely akin and related to the angels themselves in some way or other by reason of their precious nature, in so far as sensible objects can be so related. He may consider

---

[49] Cf. Josh. 5: 13–14.

that one should not attribute to the heavenly intellects, which are simple and like God in form, forms of sensible objects which are lowly and inferior, because the other method seems to be more suited to our gaining a knowledge of heavenly things and to do greater honour to the heavenly intellects. Besides, the lowly nature of the figures used may perhaps lead readers into the error of thinking that the heavenly regions are filled with large numbers of lions, horses, and similar animals, and that God's praises arc sung there in the form of lowing, after the manner of oxen, and that angels fly there like birds, and that there are other beings and forms of matter there even lowlier than those mentioned above (as for instance heavenly things are designated by stones in Ezekiel [28: 14, 16] and Job [5: 23ff.],[50] and by verdant grass in Ezekiel [34: 14][51]). Therefore, any passages of Scripture which describe images of sensible things which are of this kind [i.e. lowly], and thus are unlike heavenly things, bring down and humble the heavenly objects to a condition that is ignoble and dishonourable, and subject to passions.

If anyone thinks in the terms I have just described, I reply to him as follows. An examination of the truth teaches us that theology, in using lowly figures, makes full provision to ensure that heavenly beings suffer no injury, and that the faithful are not led astray by thinking that there are ugly or lowly forms of matter in heaven. Invisible heavenly things are represented by visible and lowly things, not just in order that our mind (which cannot directly reach out to contemplate intelligible things, but needs to be elevated by the use of figures which are familiar and natural to it [i.e. the mind]) may be led by these [objects] to an understanding of heavenly things. But there is another reason, namely that while some of the figures, although of a lowly nature, illuminate the faithful, so that they attain to knowledge of things heavenly, their lowly appearance hides the divine truth from the wicked, lest that which is holy be given to dogs. For as the Apostle says: 'knowledge is not something possessed by all' [1 Cor. 8: 7].

It is clear that the lowly nature of sensible figures of this sort does no injury to heavenly things, but rather begets a truer appreciation of them, since there are two ways of representing the invisible attributes of God and any heavenly things. One is affirmative, employing attributes which are like, as when it is said: 'God is light' [1 John 1: 5]. But the other is, so to speak, negative, employing attributes which are unlike and incompatible in the extreme, and seem to be highly incongruous in relation to God.

Thus, that element of God's nature which is beyond substance, which the Scriptures refer to as his intellect or being (thus revealing in it a rationality and wisdom which is appropriate to it, and revealing too its true essence, which is the true cause of all things that exist), they also call

---

[50] Cf. Job 6: 12, 8: 17, 14: 19, 22: 24, 28: 2, 28: 6.
[51] Ezek. 34: 14 Vulg. 'ibi requiescent in herbis virentibus'.

'light' and 'life'. By these and similar epithets, epithets which are particularly honoured among all others, they signify that God's divinity surpasses all material things, even though those figures also fall far short of the truth. For God's divinity far surpasses all substance and life, so that no light can worthily represent it, but every mind and all reasoning falls far short of any likeness to it.

The other way of making known things divine or heavenly is by negation and the removal of dissimilar qualities, as when in the Scriptures He is called: 'Invisible, indefinable, incomprehensible.'[52] All these terms signify not what He is but what He is not. The second method is more effective in bringing us to a knowledge of God. For, as we have learned secretly from the teaching of the Apostles, nothing which exists or is capable of being understood can properly be said to be God. So, all attributes can be said truly and properly to be removed from Him, but nothing can properly be affirmed regarding Him. The second way is more appropriate, proceeding by negations which are more appropriate to God. For truly we know nothing of His immaterial, incomprehensible, and ineffable infinity, which exceeds unity itself.[53]

Therefore, since all attributes of God may truly and properly be denied and removed, and nothing can properly be affirmed about Him, it is much more appropriate that the hidden secrets of divinity should be revealed through more lowly and dissimilar [i.e. from God] forms that are accessible to the senses than through more precious ones. So, when Holy Scripture designates things heavenly and divine by more lowly forms, it honours rather than dishonours them, and shows thereby that they surpass all material things in a way that is on a higher plane than this world.

But I do not think that any prudent man would deny that dissimilar figures elevate our mind more effectively than similar ones. For the infirm mind could easily be led astray by figures in a more precious form, so that it ended up by thinking that some such object existed in the sky in literal terms: for instance, that there are bright and shining beings in human form, clothed most handsomely in the most splendid attire and emitting flames of fire, which neither burn nor are harmful,[54] just because it is said in Ezekiel [1: 13]: 'their appearance is as a fire of coals, etc.' The mind could similarly be deceived when it encounters precious figures based on similarity, such as are found in the Scriptures when heavenly intelligences are designated.

Therefore, lest those who know no higher beauty than that of sensible things fall victims to this deception, the holy theologians in their wisdom,

[52] Rom. 11: 33, 1 Tim. 6: 16.
[53] Parker: 'we do not know Its [i.e. the Godhead's] superessential, and inconceivable, and unutterable indefinability' (ii. 8).
[54] Cf. Ez. 8: 2, Dan. 7: 9, 2 Macc. 3: 25 ff., Matt. 28: 3, Mark 16: 5, Acts 1: 10, Rev. 4: 4.

elevating men's minds towards the heavenly, set themselves to use comparisons that are very unlike in designating heavenly things. Thus, they do now allow our mind, which is immersed in material things, to rest content with such images, but by the ugly nature of the images, they stir up and raise that power which our mind possesses of understanding heavenly things. For it does not seem correct or consistent with truth that images which are very material and so unprepossessing can properly be compared with things heavenly and divine.

Besides, there is another reason why heavenly things are appropriately designated by the more lowly corporeal creatures. For nothing is totally deprived of a share in goodness. For Scripture says: 'God saw all that He had made, and it was very good' [Gen. 1: 31]. So, the whole range of material objects can appropriately be drawn on to designate heavenly and divine things. However, intelligent beings possess in one way those qualities which are bestowed upon sensible beings in a very different way. For instance, the rage which is assigned to irrational beings has its origin in emotion grounded in the passions, and that raging emotion is replete with every kind of irrationality. But when the quality is assigned to intelligent beings it signifies their courageous discernment and unbreakable steadfastness in retaining unchanged those good qualities which make them like God. Likewise, desire, when it is assigned to irrational beings, is an ill-considered and materialistic emotion, directed towards some object which is sensually perceived, having its origin in natural emotion or habit, unrestrained, irrationally obtaining what is being sought after by the force of the bodily appetite, and driving the whole creature towards that which is desired in sensual terms. But when we assign desire to heavenly intelligences, we understand by this name the divine love of immaterial being which rises above [the capacity of] the mind, and that longing for divine contemplation which cannot change into any other feeling, and cannot give up any of the fervour which belongs to it, a contemplation which, going beyond all substance, aims only at the embrace of the Bridegroom; is never afflicted by any anxiety—as happens with the fleshly, sensual desires, the pursuit of which is filled with anxiety, while attainment (*satietas*) is attended by remorse—and aims at that divine, most pure and ultimate splendour, which allows those who have grasped it[55] no room for error, illuminating them by the very image (*species*) of truth; and aims too at that comeliness (*decor*) that is the full expression of the beauty of the true and eternal communion with God, who makes beautiful those who contemplate and love Him.[56] In the words of the text: 'All of us, looking upon the countenance of the Lord revealed to us, are transformed into that very image, from brightness to brightness, as if by the spirit of God' [2 Cor. 3: 18].

[55] Lat. 'comprehensores', meaning those who have received this divine love.
[56] Cf. Deut. 6: 5, Prov. 4: 6, Wisd. 8: 2 ff., and of course the Song of Songs, *passim*.

I say that that desire cannot be confined or abandoned because of its strength in respect of that which it seeks, and its unchangeable relationship towards that which no circumstance can cut short. For they [i.e. souls] yearn for God purely and with a single-minded devotion (*singulariter*), and nothing can draw them away or hold them back from His love. Because God is always one and the same, equally good and beautiful, and because He possesses in Himself in their purest form every desirable quality, such as wisdom, goodness, beauty, eternity and omnipotence, and is desirable in terms of all these things; therefore He draws to Himself fully, intimately, and irrevocably all longing for His uncomprehended qualities. Likewise, when we attribute to inanimate or irrational objects inability to feel sensation or inability to reason, we show that they are deprived of sensation or reason. But when we figuratively attribute these same qualities to heavenly substances, we show that they [i.e. the heavenly substances] lie beyond our power of sensation and our reason. For we investigate immaterial things using material means, and use the senses, which are completely alien to heavenly intelligences.

It follows then from what has been said that it is not incongruous to designate the heavenly intelligences (*mentes*) by using sensible figures, even if they are of the humblest sort. All things, even material objects and the humblest of all things that exist, originate in the truly good. Thus in all their properties they possess certain echoes and representations of beauty which can be appreciated by the intellect and beauty which is beyond its understanding.[57] It is possible through all these representations to be elevated to the level of the non-material originals (*archetypias*), which are the arguments (*rationes*) of the Word, or forms (*ideae*) or exemplars. These [I have spoken about] in the book about *The Divine Names*, not indeed in the same way but in very dissimilar terms, taking properties accessible to the senses from one place and another, properties which in respect of their incongruity with intellectual things may be attributed to intellectual things, and in respect of their congruence with sensible things may be attributed to sensible things.

We find in the Scriptures that divines not only attribute to angels sensible forms, as has been said, but sometimes attribute to the very Deity nobler forms, calling them[58] 'the sun of justice' [Mal. 4: 2], 'the morning star' [Num. 24: 17] which rises in the mind when a man is justified, and 'the light' because He shines in a way which can be grasped by the intellect and which is everlasting. So the psalmist says: 'O Lord, the light of thy countenance has been stamped upon us' [Ps. 4: 7], and again: 'In Thy light we shall see light' [Ps. 35: 10]. St John [1: 1] says: 'He was the true light which illuminates every man who comes into this world'.

---

[57] i.e. there are two kinds of beauty intimated here, that which can be appreciated by the human intellect (termed *intellectualis*) and that which is beyond human intelligence (*superintellectualis*).   [58] i.e. the nobler forms.

Sometimes they attribute to Him intermediate forms (*mediocres formas*), calling God a fire. Hence, in Deuteronomy [4: 24] we read: 'The Lord your God is a consuming fire', because He illuminates without injuring, whereas fire injures and burns. They attribute to Him also the quality of water, as we read in John [7: 38, 39]: 'Streams of living water will flow from His belly. This He said of the spirit which those who believed in Him should receive.' Daniel [7: 10] also says: 'A river flowed from His face', and in Ecclesiasticus [24: 41] we read: 'I am like the river Dorix and like a water-channel.' This is said because He fills minds with life-giving streams, just as water gives material life to plants. We will say more about all this below in the fifteenth chapter.

Sometimes they attribute to God the lowest of forms, as for instance ointment. So St John says in his first epistle [2: 27]: 'His anointing teaches us about all things'; and Ecclesiasticus [38: 7]: 'The perfumier will make the sweet confection', and in the psalm [44: 8] we read: 'The Lord your God has anointed you with the oil of gladness'; and in Acts [10: 38] St Peter says: 'God has anointed him with the Holy Spirit and with power.' They attribute to Him the nature of a corner-stone, as in Isaiah [28: 16], Job [38: 6], and in Acts [4: 11]. They attribute to Him the form of a wild beast, as for instance of a lion in Hosea [13: 8]: 'I will consume them as a lion', and of a panther, in the old translation, where we have 'the cub of a lion' [Hos. 5: 14], and of a leopard: 'Like the leopard on the road of the Assyrians I will rush at them, like a she-bear whose cubs have been snatched away from her' [Hos. 13: 7]. They even attribute to Him a form which seems to be lowlier than all the others, that of a worm, which the Lord attributed to Himself in the psalm [21: 7]: 'But I am a worm.'[59]

Thus all who know God and taste of Him, who read in Scripture all that is secretly implanted in it by the divine inspiration, readily distinguish in the said imagery[60] what is heavenly and divine from imperfect and unclean material objects by (as we have already said) applying in a different sense to heavenly things those attributes which on occasion fit things accessible to our senses. In so doing they place no slur on the heavenly things. Rather they honour them by describing them, using forms that are unlike them and lowlier in their nature, so that thus the truth may be hidden from the unworthy, who despise descriptions couched in such lowly terms, and do not care to follow them up, and may be revealed to the faithful who (as we have said) diligently seek it [i.e. the truth] using a comparison of sensible objects. Since they are eager to understand the significance of the figures used, they are not allowed to stop at the sensible forms as if these had to be understood in the literal sense, for the very ugliness of the forms repels them.

[59] See the interesting use of this image made by Petrarch, *Letters on Familiar Matters*, x. 4, tr. below, p. 413.
[60] Lat. 'in dictis formationibus'.

Therefore the theologians do honour to things divine by removing from them those attributes which can truly and properly be removed from them, when they call God invisible, infinite, and the like, and by comparing Him to the lowest order of sensible things because of the familiar echoes such comparisons evoke. Thus, it is not inappropriate or harmful to the divine intellects that they should be designated by sensible forms of lowly objects as described above. Indeed, the very ugliness of the forms by which angels are described in the Scriptures, by agitating our mind, leads us to enquire into a matter which is so ambiguous, and consequently elevates us through diligent investigation of the spiritual intelligence, an investigation to which we should not be led were such an occasion not presented to us. For the ugliness does not allow our mind to rest and be content with imagery which is so patently incompatible with the heavenly substances. On the contrary, it leads it on to struggle, through careful investigation, so that it may separate out from celestial things the desiring and passionate aspects of each sensible object, and may gradually become accustomed to be stretched through the comparison of sensible objects so that it achieves an understanding of heavenly things and the ability to contemplate them. All this I have said by way of preliminary to show that heavenly substances are properly and usefully designated in the Scriptures by the forms of things which are accessible to the senses and more lowly.

After that I must define hierarchy and show in what way each hierarchy helps the intelligences placed within it. May Christ, 'My Christ', if I may call Him such, who inspires the revelation of that hierarchy, aid this discourse of mine.

But you, Timothy my son, according to the teaching of the Apostles, hear these holy sayings, as is right for someone who has been made divine by being taught divine mysteries. Hide these holy secrets, which are simple in form (*tamquam uniformia*), from the ears and the knowledge of the impure multitude. For, according to our Lord's meaning, it is not lawful to scatter before swine the beauty of pearls visible or invisible [cf. Matt. 7: 6], a beauty which is pure and lustrous, and adds beauty to men's minds.

CHAPTER XV

For the rest, giving a pause to the eye of the intellect and our contemplation of the lofty state of angels, a state difficult to contemplate, let us consider the divisible angelic forms [set out] in the Scriptures through sensible symbols (*symbola*), and the variety of their many parts. Then let us once more cast our mind's eye back from them, as from images, to examine the singleness of heavenly minds through a comparison with sensible things.

Note first of all that, according to the descriptions in sensible terms in the Scriptures and their exposition in terms of the intellect, heavenly substances are sometimes shown to rule in a hierarchical way, and sometimes to be ruled in a hierarchical way, and the last of these [heavenly substances] rule others, and the first are ruled hierarchically, and these same [substances] have, in different respects, powers which are first, middle, and last. This fact does not introduce any idea of confusion among the angelic orders. There would indeed be confusion if we were to say that any heavenly substances were ruled hierarchically by those superior to them, and hierarchically ruled the same substances by which they themselves were ruled, or again [if we were to say] that any superior substances were to rule those inferior to themselves, and yet were also ruled hierarchically by them. But if we should say that some substances rule those inferior to them, and are ruled by those superior to themselves, there is nothing out of place in that.

Therefore, following upon this, in the Holy Scriptures it is correctly shown through descriptions of sensible objects that heavenly substances are, in different respects, said to participate in first, middle, and final powers, because they are stretched out in a reflective way towards superior substances and at the same time strongly turn in upon themselves, preserving their own powers, and proceed to make provision for inferior substances by giving them a share in their own power. This is true for all heavenly substances, but for some more fully, for others in a more partial way, as has often been remarked.

Then, when dealing with the mystical interpretations of sensible forms, we must first of all ask why Holy Scripture makes use of the properties of fire more than those of any other sensible form to designate things invisible. Thus Daniel [7: 9] describes fiery wheels, and Ezekiel [1: 4–5] animals all on fire, and Matthew [28: 3] men shining like fire, and Ezekiel again [1: 13] attributes heaps of coal to heavenly substances,[61] and in Daniel [7: 10] we read of a fiery stream rushing from God's face. And again we read there: 'His throne is a flame of fire' [Dan. 7: 9]. And Scripture shows that the highest order of intelligent being is burning, because it calls them Seraphim, and attributes to them, in the purification of Isaiah [6: 6–7], the properties and effects of fire. And altogether, in designating heavenly beings, of superior or inferior rank, Scripture does particular honour to the properties of fire. So, among all sensible things, I believe that fire is the most effective in representing heavenly and divine objects. For the being of God, which is of a higher order than substance, and cannot be given a shape,[62] is symbolized (*figuratur*) by fire in many places in Scripture. For fire has many properties which can designate invisible attributes of God, in so far as this can be done through sensible images. Thus in Deuteronomy [1: 33] and in Malachi [3: 2] God is called

[61] Cf. also Ezek. 10: 2.   [62] Lat. 'non formalis'.

'a fire'. Fire, an object accessible to the senses, is itself, in a hidden way, scattered through all substances which can be sensed, and penetrates through all of them, and yet is kept separate from all of them. Its effect is of brilliant light, but in itself[63] it is hidden and unknown, unless some substance is provided, acting through which it reveals its own effective working (*operatio*). Likewise, it cannot be contained by anything because of its mobility and fineness. Likewise, its substance is such that it cannot be seen with the eyes of flesh; it is superior to all the other elements; it introduces its action into those substances in which it is implanted; it varies (*variativus*); it can transmit itself to any things which approach it in any way; it can renew itself; it can illuminate with full, unveiled light (*incircumvelate*) it cannot be penetrated by human sight. It is pure, has powers of distinguishing (*discretivus*), is unchangeable, elevating, sharply penetrating, lofty, does not admit of any humiliating subordination, is always mobile, and mobile in the same way, causes other things to move, comprehends other things but is not totally comprehended by them, has need of nothing [external to itself], secretly increases its own power, and—acting in the material with which it is supplied—it manifests by its effect the greatness of its hidden power. Likewise, it is a force which acts upon things, has power, is invisibly present in all things. When neglected it seems not to exist. But it is naturally summoned forth by the act of rubbing, as if in answer to some quest, and is suddenly revealed through its effect, and just as suddenly becomes invisible and unable to be touched once more. Likewise, it is not in the least diminished, even when transmitted in very great quantity. Anyone who chooses will be able to discover many other properties of fire which, in so far as it can be done, describe divine activities in terms familiar to us, by means of sensible images. Noting this, the divines who wrote the Holy Scriptures frequently attribute the properties of fire to heavenly substances, signifying by this their being made like God and their imitation of Him, in so far as that is possible for them.

Angels are described in human form[64] because men possess the power of the intellect, and have eyes so placed that they can freely look aloft,[65] and have an upright and straight figure, and naturally command other creatures and rule and guide them. In powers of sensation they are inferior to them [i.e. other creatures], but in mental powers, and

---

[63] i.e. when not operating in some substance. Grosseteste renders the passage thus: 'For fire that is perceptible is, one may say, in everything, and pervades everything without mingling with it, yet is distinct from other things, and at once entirely luminous and somehow hidden, unknowable in itself unless there is some matter adjacent, on which it can display its own activity' (tr. J. McEvoy, 'Robert Grosseteste on the Celestial Hierarchy of Pseudo-Dionysius: An Edition and Translation of his Commentary, chapters 10–15' unpub. MA thesis, The Queen's University of Belfast, 1967, p. 135a).

[64] Cf. Gen. 32: 24; cf. Ezek. 1: 8–10, Dan. 10: 5.

[65] Ezek. 1: 18, 9: 5, 10: 12;, Rev. 4: 6–8.

knowledge acquired through reason, and a freedom of will which cannot be coerced, they surpass all other creatures.

It is possible to create images appropriate to designate the heavenly powers seen in terms of the individual parts of the body. For instance, the human eyes are said to designate in celestial minds the very clear gaze of those minds upon the divine light. Likewise, because eyes are sensitive and flee from anything which blocks their way, and are moist, receptive of and conformable to every form [which they see], and very mobile, they signify the pure and open acceptance of illuminations sent by God, without any rejection. Likewise, the sense of smell[66] signalizes in celestial minds the ability to receive the divine sweetness which pours its fragrance over the mind, and the ability to make a sound choice among sweet odours, and avoid those that are detrimental. The sense of hearing[67] signifies the power which the angels have of sharing in and receiving in a cognitive way the divine inspiration. The sense of taste[68] signifies the ability to receive to satiety the forms of nourishment which can be taken in by the mind, and sources of increase which come from the divine nourishment. The sense of touch[69] designates the knowledge which discerns those things which help nature from those things which harm it. The eyebrows and eyelids designate the power as guards possessed by intellects which gaze upon God. Youth[70] signifies the lively power of the angels which is always in full vigour. Teeth[71] signify the divisible power of perfect light, which is thrown upon each superior mind and nourishes it, to be passed down to a lower intelligence. For every celestial intellect with providential power divides up all the light of the intellect which has been poured down upon it from above, just like a piece of dough, and multiplies it [i.e. the light] for the elevation of the lower intelligences proportionally according to the power of each.[72]

Shoulders and arms and hands[73] signify operative power, and the successful working out of that power, and the effect which that operation has on lower intelligences. The heart[74] designates the life, made in the likeness of God, which distributes in a manner befitting the good[75] its own

---

[66] Gen. 8: 21.   [67] Ps. 102: 20.   [68] Gen. 18: 5-8, 19: 3, Tobias 6: 6.
[69] Judg. 6: 21.   [70] Mark 16: 5.

[71] In Scripture this is not specifically applied to the angels, but is an obvious inference from angels' ability to eat.

[72] Here Grosseteste has: 'The teeth suggest their way of dividing the perfection of the fare that is given them, for each intellectual being, by his power of providence, divides the unifying knowledge given to him by the more divine being, into many parts, to fulfil the potential for elevation of the one below him' (ed. McEvoy, p. 172).

[73] Judg. 6: 21, Ps. 90: 12, Ezek. 10: 8, 21, Dan. 10: 6, 12: 7, Rev. 10: 5.

[74] Jer. 7: 24.

[75] Lat. 'boniformiter', cf. Greek ἀγαθοειδῶς, used not as in Plato to indicate seeming as opposed to real good, but meaning 'in the manner of the good; graciously, generously' (so McQuade's glossary, introduction, p. 126). Here Grosseteste has: 'And we can say that the heart is a symbol of their godlike life, which generously disseminates its own vital power to things under their providence' (ed. McEvoy, pp. 165a-b).

life-giving power to the elect. The breast, where resides the seat of strength and the protection of all things spiritual, designates the power of the aforesaid life-giving dispensation which comes from the heart, a courage which gives way to no violence. The back[76] signifies the joining up of all those powers which produce good works and all movements towards good, just as all the ribs spring and flow from the spine. The feet[77] represent moving power, sharply penetrating and swift, always moving in the direction of the divine. Hence we read in Isaiah [6: 2]: 'They covered his feet with two wings', where we are given to understand that the Seraphim had six wings on their feet, with which they covered the feet of the Lord (as paintings on walls depict). For the wing which carries the bird aloft, and is sharp at the tip, and keeps the bird suspended in the air, and journeys until it separates the bird far from earth, designates the power which carries the mind aloft, and sharply penetrates and moves about in heavenly and eternal regions, according to the words of Ecclesiasticus [24: 8]: 'I have circled the circumference of heaven', and separates the tip of the mind (apex mentis)[78] from everything that is of the senses. The lightness of the wings designates the power of a mind freed from everything that is earthly, and totally pure, and free from everything that drags it down as it seeks the heights.

That the heavenly minds are naked and unshod[79] signifies that they are free, and easily liberated, and indeed cannot be detained by any chance or preoccupation of the lower world, and that those eternal features which can be viewed by the senses are not added on to them, nor adhere to them, and that they are made like the divine simplicity in so far as this is possible for a created being.

But again, since Holy Scripture, which is totally one in presenting the simple truth, is made manifold[80] in the variety of its wise sayings, sometimes it shows that naked heavenly intelligences are in fact clothed. Thus we read in Zachariah [3: 4]: 'Take away his defiled garments from him', and a little later [3: 5]: 'They have put clothes upon him'; and Daniel [10: 5] says: 'I saw a man clothed in linen garments.' Sometimes Scripture shows that men carry vessels, as in Ezekiel [9: 2] and Revelation [15: 6].[81] Let us then show what garments signify, and the functions which are attributed to heavenly intelligences. For their shining and fiery raiment[82] signifies the conformity of those same minds to God, in line with the properties of fire set out above, and understood anagogically, and especially by reason of their power of giving and receiving light. The attribute of shining splendour is given to them in Mark [16: 5] and Tobias

[76] Ezek. 1: 18, Dan. 10: 5.   [77] Isa. 6: 2, Ezek. 1: 7.
[78] On the importance of this concept in Dionysian theology see E. von Ivánka, 'Apex mentis', Zeitschrift für katholische Theologie, lxxii (1950), 129–76.
[79] Cf. Gen. 18: 4 and 19: 2, where the angels' feet are bathed.
[80] Cf. Eph. 3: 10.   [81] Cf. also Dan. 10: 5.
[82] Luke 24: 2, John 20: 12, cf. Isa. 63: 1, Dan. 10: 5.

[5: 5].[83] This explanation is necessary, lest anyone should suspect that, because of such attributions, there is always some variation subject to the laws of time, and some interruption of their rest, in heavenly intelligences, which are in reality always at rest. But among them there is one simple light which, like a fountain of light, illuminates all those who are illuminated intellectually. The priestly garb[84] signifies the power of bringing angels or men to fulfil the divine wishes, which were hidden from them, and to which they had to be guided, and also [of bringing them] to holiness in the whole area of spiritual life. The belts[85] signify the power of preserving and firmly drawing together one's own virtues and spiritual graces which blossom spiritually through an increase in one's own perfection and in perfection which comes from outside—just as a belt keeps a garment trim lest it billow out, and holds in the belly, in which are the nutritive virtues—to this end that every heavenly mind may be turned upon itself, and so may be made simple by the fact that its spiritual powers are not dissipated.[86] For the belt signifies the power of the heavenly mind unceasingly, and in a seemly and unvarying (*uniformiter*) way to coil around itself, just as a belt encircles the body yet never falls. Rods[87] signify the power and prudence needed in order to rule one's subjects well and bring them to God, to guide with a sure hand whatever business has been laid on one by God, and bring it to a proper conclusion. For this is, or should be, the function of kings and judges who carry rods and sceptres. Lances[88] and axes[89] are the instruments of killing. They signify the power of separating out the wicked from the elect, or sin from a nature that is good, and of shrewdly discerning between good and good, good and better, and better and best, and of bringing one's activities to a successful conclusion. Instruments used in measuring and building[90] signify the power of initiating the virtues or a good life, or of improving and perfecting them.

In this sense must be interpreted all those attributes of God or the heavenly intelligences which relate to the elevation of lower beings and their conversion to God through the providence of superior beings. Sometimes material instruments attributed to angels designate divine judgements which are to be employed against men, while some signify divine chastisement, as Jeremiah [1: 11] says: 'I see a rod watching.' Some signify retributive justice, as in Ezekiel [chs. 1, 8–9]; some freedom from difficulties, or an end to correction, or a renewal of [God's] previous goodwill, or an accretion of new gifts, great or small, of things sensible or

[83] In the Vulgate, Tobias encounters a shining youth (*iuvenem splendidum*), who is the angel Raphael; neither of the two Greek recensions of Tobit 5: 4 mentions his splendour.
[84] Cf. Luke 24: 4.   [85] Isa. 11: 5, Ezek. 9: 2, Dan. 10: 5.
[86] i.e. are pulled in and conserved by the belt.
[87] Judg. 6: 21; cf. Isa. 11: 4.
[88] Cf. Gen. 3: 24, 2 Macc. 5: 1–3.   [89] Cf. Isa. 10: 15.
[90] Ezek. 40: 3, Zech. 2: 5, Rev. 21: 15.

things intelligible. Generally, the shrewd mind will know how to match, in terms that make them familiar, sensible symbols (*signa*) with intelligible powers.

The fact that angels are called winds[91] in the psalm [103: 3–4] signifies their swiftness in acting, a swiftness which almost without delay transmits itself to all things, and their moving force which speedily raises up lower things and lowers higher things. The angels elevate lower beings, and among them [i.e. the angels] the higher ones breathe inspiration into the lower ones, and the highest rouse the middle ones carefully to breathe divine illumination into the lower ones, sharing with them their own illuminations, according as each is able.[92]

Besides, the choice of the wind as a name, being so to speak the spirit of the air, signifies the likeness of the heavenly minds to the deity itself. For the wind expresses the image of the divine operation, as we showed in *The Symbolic Theology*, in the anagogical exposition of the four elements.[93] One of these elements is the air, which signifies the divine ways of operation in so far as it is well able to move other things and to call forth the seed from the earth, and acts speedily, and cannot be held in, and begins to move suddenly, and ceases equally suddenly, while we do not know the cause of its moving or again of its ceasing. Nor do we see how it hides itself, as is written about God in Job [9: 11]: 'If He comes to me, I shall not see Him. If He goes, I shall not be aware of it', and in John [3: 8]: 'The Spirit breathes where it wishes, and you hear its voice, but you do not know where it comes from or where it goes to.'

Angels are designated also by the name of clouds in the Scriptures.[94] For clouds are filled with the light of the sun's rays just as angels are when the divine light secretly shines upon them. The foremost angels receive the first manifestation of the divine light inwardly (without any outward show). Then they relay it plentifully to the lower angels, at second hand and according to their [i.e. the lower angels'] capacity, just as clouds receive light within themselves and relay it on down. There is another reason why clouds are compared with angels. For clouds pour out the showers which they contain in their damp folds, and through these showers the greenery of the earth bursts into bud, is given life, grows, and ripens, and thus the fruits of the earth are given life.[95] In the same way angels receiving into their own persons the abundance of the heavenly

[91] Ezek. 1: 4, Dan. 7: 2, 14: 36, Zech. 6: 5, Heb. 1: 7, Rev. 6: 1.

[92] A difficult passage in Gallus; here Grosseteste has: 'The name of winds which is given to them suggests this sharpness and their activity, which pervades things almost simultaneously, and the movement by which they pass from high to low and return to the heights again, and which raises the inferiors to the heights again, and makes the first beings go out to those beneath them, to share with and provide for them' (tr. McEvoy, p. 191a).

[93] This work of Pseudo-Dionysius' has not survived.

[94] For the association of God and His angels with clouds see: Exod. 33: 9, Numb. 12: 5; Ps. 17: 20, 98: 7, 103: 3, Isa. 4: 5, Ezek., 10: 4, 33: 9, Dan. 7: 13, Rev. 1: 7, 10: 1.

[95] Cf. Job 36: 27–31.

wisdom and holding it within them, implant it in lower beings, inflame them and make them increase, and perfect and elevate them.

As for the fact that, in Ezekiel,[96] the form of bronze and of electrum, and the forms of precious stones, are attributed to angels, that must be understood as follows. By the name of electrum, whose colour is half-way between gold and silver, and thus in a sense contains both elements, is designated, so far as the golden colour is concerned, the shining splendour in angels which never fails, which cannot be destroyed or even diminished or in any way tarnished. As regards the silver colour, it designates the heavenly brightness, which is in itself bright, and which illuminates other beings. In the case of the bronze, by virtue of its colour it has the same significance as gold or fire. As regards the various colours of precious stones: by whiteness, which is a bright shining colour, is understood the brightness of the heavenly intellects; by red, the mysteries of fire; by yellow, the mysteries of the colour of gold; by paleness, youth, that is exemption from decay, which always retains its strength. According to this manner of interpretation, each likeness has a corresponding anagogical exposition which activates our minds.

But since we seem to have dealt adequately with this subject, let us consider then how the forms of wild beasts and other animals are attributed to angels. The figure of a lion[97] among angels signifies their power in ruling others and bringing them to God, and a spiritual strength which cannot be coerced by any violent force. It also signifies that they are (in so far as they can be) made like that very hidden and ineffable divine majesty, in that they proceed to God in a very secret way, according as their path to the divine majesty is lit, and they are raised up towards it, by the most hidden light of God, just as the lion, fearing its hunters, obliterates its tracks with its tail. Therefore, we read in the psalm [76: 20]: 'thy way is in the sea, and thy paths are in many waters, and thy footsteps will not be known'. And Paul says: 'O, the depths of the riches of the wisdom and knowledge of God: how incomprehensible are His judgements, how unsearchable His ways' [Rom. 11: 33].

The figure of the ox[98] signifies vigour and strength, and the power of, as it were, opening up in furrows the minds of lower things that they may receive the gifts of heavenly grace bounteously flowing into them, and increase the knowledge of God that is in them. The horns of the ox signify defensive might and strength. For the horn protects the ox, and is stronger than flesh.

The figure of the eagle[99] signifies the royal dignity and the ascent aloft to the divine, and the swift flight of contemplation, and the power of

---

[96] Ezek. 1: 4, 26, 8: 2, 10: 1, 9; 40: 3; cf. Isa. 48: 4, Rev. 1: 15, 4: 3.
[97] Ezek. 1: 10, 10: 14; Rev. 4: 7; cf. Isa. 31: 4.
[98] Ezek. 1: 7, 1: 10; Rev. 4: 7.
[99] Ezek. 1: 10, Rev. 4: 7.

penetrating acutely, soberly, nimbly, and with wisdom to the draught of the divine sweetness which truly strengthens and nourishes. It also signifies the ability to exercise one's powers of contemplation without any let or hindrance, directly and without being turned aside, an ability which acts through the most salutary and clear-sighted elevation of one's own contemplative powers towards the most abundant and clear ray of the eternal wisdom. This ray God the Father gives forth in the fullness of spiritual light and heat, just as the sun is a full expression and source of all physical light and heat. Just so, the eagle sees its prey minutely from afar off, and flies to it swiftly and directly with wings drawn together, and gazes on the rays of the sun with sight which remains unimpaired.

The figure of horses[100] signifies that angels obey God and submit to His every wish, as the horse is managed by the use of the bridle. The white colour of horses[101] signifies that angels are dazzling white in colour, and more than any other creatures come to resemble the divine light, for white is the brightest of all colours. The black colour[102] signifies the power of concealing themselves which angels possess, because black is the obscurest of all colours. The red colour signifies a fiery and active virtue. For all the colours between black and white signify in angels the combination of shining splendour and concealment achieved by their capacity to hide their brightness and reveal what is hidden, and to join superior to inferior beings, since those that are higher in rank flow into those that are inferior, and conversely (conversive) inferior beings are elevated to reach up to superior beings.

If we were not trying to avoid excessive length in our treatment of this subject, we would have matched the particular qualities of the aforesaid creatures, and all their bodily forms and figures, with the heavenly intelligences. We could have attributed in a different sense to the heavenly intelligences those qualities which are found in the creatures, as we have done in the above examples. For example, by the furious rage which is found in animals we may understand the courage to be found in angels, a quality from which rage is very far removed and is its most distant figure (figura), and by the carnal desire of creatures we may understand the spiritual love of God which is found in angels. To put it briefly, we could have made all the bodily senses and all the manifold parts of these living creatures relate to the immaterial intellects and uniform powers of the heavenly intelligences. For the wise, what we have said, and the anagogical exposition of one form or figure which is dissimilar to the thing designated by it, are sufficient for the exposition of similar figures along similar lines.

Next we must explain that Scripture has attributed to heavenly

[100] 4 Kgs. 2: 11, 6: 17, 1 Macc. 5: 2–3, Zech. 1: 8–10, Rev. 19: 14.
[101] Rev. 19: 14; cf. Rev. 6: 2, 19: 11.
[102] Zech. 6: 2, 6, Rev. 6: 5.

substances, as being connected to them, rivers, as in Daniel [7: 10] and Ecclesiasticus [24: 35–43], and wheels, as in Ezekiel [1: 15–21],[103] and chariots, as in the Fourth Book of Kings [2: 11].[104] The fiery, whirling river, which flowed from His face, that is the face of the Ancient of Days, designates the fullness of divine light and heat, which proceeds from the Father of light, and which bounteously bestows a plentiful and unfailing supply of spiritual gifts and spiritual nourishment, from which is generated in those beings an increase of fervent and lifegiving love.

Chariots, because in their material form they are yoked up, signify the combination of grace, glory, worthiness, and all heavenly lights, which joins together those celestial intelligences which are united in the same rank or order.[105] The wheels, which raise themselves readily, which are said to pass before His face and not to turn back, and to go straight on, without turning to one side or the other, and to be raised aloft (as is clear from Ezekiel [1: 17, 21]), signify in celestial substances the power of always progressing upwards towards the divine, directly and without any deviation, so that their acts of contemplation, which move in a circular way because eternity has no boundary, are always guided upwards in an intellectual manner. A second anagogical sense can be recognized in the description of the wheels. For Ezekiel [10: 13] says: 'I heard Him call those wheels "rolling"', where the Greek translation[106] has the meaning 'revolutions and revelations'. Indeed, the heavenly intelligences, which are compared to wheels and to fire, revolve with an eternal motion round the supreme Good, and reveal what is hidden by guiding aloft inferior beings, by revealing sublime secrets, by conveying light from higher beings to lower beings.

Next, let us set forth the significance of the joy which is attributed to the angels in Luke [15: 10]. For their joy is not a thing of the senses, like our human joy, which afflicts us when it leaves us and constantly fails us. And so the joy and feasting which is attributed to the angels when the lost are found, and those who are straying turn to God and are saved, signify the exultation of the angels which conforms to the divine joy, and is abundant and unspeakable, a joy which always satisfies them. Holy men, too, sometimes deserve to taste this joy, even though they are mortal flesh, when the rays of divine illumination shine upon them.[107]

Thus what we have written about the descriptions of invisible things in sensible terms does not fully reveal these invisible things, but conveys a

---

[103] Cf. Ezek. 10: 9.

[104] A difficult passage. Grosseteste has: 'And we should examine why rivers and wheels and chariots are referred so closely to the heavenly beings' (tr. McEvoy, p. 223a).

[105] Grosseteste: 'The chariots suggest their being yoked in fellowship with the others of their rank' (ibid).

[106] Apparently a slip for 'the Hebrew text', as in the Greek original (cf. the Parker translation, ii. 65) and in Grosseteste (tr. McEvoy, p. 223a).

[107] Cf. John 16: 22, 24, 17: 13.

knowledge of them to us, and enlightens us, lest we concentrate our minds on descriptions which employ images (*imaginariae descriptiones*), seeking nothing beyond or higher than these. But let us learn from the aforesaid to investigate invisible truth in the form of other sensible figures.

But if you object that in this book I have not treated individually all the powers, functions, and images of angels which are touched on in the Scriptures, my reply is that this is indeed true. We have passed over much of this material for four reasons. A thorough treatment of celestial hierarchies is beyond the limits of our knowledge. We really need to be taught about them by someone else rather than to teach. Also, the material omitted by me can be understood from a comparison with what I have dealt with here, for it presents the same difficulties, and can be understood by employing the same method. Besides, I was concerned that I should keep my treatise within reasonable limits. Finally, I wish to respect by my silence that which is hidden from us, which surpasses our understanding.

All that surpasses our understanding must be honoured by our silence.

ROBERT GROSSETESTE

Commentary on *The Celestial Hierarchy*, Chapter xv: Extracts[108]

Our author has dealt earlier with the godlike properties of the heavenly powers. In this chapter he treats of corporeal and material symbols and shapes which signify their godlike properties. And so he recommends both himself and Timothy to rest, for a while, the mind's intellectual gaze, which has up till now been intent upon visions of the godlike properties of the heavenly powers; to descend to the broad and manifold variety of the symbols which, by corporeal forms and shapes, signify the other-worldly, immaterial properties of the angels; and to turn back once more from the symbols (*simbola*), as though from images (*ymagines*), by stripping every corporeal formation and figuration from the heavenly substances, and contemplate their simplicity and immateriality.

This is how he puts it. COME THEN Timothy, and myself too, AND FOR THE REMAINDER, that is, for the rest of our discussion of the angelic hierarchy, LET US RELAX OUR MENTAL GAZE, IF IT SEEMS RIGHT, to you that is, FROM THAT STRAIN or force, or tension, that is, from the difficult and demanding action and effort of the intellect's eye. This strain CONCERNS OF COURSE THE SUBLIME VISIONS that is, the visions of the sublime angelic properties achieved by an exalted power of the intellect free from sense-images (*phantasmata*); a strain, I say, WHICH BEFITS AN ANGEL, since the angels

[108] These extracts were specially revised for this anthology by James McEvoy from the translation in his thesis.

employ in their visions an effort of this degree, one which befits them; or because it is not fitting, just as it is not possible for us to reach the visions of the angels' properties, except by using the full strength and effort and tension of our intellect's eye. WE WILL DESCEND at length, that is, in this chapter, to contemplating lower things, by means of a lower power of the mind, TO THE BROAD BUT DIVIDED RANGE that is, that which has a great number of symbols, differing entirely from each other and divided, AND COMPOUNDED that is, the range that has the same symbols, symbols which, by the variety and number of their properties, signify in many ways those many other-worldly properties. This is the range, I say, OF THE MULTIFORM VARIETY OF THE SYMBOLIZATION OF ANGELS; for the symbols are very numerous and diverse which depict, with countless substantial and accidental forms, the multiform properties of the angels; signify, that is, by making shapes and images.

Thus, Timothy, I say, having rested our intellectual eye and descended to this range, LET US TURN BACK AGAIN FROM THEM namely from the images or symbolic formations, AS FROM FIGURES, TO contemplate, of course, THE SIMPLICITY OF THE HEAVENLY INTELLECTS. Let us return, I say, BY WAY OF RESOLUTION that is, by making an analysis of their symbols, dividing them into their parts and properties, and defining all, both symbols and their constituents, and investigating what spiritual reality can best be signified by a given bodily one, stripping every material element from the spiritual realities they signify, and in the end contemplating these with the abstract intellect. . . .[109]

He goes on to say that Scripture sometimes applies also the image of a cloud to the angels. For a cloud has light within it hidden from us, which it receives from above, from both the sun and the other heavenly bodies. It has also the matter of light hidden from us, from which the gleams of light shine forth. It pours out plentifully these manifestations of light, received for the most part from the heavenly bodies as a whole, on the things below it, though these do not receive the light so fully but rather in proportion to their capacity to receive. Moreover, the cloud is the mother of rain, and, by sending showers on the bosom of the earth it makes it [i.e. the earth] conceive, bring forth, bud, and give life, growth, and maturity to its products; so that the cloud itself has the same properties, since the cause possesses more fully and more substantially the qualities it gives to the effects. Thus these properties of the clouds symbolize the angels' properties, that is, their being immaterially filled, to overflowing indeed, with the light that is hidden from us, namely the divine light; they receive the first manifestations of this light without display, that is, humbly, and bring it down plentifully to those below, giving them the maximum amount they can take. The clouds also signify that the angels conceive

---

[109] Grosseteste's elaborate treatment of the image of fire, part of the discussion here omitted, is paraphrased by McEvoy, *Philosophy of Grosseteste*, pp. 367–8; cf. pp. 103, 110.

intelligible showers, of wisdom that is, to be poured by spiritual instruction into the capacity of the recipients; in order to bring forth, by reflection upon the instruction received, actions worthy of the teaching; to flower, through effort to extend their resolve into practice; to give life, by bringing them into act; to give growth, by directing and repeating the actions; to give maturity, by bringing them to a high point, and persevering in this; and those who pour out these showers possess these qualities in greater degree and more essentially.

Pointing this out, our author continues: BUT SCRIPTURE ALSO that is, together with the foregoing, APPLIES TO THEM namely the angels, THE APPEARANCE or image OF CLOUD, SIGNIFYING BY THIS namely, this imagery, THAT THE HOLY INTELLIGENCES, the angels, ARE FILLED IN AN UNEARTHLY WAY WITH THE HIDDEN LIGHT; BUT THAT THEY RECEIVE THE FIRST MANIFESTATION OF LIGHT TO APPEAR that is, the manifestation of divine light that reveals itself first of all. They receive it WITHOUT DISPLAY, humbly, AND CARRY IT DOWN namely the revealed light, ABUNDANTLY, TO THE SECONDARY BEINGS, the lower ones, IN A SECOND MANIFESTATION; for the very revelation of the divine light is less striking, and is present in the lower beings IN PROPORTION namely, to their receptivity; AND DOUBTLESS Scripture means by the above, namely the imagery of the cloud, THAT THEY namely the angels FLOWER, AND GIVE LIFE, GROWTH, AND PERFECTION BY THEIR INTELLIGIBLE CONCEPTION OF THE RAINS, WHICH GIVES RISE TO A RECEPTIVE WOMB WITH RICH SHOWERS, FOR LIVE BIRTHS. For Scripture represents these things, whose spiritual meaning is as given, by the cloud imagery, as being present in the angels in the way that, physically understood, they are in clouds; which conceive the rain physically and send the derivative showers to the bosom of the earth, so stimulating the earth in turn, by some natural incitement, to give birth to living plants. . . .

He goes on to comment on the reference to the angels' properties in terms of certain metals, and certain coloured stones. BUT IF that is, since SCRIPTURE REFERS THE FORM OF BRONZE AND ALLOY, AND OF COLOURED STONES TO THE HEAVENLY BEINGS, IT IS BECAUSE THE ALLOY, BEING AT ONCE GOLD AND SILVER IN FORM for the alloy is a fusion of gold and silver, REVEALS THE INCORRUPTIBLE, INEXHAUSTIBLE GLEAM, NEVER SPENT OR DEFILED, that is, the enlightenment of the heavenly beings received from above, of the knowledge and virtues, with which they gleam, without any mixture of ignorance or vice, and therefore incorruptibly, never spent, nor impoverished, nor defiled. The alloy reveals this radiance AS PRESENT IN GOLD, which is, of course, a component of it; its properties are to be radiant, incorruptible, indestructible, undiminished, and undefiled, or pure; for gold does not corrupt in the earth, for it is not consumed in the fire as other metals are, nor even diminished; it does not defile when contact occurs, as other metals do, because of its purity; and the alloy reveals THE RADIANT or clear LUMINOUS, AND HEAVENLY SHINING OF SILVER, a component, of course, of the alloy,

which has a clear, shining quality, very like the whiteness of the light of
heaven; this shining symbolizes the brightness of the angels' knowledge
and virtue; and thus the brightness of silver and the gleam of gold symbolize the same thing, unless one should say that the gleam of gold, which is
redder, refers to their knowledge as informed by a burning love, while the
brightness of silver symbolizes the light of knowledge as such, or virtue in
so far as it is directed. . . .

HOWEVER, WE MUST ATTRIBUTE TO BRONZE, OWING TO THE REASONS ASSIGNED or
given; namely that spiritual properties are symbolized by material ones,
and drawn as close to them as possible, as has been done in the foregoing
sections. For these reasons, I say, we must attribute to the bronze the
quality of either fire, or gold; that is, when Scripture refers the image of
bronze to the heavenly beings, it is using its flame-colour to signify the
same properties in them as fire does, which we remarked on earlier; and
by its kinship with gold, for it is of a golden colour, Scripture is referring
to those of their properties which the gold-component in the alloy symbolizes. Thus, the spiritual qualities of fire and gold are attributed to
bronze, spiritually understood, just as these material forms belong to it
physically understood.

WE MUST TAKE THE MANY-COLOURED FORMS or images or aspects OF STONES
TO SIGNIFY EITHER THE FORM OF LIGHT that is, the light of wisdom and virtue,
IF WHITE, since white is closer to light than the other colours; OR FIRE that
is, that spiritual quality which, as was stated above, fire signifies, IF RED
namely, if the images of the stones resemble the colour of fire; and we
must take the YELLOW images of stones to represent THE FORM OF GOLD that
is, that spiritual quality which, as we remarked above, is symbolized by
the form of gold, since gold is yellow; OR IF GREEN we should take them as
revealing YOUTH AND PRIME that is, that spiritual quality which is symbolized, as we mentioned above, by youth and prime; for in plants greenness
is a strengthener and developer. AND FOR EACH FORM, of colour that is, YOU
WILL FIND AN ELEVATING, PURIFIED NOTION that is, an explanation that will
bring you round to a spiritual understeanding, and keep us from remaining in the uncleanness of material things; an explanation, I say, OF THE
SYMBOLIC IMAGES that is, the figurative images. . . .

THAT OF THE EAGLE, the form of course, must be taken as revealing THEIR
KINGSHIP that is, the virtue of reigning; for the angels reign much more
powerfully than we do, although we are promised a royal priesthood; AND
THEIR HIGH FLIGHT that is, their motion to the heights, to God really; AND
SWIFTNESS or non-temporal movement; THEIR ALACRITY or quick, light
movement to their strengthening food, which is to the divine wisdom
which nourishes them; AND WATCHFULNESS or being always intent upon
seizing the divine lights that nourish them; AND MAKING PROGRESS that is,
straining and moving with all their might to secure their spiritual nourishment; AND INGENUITY, or prudent provision as regards the nourishment

of divine wisdom; AND THEIR LOOKING or contemplation UNHINDERED by any exterior thing, STRAIGHT that is, by a straight direction of their ray of vision, AND UNSWERVINGLY or inflexibly, untiringly, and perseveringly, AT THE PLENTIFUL AND POWERFUL RAY SENT OUT BY THE CREATIVE SUN that is, at the ray which the thearchy, or God, who is the sun of justice, and most generous illuminator of the intelligence, sends IN MOST VIGOROUS or very vigorous EXERTIONS, OF THE POWERS or potencies, OF SIGHT. For God sends a ray of His light upon the angels' powers of spiritual sight, concentrated with all their uncorrupt and untired resources, and intent on the ray itself, gazing unwaveringly at it. Thus, the form of the eagle must be taken as revealing the existence of these spiritual properties in the angels, by its bodily properties; for it is the 'royal' bird by the pre-eminence it enjoys over the other birds; it is 'high-flying' because it flies higher than the others, and 'swift' because it can fly rapidly; it has extraordinarily sharp sight, which enables it to spot its food from far off, while to pursue it, it possesses a greater speed of flight; and it is watchful and intent to perceive the food most suitable to it; and when it has sighted it [i.e. the food] not slackly but with all its might it moves to seize it, directing its movements well and aptly, by some natural prudence, to lay hold without fail of the food it needs; moreover, it sees the sun's ray shining in its [i.e. the sun's] own power, by a direct and unshaken intuition. . . .

Concluding this chapter, and the book on the heavenly hierarchy, he suggests briefly why he has collected all this, remarks that he has not mentioned all the attributes of the angels given in Scripture, and gives his reason for leaving out some of them. He says SO MUCH I HAVE TO SAY in this chapter, namely ON THE IMAGES OF SACRED THINGS that is, about corporeal forms as sacredly signifying spiritual realities. So much, I say, FALLING SHORT OF A THOROUGH or certain TREATMENT OF THEM namely the symbols, BUT LEADING US, I THINK, AWAY FROM A SLAVISH ADHERENCE TO THE IMAGES OF THE IMAGINATION. For though his suggestions on the adaptation of material realities to spiritual beings do not by any means provide a perfect statement of the spiritual nature of the intelligible beings, they do give sufficient warning to us to think, when we hear material things attributed to spiritual, not in terms of imagination and phantasy (*fantasya*), which suggests that there is something material, or with a material shape or form, in them, but that their whole reality is immaterial and other-worldly. . . .

VI

Scriptural Science and Signification: From *Alexander's Sum of Theology* to Nicholas of Lyre

FROM the thirteenth century until the end of the Middle Ages, Aristotle was 'the Philosopher'. The stimulus provided by his *libri naturales* and other recently recovered works can hardly be exaggerated. He caused medieval academics to reconsider long-established definitions of and methods in all the arts and sciences, and to analyse as never before their relationship with the queen of the sciences, theology.[1] The implications for the commentary-tradition were considerable. Aristotelian theory of causality encouraged exegetes to adopt a new type of prologue organized around the four main causes described by 'the Philosopher', an approach which encouraged new attitudes to such matters as authorship and authority, and literary style and structure. Aristotelian epistemology gave the human faculties and human perception a new dignity; late medieval scholars afforded the 'body' of Scripture, its literal sense, a corresponding dignity. A new semantics emerged. Meaning was no longer believed (as in twelfth-century exegesis) to have been hidden by God deep in the biblical text; rather it was expressed in the literal sense by the human authors of Scripture, each in his own way or ways.[2] The allegorists' obsession with *auctoritas* at the expense of the particular *auctor* receded to reveal divinely inspired yet supremely human beings who possessed their own literary and moral purposes and problems, their sins and their styles.

The present chapter offers contributions to these major developments made in the following works by some of the best minds of the thirteenth century, all associated at one time or another with the University of Paris, the centre *par excellence* for the study of theology in that period: the *Sum of Theology* begun by Alexander of Hales OFM (*c.*1186–1245) and finished by his pupils, the commentaries on the *Sentences* and Ecclesiastes, and the *Breviloquium*, by St Bonaventure OFM (*c.*1217–74), the *Sum of Theology* of St Thomas Aquinas OP (*c.*1225–74), the commentary on the Song of Songs by Giles of Rome OESA (*c.*1243/7–1316), the *Sum of Ordinary Questions* of the secular master Henry of Ghent (*c.*1217–93), and the *Literal Postill on the Bible* by Nicholas of Lyre OFM (*c.*1270–1340).[3] The main issues raised by our extracts may be outlined as follows.

---

[1] Cf. Smalley, *Study of the Bible*, pp. 292–328.

[2] Cf. Minnis, *Authorship*, pp. 72–3.

[3] For summary description of these works and relevant bibliography see ibid., pp. 91–3, 94–5, 106–7, 110–12; James A. Weisheipl, *Friar Thomas d'Aquino* (Oxford, 1974), pp. 360–2; J. G. Bougerol, *Introduction à l'étude de saint Bonaventure* (Tournai, 1961), pp. 143–5, 148–63, and, on Giles of Rome, Allen, *Ethical Poetic*, pp. 13–18, 59n., 97, 111n., 159, 160, 250.

1. *Causality in Criticism*. The 'type C' prologue, the main form in use among twelfth-century commentators, was in the thirteenth century superseded by, or assimilated to (many permutations of vocabulary being possible), the 'Aristotelian prologue', as we may term it. The *causa efficiens* or efficient cause was the author; which heading replaced, or was used in conjunction with, *nomen auctoris*. The *causa materialis* or material cause designated the literary materials which were the author's sources; this replaced or was used along with the long-established term *materia*. The *causa formalis* or formal cause was the pattern imposed by the author on his materials. Commentators spoke of the 'twofold form' (*duplex forma*), the *forma tractandi*, which was the writer's method of treatment or procedure (here the term *modus agendi* was subsumed), and the *forma tractatus*, which was the arrangement or organization (*ordo*, *ordinatio*) of the work, the way in which its author had structured it.[4]

Between 1235 and 1245 this paradigm became popular among lecturers in the arts faculty at the University of Paris, one of the first writers to use it being Robert Kilwardby, who made an early reputation as an *artista* (*c.*1237–*c.*1245) before his entry into the Dominican order.[5] It made its appearance in Scriptural exegesis in the commentaries on Mark's Gospel and the Acts of the Apostles which Hugh of Saint-Cher OP produced at Saint-Jacques, Paris, between 1230 and 1236.[6] Hugh's younger contemporary, Guerric of Saint-Quentin (who held the second chair of theology at Saint-Jacques between 1233 and 1242), was perhaps the first to apply the four causes in exegesis of the Old Testament. At the beginning of his commentary on Isaiah, Guerric describes the text's two levels of authorship in terms of the 'twofold efficient cause' (*duplex causa efficiens*): the Holy Spirit may be regarded as the 'moving' efficient cause which motivated the 'operating' efficient cause, namely the prophet Isaiah, to write.[7] Similarly, in the 'Aristotelian prologue' to his commentary on the Psalter (translated below) Nicholas of Lyre identifies the principal efficient cause as God and the instrumental efficient cause as the prophet David, who composed most of the psalms. In these cases God is regarded as the first *auctor* or the unmoved mover of the inspired text, whereas the human *auctor* is both moved (by God) and moving (in producing the text). Other books of the Bible were sometimes supposed to have had an even more complex motivation—some commentators spoke of triple and even quadruple efficient causes[8]—but what most versions of this approach have in common is the way

---

[4] Cf. Minnis, *Authorship*, pp. 28–9, 145, 148–9, and Allen, *Ethical Poetic*, pp. 68, 72–4, 80, 88, 92–3, 118, 150.

[5] For Kilwardby's early career see A. G. Judy's introduction to his edition of Kilwardby's *De ortu scientiarum* (Auctores Britannici medii aevi IV, Oxford, 1976), pp. xi–xvii; E. M. F. Sommer-Seckendorff, *Studies in the Life of Robert Kilwardby, O.P.* (Inst. hist. FF. praed., Diss. hist. VIII, Rome, 1937). Kilwardby's use of the new paradigm is discussed at length by O. Lewry, 'Robert Kilwardby's Writings on the *Logica vetus* Studied with Regard to their Teaching and Method' (unpub. D.Phil. thesis, Oxford, 1978); cf. the (to some extent outdated) article by S. Harrison Thomson, 'Robert Kilwardby's commentaries *In Priscianum* and *In Barbarismum Donati*', *New Schol.* xii (1958), 52–65.

[6] Minnis, *Authorship*, pp. 72, 78–9.

[7] See Beryl Smalley, 'A Commentary on Isaias by Guerric of St. Quentin, O.P.', *Studi e testi*, cxxii (1946), 383–97.   [8] See Minnis, *Authorship*, pp. 80–1.

in which both the divine author, God, and the human authors of Scripture are given their due. God is invoked as the guarantor of the value of a given text because He is its primary efficient cause; its *auctoritas* is thereby established beyond any possible doubt. That point having been made (with little elaboration needed), the commentator could then focus on the individual contribution of the human author or authors. Aristotelian theory of causality insisted that the causes which functioned between a given primary efficient cause and the ultimate effect had a certain amount of individual power, each thing having its distinctive and inalienable operation. In the criticism which this theory influenced, an inspired writer, being a cause which existed between the first efficient cause, God, and the effect, the scriptural text, was granted his personal purpose and procedure.[9] Consequently, the differences between the personalities of the *auctores* of the Bible and the various formal causes (i.e. styles and structures) of their works could be recognized fully.

The extracts we have translated from Nicholas of Lyre's commentary on the Psalter illustrate with supreme clarity all these principles in practice. Whereas Peter Lombard had claimed that the names which appear in the *tituli psalmorum* are there 'for the sake of the mysterious significance' rather than to designate the various psalmists (see above, p. 110), Lyre sees them as referring to real individuals. The views of Jerome and the great Jewish exegete Rashi concerning the number and names of the *auctores* of the Psalter are carefully noted.[10] Moreover, Lyre distinguishes between the authorial activities of the psalmists and the editing activity of Ezra, who is responsible for the order (or lack thereof) in which we now have the psalms. Turning to the formal cause, the distinctive *forma tractandi* of the Psalter is said to be 'the mode of praise' while the heading *forma tractatus* prompts an impressive investigation, conducted at the beginning of the commentary on the first psalm, of the way in which the psalms were brought together in a *collectio* which lacks any definite principle of arrangement. Here, Aristotelian theory of causality is working in harmony with a literalistic approach to the text—about which more later—to create a concrete and specific kind of analysis which evinces respect for the integrity of the human *auctores* of Scripture. But not all biblical texts were susceptible to such treatment. The arch-literalist Nicholas of Lyre accommodated his theories concerning scriptural language to a 'parabolic' reading of the Song of Songs,[11] and in the prologue to his commentary on that text Giles of Rome, quite predictably, emphasizes its divine *auctoritas* rather than its human author, applying St Gregory's metaphor of the inspired writer as the mere pen with which God writes.[12] Here, as in much twelfth-century exegesis (see above, pp. 70–1), allegorical interpretation and the affirmation of *auctoritas* go hand in hand. Yet when Giles turns his attention to the formal cause of the Song of Songs, a meticulous description of the ways in

---

[9] Cf. ibid., pp. 82–4.

[10] On Lyre's use of Rashi see H. Hailperin, *Rashi and the Christian Scholars* (Pittsburg, 1963), pp. 137–246.

[11] *In Cant. Cant.*, pr. (*Bib. glos.* iii. 1817).

[12] *Moralia in Job*, pr. i. 2–3 (CCSL cxliii. 8–10).

which the poem's *forma tractandi* (described as the *modus affectivus, desiderativus et contemplativus*) differs from those of the other scriptural books, is the result. Different books, it would seem, require very different handling: allegory is found in some places but not in others; the various texts have various styles and structures. In sum, awareness of the infinite variety of God and the ability-range of His creatures is the most striking aspect of the scriptural criticism conveyed by 'Aristotelian prologues'. The rich diversity of the causes of each and every book of the Bible has become the commentator's central concern.

2. *Science and Style*. At the beginning of the commentaries on Peter Lombard's *Sentences* which flowed abundantly from thirteenth-century faculties of theology, one central question occurs with great frequency, namely, what is the nature of theology, and can it in any sense be described as a science?[13] Aristotle having forced medieval thinkers to rethink their strategies for analysing the scope and hierarchy of the sciences, the issue of the exact character and status of theology became a burning one. Many different answers were offered. Albert the Great, Thomas Aquinas, and Henry of Ghent agreed at least in believing that theology was essentially a speculative science. But three of the positions represented below place the emphasis on its 'affective' and volitional aspect instead.

To take the first of these, that found in *Alexander's Sum of Theology*, the suggestion that theology cannot be scientific because the Bible is written in a 'poetic or historical or parabolical' way, a style which has no scientific basis, is dismissed with the argument that this mode of procedure is necessary because of our limited capacities, as 'blessed Dionysius' says (cf. above, Ch. V). A firm distinction is then made between theology and the 'subordinate' disciplines, the merely human arts and sciences. Biblical science has the special task of moulding the *affectus* (the disposition of the will) in accordance with piety, whence it employs the *modus* which (to take the overall view) proceeds by way of precept, example, exhortation, revelation, and prayer. On the other hand, the lesser sciences have the task of educating the intellect to know the truth, and they employ the *modus* which proceeds through definition, analysis, and deduction, these being the standard logical methods of analysis. Is the mode of sacred Scripture, then, capable of certain verification; that is, can we be sure that its doctrine is in some sense true? The answer is 'yes'—true in terms of experience and disposition rather than investigation and intellect, and according to the spiritual soul rather than the carnal soul.

---

[13] Extensive treatments of this debate are offered by M.-D. Chenu, *La théologie comme science au XIIIe siècle*, 3rd edn. (Bibliothèque Thomiste XXXIII, Paris, 1969), and U. Köpf, *Die Anfänge der theologischen Wissenschaftstheorie im 13. Jahrhundert* (Beiträge zur hist. Theol. XLIX, Tübingen, 1974); cf. Minnis, *Authorship*, pp. 119ff., R. J. Long, 'The Science of Theology according to Richard Fishacre', *Med. Stud.* xxxiv (1972), 71–98, G. H. Tavard, 'St Bonaventure's Disputed Questions *De theologia*', *RTAM* xvii (1950), 187–236. On the growing systematization of the study of theology see Chenu, 'The Masters of the Theological "Science"' in id., *Nature, Man and Society in the Twelfth Century*, pp. 270–309, and Evans, *Old Arts and New Theology*.

St Bonaventure conducted his inquiry on similar lines. In his *Sentences* commentary (written between 1250 and 1252) he attempts to reconcile the cognitive, practical, and affective aspects of theology by endorsing the idea that wisdom, which comprises both cognition and affection, exists for the purpose of contemplation but principally in order that we may become good. This places the emphasis on the affective power of the Bible, as Bonaventure's remarks in his later *Breviloquium* (written between 1254 and 1257) make clear: the authoritative doctrine of Scripture exists for the purpose of making us good, and this objective is achieved not by mere intellectual deliberation but by the correct disposition of the will. In order that the will be disposed correctly, the biblical *formae tractandi* have to move our affections (*affectus*) by examples, promises, and devotions. Therefore, Scripture has to avoid the mode of treatment which proceeds by definition, division, and synthesis. By contrast, the *Sentences* of Peter Lombard—a work which serves the Bible just as a subordinate science serves the superior one—employs the investigative mode, in order to refute the opponents of the faith, strengthen those whose faith is weak, and give pleasure to those who are perfect.

Giles of Rome was even more convinced of the importance of the affective force of the Bible. In the first book of his *Sentences* commentary (written between 1275 and 1278) he lists the three ends or objectives of theology as good works, speculation, and love (*caritas*), and concludes that only the last of these is theology's *finis* in the strict sense of the term. Since *caritas* is in the power of affection—in contrast with those speculative and practical questions which concern the intellect—the science of theology is therefore affective rather than intellectual.[14] Given this position, it is not surprising to discover that the Song of Songs, which employs the mode that is 'affective, concerned with desire, and contemplative', is of special importance to Giles. Its *finis*, love, is the same as that of 'all sacred doctrine taken as a whole', but this particular book works towards that end in a particular, specific way. Then Giles considers the possibility that, since love is a sort of action (*opus*), theology should be called a practical science. His answer is that practical science is principally directed towards exterior action (and so political sciences are called practical), but spiritual goodness is not dependent on action of that kind and therefore should not be called practical.[15]

There was, of course, never any possibility of anyone concluding that theology was simply practical, a matter of moral philosophy—that would have put it on a par with those fables of the poets which 'pertained to ethics' and with works which taught political science, like Giles of Rome's own *On the Instruction of Princes*.[16] 'In the whole field of moral teaching', Giles declares in the extract translated below, 'the mode of procedure, according to the Philosopher, is figurative and broad.' Individual matters, he continues, are variable

[14] Cf. P. W. Nash, 'Giles of Rome and the Subject of Theology', *Med. Stud.* xviii (1956), 61–92, and P. Prassel, *Das Theologieverständnis des Ägidius Romanus, O.E.S.A.* (Frankfurt, 1983), esp. pp. 69–71.

[15] Cf. Prassel, op. cit., p. 164.

[16] Written c.1285 for his pupil, the future King Philip the Fair of France.

and hence uncertain in scientific terms (as Aristotle says in the *Ethics*),[17] and therefore instruction in such matters is rightly conducted by means of a figurative style, a style which, because it is unsubtle and general and thus comprehensible to the whole populace, is the more effective in stirring the *affectus* of each and every member of the state.[18] But to reduce theology to this level would have been tantamount to denying its claim to satisfy the very highest reaches of the human intellect, such an elevated achievement being attainable only by a select few. The usual response to this problem was that anything which the *poetae et philosophi* could do the scriptural *auctores* could do better. They could be by turns cognitive, affective and practical, and the range of *modi tractandi* at their disposal was much wider than that available to pagan writers. Some books of the Bible did indeed teach moral philosophy, but others employed didactic methods far beyond the reach of any uninspired mortal, like the 'revelatory mode' as found in the Prophets and Revelation. The unique and supreme status of Scripture as the book to end (in every sense of the term) all books was thereby affirmed.

However, different positions on the question of the nature of theology entailed marked differences of opinion concerning the biblical *modi tractandi*, as may be illustrated by Henry of Ghent's attack on the claim made in *Alexander's Sum of Theology* that the overall form or mode of treatment employed in Holy Scripture has many forms and is varied. According to *Alexander's Sum of Theology* the commands, prohibitions, inductions of fear, etc. which appear in Scripture are distinct and different modes of treatment; for Henry they are different subject-matters, the mode remaining the same and uniform. *Alexander's Sum of Theology* had justified its approach by appealing to the multiform wisdom of God; Henry's reply is that a single mode of treatment can be thought of as applying to each and every aspect of God's wisdom. It is not the case that one piece of the divine wisdom is divulged in this passage and another in that; rather, in every part of Scripture the multiform divine wisdom is expressed consistently through the different senses of the text. *Alexander's Sum of Theology* had argued that various aspects of the science of theology are communicated in various ways to various people; Henry will have none of this piecemeal diffusion and diminution of the divine wisdom. Theology, he claims, is offered for our consideration in its totality to every condition of men, and each man will understand according to his capacity. Some people are content with the surface literal interpretation while others seek the spiritual understanding; the same passage can offer milk to beginners and solid food to initiates.

Behind all these disagreements with *Alexander's Sum of Theology* seems to lie

----

[17] *Eth. Nicomach.* ii. 2 (1104^{a}3–7), cf. i. 3 (1094^{b}11–14). In Grosseteste's version, tr. C. I. Litzinger, *S. Thomas Aquinas: Commentary on the Nicomachean Ethics* (Chicago, 1964), pp. 117–18, the crucial passage reads: '. . . things pertaining to actions, and relevant considerations, do not have anything fixed about them any more than the things that concern health. If this is true in the general treatment, still more uncertainty will be found in the consideration of particular cases.'

[18] For discussion of this principle, and some of its literary implications, see Allen, *Ethical Poetic*, pp. 13 ff., and Minnis (ed.), *Gower's* Confessio amantis, pp. 71–4, 115–18.

Henry of Ghent's conviction that there are no divine ideas of individuals but only of species. This is what, in essence, causes him to be less enthusiastic than the vast majority of his contemporaries concerning the theory of a literal sense of Scripture which employs different *modi tractandi* to appeal to individual human beings. One may detect the influence on Henry of the Augustinian (and ultimately Neoplatonic) notion that infinite resources of divine wisdom lurk behind each and every scriptural discourse, a notion which encourages an emphasis on the interdependence, on the spiritual level, of all the books of the Bible.[19] But adequate analysis of those and related matters would require a separate study. Enough has been said to make it clear that late medieval accounts of the styles of Scripture, far from being peripheral to the main concerns of thirteenth-century scholasticism, were in fact an integral part of a great debate, conducted among many of the best thinkers of that period, about the qualities of the highest and truest form of science known to man.

3. *Signification, literal sense, and literary sensibility.* Our translated extracts include discussions from *Alexander's Sum of Theology* and by Bonaventure, Aquinas, Henry of Ghent, and Nicholas of Lyre about the number of *sensūs* (senses, understandings) present in Holy Scripture. The authorities seem to differ on this question, two, three, four, or indeed five senses having been postulated. Yet all our schoolmen, having applied the *sic et non* technique, come to the same basic conclusion, however much they vary in emphasis: there is a single literal sense and a threefold spiritual sense (tropological/ moral, allegorical/Christological, and anagogical). Henry of Ghent's analysis is obviously based on that found in *Alexander's Sum of Theology*: he quotes the very same sources (Bede, Hugh of Saint-Victor, Augustine) and on occasion the very same passages.

The Augustinian distinction between words which signify and things which signify (cf. our discussion above, p. 66) is invoked again and again, the literal sense being supposed to involve significative words and the spiritual senses, significative things. Nicholas of Lyre, who was heavily influenced by Thomas Aquinas' exegetical theory, also uses this distinction, illustrating it with the well-worn example of the fourfold interpretation of the word 'Jerusalem', which goes back to St John Cassian (*c.*360–435).[20] What distinguishes our schoolmen's accounts from those of so many of their predecessors, however, is the way in which their analyses of scriptural signification privilege the literal sense.[21]

[19] Cf. Minnis, *Authorship*, pp. 128–9, and E. Gilson, *History of Christian Philosophy in the Middle Ages* (London, 1955), pp. 447–52, 759–62. On the Neoplatonism in Henry's exegesis see B. Smalley, 'A Commentary on the Hexameron by Henry of Ghent', *RTAM* xx (1953), p. 64.

[20] See de Lubac, *Exég. méd.* i. 190–8; O. Chadwick, *John Cassian: A Study in Primitive Monasticism*, 2nd edn. (Cambridge, 1968), pp. 101–2. Cassian's test-case of Jerusalem is cogently explained in the short 'treatise on the way a sermon ought to be composed' which Guibert of Nogent wrote (shortly before 1084) as a preface to his commentary on Genesis (PL clvi. 25 D–26A), and it occurs in the prolegomena to Genesis in the *Glossa ordinaria* (*Bibl. glos.* i, unfol., cf. PL cxiii. 63 B-C).

[See p. 204 for n. 21]

In his *Breviloquium* Bonaventure stresses the importance of having 'prior knowledge of the truth of the actual text of Holy Scripture, expressed explicitly' when investigating the meaning of the spiritual sense, and this priority is certainly operating when he codifies ideas culled from Augustine's *On Christian Doctrine* into three interpretative 'rules' or strategies. Augustine had savoured the pleasure he gained from eliciting the allegorical understanding of S. of S. 4: 2;[22] Bonaventure's point is rather that an obscure passage of that kind should be interpreted with reference to other parts of the Bible where its significative things are explained clearly in the significative words of a literal sense. Similarly, Aquinas declares that all arguments must be drawn from the literal sense alone, and not from what is said in the allegorical sense, backing up this new emphasis with a statement quoted (out of context to serve his own purpose) from Augustine's letter against Vincent the Donatist. This declaration and this *auctoritas* were reiterated with even more force by Nicholas of Lyre, in the course of an attack on those theologians who had well-nigh suffocated the literal sense with their excessive proliferation of mystical interpretations.[23] Taking Hugh of Saint-Victor's favourite metaphor of the building (see above, pp. 74, 78) a stage further than Hugh himself had ever done, Lyre argues that 'just as a building which begins to part company with its foundations is inclined to collapse, so a mystical exposition which deviates from the literal sense must be considered unseemly and inappropriate'. Lyre was exceptionally well equipped to champion the cause of the literal sense, having a knowledge of Hebrew and of rabbinic exegesis.

Nothing necessary to faith is conveyed through the spiritual sense which is not conveyed elsewhere in Scripture, clearly and openly, through the literal sense. If we push this principle, stated so clearly by Aquinas, to its logical conclusion, allegory becomes at worst redundant and at best a pleasing (and persuasive) optional extra. Theory of interpretation like this, and the exegetical practice of so many of the schoolmen, dealt a powerful blow to the status of allegorical reading of the Bible as an academic procedure.[24]

[21] Henry of Ghent, however, is something of a special case. His exegesis of the first three chapters of Genesis is certainly literalistic: see *La 'Lectura ordinaria super sacram Scripturam' attribuée à Henri de Gand*, ed. R. Macken (Louvain and Paris, 1972), pp. 41–263, and Smalley, 'Commentary on the Hexaemeron by Henry of Ghent', p. 66. But elsewhere Henry is inclined to minimize the contribution of the human authors (writers of the literal sense) to Scripture: see Minnis, *Authorship*, pp. 128–9; cf. the general argument by R. Macken, 'La théorie de l'illumination divine dans la phlosophie d'Henri de Gand', *RTAM* xxxix (1972), 82–112.

[22] *De doct. Christ.* II. vi. 7.

[23] Cf. the attack on excessive allegorical interpretation in Nicholas Trevet's Psalter commentary (written between 1317 and 1320), discussed by Minnis, *Authorship*, pp. 85–6. The ancient commentators, Trevet complains, concentrated on the profound mysteries found in allegories and, as a result, they rejected or treated perfunctorily the literal sense, in the mistaken belief that they were throwing away the rind and securing the sweet kernel. Cf. Ch. X, n. 261. Like Lyre, Trevet defends his use of Jewish exegesis, and he broke with convention in commenting on Jerome's *Hebraica* instead of his Gallican Psalter. On 12th-c. literalism relating to respect for the 'Hebrew text' see Smalley, *Study of the Bible*, pp. 101–6, 149–72, 187–8, 191–4.

[24] Cf. Smalley, *Study of the Bible*, pp. 281 ff. However, the original element in the exegesis of 'literalists' like Aquinas, Trevet, and Lyre, and the extent to which they influenced sub-

The human *auctores* of Scripture used significative words; the divine *auctor* used significative things—He, after all, was the creator of all things. The literal sense, the understanding arising from significative words, was identified as the expression of the intention of the human author. Late medieval literalistic exegesis rejected those earlier interpretations which did not pay sufficient attention to the *intentio auctoris*, but accepted those which kept close to the letter. Hence, in his commentary on Romans Aquinas can remark 'this response seems not at all to be in accordance with the intention of the author'; and elsewhere, 'this exposition is literal and according to the intention of the Apostle'.[25]

But to what extent did the authors of words know what the author of things Q was doing? This matter came to a head in late medieval analysis of prophecy: did the prophets speak with any knowledge of the significance of what they were saying? In marked contrast with earlier attitudes which tended to regard prophets and inspired writers as the passive mouthpieces for mysterious divine messages, several thirteenth-century theologians spoke up on behalf of the human beings whom God had selected. For instance, Hugh of Saint-Cher argued that there was no prophecy without knowledge,[26] the implication being, as Gillian Evans puts it, 'that the human authors of Scripture wrote / with understanding and in intelligent control of what they were saying'.[27] Similarly, in William of Auvergne's *De Legibus*, part of the vast *Magisterium divinale* which he wrote between 1223 and 1240, it is argued that 'prophetic signs, expressed by means of deeds or speech, were intended by the prophets themselves to be understood figuratively; they are the human authors' metaphors'.[28]

More and more was being claimed for the human author and the literal sense in which he expressed himself. In the extracts translated below, *Alexander's Sum of Theology*, Aquinas, and Henry of Ghent explain that all kinds of figurative language, including proverbs, parables, likenesses, ironies, and metaphors, are part of the literal sense of Scripture. If the human authors on occasion spoke openly and plainly, using words in their 'proper' or normal significations, on other occasions they expressed themselves in a figurative way, using words in 'transferred' or non-referential significations. The literal sense comprises both manners of speaking. These directions in biblical scholarship led to the appearance, in the fourteenth century, of the paradoxical term *duplex sensus litteralis*, 'twofold literal sense'. The literal sense, the sense primarily intended by the author, is *duplex*, declares William of

sequent medieval exegesis, must not be exaggerated. See de Lubac, *Exég. méd.* II/1. 238–62, II/2. 334–67.

[25] *Super epist. ad Rom.*, cap. iv, lect. 1, 331, in *S. Thomae Aquinatis super epistolas S. Pauli lectura*, ed. P. R. Cai (Marietti, 1953), p. 59; cf. P. C. Spicq, *Esquisse d'une histoire de l'exégèse latine au moyen âge* (Bibliothèque thomiste XXVI, Paris, 1944), p. 251.

[26] J. P. Torrell, *Théorie de la prophétie et la connaissance aux environs de 1230* (Spicilegium sacrum Lovaniense, étud. et doc. XL, Louvain, 1977), pp. 93, 154–5.

[27] G. R. Evans, *The Language and Logic of the Bible: The Road to Reformation* (Cambridge, 1985), p. 16.

[28] Ibid., p. 44.

Nottingham (*lector* to the Oxford Franciscans *c.*1312; d. *c.*1336).[29] There is a 'proper' literal sense, which arises from the initial signification of the language; there is also a 'figurative' literal sense, which comes from the secondary or metaphorical signification of the language, and this too is a meaning which the author intended or which can be elicited from his intention.[30] Nicholas of Lyre suggested that there was a *duplex sensus litteralis* in the passage 'I will be a father to him, and he shall be my son' (1 Chron. 17: 13). Literally, this refers to Solomon, in so far as he was the son of God by adoption in his youth, an identification confirmed by what God tells Nathan concerning Solomon in 2 Ks. 7 (see especially v. 14). Yet at Heb. 1: 5 the same passage is interpreted as referring to Christ, and Lyre argues that this too is a literal reading of the text. The problem is resolved in a way which supports rather than questions the existence of a twofold literal sense in 1 Chron. 17: 13. Since Solomon was the son of God by grace he fulfilled the prophecy less perfectly than did Christ, who was the son of God by nature.

Commentary such as this may be regarded as the high-water mark of medieval literalistic exegesis. Its widening of the breadth of the literal sense facilitated the thoroughgoing rejection of allegorical exegesis by theologians of the Reformation. 'The literal sense is the root and ground of all', declares William Tyndale in a polemical tract of the late 1520s, and goes on to claim that 'that which the proverb, similitude, riddle, or allegory signifieth, is ever the literal sense'.[31] In sum, the literal sense rules supreme over all the meaning of Holy Scripture. 'The literal sense does it', affirms Martin Luther; 'in it there's life, comfort, power, instruction and skill.' By contrast, the allegorical sense 'is tomfoolery, however brilliant the impression it makes'.[32]

Returning to the later Middle Ages, these new principles encouraged what may be described as a new kind of literary sensibility among theologians, a sensibility based on the literal rather than on the allegorical understanding of Scripture. Some of its products are offered below: Bonaventure's investigation of Peter Lombard's literary activity with reference to the respective roles of the scribe, compiler, commentator, and author; also his account of Solomon's use of different characters (*personae*) in Ecclesiastes; Lyre's elaborate description of the composition and subsequent collection of the psalms; and of course all the discussions of how the various *formae tractandi* of Scripture cater to the various needs of individual members of the audience, thereby suiting the style to the subject in the best rhetorical manner and also implementing Aristotle's

[29] See B. Smalley, 'Which William of Nottingham?', repr. in her *Studies in Medieval Thought and Learning, from Abelard to Wyclif* (London, 1981), pp. 284–7.

[30] William proceeds to equate the mystical sense (which is threefold) with the author's 'second intention'; ibid. Similarly, in his commentary on the Psalter Nicholas Trevet spoke of the literal sense of Scripture as its primary intention and the mystical sense as its secondary intention. See B. P. Shields, 'A Critical Edition of Selections from Nicholas Trevet's *Commentarius literalis in Psalterium iuxta Hebreos S. Hieronymi*' (unpub. Ph.D. thesis, Rutgers University, 1970), pp. 57–9; cf. pp. 36–7, 40–1. Cf. Minnis, *Authorship*, pp. 85–6.

[31] William Tyndale, *The Obedience of a Christian Man*, ed. H. Walter (Cambridge, 1848), pp. 304–5.

[32] Luther, *Table Talk*, ed. and tr. T. G. Tappert (Philadelphia, 1967), p. 406 (no. 5285). Both these passages are quoted by Evans, *Road to Reformation*, p. 49.

principle that moral science is concerned with particular experience. Here the *auctores* of the science of theology are being afforded a large measure of responsibility for what they said and the ways in which they said it.

4. *Authority and Fallibility.* Did the human fallibility of the *auctores* of Scripture devalue their *auctoritas?* How should the commentator cope with the unpalatable historical facts that King David, saint and supreme prophet, had committed adultery with Bathsheba and connived at the killing of her husband Uriah, and that King Solomon, the son of David and Bathsheba, had been led astray by his excessive love for women, even to the extent of worshipping strange gods? The early medieval predilection for allegorical interpretation had ensured that this problem never arose in acute form; then, the usual response was to refer matters relating to suspect authors and passages back to the divine authorship of the Bible, which guaranteed its ultimate *auctoritas* and truth. But for those later exegetes who favoured the literal-historical sense of Scripture, and were therefore interested in historical facts about the lives of its human authors, the problem was a serious one and they had to find new methods of coping with it. Two cases in point are treated below, the sins of Solomon as considered by Bonaventure in his commentary on Ecclesiastes and the sins of David as considered by Henry of Ghent at one point in his question 'Whether truth is inherent in every exposition and sense [of Scripture].'

Was Solomon unfit to be the author of Ecclesiastes? Bonaventure's key reply is that he did not write when in a state of sin but when doing penance for his sin, and therefore we can accept what he wrote with confidence. To the objection that Solomon actually committed sin Bonaventure answers that this does not destroy the wisdom in his teaching: the fault lies in his failure to practise what he preached. (This solution was offered often to a related problem which was hotly debated in the Parisian faculty of theology, namely, if a preacher is in a state of mortal sin does this devalue his preaching?)[33] Two other points, of a more conservative kind, are made by Bonaventure: God speaks through evil men as well as good men, and our belief in the Bible is dependent not as much on the goodness of any individual author as on the inspiration of the Holy Spirit who spoke through the prophets.

David's case was more complicated, and it already had occasioned a lot of debate before Henry of Ghent took it up. According to the *Glossa ordinaria*, as Henry notes, David represents Christ whereas Uriah represents the devil.[34] Here we encounter one of the fundamental paradoxes of the allegorical method: events or characters which, considered literally, are good can, considered allegorically, turn out to be bad. We have already noted that William of Conches, in his interpretation of the fable of Orpheus and Eurydice, was

[33] For discussion see Jean Leclercq, 'Le magistère du prédicateur au XIIIᵉ siècle', *AHDLMA* xxi (1946), 105–47, and A. J. Minnis, 'Chaucer's Pardoner and the "Office of Preacher"', in P. Boitani and A. Torti (eds.), *Intellectuals and Writers in Fourteenth-century Europe* (Tübinger Beiträge zur Anglistik VII, Tübingen and Cambridge, 1986), pp. 88–119.

[34] *Glossa ordinaria marginalis*, 2 Kgs. 11 (*Bib. glos.* ii. 572–5). On the two branches of the *Glossa ordinaria*, the marginal gloss and the interlinear gloss, see Smalley, *Study of the Bible*, pp. 56 ff.

able to identify Aristaeus, literally the would-be rapist who pursues Eurydice, as virtue striving to join itself to concupiscence. Similarly, in much twelfth-century exegesis David was interpreted as playing the role of Christ to Bathsheba's Church and Uriah's devil.[35] For instance, in his Psalter commentary (written between 1151 and 1158) Honorius 'of Autun' strives to assure the puzzled reader that he should not marvel at this representation, for such is the special and mysterious quality of the Bible.[36] With the decline in allegorical exegesis, however, theologians ceased to be satisfied with that kind of solution. Thus William of Auvergne, in his *De Legibus*, voiced his disquiet with the practice of having Uriah, a holy and just man, represent the devil, and the adulterous copulation of David and Bathsheba represent the most immaculate conjunction of Christ and the Church.[37] William makes the best of things by saying that one's audience will not be scandalized if the following type of similitude is decently expounded. David loved Bathsheba deeply and for her love procured the death of a man, then honoured her with regal marriage and elevated her to the royal throne; likewise, the King of Heaven loved the synagogue and, having procured the death of its Jewish magistrate, honoured it with spiritual marriage and elevated it to the kingdom of heaven. A good try, certainly, but this way out is possible only if David's adultery is glossed over and the injustice suffered by Uriah is ignored.

Henry of Ghent meets the problem of Uriah directly, declaring that the fact that David represents Christ need not entail that the devil is represented by Uriah. The solution he then offers turns on the contrast between the substance or very essence of an action and some quality or 'accident' relating to it, in this case the way in which the action was performed. Considered in terms of the way in which it was performed, no good interpretation of David's action is possible. Considered in terms of the substance of the action, one can imagine a prince having a knight put to death and taking his wife for himself: looked at from this viewpoint, a bad deed can have a good allegorical interpretation and be expounded for a good end.

One wonders if that solution really satisfied Henry. Many of his successors avoided such special pleading by approaching the problem not via allegory but via exemplification, an interpretative method which sits very comfortably with literal and historical exegesis. In their commentaries on the Psalter, Thomas Aquinas and Nicholas of Lyre expound the fiftieth psalm as David's admission of guilt and declaration of his remission. He is presented as an excellent *exemplum* of the truly penitent man who is rewarded with divine mercy.[38] The parallel with Bonaventure's treatment of Solomon is obvious.

David and Solomon, therefore, came to be regarded as *auctores* who taught by deed as well as by word. They sinned and repented; they received divine

---

[35] See B. Smalley, 'William of Auvergne, John of La Rochelle and St. Thomas Aquinas on the Old Law', repr. in ead., *Studies in Medieval Thought*, pp. 151, 165; Minnis, *Authorship*, p. 105.

[36] PL clxxxii. 283.

[37] *De legibus*, ch. xvii, in *Guilielmi Alverni episc. Paris. opera omnia* (Venice, 1591), p. 47.

[38] See Minnis, *Authorship*, pp. 107–9; cf. p. 106.

grace; their *vitae* are examples for us sinners, who may imitate their repentance of sin and hope for a corresponding remission. The theologians' recognition of the common humanity of author and audience has produced a new angle on the usefulness of the Bible.

5. *Scriptural Fiction and Truth*. The exegetes' worries about the possibility of untruth existing in Scripture extended far beyond the issue of the trustworthiness of certain authors. Statements which appear to be fabulous and false are found in the Bible: how can such things subsist in the true Word of God? And how do such passages compare with the fables of the poets, those generally acknowledged purveyors of fictions and even lies (cf. above, Ch. IV)? Many 'transferred' significations of words were being accepted as part and parcel of the literal sense: could this solution be extended to accommodate scriptural fiction? Thomas Aquinas thought so. In a passage translated below he claims that the parabolical sense is indeed contained within the literal sense, and this proves 'that nothing false can underlie the literal sense of holy Scripture'.

But there were tougher cases, such as the account in Judg. 9: 8 of the trees of the forest going forth to anoint their king. Here *Alexander's Sum of Theology* and Henry of Ghent use the argument that in such a parable there is truth in respect of the signification of things rather than the signification of words. To some extent they were influenced by Augustine's analysis of the passage from Judges in *To Consentius: Against Lying*, in which it is described as a fiction with a truthful end:

In feigning of this kind, men have attributed even human deeds or sayings to irrational animals and things without sense, in order that, by narratives of this sort which are fictitious but have true significations, they could communicate in a more agreeable manner what they wished to say. Nor is it in authors of secular literature alone, as in Horace, that mouse speaks to mouse and weasel to fox, so that by a fictitious narrative a true signification may be assigned concerning that which is being treated of; whence, the similar fables of Aesop having the same end in view, there is no man so untaught as to think they ought to be called lies: but in sacred literature also, as in the book of Judges, the trees seek a king for themselves, and speak to the olive, to the fig, to the vine, and to the bramble. Which, certainly, is all feigned in order that one may reach what is intended by a narrative which is indeed fictitious but not mendacious since it has a truthful signification.[39]

In the case of the apparently blatant lie of Jacob (recorded in Gen. 27: 24), Henry of Ghent's main source is Augustine's *On Lying*, where it is argued that Jacob's statement was in fact prophetic and directed towards the men not of his own time but of the future, who could recognize its full meaning. When something is said or done figuratively, it is no lie. Since, however, Augustine's similar treatment of the passage in *To Consentius: Against Lying* is mentioned though not elaborated upon by Henry, it may be cited here for purposes of comparison:

Concerning Jacob, however, that which his mother made him the author of, that he seemed to deceive his father, if it is examined diligently and in good faith it is not a lie

[39] *Contra mendacium*, xiii. 28 (CSEL xli. 508–9).

but a mystery. If we call such things lies then all the parables and figures which signify anything whatsoever which are not to be taken in their 'proper' meaning but in them one thing is to be understood from another, will also be said to be lies: which idea must be totally abandoned. For he who thinks this may also bring this slander to bear on tropical expressions, of which there are so many, so that even that which is called metaphor (that is, the usurped transference of any word from its proper thing [i.e. what it normally refers to] to a thing which is not proper to it) may, on this reasoning, be called a lie. For when we speak of waving corn-fields, of vines putting forth gems, of the bloom of youth, of snowy hairs, without doubt the waves, the gems, the bloom, the snow, because we do not find them in those things to which we have transferred these words from other things, shall be accounted as lies by these people. And Christ being a rock [1 Cor. 10: 4], and the stony heart of the Jews [Ezek. 36: 26], also Christ being a lion [Rev. 5: 5] and the devil being a lion [1 Pet. 5: 8], and innumerable other cases like this, will be said to be lies. . . . All these modes of speaking will be accounted lies if figurative speech or action be reckoned to be lying. But if it is not a lie when statements which signify one thing by another are related for the purpose of understanding truth, then surely not only that which Jacob did or said to his father in order that he might be blessed but also that which Joseph said as if in mockery of his brothers [Gen. 42], and David's pretence of madness [1 Kgs. 21: 13], and other similar cases, must be judged not to be lies but prophetical speeches and actions which are related for the purpose of understanding things which are true.[40]

The two scriptural passages in question, Judg. 9: 8 and Gen. 27: 24, continued to interest scholars long after the time of Henry. The tale of the trees anointing a king was cited by Pierre Bersuire in justifying his moralization of Ovid's fables on the grounds that fables had been used by both classical poets and biblical authors (cf. below, pp. 366–7), and in Boccaccio's *Genealogy of the Gentile Gods* it appears during a defence of the proposition that some pagan writers can, in a manner of speaking, be called theologians (cf. p. 438). Jacob's impersonation of Esau is one of the apparent falsehoods in Scripture discussed by Richard FitzRalph (c.1295–1360) in his highly influential *Sum of the Armenian Questions*. Here the solution offered is that Moses merely reported this and other lies without being responsible for them in any way; therefore, the truth of Scripture is secure.[41]

Returning to the thirteenth century, there were special reasons then for the schoolmen's great interest in these, and other, fabulous passages of Scripture. In the first instance, there was the influence of the Dionysian corpus, which justified even the most unlikely of comparisons, such as the deity being designated by the names of wild animals and even by the form of a worm (cf. Ch. V). Second, and also important, was the influence of certain statements in Aristotle's *Metaphysics* which afforded a measure of prestige (albeit limited). Poetry and theology were said to be connected in so far as the first poets were theologians (cf. Boccaccio's triumphant use of this passage, below, p. 437). Moreover, in the laws of the community, i.e. its traditional customs, regulations, and religious ideals, many mythical and fabulous elements were supposed to be intermixed with wisdom.[42]

[40] *Contra mendacium*, x. 24 (CSEL xli. 499–500).
[41] See A. J. Minnis, '"Authorial Intention" and "Literal Sense" in the Exegetical Theories of Richard FitzRalph and John Wyclif', *Proceedings of the Royal Irish Academy*, lxxv, sect. C, i (1975), 5–10.   [42] Aristotle, *Meta.* i. 2 (982[b]11–21), xii. 8 (1074[b]3–14).

But in the opinion of Stephen Tempier, Bishop of Paris, these ideas of Aristotle's had led certain schoolmen astray. The notions 'That the statements of the theologians are based on fables' and 'That there are fables and falsehoods in the Christian law just as in others' were among the 217 propositions which he condemned in 1277.[43] Henry of Ghent was a member of the commission of theologians which assisted Tempier.

It has been suggested that at least the proposition about fables existing in the Christian law was framed with Siger of Brabant (*c.*1240–*c.*1284) in mind.[44] If this was the case, the commission has read his commentary on the *Metaphysics* cursorily, for there he affirms that the didactic method of philosophy is superior to that of fable. However, on two counts, Siger declares, it is permissible to teach the truth in fable and metaphor. Some intelligible realities so transcend our minds that we cannot fully grasp them, and in this case some truths about the First Cause may be intimated by reference to its effects. Second, if an audience is mentally incapable of grasping the plain truth, though it is perfectly well known to the teacher, then that teacher can convey it through metaphorical language. All this, of course, is perfectly orthodox.

The proposition about theological statements being based on fables may also derive from a reading, or partial reading, of Siger, but it is equally likely that it reflects the commission's concern about a general trend among contemporary theologians. Those schoolmen who considered the possiblity that the modes of theology were in some sense poetic, sometimes practical, and even, according to some, essentially affective, could, in an atmosphere of heresy-hunting, be held to be coming dangerously close to the belief that theology rests on fable and figure. Certainly, Henry of Ghent, as we have noted already, was concerned that *Alexander's Sum of Theology* went some way towards reducing theology to moral philosophy or ethics, and ethics was, of course, the *pars philosophiae* often supposed (in the tradition of the *accessūs*) to be the province of the makers of fables, the poets. But whatever the specific target of Tempier and his advisors may have been, their attack did not bring the debate on scriptural fiction to a close. John Wyclif, writing in 1378, felt obliged to defend the truth of sacred Scripture against those who claimed that certain parts of the Bible are false, that it does not possess equal authority in all of its parts, that Christ often spoke in a merely figurative way (as when He called Himself 'the Son of God'), that the Deity was a liar, and that the Father could deceive the Son and either of them could deceive a prophet.[45]

[43] Condemned propositions 152 and 174 (1277), in *Chartularium universitatis Parisiensis*, i, ed. H. Denifle and E. Chatelain (Paris, 1889), pp. 552–3; cf. the discussion in R. Hissette, *Enquête sur les 219 articles condamnés à Paris le 7 mars 1277* (Louvain and Paris, 1977), pp. 274–5, and, more generally, J. F. Wippel, 'The Condemnations of 1270 and 1277 at Paris', *Journal of Medieval and Renaissance Studies*, vii (1977), 169–201.

[44] See A. Maurer, 'Siger of Brabant on Fables and Falsehoods in Religion', *Med. Stud.* xliii (1981), 513–30.

[45] For discussion and references see Minnis, '"Authorial Intention" and "Literal Sense"', pp. 13–14, 25–7. But, of course, one did not have to be a Wycliffite to object to the new attitude towards fables. See e.g. the attack by the English Carmelite John Baconthorpe (writing *c.*1336) on those who use falsehood to teach truth: B. Smalley, 'John Baconthorpe's Postill on St Matthew', repr. in ead., *Studies in Medieval Thought*, pp. 306–10.

But trends which held grave dangers in the minds of conservative thinkers also served to stimulate three of the most innovative literary theorists of the later Middle Ages, Dante, Petrarch, and Boccaccio. In Ch. X we shall see how they built on the 'common ground' between sacred and secular literature which had been established by several generations of theologians.

Finally, a word on the form in which most of the following discussions are written, namely, that of the scholastic question (*quaestio*) or disputation (*disputatio*). The master begins by stating a proposition with which he may or may not agree. Various arguments in favour of the proposition, and various arguments against it (*sed contra*), are then marshalled. Next comes the climax of the procedure: the master comes down firmly on one side or another, offering his own opinion. This is variously called the response (*responsio*), solution (*solutio*), or determination (*determinatio*). Finally, he addresses himself to the resolution of all the objections to the position he has espoused. But let us allow Bonaventure a word about this method, since he interprets Ecclesiastes as following the procedure of the disputation: we cannot know, he explains, 'what is accepted and what is rejected' until 'the judgement and determination is arrived at'. In reading the following *quaestiones*, therefore, it should be firmly borne in mind that only that part of the discussion which begins with the disputant's *responsio* may be taken as an account of what he personally believed.

ALEXANDER'S SUM OF THEOLOGY

Introductory Treatise, Question 1, chapter 4: Articles 1, 2, 3 and 4. i–ii[46]

The next enquiry to be made concerns the mode (*modus*) of Holy Scripture. The first question is whether the mode in Holy Scripture is art-based (*artificialis*) or scientific.[47] The second question is whether it is capable of certain verification. The third question is whether it has one single form or many forms. Then, supposing it has many forms, the fourth question is about the variety of the modes of Holy Scripture.

ARTICLE 1: WHETHER THE MODE OF HOLY SCRIPTURE IS ART-BASED AND SCIENTIFIC

First, the argument against may be made as follows.

⟨1.⟩ The way in which the poetic mode operates is not at all art-based

---

[46] Tr. from *Alexandri de Hales Summa theologica* (Quaracchi, 1924–48), i. 7–12, with the permission of Edizioni San Bonaventura, Grottaferrata (Rome).

[47] Here the terms *ars* and *scientia* are being used as synonyms: cf. Curtius, pp. 222–3. Vincent of Beauvais could claim that 'art' and 'science', and indeed 'doctrine', 'discipline', and 'faculty', mean the same thing: *Speculum doctrinale*, 1. xiii (*Speculum quadruplex*, ii. 14). Cf. Aristotle, *Meta.* i. 1 (980ᵈ21–981ᵇ12), Isidore, *Ety.* 1. i ff.; Hugh of Saint-Victor, *Didascalicon*, 11. i (ed. 23–4).

or scientific, because its mode is historical and transumptive, and these methods have no relation to any art. But the way in which theology proceeds is poetic or historical or parabolical. Therefore it is not art-based.

⟨2.⟩ Likewise, the whole way in which a science operates is by way of defining, analysing, and inferring.[48] But the mode of Holy Scripture is not thus. Therefore it is not scientific.

⟨3.⟩ Likewise, an art or science operates entirely by clear statements. But Holy Scripture operates by means of mystical statements (*sermones mysticos*). Therefore it is not art-based or scientific.

Response. It must be said that the way in which Holy Scripture proceeds is not that of an art or science which operates by means of the comprehension of human reason, but rather it proceeds through the ordering of the divine wisdom for the instructon of the soul in those matters which pertain to salvation. So Augustine in book xiv of *On the Trinity* says: 'I do not allow as part of this knowledge anything which can be known by men in human affairs where there is a very high degree of vanity or harmful inquisitiveness, but only that whereby the most wholesome faith, which leads to true happiness, is born, nourished, and strengthened.'[49] This knowledge is found in those matters which pertain to salvation.

[Against the objections.] ⟨1.⟩ To the first objection raised we must respond along the lines of the blessed Dionysius, who says in his *Celestial Hierarchies*: 'Out of consideration for our understanding theology has very artfully (*artificialiter*) used sacred poetic constructions (*formationes*) in non-material senses'. 'For it is not possible for the ray of truth to enlighten us unless it is veiled by various sorts of sacred veils for our elevation', 'since it is not possible for our mind to ascend to that immaterial contemplation of the heavenly hierarchics, unless it uses that material guidance which is suited to it'. Thus, 'there have been beautifully produced in Holy Scripture forms for those things which are without form and figures for those things which lack figures'. Therefore, 'it is most fitting to conceal divine mysteries in elaborate language and to make inaccessible to the many that true knowledge of the supernatural Intelligences which is hallowed and hidden from view. For not everyone is holy, nor have all men knowledge, as the holy writings tell us.[50] From these words of blessed Dionysius it is clear that one reason why Holy

---

[48] The *modus definitivus, divisivus, collectivus*; the last of these terms referring to the formation of syllogisms. Cf. Aristotle, *Anal. post.* i. 7 (25ᵃ38–ᵇ20), and Augustine; *De doct. Christ.* ii. xxxi. 48, ii. xxxv. 53–xxxvi. 54. For discussion and further bibliography see Minnis, *Authorship*, pp. 122–3, 144–7, and the relevant nn.

[49] *De Trinitate*, xiv. i. 3 (CCSL l(a). 424).

[50] Interspersing citations from Erigena's version of *De cael. hier.* i–ii (PL cxxii. 1040, 1038ff., 1041).

Scripture is handed down in a highly artful way (*artificialiter*) after the mode of poetry may be to meet the needs of our understanding, which is not capable of comprehending divine things. A second reason is the honour due to truth, which must be concealed from the wicked.

⟨2.⟩ To the second objection we must reply that there are two methods of achieving knowledge, one which operates through the understanding of the truth by human reason, while the other operates through the inculcation of a pious disposition (*affectus pietatis*) by means of divine instruction. The first mode must be by definition, analysis, and deduction. Such a mode must exist in human branches of knowledge because the apprehension of truth in accordance with human reasoning is unfolded through analyses, definitions, and logical arguments. The second mode must be by way of precept, example, exhortation, revelation, and prayer, because those methods are appropriate to a pious disposition. This is the mode of Holy Scripture; hence at Tit. 1⟨: 1⟩ one reads of knowledge 'according to piety'. Furthermore, the mode which uses precept is found in the Law and the Gospels, the mode using example is found in the historical books, the mode using exhortation is found in the books of Solomon and in the Epistles, the mode of revelation in the Prophets, and that using prayer in the Psalms.

Notice also that the mode employed by that type of science which has the task of moulding the affections (*affectus*) in accordance with piety is different from that employed in the type which has the task of educating the intellect alone to know the truth. The mode used to train the disposition (*affectus*) will proceed by the different ways mentioned above, for precepts, examples, exhortations, revelations, and prayers all induce desires (*affectiones*) for piety. Now, piety is 'the adoration of God', as St Augustine says in *On the Trinity*, book xii, introducing the words of Job 28⟨: 28⟩: 'Behold, piety is wisdom'. So the adoration of God is 'that by reason of which we long to see Him here and now, and believe and hope that we shall see Him'.[51] We long because of our love for Him, we believe because of our faith, and we hope because of our hope.[52] The practise of piety is taught through these three virtues.

⟨3.⟩ We must reply to the third objection that, just as it is appropriate for human knowledge to be transmitted by means of statements that are clearly understandable (*sermones manifestos*), so it is appropriate for divine wisdom to be transmitted through statements which have a hidden meaning (*sermones occultos*). For wisdom resides in the mysterious, as is said in 1 Cor. 2⟨: 7⟩: 'We speak wisdom, which is hidden in mystery.' The reason for thus concealing wisdom is threefold. For it wins merit in that it believes what it does not see. Hence Rev. 5⟨: 1⟩ says: 'I saw in the right hand of Him who was seated a book written on the inside and the outside

---

[51] *De Trin.* xii. xiv. 22, cf. xiv. i. 1 (CCSL l. 357, l(a). 421). The Septuagint text is being cited.
[52] Cf. Augustine, *De Trin.* viii. iv. 6 (CCSL l. 275).

(*scriptum intus et foris*), sealed with seven seals.' The second reason is that it stimulates study. Hence the words of Dan. 12⟨: 4⟩: 'Shut up the words and seal the book until the appointed time. For very many will pass over, and knowledge will be manifold.' The third reason is the honour due to truth, which must be concealed from the wicked. St Matthew ⟨vii: 6⟩: 'Do not give what is holy to dogs, or set pearls before swine.'

ARTICLE 2: WHETHER THE MODE OF HOLY SCRIPTURE IS
CAPABLE OF CERTAIN VERIFICATION

The next question is whether the mode of Holy Scripture is capable of certain verification, that is, whether that mode of Holy Scripture is more certain than is the mode used in other sciences.

⟨1.⟩ Understanding (*intellectus*) is more certain than faith, and understanding plays the part in other types of knowledge which faith does in this one. Therefore, the mode in other sciences is more certainly verifiable than the mode in this one.

⟨2.⟩ Likewise, that knowledge is more certain which proceeds from first principles which are in themselves clearly manifest to the understanding, than that which proceeds from first principles which are hidden from the understanding. But other sciences proceed from first principles which are in themselves clearly manifest to the understanding, while this one [i.e. theology] proceeds from first principles which are hidden from the understanding, namely principles resting on faith. So, the mode in the other sciences is more certainly verifiable.

⟨3.⟩ Likewise, the mode is more certainly verifiable in the case of that science which is transmitted by means of statements which are proper [i.e. wherein words are used in their normal, ordinary meanings] than in that which proceeds from transumptive statements.

⟨4.⟩ Likewise, that subject is more clearly verifiable which is treated of in words (*dicta*) which are univocal [i.e. having one meaning] and are expressed in a simple way than the one which is treated of in words which are of equivocal meaning and are expressed in a complex way, because from them arise judgements (*sententiae*) that are open to doubt. The end result then, is that the mode of procedure is more certainly verifiable in the case of other sciences than in the case of theology.

The contrary position. The mode of acquiring knowledge by [divine] inspiration is more certainly verifiable than that which operates by human reason. Likewise, that which is known by the testimony of the Spirit is more certain than that which is known by the testimony of created beings. Similarly, that which is known by the sense of taste is more certain than that which is known by the sense of sight. Since, therefore, the way in which Holy Scripture operates is the mode of knowing which works through inspiration, through the testimony of the Spirit, and through the sense of taste, whereas in other sciences the mode of knowing operates through reason, through the testimony of created beings, and through the sense of sight, it is clear that the mode of knowing is more certainly verifiable in theology than in the other sciences.

Response. There is certainty bred of investigation (*speculatio*)[53] and certainty bred of experience. Besides, there is certainty according to intellect (*intellectus*) and certainty according to disposition (*affectus*). Likewise, there is a certainty in terms of the spiritual soul and a certainty in terms of the carnal [lit. 'animal'] soul. I say, therefore, that the theological mode is more certain in terms of the certainty that comes from experience; and in terms of the certainty that relates to disposition, which operates through taste, as in the Psalm [118: 103]: 'How sweet are your words in my throat', etc. But it is not more certain in terms of the investigation of the intellect, which operates through sight. Likewise, for a spiritual man it is more certain, but for a carnal [lit. 'animal'] man it is less certain. 1 Cor. 2(: 14): 'The carnal [lit. 'animal'] man does not perceive those matters which come from the spirit of God. But the spiritual man discerns all things'.

[Against the objections.] ⟨1.⟩ The solution to the first objection is now clear: faith is more certain than the intellect [which operates in] other sciences by dint of the certainty that comes from disposition (*affectus*) rather than the certainty that is the result of investigation.

⟨2.⟩ In answer to the second objection we must say that there are basic principles of truth seen as truth, and basic principles of truth seen as virtue. I say, therefore, that other sciences originate in the principles of truth which are known in themselves as truth. But this science [i.e. theology] proceeds from the principles of truth seen as virtue and known in themselves as virtue, although in respect of truth those principles are hidden. So, this science [i.e. theology] belongs to virtue rather than to any art, and it is wisdom rather than a science, because it consists in virtue and the achieving of virtue rather than in study and the acquiring of knowledge. 1 Cor. 2(: 4): 'Our speech (*sermo*) does not consist in the persuasive words of human wisdom, but in the showing forth of the spirit and of virtue.'

⟨3.⟩ In answer to the third objection we must say that there is a kind of certainty possessed by the carnal [lit. 'animal'] man, who has no knowledge except that acquired by his experience of things susceptible to his senses, and there is a kind of certainty possessed by the spiritual man, who has a spirit equipped for the contemplation of things divine. Thus,

---

[53] Here *speculatio* is used in the sense of spiritual speculation, or contemplation.

the way of proceeding by means of mystical statements (*mysticas locutiones*) is not certain for the carnal man, though it is for the spiritual man. 1 Cor. 2⟨: 9⟩: 'He has revealed to us through the Spirit that which the eye has not seen and the ear has not heard, nor has it come into the heart of man. For the Spirit examines all things.' Besides, as has been said, it is the peculiar characteristic of this science to be handed down in a mysterious way and therefore in statements whose meaning is hidden. Since, therefore, the mode of hidden or mystical statements is in tune with the particular nature of that science [i.e. of theology], that mode will be more certain to the soul which is disposed towards it [i.e. theology], that is, the spiritual soul and not the carnal soul.

⟨4.⟩ In answer to the last objection we must say that there is one form of certainty in knowledge handed down through the human spirit, and a different one in knowledge handed down through God's spirit. For the former is constricted by the bounds of one single understanding (*intellectus*) through the operation of the human spirit, which only understands one thing at one and the same time. But in the latter there is no such limitation. For God's spirit, through which it [i.e. divine knowledge] has been handed down to us, is 'single yet multiple', as Wisd. 7⟨: 22⟩ says. So, the mode in Holy Scripture works in such a way that the literal sense should be single but the mystical sense multiple. This does not take away from the certainty in the soul which is disposed towards that [science of theology], namely the spiritual soul, as has already been said.[54]

ARTICLE 3: WHETHER THE MODE OF HOLY SCRIPTURE HAS
ONE FORM OR MANY FORMS

The next question to be asked is whether the mode of Holy Scripture is uniform or multiple.

[The argument] that it has many forms. ⟨*a.*⟩ Heb. 1⟨: 1⟩: 'God spoke in many different ways (*modi*) of old to the Fathers in the books of the Prophets', etc. The conclusion to be drawn from this is that there is not a uniform mode in the Old Testament.

⟨*b.*⟩ Similarly, Eph. 3⟨: 8–10⟩: 'To me, the least of all the saints, has been given the privilege of spreading abroad among the gentiles the unfathomable riches of the grace of Christ', and there follows: 'So that the manifold wisdom of God may become known to princes and powers through the Church'. From this we draw the conclusion that there is not a uniform mode in the New Testament.

⟨*c.*⟩ Likewise, there is a fourfold sense in the words of Holy Scripture, as Bede says [in the *Gloss*] at the beginning of Genesis: 'Holy Scripture

---

[54] In the response to the third objection, above.

has four senses: history, which speaks of events (*res gestae*); allegory, in which something other than the normal meaning is understood; tropology, that is, the moral form of expression, in which the ordering of men's morals is the subject; anagogy, by means of which we are led to higher things when we intend to treat of the loftiest themes and matters celestial. For instance, following the historical sense Jerusalem is a city; allegorically it signifies the Church; according to the tropological sense, that is, in terms of morals, it is the soul of any faithful Christian; according to the anagogical sense it is the life of all heavenly beings, who see God "with face uncovered" (2 Cor. 3⟨: 18⟩)'.[55] So, the ways in which Holy Scripture may be understood are manifold.

⟨*d.*⟩ In the Law the mode is that of instruction; in the historical books, it is historical and by way of example; in the books of Solomon, by way of exhortation; in the Psalms, by way of prayer; in the prophets, by way of revelations. Therefore, the conclusion is that the mode used in the books of the Old Testament is not uniform.

⟨*e.*⟩ Similarly, in the Gospels the mode is historical in terms of the account of the life and actions of Christ, while in Christ's teaching the mode is that of command and instruction. In the letters of Paul and the Canonical Epistles the mode is that of instruction, while in the Acts of the Apostles it is historical, and in the Apocalypse, revelatory. Therefore, the mode used in the New Testament is not uniform.

⟨*f.*⟩ Besides, Dionysius in his *Angelic Hierarchy* says: 'There are two kinds of holy manifestation. One proceeds appropriately by means of images which are of similar nature [i.e. akin to things divine]. The other proceeds by dissimilar forms (*formationes*) which are fashioned in a way that is altogether inappropriate and unsuitable [with regard to things divine].' Similar images are used, for instance, 'when they celebrate the eloquence of God in terms of reason and intellect and essence, declaring the divine rationality and wisdom and truly existing permanence'. Dissimilar images are used, for instance, 'when they call Him invisible, infinite, and incomprehensible, from which terms is signified not what He is but what He is not'.[56] The conclusion, then, is that there is no uniform mode of [divine] manifestation in Holy Scripture.

The contrary position. ⟨1.⟩ Rom. 15⟨: 4⟩: 'Whatever has been written has been written for our instruction.' If, therefore, for our instruction a uniform mode is better than a multiple mode, because a multiple mode confuses the understanding (*intellectus*), the consequence is that the mode of sacred instruction must be uniform.

---

[55] Actually the *Gl. ord. marg.*, Gen., pro. (Bibl. glos. i, unfol., cf. PL cxiii. 63 B-C); cf. Bede, *De tabernaculo*, 1. vi (PL xci. 410), and *In Cant. Cant. allegor. expositio*, iv (PL xci. 1142). Cf. also Henry of Ghent's citations in this passage in two parts, below, pp. 257, 260.

[56] All citations are from *De cael. hier.* ch. ii (PL cxxii. 1041).

⟨2.⟩ Likewise, our understanding is better informed by fewer facts rather than many, for the path is easier [to follow] among fewer.[57] Therefore the mode of Holy Scripture must be uniform.

⟨3.⟩ Moreover, the mode which is uniform is smoother and easier than that which is manifold. But the mode of Scripture must proceed by the smoother and clearer way. Hence, Hab. 2⟨: 2⟩ [says]: 'Write of what you have seen and explain it, so that he who reads it may run'. The consequence is that it must be uniform.

Response. It must be maintained that the mode of Holy Scripture must be manifold, and that for three reasons. The first reason relates to the effector [i.e. the author of Scripture], that is, the Holy Spirit, which is, as is said in Wisd. 7⟨: 22⟩, 'the spirit of understanding, single yet multiple'. So, in order that the mode of the effector may appear in the realm of sacred science, it must be multiple or take many forms. The second reason relates to the subject matter, which is 'the wisdom of God in its many forms' (Eph. 3⟨: 10⟩). So, in order that the mode may match the subject it too must take many forms. The third reason relates to the objective (*finis*), which is instruction in those matters which relate to salvation. The conditions (*status*) of men are manifold: in the time of the Law, in the time after the Law, in the time of prophecy, in the time of grace. Even within these periods the conditions of men are manifold. For some are sluggish in matters relating to faith, some are rebellious in matters relating to good morality, and [fall short] in different ways. Some pass their lives in prosperity, some in adversity, some in good works, some in sin. The conclusion must be drawn that the teaching of Holy Scripture, which has been ordained for the salvation of men, must employ a multiple mode, so that the mode matches the objective.

[Against the objections.] 1. To the objection that a multiple mode confuses the understanding, we must reply that this is not true. In fact it instructs the understanding. The understanding may be slow, it may be quick, or it may be moderately quick. So, the truth must be taught in different ways and in a different form to the slow, quick, and moderately quick understanding, so that what the slow intellect does not understand in one form it understands in another. Besides, the simple-minded young must be instructed in a different way from those who are fully adult. As the Apostle says in 1 Cor. 3: 1–2: 'I have given you milk to drink, not food, as you are little children in [your knowledge of] Christ. For you were not yet able for food, nor are you able now'. For this reason a mode which takes many forms is necessary.

[57] Cf. Aristotle, *Anal. post.* i. 25 (86ª33–ᵇ9), *Topica*, ii. 2 (109ᵇ14–15).

⟨2.⟩ The other objection must be resolved in the same way, by negation.[58] For the understanding is better instructed by having to cope with
fewer facts when one is concerned with the condition (*status*) of an
individual. But this is not true when we are concerned with the different
kinds of understanding arising out of differences between men and different conditions of men.

⟨3.⟩ To the objection that the mode which takes one form is smoother
and easier than that which has many forms, we must reply that this is not
true when a manifold mode is employed in revealing one and the same
thing in accordance with several different forms.

ARTICLE 4: CONCERNING THE MANIFOLD NATURE OF
THE MODES OF HOLY SCRIPTURE

The next question concerns this manifold nature.

⟨i.⟩ First of all, regarding the multiplicity to be found in the senses of
Holy Scripture.

It seems from the aforesaid authoritative quotation from Bede[59] that the
multiplicity of understanding of Holy Scripture lies in the existence of
four [senses]: historical, allegorical, tropological, and anagogical. But
objections are made against this. ⟨1.⟩ Hugh of Saint-Victor supposes that
there are only three: historical, allegorical, tropological. So he says in the
third book of his *Sentences*: 'History is the narration of events, which
consists in the primary signification of the letter. Allegory occurs when
some other event either past or to come in the future is signified by that
which is said to have happened. Tropology is when something which has
to be done is signified by that which is said to have happened.'[60] If we
follow this definition then, Bede's allocation of categories seems to be
superfluous as far as the anagogic understanding is concerned.

⟨2.⟩ Likewise, in Holy Scripture there are proverbs and parables
composed with a literal sense. Quite clearly, the mode which uses
parables is not historical or allegorical or tropological or anagogical.
Thus, there are many more ways of understanding [Scripture] than just
these four. Therefore, the aforesaid arrangement [i.e. Bede's] is
destroyed.

⟨3.⟩ Moreover, Augustine in his book *On the Usefulness of Belief* says: 'All
that part of Scripture which is called the Old Testament is set forth in four
ways: either in terms of the history, when what is written is the subject of
the teaching; or aetiologically [i.e. with reference to causes], when the

---

[58] i.e. by denying it. Cf. Aristotle, *De sophist. elen.* 18 (176ᵇ29–177ᵃ8), Ps.-Boethius, *Elen.
sophist. Arist. interp.* (PL lxiv. 1029).

[59] i.e. the passage in the *Gl. ord. marg.* cit. above in art. 3c; cf. above, n. 55.

[60] This is *De sacramentis*, i, prol. iv (PL clxxvi. 185). Cf. the references to Hugh's 'Sentences'
by Thomas Aquinas, in *Summa theologiae*, Ia 1, art. 10, ad 2um, and Henry of Ghent, *Summa
quaestionum ordinarium*, art. 16, qu. 3, both tr. below.

reason for writing is the subject of the teaching; or analogically, when the points of agreement between Old and New Testaments are taught; or allegorically, when it is taught that there are statements which must not be understood literally, but allegorically.'[61] The conclusion to be drawn from all this is that there is a single mystical sense and a threefold literal sense. But in Bede's classification mentioned above there is one literal and three mystical senses.

Response. We must assert that, since the primal Truth [i.e. God] is three-fold and yet one, the nature of the knowledge of that primal Truth is three in one. The one is the literal sense; the three, the mystical sense: the anagogical, which leads men up to the first principle [of all things, namely God]; the allegorical, which makes known the secrets of original Truth; the tropological or moral, which guides us to the supreme Good. Thus, the anagogical sense relates to the Father, the allegorical sense to the Son, and the moral sense to the Holy Spirit.

Now, the number of senses is understood as follows because there is either the literal, outer (*exterior*) meaning or the spiritual, inner (*interior*) meaning. The first of these does not multiply. But the spiritual meaning is varied, because it relates either to morals or to faith, and if it relates to faith it relates to faith on the part of God or faith on the part of man. In the first mode [i.e. relating to morals] it is moral, in the second mode [i.e. relating to faith on the part of God] it is anagogical, in the third mode [i.e. relating to faith on the part of man] it is allegorical. They can be taken in another way, so that we may say that the understanding of Holy Scripture comes from cause or from effect. From the cause, which is external, namely God, is the anagogical understanding. The understanding from effect can be twofold, either from an event which has occurred or from something which must be done. If it arises from something which must be done we have the moral or tropological interpretation. If it arises from an event which has occurred, this is understood in two ways. Either the understanding is based on the apparent meaning of the letter; that is, through the signification of the words, and this is the literal or historical understanding. 'For history is the narration of events, which is contained in the apparent meaning of the letter', as Hugh of Saint-Victor says.[62] Or else understanding is through the signification of the events described, and in this case it is allegorical, as Hugh says: 'allegory occurs when some other event either in the present or in the future or in the past is signified by that which is said to have happened.'[63]

[Against the objections.] ⟨1.⟩ Note therefore that Hugh of Saint-Victor, who postulated that the subject-matter of the Holy Scriptures is the work

---

[61] Augustine, *De utilitate credendi*, iii. 5 (CSEL xxv/1. 7–8).
[62] Loc. cit.　　　　　　　　　　　　[63] Ibid.

of man's rehabilitation,[64] postulated only three understandings of Holy Scripture which are rooted in that work: the historical, the allegorical, and the tropological.[65] But Bede, who understood the subject-matter of the Holy Scriptures as being not only the work of rehabilitation but also the reason for that rehabilitation, added the anagogical understanding, which is concerned with the cause, as the other three are concerned with the effect.[66]

⟨2.⟩ To the objection which is made about the parabolic understanding we must reply that this relates to the historical sense. But the historical interpretation is spoken of in two ways: it relates either to things or to the likenesses (similitudo) of things. Concerning things, as in actual events; concerning likenesses, as in parables. For a parable is a comparison (similitudo) of things, wherein what is meant is reached by means of the comparison of different things. So, Augustine says that as far as the parables in the Gospels are concerned, they must be understood not in terms of their actually happening but of the possibility of their happening.[67]

⟨3.⟩ To the third objection we must reply that Augustine, in his book On the Usefulness of Belief,[68] has distinguished the understanding of Scripture not according to any difference in the principle of understanding or in that which is understood, but according to the difference in the manner of understanding. So the first three senses are understood and included under the heading of the literal sense. For those three senses relate to the literal understanding in the way in which they have to be expressed. But the fourth sense embraces the three spiritual senses, and so there is no contradiction.

⟨ii.⟩ Again we ask the question whether the literal sense is founded on the truth.

For it seems at times to be founded on a lie, [as in] Judg. 9⟨: 8⟩: 'The trees of the forests went forth to anoint a king for themselves.' But that seems to be outside of what we know to be true. Job 13⟨: 7⟩: 'God does not need our lie.'

[Response.] My reply is that truth in any statement (sermo) is twofold, first in relation to that which is said, then in relation to the purpose for which it is said. We must therefore state that in parables of this sort there is truth in respect of that purpose to serve which they are spoken. For parables exist to highlight some event or thing in the interests of truth. Therefore, in this way parables are included [i.e. within the historical and

---

[64] De sacramentis, i, pr. ii (PL clxxvi. 183).
[65] See above, n. 60.
[66] Cf. the position stated at the beginning of art. 4, which refers back to art. 3c, tr. above.
[67] Contra mendac. x. 24 (CSEL xli. 499-502).
[68] See above, n. 61.

literal sense], not so much under the first signification [of the words in which they are expressed] as under the second. Thus, we must note that in historical statements there is truth as far as the signification of words is concerned, while in parables there is truth in terms of the signification of things.[69]

ST BONAVENTURE

Commentary on Peter Lombard's *Sentences*: Extracts from Exposition of the Prologue[70]

QUESTION 2: WHAT IS THE FORMAL CAUSE OR THE MODE OF PROCEDURE IN THESE BOOKS OF *SENTENCES*?

The second question concerns the formal cause or mode of proceeding (*modus agendi*). And it is said that the mode is investigative and one that enquires into secrets.

Objections against this. ⟨1.⟩ Isa. 40[: 23]: 'God brings the searchers of secrets to nothing.'

⟨2.⟩ Likewise, Prov. 25[: 27]: 'He who is a searcher of majesty will be overwhelmed by glory.'

⟨3.⟩ Likewise, Ecclus. 3[: 22]: 'Seek not the things that are too high for you, and do not search into things that are mightier than you.'

So, if the things which the Master [i.e. Peter Lombard] searches into are secrets, important things, profound and mighty, the Master is proceeding in the wrong way.

⟨4.⟩ Likewise, this is proved also by reasoning in the following way. The mode of procedure in one part of a science should be uniform with the mode of procedure in that science taken as a whole. But the mode of procedure in Holy Scripture is typological (*typicus*) and through narrative, not enquiry. Therefore, since this book [i.e. the *Sentences*] pertains to Holy Scripture, it should not proceed by way of enquiry.

⟨5.⟩ Likewise, the mode of proceeding ought to suit the material (*materia*) which the writer is dealing with. So, at the beginning of *The Old Ethics* one reads: 'discourses (*sermones*) must be investigated in a way that is in accord with the subject-matter'.[71] But the subject-matter of this body of teaching concerns belief, and that which concerns belief is above reasoning: therefore, the mode of procedure by reasonings is not suitable to this body of teaching.

---

[69] Cf. Hugh of Saint-Victor, *De sacramentis*, i, pr. vi (PL clxxvi. 185), and of course Augustine, *De doct. Christ.* I. ii. 2, 1. x. 15.

[70] Tr. from *S. Bonaventurae opera omnia* (Quaracchi, 1882–1902), i. 9–15, with the permission of Edizioni San Bonaventura, Grottaferrata (Rome).

[71] *Eth. Nicomach.* i. 3 (1094[b]11–14), cf. Grosseteste, tr. Litzinger, p. 16.

⟨6.⟩ Likewise, the mode of proceeding must be appropriate to the end (*finis*) to which that science is directed. But this science, as the Master says in the text, is directed towards the promotion of [Christian] belief[72]— and reasonings do not promote belief but make it void. Hence, Gregory says: 'Faith which depends for proof on human reason has no merit.'[73] So, such a mode is contrary to the end. Therefore, it is not appropriate. Hence, Ambrose says: 'Away with arguments when we are dealing with faith. It is the fishermen, not the experts in dialectic, who command belief.'[74] Therefore, this mode seems pointless and useless.

But against [this contrary view]. ⟨1.⟩ 1 Pet. 3[: 15]: 'Being prepared to give a reason to everyone who demands it for that faith and hope which is in you'. Therefore, since there are many who do not merely stop at demanding a reason for our belief, but actually attack it, it seems useful and appropriate to build it up with the aid of reasonings and to proceed by the investigative mode and by reasoning. Therefore, etc.

⟨2.⟩ Likewise, Richard of Saint-Victor, in his book *On the Trinity*, says: 'I believe, without a shadow of a doubt, that arguments which are not only probable, but actually necessary, are not lacking to explain anything whatsoever which has to be explained, even though these may elude our diligent enquiry.'[75] So, since our faith believes those things which are necessary, and those things contain hidden arguments, and consequently require investigation in order that they may be unravelled, it is clear that the investigative mode is particularly appropriate to this science.

⟨3.⟩ Likewise, the truth of our faith is not inferior in status to other truths. But in the case of other truths everything which can be attacked by reason can and must be defended by reason. Therefore, the truth of our faith must equally be defended by reason.

⟨4.⟩ Likewise, our faith, as it is now, is not inferior in status to what it was at the beginning. But at the beginning, when it was being attacked by the false miracles of magicians, it was defended by the real miracles of the saints. So now, when it is attacked by the false arguments of heretics, it must be defended by the true arguments of doctors.

Response. It must be said that the investigative mode is appropriate to this science. The end imposes a compulsion upon those things which are directed to that end. For, as the Philosopher [i.e. Aristotle] says, 'A saw has teeth because it is made for cutting.'[76] So, that book [i.e. the *Sentences*], because its end is to promote the faith, employs the investigat-

---

[72] Referring to Peter Lombard's prologue, 3, in *Petri Lombardi Sententiae in IV libros distinctae* (Spicilegium Bonaventurianum IV–V, Grottaferrata, 1971, 1981), i. 4.
[73] Gregory, *Homil. xxvi in Evang.* (PL lxxvi. 1197).
[74] Ambrose, *De fide*, 1. xiii. 84 (CSEL lxxviii. 37).
[75] Richard of Saint-Victor, *De Trinit.* i. 4 (PL cxcvi. 892 c).
[76] *Phys.* ii. 9 (200ᵇ5–6), cf. *De part. animal.* i. 5 (645ᵇ17–18).

ive mode. For the mode which employs reasoning or is investigative is effective in promoting the faith, and does so in three ways according to the three sorts of men. For some are opposed to the faith, some are weak in their faith, but some are perfect in the faith.

The investigative mode is effective, first of all, in refuting the opponents [of the faith]. So Augustine, in the first book of *On the Trinity*, says: 'Against the wordy, the argumentative, those who are arrogant rather than receptive, one must use Catholic arguments and likenesses suited to the defence and affirmation of the faith.'[77] Second, it is effective in strengthening those whose faith is weak. For, just as God nurtures the charity of the weak by bestowing temporal benefits on them, so he nurtures the faith of the weak through convincing arguments. For if those whose faith is weak saw that arguments in support of the truth of the faith were lacking, while those supporting the opposite abounded, no one [among them] would continue in the faith. Third, it is effective in giving pleasure to those who are perfect [in faith]. For the soul rejoices in a marvellous way at understanding what it believes with perfect faith. Hence, St Bernard says: 'There is nothing that we understand more readily than what we now believe through faith.'[78]

⟨1, 2, 3.⟩ As for the contrary view, it must be said that all those authorities[79] are understood as referring to enquiry pursued to satisfy curiosity, not to studious enquiry [of the correct kind]. For our Lord Himself said to the Jews, in John 5[: 39], 'Search the scriptures . . .'.

⟨4.⟩ As for the objection that this mode is not appropriate to Holy Scripture, our reply to this must be that this book [i.e. the *Sentences*] is related to Holy Scripture by means of a kind of subordination and not by being a principal part of it [i.e. of Scripture]. The same is true of the works of teachers which exist to defend the faith. This is clear for the following reason. Not every determination which leads to division into parts creates subordination of knowledge, but only a determination which in some way separates out knowledge creates such subordination. Hence, knowledge which relates to the straight line is not said to be subordinate to geometry (while knowledge relating to the visible line is [subordinate in this way]), for this determination leads to different principles. Holy Scripture is about belief as such; this book [i.e. the *Sentences*] is about belief as something to be understood. This determination separates out [knowledge]; 'for what we believe we owe to authority, and what we understand we owe to reason'.[80] Hence it comes about that just as there is

---

[77] *De Trin.* I. ii. 4 (CCSL I. 31).

[78] *De consideratione*, v. iii. 6, in *S. Bernardi opera*, ed. J. Leclercq, C. H. Talbot, and H. M. Rochais (Rome, 1957–77), iii. 471.

[79] i.e. the passages from Isaiah, Proverbs, and Ecclesiasticus quoted in the first three objections at the beginning of this discussion.

[80] Augustine, *De util. cred.* xi. 25 (CSEL xxv/i. 32).

one type of certainty in a superior science and another type in an inferior science, so there is one type of certainty in Holy Scripture and another in this book [i.e. the *Sentences*], and hence [in it] there is a different mode of procedure. Just as a subordinate science, when it is inadequate, returns to the certainty of the science which has subordinated it, since it is the greater, so too, when the certainty of reason is inadequate for the Master's [i.e. Peter Lombard's] purposes, he has recourse to the certainty of the authority of Holy Scripture, which surpasses all the certainty of reason.

⟨5.⟩ As for your objection that [the mode of procedure] should be appropriate to the subject-matter, it must be said that it is appropriate. As for the objection that what relates to belief is above reason, it is true that it is above reason as far as acquired knowledge is concerned. But it is not above reason that has been elevated by faith and by the [divine] gift of knowledge and understanding. For faith raises [the mind] to the point of assent, while knowledge and understanding raise it to the point where it can understand what it has believed.

⟨6.⟩ As for the objection that [this mode] is not appropriate to the end, because it makes merit null and void, it must be said that, when one agrees with reason on its own account then no place is left for faith, because [in that case] the vehement power of reason rules in the human soul. But when faith agrees [with reason] not for the sake of reason itself but on account of its love for the One with whom it agrees, then it [i.e. faith] wishes to have reasons; in that case human reason does not make merit null and void but increases the comfort we receive. And it is in the first manner that St Jerome understands, when he says that dialectical arguments, on which man principally relies, are not to be brought into [theology], because one should rely more fully on authority than on reasoning.[81]

QUESTION 3: WHETHER THIS BOOK OR THEOLOGY HAS CONTEMPLATION AS ITS AIM, OR THAT WE SHOULD BECOME GOOD; IN OTHER WORDS, IS IT A SPECULATIVE OR PRACTICAL SCIENCE?

The third question concerns the final cause. Since it has been said that the purpose of this book is to reveal things which are hidden, the question is asked whether this book has contemplation as its aim, or that we should become good. And that its aim is that we should become good is seen, etc.

⟨1.⟩ All teaching which relates to that without knowledge of which we cannot live a good life, exists so that we may become good. But this book [i.e. the *Sentences*] exists for the purpose of imparting a knowledge of the true faith, without which it is 'impossible to please God' or live a good

---

[81] Apparently a reference to the passage from Ambrose, quoted in the sixth objection at the beginning of the *quaestio*.

life, as is said in Heb. 11[: 6]. Therefore, the purpose of this book is that we should become good.

⟨2.⟩ Likewise, all knowledge which is consistent with virtue in its object, exists so that we may become good. This is obvious in itself. But this teaching [i.e. of the Lombard] is also at one with faith in its object, because it concerns matters of belief, and faith either relates to belief or is based on that belief. Therefore, etc.

⟨3.⟩ Likewise, a particular part of any body of teaching shares the same end as that body of knowledge taken as a whole. But the end of Holy Scripture taken as a whole is not only that we may become good but also that we may become blessed. And blessedness is the best state of all. Therefore, the end of this science [i.e. in the *Sentences*] is that we should become good.

Objections against. ⟨1.⟩ The Master says in his text that his end or intention (*intentio*) is 'to unveil the hidden mysteries of theological researches'.[82] But that is the concern of the man whose end is speculation. Therefore, etc.

⟨2.⟩ Likewise, that branch of knowledge, which exists so that we may become good, pertains to behaviour. But, whereas theology is about faith and morals, that book [i.e. the *Sentences*] concerns matters relating to faith, not morals. Therefore, the purpose of this work is not that we may become good.

⟨3.⟩ Likewise, every science which exists so that we may become good is practical. But every such science concerns that which results from our own action (*opus*).[83] This science, however, does not concern that which results from our own action, but that which comes from God. Therefore, its purpose is contemplation, not that we should become good.

Response. In order to understand the aforesaid, it must be noted that our intellect is capable of being made perfect by knowledge. It is proper to consider this [i.e. the intellect] in three ways: intellect in itself, or as it is extended to move the affections, or as it is extended to achieve an actual task. The intellect is extended by means of dictating and laying down rules. Because it can err, the intellect has, in line with this threefold division, likewise a threefold directive condition (*habitus*). For if we consider intellect in itself, defined thus it is truly speculative and is brought to perfection by the condition which exists purely for the sake of contemplation and which is called 'speculative knowledge'. But if we consider it as being created in order to be extended to achieve some task, it is brought to perfection by the condition which exists so that we may become good; and this is practical or moral knowledge. But if in some

---

[82] Pr. 2 (ed. cit. i. 3).

[83] Cf. Aristotle, *Eth. Nicomach.* ii. 2 (1103ᵇ26–31); cf. Grosseteste, tr. Litzinger, p. 117.

middle way it is considered as being created to extend to moving the affections, considered thus it is brought to perfection by a condition which lies between the purely speculative and the practical, and which embraces both. This condition is called wisdom, and it expresses both cognition and affection. As Ecclus. 6[: 23] says: 'For the wisdom of doctrine is according to her name.' So, this condition exists for the purpose of contemplation, and also that we may become good, but principally that we may become good.

Such is the knowledge handed down in this book [of the *Sentences*]. For this knowledge aids faith, and faith is present in the intellect in such a way that, in so far as one can speak about its [i.e. the intellect's] reason for existence (*ratio*), it is created to move the affections. This is quite clear. For the knowledge that Christ died for us, and similar intimations, moves a man to love, unless he is a hardened sinner. But the knowledge that a diagonal is asymmetrical with a side does not move anyone to love. Therefore, it must be conceded that this science [of theology] exists in order that we should become good.

⟨1.⟩ As for the objection that it [i.e. theology] exists for the purpose of revealing hidden secrets, it must be said that its essential function (*status*) does not lie therein, because that revelation disposes [minds] to affection.

⟨2, 3.⟩ As for the objection that it does not relate to morals or that which proceeds from our own action, the reply to that is now clear. For he himself [i.e. Peter Lombard] speaks of that which, properly speaking, exists in order that we may become good as being something practical.

QUESTION 4: WHAT IS THE EFFICIENT CAUSE OR AUTHOR OF THIS BOOK?[84]

Finally, in the interests of greater clarity the question of the efficient cause can be raised. This is said to be Master Peter the Lombard, Bishop of Paris. But it is clear that he should not be called the author (*auctor*) of this book [for the following reasons].

⟨1.⟩ He alone ought to be called the author of a book who is the teacher or originator (*auctor*) of the doctrine contained in it. But, as Augustine says in his book *On the Master*, 'Only Christ is our teacher.'[85] Therefore, he alone ought to be called the author of this book.

⟨2.⟩ Likewise, as the Philosopher [i.e. Aristotle] says in *The Old Ethics*, 'Not everyone who produces something which is grammatical or musical should be called a grammarian or musician, for he may well produce such things by chance, or with someone else putting in his ideas or dictating

---

[84] Cf. the discussion in Minnis, *Authorship*, pp. 94-5.
[85] *De magistro*, xiv (CSEL lxxvii. 20-1).

them.'[86] But the Master himself [i.e. Peter Lombard] put together this work from the teachings of others, as he himself says in the text: 'in this work you will find the examples and the teaching of greater men [than I]'.[87] So, he ought not to be called the author.

If you say that here [i.e. in the *Sentences*] there is to be found not only the teachings of the holy Fathers but also his own teaching, by reason of which he ought to be called the author, against this [I say]: the person who is more important and more worthy of respect ought to be called the author. But the Master says that 'his own voice has been heard only for a short time, and that not outside his native shores'.[88] Therefore, that book should not be said to be by the Master.

Objections against this. It is clear that God did not write this work with His own hand. So it had another author, a created being. But one cannot think of any other such except the Master.

Likewise, if the Master's own testimony is accepted in this matter, he himself says in his text: 'We have put together this volume with much labour and sweat with God's help.' So, it seems that he was the author of the present book.

Response. To understand the above we must note that there are four ways of making a book. For someone writes out the words of other men without adding or changing anything, and he is called the scribe (*scriptor*) pure and simple. Someone else writes the words of other men, putting together material, but not his own, and he is called the compiler (*compilator*). Someone else writes the words of other men and also his own, but with those of other men comprising the principal part while his own are annexed merely to make clear the argument, and he is called the commentator (*commentator*), not the author. Someone else writes the words of other men and also of his own, but with his own forming the principal part and those of others being annexed merely by way of confirmation, and such a person should be called the author (*auctor*). The master falls into this [last] category, for he sets out his own opinions (*sententiae*) and buttresses them with the opinions of the holy Fathers. So, he ought to be called the author of this book [i.e. the *Sentences*].

⟨1.⟩ As for the objection that only Christ is the teacher and author, we must say that, to quote Augustine in his *On Christian Doctrine*, teaching can mean one of two things,[89] just as 'making someone see' can be taken in

---

[86] *Eth. Nicomach.* ii. 4 (1105ᵃ22–3); cf. Grosseteste, tr. Litzinger, p. 128.

[87] *Sent.*, pr. 4 (ed. cit. p. 4).

[88] Ibid.

[89] Bonaventure's editor suggests this is a *sententia* gleaned from the prologue to Augustine's *De Doct. Christ.*

two different ways. For the person who restores a man's sight makes him see in one way, while he who points out with his finger that which is already visible makes him see in another way. God does the first; man, the second. In the same way, the man who presents and reveals the knowledge which he has in his soul in word or writing is doing something quite different from He who imprints the condition (*habitus*) of knowledge [on men's souls]. Each is called a teacher and author, but God is the more principal one. The same is true of the book [i.e. the *Sentences*] set before us.

⟨2.⟩ As for the objection that the Master wrote the book but another supplied the matter, we must say this. Someone cannot be denied the authorship of a book for which someone else has supplied the material just because he has learned its material from someone else—for if that were so there would be few teachers or grammarians—but only if his knowledge is completely derived from another to the extent that he does not possess within himself the condition (*habitus*) of knowledge. An example is those who themselves use good Latin, because others have spoken [the words] to them, but are ignorant of the art of the language. But this was not the case with the Master [of the *Sentences*]. For he composed this book from the knowledge which he had acquired over a long period of time and with much effort, and used the teachings of the Fathers to buttress his own opinions (*sententiae*). The fact that there are many statements by other writers to be found in his work does not detract from the authorship (*auctoritas*) of the Master, but rather confirms his authorship and commends his humility.

Commentary on Ecclesiastes: Extract from the Prologue[90]

CONCERNING THE FOURFOLD CAUSE OF THIS BOOK

So it is clear what is the end (*finis*) of the book of Ecclesiastes.[91] Since 'an end imposes its compulsion upon those things which contribute to that end',[92] and the end of this book is contempt of the things of this present world, in treating of them he shows not their attractive features but those which make them despised. They attract men when they appear to be good, but are despised when they appear to be vain. Therefore, it follows from this that the material (*materia*) of this book is the vanity of the things of this present world, or rather, to put it more correctly, those qualities which make them vain. For the author proves that vanity is an attribute existing in things, first of all putting forward his argument, secondly

[90] Translated from *Bonaventurae opera*, vi. 5–6, 7–8.

[91] Bonaventure's treatment of the *modus procedendi* of Ecclesiastes both here, and in question 3 following, is heavily indebted to Gregory the Great, *Dialogi*, iv. 4 (PL lxxvii. 321–5).

[92] Cf. Aristotle, *Phys.* ii. 9 (199ᵇ34–200ᵇ8).

proving it, and thirdly drawing his conclusions. So he proceeds by persuading and by proving the existence of that threefold vanity which we spoke of above: vanity of nature, of guilt, and of misery. From this his mode of proceeding, or form (*forma*), is clear. This mode of proceeding is unique among all the other books.[93] For he proceeds like an arranger (*concionator*), setting forth the opinions of various people—at one point that of a wise man, at another that of a foolish man—so that out of these many opinions one clear vision of the truth may dawn in the minds of his hearers.

The efficient cause (*causa efficiens*) of this work clearly follows from what has been said above. For in this book we are taught to despise pleasure, wealth, honours, and human preoccupations, as being forms of vanity. No one who talks about the contempt of such things has any credibility unless he actually has experienced them himself. For a poor man, who has never had wealth, has no credibility when he speaks of the contempt of wealth, because 'he has not experienced it' and therefore 'knows nothing about it' [Ecclus. 34: 10]. The author [of this book] had to be the sort of person who had experienced all of these things; in other words, someone who was powerful, wealthy, fond of luxury, and of an enquiring mind or wise. We have not read or heard of anyone who had these attributes to such a high degree as Solomon. Therefore, he was far more suitable than anyone else to be the author of this book. It is clear, then, what is the material cause, the formal cause, the efficient cause, and the final cause, of this book.

Four subsidiary questions can be asked, each relating to one of these four causes. . . .[94]

Question 3: Concerning the Mode of Proceeding in this Book

Likewise, a question arises concerning the mode of proceeding. For it has been said that the author proceeds and speaks through two different characters (*personae*), that of the foolish man and that of the wise man.

Objections against this. ⟨1.⟩ As Ecclus. 20[: 22] puts it, 'a parable coming out of a fool's mouth shall be rejected'. Therefore, an opinion put in the mouth of a fool is not to be heeded. So, if the meaning of the sacred books is to be heeded, the writer should not speak in the character (*persona*) of a fool.

⟨2.⟩ Likewise, statements made in the character of a foolish and carnal man must be rejected, but it is not known, when the writer speaks,

---

[93] i.e. this *modus* distinguishes it from the other biblical books attributed to Solomon in the Middle Ages, Proverbs, the Song of Songs, Wisdom, and Ecclesiasticus. On Solomon as *contionator* ('preacher'), cf. Abelard, tr. above, p. 90, and n. 72, and Giles of Rome, tr. below, p. 245, and n. 132.

[94] Questions 1 and 2, concerning the end and the material of Ecclesiastes respectively, are here omitted.

whether he is saying this in his own person or in the character of someone else. So, one does not know what should be believed in this book and what should be rejected. Therefore, the teaching of this book is a path leading to error. But the canonical books ought to purge error. This book, therefore, should be removed from the canon.

Response. ⟨1.⟩ It must be said that to say something in the character of a foolish or carnal person has two possible purposes: either to win approval for what is said or to castigate it and show that it is vain. The first of these is not conducive to a knowledge of the truth, but the second is, just as if someone wanted to castigate some error and first of all explained what it is, then demolished it. That is the mode adopted by the writer [of Ecclesiastes], not the first mode. Consequently, he should not be criticized, but rather commended, for attacking those things which deserve to be attacked.

⟨2.⟩ As for the objection that it is not possible to know when he is speaking in his own person, we must state that the other [i.e. the rejected] side of a disputation (*disputatio*) cannot be known until the judgement (*sententia*) and decision (*determinatio*) is arrived at, for in the solution (*solutio*) it becomes known what is accepted and what is rejected. So, I submit that Ecclesiastes proceeds by using the method of a disputation right up until the end of the book. At the end he [i.e. the author] gives his verdict, when he says: 'Let us all hear together the conclusion of the discourse. Fear God, and know that God will bring you to judgement for every sin you have committed' [Eccles. 12: 13–14]. In these words he condemns all the opinions of the foolish, the carnally inclined, and the worldly. So, everything which is in accord with this judgement he speaks in his own person, and everything which is at odds with it [he speaks] in the characters of others. And so that book cannot be understood unless attention is paid to its totality.

Question 4: Concerning the Efficient Cause of this Book

Last of all, we may consider who was the efficient cause [of this book]. As has been said, this was Solomon. It would seem that such a man as he was was unfit to be the author of such a book [for the following reasons].

⟨1.⟩ Because he himself was a sinner and a man of carnal desires. But when a man of carnal desires preaches spirituality he gives ground for scandal rather than edifies his hearers. So, that book [of Ecclesiastes] tends to produce scandal rather than edification.

⟨2.⟩ Likewise, we read in the Psalm [49: 16]: 'But to the sinner God has said: "Why do you declare my acts of justice?"' Therefore, if Solomon was a sinner he sinned in recounting God's just acts.

⟨3.⟩ Besides, a good author encourages belief, and hence his text possesses a strength arising from his authority. Therefore the evil author encourages no belief. But the purpose of the books of Holy Scripture is to encourage belief. Therefore, etc.

Response. The answer we must give to this is that, ⟨1.⟩ according to Jerome[95] and to the Jewish tradition, that book was written by Solomon when doing penance. God does not cast out those who repent, but receives them. In the light of this, Solomon was not in a reprehensible state when he wrote this book.

Alternatively, it can be replied that the Holy Spirit speaks that which is true and good not just through the mouths of good, but also of evil men. Wherefore, our Lord says in the Gospel: 'do all things that they say to you, but do not do the things they do' [Matt. 23: 3]. Thus, he prophesied in the very plainest of terms through the mouth of Balaam, and likewise said many good things through the mouth of Solomon, carnally inclined though he was.

⟨2.⟩ As for the objection that he committed sin, we must reply that the gift of wisdom was entrusted to him more than to all other men. Because he was under obligation not to hide the talent entrusted to him by the Lord[96] he had to teach the people of the Lord by words and by his writing, particularly as he had been ordained to rule over them. Therefore, his sin was not in teaching, but in not behaving as he ought.

⟨3.⟩ As for the objection that one should not believe a book when the author is not worthy of being believed, I reply as follows. We believe the prophets because they have not spoken as from themselves but through the Holy Spirit. It is the same with all the books of Scripture, for they were written at the inspiration of the Holy Spirit. Therefore, the goodness of an individual does not make for greater or lesser belief if we are to suppose that he has spoken through the Spirit. We are all agreed that Solomon was filled with the spirit of wisdom, as is clear from 3 Kgs. 3[: 5]. Therefore, the Church accepts his books without hesitation.

Breviloquium: Prologue, Sections 4–6[97]

4. ON THE DEPTH OF HOLY SCRIPTURE

Finally, Scripture has depth, which consists in its having several mystical understandings. For, besides its literal meaning, in many places it can be interpreted in three ways, allegorically, morally, and anagogically. Allegory occurs when by one thing is indicated another which is a matter of belief. The tropological or moral understanding occurs when by something which has been done in the past something else, which we must do,

[95] Jerome, *Comment. in Eccles.* i. 12 (CCSL lxii. 258).
[96] Cf. Matt. 25: 14ff., Luke 19: 12ff.
[97] Tr. from *Bonaventurae opera*, v. 205–8. Cf. the translation of the entire *Breviloquium* by José de Vinck, *The Works of Bonaventure*, ii: *The Breviloquium* (Paterson, NJ, 1963).

is indicated to us. The anagogical meaning, being a 'leading upward', occurs when we are shown what it is we should desire, that is, the eternal happiness of the blessed.

It is right and proper that Scripture should have this threefold sense over and above the literal sense. For in this way it is appropriate to the subject-matter of Scripture, its hearer or pupil, its origin, and its end.

It is appropriate to the subject-matter, because that is doctrine which concerns God, Christ, the works of redemption, and belief. For, in terms of being, its subject is God; in terms of virtue, Christ; in terms of the action described, the works of redemption; and in terms of all these things together its subject is belief itself. Now, God is threefold and also one, one in substance and threefold in persons. Therefore, Scripture, which is concerned with Him, has within the unity of the literal text the threefold understanding. Though Christ the Word is one, all things are said to have been 'made by him' [John 1: 3], and all things shine forth in his person, so that His wisdom at one and the same time has one and many forms. Similarly, though the works of redemption are many, they all look towards the original offering of Christ. Finally, belief as such gives forth its light in different ways according to the different states of believers. So, because Scripture meets all the above requirements, it gives us a manifold meaning in the one text.

This manifold meaning of Scripture is appropriate to the hearer. For no one is a fitting hearer of Scripture unless he is humble, pure, faithful, and attentive.[98] So, under the shell of the obvious literal meaning are hidden mystical and profound understandings, to humble pride, so that the profound truths hidden within the humble letter of the text may abash the arrogant, keep out the unclean, drive away the deceitful, and arouse the idle to an understanding of the mysteries.[99] And, because the recipients of this teaching do not belong to any one class (genus) of people, but come from all classes—for all who are to be saved must know something of this teaching—Scripture has a manifold meaning so that it may win over every mind, reach the level of every mind, rise above every mind, and illuminate and fire with its many rays of light every mind which diligently searches for it.

The manifold meaning of Scripture is also appropriate to its origin. For it comes from God, through Christ and the Holy Spirit who spoke by the mouths of the prophets and the others who put this doctrine into writing. For God speaks not with words alone, but also through deeds (facta), because with Him to say is to do, and to do is to say. All created things, being the results of God's action, point the way to their cause. So, in Scripture, which has been handed down to us by God, deeds no less than

---

[98] Cf. Augustine, De doct. Christ. II. xli. 62 ff.
[99] Ibid. II. vi. 7 ff., cf. Clement of Alexandria, Stromateis, vi. 15 (GCS lii. 489–90; PG ix. 339–58).

words must have meaning. Christ the teacher, though humble in His humanity, was elevated in His divine nature. So, it was fitting that both He and His teaching should be humble in word and profound in meaning so that, just as Christ was wrapped in rags,[100] so the wisdom of God in the Scriptures should be wrapped in humble images. Moreover, the Spirit gave enlightenment in various ways, and provided revelations in the hearts of the prophets. No mind can remain hidden from Him, and He was sent to teach the truth in its entirety. Hence, it fitted in with His teaching that several meanings should be hidden in the one passage [of Scripture].

This is equally appropriate to the end of Scripture. For Scripture was given so that through it man might be guided in the things he must know and what he must do, so that he might come at last to the things for which he should hope. Because all creatures have been made to serve man on his journey to his heavenly homeland, Scripture takes on the various aspects of creatures, so that through them it may teach us that wisdom which guides us to eternal life. Man is not guided to eternal life unless the intellect comes to know what we can accept as being true, and that part of us which performs actions does the good which has to be done, and the affective part of our nature longs to see God and love and enjoy Him. Thus, Holy Scripture, given to us by the Holy Spirit, takes up the book of God's creation, making it relate to its [i.e. Scripture's] end through the threefold manner of understanding: the tropological meaning enables us to know what we must resolutely do; the allegorical meaning, what we must truly believe; the anagogical meaning, what we must desire for our [eternal] delight. In this way, cleansed by virtuous deeds, illuminated by the bright rays of faith, and made perfect by burning love, we may come at last to the prize of eternal happiness.

5. ON THE MODE OF PROCEDURE OF HOLY SCRIPTURE

Among all the many kinds of wisdom which are contained in the width, length, height, and depth of Holy Scripture, there is one common way of proceeding: by authority. Grouped within it are the narrative, preceptive, prohibitive, exhortatory, instructive, threatening, promising, supplicating, and laudatory modes. All these modes come within the scope of that one mode, proceeding by authority, and quite rightly so.

This doctrine exists in order that we should become good[101] and be redeemed, and this is not achieved by deliberation alone, but rather by a disposition of the will. Therefore, Holy Scripture had to be handed down to us in whatever way would dispose us best [to goodness]. Our affections

---

[100] Cf. Luke ii: 7.
[101] Cf. Aristotle's description of the end of moral science, in *Eth. Nicomach.* ii. 2 (1103ᵇ26–8); cf. Grosseteste, tr. Litzinger, p. 117.

are moved more strongly by examples than by arguments, by promises than by logical reasonings, by devotions than by definitions. Scripture, therefore, had to avoid the mode of proceeding by definition, division, and inferring to prove the properties of some subject, as do the other sciences.[102] It had rather to adapt its own modes to the various dispositions of men's minds which incline those minds differently. Thus, if a man is not moved to heed precepts and prohibitions, he may at least be moved by the examples narrated; if someone is not moved by these, he may be moved by the benefits which are pointed out to him; and if he is not moved by these, he may be moved by wise warnings, by promises which ring true, by terrifying threats; and thus be stirred to devotion and praise of God, and thereby receive grace which will guide him to the practice of virtuous works.

These narrative modes cannot proceed by way of certainty based on reasoning, because particular facts do not admit of formal proof.[103] Therefore, lest Scripture should seem doubtful, and consequently should have less power to move [men's minds], instead of certainty based on reasoning God has provided it with certainty based on authority, which is so great that it rises high above the most acute human mind. The authority of him who can deceive or be deceived is not absolutely certain, and there is no one who cannot be deceived and who is himself incapable of deceiving except God and the Holy Spirit. This is why Holy Scripture, in order that it should be perfectly authoritative, as it should be, was handed down not through human enquiry but divine revelation. Consequently, nothing in Scripture should be dismissed as useless, nothing scorned as false, and nothing rejected as unjust. For the Holy Spirit, its author, perfect in every respect, was incapable of saying anything false, superfluous, or trivial. This is why 'heaven and earth shall pass away' [Matt. 24: 35] but the words of Holy Scripture will not pass away without being fulfilled. 'For until heaven and earth pass away not one jot or one tittle shall pass of the law, till all be fulfilled' [Matt. 5: 18], as our Saviour affirms. 'He therefore who shall break' the laws taught by Scripture 'and shall so teach men shall be called the least in the kingdom of heaven. But he that shall do and teach, he will be called great in the kingdom of heaven' [Matt. 5: 19].

6. ON THE MODE OF EXPOUNDING HOLY SCRIPTURE

Just as Scripture has this special mode of procedure, so it must be understood and expounded in its own special mode, to fit in with the way in

---

[102] The *modus definitivus, divisivus, collectivus*; cf. the function of this phrase in *Alexander's Sum of Theology*, tr. above, p. 213.

[103] Cf. Aristotle, *Anal. post.* i. 14 (79ᵃ17–32).

which it proceeds. For, since it hides several meanings under a single text, the expositor must 'bring forth that which is hidden into the light' [Job 28: 11], and, having brought it forth, explain it, using another part of Scripture which is more open to understanding. For instance, if I were expounding the words of the Psalm [34: 2], 'Take hold of arms and shield, and rise up to help me', and wanted to explain what is meant by the divine arms, I will say that this means God's truth and goodwill. We must use an explicit passage of Scripture to prove that this is so. For elsewhere it is written: 'You have crowned us, as with a shield of your good will' [Ps. 5: 13], and again: 'His truth will compass you with a shield' [Ps. 90: 5]. No one can easily reach this standard of exposition unless he is thoroughly familiar with the text and commits the text and its literal sense to memory. Otherwise he will never have any real capacity to expound the Scriptures. The man who is too proud to learn the elements which go to make up a word can never understand the meaning of words or correct grammatical construction. Just so, he who scorns the letter of Holy Scripture can never rise to interpreting its spiritual meanings.

The interpreter must also note that one should not look for an allegorical sense everywhere, and that not everything should be given a mystical interpretation. In this connection it must be noted that Holy Scripture has four parts. One is that in which, as interpreted literally, it deals with the forms of being in this world and through them signifies our redemption, as is clear from the description of the Creation. Another is that in which it deals with the actions and journeyings of the people of Israel, and uses them to signify the redemption of the human race. A third is that in which, in plain words, it signifies and expresses all that concerns our salvation in terms of faith or morals. The fourth is that in which it foretells the mystery of our salvation, partly in plain words and partly in words which are enigmatic and obscure. In consequence, a single, uniform method of exposition should not be used in explaining these various parts of Scripture.

In explaining Holy Scripture the interpreter should be guided by three rules taken from St Augustine's *On Christian Doctrine*.[104] The first is this. Where the primary signification of the words denotes things which are part of God's creation, or individual acts which occur in human society, in the first instance they refer to the facts signified by the words and then [secondly] to the mysteries of our redemption. But where the primary signification of the words expresses some aspect of faith or love, then one has no need to look for any allegorical meaning.

The second rule is this. When the words of Scripture signify things which are part of creation, or part of the life of the people of Israel, there

---

[104] With the following discussion cf. Augustine, *De doct. Christ.* III. x. 14 ff., also II. vi. 7, ix. 14 ff.

the interpreter must use some other part of Scripture to find out what
each thing signifies, and then elicit the meaning of that [passage] using
words which plainly signify some truth of our faith or of some correct
principle of morality. For instance, if the text says 'the sheep bring forth
twins' [S. of S. 4: 2], the interpreter must show that here 'sheep' signify
men, and 'twins', two kinds of love.

The third rule is as follows. When a certain passage of Scripture has a
possible literal and spiritual meaning, the interpreter ought to judge
whether that passage relates to the literal or to the spiritual meaning—if,
that is, it cannot be accepted in both senses. But if it can be accepted in
both senses, then it ought to be given both a literal and a spiritual
interpretation. If it is capable of only one interpretation, then it must be
interpreted spiritually. Instances of this are the statements that the law of
the sabbath has perpetual force [Exod. 12: 16ff.], that the priesthood is
eternal [Exod. 40: 13; Numb. 25: 13], that [the children of Israel's]
possession of the land is perpetual [Gen. 17: 8], that the covenant of
circumcision has everlasting force [Gen. 5: 13]. All of these statements
ought to be understood in their spiritual sense.

Related to the way in which one advances through the forest of Holy
Scripture by hacking with an axe and thus laying it open, is the need to
have prior knowledge of the truth of the actual text of Holy Scripture,
expressed explicitly. In other words, one needs to know how Scripture
describes the beginnings, progress, and final end of the two groups of
people who confront each other from opposing sides: the good, who
humble themselves in this world, so that they are exalted for ever in the
world to come, and the wicked, who exalt themselves in this world, so that
they are eternally crushed.[105]

Scripture, then, deals with the whole universe: high and low, first and
last, and all that lies between. It takes the form of an intelligible cross, on
which the whole fabric of the universe can be described and in some way
or other seen in the light of the mind. To gain an understanding of this
one must know about God, the origin of all things, about the creation of
those things, the fall, the redemption by the blood of Jesus Christ, the
reformation through grace, healing through the sacraments, and finally
the retribution through punishment and reward in the form of everlasting
glory.[106]

---

[105] Cf. Matt. 23: 12.

[106] The remainder of the sixth part of the prologue comprises Bonaventure's commendation of his own *Breviloquium*, written at the request of his colleagues as a brief summary
of true theology, offering teaching which 'has been handed down in such a diffuse state in the
works of the Saints and doctors that it cannot be read or heard by those who come to be
taught in the subject of Holy Scripture even if they devote long periods of time to their
studies'.

THOMAS AQUINAS

The Sum of Theology: 1a 1, Articles 9 and 10[107]

ARTICLE 9: SHOULD SACRED WRITING USE METAPHORICAL OR SYMBOLICAL LANGUAGE?

The ninth [article]. ⟨1.⟩ It seems that sacred writing should not use metaphors. For what is appropriate for a lowly type of instruction does not seem to be appropriate for this one, which holds the supreme place among all others, as has already been said. To proceed using various likenesses and images is appropriate for poetry, which however is the most lowly among all methods of instruction. So it is not appropriate for this science [i.e. theology] to use likenesses of this sort.

⟨2.⟩ Besides, this type of instruction seems to have as its end the elucidation of the truth; and so a reward is promised to those who thus elucidate it, in Ecclesiasticus [24: 31]: 'Those who explain me will have life everlasting.' But the truth is actually obscured by likenesses of this sort. Therefore, to impart divine truths in the guise of likenesses of corporeal things is not in keeping with this type of instruction.

⟨3.⟩ Besides, the nobler the creatures are the closer they approach God's likeness. So, if any of these creatures were metaphorically to be applied to God, then such a metaphorical application should be drawn from the superior rather than the lowest sort of creatures. But such examples are often found in the Scriptures.

But on the other hand there are the words of Hosea [12: 10]: 'I have multiplied visions for their benefit, and, through the prophets, have given them comparisons.' But to impart something under the guise of imagery is metaphorical usage. Therefore, it is appropriate for sacred instruction to use metaphors.

Response. It must be said that it is appropriate for sacred writing to teach that which is divine and spiritual under the guise of comparison with corporeal objects. For God makes provision for all things in a way that suits their nature. It is natural for man to reach intellectual things by means of sensible things, because all our knowledge originates in sensation. So it is quite appropriate that in Holy Scripture spiritual things are imparted to us under the guise of metaphors taken from corporeal things. As Dionysius says in the first part of his *Celestial Hierarchy*, 'The divine ray cannot shine upon us in any other way except wrapped up in a large number of sacred veils.'[108]

---

[107] Tr. from Aquinas, *Summa theologiae*, i (1a 1), ed. T. Gilby (London and New York, 1964), pp. 32–40, with the permission of Eyre and Spottiswoode, London.

[108] Dionysius, *De cael. hier.* i. 2 (PG iii. 121). Generally, Aquinas preferred the translation of ·

Holy Scripture is set before all of us together: in the words of Romans [1: 14], 'I am a debtor to wise and foolish alike.' It is therefore appropriate that spiritual things should be set before us under bodily likenesses, so that at least in this way even the uneducated, who are not able to understand intellectual truths in their pure form, may be able to understand Holy Scripture.

⟨1.⟩ To the first [objection] it must be replied that poetry employs metaphors for the sake of representation, for this is something which naturally gives men pleasure. But sacred instruction uses metaphors because they are necessary and useful, as we have said.

⟨2.⟩ To the second [objection] it must be said that the ray of divine revelation is not destroyed by the sensible images with which, as Dionysius says, it is veiled. But it remains rooted in its own essential truth, so that the minds to which it is revealed are not permitted to remain in the realm of images, but it raises them up to a recognition of intellectual truths, and others too may then receive instruction about these [truths] from those to whom the revelation has been made. In fact, truths which are taught under the guise of metaphor in one part of Scripture are explained more explicitly in other parts. Also, the disguise afforded by the images is useful in stimulating serious students and as a defence against the mockery of infidels, concerning whom St Matthew [7: 6] says: 'Do not give what is holy to dogs'.

⟨3.⟩ To the third [objection] it must be said that, as Dionysius teaches, it is more fitting that divine truths in the Scriptures should be imparted to us in the guise of figures drawn from base objects rather than noble objects.[109] There are three reasons for this. First of all, this method is better able to free the human mind from error, for it is clear that these expressions cannot in the proper meaning of their words be used about divine things, whereas there could be more room for doubt if divine things were described in the guise of figures drawn from noble objects, especially in the minds of those who can think of nothing nobler than physical beauty. Second, this method fits in better with the kind of knowledge we have of God in this life. For from it we see more clearly what He is not than what He is. Therefore, likenesses drawn from those things which are furthest removed from God give us a truer estimation of God, showing that He is far above any words or thought we may use to describe Him. Third, by such means as these, divine truths are concealed from the unworthy.

John the Saracen (c.1167) as being the better one. See Chenu, *Toward Understanding St. Thomas*, p. 229.

[109] *De cael. hier.* ii. 2 (PG iii. 136).

ARTICLE 10: WHETHER ONE PASSAGE OF HOLY SCRIPTURE CAN HAVE SEVERAL SENSES

The tenth [article]. ⟨1.⟩ It appears that one and the same passage of Holy Scripture does not have several senses, namely the historical or literal, the allegorical, the tropological or moral, and the anagogical. For the presence of several senses in one scriptural text produces confusion and deception, and removes any firm basis from argument. Hence, the large number of basic propositions does not result in reasoned argument, but fallacies. But Holy Scripture ought to be effective in revealing the truth without any fallacy whatever. Therefore, several meanings ought not be assigned to one passage.

⟨2.⟩ Besides, Augustine says that 'that part of Scripture which is entitled the Old Testament is interpreted in a fourfold way, namely, according to history, to aetiology,[110] to analogy,[111] and to allegory'.[112] These four appear to be quite different from the four senses mentioned above. Therefore, it does not seem right that the same passage of Holy Scripture should be interpreted according to the four abovementioned senses.

⟨3.⟩ Moreover, as well as the above-mentioned senses we find the parabolic sense, which is not included in those four senses.

But on the other hand, St Gregory says: 'Holy Scripture transcends all other branches of knowledge in the way it expresses itself, because it narrates an event and reveals a mystery in one and the same discourse.'[113]

Response. We must acknowledge that God is the author of Holy Scripture. It lies within His power, not only to provide words to convey a required meaning—something which men can do too—but also to provide the things themselves [to which the words refer]. Therefore, though in every branch of knowledge words have meaning, this science has this special property, that the things meant by the words also themselves have meaning. That first meaning, whereby the words signify things, belongs to the first sense, which is the historical or literal sense. That meaning, whereby the things signified by the words in turn signify other things, is called the spiritual sense, and this is based upon the literal sense and presupposes it.[114]

This spiritual sense is divided into three. For, as the Apostle says in Hebrews [7: 19]: 'the Old law is the figure of the New Law', and the New Law, as Dionysius says, is the 'figure of the glory that is to come'.[115]

---

[110] Lat. 'aetiologiam', i.e. the indication of the cause at work.
[111] Lat. 'analogia', i.e. the resemblance of attributes or relations.
[112] De util. cred. iii. 5 (CSEL xxv/i. 7–8).   [113] Moralia in Job, xx. i. 1 (CCSL cxliii A. 1003).
[114] Cf. our treatment of the distinction between significative words and significative things above, pp. 66, 203ff.
[115] De Ecclesiastica hierarchia, v. 2 (PG iii. 501).

Besides, in the New Law the actions done in the person of Our Head [i.e. Christ] are indications of what we should be doing.

The allegorical sense is that whereby those things which are of the Old Law signify the things of the New Law. The moral sense is that whereby those things which are done in the person of Christ or those things which prefigure Christ are guides to what we ought to be doing. But in so far as they signify what lies ahead in eternal glory, that is the anagogical sense.

But because the literal sense is that which the author intends, while the author of Holy Scripture is God who comprehends everything all at once by His understanding, it seems consistent with this that, as Augustine says in the twelfth book of *The Confessions*, there should be several meanings in one passage of Scripture, even when interpreted literally.[116]

⟨1.⟩ So, to the first [objection] we must say that the fact that there is more than one meaning does not create ambiguity or any kind of mixture of meanings. For as we have said above, those meanings are many, not because one word has many meanings but because the actual things signified by the words can be signs of other things. So, no confusion results from this in Holy Scripture, since all the senses are based on one, namely the literal sense. All argument must derive from this alone, and not from what is said in the allegorical sense, as Augustine says in the letter against Vincent the Donatist.[117] For no part of Holy Scripture loses any of its force because of this, for nothing necessary to faith is contained within the spiritual sense which Scripture does not openly convey elsewhere through the literal sense.

⟨2.⟩ To the second [objection] we must say that these three [senses]—history, aetiology, and analogy—all relate to the one literal sense. For history is when, as Augustine explains, something is presented to the reader in a straightforward way.[118] Aetiology is when a cause is indicated for what has been said, as when Our Lord gave a reason why Moses allowed men to divorce their wives, namely, the hardness of their hearts.[119] Analogy is when the truth of one passage of Scripture is shown not to be inconsistent with the truth of another. Only allegory is placed among those four to stand as a representative of the three spiritual senses. Thus, Hugh of Saint-Victor includes the anagogical sense within the category of the allegorical, and postulates only three senses in the third book of his *Sentences*, namely the historical, allegorical, and tropological.[120]

⟨3.⟩ To the third [objection], we must say that the parabolical sense is contained within the category of the literal sense. For something can be

---

[116] *Conf.* xii. xxxi. 42 (CCSL xxviii. 240–1).
[117] *Epist.* xciii. viii. 24 (CSEL xxxiv. 469–70).
[118] Ibid.   [119] Cf. Matt. 19: 8.
[120] Actually the *De sacramentis*, i, prol. iv (PL clxxvi. 184). Cf. the same entitling in *Alexander's Sum of Theology*, noted above, n. 60.

given both its own proper meaning and also a figurative meaning by words. And the literal sense is not itself a figure, but rather that which is designated by the figure. For when Scripture names the arm of God, the literal sense is not that God has a physical limb of this kind but rather that he has that which is signified by this limb, namely, effective power. It is clear from this that nothing false can underlie the literal sense of Holy Scripture.

GILES OF ROME

Commentary on the Song of Songs: Prologue[121]

'Let your voice sound in my ears: for your voice is sweet and your face comely', S. of S. 2[: 14]. According to present practice, at the beginning of any book two questions must be distinguished: first, what is the title of the book, and secondly, what are the causes of the work. The aforementioned authority,[122] which is found in the S. of S. 2[: 14], refers us to both questions, when expounded in two different ways. For if the words of the above-mentioned authority are those of a spouse to his beloved (that is, of Christ to the Church) then they tell us what the title of the book is. But if they are to be interpreted as referring to Christ [alone], then they tell us what are the causes of the work.

That book is entitled *The Song of Songs*, as can be seen from the *Gloss*.[123] But the song which we learn about in this book is not corporeal or sensible, but rather to be grasped by the intellect and according to the spirit. For we say that there are two kinds of words, exterior and interior, or sensible words and intellectual words, as is clear from Augustine, in book xv of *The City of God*, where he calls thoughts the expressions (*locutiones*) of the heart.[124] In the case of exterior expressions which have been articulated in accordance with harmony (*melodia*) and proportion, the result is a song which can be appreciated by the senses. Likewise, in the case of interior expressions, and also affections directed towards God in accordance with proportion and due order, a spiritual harmony is the result, and a kind of song which can be appreciated by the intellect. For we should not restrict the noun 'song' so that it applies only to tones (*voces*) which can be grasped by the senses. For Boethius, in his *On Music*, shows that after some fashion a musical proportion exists between all things, inasmuch as all things have been constructed in a certain proportion to each other, in a harmonious pattern.[125] Likewise, St Augustine, in

---

[121] This translation is based on two editions in which the work is falsely attributed to Aquinas: *Thomae de via Caietani in parabol. Salom., etc. commentaria; d. Thomae Aquinatis in librum Salomonis expositio* (s.l., 1545), fos. 194ʳ–196ʳ (incorrectly numbered); *Thomae Aquinatis opera omnia* (Parma, 1852–72), xiv. 387–9.

[122] i.e. the opening quotation from the Song of Songs, an 'authority' being an extract from an author.   [123] *Gl. ord.*, S. of S., pr. (*Bib. glos.* iii. 1815).

[124] Actually *De Trinitate*, XV. x. 18 (CCSL 1A. 484–5), as James Simpson has pointed out.

[*See p. 244 for n. 125*]

the sixth [book] of his *On Music*, extends musical numbers to apply to the activities of the soul.[126] For he enumerates the actions of the soul itself in accordance with five kinds of numbers which he himself has distinguished in the second chapter of the said book,[127] namely judicial (*judiciales*), advancing (*progressores*), reacting (*occursores*), memorial (*recordabiles*), and harmonious (*consonales*).[128] In fact, everyday usage permits of the expression 'song', meaning something clearly stated, in exactly the same way as in the geometricians' manner of speaking. When they want to prove something geometrically they say: 'As such and such a proposition sings', if some proof is clearly produced in that proposition.

Because every heart is open to God and every will speaks to Him, and the thoughts and affections of the will do not deviate from that harmony and those proportions which men follow in striving to achieve good works grounded in virtue, they [i.e. those thoughts and affections] can be called a kind of song. A song of that kind is sung here, for here are expressed the proper affections and thoughts of any individual holy soul, or even of the whole Church, through which it [i.e. the soul] is striving to taste the divine sweetness and to have intercourse with its spouse. And if we wish to speak by way of a comparison (*adaptatio*), we can say that God has two ears, one of anger and one of mercy. Through the ear of anger He hears a shout; as He said to Cain: 'The voice of your brother's blood cries out to me from the earth', Gen. 4[: 10]. Through the ear of mercy He is said to hear melodies (*cantilenae*), that is, affections, thoughts, prayers, and desires of devoted minds. And because it is sweet to God to hear such songs, and He takes delight in holy souls as a good father does in good children, He invites the pious soul or the Church as a whole to take part in this kind of singing: 'Let me hear your voice sound in my ears', and He adds the reason: 'For your voice is sweet and your face comely.' For the song of anyone is sought after for these two reasons: first of all, for itself, that is, when the song is sweet and pleasant; secondly, because of the singer, as happens if she should have a comely face. For it is likely that he who is pleased by the singer's face takes all the greater pleasure in her singing. Christ takes pleasure in the pious soul in both ways: that is, by reason of its song, that is, the goodness of its affections and thoughts, and by reason of its grace, for when the grace of God dwells in the very essence of the soul it makes that soul good, and its works pleasing to God. It is obvious, then, that if the aforesaid words are those of the spouse to

[125] See Boethius' definition of *musica mundana* in *De musica*, I. ii, ed. G. Friedlein (with *De arithmetica*, Leipzig, 1867), pp. 187–8 (PL lxiii. 1171–2).

[126] Augustine, *De musica*, vi (PL xxxii. 1161–93), esp. cap. vi (tr. R. C. Taliaferro, *On Music (De Musica)*, in *Writings of St Augustine*, ii (The Fathers of the Church, New York, 1947), pp. 342–79); cf. the helpful summary of Augustine's argument in W. F. Jackson Knight, *St Augustine's De Musica: A Synopsis* (London, 1949), pp. 85–124.

[127] i.e. *De musica*, vi. ii (PL xxxii. 1163–4, tr. Taliaferro, pp. 325–8).

[128] In Augustine's list (PL xxxii. 1172) the final term is 'sonantes' (the 'sounding' kind of number) rather than 'consonales', as in the two early printed editions of Giles's text here used.

the beloved they designate the title of this book, which is called the Song of Songs, because a melody such as this is excellently intimated here. For the genitive plural, coupled with the nominative, are used to denote some outstanding quality, as in 'King of kings, and Lord of lords' (Rev. 19[: 16]).

But if we wish to expound the aforesaid words so that they are the words of the Church speaking to Christ, they designate for us the causes of the work, even though the sequence of the text may seem to contradict this. But in so far as it does not diverge from true belief such an interpretation is not to be rejected. For a passage of Scripture is given not only a literal meaning (*sensus literalis*), which is always continuous, but also a mystical one, which should not be continuous. Following this principle, then, we must say that the material cause (*causa materialis*) and the efficient cause (*causa efficiens*) are denoted in the words 'Let your voice sound in my ears'; the formal cause (*causa formalis*) in the words 'for your voice is sweet'; the final cause (*causa finalis*), when the words 'and your face comely' are added. The spouse and his bride, that is, Christ and the Church, or Christ and the pious soul, is the material of this book, as is mentioned by the *Gloss*.[129] So, if the bride says to the spouse 'Let your voice sound in my ears' we have both the material cause and the efficient cause. For the spouse, who is the true God, besides being the subject or material of sacred doctrine, is also principally the efficient cause[130] of this science. We do not need to trouble about the instrumental cause, for causes of this sort, in terms of teaching, are regarded as instruments, just like the pen of a scribe. In the words of Ps. 45[: 2]: 'my tongue is the pen of a scribe who writes swiftly.' Therefore, just as it would be over-scrupulous, when enquiring into the authorship of any book, to ask with what pen that book had been written, so in one way it seems to be over-scrupulous for anyone to be much concerned with enquiring into the instrumental causes of Holy Scripture.[131] For if there is general agreement that the book truly originated from the Holy Spirit, there is no point in taking great trouble to discover any other author. But if the other view is taken, and it is felt that we should expend effort on this question, then we assert that Solomon was such a cause [i.e. the instrumental cause] of this book.

According to the *Gloss*, he [i.e. Solomon] had three names and wrote three books to correspond to the number of names. For he was called Solomon, that is, 'peaceloving'; Idila, that is, 'beloved'; and Ecclesiastes, that is, 'the preacher'. In that he was peaceloving, he wrote the book of Proverbs; in that he was beloved, he wrote the book of Songs [i.e. the Song of Songs]; and in that he was a preacher (*concionator*) he wrote the book of Ecclesiastes.[132]

When we add the words 'your voice is sweet', that gives us the formal

---

[129] *Gl. ord.*, S. of S., pr. (*Bib. glos.* iii. 1816).
[130] Lat. 'Est etiam principaliter causa efficiens huius scientiae'.
[131] Cf. Gregory, *Moralia in Job*, pr. i. 2–3 (CCSL cxliii. 8–10).
[132] *Gl. ord.*, S. of S., pr. (*Bib. glos.* iii. 1815). Cf. n. 93 above.

cause. For it has been usual to distingush two kinds of form: the form of treatment (*forma tractandi*), which is the mode of procedure, and the form of the treatise (*forma tractatus*), which is the way in which the chapters are ordered in relation to each other.[133] The mode of procedure in other sciences is by way of proof or disproof, but in sacred doctrine, particularly in the Canon, it seems to be derived from inspiration or revelation. For a treatise of this sort[134] relies on revelation rather than proof. The mode in this book in particular seems to be affective, concerned with desire, and contemplative. So, the *Gloss* observes that the mode of this book is to show with what desire the limbs cling to the head, and strive to please Him, and with what affection the spouse loves the Church.[135] Hence, the mode of proceeding is aptly denoted by a sweetness of this sort, when [the text] says 'your voice is sweet', for a feeling of satisfaction (*complacentia*), affection, and desire imply a certain sweetness characteristic of love.

Moreover, the form of the treatise can be ascertained from this, for it must be such as is required by the mode of proceeding. Or rather, because the order of the chapters in relation to each other, if properly understood, soothes the mind and gives it pleasure, it is quite appropriate that the form of the treatise is understood by the word 'sweetness'.

The final cause is ascertained when the words 'your face is comely' are added. Therefore, the end of this book, as stated by the *Gloss*, is love (*dilectio*), in the way in which the beloved experiences love.[136] Since the main source of this love is the comeliness of the face of the bridegroom, such an end is most aptly referred to in the words 'your face is comely'.

Seeing that love is the ultimate goal in all Holy Writ, perhaps someone might wonder how the love of God is the end of this book in a different way to its being an end of all sacred doctrine taken as a whole, and also whether, seeing that the end of this science is action (*opus*), it can be called a practical science. To clarify these points it should be noted that in physics, taken as a whole, the end is to know the moving body in so far as it is mobile. But in books which cover only parts of the science, this kind of end is narrowed down. For instance, in the *Physics* the end is not the knowledge of a moving body in some kind of special way, but absolute knowledge of such a body, not narrowing it down to this or that aspect. But in the *On Generation* such [a specialized] knowledge is the end, as the formal aspect of the moving body is focused on, and in the *On Heaven*, where its position is focused on; and similarly in the other books the end is knowledge of such a body in a specific sense. In exactly the same way, in ecclesiastical doctrine the love of God, taken in its universal aspect, is the

---

[133] In the Parma edition the terms *forma tractandi* and *forma tractatus* are here inverted; we follow the correct reading of the 1545 ed., fo. 195ᵛ.

[134] i.e. of a treatise in the science of sacred doctrine.

[135] *Gl. ord.*, S. of S., pr. (*Bib. glos.* iii. 1816).

[136] Ibid.

end, in whatever way we may be led on to that love. But in the books which cover parts of the whole this purpose is made more specific. For instance, in Genesis it is made specific in that we are drawn to that love by a consideration of God's power. For there it is shown how God created heaven and earth, and brought all things from nothing into being. But in this book [i.e. the Song of Songs] we are particularly drawn to love of God by a consideration of God's benevolence, and by pondering the depth of the affection which Christ shows towards the beloved, and with what great desire the pious soul should be moved to taste the divine sweetness. If we consider all this with due attention, then it seems appropriate that the love of God should be assigned as the end of a book of this sort, even though this is the end of Holy Writ taken as a whole. For this book encourages us to the love of God and our neighbour in a particular way.

In response to the second question it must be said that this science is described as promoting the love of and affection for God, as we clearly proved in our questions upon the first book of the *Sentences*.[137] And if for this reason someone should wish to call it a practical science, because love is a sort of action, let him keep his opinion but correct his language. For a practical science is principally directed towards exterior action. That is why political sciences are called practical, and *polities*, that is, goodness, is dependent on our actions, for, according to the Philosopher [i.e. Aristotle], we become good because we perform good actions, and like mental conditions (*habitūs*) are begotten from like actions.[138] But because spiritual goodness is not dependent upon exterior actions but rather upon the condition and works of charity, Holy Writ, which is directed towards this sort of goodness, should not be called practical. The science which is directed towards speculation is not called practical, even though to speculate is a kind of work, but instead derives its name from speculation, and is called 'speculative'. Likewise, theology, which is directed towards the affection or love of charity (because works of this sort are not exterior), must derive a special name from these qualities [i.e. affection and love] and must be described as affective and concerned with love, and not as practical. Having considered all this, let us now proceed to the exposition of the text.

---

[137] *In I Lib. sent.*, prologi questio 3, art. 4, resolutio (*Commentarium b. Aegidii Romani in primum librum Magistri sententiarum* (Cordova, 1699), p. 31).

[138] *Eth. Nicomach.* ii. 1 (1103ᵃ11–ᵇ25), cf. i. 1–2 (1094ᵃ1–22); cf. Grosseteste, tr. Litzinger, pp. 117–19, cf. pp. 5–6. Cf. Giles's *Sentences* commentary, *In I Lib. sent.*, prol. qu. 3, art. 4, resolutio, ad 3um (ed. cit. p. 31).

On the Instruction of Princes: Book I, Chapter i[139]

WHAT THE MODE OF PROCEDURE IS IN THE INSTRUCTION OF PRINCES

In every subject the scope of the discussion should fit in with the requirements of that subject, and should be neither more or less than necessary, according to the Philosopher [i.e. Aristotle] in the *Metaphysics*, book vii.[140] So, if our purpose is to teach the art and knowledge of princely or royal government, in order that my account does not take in a wider area than the present task requires, I must first of all consider the mode of procedure in this art. It must be understood, therefore, that in the whole field of moral teaching the mode of procedure, according to the Philosopher, is figurative and broad (*grossus*).[141] For in such matters one should make one's way by use of types and figures, for moral actions do not fall completely within the scope of narrative.

We can show by using three approaches that the mode of procedure in this science should be figurative and broad. The first approach is taken from the standpoint of the subject-matter (*materia*) with which an art of this sort is concerned; the second, from the standpoint of the end-purpose (*finis*) which is being pursued in this art; the third, from the standpoint of the audience (*auditor*) who is to be educated by means of an art such as this.

The first approach is as follows. The body of knowledge which relates to princely rule is concerned with human actions and is included within the moral sphere (*morali negocio*). The subject-matter of morals, as has been said, does not admit of detailed and thorough scrutiny, but concerns individual matters, matters which, as is shown in the *Ethics*, book ii, are very uncertain [in scientific terms] because of the variability of their nature.[142] Therefore, the individual actions which are the subject-matter of this work show that we must proceed by way of figures and types. The Philosopher seems to touch on this principle in the first book of the *Ethics* when he says that it will be a sufficient discussion of moral matters if an explanation is made in keeping with the subject under discussion. Wherefore he adds that it is the mark of an educated man to seek that amount of exactness in each kind which the nature of the subject admits. For the nature of morality appears to be quite the opposite to that of mathematics.[143] For mathematical proofs are exact in the first degree of exactness, as the Commentator [i.e. Averroes] says in [expounding the]

---

[139] Tr. from *D. Aegidii Romani . . . de regimine principum libri iii* (apud Antonium Bladum, Rome 1556), fos. 1ʳ–5ʳ.

[140] Cf. *Meta.* vii. 15 (1039ᵇ20–1040ᵃ7).

[141] *Eth. Nicomach.* i. 3 (1094ᵇ19–21), cf. Grosseteste, tr. Litzinger, p. 16.

[142] *Eth. Nicomach.* ii. 2 (1104ᵃ1–2), cf. Grosseteste, tr. Litzinger, pp. 117–18; cf. above, n. 17.

[143] *Eth. Nicomach.* i. 3 (1094ᵇ25–7); cf. Grosseteste, tr. Litzinger, p. 16.

second book of the *Metaphysics*.[144] But moral arguments are superficial and broad. It is the function of geometry not to persuade but to prove [propositions]. But it is the function of an orator and politician not to prove but to persuade.[145] Hence [Aristotle] writes in the first book of the *Ethics* that it is equally wrong to accept a mathematician giving merely persuasive arguments and to seek an exact proof from an orator.[146]

The second approach is from the standpoint of the end-purpose which is intended in this art. For, as [Aristotle] writes in the second book of the *Ethics*, we undertake moral study not for the sake of abstract contemplation, nor to gain knowledge, but in order that we may become good.[147] Therefore, the end in this science is not to gain knowledge concerning its own matter, but [moral] activity; it is not truth but goodness. Since subtle arguments, therefore, are more effective in illuminating the intellect, while those that are superficial and broad are more effective in stirring and firing the affections (*affectus*), in the speculative sciences, where the main aim is the illumination of the intellect, one must proceed by way of proof and in a subtle manner, but in moral matters, where the goal is an upright will and that we should become good, one must proceed by persuasion and the use of figures. Whence [Aristotle] says[148] in the first book of the *Ethics*, that moral matter, being lovingly devoted to such things and basing its discussions on such things, and concerned with those things which are of the greater frequency, expresses truth in a broad and figurative way.[149]

The third approach is from the standpoint of the audience which is to be instructed in this art. For though the title of the book is *On the Instruction of Princes*, all of the populace is to be instructed by it. For, although not everyone can be a king or prince, everyone ought to do his best to see that he becomes the sort of person who would be worthy to be a prince or

---

[144] Averroes, *In Meta. Arist.* ii. 3 (995ᵃ6), in *Aristotelis Metaphysica cum Averrois Cordubensis commentaria* (Venice, 1574), fo. 35ʳ.

[145] In the commentary on Aristotle's *Rhetoric* (recently tr. by William of Moerbeke) which Giles of Rome wrote around 1280, it is argued that rhetoric serves the need of the practical intellect; specifically, of the man who uses his reason to discover and practically promote the common good of society. Consequently, rhetoric will be the proper instrument of the statesman in carrying out his task of persuading those under his government to perform those actions which serve the common good. The rhetorician must be able to deal directly with the most particular of practical issues, and concern himself with disposing arguments so as to arouse the passions; he must speak in a way which will appeal to the capacity even of the simplest and most uncultivated hearer. *Rhetorica Aristotelis cum Egidii de Roma commentariis* (Venice, 1515), fos. 1ʳ–4ᵛ, 8ʳ. Cf. the helpful summary by Brother S. Robert, 'Rhetoric and Dialectic: According to the First Latin Commentary on the Rhetoric of Aristotle', *New Schol.* xxxi (1957), 484–98, esp. pp. 494–5. See also Giles's short question *De differentia rhetoricae, ethicae et politicae*, ed. G. Bruni, *New Schol.* vi (1932), 1–18, partly tr. in J. M. Miller, M. H. Prosser, and T. W. Benson, *Readings in Medieval Rhetoric* (Bloomington, Ind., and London, 1973), pp. 265–8. The notion that rhetoric seeks to move rather than prove was quite commonplace; cf. Robert Kilwardby's view, as described by Sharp, 'The *De ortu scientiarum*', p. 27.

[146] Cf. above, n. 143.   [147] Cf. above, n. 101.

[148] Reading 'dicens' for the text's 'dicentes'.   [149] Cf. above, n. 141.

king. This cannot be achieved unless the tenets which are to be related in this work are known and observed. So, in a sense the populace as a whole forms the audience for this art. But only a few are endowed with acute understanding; hence the remark in the third book of the *Rhetoric* that the larger the population the farther are they from understanding.[150] So, the audience for these moral matters is simple and unsophisticated (*grossus*), as I showed in [my commentary on] the first book of the *Rhetoric*.[151] Since, therefore, the populace as a whole cannot understand subtleties, one must proceed in the sphere of morals in a figurative and broad way. According to the Philosopher in his *Politics*, the subject ought to know and to do what his lord ought to know and to command.[152] If, therefore, by means of this book, princes are instructed how they should conduct themselves, and how they should govern their subjects, this teaching must reach out to the population, so that it knows how it ought to obey its princes. But since, as I have already touched on, this cannot be achieved except by arguments which are superficial and appeal to the senses, therefore the mode of procedure in this book ought to be broad and figurative.

HENRY OF GHENT

The Sum of Ordinary Questions: Extracts from Articles 14 and 16[153]

ARTICLE 14: CONCERNING THE MODE OF IMPARTING THEOLOGY

There follows a discussion of the cause this science in terms of its formal cause (*causa formalis*). Because in the case of the sciences there is a twofold form, the form of treating the subject (*forma tractandi*), and the form taken by the treatment itself (*forma tractatus*), this is therefore a twofold question; first of all concerning the form of treating the subject, then the form taken by that treatment. And because, in a science, the form of treating the

---

[150] *Rhet.* iii. 18 (1419ᵃ17–18), tr. R. McKeon, *The Basic Works of Aristotle* (New York, 1941, repr. 1968), p. 1449: 'You cannot ask a series of questions owing to the incapacity of the audience to follow them.' In his commentary on this passage Giles explains that the audience of rhetorical orations is supposed to be *grossus*, and so the enthymemes must be suited to the capacity of the minds of such 'gross' people. *Rhet. Aris. cum Egidii comm.*, fo. 117ʳ; cf. *Rhet.* i. 1 (1355ᵃ14–19) and i. 2 (1357ᵃ3–4), and also the relevant discussion in the 13th-c. Parisian *quaestio* on the nature of poetry below, pp. 309–10.

[151] *Rhet. Aris. cum Egidii comm.*, fo. 1ᵛ.

[152] *Politica*, iii. 4 (1277ᵃ25–ᵇ7).

[153] Our translation is based on two early printed editions, *Summae quaestionum ordinariarum theologii recepto praeconio solennis, Henrici a Gandavo* (in aedibus J. Badii Ascensii, Paris, 1520), fos. xcixᵛ–cᵛ, cvʳ–cviᵛ, cviiᵛ–cviiiʳ, and *Magistri Henrici Goethals a Gandavo . . . Summa in tres partes praecipuas digesta* (apud Franciscum Succium, Ferrara, 1646), i. 247–9, 263–5, 268–9.

subject is the same thing as the way in which the author proceeds (*modus agendi*), which consists in imparting [the material] and expounding it, there are two questions concerning this; first, concerning the manner of imparting this science, and secondly, concerning the manner in which it is expounded. The question regarding the imparting of the science is twofold; first, whether the mode of imparting this science should have many forms or only one; secondly, whether that mode proceeds by argument or by narration.

Question 1: Whether the Mode of Imparting this Science should have Many Forms or only One

As regards the first point, the first argument is that the mode (*modus*) of this science should have many forms rather than just one.

⟨1.⟩ Heb. 1[: 1]: 'God formerly spoke to the holy Fathers in many forms and using many methods.' That 'speaking' is the enunciation of this science, which is related to the way in which it is imparted. Therefore the way in which this science is imparted takes many forms, and not just one.

⟨2.⟩ Eph. 3[: 10]: 'The manifold wisdom of God may be known through the agency of the Church, to principalities and powers.' But something of this sort [i.e. wisdom] does not become known to people except as a result of the manner in which it is imparted. Therefore, etc.

⟨3.⟩ Against this view. The mode of [imparting] a science ought to be on a level that is adapted to the listener (*auditor*), for otherwise it would not give him instruction, and also the subject-matter (*materia*), for otherwise it would be incongruous. But the mode which has only one form is better suited than that which has many to the fleshly understanding, which is being offered the milk of faith in the authoritative text of Scripture. For that understanding is more readily instructed by the uniform mode and is more confused by the mode which employs many forms, for it makes more headway when faced with fewer alternatives. Likewise, the mode which uses one form suits the subject-matter better than that which uses many. For that subject-matter is itself very simple and has one form, as we have said above, concerning the oneness of this science. Therefore, etc.

⟨4.⟩ Some people say that the mode of imparting this science should employ many forms, both because the wisdom of God has many forms and it is this wisdom which ought to be transmitted in this science, and also because the human condition takes many forms and that science ought to be adapted to these. For, they say, those who could be instructed by only one way, and only one mode, could not be instructed by another way, but different people are instructed in various ways about various things, so that a mode that suits one does not suit the other. Therefore, the mode used by this science must be manifold. And they distinguish these modes by this criterion, that Holy Scripture sometimes commands, sometimes forbids, sometimes permits, sometimes gives advice, sometimes threatens, sometimes promises, sometimes strikes terror in the reader, sometimes exhorts, sometimes reveals mysteries, sometimes narrates events, and performs other functions of this sort. So, in line with this, the mode used by Holy Scripture is to give advice to one person, to prohibit another, to give freedom of action to another, and so on.

⟨5.⟩ It is clear that their statement is defective as regards both what is said and the rationale behind what is said. [It is defective] as regards what is said, namely that the mode of this science is manifold particularly because it gives orders and therefore is command-giving, it prohibits someone [from doing something] and therefore it is prohibitive, and has other qualities of this sort. That diversity does not lie in the mode of treating or handing down this subject-matter, but in the subject-matter which is treated of. For at one moment it hands down precepts, at another deals out prohibitions, at another sets before the reader grounds for fear, or hope, or similar things of this sort. So, if all these differences could be given as grounds for calling the mode of this science manifold, then likewise the mode of any other science could be called manifold because of the different elements of its subject-matter. This cannot be. For the same mode of scientific treatment can well be used in treating different subjects, either terrifying, forbidding, and similar things of this sort. Consequently, the mode of treating a subject by reasoning or argument is precisely the same in different sciences, following the different subjects which are being dealt with.

⟨6.⟩ Their argument is also defective as regards the rationale behind what is said. It is true that God's wisdom is manifold and the human condition is manifold. But this is no reason why the mode employed by this science should be manifold. A manifold mode should not be adduced because of the manifold nature of God's wisdom. The one mode of treatment can be applied to each and every aspect of God's wisdom, even if different aspects of God's wisdom were to be treated in different parts of that science of theology; for instance, in one place the wisdom which moves Him to issue commands, and in another the wisdom which causes him to prohibit, and other similar aspects, as referred to above. Here one piece of the manifold science of God is not taught in one place, and another part in another, but in each discourse (*sermo*) concerning this science [i.e. theology] a manifold knowledge of God is gained in accordance with the multiplicity of textual meaning (*sensus*) and of exposition. This will be dealt with later.

Likewise, the mode of this science cannot be manifold simply because of the manifold nature of the human condition. For in that case, that science would have to be passed on to one sort of men in one place, and to another sort in a different place, and not in its totality in all places. Thus, it would not be offered in its totality everywhere to every condition of men. This is quite false, as will be clear from what follows. Since this [science] is offered for consideration in its totality everywhere to every condition of men, one should in no way claim that there should be a different mode of imparting that knowledge because of the different conditions of men, so that often a science that is one whole should be dealt with in different ways, which is absurd.

⟨7.⟩ So we must argue on another tack. That science [i.e. theology], like any other, is handed down for the sole purpose of becoming known to man, to meet whose need it has been handed down, as the Apostle says in Rom. 15[: 4]: 'Whatever has been written has been written for our instruction', and St Augustine, *On John*, with special reference to this science, says: 'Above all we ought to try to know God's words, for why were they spoken if not that they be known?'[154] It is, therefore, essential that the mode of handing down this science, as with any other science, must match the way in which knowledge is acquired, so that the subject may be dealt with in such a way that men may be able to acquire knowledge of it more readily.

I have spoken above about the mode of acquiring knowledge in the sciences. This desired goal is pursued from the starting-points of the nature of the subject-matter, the peculiar nature of the science itself, and the situation of the person who possesses that knowledge. The subject-matter of this science, as will be stated below, is the universe as seen in the work of creation and of the renewal of creation. The peculiar attribute of this science is to build the foundations of the spiritual dwelling in those matters which belong to the faith. The situation of the person who possesses that knowledge corresponds to the various positions which men occupy—as far as concerns their intellect (*intellectus*) and affections (*affectus*)—in relation to their perception of the truths which constitute this science. This science is not able to cover all the individual things which relate to its subject-matter individually and separately, and to teach the elements of Christian belief in a way that exactly suits all the various conditions that men find themselves in. Therefore, the appropriate mode for this science is not that all the individual things relating to it should be treated separately, and receive different treatment as is best suited to various people, and in so far as [the teachers] can impart information in different ways about different aspects of Christian belief. But the mode used ought to be such that disparate teachings (*sententiae*) concerning different subjects and different tenets of belief should be contained in one and the same discourse (*sermo*), and that these should be tailored to suit various conditions of men, so that the man who cannot assimilate more may be content with the surface literal interpretation, but the man who can may seek the spiritual understanding underneath the literal one, depending on the

154 *Tract. in Ioh.* xxi. 12 (CCSL xxxvi. 219).

progress he has made. This is exactly what St Augustine says in the twelfth book of the *Confessions*, when he approves the mode of imparting Holy Scripture. There he is speaking particularly about the books of Moses, and most particularly Genesis. But what he says applies generally to Scripture as a whole: 'My God, I cannot believe that thy faithful servant Moses had fewer gifts than I myself should wish to be given me from thee, if I had been born at the same time, and put in such a position, so that by the service of my heart and tongue writings would be vouchsafed which should benefit all humanity so long afterwards, and throughout the whole world would surpass by their lofty authority all false and arrogant thinking. If I had been Moses at that time, and thou hadst given me the task of writing the book of Genesis, I should have wished to be granted such a skill in writing, and such a style of putting together my discourse, that those who are not yet able to understand them would not reject thy words as far beyond their capacity and those who could grasp them would find that whatever truths they had arrived at in the course of their own thinking were not omitted in the few words of thy servant. And if someone else saw another meaning in the light of truth, that meaning too would not be absent in these same words of mine. A spring is more abundant when located within narrow confines, and provides a flow of water over a wide area with more channels than does any one stream, drawn from that spring, and flowing through many different places. In the same way, the account of thy steward [i.e. Moses],[155] which is destined to help many future preachers, in the limited compass of a few words gushes forth streams of limpid truth. From this each may draw off for himself whatever truth he can regarding these matters [i.e. the Creation], each expressing different opinions in more lengthy and more discursive phrases.'[156]

⟨8.⟩ So it is a completely wrong view which some hold, that the mode of this science ought to take many forms so that in one way and in one place the truth may be taught to the backward, and in a different way and in another place to the moderately intelligent person, and again differently in yet another place to the subtle intelligence. For they say that those who are young [in the faith] and still imperfect must be educated in one way, and those whose faith is mature and perfect in another, in the words of the Apostle at 1 Cor. 3[: 1–2]: 'As you are still infants in Christ I have given you milk to drink, rather than solid food, for hitherto you were not able to eat this. But even now you are not able.' It is indeed quite true that these two groups are to receive different kinds of instruction. But this is achieved by the two groups' receiving the exposition of the Scriptures in two different senses, not because two different texts of Scripure are offered them for their consideration. In fact, all Scripture is offered on a common basis to all men for consideration, and it adapts itself to each

---

[155] Cf. 1 Cor. 4: 1, Tit. 1: 7.
[156] Augustine, *Confessiones*, XII. xxvi. 36–7 (CCSL xxvii. 236–7).

according to his capacity to understand. Hence, as St Augustine puts it, one text must not be offered to those who are perfect in the faith and another text to beginners, [but texts must be offered] to all in common, so that each may take it in according to his capacity.[157] So the same teaching is presented to all, but, because of their different capacities, for some it serves as the milk of faith only, while to others it is solid food, for they, with the help of faith, can get some understanding of the text, as we will explain later.

⟨9.⟩ To assemble together in compendious form and in simple language a large number of teachings (*sententiae*) concerning diverse topics and fitting in with diverse topics, and to proceed in this way through all the constituent parts of a science, means adhering to absolute uniformity in the mode of handing down the science and describing it. Therefore, it must be said without reservation that the manner of handing on this Scripture is one characterized by the utmost simplicity and oneness of form. That oneness is all the more marked in that there is greater unity in the subject which it deals with than there is in the other sciences, as we found earlier on.

⟨10.⟩ In answer to the first objection, namely that in this science God has spoken variously and in many ways, we must reply that that variety of ways does not relate to the mode of treating the material or of assembling the constituent parts of this science, but to the mode of revealing what was to be written for the benefit of different kinds of people and in different ways. As the *Gloss* says at that point [i.e. on Heb. 1: 1]: '[God spoke] in many ways, that is on many occasions, and to many men, namely Abraham, Isaac, and Jacob, and to others, and spoke often to these men in many ways, that is in many kinds of communication, for he spoke sometimes through the medium of dreams as he did to Daniel, sometimes with his own unveiled and direct (*apertus*) voice as he did to Moses, sometimes through inspiration within a man as in the case of David.'[158] Or, as another gloss says: 'In many ways, that is by means of many different kinds of converse (*locutio*), for example through dreams, or cases of inspiration, or unveiled and direct utterances (*apertas voces*), telling what the future would be in many ways, that is through various mysteries.'[159] But all these different ways are contained within the one and the same mode of handing down this science. So the statement that used to be made, that in the prophets the mode of this science is revelatory, is absolutely untrue. For that does not relate to the manner of writing down what has been revealed, but only to the manner of understanding what is to be committed to writing.

[157] Id., *Tract. in Ioh.* xcviii. 3 (CCSL xxxvi. 577–8), from which Henry takes the following metaphors of milk and solid food.

[158] *Gl. ord. marg.*, Heb. 1: 1 (*Bib. glos.* vi. 792).

[159] Ibid. (*Bib. glos.* vi. 793).

So, because those who wrote whatever has been written in this science gained their knowledge of these things through revelation, if you went by the above dictum then you would be forced to say that every part of that science [of theology] used the revelatory method, and it is clear how foolish it would be to say this.

⟨11.⟩ To the second point, that this is 'the manifold wisdom of God' [Eph. 3: 10], we must reply that this is true, not in terms of the mode used in handing down this science but of its contents. For in this science God's wisdom is clearly portrayed in marvellous acts. So the *Gloss* says at that point [i.e. on Eph. 3: 10]: 'because in the Greek text the word is "manifold [wisdom]", not just diverse, but marked off by great diversity'.[160] Let us consider then in what way it has many forms. Christ is a being immeasurable, but He is conceived. He wails, an infant, in the crib, but is praised by angels in the sky. Herod persecutes Him, but the magi adore Him. The Pharisees ignore Him, but the star shows [His coming], etc., and similar things.

ARTICLE 16: CONCERNING THE MODE OF EXPOUNDING THIS SCIENCE IN RESPECT OF ITS EXPOSITION

Question 3: Whether solely a Fourfold Exposition is to be sought after in this Science

Concerning the third question it is argued that Holy Scripture should have only two [senses].

⟨1.⟩ For Dionysius says in his *Heavenly Hierarchy*: 'Divine revelation is twofold.'[161] But revelation of the divine is effected by the expositions of this science. Therefore, etc.

⟨2.⟩ It is argued that there are only three [senses]. For Hugh [of Saint-Victor], in book iii of his *Sentences*, says: 'There are three modes of Holy Scripture: history, which is the narrative of events; allegory, when some fact has another, quite different significance; tropology, that is speaking in moral terms, in which the subject is the right ordering of men's morals.'[162]

⟨3.⟩ It is argued that there are four [senses]. For Bede, in the *Gloss* on Genesis, says: 'There are four guidelines (*regulae*) for Holy Scripture: history, which speaks of events; allegory, in which some fact has another, quite different meaning; tropology, that is speaking in moral terms, in which the subject is the right ordering of morals; anagogy, that is the spiritual interpretation, which leads to the heights of heaven when we are

---

[160] *Gl. ord. marg.*, Eph. 3: 10 (*Bib. glos.* vi. 543).
[161] *De cael. hier.* ii (PL cxxii. 1041); cf. *Alexander's Sum of Theology*, Introd. treat., qu. 1, ch. 4, art. 3⟨f⟩, tr. above, p. 218.
[162] *De sacramentis*, pr. iv (PL clxxvi. 184–5).

intending to treat of lofty and celestial matters. For Holy Scripture is carried along on these four senses as if by four wheels.'[163]

⟨4.⟩ It is argued that there are five [senses]. For Augustine, *On the Usefulness of Belief*, likewise lists four modes, and in discussing them touches on an extra one, not one of the four. He says: 'All those who have an earnest desire to get to know that part of Scripture which is called the Old Testament will find that it is divided in four ways, in terms of history, etymology [*sic* for aetiology], analogy, and allegory.'[164]

⟨5.⟩ It is argued that there are many more [senses]. For just as Holy Scripture is sometimes expounded historically, sometimes tropologically or allegorically or anagogically, so sometimes it is expounded in terms of parable, sometimes ironically, and in several other modes according to the different figures of speech.

⟨6.⟩ We must reply to this in the words of St Augustine, in the first book of *On Christian Doctrine*: 'The fulfilment and end of the Law and of all divine Scriptures is love.'[165] Man cannot love what he does not believe in. Besides, if he believes and loves he makes his belief effective by acting on it, so that he hopes that he will succeed in reaching the object of his love. For faith, hope, and love are the three weapons with which all knowledge, and all prophecy, fight. 'Wherefore, when anyone has come to understand that the goal of God's commandment is love that proceeds "from a heart that is pure, a clear conscience and faith that is sincere", and if he determines to relate the entire process of understanding the divine Scriptures to those three things, then he may approach the task of treating of the Scriptures with confidence.'[166] The things which belong to the realm of hope and love do not fall within the bounds of this science, except in so far as they also belong to the realm of faith. So this science is called the science of faith. For whatever subject is dealt with within the bounds of that science must be expounded in such a way that it is made to point towards the rule of faith. As Augustine says in book xv of *The City of God*, 'Even if these things which are to be expounded here differ in many ways, they must be brought back to the undivided concord of the Catholic faith.'[167]

That whole science contains only three things which are laid down in order to achieve three good ends in this life: things to be believed, so that we may believe them; things to be loved, so that we may love them, and

[163] *Gl. ord. marg.*, gen., pr. (*Bib. glos.* i, unfol. — PL cxiii. 63 B); here not attributed to Bede. Cf. the use of most of this passage in *Alexander's Sum of Theology*, tr. above, pp. 217–18, and n. 55; see further the continuation of the passage attributed to Bede, tr. below, p. 260.

[164] *De util. cred.* iii. 5; cf. Aquinas' use of this passage in his *Sum of Theology*, 1a 1, art. 10, 2, tr. above, p. 241. Here, and later in the discussion, the two printed editions of Henry's work have 'etymology' for 'aetiology', i.e. the indication of the cause at work (cf. above, n. 110), an obvious case of a more common term being substituted for a more difficult one.

[165] *De doct. Christ.* 1. xxxv. 39.

[166] Ibid. 1. xi. 44, quoting 1 Tim. 1: 5.   [167] *De civ. Dei*, xv. xxvi.

things to be hoped for, so that we may hope for them. And Holy Scripture treats of all these things, as for example it treats of those things which belong to the realm of faith. For there is faith in those things which are to be believed, loved, and hoped for. So every exposition of Holy Scripture must be aimed towards these three, in accordance with the rule of faith, namely that things worthy of belief be believed, things worthy of love be loved, and things worthy of hope be hoped for.

⟨7.⟩ Therefore, Holy Scripture imparts a knowledge of what can be believed and loved, and what must be hoped for, not so much by describing to us those things in themselves in a literal fashion as by conveying them by means of certain things done and undertaken, which it recounts. For that science speaks not in words alone like others, but speaks also by things.[168] However, the knowledge of those things cannot be conveyed by means of what was done and undertaken, unless the knowledge of those undertakings themselves can be assumed. Therefore, to begin with, we need to make a twofold exposition of Holy Scripture. One exposition is necessary to ascertain the truth in the facts and events, which themselves suggest other meanings to us. This first exposition is called the historical or literal one, and the spiritual exposition must be based upon it. The other exposition has as its purpose to ascertain the knowledge which the facts and deeds supply for us to understand. This is called the spiritual or mystical exposition. It is because of that twofold exposition that the following words are spoken about the strong woman, who personifies the Church, in the last chapter of Proverbs [31: 21]: 'The snow and frost will not make her to fear for her household, for all her household are clothed in garments of double thickness'. 'The servants of her household' are teachers of Holy Scripture, who are protected by garments of double thickness, that is the twofold exposition of Holy Scripture, viz. historical and mystical. So she will not fear for her house, that is for Holy Scripture, in contemplating which she takes her rest, at the hands of the frosts and snow, that is the deviation of heretical wickedness. For whenever some absurdity is introduced by heretics in the literal sense, we must immediately have recourse to the sound spiritual interpretation.

⟨8.⟩ The facts and events found in this science of faith provide us with material as a basis for [spiritual] understanding only in such areas as that science wishes to inform us of, namely what we should believe, what we should love, and what we should hope for. All spiritual exposition of this science according to the rule of faith ought to be directed towards these [three] areas. So the spiritual exposition is threefold, and only threefold. One interpretation is to teach us through the facts and events what we are to believe, the second is to teach us what we are to love, and the third what we are to hope for. The first is the allegorical, the second the tropological, the third the anagogical.

[168] Cf. Augustine, *De doct. Christ.* i. ii. 2, ii. x. 15.

The allegorical exposition is that which among the essential elements of our belief teaches the hidden sacraments of primal truth, upon which, through faith, the Church of Christ is founded. Therefore, the allegorical interpretation is centred on Christ and the Church, because within the trinity of divine persons the knowledge of essential elements of belief is likened to the Son, because wisdom is assigned to Him as His particular attribute.

The tropological exposition is that which in those spheres where we should exercise our love shows us the stimuli to the love of the supreme Goodness, stimuli by which, through love, morality and a pattern for living may be established within us. Therefore, the tropological exposition always has in view the formation of the virtues in the just soul, and is linked to the Holy Spirit, because goodness is assigned to Him as His particular attribute.

The anagogical exposition is that whereby, in the realm of future expectations, we are shown the immeasurable joy of everlasting bliss, that bliss which hope encourages us to grasp. For the anagogical exposition looks to the heavenly rewards in the life everlasting and is linked to the Father, because eternity is His particular attribute.

However, one should add the reservation that the threefold mystical exposition, based on the simple historical exposition, in a sense perfectly reflects the trinity of the divine persons rooted in a unity of being, upon which the truth of faith in this science is based.

⟨9.⟩ We understand the words of Prov. 22[: 17–21] to apply to these three types of spiritual exposition: 'Apply your heart to my teaching, so that you may have confidence in the Lord. That is why I have revealed it to you, and described it in three ways, so that I might show you certainty, and the words of truth.' In truth, the confidence of the Church is based on the reliability of the authority of Holy Scripture, as stated above, and this, in its spiritual interpretation, never wavers. Augustine is speaking at one and the same time about those four senses and types of exposition of Holy Scripture at the beginning of his work *On Genesis*. 'In all the holy books one ought to consider what eternal truths are conveyed to us in them': he refers here to the anagogical sense. Concerning the historical sense he adds: 'what actions are narrated'. Concerning the allegorical sense: 'what future events are foretold', and concerning the tropological sense: 'what course of action we are advised to follow'.[169]

Paul writes about these [senses] in 2 Tim. 3[: 16]: 'Every part of Scripture, being divinely inspired, is useful for teaching.' The *Gloss* adds: 'Those who are ignorant'. This relates to the historical sense in which first of all they are to be instructed. [Paul continues:] 'useful for debating'. The gloss is: 'that is, for winning men over from evil'. This relates to

---

[169] *De Genesi ad litteram*, 1. i (CSEL xxviii. 3); cf. *Gl. ord. marg.*, Gen., pr. (*Bib. glos.* i, unfol. — PL cxiii. 63 c).

allegory, by which heresies are to be condemned. [Paul continues:] 'useful for correcting'. The gloss is: 'those who persist in evildoing'. This relates to tropology, by which vices are held in check. [Paul continues:] 'useful for educating'. The gloss is: 'those who are penitent'. This relates to anagogy, which hastens the journey to the celestial regions.[170]

Bede also gives an example of these senses in the *Gloss* on the beginning of Genesis. He writes: 'Jerusalem interpreted historically is a city, allegorically it signifies the Church, tropologically the faithful soul, anagogically the life of those who dwell in heaven.'[171] Hence St Augustine, when he considers the simplicity of the literal interpretation of this science when it is taken in the historical sense, and the depth of meaning when it is taken in the spiritual sense, says in book ii of the *Confessions*: 'Behold, the surface of thy Scriptures lies before us, flattering us. But their profundity is marvellous. My God, to gaze into them inspires dread.'[172] For there is in it, as Wisd. 7[: 22] says, 'the spirit of understanding, holy, unique, yet manifold'.

⟨10.⟩ So, to put it briefly, it must be said that there are four senses of this science, and there cannot be more than four. It follows from this that the exposition of the science can be fourfold only, and can have neither more nor fewer senses.

⟨11.⟩ To the first objection, namely that the science is twofold according to blessed Dionysius, we must admit that the method of revealing things divine is twofold. One part relates to the manner of describing for our benefit matters divine through the literal sense of this science. The other relates to the method of interpreting what is written in that science about matters divine. Dionysius is speaking about the first method of revelation and that is purely twofold. For, as he says at the beginning of *The Celestial Hierarchy*, 'Matters divine cannot be revealed to us except when enveloped in sacred veils, and those veils are taken from the elements of God's creation which we recognize.'[173] Created things have some properties which presuppose a certain nobility in their nature and are more in keeping with God than with His creatures, thus goodness, wisdom, and suchlike qualities. But there are other things which it is quite unworthy to attribute to God if they retain their own usual meaning. But they can be attributed to Him if a simile is used. For instance, He can be said to have eyes, a hand, and similar attributes. And it is in these terms that Dionysius speaks of a twofold way of revealing divine truths. One of these ways he calls congruous, as when they are made known by means of qualities which are found in created beings but are more properly found

---

[170] *Gl. ord. marg. et interlin.*, 2 Tim. 3: 16 (*Bib. glos.* vi. 751).
[171] *Gl. ord. marg.*, Gen., pr. (*Bib. glos.* i, unfol., cf. PL cxiii. 63 c). Cf. above, nn. 55 and 163.
[172] *Conf.* xii. xiv. 17 (CSEL xxvii. 224).
[173] *De cael. hier.* i (PL cxxii. 1038). With the following argument about the 'twofold way of revealing divine truths' cf. ibid., ch. ii (cols. 1039 ff.).

in God. The other he calls incongruous, when they are made known by means of qualities found in created beings, but unworthy of God, properties which cannot be attributed to Him except by a certain transfer to a figurative signification (*translatio*). But these two methods have nothing whatever to do with the different senses or types of exposition. In fact, both pertain to the historical sense, for by these methods divine truths are revealed to us in Scripture. For all metaphor and parable pertains to the historical sense, as I will discuss presently.

⟨12.⟩ In response to the second objection, that Hugh [of Saint-Victor] only enumerates three types of exposition, we must reply that Hugh is only speaking of those expositions which are grouped round the subject-matter (*materia*) of Holy Scripture. Now, according to Hugh himself, the subject-matter of Holy Scripture is the work of man's restoration to grace, and only that,[174] and this work is carried on in the Church Militant. But it [i.e. the subject-matter] is not the work of man's glorification, which is carried on in the Church Triumphant. Therefore, since the anagogical sense relates to the Church Triumphant, while the other three senses relate to the Church Militant, as is clear from what we have said, this is the reason why he enumerates only those three senses and omits the fourth.

Strabo did exactly the same in the *Gloss* on the penultimate chapter of Exodus.[175] He says: 'Holy Scripture, which is made up of a historical, moral, and allegorical constituent, cannot be broken by any heretical dogmas, for "a threefold rope is difficult to break" [Eccles. 4: 12].'[176]

⟨13.⟩ As for the argument that Augustine makes etymology [*sic* for aetiology] a [fifth][177] sense as well as the four already mentioned, it must be stated that in that passage[178] Augustine does not set out in any way to distinguish the senses and ways of expounding Scripture, but rather to set out the different ways in which Scripture is treated, and particularly ways in which the literal meaning of the Old Testament is taken up in the New, so that by this means he may show that the Old Testament is not contrary to the New. 'For all Scripture which is given the name of "Old Testament" is divided in a fourfold manner', that is after the way in which it is treated in the New Testament, according to the four manners in which the statements of the Old Testament are taken up in the New, 'viz. historically, etymologically [*sic* for aetiologically], anagogically [*sic* for analogically], allegorically.[179] They are taken up historically when we are

---

[174] Hugh of Saint-Victor, *De sacramentis*, i, pr. ii (PL clxxvi. 183).

[175] The *Glossa ordinaria* was not the work of Walafrid Strabo: see Smalley, *Study of the Bible*, pp. 56–66. The central figure was in fact Anselm of Laon.

[176] *Gl. ord. marg.* Exod. 38: 21 (*Bib. glos.* ii. 893).

[177] This mistake occurs in both editions; cf. above, n. 164.

[178] Augustine, *De util. cred.* iii. 5 ff. (CCSL xxv. 7 ff.), quoted and paraphrased in the ensuing discussion. Cf. above, p. 257 and n. 164; also p. 241.

[179] These and the following confusions occur in both the early printed editions of Henry's work.

taught in the New Testament what was written or said in the Old. They are taken up etymologically [*sic* for aetiologically] when it is shown' in the New Testament 'what the underlying cause is for something being said or done [in the Old]; anagogically [*sic* for analogically], when it is shown that the two testaments do not contradict each other; and allegorically when it is taught' in the New Testament 'that certain statements made' in the Old Testament 'must not be taken literally. Christ and the Apostles used the Old Testament in the New in these ways.' Just so Augustine clearly declares, using examples, that the history of the Old Testament, its etymology [*sic* for aetiology], anagogy [*sic* for analogy], and allegory are all found in the New Testament. 'For history is involved when Christ was accused because His disciples had plucked ears of wheat on the Sabbath. He said: "Have you not read what David did when he was hungry, and those who were with him, how he entered the house of God and ate the shewbread, which it was unlawful for anyone except the priests to eat" [Matt. 12: 3ff.]. Etymology [*sic* for aetiology] is involved when Christ had laid down that a woman should not be divorced unless she had committed fornication, and He was reminded that Moses had permitted divorce when a bill of divorce had been given. But Christ said: "Moses did this out of consideration for the hardness of your hearts" [Matt. 19: 8].' St Augustine does not give a separate example of analogy, but one could cite what Christ said in John 5[: 46]: 'If you believed Moses you would believe me also', for these words reveal the congruity of the Old and New Testaments. Our Saviour uses allegory drawn from the Old Testament when he says: 'This generation seeks a sign, and the only sign it will be given will be that of the prophet Jonah. For just as Jonah, etc. [Matt. 12: 39–40].' There[180] Augustine interprets allegory in a wide sense to mean every spiritual interpretation of the words of the Old Testament, so that it embraces the three mystical senses of expounding Holy Scripture.

⟨14.⟩ To the final objection, that there are many other senses and ways of expounding Scripture, namely by parable, irony, and metaphor and other such ways, we must reply that all those ways of expounding Scripture are reducible to the historical exposition. For the historical truth is sometimes expressed in the straightforward language appropriate to historical narrative, but sometimes in language that is figurative and employs 'transferred' speech (*sermo translatus*), and variously according to the various different kinds of figures of speech. Hence the parables in the Gospels relate to the historical sense, and likewise their exposition is the exposition of history. And the metaphor about how the trees chose themselves a king (Judg. 9[: 8]), relates to history, and other similar things of this sort.

[180] i.e. in the same part of *De utilitate credendi* that Henry has been discussing above. Cf. above, nn. 164, 178.

Question 5: Whether Truth is Inherent in Every Exposition and Sense

As regards the fifth issue it is argued that truth is not inherent in every sense of Holy Scripture.

⟨1.⟩ Thus, in Judg. 9[: 8] we read: 'The trees of the forest went forth to anoint themselves a king.' Which is quite at variance with the truth.

⟨2.⟩ Secondly, in Gen. 27[: 24] [we read]: 'Jacob said to Isaac his father: "I am Esau your first-born."' There the Scripture retains a blatant lie (or so it seems) and treats it as if it were true.

⟨3.⟩ Thirdly, in 2 Kgs. 11[: 2ff.], concerning the affair of David and Uriah, in which David injured Uriah, and Uriah suffered the injustice, the mystical sense says, according to the *Gloss*,[181] that David is the figure of Christ, and Uriah the devil. But this simply cannot be a true allegory (*mysterium*), for the cause of understanding one opposite is not given by another. Therefore, etc.

⟨4.⟩ Fourthly, in Gen. 19[: 2], when Lot asked the angels to stay in his house they replied: 'Not at all, we will stay in the street', which however they did not do, and so they lied, and Holy Scripture lies in that text.

⟨5.⟩ Fifthly, in Gen. 20[: 3] the Lord said to Abimelech: 'You will die because of the woman you have taken', and yet he did not die, and so Holy Scripture lies in that text.

⟨6.⟩ Sixthly, in Exod. 1[: 17–19] the midwives lied to avoid having to kill the Hebrew babies, a lie which God approved of and rewarded, and so, etc.

⟨7.⟩ In opposition to this view, since any exposition of Holy Scripture proceeds in accordance with the rule of faith, and no falsehood can be inherent in that faith, because it is founded on primal truth, as was shown above, therefore [truth is inherent in every sense].

⟨8.⟩ We must reply to this view [i.e. the view that certain passages of Scripture lie] by saying that the words of Holy Scripture are none other than the oracles of God and testimonies of the eternal truth. And therefore they must be expounded in such a way that they may be recognized and understood to be such. Hence Christ, the originator (*auctor*) and principal expounder of Scripture, said: 'I have come into the world to bear witness to the truth' [John 5: 33]. But the eternal truth does not seek to have any kind of falsehood bearing witness to it. Therefore, it follows of necessity that truth is inherent in this science in all its expositions and senses. Hence the words of Job 13[: 7]: 'Surely God does not require your lying testimony, that you should talk deceitfully on His behalf?' The *Gloss* [comments]: 'Truth does not need to be supported by falsehood etc.'[182] Job continues [5: 8]: 'Surely you have not received His features and are trying to judge in His place?' The *Gloss* [comments]: 'To receive the features of God is to take upon oneself His authority in judgement.'[183]

[181] *Gl. ord. marg.*, 2 Kgs. 11 (*Bib. glos.* ii. 572–5).
[182] *Gl. ord. interlin.*, Job 13: 7 (*Bib. glos.* iii. 159–60).   [183] Ibid.

The extent to which Holy Scripture everywhere contains the truth has been sufficiently discussed above. But Augustine puts this in a specific way at the beginning of his book *On Predestination and Grace*: 'Every reader who approaches Holy Scripture with the intention of expounding it, when troubled by some discordant opinion expressed in the sacred writings, must with faith that is sure and unshaken steadfastly believe that truth is nowhere absent [in Scripture], even though understanding does not readily come to those who seek answers, simply because of the immensity of the subject.'[184]

⟨9.⟩ To the first text cited by way of objection, the one drawn from the book of Judges, we must reply that the rule laid down by Augustine provides that, whenever the text literally interpreted can have no true historical meaning, then recourse must be had to the mystical sense, and the passage must be expounded not in its proper [i.e. normal] meaning but figuratively. So, that text has no true historical sense of its own, but the words are put there figuratively for the sake of the mystical sense, and the passage ought to be understood metaphorically. This is how Isidore expounds it in the *Gloss*, for he understands the trees as signifying men according to the allegorical sense of the text.[185] In such metaphors and parables the truth about the signification of the things described in the passage is discovered, just as in straightforward historical accounts truth is expressed in normal language and is revealed by the signification of the words. For in that science not only do words signify, but also certain things signify certain other things, as will be related below.

⟨10.⟩ To the second text, drawn from the book of Genesis, we must reply that Jacob and Esau do not represent their own persons, but rather what is signified by those persons. So, taking the persons into consideration, that passage could be regarded as true. It is certainly true as far as what is signified by those persons is concerned. So Augustine, in book xvi of *The City of God*, says: 'What is that guile on the part of a simple man [i.e. the shepherd Jacob], what means that fabrication of one who is nevertheless not lying, unless it is a profound mystery of truth?'[186] And in the book *On Lying* he speaks of such passages of Holy Scripture in the following terms: 'Those who believe that one must lie when it is useful cite various testimonies to support their view. For they recall that when Sarah laughed she denied that she had laughed; that Jacob, when asked by his father, had replied that he was his elder son Esau, and many other instances of the same sort. They recall lies told by men whom you would not dare to blame.'[187] He answers them in the following terms: 'Examples of lies have been produced from writers of former times, and there every

---

[184] Cf. ps.-Augustine, *De praedestinatione et gratia*, i (PL xlv. 1666–7).
[185] *Gl. ord. marg.*, Judg. 9: 8 (*Bib. glos.* ii. 215).
[186] *De civ. Dei*, xvi. xxxvii (CCSL xlviii. 542).
[187] *De mendacio*, v. 5 (CSEL xli. 419–20).

event is capable of being given a figurative interpretation. But whatever is done or said with a figurative significance is not a lie. For every act of speech is to be referred to that which it states. But everything that is done or said figuratively states what it signifies to those for whose understanding it was put forth. So we must believe that those who are said to have deserved the authority of prophets in prophetic times did all the things they are said to have done for a prophetic purpose, and that, likewise, whatever happened to them happened for a prophetic purpose, so that all might be considered to have been committed to tradition and to writing by that same prophetic spirit.'[188] So what Jacob said, he said in the first stage of the Church, which was more exalted and held in greater esteem among the first Fathers [i.e. of the Church] than the synagogue of the Jews, which is represented by Esau. This is how Augustine expounds the passage, when talking about the same material in his *Against Consentius*.[189]

⟨11.⟩ To the third text, drawn from the book of Kings, we must reply that we must consider two aspects in the above-mentioned deed, namely the substance of the action (*substantia facti*), and the quality of the action (*qualitas facti*) or the way of doing it. In terms of the quality of the action no true exposition in a good sense can be had, but in terms of the substance of the action it can indeed have a true exposition in a good sense, because the substance of the action may well signify in a good sense. For it can be that a prince orders the death of a knight and takes his wife for himself, and for this reason there would be no contradiction in an evil action having an allegorical interpretation that is good, and being expounded for a good end, as the *Gloss* has in fact expounded it in that passage.[190]

⟨12.⟩ To the fourth and fifth objections, and to all similar examples found in Holy Scripture, we must reply that all are understood to have been spoken subject to a condition understood [by the reader]. Hence, the angels would not have entered in to Lot's house had he not immediately addressed them, and the angels understood his words in unconditional terms. And in the same way the Lord warned Abimelech that he would die unless he quickly gave back the woman he had taken, and this follows in the text: 'Give back the woman to her husband and you will live. But if you do not give her back you will die' [Gen. 20: 7].

⟨13.⟩ To the sixth passage, about the midwives, we must reply that Holy Scripture sets before us not only the deeds and characters of the just, which it uses to encourage us to imitate them, but also men's weaknesses and sins, which it uses to instil fear into us. So, contrary to the assertion of some that such lies are not sins, Scripture sets before us a deceit as an example which it does not recommend us to imitate, but rather relates to show us what a severe punishment is incurred even by

---

[188] Ibid. v. 7 (CSEL xli. 421).
[189] *Contra mendacium*, x. 23–4 (CSEL xli. 497–502).
[190] *Gl. ord. marg.*, 2 Kgs. 11 (*Bib. glos.* ii. 573).

such a pious falsehood. As St Gregory says at this point in the *Gloss*: 'Many try to assert that this kind of lie is not a sin because the Lord built them [i.e. the midwives] houses; in this reward it becomes clear rather what is deserved by the guilt of lying. For the reward of their kindly deed, which could have been stored up for them in the life hereafter, was commuted into a reward here on earth because of the guilt they had incurred by lying.'[191]

So, in brief, whatever lies are found in Scripture, it does not proffer to us as being true by positively asserting (*asserendo*) their truth and commending them, but in reporting (*recitando*) them in the text solely for our instruction.

NICHOLAS OF LYRE

Literal Postill on the Bible: Extracts from the General and Special Prologues, and from the Commentary on the Psalter[192]

THE GENERAL PROLOGUE: EXTRACT

... But this book [i.e. the Bible] has this special quality, that one text (*litera*) has several senses (*sensūs*).[193] The reason for this is that the principal author of this book is God Himself, who not only has the power to use words to signify—something which men can do, and do—but also uses the things signalled by the words to signify other things. And it is the common intention of all books that their words should signify something, but it is a special quality of this book that the things signified by the words should signify something else. We understand by the first signification, which is that conveyed by the words, the literal or historical sense. We understand by the second signification, which is that conveyed by the things, the mystical or spiritual sense. This is in general threefold. If the things signified by the words are taken as referring to the essential elements of belief to be found in the New Law, this is understood to be the allegorical sense. If they are taken as referring to those things which

---

[191] *Gl. ord. marg.*, Exod. i: 20 (*Bib. glos.* i. 482).

[192] Tr. from *Biblia sacra cum Glossa ordinaria et Postilla Nicolai Lyrani* (Lyon, 1589), i, unfol., iii. 415–16, 433–4.

[193] Lyre's General Prologue begins with the text 'All these things are the book of life' (Ecclus. 24: 32). The Book of Life, or Holy Scripture, is said to have four excellent qualities by which it surpasses all other writings: its singular eminence (its wisdom is superior to philosophical knowledge), its universal relevance, its mirroring capacity, and its efficacy in winning salvation. Our selection begins towards the end of Lyre's discussion of the third excellent quality. The prophets, he says, have read something in the mirror or book of divine knowledge, and they have transmitted this knowledge for the sake of us lesser mortals. Then Lyre proceeds to argue that the Bible transcends all other books, books written by merely human agency, in a way which is reminiscent of Aquinas, as tr. above, p. 241.

we ourselves must do, this is the moral or tropological sense. But if they are taken as referring to that which we must hope for in our future blessed state, this is the anagogical sense. This word is derived from *ana*, which means 'up', and *goge*, which is 'leading'. Hence the verse: 'The letter teaches history; allegory, what you must believe; the moral sense, what you must do; the anagogical, your future destination.'[194]

The word 'Jerusalem' can be taken as an example of these four senses.[195] According to the literal sense it signifies a certain city which was formerly the capital of the kingdom of Judea, which was first founded by Melchizedek and afterwards enlarged and fortified by Solomon. According to the moral sense it signifies the faithful soul, and Isa. 52[: 2] is in line with this interpretation: 'Arise, Jerusalem, etc.' According to the allegorical sense it signifies the Church Militant, and Rev. 21[: 2] is in line with this interpretation: 'I saw the holy City, the New Jerusalem, coming down from heaven, like a bride adorned for her husband.' According to the anagogical sense it signifies the Church Triumphant, and in line with this we read in Gal. 4[: 26]: 'That Jerusalem which is above is free, which is our mother'. Just as one word was used as an example [here], so a passage (*oratio*) could have been used, or several just as easily as one.

So, Ezek. 2[: 9] speaks of this book which has several senses concealed underneath the one text: 'Behold a hand was put forth to me in which was a book rolled up, and He opened it before my eyes, and it was written on the inside and on the outside'; and Rev. 5[: 1]: 'I saw on the right hand of Him that sat upon the throne a book written on the inside and on the outside.' The writing on the outside is the literal sense, which is the more obvious one and is more immediately signified by the words. But the writing on the inside is the mystical or spiritual sense, which is more hidden, and is denoted by the things signified by the words, as was mentioned above. This explains the third excellence [of Holy Scripture].

Regarding the fourth [excellence of Holy Scripture], by which is denoted efficacy in winning salvation, when the text says 'of life'[196] we must consider that, as was said at the beginning, no other written text except the Scriptures leads directly to the blessed life, which is the only life in the unqualified sense of the word, since it is totally untouched by death. Therefore, the Saviour, speaking in John 5[: 39] of the efficacy of this Holy Scripture, said to the Jews who were skilled in the knowledge of the Law: 'Search the scriptures, in which you think that you have eternal life.' Regarding this, it must be understood that this word 'you think', which implies a false opinion or at least some doubt as to the truth, does

---

[194] This famous distich has been attributed to Augustine of Dacia (d. 1282): see F. Châtillon, 'Vocabulaire et prosodie du distique attribué à Augustin de Dacie sur les quatre sens de l'écriture', in *Mélanges offerts au père Henri de Lubac*, ii. 17–28.

[195] See above, p. 203 and n. 20.

[196] From Ecclus. 24: 32, 'All these things are the book of life', quoted at the beginning of this prologue. Cf. above, n. 193.

not refer to Holy Scripture itself, which contains nothing that is false, as is clear from what has been said above. Likewise, there is no doubt that it leads to the blessed life, since it is instrumental in bringing us to eternal bliss, as is clear from the words of St Augustine quoted above. But it refers to the scholars, skilled in knowledge of the law, who expounded Holy Scripture wrongly and lived evil lives, because of which they were rightly to be deprived of the opportunity to obtain eternal bliss, which is the end (*finis*) of this science [of theology]. Those who understand Scripture correctly and live a holy life in accordance with that correct understanding, beyond all doubt obtain eternal bliss. As Ecclus. 24[: 31] says: 'Those who elucidate me will have eternal life.' Holy Scripture is elucidated when it is truly expounded and is put into practice in the form of a holy life. For this text [i.e. Scripture] excels all others and contains the perfect forms of both practical and speculative sciences. Consequently, through gaining knowledge of its truth and the working-out in action of its goodness, it leads to that blessed life which I pray that He who lives and reigns world without end may grant us.

HERE BEGINS THE SECOND PROLOGUE, CONCERNING
THE INTENTION OF THE WRITER AND THE MODE
OF PROCEEDING

'I saw in the right hand of Him that sat upon the throne a book written on the inside and on the outside' (Rev. 5[: 1]). As was said in the preceding prologue, this book is Holy Scripture, which is said to be written on the outside in terms of the literal sense of the text, and on the inside in terms of the mystical and spiritual sense. It [i.e. the mystical and spiritual sense] is, generally speaking, divided into three categories, as I have already said. Yet in each of these, the number of mystical meanings in any particular place can be multiplied. But all presume the literal sense as a kind of foundation. So, just as a building which begins to part company with its foundations is inclined to collapse, so a mystical exposition which deviates from the literal sense must be considered unseemly and inappropriate, or at any rate less seemly and less appropriate, than other interpretations. So, those who wish to make headway in the study of Holy Scripture must begin by understanding the literal sense, particularly since any argument that is used to prove or explain a doubtful point can only be based on the literal sense, and not on the mystical sense, as Augustine says in his letter against Vincent the Donatist.[197]

One should, moreover, bear in mind that the literal sense, which should be our starting-point, as I have said, seems to be greatly obscured in these modern times. This is partly through the fault of scribes who,

---

[197] *Epist.* xciii. viii. 24 (CSEL xxxiv. 469–70). Cf. Aquinas' use of this passage in his *Sum of Theology*, Ia i, art. 10, ad 1um, tr. above, p. 242.

misled by similarities between letters, have in many places written something which differs from the true reading of the text (*veritas textus*). Partly it
is the fault of lack of skill on the part of correctors, who in several places
have punctuated where they should not, and have begun and ended verses
where they should not begin or end, and for this reason the meaning of the
text (*sententia literae*) is inconstant,[198] as will be apparent, for this is something which I will have to discuss in the appropriate places, God willing.
Partly it is due to the manner of our translation. For often the translation
has something quite different from the meaning of the Hebrew text, as
Jerome explains in his book *On Questions concerning the Hebrew Text* and in
several other places.[199] Other commentators on Holy Scripture say the
same in their sermons or writings. Yet, according to Jerome in his second
prologue on Genesis[200] and in many other places, in order to obtain the
true text in the Old Testament one must have recourse to the Hebrew
manuscripts. But in so doing one should be very wary of those passages of
Old Testament scripture which speak of the divinity of Christ and the
consequences which follow from that. For the Jews have corrupted some of
these to defend their own erroneous doctrine. I have, in part, explained
this in a question on the divinity of Christ, and will explain it more fully,
with God's help, when such passages crop up. In those passages where it is
unlikely that they have altered something, since they have had no specific
reason for so doing, there appears to be no danger. As Jerome says, in such
cases it is safer to have recourse to the Hebrew text, as being the original, in
order to make it clear which is the true text.[201]

One should also understand that the literal sense of the text has been
much obscured because of the manner of expounding the text commonly
handed down by others. Although they have said much that is good, yet
they have been inadequate in their treatment of the literal sense, and have
so multiplied the number of mystical senses that the literal sense is in
some part cut off and suffocated among so many mystical senses. Moreover, they have chopped up the text into so many small parts, and brought
forth so many concordant passages to suit their own purpose,[202] that to

---

[198] On the significance of this statement for the history of punctuation, see M. B. Parkes,
'Punctuation, or Pause and Effect', in J. J. Murphy (ed.), *Medieval Eloquence: Studies in the
Theory and Practice of Medieval Rhetoric* (Berkeley and Los Angeles, 1978), pp. 131 ff.

[199] *Liber Hebraic. quaest. in Gen.*, pr. (CCSL lxxii. 1-2).

[200] i.e. the *Praefatio S. Hieronymi in Pentateuchum, ad Desiderium* (PL xxviii. 177-84), which
became incorporated into the *Glossa ordinaria* and known as Jerome's second prologue to
Genesis. Cf. below, n. 204, on the 'common set' of Bible prologues.

[201] See esp. the passages cit. above, nn. 199-200.

[202] The sense of this passage seems to be that, thanks in part to the new Bible concord-
ances, which greatly facilitated the collection of supposedly parallel passages of Scripture,
some clerics are selecting and juxtaposing texts which are quite divorced from their contexts,
thereby obscuring the literal sense of their citations. On late-medieval Bible-concordances
see esp. R. H. and M. A. Rouse, 'The Verbal Concordance to the Scriptures', *AFP* xliv
(1974), 5-30.

some degree they confuse both the mind and memory of the reader and distract it from understanding the literal meaning of the text. As I wish to avoid these and similar faults, with God's help I intend to concentrate on the literal sense, and to interpose a very few brief mystical explanations on occasion, but not very often. Likewise, my intention is to cite the statements not only of Catholic but also of Jewish teachers, and especially Rabbi Solomon,[203] who among all the Jewish exegetes has put forward the most reasonable arguments, in order to illuminate the literal meaning of the text. I shall also sometimes, though very rarely, include some teachings of the Jews which are very absurd, not in order that they should be adhered to or followed, but that they may show the prevalence of blindness in Israel, as St Paul says in Rom. 11[: 7–10]. So, one must not adhere to the teachings of the Jews except in so far as they are in accord with reason and the true literal meaning.

Likewise, I shall omit the prologues [of Jerome and others] and start from the beginning of Genesis, for I believe that the rest of my life is not long enough to allow me to expound the whole of Holy Scripture, and so I do not want to waste time in expounding the words of St Jerome or any other teacher. Furthermore, in my opinion, the aforesaid prologues contribute little to the understanding of the books which follow.[204] Besides, another brother of my own order, Brito, has expounded the prologues to the Bible very adequately,[205] and his work is generally available, so that it seemed to me unnecessary to set about expounding these prologues for a second time. I have, however, written commentaries on the prologues to some of the books. I wrote these before I took the book of Genesis as the starting point for my commentary.

Finally, since I am not so well versed in Hebrew and Latin as to avoid displaying my inadequacy in many respects, I assert that my purpose is never to give an authoritative or definitive opinion, except on those matters which have clearly been established by Holy Scripture or the authority of the Church. All other statements may be accepted as having been made within the context of the schools and in the manner of the exercises [undertaken there]. I therefore submit all my past and future statements to the correction of Holy Mother Church and of all wise men, asking the reader to correct my work in a spirit of devotion and love. . . .[206]

---

[203] i.e. Rashi. On Lyre's debt to Rashi see H. Hailperin, *Rashi and the Christian Scholars* (Pittsburg, 1962), pp. 137–246.

[204] Here Lyre refers to the prologues by diverse hands which, through a process of accretion, had come to introduce the various scriptural texts and were standard in the so-called 'Paris Bible'. For a convenient listing see N. R. Ker, *Medieval Manuscripts in British Libraries*, i: *London* (Oxford, 1969), pp. 96–7. See further S. Berger, *Les Préfaces jointes aux livres de la Bible dans les manuscrits de la Vulgate* (Mémoires de l'Académie des Inscriptions et Belles-Lettres, 1er ser. XI, Paris, 1902), 1–78. For the 'Paris Bible' see H. Denifle, 'Das Exemplar Parisiense', *ALKM* iv (1888), 277–92.

[205] For William Brito's exposition of the prologues in the 'Paris Bible' see F. Stegmüller, *Repertorium biblicum medii aevi* (Madrid, 1949–61), ii. 404–9 (items 2824–72).

[See opposite page for n. 206]

COMMENTARY ON THE PSALTER

The Prologue: Extract

'A great prophet has arisen among us' (Luke 7[: 16]). Although the book of Psalms is included among the holy writings (*agiographia*) by the Jews, among the Latins it is placed in the category of prophetic books. This is not without reason, for David, who composed the Psalms, or at any rate most of them, is called not only a prophet but the most outstanding among the prophets, as we read at the beginning of the *Gloss* on the book of Psalms.[207] So, the words quoted above, 'A great prophet, etc.', may appropriately be applied to him. In that text one can see indicated the four causes of this book: the efficient, material, formal, and final causes. The efficient cause can be subdivided in two, namely the principal cause and the instrumental cause. The principal cause is God Himself, who reveals the mysteries described in this book. The instrumental cause is David. According to Augustine, all the contents of this book were revealed to him, and written down by him. But according to Jerome, Hilary, and all the Jewish teachers, David did not write all the psalms but the greater part of them.[208] Some of the psalms were written by various other people—Moses, Solomon, and others—and this will be clear presently, when we go through the titles of the psalms. But the psalms written by David and others were collected and gathered together into one book. It is called the book of Psalms, and was given this name by the scribe and prophet Ezra, or by some other holy prophet, whoever he was, as Jerome says in his prologue to this book, which is not commonly found in present-day Bibles.[209] But our teachers in general hold the view that Ezra, who restored the law which had been burnt by the Chaldeans, collected together into this single volume psalms composed by various hands. He is not, however, called the author (*auctor*) of the book, or the instrumental efficient cause. That is David himself, who composed the greater part of the psalms, for a whole gets its name from its greater part. Now, this twofold efficient cause, that is, the principal cause and the instrumental cause, is referred to by the word 'prophet'. For two factors come together to bring about the act of prophecy: God, who touches the

---

[206] Lyre rounds off this second prologue with a summary of the seven 'Tyconian Rules' for the interpretation of Scripture, on which see F. C. Burkitt, *The Book of Rules of Tyconius* (Cambridge, 1894). They are found in, for example, Augustine, *De Doctrina Christiana*, III. xxx. 42–xxxvii. 56, and in Hugh of Saint-Victor, *Didascalicon*, v. iv (Buttimer, pp. 97–102, tr. Taylor, pp. 122–5).

[207] *Gl. ord. marg.*, Ps., proth. (*Bib. glos.* iii. 427 B-C).

[208] On this debate see above, pp. 71, 110 and esp. Ch. III, n. 137. Cf. n. 220. For Hilary's position see his *Tractatus super psalmos*, instructio psalmorum 1–3 (CSEL xxii. 3–5).

[209] Rather a free interpretation of Jerome's statement in his *Hebraica* prologue: *Praef. in lib. ps. iuxta Heb. verit.* (PL xxviii. 1123A). Lyre's point is that this is not one of the 'standard set' of prologues found in the Paris Bible, on which see above, n. 204.

mind of the prophet, or raises it to the comprehension of divine knowledge, and the mind of the prophet, which is thus touched or illuminated.
For the action of the motivating force [i.e. God] and the reaction of the
thing moved by it must be simultaneous. Hence, God says in Num.
12[: 6]: 'If any among you is a prophet of the Lord, I will appear to him in
a vision, or I will speak to him in a dream.' This text refers to the two
methods of prophecy, to which all other methods of prophecy can,
properly speaking, be reduced, as will become clearer at a later stage. One
occurs during the waking hours, and this is referred to by the words 'I will
appear to him in a vision'. The other occurs during sleep, and this is
referred to by the words 'or I will speak to him in a dream'. For in both
kinds of prophecy God as the principal agent and the mind of the prophet
as the instrumental agent come together. This is clear from the words 'I
will appear to him in a vision', that is, revealing to him supernatural truth
in his waking hours. Or, 'I will speak through a dream', revealing hidden
things to him. So, first of all, it is clear what the nature of the efficient
cause is.

Second, the material or 'subjective' cause is referred to by the word
'great'.[210] To understand this it must be appreciated that a prophet is
called 'great', and his prophecy a 'great' prophecy, in two senses. One
sense is in terms of intensity (*intensive*). This tends to occur rather in
proportion to the powers of cognition present in the prophet. And by this
definition David is called a great prophet. So, at the beginning of the
Gloss on that book, we read: 'Other prophets prophesied through images,
and words which concealed their meaning. But David prophesied solely
through the inspiration of the Holy Spirit without any external aids.'[211]
This is the most excellent method of prophecy, as will be seen more
clearly when we deal with degrees of prophecy. But this kind of greatness
in prophecy really pertains to the formal cause, which consists in a work's
mode of treatment rather than to the cause discussed in terms of subject-
matter.[212]

Greatness in a prophet or in prophecy can be interpreted in another
way, namely in terms of extent (*extensive*), that is, when it stretches out to
include more subjects. This concerns the 'subjective' or material cause.
And by this definition the prophecy contained in this book is called 'great'
because in a certain sense it reaches out to embrace everything which is
contained in Holy Scripture. According to Cassiodorus, commenting on
this book, Christ in His totality, in terms of both his head and his limbs, is
the subject in the whole of Holy Scripture, if we accept that the 'subject' is
the same thing as the material of the book. And likewise, according to
Cassiodorus, Christ in His totality is the material of this book [i.e. the

[210] Lat. 'subjectiva', i.e. the cause in terms of subject-matter.
[211] *Gl. ord. marg.*, pron. (*Bib. glos.* iii. 427 B-C).
[212] Cf. above, n. 210.

Psalter], but in a different way from Holy Scripture taken as a whole, because here [i.e. in the Psalter] the subject or material is expressed through the mode of praise. For this reason it is called the book of Psalms, that is, of songs of divine praise. For this reason also it is commonly said by other teachers that it contains within itself the whole of Holy Scripture expressed through the mode of divine praise. So, regarding the magnitude of the material of this book one can say: 'I will go and see this great sight' (Exod. 3[: 3]). This is the speech of Moses, whose name in translation means 'drawn out of the waters'. For no one is fit to consider the truth contained in this book unless he has been 'drawn out of the waters' of the desires of this present life. So, Isa. 28[: 9] says: 'Whom will He (that is, the Lord) make to understand what He has heard?' And the prophet replies: 'those who have been weaned from the milk and drawn away from the breasts', that is, the desires of the body.

Third, in the passage cited,[213] the formal cause is referred to when it says: 'has risen'. Regarding the formal cause one must understand that the form is twofold: the form of the treatise (*forma tractatus*) and the form of the treatment (*forma tractandi*). The form of the treatise is the manner of division of the book. We shall talk about this later in the course of the book. But the form of the treatment is the mode of proceeding, which in the work under discussion is the mode of praising God, as has been said. For whatever is contained in this book is put there through the mode of praise of God. Praise of God is a prayer or kind of prayer. According to Damascene, prayer is the ascent of the mind to God.[214] This ascent is referred to in the word 'has arisen'. Wherefore we read in Ps. 56[: 9]: ARISE, MY GLORY, ARISE MY PSALTERY, etc.' Glory is clear knowledge (*notitia*) combined with praise. David's power of cognition contained in this book was very clear, as far as prophetic cognition goes, as has already been touched on in part and will be touched on more fully subsequently. It is described through the mode of praise of God, as has already been said, and therefore is aptly called 'glory'. Wherefore David says ARISE, MY GLORY, and adds ARISE MY PSALTERY AND HARP (*CITHARA*). For some of the psalms written by him were sung to the accompaniment of the musical instrument called the psaltery, and some to that of the harp (as will be seen in due course), just as nowadays some songs or notes are more properly sung to the accompaniment of the vielle (*lyra*) and other instruments.

Fourth, the final cause is touched on when the text says: 'among us', that is, 'to serve our advantage and promote our salvation'. For man, because he is able to comprehend God[215] through cognition and through love, is ordained to a supernatural end, according to the words of Isa. 64[: 4]: 'For eye has not seen, nor ear heard, and it has not come into the

---

[213] i.e. the biblical text cited at the beginning of Lyre's Psalter prologue, Luke 7: 16.
[214] Damascenus, *De fide orthodoxa*, III. xxiv (PL xciv. 1090 D).
[215] Lat. 'capax Dei'.

heart of man what God has prepared for those who love Him.' Because no one can aim at a goal which is totally unknown, it was necessary that some things should be revealed by God to man, which might guide him to his supernatural end. Holy Scripture, divinely revealed, belongs to this category, and so the holy Apostle says of it: 'All that has been written has been written for our doctrine, that through patience and the consolation afforded by the Scriptures we might have hope' (Rom. 15[: 4]), and this hope is the sure expectation of our future bliss.

Now, the book of Psalms contains the whole of Holy Scripture expressed through the mode of praise. Consequently it is eminently useful for the whole Church in creating hope and in achieving future bliss.[216] We can say this about it: 'He has raised up a horn of salvation for us in the house of His servant David' (Luke 1[: 69]). For the holy and blessed God has raised up for us 'the horn of salvation', that is, Holy Scripture, which is efficacious in acquiring salvation. And this is that part of Scripture which contains the book of Psalms, as has been said. [We can say] 'in the house of His servant David', because David was, for the most part, the author of this book. If this book is retained in our heart and fulfilled in our actions, we shall have in this world God's grace, and in the world to come glory, which glory may He grant us who is blessed world without end. . . .[217]

Exposition of Psalm I: Extract

BLESSED IS THE MAN [1] St Augustine tells us that David was the author of all the psalms. But Jerome is of the opposite opinion, and we must include his view, since he made a more thorough study of Holy Scripture.[218] In his prologue on the Psalms he names ten authors of the psalms: David, Moses, Solomon, the three sons of Korah, Asaph, Ethan, Heman, and Jeduthun.[219] Besides these he mentioned several others. For psalms were written by several holy prophets whose names are not known. So, some psalms are without a title, while others have a title but do not give the names of their authors, as will appear in the course of our commentary. Likewise, Rabbi Solomon, commenting on the beginning of the book of Psalms, names ten authors: Melchizedek, Abraham, Moses, David, Solomon, and Asaph, the three sons of Korah, and Jeduthun. Thus, in some respects he differs from Jerome, because he inserts Melchizedek and Abraham among the authors of psalms, and omits Heman and Ethan. You will see which of these views corresponds more nearly to the truth in the course of our commentary, in the appropriate places.

---

[216] i.e. happiness in the life to come.

[217] Lyre then appends a *quaestio* on the subject, 'whether or not David was the most excellent of the prophets'.

[218] See the references in Ch. III, n. 137.

[219] The *Hebraica* prologue (PL xxviii. 1123A).

And so, someone might well take the view that this book of Psalms could be divided according to authors. But this cannot conveniently be done. For the psalms that belong to one author are not separated to one side, since several of the psalms written by others are inserted in among the psalms of David, and several psalms of David are inserted among those other psalms, as we shall see. Likewise, after Ps. 71, at the end of which is placed in Hebrew 'Here end the psalms of David son of Jesse', there follow several psalms which have been provided with a title by David himself, giving the impression that he is the author. According to Jerome in his prologue on the Psalter, the reason for this is that psalms which had been composed by various authors were gathered together into one book long after they had been written, and were written out in the order in which they were found. The result is that some of the psalms which had been composed earlier were written [into the book] later, because they were discovered later. The same is true for the individual authors too. For all the psalms written by one particular author were not found all at the same time, nor yet immediately one after the other. But some psalms were found in the middle of the work of other authors. So, that book [i.e. the Psalter] cannot be divided according to any fixed order of authors or of the respective times of composition, as is clear from what has been said.

Neither can it be divided according to the various subjects treated. For the same matter is often touched on in different psalms, and in psalms by different authors, and psalms widely separated from each other. Conversely, on occasions various subjects are treated in one and the same psalm. Thus, I cannot very well see how this book could be divided artificially (*artificiose*), except in some general way. For first there is the preface, then the execution of the work, and thirdly the conclusion that has principally been aimed at. The second part begins at the beginning of the second psalm, and the third at the beginning of Ps. 145[: 2]: PRAISE THE LORD, O MY SOUL. For the intention of this book is the praise of God.

As regards the first psalm, it must be understood that this psalm has no title in the Hebrew text. Jerome confirms this in the prologue to the psalms.[220] So, if in any books one finds the title *A psalm of David* this would appear not to be a true attribution, but a wilful insertion on someone's part. It would seem more likely that this psalm was composed by the person who collected the psalms together and edited them in the form of this book. According to the general and more likely view this was Ezra, as we mentioned above. He prefaced his collection (*collectio*) with this psalm

---

[220] Perhaps a reference to the Psalter prologue in the *Glossa ordinaria*, where Jerome's views are given: *Gl. ord. marg.*, Ps., proth. (*Bib. glos.* iii. 428F); see further the statement (not attributed to Jerome) in *Gl. ord. marg.*, Ps. 1 (*Bib. glos.* iii. 433). Cf. Jerome, *Breviarium in psalmos* (PL xxvi. 823B).

as a kind of prologue.[221] But it is regarded as a psalm in the true sense, being closely joined to the others. For we read in Acts 13[: 33]: 'As was written in the second psalm [Ps. 2: 7], THOU ART MY SON. TODAY I HAVE BEGOTTEN THEE', and this is found in the psalm immediately after [Ps. 1]. This [psalm] could not truly be called 'the second' unless the other one was the first. It [i.e. the first psalm] deserves to be reckoned among the psalms since Ezra had the spirit of prophecy, and his book takes its place among the canonical Scriptures.

So, in this psalm, which performs the function of a prologue, Ezra encourages us to study Holy Scripture, which in this book adopts the mode of praise of God. This he does in two ways: first, by excluding from [the minds of] the faithful perverted doctrine; secondly, by enclosing within their minds sound, Catholic doctrine, in the words BUT IN THE LAW [v. 2].

---

[221] On the possible significance of Lyre's use of the term *collectio*, in contradistinction with the term *compilatio* (which implies orderly arrangement of some kind), see Minnis, *Authorship*, pp. 97, 152–3.

VII

Placing the *Poetics*:
Hermann the German; An Anonymous Question
on the Nature of Poetry

WHEN Aristotle came to the West he did not travel alone: he had many companions, the most important being Averroes (Ibn Rushd) of Cordova in Islamic Spain, who lived from 1126 until 1198. This Arab scholar became known simply as 'the Commentator' on the Philosopher.[1] The consequence of greatest concern to historians of literary theory and criticism is the fact that it was Averroes' interpretation of Aristotle's *Poetics* which dominated the scholarship on that text for over four centuries—until, according to O. B. Hardison, the study published by Ludovico Castelvetro in 1570.[2] The form in which Averroes' main exposition of that work, the so-called 'Middle Commentary' on the *Poetics*, was best known was in the Latin translation made in 1256 by Hermann the German, a monk living in Toledo.[3]

Twenty-three manuscripts collated in the *Aristoteles Latinus* preserve Hermann's Averroistic *Poetics* in several forms: there are five manuscripts of the complete text, fifteen of abridgements, and three of compendia.[4] One manuscript, Paris, Bibliothèque nationale, MS Lat. 16709, includes a glossed

[1] The bibliography on the Arab transmission of Aristotle is immense; on the reception of the *Poetics* in particular see J. Tkatsch, *Die arabische Übersetzung der Poetik des Aristoteles und die Grundlage der Kritik des griechischen Textes* (Vienna, 1928–32); F. Gabrielli, 'Estetica e poesia araba nell'interpretazione della poetica aristotelica presso Avicenna e Averroè', *Rivista degli studi orientali*, xii (1929/30), 291–331; F. Lehner, 'An Evaluation of Averroes' Paraphrase on Aristotle's *Poetics*', *The Thomist*, xxx (1966), 38–65; O. B. Hardison, 'The Place of Averroes' Commentary on the *Poetics* of Aristotle in the History of Medieval Criticism', *Medieval and Renaissance Studies* IV, ed. J. Lievsay (Durham, NC 1970), pp. 57–81; Vicente Cantarino, 'Averroes on Poetry', in G. L. Tikku (ed.), *Islam and its Cultural Divergence: Essays in Honor of G. E. von Grunebaum* (Urbana, Ill., 1971), pp. 10–26.
[2] *Classical and Medieval Literary Criticism: Translations and Interpretations*, ed. A. Preminger, O. B. Hardison, and K. Kerrane (New York, 1974), p. 348.
[3] On Hermann's life and works see G. H. Liquet, 'Hermann l'Allemand (†1272)', *Revue de l'histoire des religions*, xliv (1901), 417–22; W. F. Boggess, 'Hermannus Allemannus's Rhetorical Translations', *Viator*, ii (1971), 227–50; Weinberg, *History of Literary Criticism*, pp. 351–61; J. B. Allen, 'Hermann the German's Averroistic Aristotle and Medieval Poetic Theory', *Mosaic*, ix/3 (1976), 67–81, cf. id., *Ethical Poetic*, pp. 19, 22–30, 87, 120–6. The fullest and most penetrating study of Hermann's translation of Averroes' 'Middle Commentary' on the *Poetics* is by H. A. Kelly, 'Aristotle–Averroes–Alemannus on Tragedy: The Influence of the *Poetics* on the Middle Ages', *Viator*, x (1979), 161–209. O. B. Hardison has translated the complete work in *Classical and Medieval Literary Criticism*, pp. 349–82, with an introduction based largely on his 1979 article (cit. above, n. 1). Averroes' commentary has recently been translated from the Arabic by C. E. Butterworth, *Averroes' Middle Commentary on Aristotle's Poetics* (Princeton, 1986).
[4] W. F. Boggess, 'Aristotle's *Poetics* in the Fourteenth Century', *SP* lxvii (1970), 279–82. On a MS which was not included in the *AL* collation, see ibid., p. 279 n. 5. In addition, a fragment of a MS of the complete text is in the possession of Professor Ralph Hanna.

text of the translation along with an anonymous question on the nature of poetry, which takes its point of departure from Hermann (this is translated in full below). W. F. Boggess's study of this manuscript evidence concludes that the University of Paris was probably the centre in which, in the late thirteenth or early fourteenth century, Hermann's translation underwent a recension which was the state in which it was taught and studied during the fourteenth century.[5] But it should be noted that the schoolmen rarely studied it in its entirety: in 1307 Bartholomew of Bruges gave a lecture course on it, which is extant in a single manuscript—indicative of a very limited circulation.[6] Hermann's *Poetics* exercised an influence rather in extracts. Various schoolmen quoted it quite out of context and in conjunction with authorities of a very different nature (see for example Aquinas' use of its statement that men naturally take delight in representation, above, Ch. VI), and it was excerpted in many *florilegia*, including the *Parvi flores* or *Auctoritates Aristotelis*, a highly popular students' aid.[7] More elaborate use of the Averroistic *Poetics* was made by Benvenuto da Imola, who in the late fourteenth century analysed the structure of Dante's *Divine Comedy* on the basis of Hermann's contention that all poetic discourse is either praise or blame (on which more later). Many Italian humanists and their opponents knew the work too, including Giovannino of Mantua, Salutati, Savonarola, Robortello, Segni, Maggi, and Lombardi. In 1481 it was published in Venice by Philippus Venetus.[8]

What kind of work, then, is Hermann's Averroistic *Poetics*? After finishing his translation of Aristotle's *Rhetoric*, Hermann tells us, he turned his attention to the *Poetics*, but found that task fraught with difficulties 'because of the diversity of the system of writing poetry in Greek and Arabic and because of the difficulty of the vocabulary'. Not trusting himself 'to be able to make a full translation of this work for Latin-speaking readers' he turned to the commentary in which Averroes had explained what he could understand of the *Poetics*, and 'translated the commentary as well as I could into Latin'.[9] Hermann's work presents a fascinating case to those interested in reception-criticism. Considered as a translation of what Aristotle actually said (according to the conclusions of modern research) it must be judged a failure, although Hermann's critics should note that he was following the best scholarship available to him. But considered in medieval terms it makes a lot of sense, for reasons which this introduction must try to explain, particularly in view of the fact that most modern studies of the Averroistic *Poetics*—even the most sympathetic—

---

[5] Boggess, 'Aristotle's *Poetics*', p. 284.

[6] For discussion and partial edition of this work see G. Dahan, 'Notes et textes sur la poétique au moyen âge', *AHDLMA* xlvii (1980), 220–39; cf. Kelly, 'Aristotle–Averroes–Alemannus on Tragedy', pp. 175, 178–81. For the life and writings of Bartholomew, who died c. 1356, see C. H. Lohr, 'Medieval Latin Aristotle Commentaries, Authors A–F', *Traditio* xxiii (1967), 375–7. A Paris-trained Swedish scholar, Matthias of Linköping, expounded Hermann's 'Middle Commentary' in his *Poetics* (finished between 1318 and 1332). See S. Sawicki, '*Poetria* och *Testa nucis* av magister Matthias Lincopensis', *Samlaren*, NS xvii (1936), 109–52. Birger Bergh's edition of this work is forthcoming.

[7] See Boggess, 'Aristotle's *Poetics*', pp. 280–2, 284–94.

[8] *Classical and Medieval Literary Criticism*, pp. 347–8.

[9] Ibid. p. 349.

have comprised some misunderstanding of what Hermann actually said. It is significant that the impressively accurate translation of the *Poetics* which William of Moerbeke made in 1278 was largely ignored by medieval thinkers:[10] they preferred to understand the text within the ideological context in which Averroes had located it. That context made it easier for them to place the *Poetics*, in other words to classify it within their hierarchies of the sciences and to relate it to long-established notions concerning the rhetorical methods and ethical aims of poetry.

Poetry as part of logic. The classification of poetry had always been a problem for philosophers.[11] Faced with Horace's *Art of Poetry*, an anonymous commentator declared that it pertains to ethics because it is about behaviour, albeit the behaviour appropriate to the poet (an awkward over-specification of the standard *ethice supponitur* analysis); or indeed it pertains to logic, because it is about language: 'it guides us to a knowledge of correct and elegant style . . .' (see above, p. 33). Grammar was, of course, the medieval discipline comprising the classroom study of poetry, and William of Conches must have had this in mind when he declared that grammar may be regarded as a branch of eloquence, the others being dialectic and rhetoric, 'but alternatively, to remove all dispute, the category to which grammar belongs may be called logic' in so far as it is an art of language, 'logic applied through the medium of words' (see above, p. 132). John of Salisbury certainly believed that poetry belonged with grammar, despite its relation to rhetoric, but reported a different viewpoint: 'so closely does it cleave to the things of nature that several have denied that poetry is a subdivision of grammar, and would have it be a separate art. They maintain that poetry no more belongs to grammar than it does to rhetoric, although it is related to both, in as much as it has rules in common with each.'[12] Hermann the German claims that, although Cicero made rhetoric part of civil [i.e. practical] philosophy and Horace 'treated poetry rather as it pertains to grammar', the correct view is that the *Rhetoric* and the *Poetics* are parts of logic. No one will doubt this, he declares, 'who has read the books of al-Fārābī, Avicenna, and Averroes, and various others'.[13]

Hermann was perfectly correct in his statement about the position held by the Arab interpreters of Aristotle. Following the Greek commentators on Aristotle, they had believed that the *Rhetoric* and the *Poetics* were the seventh and eighth parts of the *Organon* respectively, preceded hierarchically by the six familiar treatises on logic proper. This view is inherent in Avicenna's commentary on the *Poetics* (*c.* 1020), a major source of Averroes' ideas on literature, and in Averroes' 'Short' and 'Middle' commentaries on the same text (he is

[10] Cf. Boggess, 'Aristotle's *Poetics*', p. 278; text ed. by L. Minio-Paluello, *De arte poetica, cum Averrois expositione* (Corpus philosophorum medii aevi: Aristoteles Latinus XXXIII, 2nd edn., Brussels, 1968), pp. 3–37.

[11] Cf. *Classical and Medieval Literary Criticism*, pp. 278–82; Hardison, *The Enduring Monument*, pp. 3–23.

[12] *Metalogicon*, I. xvii, tr. D. D. McGarry (Berkeley and Los Angeles, 1955), pp. 51–2.

[13] *De arte poetica cum Averrois expositione*, ed. Minio-Paluello, p. 41; cf. Hardison, 'Averroes' Commentary', p. 78.

supposed not to have produced a 'long' commentary).[14] It is also found in an earlier work, Abū Naṣr al-Fārābī's *Catalogue of the Sciences* (mid tenth century). Here the art of demonstration, as taught in the *Prior* and *Posterior Analytics*, is placed at the very centre of the logical scheme; its characteristic discourse is scientific and it employs syllogisms which proceed from true and necessary premisses (as in metaphysics). The *Categories* (known as the *Praedicamenta* in the Latin West) and the *On Interpretation* (known as the *Perihermenias*) are 'introductions' and 'ways into demonstration', while the other four works, the *Topics*, *Sophistic Refutations*, *Rhetoric*, and *Poetics*, offer 'appendages and tools which are more or less useful to the process of "judicative logic", which induces necessity and truth'. The first of these in order of rank is the *Topics*, which teaches dialectic. Its discourse concerns probable or contingent things (e.g. ethical matters), its purpose is to bring about strong opinion, and it employs syllogisms which follow from generally accepted premisses. Next comes sophistic refutation, which is concerned with deceptive discourse and has as its characteristic device the apparent syllogism. This is followed by rhetoric, which seeks to persuade and employs the enthymeme and the example.[15] Last comes poetics, which has imaginative representation as its purpose and the imaginative syllogism as its device.[16]

Al-Fārābī's *Catalogue* was the dominant influence on the treatise *On the Division of Philosophy*, written shortly after 1150 by Dominicus Gundissalinus, one of the group of translators gathered together by Archbishop Raymond of Toledo (1126–51). Moreover, it was translated into Latin twice in the twelfth century, first by Gerard of Cremona and later by John of Seville. Its doctrine is constantly echoed by the schoolmen, as in Vincent of Beauvais's *Speculum doctrinale* and Thomas Aquinas' commentary on the *Posterior Analytics*.[17]

By such means the idea that poetry was part of logic was firmly established in scholasticism. Our anonymous question on the nature of poetry makes clear the lines along which discussion of this subject were usually conducted. Poetry constitutes a special part of logic, as is revealed by a comparison of the *Poetics* with all the other books of the *Organon*. Special attention is paid to the relationships between the three arts at the bottom of the logical scale, poetry,

[14] See I. M. Dahiyat, *Avicenna's Commentary on the Poetics of Aristotle: A Critical Study with an Annotated Translation of the Text* (Leiden, 1974), esp. his discussion of 'The Context Theory of Poetry', pp. 12–20. Averroes' 'Short' commentary on the *Poetics*—not known to the Latin West—has recently been translated and discussed by C. E. Butterworth, *Averroes' Three Short Commentaries on Aristotle's Topics, Rhetoric and Poetics* (Albany, NY, 1977), pp. 34–41, 81–102. For Butterworth's translation of Averroes' 'Middle Commentary' see above, n. 3.

[15] Cf. Aristotle's *Rhetorica*, i. 1 (1355ᵃ6–14), i. 2 (1356ᵇ4–6).

[16] Cf. Hardison, *The Enduring Monument*, p. 13, Dahiyat, *Avicenna's Commentary*, pp. 15–20; Dahan, 'La Poétique au moyen âge', pp. 175 ff.; Weisheipl, 'Classification of the Sciences', pp. 68–70. On al-Fārābī's views on poetry see further A. J. Arberry, 'Fārābī's Canons of Poetry', *RSO* xvii (1938), 267–78; cf. Dahiyat, *Avicenna's Commentary*, pp. 15–20.

[17] Cf. Hardison, *The Enduring Monument*, pp. 11–12; Dahan, 'La poétique au moyen âge', pp. 187 ff., Weisheipl, 'Classification of the Sciences', pp. 70–2; see further, H. Hugonnard-Roche, 'La Classification des sciences de Gundissalinus et l'influence d'Avicenne', in J. Jolivet and R. Rashed (eds.), *Études sur Avicenne* (Paris, 1984), pp. 41–75 (esp. pp. 58–9). Cf. Vincent of Beauvais, *Speculum doctrinale*, i. xvii, iii. iii (*Speculum quadruplex*, ii. 16–17, 213–14).

rhetoric, and sophistic. Because of the large number of people addressed in rhetorical discourse only the example and the enthymeme may be used (cf. Giles of Rome's claim that 'in the whole field of moral teaching the mode of procedure, according to the Philosopher, is figurative and broad (*grossus*)', since 'the populace as a whole cannot understand subtleties': above, p. 250).[18] By contrast, in poetry it is the individual's imagination and faculty of desire which is appealed to, and imaginative syllogism is appropriately used because everyone is especially fond of 'his own instinctive estimations and relies particularly on his own imaginings'. Since, however, the good of the whole populace is more important than the good of the individual, poetry must be placed after rhetoric. A similar statement is found in the prologue to the commentary by Bartholomew of Bruges on Hermann's Averroistic *Poetics*.[19] However, according to our anonymous *artista*—here paralleling Aquinas' teaching in his commentary on the *Posterior Analytics*[20]—poetry comes before sophistic, since the right process of reason is, in some sense, the aim of poetry, whereas sophistic is concerned with wrong processes of reason, with mere sophistry. Another Paris schoolman, Jean Buridan (*c.* 1300–58), held a somewhat different view of the order of the branches of logic, but he certainly agreed with the belief of our anonymous *artista* that poetry 'is closely linked to rhetoric'. The *Rhetoric* and the *Poetics* comprise the 'supportive and instrumental part' of logic, he argues in his commentary on the *Nicomachean Ethics*; the knowledge imparted by those two books 'is not simply logic, nor simply moral science, but moral logic'.[21] Poetry as much as rhetoric is a valuable instrument for the use of moral philosophy. From such accounts it emerges that the poet is supposed to be concerned ultimately with what is true and right. Poetry has become the concern of philosophers in a way which twelfth-century friends of the Muses like William of Conches and Bernard Silvester could never have predicted (cf. above, pp. 118–22).

---

[18] In the commentary on Aristotle's *Rhetoric* which Giles wrote *c.* 1280 (cf. Ch. VI, n. 145), the statement 'rhetoric is subservient (*assecutiva*) to dialectic' is interpreted as meaning that the two disciplines are distinct and rhetoric is the inferior, because it serves the needs of the practical intellect while dialectic is an instrument of speculation. Cf. Brother S. Robert, 'Rhetoric and Dialectic', pp. 484–98; see further Giles of Rome's *quaestio* on the differences between rhetoric, ethics, and politics, ed. G. Brunl, *New Schol.* vi (1932), 1–18, partly tr. in Miller *et al.*, *Readings in Medieval Rhetoric*, pp. 265–8. In his essay 'The Scholastic Condemnation of Rhetoric in the Commentary of Giles of Rome on the *Rhetoric* of Aristotle', *Arts libéraux et philosophie au moyen âge*, Actes du Quatrième Congrès international de philosophie médiévale (Montreal and Paris, 1969), pp. 833–41, J. J. Murphy tentatively suggests that Giles's statements on rhetoric amount to a condemnation of that subject, but in fact Giles is applying to this newly recovered text a long-established view concerning the subordination of rhetoric to logic, which is well documented by R. McKeon, 'Rhetoric in the Middle Ages', pp. 260–96. Aristotle himself declared that 'rhetoric is an offshoot of dialectic and also of ethical studies', *Rhetorica*, i. 2 (1356ª25–6).

[19] Ed. Dahan, 'La poétique au moyen âge', p. 224.

[20] Lect. i, prol., in Aquinas, *Exposition of the Posterior Analytics of Aristotle*, tr. P. Conway (Quebec, 1956), pp. 5, 7.

[21] *Questiones in decem libros Ethicorum Aristotelis ad Nicomachum*, prologus (Oxford, 1637), pp. 1–3; discussed by Dahan, 'La poétique au moyen âge', pp. 182–3.

From imitation to affective imagination: poetry as praise or blame. In ch. iv of the *Poetics* Aristotle had said that there are two causes for the origin of poetry, both rooted in human nature.[22] First, the instinct for imitation is inherent in man from his earliest days: being the most imitative of creatures, he learns his earliest lessons by imitation; also inborn in us is the instinct to enjoy works of imitation. Secondly, a feeling for music and rhythm is also natural to us. Averroes produces a simplified but clear enough version of that second cause, but markedly alters the first, which becomes a defence of exemplification: examples are used in teaching, so that what is said may more easily be understood because of the moving power of the imagery involved.

Aristotle had proceeded to give a very succinct account of the development of poetry along two different channels: in early times the more serious-minded poets represented noble actions and the deeds of noble persons while the more trivial-minded wrote about the lower sort of people, thus creating a distinction between panegyric and invective. Averroes seizes on this idea to the exclusion or the considerable modification of much else. One kind of poetry praises and extols good and fine deeds, while the other kind castigates and blames base and dishonourable deeds. Indeed, Averroes' very first comment on poetry (as rendered by Hermann) is the firm declaration, 'Aristotle says: Every poem, and all poetic utterance, is either praise or blame'. But no such statement occurs in ch. i of the *Poetics*—or anywhere else in Aristotle's text for that matter. Here we have an Arab interpolation which is assimilating poetry to epideictic rhetoric, i.e. the branch of that subject which is concerned with the praising or blaming of some particular person.[23] This emphasis is at the very centre of Averroes'—and therefore of Hermann's—affective and audience-oriented understanding of the *Poetics*.

The crucial point to grasp is that the concept of imitation (*mimesis*) has largely been replaced with that of imagination (*imaginatio*) or imagistic 'likening' (*assimilatio*), representation of a kind which arouses the emotions of the audience in a way which encourages them to follow virtue and flee from vice. 'Imagination' here has nothing to do with the Romantic notion of 'creative imagination'; it designates both image-making (as in representing reality) and the emotive effect which such images have on an audience. This is, of course, utterly consistent with Averroes' insistence that poetry is part of logic. In place of the intellectual assent demanded by scientific demonstration, poetic representation elicits psychological assent; its imaginative syllogisms seek to move rather than prove (cf. our discussion of biblical *formae tractandi* in relation to the different spheres of intellect and affection, in the previous chapter). The Arab theorists, as Dahiyat says, leave no doubt about their view of the affective nature of poetic representation:

[22] As representative of the modern understanding of the *Poetics*, here, as elsewhere in this section, we use *Ancient Literary Criticism*, ed. D. A. Russell and M. Winterbottom (Oxford, 1972), pp. 85–132, and *Aristotle, Horace, Longinus: Classical Literary Criticism*, ed. T. S. Dorsch (Harmondsworth, 1965, repr. 1967), pp. 31–75.

[23] Cf. Cicero, *De inventione*, I. v. 7: *Ad Herennium*, II. ii. 2.

... the effect is of a 'kinetic' movement of desire or avoidance, a psychological tendency towards acceptance or rejection of a moral action. Poetry is directed towards moving an audience with whom logical reasoning may not be effective.[24]

In order that poetry should be effective, therefore, the affective aspect of imitation—or imaginative representation, to use the Arab substitute—must be dominant in its purpose.

What has happened to the beginning of the *Poetics* now becomes more clear: we are faced not with a jumble of misunderstandings but with a distinctive and consistent interpretation. In his second chapter Aristotle had said that 'since imitative artists represent men in action, and men who are necessarily either of good or bad character ..., these men must be represented either as better than we are, or worse, or as the same kind of people as ourselves'.[25] Comedy, he continues, represents men as worse than they are; tragedy, as better. The Arabs gave this a rhetorical and ethical twist. Avicenna argues that the aim of every representation is 'either amelioration or depreciation', for something is represented 'either to be made better or worse'. 'The Greeks intended, by means of speech, to induce or represent action. Sometimes they did this by means of oratory, sometimes by means of poetry.'[26] Similarly, al-Fārābī said that poetry is 'composed of things that aim at imaginative assent to the given matter ... and result in seeing it as better or worse, more beautiful or more ugly, more dignified or base'.[27] Vincent of Beauvais credits him with the theory that poetic discourse makes the hearer 'image something as fair or foul which is not so in reality, so that he may believe it and shun or desire it. Although certainly it is not so in reality, the minds of the hearers are roused to shun or desire what they image.'[28] Here the notion that affective imagery need not have any depictive function, any necessary connection with anything in reality, is very much to the fore. It also appears in Thomas Aquinas' version of the same doctrine. In contrast with dialectic and rhetoric, he says, in poetics 'one's conjecture alone' inclines us to assent to one of two opposed viewpoints 'because of some representation, as when a man is brought to abominate some food if it is presented to him under the form of something abominable'.[29] The good end, it would seem, justifies the somewhat dubious—because illusory—means.

Hermann's Averroes declares that since all likening (*assimilatio*) involves what is either becoming or base, the art of poetry must have as its purpose 'the pursuit of what is becoming and the rejection of what is base'. Good men are to be praised and evil men are to be blamed, whence tragedy is defined as 'the

---

[24] Dahiyat, *Avicenna's Commentary*, p. 19.

[25] Aristotle, *Poetics*, ii (1448ᵃ1–5, tr. Dorsch, p. 33).

[26] Avicenna, *Poetics*, ii. 10–11, tr. Dahiyat, p. 74.

[27] Quoted by Dahiyat, p. 18.

[28] *Spec. doct.* iii. cix (*Speculum quadruplex*, ii. 287). Cf. the doctrine of Aristotle's *De anima*, 427ᵇ23–4, as tr. by William of Moerbeke, that 'in imagining it is as though we were regarding in a picture things arduous or encouraging' (tr. Foster–Humphries, p. 376). See also C. S. Baldwin, *Medieval Rhetoric and Poetic to 1400* (London, 1928; repr. Gloucester, Mass., 1959), pp. 175–6.

[29] *Exposition of the Post. Anal.*, lect. i, prol., 6 (tr. Conway, p. 5).

art of praise' and comedy, which is reduced to satire, is defined as 'the art of blame' or vituperation.[30] But Averroes is not interested in the idea of poetry as a sort of pious fraud. He emphasizes the connection between representation and reality, between art and nature. In nature are to be found the origins of poetic recommendation and dissuasion, of praise and blame. Good men and evil men certainly do exist. One type of poet inclines towards representation of the former; another type, towards representation of the latter. In the first case men who are better than usual are depicted and shown to be praiseworthy; in the second, men who are worse than usual appear and are duly shown to be blameworthy. The implication is that the function of most poetry is not simply to image nature passively but to heighten or exaggerate certain natural qualities relating to what is fair and what is foul, in order to condition an audience's response to whatever is thus represented. But such imaginative heightening is not the same as false representation. The poet does not have the licence to create pure fictions—a point made in no uncertain terms in the section of the Averroistic *Poetics* which corresponds to ch. ix of Aristotle's work. There the poet is denied the use of impossible and invented fables such as those composed by Aesop. That statement would, doubtless, have surprised those readers who regarded as a commonplace the notion that poetic fiction comprised events neither true nor probable (cf. above, p. 113) and who respected the genre of moral fable. But Averroes is following Aristotle's point that imitation which keeps within the realm of the possible is more credible than that based on things which have never happened nor are ever likely to happen. When the represented actions 'are possible and seem real', declares Averroes, 'they have greater power to persuade'. He returns to this idea in the section that corresponds to ch. xiv of the *Poetics*, to say that when a fictional account is obviously based on suspect material it will not produce the intended effect; 'a statement which someone has not really believed will not move him to fear or pity'.

It would seem, then, that for Averroes the art of poetic representation is firmly rooted in nature, and the poet's affective imaginations should not be so fantastic that they sever themselves from that root. To apply a statement which Thomas Aquinas used in a different context, 'works of art necessarily imitate the works of nature, and the processes of art are modelled upon those found in nature'.[31] But it is crucial to realize that the verisimilar image-making to which Averroes strives to reduce fiction has its *raison d'être* not in any aesthetic principle but rather in its psychological appeal.

The transformation of tragedy. Our second, and major, extract from Hermann's translation of Averroes' 'Middle Commentary', which corresponds roughly to chs. vi–xiv of the *Poetics*, illustrates the way in which Aristotle's discussion of

---

[30] On medieval theory of satire see above, pp. 116–18. See further Butterworth, *Averroes' Middle Commentary*, pp. 13–14, who believes that Averroes' understanding of poetry in terms of praise and blame 'derives more from the rank he ascribes to poetry in the hierarchy of knowledge than from his misapprehension of what Aristotle means by tragedy and comedy'.

[31] *Commentum in libros politicorum*, lib. I, lect. i, in Aquinas, *Selected Political Writings*, ed. A. P. D'Entreves, tr. J. G. Dawson (Oxford, 1959), p. 195.

tragedy has been transformed by cultures which were ignorant of Greek plays and had only the haziest notions concerning the staging conditions of the classical theatre. Three aspects of this transformation will be discussed here because of the difficulties they may present to those who know well the *Poetics* as represented by modern scholarship: what Averroes did to catharsis, to the six parts of tragedy, and to the concepts of reversal, discovery, and the two kinds of plot, complex and simple.

In place of Aristotle's cryptic description of the essential structure of tragedy and the cathartic or purgative emotional effect which it brings about in the audience—

Tragedy, then, is a representation of an action that is worth serious attention, complete in itself, and of some amplitude, in language enriched by a variety of artistic devices appropriate to the several parts of the play, presented in the form of action, not narration, by means of pity and fear bringing about the purgation of such emotions.[32]

—is a definition of the general moral relevance and the morally stimulating effect which any given product of 'the art of praise' should have:

And the end in respect of substance, or what makes intelligible the substance, of the art of praise is that it should be the likening and representation of a full (*complete*), voluntary and virtuous action which has universal efficacy (*potestas*) in relation to virtuous actions, and not just a particular efficacy in relation to any specific virtuous actions whatever. A representation, I add, which arouses in souls certain passions which moderate themselves [*or* which moderate the souls] to feel pity or be fearful or to other similar passions which the representation induces and stimulates by what it images in the form of virtuous men concerning decency and corruption.[33]

Pity, fear, and such virtue-provoking feelings are to be positively aroused by tragedy, not over-stimulated and thence purged by it. The rather awkward statement about the represented action having to be universal rather than particular in its significance has, of course, nothing to do with Aristotle's remark about the artistic structure of tragedy. Averroes' point seems to be that the action in question, being voluntary, virtuous, or noble and 'full' (in the sense of having amplitude rather than being minor or narrow and hence possessing little impact or consequence in behaviour), has a widespread moral and didactic import, not merely showing a specific virtue of one

---

[32] Aristotle, *Poetics*, vi (1449ᵇ23–8; tr. Dorsch, pp. 38–9).

[33] W. F. Boggess, 'Averrois Cordubensis Commentarium medium in Aristotelis poetriam' (unpub. Ph.D. thesis, University of N. Carolina, 1965), p. 16. Cf. the generally similar rendering in Kelly, 'Aristotle–Averroes–Alemannus', p. 165. In his translation of the original Arabic text of Averroes, Butterworth renders this passage as follows: 'The definition that makes the substance of the art of eulogy understood is: it is a comparison and representation of a complete, virtuous voluntary deed—one that with respect to virtuous matters is universal in compass, not one that is particular in compass and pertains only to one or another virtuous matter. It is a representation that affects souls moderately by engendering compassion and fear in them. It does this by imitating the purity and immaculateness of the virtuous' (*Averroes' Middle Commentary*, p. 73). Cf. Dahiyat's translation of the same passage of Averroes, *Avicenna's Commentary*, p. 86 n. 1.

individual but revealing the nature of virtuous action in general.[34] An aesthetic poetic has been replaced by a rhetorical–ethical one.

This is the principle which also governs Averroes' transformation of at least some of the six parts of tragedy as identified by Aristotle (with which our second extract begins). Aristotle's category of 'plot' is replaced with 'fictional language' (*sermo fabularis*), this being the principal and fundamental part of tragedy. By this is meant the full imaginative representation of something, which gives pleasure to the beholder. Even though a man may derive no pleasure from seeing a certain thing as it exists in nature, he may well be delighted by its representation in painting and colours: this is the reason why men employ the art of painting and description. A similar point is made a little later:

Just as the skilled painter depicts something as it is in reality (*in sua existentia*) so that he can represent anger and derision and sloth by his painting—although the characteristics of these are primarily of the soul [rather than of the body]—in the same way the poet in his representation should depict and form the thing as it is in itself and to the best of his ability, so that he imitates and expresses the actions and habits of the soul.[35]

The truest poetry, it would seem, is very definitely not the most feigning (cf. above, p. 121). Fiction should keep within the realm of the possible and confine itself to verisimilar image-making, in the manner already discussed.

'Character' becomes *consuetudo*, a term difficult to render succinctly in English. Basically, it means 'habit', 'custom', or 'normal practice'; in this context it designates those typical patterns of behaviour which are common to many men and not simply the personal eccentricities of some individual.[36] (Here, it should be noted, the meaning of Aristotle's concept is being conveyed accurately.) Clearly, this emphasis is of a piece with Averroes' statement, as quoted earlier, that tragedy represents action which has universal relevance to many virtuous actions rather than merely specific relevance to some particular virtuous action. Tragedy is concerned with character-types, especially those which exemplify 'honourable characteristics and praiseworthy actions and ennobling beliefs'.

'Expression of thought' becomes belief or credibility (*credulitas*) in the sense of the imitated action being made convincing: the tragic poet must show what something is or is not in such a way that the audience believes it. Whereas rhetoric urges us actually to do something, poetry 'urges us to adopt some belief only, urges us to believe that something is or is not true, but not to seek it or reject it'. This statement sits rather uneasily with Averroes' earlier remarks concerning the emotive effects of poetic imagery, the psychological

---

[34] Cf. Avicenna, *Poetics*: 'Tragedy is an imitation of an action complete and noble, and elevated in rank; in very appropriate speech, not devoted to every part; affecting the particulars not with respect to quality but with respect to action—an imitation which moves souls to mercy ["pity"] and piety ["fear"]' (tr. Dahiyat, pp. 88–9, and see his important nn., pp. 88–9 nn. 5–6, 89 n. 1, and 85–7 n. 1).

[35] In the section of Averroes' commentary corresponding to ch. xv of Aristotle's *Poetics* (ed. Boggess, p. 47; tr. Hardison, p. 365).

[36] Cf. Allen, *Ethical Poetic*, p. 26.

assent demanded by imaginative syllogisms. The Arabs had assimilated poetics to rhetoric to such an extent that any such attempt to distinguish between them on the basis that the former 'advances an opinion that a thing is or is not, without an appeal for desiring or avoiding it' whereas the latter 'urges an attitude' (to cite Avicenna's version of the doctrine)[37] strikes one as something of an inconsistency. Here the tension between an aesthetic poetic and a rhetorical–ethical one is obvious.

'Diction' becomes metre or measure (*metrum seu pondus*), 'song' becomes musical intonation (*thonus*), and spectacle becomes 'viewing' or 'regarding' (*consideratio*). The last of these concerns the way in which the represented action strikes the audience. 'It is the process of showing the appropriateness of that belief (*credulitas*) by which a man appears as praiseworthy'; in other words, the audience must be confirmed in their conviction that the tragic heroes are indeed worthy of praise. In this regard the persuasive speech characteristic of rhetoric must not be used (cf. the discussion of *credulitas* above). Moreover, poetry does not use arguments and philosophical speculations (of the kind, presumably, which are characteristic of the higher branches of logic), and neither does it depend on those facial expressions and gestures which orators use to emphasize their points (cf. the similar comment in the section corresponding to the *Poetics*, ch. ix). Tragedy must present its subject to the view of its audience by 'representational language' alone.

Finally, a word on what Averroes did to the notions of 'reversal' and 'discovery'. The former becomes 'indirect' or 'circular' imagination (*circulatio*); the latter, 'direct' imagination or recognition (*directio sive directiva significatio*). Moreover, 'simple plot' is replaced with 'simple imitation' (*imitatio simplex*) and 'complex plot' with 'compound imitation' (*imitatio composita*). Here as so often in the Averroistic *Poetics* we are dealing with substitutions not of individual terms but of complete structures of argument. What Aristotle had said was that a simple plot represents a simple action, i.e. one 'which is single and continuous' and in which 'the change of fortune comes about without a reversal or discovery', whereas 'a complex action is one in which the change is accompanied by a discovery or a reversal, or both'.[38] What Averroes is saying is that indirect imagination is representation of what is to be blamed whereas direct imagination is of what is to be praised. Simple imitation occurs when one or the other, either indirect or direct imagination, is used; compound imitation when both are used, beginning with the blameworthy and ending with the praiseworthy, or vice versa. Compound imitation is preferable to simple imitation, and within compound imitation the kind which begins with indirect imagination and ends with direct imagination is the better procedure.

These principles were applied in a most interesting way in Benvenuto da Imola's commentary on the *Divine Comedy*. This poem is said to begin with representation of blameworthy sinners in Hell, to proceed with representation of the inhabitants of purgatory, who, while to some extent blameworthy, have some redeeming qualities and prospects, and to end with people who, having

[37] Avicenna, *Poetics*, vi. 20 (tr. Dahiyat, p. 94).
[38] Aristotle, *Poetics*, x (1452ᵃ16–18, tr. Dorsch, p. 45).

received their heavenly reward, are unqualifiedly worthy of praise and emulation. The whole work, then, is a particularly elaborate example of compound imitation, Dante being the supreme master of the art of praise and blame: 'no other poet ever knew how to praise or blame with more excellence. . . . [Dante] honoured virtue with encomia and lacerated vice and vicious men.'[39] Benvenuto has evaluated the *Divine Comedy* in accordance with the highest canons of poetic excellence known to him, and found it to be very good.

At the end of the short story 'Averroes's Search', in which Averroes' struggle to understand the Aristotelian notions of tragedy and comedy is portrayed sympathetically, Jorge Luis Borges writes:

I remembered Averroes who, closed within the orb of Islam, could never know the meaning of the terms *tragedy* and *comedy*. I related his case; as I went along, I felt what that god mentioned by Burton must have felt when he tried to create a bull and created a buffalo instead. I felt that the work was mocking me. I felt that Averroes, wanting to imagine what a drama is without ever having suspected what a theatre is, was no more absurd than I, wanting to imagine Averroes with no other sources than a few fragments from Renan, Lane and Asín Palacios.[40]

Unfortunately, too many readers of Averroes' 'Middle Commentary' on the *Poetics* have come determined to find a bull and have not appreciated that they are looking at a buffalo instead. Much work remains to be done on Hermann's translation of the Averroistic *Poetics*, a good start having been made by O. B. Hardison, J. B. Allen, and H. A. Kelly. The recent appearance of a proper critical edition of the Arabic text of the 'Middle Commentary',[41] together with the English translation thereof by C. E. Butterworth, have paved the way for, among other things, a full analysis of Hermann's translation techniques; such a study would reveal the extent to which Hermann discerned the shape of Averroes' buffalo. The circulation and significance of the abridgements of Hermann's translation, and the extracts from it which were transmitted in *florilegia*, richly deserve further investigation. Indeed, a full study of the influence exercised by Arab poetics in general in the later Middle Ages and the Renaissance is long overdue. Only when all this is done can we 'imagine' Averroes with adequate sources and afford his 'Middle Commentary' its proper place in the reception-history of Aristotle's *Poetics*.

---

[39] Cf. Hardison, *Classical and Medieval Literary Criticism*, pp. 346–7.
[40] *Labyrinths* (repr. Harmondsworth, 1981), pp. 187–8.
[41] *Talkhīṣ Kitāb al-Shiʿr* [Abridgement of the Book of Poetry], ed. C. E. Butterworth and A. Haridi (Cairo, 1985).

HERMANN THE GERMAN

Translation of Averroes' 'Middle Commentary' on Aristotle's *Poetics*: Extracts[42]

[CHAPTER i][43]

. . . Aristotle says: Every poem, and all poetic utterance (*oratio poetica*), is either praise (*vituperatio*) or blame (*laudatio*). This is clear from an inductive examination of poems, and essentially of those poems which deal with matters relating to the human will, that is, nobility and baseness. This is also the position in the representational arts which follow the lead of poetry, for instance the striking of the lyre or psaltery, or blowing into a flute or pipe, and the skilful use of the dance. For these arts naturally correspond to these two intentions [i.e. praise and blame].

Poetic forms of speech are based on images. There are three modes of imagination and of 'likening' (*modi ymaginationis et assimilationis*). There are two simple modes, and the third is a compound of those two. One of the two simple modes is the 'likening' of one object to another and its exemplification in terms of that object. This is achieved in all languages by words peculiar to that language, for instance *quasi* or *sicut*, or similar words which are called particles of comparison, or else by adopting that which is 'like', together with the thing to which it is compared, or in place of it. And in this art this process is called 'a trope' (*concambium*). An example of this is when a certain poet said of a very generous man: 'He is a sea flooding in from every quarter and, with overflowing abundance, replenishing the needs of those who come to him.'[44]

---

[42] We have based our translation on the edition which is most easily available, that by Minio-Paluello, pp. 41–5, 48–57, with the permission of Desclée de Brouwer, Paris. This is based on five MSS and the 1841 printed edition. We have also consulted the edition, based on all the MSS (except the fragment now in the possession of Professor Hanna, on which see n. 4), by W. F. Boggess (cit. above, n. 33). Only a single MS and the 1481 edition were used by L. L. Bronson, 'An Edition of Averroes' *Commentaria media* on Aristotle's *Poetics*, translated by Hermannus Alemannus' (unpub. Ph.D. thesis, Rutgers University, 1970).

[43] In order to facilitate comparison between Aristotle's *Poetics* and Hermann's translation of the 'Middle Commentary' we have inserted the chapter-divisions of the former. In this we follow Kelly, 'Aristotle–Averroes–Alemannus', p. 164 n. 10, rather than those inserted by Hardison in his translation (cit. above, n. 3).

[44] Abū Tammām, on whom see H. A. R. Gibb, *Arabic Literature: An Introduction*, 2nd edn. (Oxford, 1963), pp. 12, 24–5, 85, 91, 164. Butterworth renders the original Arabic as 'he is the sea from whatever direction you come to him', and explains that the generosity of the Sultan being praised here is likened to the boundlessness of the sea. Thus, 'the sea' is substituted for the generous man. *Averroes' Middle Commentary*, p. 60 and n. 9. On Hermann's citations of Arab poets see W. F. Boggess, 'Hermannus Alemannus' Latin Anthology of Arabic Poetry', *JAOS* lxxxviii (1968), 657–70. Averroes was determined to compare Arabic and Greek poetry, in line with his declared intention of extracting from the *Poetics* only those 'universal rules' which 'are common to all or most nations, for much of its contents are either rules particularly characteristic of their [i.e. Greek] poems and their customs therein' (tr. Butterworth, p. 59). Avicenna, in marked contrast, did not attempt such a harmonization. See Dahiyat, *Avicenna's Commentary*, pp. 11–12.

You must understand that the forms (*species*) which our modern writers call substitution (*transumptio*) and figurative usage (*translatio*) fall within this category, as for instance we read: 'the meadow is smiling', 'the shore is ploughed', and as a certain poet writes: 'there are mares which in their early years have not yet experienced the saddle or bridle, and camels which have not yet carried saddle-bags'.[45] But those figures can most properly be called tropes which have been created from the attributes of an object, or the characteristics which go with it.

Substitution (*transumptio*) is a trope based on proportion. For instance, when the proportion of one thing to a second is the same as that of a third thing to a fourth, then the name of the third thing is substituted for the first, and vice versa. The various origins of this sort of trope have already been dealt with in the *Rhetoric*.

The second simple mode is when the comparison is reversed, as when you say: 'the sun is like this woman' or 'the sun is this woman', not 'this woman is like the sun' or 'this woman is the sun'. The third mode of poetic discourse is a compound of these two.

Aristotle says: Just as certain men are naturally made in the likeness of certain others, and imitate them in their actions—for instance, some model themselves upon others in colours, form, and the voice, and this occurs either through skill, or through habit on the part of the persons who are making the images, or from long practice in this field—so we also find in men representation arising naturally through the medium of speech.

In poetic discourse imagination and representation is produced by three things: the harmonious sound, the measure, and the 'likening' itself. Each of these is sometimes found alone without another; for example, there is the sound of the flute or pipe, and the rhythm in dancing. Representation or imitation occurs in speech, that is, in discourses which represent or imagine, without metre or rhythm. Sometimes these three elements are found together. This is found among us [i.e. the Arabs] in the kind of so-called song recently discovered or invented by the inhabitants of that island [i.e. the peninsula, Spain], in that language, that is, Arabic.[46] For these are poems which have developed naturally, which include both these two elements.[47] Natural forms are found only among

---

[45] Bahā' al-Dīn Zuhayr (d. 1258), on whom see Gibb, *Arabic Literature*, pp. 130–1, 170, and Boggess, 'Alemannus' Latin Anthology', pp. 665–6. Butterworth renders the Arabic as 'the horses of youth and its trappings have been removed', and explains: 'The horses and trappings stand for the activities and pastimes of youth, especially making war and love; when one becomes too old for such things, it is as though they had been taken away'.

[46] i.e. the Mozarabic *muwashshaḥ* (strophic poem) and *zajal* (amatory ode), on which see Butterworth, pp. 63–4, esp. nn. 19–20, and Gibb, *Arabic Literature*, pp. 44–5, 60–2, 109–12, 135, 150.

[47] i.e. both mimetic speech and music. Here Hermann's rendering differs markedly from the original Arabic (tr. Butterworth, pp. 63–4).

peoples who live according to nature. Indeed, harmony (*simphonia*) or melody (*consonantia*) does not exist in Arabic poetry, but either metre on its own or metre and representation.

This being so, there are three arts which are imaginative, or which create the effect of imagining: the art of rhyme, the art of metre, and the art of composing discourses which represent [objects]. This is the aspect of the art of logic which is dealt with in this book [i.e. the *Poetics*]. Aristotle says: Often, in those discourses which are called poems, no element of poetic intention is found, save only the metre. Examples are the Socratic discourses in metre, and the discourses of Empedocles on natural philosophy, in contrast to what is contained in the poems of Homer. For in them [i.e. Homer's poems] one finds both elements together.

Aristotle says: So it is not right that a work should be called a poem in the true sense unless it combines these two elements. For otherwise they should more properly be called discourses of one sort or another, rather than poems. Likewise the writer who composes discourses in metre on natural history should be called a maker of discourses rather than a poet. Likewise the imaginative discourses made up of mixed metres are not poems. Aristotle has related how there are found among the Greeks poems made up of rhythms or mixed metres. But these are not found among us [i.e. the Arabs]. It is clear now from what has been said how many ways of representation there are, and from what arts representational works are put together in words in such a way that they attain their end.

[CHAPTER ii]

Aristotle says: Since those who make representations and likenesses have as their purpose, by this activity, to urge men on to certain actions which are voluntary, and to dissuade them from others, it will of necessity be virtues or vices which they urge by their acts of representation. For every action and every trait of character is concerned only with one of these two, virtue or vice. It therefore follows that good and virtuous men only represent virtue and the virtuous, while evil men represent evil and evildoers. And since, without exception, all comparison and representation occurs through showing what is becoming or unbecoming or base, clearly this can have no other purpose than the pursuit of what is becoming and the rejection of what is base. It must then follow that there are imitators (*representatores*) of the virtues, that is, those who incline naturally to those traits which are represented by those who are more noble and of better character, and imitators of vices, who are less perfect and closer to evil than they are. Praise and blame—that is, praise of good men and blame of evil men—have their origins in these two kinds of men.[48] For this reason,

---

[48] Butterworth translates the original Arabic as follows: 'those who make representations of the virtues—I mean, those who are naturally inclined to make representations of them—

some poets are successful in praising, but not in bestowing blame. Conversely, others are successful in bestowing blame rather than praise.

So, in every 'likening' these two different ingredients should be found, that is, praise of what is good and condemnation of what is evil.

[CHAPTER iii]

These two different categories are found only in 'likening' and representation achieved through the medium of language, not that which is achieved through metre nor that which is achieved through rhyme.

'Likening' achieved through the medium of language is found in three different forms. There is 'likening' which has as its purpose the comparison of the thing compared with that which bears a similarity to it, without showing what is good or base, the sole purpose being to bring out the comparison. This kind of 'likening' is well suited to be altered or modified in the direction of either of the two extremes. In other words it is sometimes modified to show goodness by strongly emphasizing it, and sometimes to show evil by strongly representing it.

Aristotle says: Such was the path taken by Homer. For he, in his comparisons, proceeded to express virtue and baseness by comparing like features.[49] The effectiveness (*bona operatio*) of some poets consists in simply making an unadorned comparison, and of others in showing good and evil, and of yet others in a combination of both, as we find in Homer. And he, that is, Aristotle, takes individual examples of each kind from the poets who were famous or notorious among the Greeks and in their various jurisdictions, and of their use of each of the three kinds of comparison.

It will not be difficult for you to think up examples in Arab poetry, although, as Abū Naṣr al-Fārābī says, their poems are mostly concerned only with the various pleasures of life.[50] The kind of poetry which they

must necessarily be more virtuous and those who make representations of the vices naturally more deficient and more proximate to vice. Eulogy and satire—I mean, eulogizing the virtues and satirizing the vices—arise from these two sorts of people' (p. 66). Here Avicenna places a rather different emphasis: 'Every action is either base or noble. Since they [the Greeks] practiced the imitation of actions, some proceeded to imitate them for pure similitude, neither for amelioration nor depreciation. Every imitation and similitude, however, was implicitly prepared towards amelioration or depreciation, or, in general terms, towards encomium or invective. Their practice was [similar to] that of the painters who painted the angel in a beautiful form and Satan in an ugly form' (tr. Dahiyat, p. 75).

[49] Averroes' point here, which is rather obscured by Hermann, is that there are three kinds of linguistic 'likening': praise, blame, and mere comparison or congruity without any element of praise or blame being added. Some poets excel only in comparison, others in either praise or blame—but Homer excels both in comparison and in praising and blaming (tr. Butterworth, pp. 66–7). In Avicenna's view, by contrast, Homer 'mostly imitated noble deeds alone' and therefore is the encomiastic poet *par excellence* (tr. Dahiyat, p. 76).

[50] Referred to by Hermann as Abunazrin Alfarabius. According to Butterworth, p. 67 n. 9, 'This statement is apparently taken from a work that has not survived'; but cf. the discussion by Avicenna, *Poetics*, x. 10 (tr. Dahiyat, p. 74).

call elegy is simply an incitement to the sexual act, which they disguise and dignify by the name of love. So, children should be discouraged from reading such poems, and should be instructed and rehearsed in poems which urge them on to acts of bravery and generosity, or liberality. For in their poems the Arabs inculcate these two virtues alone, out of all the virtues, and not only because they are virtues, but because through them are acquired honour and a high reputation.

The kind of poem in which comparison alone is aimed at is found often in their [i.e. Arabic] poetry. So they often introduce the properties and characteristics of metals and similar materials, and things which grow in the earth, and animals. But the Greeks do not employ many such comparisons in their poems except in so far as they intend through them to convey proof and precept for the encouragement and pursuit of the virtues, and the rejection of the vices, or to convey other kinds of good qualities, either in terms of acts or of knowledge.

From this it is clear that the various kinds of 'likening' have three roots and three differences. It is also clear what those three differences and those three kinds of comparison are. It is clear, when various poems are examined, that there certainly is not a fourth kind of comparison, nor a fourth kind of difference.

[CHAPTER iv]

Aristotle says: There seem to be two causes for the origin of poetry naturally implanted in men. First of all, the tendency to 'liken' one thing to another and to represent one thing by another is naturally to be found in man from birth. Indeed, this act of comparing and representing is found even in infants, and is peculiar to man among all animals. The reason is that, among all the other animals, man alone takes pleasure in the 'likening' of things which he has already received in his mind, and in representing or imitating them. An indication of this—that man instinctively rejoices and takes pleasure in 'likening'—is that we derive pleasure from the representation of some things which we do not enjoy when we experience them. This occurs most notably when the representation expresses very subtly the thing represented, as happens in the configuration of many animals achieved by skilled sculptors or painters. This is why we use examples in teaching, so that what is said may more easily be understood, because of the moving power of the images. For the mind will more perfectly assimilate teachings as a result of the pleasure which it takes in examples. So learning is not a prerogative of philosophers alone, but of all other men, who share it with philosophers in some degree.

For we find that learning naturally passes from one man to another through the relationship which a teacher has to his pupil. Since imitations which are meant as examples are nothing other than 'likenings' made to

things which we have already experienced, it is clear that the only reason
for employing them is that what is said may be understood more quickly
and easily. It is understood more quickly through the use of 'likenings'
because of the pleasure derived from the image of the thing which they
represent. This is the first cause of the origin of poetry.

The second cause is the pleasure which man naturally takes in metre
and harmony. Harmony (*simphonia*) is adapted to the metre by those who
have the natural ability to hear and judge metres and harmonies. So the
pleasure which the soul takes in representations and in metres and harmonies was the cause of the invention of the art of poetry, above all among
men whose talent in this field was pre-eminent.

And so, when human beings began to gather together and constitute a
social group, the art of poetry had its origin among them. But its development was a gradual one, for at first they discovered only a small part of it,
and after that some more, until finally perfection in the art was attained in
this way. The various kinds [of poetry] reached perfection according to
the greater or lesser capacity of every sort of man to enjoy this or that kind
of poetry. For example, noble and virtuous souls instinctively invented
the art of writing poems to praise and extol good and fine deeds. Souls
which had less nobility in them than these invented poems to castigate
and blame base and dishonourable deeds. However, it is necessary for the
writer whose intention is to blame evil men and evil deeds to praise and
extol good men and good and virtuous deeds, so that by this means evil
and base deeds may be thrown into sharper relief, when he tells of them
and places the opposite qualities in juxtaposition to them. . . .

[CHAPTER vi]

. . . Aristotle says: Tragedy, that is, the art of praise, should have six parts,
namely representative fictional language (*sermo fabularis*), typical characteristics (*consuetudo*), metre or measure (*metrum seu pondus*), belief (*credulitas*), regarding (*consideratio*), and musical intonation (*thonus*). An
indication of this is that all poetic discourse is divided into 'likening' and
the means whereby 'likening' is made. These [means] are three in
number: representation, metre and music. And there are three things
which are 'likened' in the poetry of praise: typical characteristics, belief,
and regarding, which [i.e. regarding] is the process of proving a belief to
be true.

So, tragedy must have six parts. The more important parts of a poem
which bestows praise are typical characteristics and belief. For tragedy is
not an art representing men as they strike us individually, but rather
represents their honourable characteristics and praiseworthy actions and
ennobling beliefs. 'Typical characteristics' embrace actions and morals.
Therefore, 'typical characteristics' are included as one of the six parts,

and thus its presence among them gives grounds for including actions and morals in that category. 'Regarding' is the process of showing the appropriateness of that belief [or credibility] by which a man appears as praiseworthy. That is not found at all in the poems of the Arabs, but it is found in the writings of the law [i.e. the Koran]. This [i.e. regarding] is represented by three things—typical characteristics, belief, and signification—through using three things which enable representation to take place, namely imaginative speech, metre, and musical intonation.

As Aristotle says: The parts of the fictional speech which make it representational are two in number. For all representation marks out its proper place [i.e. the category under which it falls] by representation of what is contrary and afterwards is changed to conform with its own purpose. This is the method which the Greeks call 'indirect' (circulatio). Or else it mentions the thing itself, making no mention of its contrary. This is what the Greeks call '[direct] signification' (significatio).[51]

The principal and fundamental part of these [six] parts is fictional language. The second most important part is 'typical characteristics': originally that was the part upon which representation was employed; in other words, that was the part which was represented. Indeed, representation or imitation is the foundation or sustenance in this art, because no pleasure is derived from mentioning a thing which we want to, without it being represented. But when it has been thus represented, the result is pleasure and it becomes acceptable. So, frequently a man derives no pleasure from seeing the form of something which exists in nature, and yet does take pleasure in its representation and re-creation through the medium of painting and colours, and this is the reason why men employ the art of painting and description.

The third part of tragedy is 'belief' (credulitas), that is, the ability to represent a thing in terms of what it is and is not. This is similar to what rhetoric tries to achieve in its attempt to prove that a thing is or is not, except that rhetoric attempts to achieve this end through persuasive speech, and poetry through representational speech. And this form of representation is found also in writings of the law. Aristotle says: The lawgivers at Sparta were content to strengthen the beliefs in the minds of

---

[51] Cf. chs. x–xi (below, pp. 301–3). On Averroes' replacement of 'reversal' and 'discovery' with circulatio and directiva significatio see the introduction to this section, pp. 287–8. Butterworth renders the Arabic as follows: 'every representation is prepared either by starting with a representation of its contrary and then pasing to its proper representation—and this was known among them as reversal—or the object itself is represented without the representation of the contrary taking place—and this is what they used to call discovery' (p. 77). Avicenna has this to say: 'The parts of a fiction are two. Reversal is the transition from one [state of] affairs to its opposite—it resembles what we now call antithesis. But in their [i.e. Greek] tragedies, it was used as a gradual transition from a bad to a beautiful state by depreciating the bad one and ameliorating its opposite. This is analogous to refutation, adjuration, and proof. The second part of the fiction is recognition, which is ameliorating the beautiful state, not by depreciating its opposite' (tr. Dahiyat, p. 93).

men, using a poetic way of speaking, until later generations began to discover the paths of rhetoric. The difference between a poetic speech, which inculcates and urges us to belief, and one which inculcates and urges us to morals, is that the speech which urges us to morals urges us to action, and to do something, or to reject or withdraw from something. But speech which urges us only to adopt some belief urges us to believe that something is or is not true, but not to seek it or reject it.

The fourth part is 'metre or measure'. For it to be perfect it must be appropriate to the purpose or intention. For at times a certain measure is appropriate to one purpose and not to another. The fifth part, which consists in harmonious proportion (*ordo*), is 'musical intonation'. This does more than any of the other parts [of tragedy] to make an impression on the soul and work upon it.

The sixth part is 'regarding',[52] that is, the argument or proof of what is correct belief or correct behaviour, without using persuasive speech. For this last is not suitable or appropriate to this art [of poetry], but [poetry] operates by the use of a representational mode of speech. Indeed, the art of poetry does not consist in arguments or in philosophical speculation, and this is particularly so of tragedy. So, a poem of praise does not employ the art of gesticulation, nor that of adopting [appropriate] facial expressions in the way that rhetoric does.

Aristotle says: The scientific art which shows and teaches us from what elements and how poems are composed, is more important and perfect than the actual making of the poems themselves.[53] For every art which instructs, and which contains, subordinated to it, the principles whereby it performs its functions, is more important than those things which are subordinated to it.

---

[52] *Consideratio*, i.e. viewing, regarding, proof; here replacing Aristotle's 'spectacle' or stage-effect, which, he declared, 'has the least to do with the playwright's craft or with the art of poetry. For the power of tragedy is independent both of performance and of actors, and besides, the production of spectacular effects is more the province of the property-man than of the playwright' (tr. Dorsch, p. 41). Butterworth renders the Arabic thus: 'The sixth part is spectacle—I mean, giving argument for the correctness of a belief or the correctness of a deed, not by means of a persuasive statement for that is not appropriate to this art, but by means of a representative statement. Indeed, the art of poetry and especially the art of eulogy, is not based on proving and disputing. That is why eulogy does not use the art of dissimulation and delivery the way rhetoric does (pp. 77–8). Avicenna defines 'viewing and proof' as 'that which fixes in the soul the import of diction and the necessity of its acceptance, in order to alleviate grief and produce the emotion proper to tragedy. It is not a matter of art; i.e. the [means of] persuasion mentioned in the *Rhetoric* are not proper to poetry. Tragedy is not based on argumentation and competition, nor on the player's art' (*Poetics*, vi. 22, tr. Dahiyat, p. 95).

[53] Averroes differs from Avicenna here: whereas the former is saying that poetic theory is 'superior' to the actual composition of poems, the latter declares that 'The art [of persuasion] is superior to poetry', reiterating the hierarchical relationship between these two branches of logic (tr. Dahiyat, p. 95).

[CHAPTER vii]

So, since we have said what tragedy is and what its components are, and how many parts it has, and what they are, let us discuss those elements which make for beauty and excellence in the constituent parts of poetry.[54] For we must discuss this both in the case of tragedy and in that of other forms. For these elements are the first causes and basis for the existence of such forms.

The bases from which the arts arise fall into two categories. Some are necessary to the arts, while others make them complete and improve them.

So we will say that tragedy must fulfil the end purposes towards which it operates, so that in 'likening' and representation it may attain whatever end it is naturally capable of. This will be achieved by several means, of which one is that the work aimed at should have a certain fixed size which makes it whole and complete. That is whole and complete which has a beginning, a middle, and an end. The beginning comes before the main subject, and it must not be mixed up with the matter to which it forms the beginning. The ending goes with the matter to which it forms the conclusion, and not before. The middle is both 'before' and 'with'. So it is more important (*melius*) than either end [of the tragedy], for the middle is found in the place which is between 'that which precedes' and 'that which is placed after'. For in war this place is given to those who are brave, that is, the place between where the timid are positioned and that where the bold and headstrong are put. This is the middle part. And so the good part in any writing is the middle, and it is that part which is derived from the two extreme parts, but they are not derived from it. Moreover, the middle of a work should not occupy a middle place solely in terms of the composition and order of the work, but also in terms of size and excellence. When this is the case, the work thus undertaken must of necessity have a beginning, a middle, and an end, and each of these parts must be of a size proportionate to the others. Likewise, the complete whole made up of those three parts must have a carefully determined size, and must not be on an indeterminate scale.

For excellence in a composition arises from two elements, one of which is order and the other size. For this reason, when speaking of an animal which is small in comparison to other individual members of its own species, we do not say that it is good or beautiful.

Arrangement in poetic discourse is just like arrangement in teaching (*doctrina demonstrativa*). For if a discourse which is aiming to teach is shorter than it should be, it obscures the meaning, and if it is too long it

---

[54] Here Averroes follows Aristotle fairly closely, stressing the importance of the progression from beginning to middle to ending, and considering the middle as the most important part of tragedy.

will be difficult to retain in the memory and will cause the student to forget it. Therefore, arrangement has a role to play in this, just as it has in the viewing of anything which can be grasped by the senses. For the view will be good when the distance between the person who views it and the object which is to be viewed is well judged, and that object is not too near or too remote. What happens in the sphere of teaching also happens in poetic discourses. Thus, if a laudatory poem is briefer and more compressed than the subject to be praised demands, it will not completely fulfil its function of bestowing praise. But if it is too prolix, then its various parts cannot be retained in the memory of the audience. The result will be that, by the time they have heard the final parts, they will have forgotten the earlier parts.

Rhetorical discourses used in controversy to confirm or refute do not have a naturally determined length. This is why men need to measure the time of a debate between adversaries either by a device operated by the dripping of water, as was the custom among the Greeks, since they relied only on enthymemes, or by fixed adjournments, as is our custom. For in deciding lawsuits we rely solely on facts outside the argument of the case to convince us of its truth. So, if tragedy consisted in the juxtaposition of arguments, some measurement of the time taken up by each argument in it would be needed, either by marking off the hours of a water-clock or by some other means. Since this is not the case, then the art of poetry had to have a natural limit, just as is found in the case of the natural sizes of things which exist in nature. For all things that are born into the world grow to a certain size predetermined by nature, unless prevented at birth by some adverse circumstances. This must also be true in the case of poetic discourses, and particularly in the two kinds of representation, one of which is achieved by a change from representing the opposite of something to representing the thing itself, and the other by representing the thing itself without reference to its opposite.

[CHAPTER viii]

Aristotle says: The structure of a poem is made attractive and beautiful if it is not drawn out by telling of all the things which happen to the one thing (*res*) which that poem aims to describe. For many things happen to a single thing, and a single thing has many incidental properties.

He also says: It seems that not all poets continue with the one thing (*res*); in fact, they change from one thing to another and Homer is the only poet who so continues [i.e. with the one thing].[55] And you will find this

---

[55] Here Aristotle is saying that a plot does not possess unity merely because it is about one man, since 'Many things . . . may happen to one man, and some of them will not contribute to any kind of unity, and similarly he may carry out many actions from which no single unified action will emerge' (1451ᵃ16–19, tr. Dorsch, pp. 42–3). Those who compose a *Heracleid* or

[changing from one thing to another] often in Arabic poetry, and in new or modern poems,[56] and particularly in eulogies.[57] When they [i.e. the Arabs] have some subject to praise, for instance a vigorous horse or a precious sword, they digress from the subject and dwell at excessive length on the praise of any [other] subject which presents itself as praiseworthy.

And to sum up, in this matter art must imitate nature, so that everything it does it should do in terms of one purpose (*propositum*) and aiming at one end. This being so, 'likening' and representation must have one end in view, and the subject which they aim to describe should be one, and its parts must have a precisely defined magnitude, and should have a beginning, a middle, and an end, and the middle should be the best part. For things which depend on the arrangement [of their parts] for their very existence, and also owe their effectiveness (*bonitas operationis*) to proper arrangement, do not function as they should if they are deprived of proper arrangement.

[CHAPTER ix]

Aristotle says: It is clear from what has been said about the purpose of poetic discourse that representations arrived at by means of false and invented fictions are not part of the work of a poet. These are what are called proverbs and exemplary tales (*exempla*), like those in Aesop and similar fabulous writings. So, it is not a poet's business to speak other than in terms of objects which exist or which can exist. Such things are to be aimed at or rejected, or an appropriate comparison drawn from them, as was said in the chapters on kinds of representation. The task of composing proverbs and fables is not the same as that of a poet, although men compose proverbs and invented fables of this sort in metre. For, although they both use metre, the purpose of both proverbs and fables is achieved through the stories themselves, and would be achieved even if metre were absent. It is a kind of instruction in prudence which is acquired through such invented stories. But it is only through metre that the poet attains his end by imaginative stimulation. Thus, the writer who makes up invented proverbs and fables invents or imagines individual things which

a *Theseid* in the belief that writing about a single person is all that is required to achieve unity, are mistaken; the poet must present the represented action as a unified whole with its various incidents properly arranged. Homer acted rightly, by constructing his *Odyssey* and *Iliad* around a single action, and not putting in everything that happened to his heroes. Hermann's use of the one bald term *res* in the sentence about Homer, the same term used in the first two sentences in this chapter, quite obscures this point. Cf. *Averroes' Middle Commentary*, tr. Butterworth, p. 82. Avicenna is much clearer (tr. Dahiyat, p. 99).

[56] On the periods or classes generally recognized in Arabic literary theory, see Butterworth, pp. 22–3 n. 25, 82–3 n. 12.

[57] i.e. the *qaṣīdah* (formal classical ode), on which see Gibb, *Arabic Literature*, pp. 13–31, 42–3, etc.; Butterworth, p. 80 n. 3.

do not exist at all in reality, and gives them names. But the poet gives
names only to those things which already exist. And perhaps poets speak
in universal terms. Therefore, the art of poetry is closer to philosophy
than is the art of inventing proverbs. This is what Aristotle himself says
concerning the conventions of the Greeks in their poetry, which appears
to imitate nature, and so [concerning poetry] among foreign peoples who
live according to the rules of nature.

Aristotle says: The writer who has to work in tragedy or the art of praise
must be most careful to ensure that the subjects which he draws on for his
imitative representation actually exist in nature, and are not invented fictions for which he has made up names. For poems of praise have as their
purpose the encouragement of acts of the will. When such acts [i.e. acts
represented in poetry] are possible[58] and seem real they have greater
power to persuade, in other words to promote poetic belief which moves
the mind to pursue something or reject it. Only rarely in tragedy are
names invented and given to things which do not exist in nature, as for
instance when poets sometimes depict generosity as something which has
a separate existence,[59] and then go on to attribute to it acts appropriate to
a generous person, and make a representation of it, and multiply songs in
its praise. This is a kind of imaginative stimulation. Even if this approach
is sometimes effective to no small degree because of the similarity of the
acts and passions of such an invented thing to things which really exist in
nature, yet one should not rely on such means in tragedy. For this kind of
imaginative stimulation is not something which appeals to every temperament. On the contrary, most people mock or deride it, and have no high
opinion of it.

The good [poetic] qualities discussed in this chapter [of Aristotle's] are
exemplified among Arab writers by the words of al-A'shā,[60] though they

---

[58] The key concept throughout this discussion is 'what is possible': poetic representation
may appropriately include those things which *can* exist as well as those things which actually
do exist. Cf. Cicero, *De invent.*, i. xix. 27 (on *argumentum*), i. xxi. 29 (*probabilis narratio*); *Ad
Herennium*, i. viii. 13 (*argumentum*); Macrobius, *In somn. Scip.* i. ii. 9 (*narratio fabulosa*), and
Isidore, *Ety.* i. xliv. 5 (*argumentum*). Averroes' statement that 'made-up stories are not lacking
in poetry' (see below, p. 301) should be taken in this sense; it does not contradict the statement made at the beginning of this chapter that 'false and invented fictions are not part of the
work of a poet' since what is being denigrated there is utterly fictitious depiction of the
impossible.

[59] Here Averroes is thinking of personification allegory, and uses the personification of
Generosity as an example. This method may be used and may be effective, he thinks, but it
should not be relied on, since it appeals only to a minority. Cf. Avicenna, *Poetics*, ix. 16 (tr.
Dahiyat, p. 101).

[60] Referred to by Hermann as Alaschei. Cf. Boggess, 'Alemannus' Latin Anthology', p. 660.
Hermann seems to have missed Averroes' point here, which is that in the al-A'shā passage,
confusingly abridged in his translation, Generosity is being personified. Butterworth, p. 85,
renders the full quotation as follows: 'Upon my life, watchful eyes have perceived a fire's light
burning on the rise; Blazing for two cold men seeking its warmth, Generosity and al-
Muḥalliq, night-long at the fire; Having sucked milk from the breast of a single mother, they
swore by her dark nipple never to become sundered.' Here the poet is praising the generous

do not incite to virtue. He is such a poet [as Aristotle describes], and says as follows: 'By my life, many eyes have appeared gazing on the light of a fire kindled upon the hills so that two cold people, spending the night underneath its fiery glow, grew warm from its radiance.'

This being the case, it is clear that a poet is not a poet unless he uses fictions and metres and measures in such a way that he is successful in producing 'likenings' and imitative representations. He does not employ 'likenings' except for matters relating to the will which exist in nature. It is part of his task to imitate and represent, not just things which exist, but also those things which it is thought can exist. In so doing he will be a poet no less than if he does this for those things which do in fact exist. Nothing prevents him from taking and using those [possible] things as he uses things which exist here and now. So, made-up stories are not lacking in poetry which is intended to stimulate the imagination.

Nor does the skilled and perfect poet need to fill out his representation through external aids such as dramatic gestures and facial expressions. Only those poets who pose as poets, though they really are not, use these. Genuine poets do not use them, except when they want to counter the practice of false poets; they do not use them at all to attack skilled poets.

Sometimes perfect poets are forced, as time and place may require it, to avail themselves of the use of those things which are external or lie outside the central basis of poetry. This is because imitation or representation is not everywhere achieved by the imitation of things which are complete, so that their imitation may be definite and complete, but by imitation of things which are imperfect, so that it is difficult to imitate them purely in terms of speech. So, external means are an aid to their imitation, particularly when the intention is to imitate belief[s]. For it is difficult for these things to be expressed by way of images, when they are neither actions nor substances.

Sometimes these external aids are mingled with poetic images. If this happens by chance, without being intended, it will be a source of wonder, for events which in their very nature happen by chance are marvellous.

[CHAPTER X]

Aristotle says: There are many kinds of poetic discourse whose excellence consists in simple imitation (*imitatio simplex*) without many variations. There are, too, many whose excellence consists purely in the variety of their 'likenings' and imitations. For exactly the same holds good for 'likenings' as for other activities. Just as some activities are effected by one simple act, and some by a complex act, so too with imitation or representation. Simple imitation is that in which one of the two kinds of imagination is used, either

hospitality of al-Muḥalliq, described by Butterworth as 'an otherwise poor and unknown man with several daughters whose marriages he despaired of being able to arrange'.

the kind which is called 'indirect' (*circulatio*) or the kind which is called 'direct' or 'direct designation' (*directio sive directiva significatio*).

Compound imitation (*imitatio composita*) is that in which both kinds are used, this being achieved either by beginning with the indirect kind and ending up with the direct kind, or beginning with the direct kind and ending up with the indirect kind. For it makes a great difference whether you begin with the indirect kind and end with the direct, or begin with the direct kind and end with the indirect.

[CHAPTER xi]

Aristotle says: And I mean by the indirect kind imitation of the opposite of that which it is intended to praise, so that the soul first of all rejects and abhors it [i.e. the opposite of what is to be praised], and then there is a change from this to the imitation of that which is to be praised. For instance, when someone wants to imitate or represent success and those people involved with it, he begins first of all by imitating failure and those people who are involved with it [i.e. failure], then a change takes place to the imitation of success and those people involved with it [i.e. success]. This effect will be achieved by representing the opposite of that [which it is intended to praise], whereby those people involved with failure are represented. But the direct kind is imitation only of the thing itself.

Aristotle says: The more elegant of the direct methods is that which is combined with the indirect method. He adds: Sometimes the direct and indirect methods are employed in respect of animate and inanimate objects, not in the way they are used when the goal is action or rejection [by the audience], but in the way they are used simply to stir the imagination. I call this 'accurate imitation' (*convenientia*).

The kind of direct comparison he mentions here is the sort more used in Arabic poems, namely the direct method combined with the indirect, applied to inanimate objects. For example, there is the passage in al-Mutanabbī[61] as follows: 'As often as were your visits to hidden entrances, when all were asleep, visits more furtive than those of wolves, so often did I visit them and the darkness of the night interceded for me, and I returned, and the brightness of the dawn met me.' The first part of the poem is the direct method, while the second is the indirect method. Since these two stanzas embrace the two manners of imitation the result is elegant and beautiful.

[61] Abu'l-Ṭayyib al-Mutanabbī (d. 956), here referred to by Hermann as Abytaibi. See Boggess, 'Alemannus' Latin Anthology', p. 660, cf. p. 669; also Gibb, *Arabic Literature*, pp. 91–2. Butterworth translates the Arabic verses as follows: 'Many a stealthy visit shrewder than the wolf's did I make to you among the Bedouins as they slumbered; I slip among them while night's blackness intercedes for me, and I turn back as dawn's whiteness tempts them to me' (p. 88). 'The inanimate things used here', Butterworth explains (n. 26), are 'the blackness of night and the whiteness of dawn'.

Aristotle says: In the case of human subjects the direct method and the indirect method are used only in enquiry and refutation. This kind of directness is that which moves the soul sometimes to feel pity and sometimes to fear. This is what is needed in the art of praising laudable and noble human acts and of blaming base and ugly acts.

Aristotle says: These two parts which we have described are parts of tragedy. There is here too a third part, that which generates animal passions, namely pity and fear and sadness. He includes among these passions all events that inspire pity, such as dangers experienced by friends, the deaths of relations, and other similar circumstances that are wont to happen to men. For these are the things which induce pity and fear. This is a large element in those parts of a poem through which men are incited to acts which deserve praise, and to the praising of which the poem is directed.

[CHAPTER xii]

Aristotle says: So, having described the parts of tragedy in qualitative terms, I must now speak of its parts in quantitative terms. He mentions in this account the parts which are particular to their own [i.e. Greek] poems. Three of these parts are found also in Arabic poems. The first part is that which appears in Arabic poems after the manner of a rhetorical exordium. This is the part in which they mention houses or noble buildings and ruins and remains. After that come preliminary remarks (*preludia*) and consolations (*solatia*). The second part contains the actual praise. The third part corresponds to the conclusion in a rhetorical work. A great deal of this part among the Arabs is either invocation and entreaty on behalf of the person they have praised, or else a commendation of the poem written in praise of him.

The first part is more conspicuous and widely appreciated than these latter parts. Consequently, they call the transition from the first part to the second a 'follow-on'. Perhaps they may proceed directly to the praise, leaving out the exordium, as Abū Tammām says: 'Certainly I should be too timid both to speak and act', and al-Mutanabbī: 'Every man enjoys what he has been accustomed to all this life, and the lance of Saif al-Dawlah has been accustomed to pierce his enemies.'[62]

---

[62] On Abū Tammām, here referred to by Hermann as Abuteminin, see Boggess, 'Alemannus' Latin Anthology', p. 661. On al-Mutanabbī see previous n. Butterworth translates Abū Tammām's statement as 'It is easy for us to speak and for you to act', explaining that this is the opening half-verse of an ode in praise of al-Zayyāt, a man of letters and poet. The quotation from al-Mutanabbī, being the opening half-verse of an ode in praise of Saif al-Dawlah, is rendered 'From his lot in life each man has what he is accustomed to'; in a note Butterworth supplies the rest of the verse, which means 'And the custom of Saif al-Dawlah is to thrust at the enemy' (p. 91).

[CHAPTER xiii]

And after he has enumerated all the parts of a poem in their [i.e. Greek] terms, Aristotle says: We have now set out the parts of tragedy seen in both quantitative and qualitative terms. Next we will give an account of the sources from which is derived the effective operation of the art of praise, that is, tragedy. We will add that to what has preceded.

As we have said, laudatory poems should not be made up from simple imitations only, but from combinations of the different types, that is, from direct or indirect kinds and from imitations which move the emotions, and are conducive to feelings of fear or pity, thus moving men's souls. For odes, that is, laudatory songs, which have as their purpose to impel men to virtue, must be made up from representations of virtue, and of things which inspire fear, and those which produce a sad frame of mind, which thus result in a disturbance of the emotions, for instance undeserved misfortunes befalling the good. For in this way there is provided a strong stimulus to the soul to receive virtue.

For when a poet changes from representation of a virtue to representation of that which is not a virtue, or from representation of a virtuous person to representation of one who is not, he is not doing anything to arouse a man or stimulate him, through terror, to practise the virtues. For such a change does not induce an intense love of the virtues, nor does it induce fear, and both of these should be found in laudatory poems. This is achieved when there is a change from the representation of virtues to the representation of misfortunes, and evil happening to the good and deserving, or when there is a change from this to a representation of those who abound in virtue. No doubt such representations arouse men's minds, and make them more receptive to virtues.[63] You will find many representations of accidents that befall men in the words of the law, which are like those that Aristotle has described. For such are laudatory discourses which incite to praiseworthy acts, for instance, the one that is introduced relating to the story of Joseph and his brethren,[64] and other similar stories based on past events, which are called 'hortatory examples'.

Aristotle says: Pity and compassion occur when we are told of misery and misfortune unjustly befalling someone who has not deserved it. Fear and panic occur when these events are recounted, because the hearers imagine the harm which must befall those who are less worthy—for those

---

[63] In this chapter Aristotle had argued that the best tragic situation is that in which the chief character represents a mean between the extremes—someone who is not conspicuous either for virtue or vice, and whose fall from prosperity into misery is due not to depravity but rather to some error.

[64] The story of Joseph and his brethren is told in the Koran, xii. 1-111. On Averroes' attitude to the Koran see M. Fakhry, 'Philosophy and Scripture in the Theology of Averroes', *Med. Stud.* xxx (1968), 78-89.

that hear these accounts realize that *they* are less worthy. Sadness and pity are the result of these accounts because the calamity befalls someone who did not deserve it. When the virtues are simply alluded to, that does not inflict fear of losing them on the soul, or pity or love. So, he who wishes to urge men on to imitate the virtues must occupy part of his representation with matters which induce sadness and fear and pity.

Aristotle says: So, in terms of poetic art, those laudatory poems are regarded as good and excellent which have in their composition a narration of virtues and of events which inspire sadness and fear and move men to pity and compassion. He also says: For this reason, those who criticize the author who includes as part of his poem fictitious tales or those based on history, and the things they indicate to us, are in error. For these things are useful in laudatory poems. For things which move men to anger are introduced into the branch of poetry which praises warlike events. Anger, indeed, is a kind of sadness and emotional upset accompanied by an intense desire for vengeance. This being so, the recounting of the death of relations and similar misfortunes, happening to brave and virtuous men, moves and arouses in men an intense desire for what is good, and a love of virtue, and fear, lest in some way they be deprived of the benefits of virtue.

Some writers have included a representation of vices or weaknesses in laudatory poems, because that is a kind of 'indirect method'. But blame and denigration of failings pertains to satire more than to tragedy. So they should not be represented in tragedies as directly relating to the principal intention of the author, but through the 'indirect method'. When mention is made of failings in a laudatory poem this cannot be excused unless mention is also made of the enemies [of the virtuous] and of those who are an object of hatred. A laudatory poem is composed solely for the purpose of recalling the deeds of friends and of those we love. But enemies of enemies and friends of friends are not mentioned in poems of praise or of blame, since they are not friends or enemies.[65]

[CHAPTER xiv]

Aristotle says: Fictional invention intended to inspire grief or fear must be invention that is 'set before our eyes', so that it may convince us, as if

---

[65] i.e. they are not directly connected with each other. Here Aristotle had said that the kind of ending in which enemies became friends is unsatisfactory. Averroes brings in material from the *Poetics*, xiv (under the influence of Avicenna's paraphrase of the relevant passage; tr. Dahiyat, pp. 107–8), in which Aristotle had said that there was nothing pitiable in the action of a man injuring his enemy (except for what happens to him in itself) or of men who are indifferent to each other, but when the sufferings involve those who are dear to one another, then we have the ideal tragic situation (tr. Dorsch, p. 50). The point made by Hermann's Averroes seems to be that if failings are mentioned in a tragedy they should be clearly related to those characters who are the enemies of the virtuous. Cf. the statements in his version of the *Poetics*, xiv, translated below.

we had actually seen the event happen.[66] For when a fictional account is untrustworthy and is clearly made up on the basis of doubtful material, it will not produce the effect (*actio*) which it was intended to produce. For a statement which someone has not really believed will not move him to fear or pity. The phenomenon referred to here by Aristotle is the reason why many of those who do not believe the words of the law become wicked and depraved. For men are naturally moved by either one of two modes of discourse, demonstrative and non-demonstrative. The kind of depraved person mentioned above is prevented from being moved[67] by either kind of discourse in those matters which lie within the realms of the law.

Aristotle says: Some poets introduce into their tragedy a representation of things through which they seek to arouse wonder only, but nothing which will produce fear or sorrow. You will find much that is similar to all this in the writings of the law [i.e. the Koran], whereas poems which praise the virtues are not found in Arabic poetry, and in our time only in writings of the law. Aristotle says: Tragedy has no share in that effect [i.e. wonder] at all. For the goal of poetry is not just any sort of pleasure, but that kind of pleasure which is achieved by the arousing of the virtues through representation. This is the kind of pleasure which pertains to tragedy.

He also says: It is well known what are the things which cause pleasure by being represented, without this representation giving rise to pain or fear. One can see what things cause sadness, grief, and fear, mixed in with pleasure, by asking which experiences, among all those that can befall men, are hard to cope with and severe, and which are small and trivial and do not occasion a great degree of sadness or fear. Among the former are misfortunes which friends suffer at the hands of friends, as a result of voluntary actions, for instance the killing of relations and their suffering, danger, and loss, and other misfortunes of this sort, but not anything which happens to enemies at the hands of their enemies. For no one feels sorrow or is injured or experiences fear because of an injury inflicted by enemies to the same extent he feels sorrow and is offended by an injury inflicted on him by friends. And even if he suffers some pain as a result of the former, it is not so intense as the pain suffered from an injury inflicted by those who are near and dear to him, like the killing of one brother by another or a father by a son or a son by a father.[68] So the account of Abraham being ordered to sacrifice his son, who was very dear to him,

---

[66] Here Averroes returns to the notion of *credulitas* (cf. his version of *Poetics*, vi, above); i.e. the represented action must be made convincing. Cf. Avicenna: 'The fiction should not seem implausible and, consequently, become rather hard for imaginative assent . . .' (tr. Dahiyat, p. 107).

[67] i.e. prevented by his own depravity.

[68] Cf. above, n. 65.

arouses pity to a high degree, and its final emotive effect will be grief, pity, and fear.[69]

Aristotle says: Indeed, praise should only be bestowed upon those acts which are noble, and originate in free will and knowledge.[70] For some acts are the result of free will and knowledge, while others are not, and yet others are the result of knowledge without free will, or free will without knowledge. Likewise, some acts are effected by agents who are known, others by agents unknown. When an act has not originated in free will or knowledge it should not be regarded as a fit subject for praise. Likewise, when an act has been initiated by unknown agents, for that should be classed among fictions rather than among poems. In that case, it should not be the subject of representation. Acts which have beyond all doubt originated in free will and knowledge, and which are performed by known agents, are the most worthy subjects of praise and outright commendation.

Aristotle says: We have now said enough on the subject of proper selection of the matter from which poems are put together, and how they are to be put together.

A QUESTION ON THE NATURE OF POETRY[71]

⟨1⟩ Question. Whether poetry differs from other parts of logic.

First of all, [it is said] not to differ from rhetoric, because they are both directed towards the same end, namely, that virtuous acts should be pursued and vices shunned, as is clear by the way of proceeding which they both share.

Likewise, the way and mode of procedure is the same in both cases [i.e. in poetry and logic] in as much as they both proceed by syllogisms based on symbols (*signa*) and by discourses intended to affect the emotions, as is clear from the second discussion of this second book [of the *Poetics* as translated by Hermann the German].[72]

Likewise, it does not seem to differ from treatises on subject-matter (*topica*), because both are concerned with things that do not fall under necessary laws.[73]

---

[69] The story of Abraham and his son Isaac is told in the Koran, xxxvii. 98–113. Cf. above, n. 64.

[70] Cf. the importance of the voluntary nature of the action in Averroes' version of the doctrine of catharsis, cited and discussed above, pp. 285–6.

[71] Tr. from G. Dahan, 'La poétique au moyen âge', pp. 214–9, with the permission of G. Dahan and Librairie Philosophique J. Vrin.

[72] *De arte poetica cum Averrois expositione*, ed. Minio-Paluello, p. 64; 'Averrois Cord. comm. med.', ed. Boggess, pp. 61–2; tr. Hardison in *Classical and Medieval Literary Criticism*, pp. 371–2. Cf. Aristotle's *Rhetorica*, ii. 1–18, 20–6 (1377ᵇ–1392ᵃ, 1393ᵃ–1403ᵇ).

[73] Literally 'are concerned with contingent things'.

Likewise, it does not differ from demonstrative logic, because demonstrative logic argues to a delimited effect simply from delimited causes: the nature of poetry is the same, as is clear from the course of this first book [of the *Poetics*].[74]

The opposite position [i.e. that poetry does differ from the other parts of logic] is clear from Aristotle and his commentator [i.e. Averroes], in his second book [of the *Poetics*], in the first chapter about the appropriate size of poems.[75]

The response to the question is that poetry differs from each one of the parts of logic, and constitutes a special part of logic.

⟨2⟩⟨a⟩ To prove this it must be noted that logic as a whole is concerned with concepts formed through the action of reason in its acts.[76] Therefore, since the sciences are divided up by their various objects (as is said in book iii of *On the Soul*),[77] that is, the sciences are distinguished as a consequence of the division of their objects, it is reasonable that the parts of logic should be distinguished according to the concepts expressed in words which correspond to the acts of the reason. Let us leave aside the act of the intellect which apprehends simple facts, and the act which in turn synthesizes or analyses the fact that has been thus apprehended, and the act which moves back and forward by argument from one thing to another under a common heading, and the concepts expressed in words corresponding to these acts, which are treated in the books of the *Praedicamenta*, the *Perihermenias*, and the *Prior Analytics*.

⟨b⟩ We can then say about the argumentation back and forward of the reason in particular that, either the intellect guides the movement of its argument and forms concepts compatible with the argument that has been so directed, in so far as the reason is distinct from the lower powers of the soul; or else, just as is done by them [i.e. the lower powers] in their actions, sometimes it moves those lower powers, and sometimes it is moved by them, as is clear from the third book of *On the Soul*, in the chapter on moving power.[78] As regards the first way of directing its acts, the intellect is called speculative; as regards the second, it is called practical. The matters on which the intellect speculates are sometimes necessary,[79] sometimes contingent.[80] The concept which is called

---

[74] i.e. poetry aims at achieving a determined effect (namely, to arouse an emotion), proceeding from precise causes (namely, poetic arguments); cf. the part of Hermann's translation which corresponds to *Poetics*, iii–iv, tr. above, pp. 292–4 (ed. Minio-Paluello, pp. 44–5; ed. Boggess, pp. 9–12).

[75] i.e. in the part of Hermann's work which corresponds to *Poetics*, vii; tr. above, pp. 297–8 (ed. Minio-Paluello, p. 50; ed. Boggess, pp. 26–7).

[76] For discussion of this doctrine see Dahan, 'La poétique au moyen âge', p. 210.

[77] *De anima*, iii. 8 (431ᵇ); cf. Moerbeke, tr. Foster–Humphries (op. cit. n. 28), p. 453.

[78] *De anima*, iii. 10 (433ᵃ); cf. Moerbeke, tr. Foster–Humphries, pp. 468–9.

[79] Matters relating to logical, physical, and metaphysical necessity; fixed laws.

[80] The results of free choices or accidental causes.

demonstrative syllogism corresponds to the direction of the process of reasoning as regards necessary matters, and knowledge of this concept is imparted in the book of the *Posterior Analytics*. The topical syllogism corresponds to the direction of the process of the speculative intellect as regards contingent matters, and this is taught in the eight books of the *Topics*.

⟨c⟩ As regards the direction of the act of the intellect in its practical form, such a distinction between the necessary and the contingent is not appropriate, since all those matters in relation to which the intellect is practical are contingent, and may or may not occur. And therefore one must divide up the logical concepts which correspond to acts of the practical intellect according to the different sorts of contingents in relation to which a man is acting. Man acts as regards both himself and others through an understanding that combines imagination and the faculty of desire.[81] Therefore, to make the logic complete, one must teach the method whereby the faculty of desire might be guided by reason, in relation to both himself and others. The persuasion of rhetoric, or rhetorical logic, relates to the act of the intellect in respect of the faculty of desire in so far as it is directed towards others. For it, because of the large number of people whom anyone addresses, is cut down to the example and the enthymeme.[82] Therefore, because men live with each other through mutual trust, that is called persuasion which is intended to produce trust in another. But poetic persuasion relates to the act of the intellect in respect of the faculty of desire through which a man is guided in himself. Because everyone has most trust in his own instinctive estimations and relies particularly on his own imaginings, poetic discourse or poetic syllogism is therefore called by the Philosopher 'imaginative'.[83]

⟨3⟩ Because all things which relate to the life of a community have to be watched over by judges and rulers, and those things are concerned with the act of justice—an act which in a sense is judicially dispensed, with some degree of compulsion, to inferiors by superiors—therefore rhetorical persuasion is said most of all to have its place in the sphere of judicial acts. But in his own private domain any person is his own judge and master, providing he does not annoy those with whom he lives. So, poetic composition relates to acts which are private and more on the voluntary

---

[81] Cf. the passage from *De anima*, iii. 10 (433ᵃ), cit. above, n. 78.

[82] Cf. above, n. 15, and Giles of Rome's commentary on the texts there cited, *Rhet. Aris. cum Egidii comm.*, fos. 2ᵛ–4ᵛ, 8ʳ, part of the argument of which is summarized by Brother S. Robert, 'Rhetoric and Dialectic', pp. 494–5. Cf. Ch. VI, n. 150, and the extract from Giles's *On the Instruction of Princes* tr. above, pp. 248–50, with which the present text should be compared; also the similar view of Robert Kilwardby, as summarized by D. E. Sharp, 'The *De ortu scientiarum* of Robert Kilwardby (died 1279)', *New Schol.* viii (1934), 26–7.

[83] No statement of this kind is found in Aristotle's authentic works; it seems to refer to the transformation, in the Averroistic tradition, of the notion of imitation: 'Poetic forms of speech are based on images' ('sermones poetici sunt ymaginativi'). Cf. above, p. 289.

side. So, because a man is most praised for voluntary acts if these are
honourable,[84] and reviled if they are dishonourable, the major part of
poetic discourse is concerned with praise and blame, as the Philosopher
writes in the first chapter of this first book [of the *Poetics*].[85]

⟨4⟩[86] But because, as well ordained laws teach us, it is required for the
common good that no one should mismanage what is his own, and that
even the public good is shared in by the good of each community,[87] therefore rhetorical persuasion in some way descends to the bestowal of praise
and vituperation, while poetic composition sometimes rises to the level of
judicial acts. And it is no wonder that one part of the mode of proceeding
relating to acts of the practical intellect mingles with the other part,
because of the close interconnection between the two objects to which
they [i.e. the two parts of the mode of proceeding] are applied. For even in
speculation relating to contingents,[88] in some sense—even though only
feebly—there is proof (*demonstratio*), while sometimes we introduce an
opinion topically (*topice*) even though it concerns an outstanding necessity, as the Commentator writes on the first book of *Concerning Heaven and
Earth*, where Aristotle puts forward [the theory of] the eternity of movement on the evidence of others.[89] In fact—and this may seem even more
amazing—the speculative faculty descends to the practical, since we are
taught in the second book of the *Posterior Analytics* how in practical
matters proof has to be made starting with the end-purpose.[90] But this

---

[84] i.e. he wins poetic praise for honourable actions which he is not obliged to perform by
law.

[85] i.e. the part of Hermann's work which corresponds to ch. i of Aristotle's *Poetics*, tr.
above, p. 289 (ed. Minio-Paluello, pp. 42–3; ed. Boggess, pp. 3–7).

[86] Because of the difficulties presented by this section we offer the following breakdown
and elaboration of its main arguments. (1) As the two parts of the mode of logical procedure
relating to acts of the practical intellect (which acts fall within ethics and politics), rhetoric
and poetic are interconnected to the extent that it is difficult to distinguish the two. (They will
be distinguished in part ⟨5⟩ of the *quaestio*, below.) (2) Rhetoric concerns acts affecting the
common good and acts that may be subject to legal judgements: the rhetorician must attempt,
by persuasion, to (for example) change the mind and heart of a wrongdoer, or to influence the
decision of a judge. Hence, praise and blame are central to its operations (as Cicero makes
clear in *De inventione*). (3) Some sort of *demonstratio* is sometimes adduced even with regard to
free acts (contingents); sometimes a purely topical approach is made to matters that in themselves must be (or must not be) the case. The example of Aristotle is noteworthy, for he
approaches the matter of the eternity of the world demonstratively, for the most part, yet at
one point he makes a topical approach to it. (4) The speculative and practical intellects cannot be rigidly separated, either in logic or in the sciences of reality. As regards the latter,
building, for example, includes mathematics, which is theoretical, whereas metaphysics
(theoretical) could be approached in the hope of obtaining direction concerning one's way of
life (practical).

[87] i.e. the more restricted community, family, etc.

[88] Cf. above, n. 80.

[89] Cf. Averroes, *Comm. in De caelo*, i. 10 (279ª4–280ª34), in *Aristotelis omnia opera ... Averrois
Cordubensis in ea opera omnes commentarii* (Venice, 1560–2), v. 73ᵛ–74ʳ.

[90] Here Dahan refers us to Averroes' *Epitome in libros logicae Aristotelis*, in *Aristotelis opera*, ii
(Venice, 1562), fo. 61ʳ.

exchange of roles and reciprocity is found not only in the case of the method of cognition and the process of reasoning which logic teaches. Indeed, in the sciences of reality too, a specifically practical science (such as building or any similar one) could be learnt with a speculative end in view, since it contains something of speculation; and a specifically speculative science (such as metaphysics) could be learnt with a practical end in view, as for instance if someone, having through metaphysics learnt matters relating to what he was doing, were to think that he would thereby carry out that business more wisely.

⟨5⟩ If the matters which I have up to now treated diffusely are considered, three things become apparent: first of all, what the art of poetry has as its subject; secondly, how it differs from all the other arts and sciences, and third, what degree of necessity, order, and usefulness obtains among the parts of philosophy. For it has for its subject a concept formed by the act of reason, a concept which answers to the process of practical reason relating to the acts of a man concerning himself—although, as has been said, it can be extended to certain other things.

And from this, secondly, the answer to what was the principal question is clear, that it does indeed differ, and how it differs, from the individual parts not just of logic but of philosophy as a whole. For it differs from all sciences of reality because it does not delimit any one thing for itself, but deals with a method of treatment which is applicable to many things.[91] Therefore, it is regarded as a part of logic. But it differs from the more basic parts of logic such as the *predicamenta*, the *perihermeneias*, and the prior analytics.[92] For the teaching imparted here [i.e. in poetry] in some way settles the things which are treated in these other [parts of logic]. It differs from the science of the posterior analytics and the topics, for poetry is more applicable to moral realities where they [i.e. the analytics and topics] are more applicable to speculative objects. It differs from both [these sciences of logic][93] in its degree of certainty.

But it differs from rhetoric because, even though both sciences teach the pursuit of virtuous ways and the avoidance of evil ones, rhetoric lays down guidelines in relation to actions which are subject to justice, and to compulsion, but poetry in relation to acts that are more of a voluntary nature. Rhetoric is more concerned with the way of living with special reference to the other [person], poetry more with reference to the self. Rhetoric begets trust,[94] but poetry esteem, as will be clear below. The

[91] See esp. Giles of Rome's commentary on the *Rhetoric*, i (*Rhet. Aris. cum Egidii comm.*, fos. 6ᵛ–7ʳ).
[92] Here the writer seems to intend branches of logic rather than the Aristotelian works so named, the *predicamenta* being the highest predicates applicable to real things or individuals and the *perihermeneias* comprising the study of propositions.
[93] i.e. it differs from the *predicamenta*, *perihermeneias* and prior analytics on the one hand, and from the posterior analytics and the topics on the other.
[94] i.e. credence; the successful orator is believed.

purpose of rhetoric is to make the opposing side abandon vice by van-
quishing it. But the purpose of poetry is to win its listeners to the practice
of virtue through praise and encouragement.

So, if poetry should happen to employ a tone of reproving rebuke in
order that thus it may recall men from vice, it does so in imitation of the
satirists and not following its own poetic purpose. If, moreover, it should
happen to persuade its hearers to believe the story it tells by employing
emotional language, it does so through having an affinity with rhetoric.

From all this, then, the relationship of poetry to the other parts of logic
is clear. For, since in some sense the right process of reason is aimed at
[in poetry], as far as the subject-matter to which it is applied permits, it is
clear that, along with the other parts of logic which observe the correct
process of reason, it precedes the book *On Sophistic Refutations*, in which
we are taught to avoid sheer sophistry and the failures of each process of
the reason, but [it] comes after all the others on the scale of certainty. But
in particular it comes after the book of the *Rhetoric* and is immediately
joined to it. It is indeed closely linked to rhetoric, since it may be directed
to the same common end. But it comes after rhetoric, because the
common good, which is aimed at by means of rhetoric, is more important
than the good of the individual, which is aimed at by means of poetry. Just
as twisted pieces of wood are guided so that they may become straight, as
is clear from the second book of the *Ethics*,[95] so it would seem that citizens
have to be drawn away from injustice by means of judicial acts, which is
achieved by rhetoric, and then and only then are [they] to be encouraged
by means of poetic praises to the practice of virtues which relate to individuals.

It is likewise clear from what has been said that rhetoric is not an
adequate method of proceeding in moral matters. Therefore, the added
help which poetry contributes to complement logic would appear to be a
useful and necessary part of it.

And although the parts of logic which can be applied to a subject which
can form the basis of speculation may be more honourable and more
exact, yet those parts which guide morality appear to be more useful to
the common life of the populace. For among ordinary folk error arises
more often from a perversion of desire than from *naïveté* of understanding. And, among the parts of logic which can be applied to morality,
rhetoric is more worthy and divine, for it concerns more closely the common good. For, although in a judicial action the end in view may be victory for one side [or the other], yet this is an instrument in urging the
common good of all citizens. But poetry seems more useful for educating
anyone individually to live by what is right, in matters where the rule is
not a legal obligation. For worst of all is the man who employs malice
against his true self, as is written in the fifth book of the *Ethics*.[96]

[95] *Eth. Nicomach.* ii. 9 (1109^{b}5–7).   [96] Ibid. v. 3 (1130^{a}5–7).

⟨6⟩ Thus, the difference between poetry and all the other parts of philosophy is clear, which was the principal matter under discussion. This difference enables us to answer the [four] objections.[97]

In answer to the first [objection], we say that the arts are not differentiated by the ends which they have in common but by their own particular ends, and those which relate most closely to them, as is clear from the preface to the first book of the *Ethics*.[98] But the particular ends proper to rhetoric and poetry are distinguished, as is clear from what has already been said, even though they share a common end.

A similar reply is made to the second [objection].

A similar reply is made to the third [objection]. It must be said that the two sciences are not applied to the same goal specifically, nor in the same way, as has been seen, although the one may be applied to the field of the other reciprocally, as has been said.

The fourth [objection] must be solved by applying an old solution. For poetry, like any art that can be applied to another [art], can be considered as teaching the ways in which the subordinate type can be affected, just like the proofs which teach the nature of the demonstrative syllogism and the ways in which it can be affected. In another way it can be considered as using (*utens*), and in this way it differs completely from the demonstrative part of logic in degree of certainty, as has been said: demonstrative logic, applied to other things, becomes instrumental in making a science about them; but poetic logic produces a certain weak attraction which merely inclines someone to desire something or to avoid something.

---

[97] i.e. the four statements, made at the beginning of this *quaestio*, to the effect that poetry does not differ from the other parts of logic.

[98] *Eth. Nicomach.* i. 1 (1094ᵃ1–18).

VIII

Updated Approaches to the Classics: William of Aragon, Nicholas Trevet, Giovanni del Virgilio, and Pierre Bersuire

HENRI D'ANDELI'S worries that grammar (and hence the study of the classics) had been ousted by logic were somewhat exaggerated, as is witnessed by the materials collected in this chapter. The classification of poetry under logic (which has been described in Ch. VII) was generally accepted and developed in commentaries on the classics produced in the late thirteenth century and in the fourteenth century. For instance, an anonymous Ovid commentary explains that in general the *forma tractandi* comprises a 'fivefold mode, that is, dividing, defining, providing examples, proving, refuting, and inferring', while in particular the *Metamorphoses* has a threefold mode, 'that is, dividing, defining, and providing examples'.[1] Similarly, Giovanni del Virgilio describes Ovid's mode of treatment in that work as being multiple because it 'offers definitions, is discursive and inferential', and so forth. Here logical concepts are being employed in a loose sense, certainly, but without any feeling that their application is incongruous.

These comments form part of the discussions of the formal causes of literary texts: the 'Aristotelian Prologue' (as defined above in Ch. VI) is frequently found at the beginning of expositions of the classics. Two sophisticated examples, by Nicholas Trevet and Giovanni del Virgilio, are offered below. Within the new conceptual frameworks many traditional glosses continued to be transmitted—Giovanni del Virgilio's account of the 'three forms of metamorphosis' being a case in point—and certain interpretative systems which were well established in the twelfth century received further adaptation and amplification, as in the fourfold method of interpreting pagan fables used by Pierre Bersuire. In these and other respects the impression given is one of continuity rather than of demise or sharp diminution. Until more work is carried out on the scale and provenance of such scholarship as did exist, and also on the influence of certain popular 'classicizing' reference-books, Bible commentaries, and *exempla* collections, and of course the mythographies, we should be wary of following Henry d'Andeli down the path of gloomy generalization.

However, there does seem to have been a shift of emphasis within the commentary-tradition, as new textbooks, often the work of medieval writers, were introduced into the grammar curriculum, books like the *De contemptu mundi* (falsely ascribed to St Bernard), the *Tobias* of Matthew of Vendôme, the *Parvum doctrinale* or *Liber parabolarum* of Alan of Lille, and the *Floretus Sancti Bernardi*.[2] The large corpus of glosses on the 'teaching-collections' (such as the

[1] Cit. Allen, *Ethical Poetic*, p. 73.
[2] On these texts see N. Orme, *English Schools in the Middle Ages* (London, 1973),

sex auctores and *octo auctores*) has largely been neglected in our day, medievalists being attracted rather by the commentaries on the classics, although it is clear that they offer a major source for our study of the fundamental literary attitudes and ideas in vogue during the later Middle Ages. To the historian of literary criticism a commentary on, say, Alan of Lille's *Liber parabolarum*[3] may yield information as fruitful as that which he may discover in a commentary on Ovid. This major caveat having been entered, we may now proceed to illustrate the way in which the classics (Boethius' *Consolation of Philosophy* having been included among their ranks, in deference to medieval sensibilities) were interpreted in the later Middle Ages.

We offer below two updated approaches to *The Consolation of Philosophy* and two to the *Metamorphoses*, and also an application of the latest conceptual frameworks and analytical techniques to works which no medieval scholar had commented on before, the tragedies of the younger Seneca. The first scholar represented below, William of Aragon, is a shadowy figure. Recently it has been discovered that the prologue to his Boethius commentary was drawn on in the prologues to two Old French translations of *The Consolation of Philosophy*. The first version, edited by R. Schroth and judged by K. Atkinson to come from somewhere in medieval Hainault (probably the region of Mons), was produced in the late thirteenth century, and the second, by Jean de Meun, is generally supposed to have been completed shortly before his death in 1305.[4] Hitherto most scholars, following Pierre Courcelle, had assumed that William of Aragon had written his commentary in 1335; this dating depends on a misreading of the colophon in the only manuscript of the work known to Courcelle, Erfurt, Wissensch. Bibl., Amplon. F. 358.[5] Supporting evidence for the earlier dating of William of Aragon is afforded by M. L. Colker's analysis of another work attributed to him, the *De nobilitate animi*: on the basis of internal evidence and the dates of its manuscripts he assigned it to the 'second half of the thirteenth century'.[6] William may have had some interest in the vernacular—the *De nobilitate animi* contains Latin translations of extracts from troubadour poets[7]—but the

pp. 103–4. See further Tony Hunt's study of the vernacular glosses appearing in the school books, *Teaching and Learning Latin in 13th Century England: Texts and Glosses* (Woodbridge, 1991).

[3] On this text, with special reference to its Old French translators, see T. Hunt, 'Une traduction partielle des *Parabolae* d'Alain de Lille', *Le Moyen Âge*, lxxxvii (1981), 45–56; id., 'Les Paraboles Maistre Alain', *Forum for Modern Language Studies*, xxi no. 4 (1985), 362–75.

[4] See R. Crespo, 'Il prologo alla traduzione della *Consolatio philosophiae* di Jean de Meun e il commento di Guglielmo d'Aragonia', in W. den Boer *et al.* (eds.), *Romanitas et Christianitas: Studia I. H. Waszink oblata* (Amsterdam and London, 1973), pp. 55–70; R. Schroth, *Eine altfranzösische Übersetzung der 'Consolatio philosophiae' des Boethius (HS Troyes 898)* (Bern and Frankfurt, 1976), pp. 80–3.

[5] P. Courcelle, *La Consolation de la philosophie dans la tradition littéraire: Antécédents et postérité de Boèce* (Paris, 1967), pp. 321–3, 414; followed by C. I. Terbille, 'William of Aragon's Commentary on Boethius' *De consolatione philosophiae*' (unpub. Ph.D. thesis, University of Michigan, 1972), i. 24–5.

[6] M. L. Colker, 'De nobilitate animi', *Med. Stud.* xxiii (1961), 50. For the identification of William of Aragon as its author see M. Thomas, 'Guillaume d'Aragon auteur du *Liber de nobilitate animi*', *BEC* cvi (1945/6), 70–9.

[7] See A. Thomas, 'Le *Liber de nobilitate animi* et les troubadours', *Studi medievali*, NS ii (1929), 163–72.

Old French Boethius prologues seem to be following William's Latin rather than the other way round. In the present state of our knowledge, then, we can tentatively claim William of Aragon as the first 'Aristotelian' commentator on Boethius, a position which for long has been allocated to Nicholas Trevet, the other Boethian commentator represented below.

The Dominican Nicholas Trevet (d. *c.* 1334), who studied and taught at Oxford (*c.* 1303–7, and again in 1314), Paris, and London, was an exceptional classicist.[8] Apart from the younger Seneca's tragedies, no medieval scholar had tackled before the elder Seneca's *Declamations* (i.e. *Controversiae*), Livy's *Ab Urbe condita*, or Augustine's *De civitate Dei*. In addition, he expounded the Psalter[9] and the pseudo-Boethian *De Disciplina scholarium*, and perhaps wrote on Cicero, Juvenal, and Virgil's *Aeneid* (these last commentaries having been lost). Recently a commentary on Virgil's *Bucolics* has been attributed to him.[10] The range of his scholarship is as unusual as is its quality.

Turning now to our updated approaches to Ovid, Giovanni del Virgilio's reading of the *Metamorphoses* is a symptom of cultural change in late medieval Italy. 'We find hardly any commentary on a Latin poet or prose writer composed in Italy prior to the second half of the thirteenth century,' as P. O. Kristeller says; that was the period in which classical scholarship, inspired by French precedents, began to put down strong roots in Italian soil.[11] 'It was only after the beginning of the fourteenth century that the teaching of poetry and the classical authors became firmly established in the Italian schools and universities,'[12] and Giovanni del Virgilio was one of the first of the new generation of classicists. In November 1321, at the request of the student body, he was hired by the city government at Bologna to give lectures on Virgil, Statius, Lucan, Ovid, and on any other authors (not exceeding two per year) that the students might nominate. In April 1323 Giovanni was assaulted and wounded; he moved to Cesena. Back in Bologna by March 1326, he does not appear to have taken up teaching again, and nothing is known of his whereabouts after 1327.[13] The appellation 'del Virgilio' was earned when Giovanni became known as an admirer of and commentator on Virgil. Although this commentary has not survived, the Dante commentator Benvenuto da Imola

---

[8] On Trevet's life and works see A. B. Emden, *A Biographical Register of the University of Oxford to A.D. 1500* (Oxford, 1957–9), pp. 1902–3; R. J. Dean, 'The Life and Works of Nicholas Trevet with special reference to his Anglo-Norman Chronicle' (unpub. D. Phil. thesis, University of Oxford, 1938); ead., 'The Earliest Known Commentary on Livy', *Med. et hum.* iii (1945), 86–98; F. Ehrle, *Nikolaus Trivet, sein Leben, seine Quodlibet und quaestiones ordinarie* (*BGPTM*, suppl. ii, Münster, 1923); B. Smalley, *English Friars and Antiquity in the Early Fourteenth Century* (Oxford, 1960), pp. 58–65.

[9] Ed. B. P. Shields, *Comment. lit. in Ps.*

[10] See A. A. Nascimento, 'Um comentador medieval das Bucólicas de Virgílio: Nicolau Trivet', *Euphrosyne*, xi (1981/2), 180–6. But this attribution has proved to be controversial.

[11] 'Humanism and Scholasticism in the Italian Renaissance', in *Renaissance Thought and its Sources*, p. 96; cf. Greenfield, *Humanist and Scholastic Poetics*, pp. 18 ff.

[12] Kristeller, 'Humanism and Scholasticism', pp. 96–7.

[13] These biographical details follow F. Ghisalberti, 'Giovanni del Virgilio espositore delle *Metamorfosi*', *Giornale Dantesco*, xxxiv (1933), 1–5; Guido Martellotti, 'Giovanni del Virgilio', in *ED* iii. 193–4.

does refer to one of Giovanni's glosses on Virgil.[14] It seems reasonable to assume that his writings on Ovid, which took the form of two closely related commentaries, the *Expositio* and the *Allegorie*, date from roughly the same period as his Ovid lectures, namely 1322–3. The two texts may have been written in parallel, since at one point in the *Expositio* Giovanni refers us to a relevant passage of the *Allegorie*, and, of course, it was customary to follow a literal exposition with an allegorical one.[15] Giovanni also entered into poetic correspondence with a certain ser Nuzio of the Marches, an exchange known as the *Diaffonus*, and with the celebrated Paduan proto-humanist Albertino Mussato. Several other Latin verse exchanges are attributed to him, along with an epic fragment (43 hexameters) and an epitaph for Dante,[16] and he is also credited with an *ars dictaminis* which he would have employed in his work as a university teacher.[17] Nowadays he is chiefly remembered for his exchange of eclogues with Dante (see below, p. 440).

The world of the Benedictine monk Pierre Bersuire (who died in 1362)[18] was a very different one, although there was one point of contact. Some time just before 1340, Bersuire, then a member of the household of the papal vice-chancellor Pierre des Prés, visited Francis Petrarch, then living near Avignon.[19] Petrarch was composing his *Africa*, and was sufficiently impressed by his guest (whom he later described as 'a man distinguished in religion and in letters')[20] to allow him not only to see the work in progress but also to copy from it a passage for his own use.[21] Since *c.* 1320 Bersuire had been working on an amplified and moralized version of the *De proprietatibus rerum* which Bartholomaeus Anglicus had compiled in the third decade of the thirteenth century.[22] At Avignon he

---

[14] See Ghisalberti, op. cit., pp. 3–4; Martellotti, p. 193.

[15] For the cross-reference see Ghisalberti, op. cit., p. 5. Three of the four *Expositio* MSS listed by Ghisalberti also contain (in later folios) a text of the *Allegorie*. Six further MSS contain texts of the *Allegorie*, and seven others draw upon the *Allegorie* for marginal glosses (ibid., pp. 39–42).

[16] For texts and translations, see P. H. Wicksteed and E. G. Gardner, *Dante and Giovanni del Virgilio* (Westminster, 1902); E. Bolisani and M. Valgimigli, *La Corrispondenza poetica di Dante Alighieri e Giovanni del Virgilio* (Florence, 1963).

[17] This was discovered at Naples by P. O. Kristeller, 'Un *ars dictaminis* di Giovanni del Virgilio', *Italia medioevale e umanistica*, iv (1961), 181–200.

[18] On Bersuire's life and works see F. Ghisalberti, 'L'Ovidius moralizatus di Pierre Bersuire', *Studi Romanzi*, xxiii (1933), 5–136; R.-A. Meunier, 'L'humaniste Pierre Bersuire', *Bulletin de la Société des Antiquaires de l'Ouest*, 3rd ser., xiv (1948), 511–32; C. Samaran and J. Monfrin, 'Pierre Bersuire', *HLF* xxxix (1962), 259–450; J. Engels, 'Berchoriana, I', in *Vivarium*, ii (1964), 62–124; also M. Twycross's review of the Engels Bersuire edition in *Medium Aevum*, xxxvii (1968), 320–3.

[19] On this meeting see esp. E. H. Wilkins, 'Descriptions of Pagan Deities from Petrarch to Chaucer', *Speculum*, xxii (1957), 511–22.

[20] *Lettere senili*, xvi. 7, ed. G. Fracassetti (Florence, 1869–70), ii. 504. Here Bersuire is referred to as 'Peter of Poitiers', as in the two *Letters on Familiar Matters* which Petrarch addressed to him (tr. S. Bernardo, *Francesco Petrarca: Rerum familiarium libri xvii–xxiv* (Baltimore, Md., and London, 1985), pp. 240–53).

[21] i.e. Petrarch, *Africa*, iii. 138–264; see *Petrarch's Africa*, tr. T. G. Bergin and A. S. Wilson (New Haven, Conn., and London, 1977), pp. 45–9.

[22] John Trevisa's Middle English translation of Bartholomaeus has recently been edited by M. C. Seymour *et al.*, *On the Properties of Things* (Oxford, 1975).

produced what was to become the fifteenth book of the *Moral Reduction*, a moralized *Metamorphoses*; a moralized Bible was to form the sixteenth and last book. Bersuire was dissatisfied with the Avignon version of book xv, possibly completed by 1340. By 1350 he was living in Paris and had access to the Old French *Ovide moralisé* (written between 1316 and 1328)[23] and John Ridevall's *Fulgentius metaforalis* (before 1333); material from these two works was incorporated into the second redaction (or the 'Paris text') of his *Ovid Moralized*, which must have been completed by 1362, the year of Bersuire's death.[24] This part of the *Moral Reduction* circulated independently of the rest of the work, which it far outstripped in popularity. In 1509 Jodocus Badius Ascensius revised and printed the Avignon version, under the name of Thomas Waleys.[25] The second redaction may have been the main source of the portraits of the pagan deities included in Chaucer's *Knight's Tale*, and John Gower and John Lydgate seem to have known Bersuire's work in some form.[26]

Boethius Aristotelianized. 'Let us not impute to Boethius the crimes of the Platonists', exclaims William of Aragon, 'for he knew Aristotle very well.'[27] His commentary on *The Consolation of Philosophy* is an original work which attempts to break away from the tradition of Neoplatonic interpretation which came to him through glosses deriving from William of Conches (on whom see above, pp. 118–22). Neither was he content to simply follow the standard corpus of historical, mythical, and scientific explanations which had been handed down from one generation of scholars to the next; often he engaged in fresh research on new sources. His efforts, however, do not seem to have been much appreciated in the later Middle Ages, since only five manuscripts have so far come to light. By contrast, Nicholas Trevet's Boethius commentary, which is in many respects a thorough revision and updating of William of Conches's commentary on the same author, was something of a best-seller and survives in over a hundred manuscripts.[28]

According to Courcelle, Trevet plagiarized William's commentary on the *Consolation*, and in those few glosses which are truly his own he substituted Aristotelian interpretations for William's Neoplatonic statements with an 'unconcealed contempt' for the earlier scholar.[29] But the notion of plagiarism, which has its roots in post-Romantic notions of literary individuality, is

[23] On the *Ovide moralisé* see esp. Demats, pp. 61 ff.

[24] The first chapter of the Paris text, parts of which we translate below, has been edited and published by J. Engels and the Instituut voor Laat Latijn of Utrecht, *Petrus Berchorius, Reductorium morale, liber xv: Ovidius moralizatus, cap. i: De formis figurisque deorum* (Werkmateriaal III, Utrecht, 1966).

[25] Republished by J. Engels and the Instituut voor Laat Latijn of Utrecht, *Reductorium morale, liber xv. naar de druk van 1509; Metamorphosis Ouidiana moraliter a M. Thoma Walleys . . . explanata* (Werkmateriaal I–II, Utrecht, 1960–2).

[26] See M. Twycross, 'The Representation of the Major Classical Divinities in the Works of Chaucer, Gower, Lydgate and Henryson' (unpub. B. Litt. thesis, University of Oxford, 1961); ead., *The Medieval Anadyomene: A Study in Chaucer's Mythography* (Medium Aevum Monographs NS I, Oxford, 1972).

[27] *Comm. in De cons. phil.* III met. ix, in Terbille, ii. 135, cf. p. 129.

[28] Cf. Minnis, 'Aspects of the Medieval French and English Traditions', pp. 314, 318.

[29] Courcelle, *Consolation*, p. 319; echoed by Friedman, *Orpheus in the Middle Ages*, p. 110.

inappropriate to medieval traditions of commentary, in which each new generation of students sought to augment the doctrine channelled by their masters. And Trevet, as C. Jourdain declared as long ago as 1862, was by no means hostile to Neoplatonic ideas.[30] The strongest statement we have managed to find by Trevet concerning the 'Commentator' (as he refers to William of Conches, whose identity he seems not to have known) is that he and 'the expounders of the *Timaeus* . . . wrongly state (*fingunt*) that the World Soul is called the Holy Spirit'.[31] This can hardly count as 'contempt' since the *anima mundi* was that part of Plato's teaching which gave William the most trouble, being the most resistant to Christian interpretation: William himself had changed his mind on the subject on several occasions.[32] When Trevet identified the World Soul with the motive power of the twin heavenly spheres, he was carrying on a refining and ameliorizing process which had already gone a long way in the twelfth century. Although Trevet was thoroughly conversant with Aristotelian doctrine there is nothing in his entire commentary which corresponds to William of Aragon's attack on the *crimina Platonicorum*.

William of Aragon displays his credentials at the outset by commencing his prologue with a quotation from 'the Philosopher', Aristotle. This represents a secularization of a technique established by twelfth-century scriptural exegetes. Theologians like Peter Comestor, Peter of Poitiers, and Praepositinus had used what Beryl Smalley has called the 'sermon type' prologue: this begins with a text from the Bible, which is then applied to the contents of the book under discussion, just as preachers cited a scriptural passage at the beginning of their sermons.[33] This practice was standard in scriptural commentaries for at least the next two centuries, and secular commentaries were often introduced with a quotation from some major secular authority. Interestingly, Giovanni's *Expositio* of Ovid and Bersuire's *Ovid Moralized* both begin with a biblical quotation: honour is being bestowed on the pagan *Metamorphoses* by having it reflect, as it were, something of the glory of scriptural authority—a point to which we shall return.

The Boethius prologue of William of Aragon falls into two major parts. The second part, the 'intrinsic' discussion or the prologue concerning the book itself, offers a *vita auctoris* and a discussion of *intentio*, *utilitas*, and *modus tractandi* (the 'type C' prologue paradigm, as defined above, pp. 13–14, here being the determining factor rather than the type based on the four causes).[34] The *modus tractandi* analysis is of special interest as a development of the medieval theory of *persona*, a theory which we have already encountered in St Bonaventure's commentary on Ecclesiastes (cf. above, pp. 231–2). Boethius is said to

---

[30] 'Des Commentaires inédits', p. 66.

[31] *Comment. in De cons. phil.* III met. ix, studied in the unpub. edition by the late E. T. Silk. We are grateful to Professor Silk for providing a typescript of this edition for our use in the present anthology.

[32] Cf. Southern, *Platonism, Scholastic Method, and the School of Chartres*, pp. 21–5.

[33] Smalley, 'Peter Comestor on the Gospels', pp. 109–10; cf. Minnis, *Authorship*, p. 64.

[34] Jean de Meun's Old French version of this prologue is discussed with reference to *accessus* tradition by Glynnis Cropp, 'Le Prologue de Jean de Meun et *Le Livre de Boece de Consolacion*', *Romania*, ciii (1982), 278–98.

play the part of the troubled and passionate man, the sufferer, while Dame
Philosophy plays the part of the one who follows intelligible goods, the healer:
thus, the author speaks through two characters.[35] The first part of William's
introduction is an early example of an Aristotelian 'extrinsic prologue' which
views the hierarchy of goods—a subject discussed at length in books ii and iii of
the *Consolation*—in the light of Aristotle's teaching that all things seek the good
or final perfection which is appropriate to them.

Man's quest for the good is the subject of the Orpheus metre (book iii, met.
xii) as interpreted by William of Aragon, an exposition which differs in several
respects from the one which William of Conches had offered before him and
the one which Trevet (heavily influenced by William of Conches) was to offer
subsequently. For William of Conches Orpheus represented wisdom and eloquence whereas Eurydice was 'that natural concupiscence which is part of
every one of us'. Aristaeus, who stands for virtue (*ares* meaning 'excellence'),
pursued Eurydice because excellence always tries to raise human desire aloft
to earthly things. 'But Eurydice fled Aristaeus because desire struggles with
virtue, wishing its own pleasure which is contrary to the way of excellence.'[36]
Trevet updated this approach by interpreting Orpheus as the intellect (*intellectus*), which is taught in wisdom and eloquence, and Eurydice as the affections or disposition (*affectus*) of the will. Orpheus' ascent from the underworld
represents the difficult process wherein the affections 'must be drawn up
through the many delights which impede virtue when it would ascend'.[37] By
contrast, William of Aragon goes back to Fulgentius' etymology, which interprets Eurydice as 'good judgement',[38] and puts all the blame on the serpent
(representing debased desire) which bit her. The result is that here the
heroine gets a far better press than that afforded by the tradition channelled by
William of Conches and Trevet. But William of Aragon has to pay a price: he
must leave the moral sense of the ending of the story unexplained, presumably
because of the difficulty of finding anything blameworthy about eloquence
looking back at good judgement.[39] But medieval moralization, we should
remember, need not cover every detail of the fable which it is interpreting.
Incidentally, it is William of Aragon, and not Trevet (as J. B. Friedman suggested),[40] who seems to have been the first to introduce the serpent into commentary on the Orpheus metre from the Ovidian and Virgilian versions of the
legend.

[35] For Jean de Meun's translation of this interesting passage see the edition of *Li Livres de
confort* by V. L. Dedeck-Héry in *Med. Stud.* xiv (1952), 171. For his part, Nicholas Trevet distinguished between the *persona indigens*, the person in need of consolation, and the *persona
afferens*, the person effecting that consolation. The first metre of *De consolatione philosophiae* is
said to present the former, i.e. the sorrowing Boethius lamenting his misery in elegiac verses,
whereas the first prose presents the latter, i.e. Dame Philosophy.

[36] See Friedman, *Orpheus in the Middle Ages*, pp. 106–7, and cf. above, p. 121.

[37] See the text printed by Denton Fox, *The Poems of Robert Henryson* (Oxford, 1981),
pp. 385–6; cf. Friedman, *Orpheus in the Middle Ages*, pp. 110–2.

[38] *Mit.* iii. 10 (ed. Helm, p. 77; tr. Whitbread, p. 96).

[39] But it must be emphasized that Giovanni del Virgilio did manage to find just that in his
Allegorie: see Friedman, *Orpheus in the Middle Ages*, pp. 122–3.

[40] Ibid., p. 114.

The Fulgentian interpretations of the main characters in the Orpheus story are followed by Giovanni del Virgilio as well, in his *Allegorie* on the *Metamorphoses*, and the serpent is identified, quite predictably, as the devil.[41] Pierre Bersuire, with typical thoroughness, affords many interpretations of Orpheus, in both good and bad senses, ranging from his being Christ who leads the human soul to Himself and reverses man's fall from Eden, to being a sinner who lost his soul by the temptation of the devil when 'she' was applying her mind to the flux of earthly things.[42]

Ovid Allegorized. Giovanni del Virgilio and Bersuire, in their different ways, developed the system of secular allegory which had been well established by twelfth-century French grammarians (see above, Ch. IV), and consolidated its prestige by reference to the highest of all authorities, God, and the divinely inspired *auctores* of Scripture. Giovanni applies to his pagan text the notion of the 'double efficient cause' which for generations had been used in Bible commentaries (cf. above, pp. 198–9). The 'moved' efficient cause is of course Ovid, who wrote the *Metamorphoses*, while the 'moving' efficient cause was God Himself, as Prime Mover. This position represents an interesting halfway point between the Thomistic segregation of scriptural metaphor from imaginative poetry ('the most lowly among all methods of instruction') on the one hand, and on the other the claim by later Italian scholars that literature was the result of exceptional, God-given gifts (as in the cases of Petrarch and Boccaccio) or even of divine inspiration (as in the cases of Mussato and Salutati).[43]

In his account of the 'moved efficient cause' of the Ovidian text Giovanni shows a marked interest in piecing together the life, times, and writings of his pagan author. Such an interest was shared by Arnulf of Orléans, the Ovidian commentator Giovanni owes most to. In Arnulf, however, this interest was developed sporadically through a number of prologues; in Giovanni it is concentrated into one continuous account that deserves to be termed 'biographical' in the strict sense of that term. Giovanni's Ovid biography was to be much appreciated by such later commentators as Benvenuto da Imola and Boccaccio; and this increased interest in biography as an aspect of commentary was to be vigorously developed by Boccaccio in his writings on Petrarch and Dante. Humanist scholars would also concern themselves with another, related theme that runs through Giovanni's prologue right to its concluding words on final cause: fame. Giovanni's friend Mussato had already received the poet's laurels at Padua; Petrarch was to be crowned in Rome in 1341, and several lesser talents would be similarly honoured thereafter. Giovanni's account of Ovid's thirst for fame is not without its ironic reservations, however: according to one account (Giovanni reports) Ovid grew so famous that he was suffocated by a crowd of admirers!

[41] Ibid., pp. 122–4.
[42] Ibid., pp. 126–32.
[43] Cf. Thomas Aquinas, *Sum of Theology*, Ia I, art. 9, tr. above, pp. 239–40; also above, pp. 9–11, and below, pp. 387–92, and the discussion by Hardison, *The Enduring Monument*, pp. 6–7, 11–18, and Greenfield, *Humanist and Scholastic Poetics, 1250–1500*, pp. 50ff.

Giovanni rounds out his prologue in familiar fashion by considering the work's title and the part of philosophy to which it belongs. He begins his literal exposition by analysing the opening verses of *Metamorphoses*, book i in minute detail. This is said to begin with a statement of purpose (ll. 1–2) and an invocation (ll. 2–4) before proceeding with its *narratio*, which may be divided into fifteen parts since it contains fifteen metamorphoses. The first of these is divided into two parts: chaos into elements, earth into man. The first of these two is divided again, and a detailed scientific explanation is offered for each subdivision. Following a series of disquisitions on scientific and geographical phenomena, Giovanni comes to his first human figure, Prometheus, and switches to a paraphrastic method that he adheres to for the remainder of the *Expositio*. The habit of making *divisiones* in the material is dropped after the first book. F. Ghisalberti argues that such a 'paraphrastic reduction of the story' does not merit the name of commentary.[44] But paraphrase is a perfectly legitimate aspect of commentary pursued at the literal level.

Giovanni's *Allegorie* alternates prose and verse. Each account of a *transmutatio* or metamorphosis opens in prose before switching to verse for anything between two and eighteen lines. Giovanni sometimes switches back to prose after several lines of verse, and he may then return to prose after that. Sometimes he assigns only a few lines of prose to a metamorphosis and does not employ verse at all. The chief source of Giovanni's prose is Arnulf of Orléans. He evidently worked with an Arnulfian manuscript on his desk; many of his allegorical expositions are straightforward expansions of Arnulf. Sometimes, however, Arnulf is put aside in favour of Fulgentius, the Vatican Mythographers, or John of Garland. It was, in fact, Garland's *Integumenta Ovidii* that provided the chief inspiration for Giovanni's verses.[45] But, although he relies heavily upon such sources, Giovanni does come up with some interpretations of the *Metamorphoses* that are, apparently, original. For example, the Giants (i. 152) are taken to represent men who run after riches, refusing to acknowledge God's existence. God strikes them down with a thunderbolt; they are transformed into apes, and hence rendered laughable and repellent. In general, Giovanni tends to favour allegorical accounts which have a highly accentuated religious content.

Prose is used to establish the most plausible account of a given metamorphosis; Giovanni then attempts to capture the essence of this account (and hence render it more memorable) in a few lines of verse. He must have read Arnulfian comments to which Latin verses (by John of Garland and others) had been added as marginal glosses, and evidently hit upon the idea of fusing both kinds of exposition into one continuous account. This decision to draw marginal glossing into the main body of the commentary parallels that taken by Guido da Pisa in his commentary on Dante (see below, pp. 447–9). Parallels between Guido and Giovanni (who were exact contemporaries) go

---

[44] See Ghisalberti, 'Giovanni del Virgilio', p. 10. Ghisalberti provides selective snippets from the *Expositio* in the introduction to his edition of the *Allegorie* (pp. 19–29).

[45] Giovanni borrows verses, distichs, or phrases from John of Garland on a number of occasions; ibid., pp. 35–6. John's text was edited by Ghisalberti (see ch. IV, n. 53).

further than this, however. Both writers were highly erudite Latinists: but neither of them is unremittingly serious. Giovanni, for example, finds space for a number of salacious anecdotes when describing pagan gods and goddesses. Modern critics have been somewhat disturbed by such frivolity in a man who corresponded with Dante.[46] Giovanni himself, however, saw stylistic and intellectual versatility as one of Dante's greatest strengths: his celebrated epitaph for Dante speaks of the poet as being at once 'the glory of the Muses' and 'the author most dear to the populace'.[47] Boccaccio maintained that Giovanni's was the best of the epitaphs known to him and he made it an integral part of his Dante biography. Boccaccio himself, of course, never enforced a rigid separation between learned commentary and story-telling. Perhaps modern critics are sometimes more narrow-minded and convention-bound than their medieval counterparts.

Pierre Bersuire did not attempt to claim God as the prime mover of the *Metamorphoses*; his innovative allegorizing was daring in a different way. St Paul's attack on fables in 2 Tim. 4: 4 is taken in the sense that, because people have turned away from the obvious truth and become interested in fables, the truth which those fables contain must be made manifest. Holy Scripture itself tacitly admits this principle when it concocts 'fables to demonstrate some truth'. Here Bersuire is taking an argument from St Augustine's *Against Lying* and standing it on its head: the Saint had certainly not been speaking in defence of the moral sense of classical literature.[48] Having twisted the waxen noses of his authorities in the direction which pleases him,[49] Bersuire proceeds to interpret the pagan deities as they were 'painted' by the ancients, and then moralizes all fifteen books of the *Metamorphoses*.

This notion of 'painting' goes back to the *Mythologiae* of Fulgentius at least; in his moralization of this work John Ridevall had used it extensively.[50] Ridevall, and Bersuire after him, were thinking of literary images rather than of visual art, whether paintings or statues: each and every 'picture' was the work of the poets (*pingitur a poetis*). These images are allegorized in a way

---

[46] Wicksteed–Gardner, *Dante and Giovanni del Virgilio*, p. 314, speak of Giovanni's Ovid commentary as something which 'falls in every respect below the level we should expect in Del Virgilio's work' (p. 314); it exemplifies a 'child-like style of allegorizing that asks no questions and is troubled by no anachronisms' (p. 316). Cf. Ghisalberti, 'Giovanni del Virgilio', pp. 9–10, 29–30.

[47] 'Gloria musarum, vulgo gratissimus auctor.' See *Trattatello in laude di Dante*, red. I, § 91, ed. P. G. Ricci in Boccaccio, *Opere*, iii. 459–60, where Boccaccio quotes the fourteen-line epitaph. Boccaccio there speaks of Giovanni as a 'most famous and great poet who had been a very special friend of mine'.

[48] *Contra mendacium*, xiii. 28 (CSEL xli. 511); cf. our discussion above, pp. 209–11.

[49] Here we borrow an idiom from Alan of Lille, who declared that an authority 'has a wax nose, which means that it can be bent into taking on different meanings' (PL ccx. 333A); cf. the discussion in Chenu, *Toward understanding St Thomas*, pp. 144–5.

[50] For discussion of the classicizers' 'pictures' see Smalley, *English Friars and Antiquity*, pp. 112–18, 123, 146–7, 165–83; F. Yates, *The Art of Memory* (repr. Harmondsworth, 1969), pp. 106–8; J. B. Allen, 'Commentary as Criticism', pp. 25–47; N. F. Palmer, '"Antiquitus depingebatur". The Roman Pictures of Death and Misfortune in the *Ackermann aus Böhmen* and *Tkadleček*, and in the writings of the Classicizing Friars', *Deutsche Vierteljahrsschrift für Literaturwissenschaft und Geistesgeschichte*, lvii (1983), 171–239.

which is encyclopaedic and structured. Arnulf of Orléans had approached the fables in the *Metamorphoses* allegorically, morally, and historically. Bersuire develops these twelfth-century categories into a comprehensive interpretative system which provides his putative audience of preachers with a moral for every conceivable occasion.

The four senses of poetic fiction according to Bersuire (*litteraliter*, *naturaliter*, *historialiter*, *spiritualiter*) are quite different from the four senses of Scripture according to the theologians. The literal reading is an astronomical/astrological one. Thus, Saturn, the first of the gods, is the first of the planets; he eats his sons in the sense that anyone who is born under Saturn rarely lives.[51] Mars is the hot and dry planet which governs a choleric disposition in man, while Diana or the moon, the seventh planet, is the source of all moisture (see the passages translated below). But, as Bersuire admits in the prologue to the *Ovid Moralized*, he has only 'very occasionally' provided this kind of interpretation. He had, after all, reiterated the planetary lore of Bartholomaeus Anglicus in the fifth book of the *Moral Reduction*. Naturally, the deities can be understood in terms of natural elements and processes. Juno signifies the upper air, which gives birth to Vulcan, i.e. the fire which we mortals have here on earth; Saturn is all-devouring time. The historical interpretation has its rationale in the euhemeristic theory of the origin of the gentile gods: historical personages like Saturn and Jupiter, with the passage of time, had come to be worshipped as gods, either through fear, misplaced reverence, or misunderstanding of their true nature.[52] The story of Perseus and the Gorgon may therefore be understood as a mythologized account of how a valiant soldier conquered a princess called Gorgona and used her riches to raise an army with which he conquered Atlas, the king of Africa. Exposition of the allegorical sense of fables entails moralization, and here Bersuire's imagination takes wing as he offers alternative interpretations both *in bono* and *in malo*. Diana, for example, may be taken as representing the Virgin Mary, the archetypically wicked woman, or Avarice. Bersuire seems to have been unable to think up an interpretation *in bono* for Mars, however, and contents himself with two explanations *in malo* (as worldly princes and tyrants, and as Discord). Such enthusiastic classicism is appealing, even if one wonders how many practising preachers found that it met their needs.

The Literal Significance of Senecan Tragedy. Nicholas of Prato, an Italian Dominican cardinal and dean of the Sacred College, urged Trevet (in the letter translated below) to make Seneca's tragedies accessible to the reader by clearing up obscurities, and in particular by explaining the fables which form the framework of the dramas. And this is precisely what he did, although, as he explains at the outset, in order to avoid prolixity he has not fully pursued all the *fabularum integumenta*. The result is a generally literal commentary, which

---

[51] *Ovidius moralizatus*, ed. Engels, p. 5. Cf. the discussion in A. J. Minnis, *Chaucer and Pagan Antiquity* (Cambridge, 1982), p. 14.

[52] See Cooke, 'Euhemerism'; also Twycross, 'Representation of the Major Classical Divinities', pp. 32–80.

concentrates on construing Seneca's Latin and providing plot-summaries of the stories to which allusion is made. Working off a single and deficient manuscript, which offered a text of the *A* family (whereas modern texts of Seneca make large use of manuscript *E*) and (apparently) not knowing any version of the *Poetics*, Trevet made the best he could of his limited resources.

Trevet's conception of Seneca's aims and methods is of particular interest. The 'final cause' of the *Hercules furens* is said to be to delight the audience— perhaps a surprising claim on the face of it, but, as Glending Olson has ably demonstrated, medieval physicians, philosophers, and poets often declared their belief that pleasure is necessary to the mind as sleep is to the body, and that the pleasures of literature can promote in us an inner harmony that fosters physical and mental health.[53] Alternatively, Trevet continues, the book can 'in a certain manner' (that qualification is significant) be classified under ethics, in which case 'its end is the correction of behaviour by means of the examples set out here'. One can understand why Trevet would wish to claim this objective for a famous philosopher who was supposed to have corresponded with St Paul. Having 'moved in the lofty realms of virtue' Seneca turned to fables in order to 'instil into tender minds ethical teachings' while 'at the same time amusing'. But the views of St Augustine on the classical theatre[54] proved something of a stumbling-block for this approach, as Trevet's General Prologue indicates. There the saint's condemnation of 'mythical' or 'poetic' theology, 'which relates to the theatre',[55] is admitted, but presented in the best possible light. Augustine, it is emphasized, was more critical of 'civil' theology which took place in temples—and in stating this position he cited the authority of Seneca himself. Better to imitate pagan rites, as in the theatre, than actually to perform them, as in temples! Trevet quickly passes on to consider the different parts of 'poetic theology', namely comedy and tragedy.

As a man of his time, he has a limited and confused notion of classical drama as performance art, whether on the stage or for recitation.[56] Hence, in the prologue to the *Hercules furens* a 'scene' (*scena*) is defined, in a way which elaborates on Isidore of Seville,[57] not as a division within a play but rather as a small edifice in the middle of the theatre in which the poet stood and recited

[53] See G. Olson, *Literature as Recreation in the Later Middle Ages* (Ithaca, NY, and London, 1982); more specifically, see Hugh of Saint-Victor's generally favourable attitude to theatrics (including gymnastics, dances, games, etc.) as expressed in *Didascalicon*, II. xxvii, where such entertainments are described as having been numbered 'among legitimate activities' by the ancients 'because by temperate motion natural heat is stimulated in the body and by enjoyment the mind is refreshed' (tr. Taylor, p. 79).

[54] See esp. *De civ. Dei*, I. xxxi–xxxii; II. viii–xiv, xxvii; VI. v–vi, for views quite the contrary of Hugh of Saint-Victor's as cited in our previous n. Similarly, Robert Kilwardby dismisses the theatrical art as being indecent and cruel, and therefore unfit for Christians. See D. E. Sharp, 'The *De ortu scientiarum* of Robert Kilwardby', 19.

[55] *De civ. Dei*, VI. v–vi.

[56] For medieval notions of classical theatre see the excellent article by M. H. Marshall, 'Theatre in the Middle Ages: Evidence from Dictionaries and Glosses', *Symposium*, iv (1950), 1–39, 366–89.

[57] *Ety.* XVIII. xliii. Cf. Boccaccio's use of this discussion in the *accessus* to his commentary on Dante, tr. below, p. 508.

his verses; outside were the actors who mimed the various events, adapting their gestures to suit the characters in whose persons the poet was speaking. A little earlier, Trevet refers us back to the account of the 'dramatic mode' provided in his General Prologue, this being a version of the commonplace distinction between three *scripturae characteres* or *modi recitandi*, the exegematic, the dramatic, and the mixed, which we have already encountered in an Introduction to Ovid's *Epistles* (cf. above, p. 23). In the *modus dramatis* the poet does not speak *in propria persona* but only through the characters he has created. Seneca is said to write in this dramatic way (specifically, in the tragic mode); moreover, his subjects are also tragic since they comprise the misfortunes of great men. Here Trevet is accommodating yet another piece of Isidoran lore,[58] a notion best known to students of literature in Chaucer's formulation:

> Tragedie is to seyn a certeyn storie,
> As olde bookes maken us memorie,
> Of hym that stood in greet prosperitee,
> And is yfallen out of heigh degree
> Into myserie, and endeth wrecchedly.

(The Prologue of the Monk's Tale, *Canterbury Tales*, VII. 1973–7).

But if Chaucer knew Isidore's definition (which, incidentally, Trevet had cited in his Boethius commentary, a work which Chaucer certainly knew),[59] there is no evidence that he knew Trevet's commentary on Seneca.[60] The latter circulated far more widely in France and Italy than in England, perhaps to some extent owing to the Italian patron who requested Trevet to expound Seneca.[61] In his Dante commentary Pietro Alighieri provided an account of the ancient theatre which is taken in part from Trevet's explanation of *scena* in his commentary on the *Hercules furens*,[62] as cited above.

Finally, a word on what Trevet did to Seneca's *Agamemnon*. In that play Seneca is not, in the main, aiming to teach men or correct their false values. He is, however, underlining certain ideas, and presenting them to his audience for their consideration, and these ideas do have an indirect bearing on human behaviour. These are old and hackneyed themes, for they occur as far back as the *Agememnon* of Aeschylus, though it should be noted that the most recent editor of that earlier play sees no evidence that Seneca used or was even

[58] *Ety.* xviii. xlv.

[59] Cf. Minnis, 'Aspects of the Medieval French and English Traditions', pp. 336–7, and see the relevant passage in his *Boece* II pr. 2, 70–2, discussed by Minnis, *Chaucer and Pagan Antiquity*, p. 27.

[60] *Pace* John Norton-Smith, *Chaucer* (London and Boston, 1974), pp. 165–9, who contends that Chaucer knew Trevet's Seneca commentary but fails to offer any substantial evidence.

[61] See R. Weiss, 'Notes on the Popularity of the Writings of Nicholas Trevet O.P. in Italy during the First Half of the Fourteenth Century', *Dom. Stud.* i (1948), 261–5; cf. R. J. Dean, 'Cultural Relations in the Middle Ages: Nicholas Trevet and Nicholas of Prato', *SP* xlv (1948), 541–64; ead., 'Life and Works of Trevet', pp. 171, 232–4, and *Medium Aevum*, x (1941), 161–8.

[62] See E. Franceschini, 'Glossi e commenti medievali a Seneca tragico', *Studi e note di filologia latina medievale* (Milan, 1938), pp. 11–12; cf. J. B. Bowden, *An Analysis of Pietro Alighieri's Commentary on the Divine Comedy* (New York, 1951), p. 50.

familiar with it. In Seneca's *Agamemnon* the fall of Troy, the captivity of the royal princess Cassandra, and the death of Agamemnon himself are all used to illustrate the impermanence of human power, which is stressed by the chorus (l. 57 onwards) and can be summed up by the epigrammatic words of Strophius, 'no happiness is of long duration' (l. 928). Another very obvious theme is that of vengeance: the vengeance exacted by Clytemnestra for Agamemnon's sacrifice of her daughter, and the vengeance which will be exacted on her in turn by Orestes. But Seneca's play is primarily a study of characters and how they react to each other: for instance, how the resolutely evil Aegisthus persuades Clytemnestra, who is wavering, to join in killing her husband. As R. J. Tarrant has put it succinctly in the introduction to his edition, much of the play is concerned with the reactions of the characters to Agamemnon's death.[63] Probably this is why Agamemnon himself is such an unimportant character. As in all his plays Seneca never misses a chance to introduce rhetorical features by stressing the extreme and bizarre elements in the situation.

Trevet does not comment on rhetoric and characterization. Nor does he have much to say on the ethical import of the play, as one might expect of him from his remarks in the letter to Nicholas of Prato and in the prologue to the *Hercules furens*, where he declares that the book can 'in a certain manner be placed in the category of ethics'. Throughout the commentaries from which extracts are translated below he limits himself to explaining very closely the mythology and construing the text phrase by phrase. Above all, he is uninterested in the allegorical meaning of the fables.

Sometimes words and phrases are misunderstood. For instance, at ll. 593–4, 'impotens procella Fortunae' (the *A* reading) actually means 'uncontrollable storm of Fortune', but Trevet—somewhat perplexed, one imagines—glosses it as 'Fortune, which is here called powerless because she makes all who give way to her powerless to live good lives'. In the same line, 'hunc [portum] nullus terror movet', he explains *movet* as 'removes', 'takes away', but the correct meaning is 'disturbs'. A minor mistake in interpretation occurs at ll. 753–5: 'haec hodie ratis ... regias animas vehet, victamque victricemque', meaning 'today this boat [i.e. the boat of Charon] will carry royal souls, the vanquished and the victor'. 'The vanquished' refers, not to Priam as Trevet would have it (for Priam is long since dead), but to Cassandra herself, who will be killed with 'the victor', Agamemnon. Again, at l. 756 the 'levis turba Phrygum' is 'the shadowy [i.e. ghostly] throng of the Trojans', not 'the thin [i.e. sparse] throng' as Trevet interprets. Very occasionally Trevet gets the *historia* and mythology wrong. Thus he calls Patroclus 'Protesilaus' at l. 619, and at l. 651, where reference is made to 'walls made by the hands of divine beings', he does not spot the reference to Poseidon/Neptune and his part in the building of Troy.

But these failures to interpret correctly are all small, and localized, and indeed are often the sort of mistakes that even a modern editor or translator might make. What we do not find in Trevet's commentary on Seneca are basic

[63] *Seneca: Agamemnon*, ed. R. J. Tarrant (Cambridge, 1976), p. 4.

misinterpretations running right through his treatment of the text, as found, for example, in William of Conches's interpretation of *The Consolation of Philosophy* IV, met. iii and in our anonymous commentary on Juvenal's Fourth Satire (both translated above, Ch. IV). To some extent this is due to the relatively narrow scope of the commentary, as described above, but more importantly it is a reflection of Trevet's exceptional abilities as a scholar. His achievement in making clear the literal significance of Senecan drama was considerable. Nicholas of Prato's fulsome praise of this 'classicizing friar' was, in our opinion, quite justified.

WILLIAM OF ARAGON

Commentary on Boethius, *The Consolation of Philosophy*:
Prologue and Exposition of Book III, metre xii

THE PROLOGUE[64]

As the Philosopher says in the first book of the *Politics*, all things seek the good.[65] This is proved not only by the authority of the Philosopher, but by reason and the clear evidence of experience. I say 'by reason' because since any natural desire is directed towards that which is like itself, since that is conducive to preserving and perfecting that desire, and shuns the opposite since that is harmful, it follows that, since all entities are good, all things seek the good as being the perfection of their own natures, or the means of preserving their own perfection, and shun the opposite as being unsuitable and harmful. Our experience clearly teaches us the same lesson with regard to living things, and we shall find the same to be true in the case of all beings to a greater or less extent. For if a plant is planted on the dividing line between two soils, of which one is rich and good and the other poor and bad, we shall find that it will send all its roots into the good soil and as far as it can will avoid the bad soil. We also see that small trees placed under big ones lean towards the light as if towards the good — for sunlight is the father of plants, as is said in [Aristotle's] book on plants[66] — and avoid shade as being harmful. We see the same to be true in the case of animals. For wild animals become domesticated as a result of kind treatment, but if they are badly treated domestic animals become wild. This is even more evident in the case of human beings, for one human being loves another and follows him because of the acts of kindness which he has experienced at the hands of that other person. But conversely, one man shuns another because of acts of injustice and

---

[64] Tr. from Crespo, 'Prologo', with the permission of Professor Crespo and Noordhollandse Uitgeversmaatschappij, Amsterdam.

[65] Aristotle, *Politics*, i. 1 (1252ᵃ4).

[66] Ps.-Aristotle, *De plantis*, i. 2 (817ᵃ28), quoting (and repudiating) Anaxagoras.

wrongs inflicted on him by that other person, and all bonds of friendship and association are dissolved. You can also see the same characteristic appearing in a proportionate degree in other beings. For the inclination to get nearer to the good is innate in all things, as for instance the elements, which are drawn by their own natural properties to their proper place[67] as ensuring their survival, and shun a place that is not their own as being harmful. So it is clear that all beings seek the good.

But even though this is so, the human race is very much out of step with other kinds of creatures. For other creatures seem to seek and pursue what is good for them following a fixed pattern and without deviation. But man seeks and is moved towards the good in a haphazard and confused way. For different people are moved and direct their efforts towards different goods, and this reveals human error and the imperfection of the human race. So man alone, out of all other creatures, needs practice in acting and needs to be taught in the matter of exercising his choice so that he may be brought closer to what is good for him by a direct route and without deviation.

The cause of this deviation and imperfection is that man's good is an intelligible good to the knowledge of which man comes first of all through sensation. Because there are many different kinds of good which can be perceived through the senses, man easily abandons the one that is good for him and chooses one that is inappropriate, and he believes that that is good in absolute terms which is good only in respect of some particular circumstance,[68] and judges to be particular to himself that which is common, and regards as good in itself that which is good only by dint of some feature which is non-essential in its nature.[69] For man spends a long time being nurtured in a world of sensible goods before he is raised to an understanding of intelligible goods. So he must be educated by teaching and by experience of many kinds in order that he may arrive at the stage where he can distinguish between the various goods and knows how to choose the true, supreme, and perfect good from among those which are imperfect and only seem to be good. When he has reached this stage, he will rejoice and take pleasure in the things he ought to, and will not grieve over that which reason tells us we should not grieve over. For many are found wanting in this matter, and we see that they have not reached the above-mentioned stage of being able to distinguish [i.e. between the various goods]. Frequently they grieve at those things which, if they followed reason, should give them pleasure, and conversely they rejoice at things which sadden reason. Hence the life of such men is besprinkled with many bitter experiences. For they are preoccupied with sensible goods, and in these there is no pleasure unmixed with grief, and they do not remain the same, since their goodness is constantly changing.

[67] i.e. in the order of things in the universe.
[68] Lat. 'quod est secundum quid bonum'.
[69] Lat. 'quod est per accidens in natura'.

It is to help such people that I decided to lecture on (*legere*) Boethius' book on *The Consolation of Philosophy*. Boethius wrote this book to console himself, but those things which are disputed in it clearly teach each of us to distinguish between the various goods and show which good men ought to direct their hearts and minds towards, and if men are granted an abundance of other goods, it shows us what use we should make of them. So, this is a book that is not just moderately useful, but is most valuable. For out of all the books which have ever been written this is considered the most effective in helping us to spurn transitory goods which present to our view an image of spurious happiness, and to choose those goods which are permanent, which guide us and educate us on the path towards true happiness.

Be it understood, then, that Boethius was an outstanding philosopher among Latin writers, and was distinguished by his possessing all the characteristic traits of a philosopher. Among the Romans—for he was a Roman—his noble birth made him distinguished, but indeed he outshone all others in true nobility of character. For he was of the family of Manlius Torquatus, a brave warrior, who leaped into a chasm, fully armed and on horseback.[70] This yawning chasm appeared in the city and a loud voice demanded the sacrifice of one man from the community, otherwise it would undermine the whole city. When Manlius Torquatus, who had a deep love of his country, heard this, he armed himself and made ready his horse, and leapt into the chasm. The chasm closed over Torquatus and engulfed him, and the city was freed from this very serious danger. According to one account, Boethius belonged to the same family. In no way did he fall short of the standards set by the aforesaid Torquatus. Because of his devotion to his country he incurred the hatred of Theodoric, a Goth and king of the Romans in Boethius' day. So, when King Theodoric was acting tyrannically against the interests of the state in several matters and continually finding Boethius opposed to him, sheer wickedness and iniquity prompted him to engineer Boethius' death. Since he could not find any just cause for this, he forged letters, allegedly sent to Boethius from the Emperor at Constantinople, taking the form of a reply, addressed to Boethius, to a supposed invitation from the Romans.[71] Therein he [i.e. the Emperor] promised to give every sort of help to the Romans against the tyranny of Theodoric. These letters gave Theodoric the chance to fabricate a reason for killing Boethius, and so, without Boethius himself knowing anything about it, the aforesaid wicked king had him condemned to exile. Then Boethius, though innocent, was taken to the city of Pavia and imprisoned, and his true virtue suffered under the false imputation of vice malevolently levelled at it. But, as the Philo-

---

[70] The hero of the gulf was not Manlius Torquatus but M. Curtius: the Manlii Torquati are not heard of after Augustus' time.

[71] Cf. *De cons. phil.* 1. pr. iv (ed. Tester, p. 152).

sopher says in the first book of the *Ethics*, he who is truly good sustains
the vicissitudes of fortune most creditably and wisely, even when he
suffers many serious misfortunes, not because he is impervious to pain
but because he is brave and heroic.[72] Therefore, Boethius, who had
always lived a truly good life, composed this book, which is entitled *The
Consolation of Philosophy*, in which he shows that he sustains his own
[mis]fortune most creditably and with great wisdom, and that, brave and
heroic though he may be, he is all too well aware of his own suffering, as
is clear from his manner of literary treatment (*modus tractandi*).

To clarify this point, we must recall what we touched on above,
namely, that man at first, and for a very long time, is nurtured in a world
of goods which are sensible and external to himself. So, it is part of the
human condition to feel intensely, and grieve over, misfortunes which
occur in relation to those goods. But when he has been raised to [an
understanding of] intelligible goods, he sustains creditably and wisely
the changing fortunes of such goods [i.e. the inferior, sensible goods]
and thus passes into a godly life. So, according to this argument,
humanity is divided into two groups; that part of mankind which is
motivated by passions rooted in the senses, and that which is elevated
by intelligible goods through divine influence. But because philosophy
alone raises us to the level of intelligible goods, through God's boun-
teous gift, Boethius has given himself the part of a man who is troubled
and motivated by passions rooted in the senses, and introduces the
figure of Philosophy in the part of a man who follows intelligible goods.
So, speaking in his own part he displays his afflictions and the reasons
that lie behind them, and speaking in the part of Philosophy he brings
forth arguments which eliminate these sources of grief and show us
where we can find comfort. So, this book is said to be about the consolation offered by philosophy.

This mode of treatment is called didactic (*didascalicus*) in terms of
genre, in which two characters are feigned, one who is taught and the
other who teaches, or one who is suffering and the other who heals. In
this work, the two characters of the sufferer and the healer are united in
one person [i.e. Boethius], because pain and mental turmoil arising out
of misfortunes are due to the weakness of the mind, while consolation
and a will to resist in these misfortunes are due to the perfecting of the
intellect and its goodness, in which qualities consist nothing less than
the healthy state of our mind. And so, Boethius in his book proceeds as
follows.

[72] *Eth. Nicomach.* i. 10 (1100ᵇ30–3).

With reference to this, it must be noted that the philosophers here touched upon various kinds of happiness which dispose us towards that final and perfect state of happiness. Hence someone says: 'Happy is the man who has been able to discover the causes of things',[74] because through this knowledge he is very well disposed towards acquiring knowledge of the highest good. Another says: 'Happy is the man who has had no experience of prosperity. Anguish is the outcome of unalloyed prosperity'.[75] For prosperity in this world[76] inflicts pain in the course of acquiring possessions, and in holding on to them once they have been acquired, and even greater pain if possession of them is prolonged,[77] and distract men from consideration of the highest good. Therefore[78] Ptolemy, in the proverbs of his *Almagest*, says: 'Happy is he who does not care in whose hand is the world.'[79] The words: 'Happy is the man made cautious by other peoples' dangers'[80] can be expounded to the same effect. For we can acquire these kinds of happiness which dispose us [to supreme happiness] in two ways, either through that which befalls in our own case, or through that which we see befalls in the case of others. Although the man who is educated towards the good by that which befalls himself may be happy, the man who is taught and educated towards the good by that which befalls others is said to be happier, because his training is quicker and better. For we can observe much in the case of others in the course of a brief period which we cannot see in our own case even over a long period. Therefore: 'Happy is the man made cautious by other peoples' dangers', for he is disposed in the opposite direction to the dangers and stumbling blocks which he sees appearing in the lives of others, and so he progresses more freely to the supreme good.

When Boethius says FORMERLY [THE THRACIAN POET MOURNED: 5–6] he is referring to the fable of Orpheus. To make this easier to understand, note that the story of Orpheus, referred to here, is as follows. Eurystus [*sic* for Aristaeus], the brother of Orpheus, was once pursuing Eurydice, the wife of Orpheus, across a meadow in order to ravish her.[81] In the course of her

---

[73] Tr. from Erfurt, Wissensch. Bibl., Amplon. F. 358, fo. 16ʳ⁻ᵛ (= *E*), which we collated with the text in Cambridge, University Library, MS Ii. 3. 21, pt. 2, fos. 71ᵛ–72ᵛ (= *C*). A transcription of the passage in *E* is provided by Terbille, 'William of Aragon's Commentary', ii. 136–41.

[74] Virgil, *Georgics*, ii. 490.

[75] Attributed to Henry of Settimello by H. Walther, *Proverbia sententiaeque Latinitatis medii aevi* (Carmina medii aevi posterioris Latina II/1–6, Göttingen, 1963–9), iii. 524 (no. 19459).

[76] mundane *C*; ruinam *E*.

[77] producantur *E*; perdantur *C*.

[78] ideo *C*; secundo modo *E*.

[79] Not found in Ptolemy's *Almagest*.

[80] *Proverbia sententiaeque*, ed. Walther, ii. 52 (no. 8952).

[81] per pratum quadam vice *C*; per peccatum quiddam vitae *E*.

flight she was bitten [by a snake, died, and was snatched away to the shades below. When Orpheus learned of the death][82] of his wife he grieved deeply and, taking his lyre, he began to play it, and to seek her first of all throughout the whole world. Because he did not find her there, he descended to the shades below, still playing his lyre. While he was seeking her in the world he played the lyre so well[83] that he caused the woods, normally immovable, to run, and the waves, which are normally in constant motion, to stand still. The doe consorted with lions fearlessly, and the hare ceased to fear even the dogs. This he did in the upper world. But because he did not find his wife there, the ardour[84] of his passion caused him to descend to the lower world. There, first of all Cerberus, the door-keeper of the nether regions, was captivated by his song, and the goddesses who punish crimes[85] joined Orpheus in his lamentation. The wheel to which the head of Ixion was nailed ceased to revolve. Tantalus no longer suffered from thirst, and the vulture ceased to pull at the liver of Tityus. Consequently, Pluto, the god of the underworld, said: 'We are conquered. So let us give him his wife. For by his song he has paid a sufficient price for her. But let it be on this condition. Let him not look back before he has left the underworld. Otherwise he will lose her irrevocably.' But when Orpheus had come out with his wife, and was near the boundary of the realm of darkness, he looked back at her, saw the shades, and lost his wife, and she was dragged back to the underworld.

According to Fulgentius in his book *On the Nature of the Gods* the moral sense of this fable is as follows.[86] Orpheus means 'he who speaks'. For he is said to be, as it were, 'the voice of the mouth (*phonos oris*)'. Eurydice is 'good judgement', or 'good works'. She is fittingly called the wife of Orpheus because it is the function of him who is eloquent, by teaching or giving good advice, to explain good works and good judgements. The word Eurystus comes from *eu*, which means 'good', and *ares*,[87] which means 'virtue'. Thus Eurystus means 'he who is virtuous to good effect'.[88] For it is the function of the virtuous man to pursue good works and enact good judgements. Therefore, Eurystus is said to have pursued Eurydice across a meadow,[89] that is, he sought her throughout the world, but was

---

[82] Only in *E*; passage omitted in *C* because of eyeskip.

[83] *C* adds 'so sweetly and so pleasantly'.

[84] *fervore C; furore E*.   [85] i.e. the Furies.

[86] *Mit*. iii. 10 (tr. Whitbread, p. 96): 'Now this legend is an allegory of the art of music. For Orpheus stands for *oreafone*, that is, matchless sound, and Eurydice is deep judgment.' It should be noted, however, that the moralization of this fable as found in William of Conches' exposition of the same metre (cf. above, p. 320) is a major influence on the following discussion. William of Aragon, like William of Conches before him, is interested in morality rather than music.

[87] *ares C, aris E*.

[88] *Mit*. iii. 10 (tr. Whitbread, p. 97): 'Eurydice was desired by the best, that is, by Aristaeus—for *ariston* is the Greek for best . . .'.

[89] *pratum C, peccatum E*.

not able to lay hands on her because she was bitten by a snake and was snatched away down to the underworld. Good works or good judgement are said to be bitten by a snake whenever they are tainted by some debased desire, which we understand by the serpent. And they are said to be dragged down to the underworld because they have been infected on account of some earthly good. For when good judgement and good works are ordered with the supreme good as their end they are not bitten by the serpent, but are carried straight to God by having as their end love, and the desire to please God, this being the ultimate end to which they are ordered. Just so, when they are distorted by base desire, they are directed to some earthly good, and have this as their ultimate end. And this does not happen without some vice[90] ensuing.

Orpheus, then, whose name means 'eloquent', is the wise man who grieves at the debasement of judgements and good works. He takes up his lyre, that is, he puts right[91] and corrects debased desires throughout the whole world by his eloquence and learning. He does this first of all in respect of those things brought forth[92] by the shortcomings of our sensible appetite with regard to external actions. This is indicated by the fact that he forced woods[93] to run, and waters to stand still, and that the doe lay down side by side with lions without fear and the hare did not fear the dog. For the eloquent man's wisdom represses all such desires [by means of the very sweet eloquence of the wise man][94] and draws them towards the mean of virtue. The woods denote rude and uncouth men; the waters, the volatile and soft. The doe and lions, and the hare and dog, we understand to refer to men who are unlike [in their manners and in their life],[95] who, being enthralled by dissimilar passions, cannot live together satisfactorily. But when drawn to the mean of virtue they do live together well.

Secondly, he does this in respect of those things in which we fall short in terms of our inner meditation. This we must understand by the descent of Orpheus to the shades below. In the course of this, first of all Cerberus is beguiled by his song. He [i.e. Cerberus] is the door-keeper of the lower world. We understand him to represent the three appetites within us, namely, of anger, of desire, and of the will. Unless these are governed and educated by the truth of intellectual knowledge, they open up the lower world for us by drawing us down towards earthly things and by initiating[96] debased fantasies and thoughts. But they are educated by goodness and enlightened[97] by true teaching, so that they seek only that which is good in itself. This is the meaning of Cerberus being captivated by Orpheus' song.

[90] vicio C; iudicio E.
[91] Lat. 'explicans', literally 'sorting out, disentangling'.
[92] ostendunt C; E unclear (Terbille suggests 'habent').
[93] silvas C; silva E   [94] Only in C.
[95] Only in C.   [96] movendo C; modi E.
[97] luminantur E; limitantur C.

So, in this matter[98] Boethius does two things. First, he shows what Orpheus does in the underworld. Secondly, he shows what is done to Orpheus by the powers of the underworld as a result of this, beginning AT LAST WE ARE CONQUERED, etc. [40].

Regarding the first point, he mentions four consequences which happened among the dwellers of the underworld as a result of the sweetness[99] of Orpheus' song, after the gates were opened. In the first instance the avenging goddesses of the underworld who punish crimes began to wail, feeling pity [for Orpheus]. It must be noted that after desire come affections and thoughts concerning the thing desired. But when we are unable to fulfil these, they torment us in many ways.[100] They are said to punish crimes because they torment us immediately, even while we are [only] thinking about those crimes, acting upon us in a frenzied way. So, the poets call them furies, and tell us that there are chiefly three in number. The first of these is called Allecto, that is, 'unstoppable'; the second, Tisiphone, that is, 'who imposes her voice'; the third, Megaera, that is, 'great quarrelling'. For through the action of the first we form notions without cease, through the action of the second we break forth into speech, while by the action of the third we instigate quarrels. These then, vanquished by Orpheus' song, began to lament. This denotes grief and repentance for crimes committed, when we recognize that we have erred.

The second thing he mentions is that the wheel to which Ixion's head was fixed ceased to rotate. It must be noted that Ixion was the confidant of Jupiter and Juno, who—because of his desire for honour and [divine] power[101]—wished to lie with Juno. Therefore the Giants [sic for the Centaurs] are said to have been begotten by his sperm, which poured over the earth. When the gods learnt of this they fixed his head to a wheel as punishment for a crime of such enormity. This was very well said. For those who place their hope of the supreme good in such things are always moved like a wheel. For if [human] fame and power[102] rise in one direction they fall in another, and if they [i.e. fame and power] are raised from one point [on the wheel] they are pushed down from another.

The third thing he mentions is that Tantalus was no longer thirsty, for the excellence of Orpheus' music had taken away his thirst. This is because by the excellence of virtue all excesses arising from avarice and any other desire are removed.

The fourth thing he mentions is that the vulture, sated by Orpheus' airs or melodies, ceased to pull at the liver of Tityus. Tityus had been condemned to this punishment among the shades of the underworld

[98] i.e. Orpheus' visit to the underworld.
[99] dulcedine C; delectione E.
[100] multipliciter C; E unclear (Terbille suggests 'magis').
[101] dominii C; divini E.
[102] dominium C; enim E (Terbille emends to 'detrimentum').

because he had accosted Latona, in an attempt upon her honour. In this
we note those who are libidinously disposed towards every sort of lust.

These are the more notable vices designated in this fable. But it contains this truth relating to all vices, that by the excellence of virtue, and by
wisdom, all vices are corrected.

NICHOLAS TREVET

Commentary on Boethius, *On the Consolation of Philosophy*:
Extracts[103]

EXPOSITION OF BOOK II, METRE V

O TRULY HAPPY The fifth metre is called a paroemiac after its inventor,[104]
and anapaestic from its predominant foot. It is a dimeter, that is a catalectic line of four feet, wanting one syllable. For only one syllable of the
fourth foot is left to follow the other three. The line consists, then, of three
anapaests with one syllable left over. It allows a spondee in the first and
second place, but never in the third.

Just as Philosophy has been inveighing against riches, so here she commends the primal age of the world, when there was no lust for wealth, and
laments the present age, which is dominated by greed and desire for
wealth.[105] At this point it should be noted that the poets distinguished four
ages of the world, using the comparison with four metals to describe them.
They imagined a first age in which men lived primitive and innocent lives,
and they called this the golden age, under Saturn. They imagined a second
age when men, though still uncivilized, lived in a rather more sophisticated
way. For then they began to live in houses and cultivate the land. This they
called the silver age, under Jupiter, because there was less innocence in that
age than previously. The third age they imagined was the bronze age, when
men, because of their preoccupation with possessions, began to push other
men aside, and yet they were not entirely enslaved by wickedness. But the
fourth age they called the age of iron, when greed and human wickedness
were so rife that neither trust nor justice remained on the earth. Hence
Ovid, in his description of these ages in the first book of the *Metamorphoses*,
says of justice: 'last of all the heavenly beings the maiden Astraea abandoned the earth which reeked of slaughter'.[106]

---

[103] Tr. from the complete but unfinished edition of Nicholas Trevet's commentary on *De consolatione philosophiae* on which Professor E. T. Silk was still working at the time of his death.

[104] In fact, it comes from παροιμία 'proverb', since some pithy sayings were couched in it.

[105] On the origins and development of the idea of the golden age see esp. Bodo Gatz,
Weltalter: Goldene Zeit und sinnverwandte Vorstellungen (Hildensheim, 1967); Harry Levin, *The
Myth of the Golden Age in the Renaissance* (London, 1969); A. V. C. Schmidt, 'Chaucer and the
Golden Age', *Essays in Criticism*, xxvi (1976), 99–115.

[106] *Metamorphoses*, i. 149–50.

Boethius is here speaking of the first and last of these ages, and accordingly is doing two things in this metre. First of all he commends the first age. Then he laments the age we live in, which is the last, when he says WOULD THAT [23]. So he says THAT FORMER AGE WAS TRULY HAPPY [1] that is, WAS CONTENT WITH THE FAITHFUL HARVEST OF THE FIELDS [2], no doubt because men did not falsely overstep the boundaries of fields to enlarge their own possessions; AND WAS NOT RUINED BY SLOTHFUL LUXURY [3] that is, was not a slave to luxury, and he aptly calls LUXURY SLOTHFUL, for how much are idleness and slothfulness the causes of luxury! This prompts Ovid to say in his *Remedy for Love*: 'if you remove leisure then Cupid's darts lose their force', and again: 'Do you ask why Aegisthus became an adulterer? The answer is not hard to find: he had time on his hands.'[107] There are three sorts of luxury, as Boethius teaches in his work *On the Training of Students*: luxury in sexual matters, luxury in matters of food and drink, luxury in the choice of clothing.[108] He clearly shows us in the same work how a man is led to ruin by any one of these forms of luxury.

THIS (understand 'age') BROKE ITS FAST LATE IN THE DAY [4], because they used to dine late waiting until they were hungry before so doing; ON EASY ACORNS [5], because they were easily found and could be prepared for use without difficulty; DID NOT KNOW [6] 'knew not',[109] that is the men of that age did not know HOW TO MINGLE that is, to mix THE GIFT OF BACCHUS that is, draughts of wine, because Bacchus is said to be the god of wine WITH LIMPID [7] that is, clear HONEY to make mulled wine and claret as is done nowadays; NOR [8] understand 'did they know how to' MIX THE WHITE FLEECES OF THE SERES that is, of that people WITH TYRIAN POISON [9] that is, with the blood of shellfish which is used in dyeing cloth purple. These are found in great quantity round Tyre. He calls this dye poison because,[110] just as poison turns bodies black, so purple cloth is dyed by the black blood of the shellfish. Note that according to Isidore in book ix of the *Etymologies*, in the chapter on names of foreign peoples, the Seres are a race, dwelling in the east, who derive their name from the town they inhabit, and among whom wool is woven from the trees.[111] He also says, in book xix, in the chapter on kinds of wool, that *sericum* ['silk'] is so called because the Seres were the first to send it to us. For it is said that there are worms there who spin out the threads all around trees. These worms are called *bombices* in Greek.[112] So here Boethius calls the threads produced by those worms WHITE FLEECES.

---

[107] *Rem. amor.* 139, 161–2.

[108] *De disc. scol.* ii. 7–14, ed. Olga Weijers, *Pseudo-Boèce, De disciplina scolarium* (Leiden, 1976), pp. 101–4.

[109] Trevet is explaining the syncopated form *norant* for *noverant*.

[110] *Venenum*, though it usually means 'poison', sometimes, as here, means 'dye'. Trevet seems aware of both meanings.

[111] *Ety.* ix. ii. 40.

[112] *Ety.* xix. xvii. 16; xxvii. 5.

Résumé: so, as I have said, men did not possess such pleasing and highly prized [objects] in that age, but lived innocent and primitive lives. For they did not sleep in painted beds but THE GRASS GAVE THEM HEALTHFUL SLEEP [10], THE GLIDING RIVER HEALTHFUL DRINK [11], WHILE THE TALLEST PINE-TREE PROVIDED SHADE [12]. For houses and carefully constructed buildings had not yet been invented. AS YET [13] NO STRANGER, that is anyone living at that time, for everyone remained in his own country; PLOUGHED THE DEEP WATERS OF THE SEA, because ships had not yet been invented; HAD VIEWED UNKNOWN SHORES WITH MERCHANDISE COLLECTED FROM EVERY QUARTER [14–15] that is, foreign merchandise, brought from abroad; THEN [16] that is, in those days THE CRUEL WAR-TRUMPETS that is, trumpets or horns which call men to war, called *classica* from the verb *calo* 'I call'[113] WERE SILENT, for as yet those vices which incite men to war were not rampant NOR HAD BLOOD, SHED IN BITTER FEUD, STAINED THE HORRID ARMS [17–18],[114] for arms had not yet been invented, because there was nothing which could serve as the fuel for wars; hence he says FOR WHY? [19] that is, 'for what reason?', why did an enemy in his madness wish to be the first to attack, when they saw SAVAGE WOUNDS, AND NO REWARD [21–2], that is, FOR BLOOD spilt, for there was nothing for which men might fight.

Then, when he says WOULD THAT [23] he laments the present time, saying WOULD THAT OUR TIMES that is, the conditions that prevail in our time, WOULD NOW RETURN TO THOSE ANCIENT WAYS [24], but—and this we must deplore—it is not so, but rather LOVE OF POSSESSING [25] that is, greed (*cupiditas*), BURNS FIERCER THAN THE FLAMES OF ETNA, because many of the evils that befall the human race have their origin in that. ALAS. WHO WAS HE WHO FIRST DUG UP THE MASSIVE WEIGHT OF HIDDEN GOLD AND THE GEMS WHICH WISHED TO LIE HIDDEN? [27–30] because it is their nature to be hidden in the ground. I say that THE MASSIVE WEIGHT OF GOLD and GEMS are the PRECIOUS PERILS, because many incur danger because these things are so precious.

EXPOSITION OF BOOK III, METRE vi

EVERY SORT OF MAN This is the sixth metre, a mixed one. It consists of an alcmanic—a dactylic hypercatalectic trimeter—followed by a pherecratean. The first line is called alcmanic from its inventor, dactylic because this is the predominant foot, a 'trimeter' from the number of feet, and hypercatalectic, that is, with an extra syllable over and above the three feet.[115] It allows a spondee in place of the dactyl anywhere in the

---

[113] Cf. *Ety.* XVIII. iv. 5.

[114] Most MSS of Boethius here read 'horrida arva', 'the uncultivated fields'. Trevet obviously saw a MS which read 'horrida arma'.

[115] In this metre Boethius is, as often, experimenting with what Raven, *Latin Metre: An Introduction*, p. 132, calls a 'startling mixture of lines'. Thus, each of Boethius' long lines consists of two classical metres joined together. The first is nowadays described as a dactylic tetrameter catalectic, i.e. a 'colon' consisting of four dactylic feet (which can be replaced by

line. The pherecratean has already been discussed earlier, in the second metre of the second book. Note that in this poem an anapaest sometimes replaces the first spondee, though this is against the rule laid down in the *Centimetrum* [of Servius].

In this metre Boethius shows that all men are noble except the wicked.[116] For, since nobility is a quality of excellence owed to origin, and this [quality] is manifest in man alone, it must be particularly regarded in terms of [that aspect of] man's origin by dint of which he is man. Since there are two elements in man, the soul and the body, it is clear that a man is not a man by reason of his body, but by reason of his soul, through that part which makes him a rational being. But the souls of all men share the same origin, for all souls come from God. Therefore, judging by this criterion all men are equally noble. The only ignoble ones are those who fall away from their original state.

The soul is brought into the world in the likeness of God. Therefore, the only ones who lose their nobility are those who obscure that likeness to God which they have at birth by contracting evil ways. Hence Boethius says EVERY SORT OF MAN [1] that is, in general terms all mankind, rich and poor, of every degree, living on this earth, RISES FROM A SIMILAR BEGINNING, that is, because all men, in terms of the soul, come from the one Creator. So he adds FOR THERE IS ONE FATHER OF ALL THINGS [2] that is, one Creator. ONE BEING LOOKS AFTER ALL THINGS, that is by guiding them. Besides, lest it should be thought that that Father was ignoble and in consequence all who have their origin in Him were also ignoble, he adds a certain grandeur to God's power by describing it in what follows. HE [3] that is, the one and only Father, of whom we are now speaking, GAVE THE SUN ITS RAYS, that is its radiant nature, or in other words its shining brightness; AND GAVE THE MOON HER HORNS, that is, the nature which makes her sometimes appear to be horned. (The reason for this has been given above in the fifth metre of Book I.) HE ALSO [4] that is, the Father PEOPLED THE EARTH WITH MEN, that is caused men to dwell on the earth. For the nature of his [i.e. man's] body demanded this. HE GAVE THE SKY ITS STARS for its

spondees), wanting the final syllable. This clearly adds up to the same thing as Trevet's description of the line as a hypercatalectic trimeter, 'that is, with an extra syllable over and above the three feet', so that his description of this first part of the long line, though now obsolete, is correct. The second part of Boethius' long line is an ionic dimeter and not, as Trevet says, a pherecratean, but these types of line are easily confused. The basic form of the ionic dimeter is ∪∪ – – | ∪∪ – –. If the short syllables of the first metron are contracted, and none of the other permissible variants is admitted, the verse could be mistaken for a pherecratean – – | – ∪∪ – | – in which the first syllable of the base had been resolved to give ∪∪ –. This resolution of the first syllable before a long second was not in fact permissible, a fact Trevet cannot be blamed for not knowing.

[116] Useful introductions to, and bibliographies on, the important concept of nobility or gentility are provided by G. M. Vogt, 'Gleanings for the History of a Sentiment: *Generositas virtus non sanguis*', *JEGP* xxiv (1925), 102–24, and Marvin L. Colker's introductory comments to his edition of William of Aragon's *De nobilitate animi*, in *Med. Stud.* xxiii (1961), 47–9.

adornment. HE [5] that is, the Father ENCLOSED IN [HUMAN] LIMBS MINDS BROUGHT DOWN FROM THEIR LOFTY DWELLING that is, the limbs of the body. Boethius is speaking in the Platonic manner here. However, in order to have a right (*sanum*) understanding [of this matter], one must not think that souls have been created in heaven and glide down from there into bodies, as Plato appears to say, and as do some of his followers, notably Macrobius, as is clear from the first book of *On the Dream of Scipio*. Instead, the souls have been created in the actual bodies.[117] So, when Boethius says here BROUGHT DOWN FROM THEIR LOFTY DWELLING this must be understood as meaning that the 'dwelling place' of a thing (*sedes rei*) is the potentiality in which that thing exists before it comes forth into being. Because matter is the lowest of the various states of being, those things which lie within the power of matter originate from the lowest abode. But those things which do not lie within the power of any material thing but only within the power of Him who made them, namely God, who is the highest being, are said to originate from a lofty abode. More will be said on this subject later, [in the commentary on] metre ix.

THEREFORE HE IS THE AUTHOR OF ALL MORTALS AS HIS NOBLE OFFSPRING [6] that is, men. WHY [7] that is, to what end? DO YOU TRUMPET ABROAD, that is noisily boast OF YOUR GRANDFATHERS AND GREAT-GRANDFATHERS? IF YOU CONSIDER GOD YOUR CREATOR—QUE stands for *et*, 'and'; YOUR ORIGIN this is the figure which is called zeugma;[118] NO MAN IS DEGENERATE, UNLESS HE ABANDONS HIS OWN BIRTHRIGHT BY SINNING [8–9] that is, the likeness of God which he inherited at birth; by cherishing evil. Therefore, it is through vice that man becomes ignoble, while he is ennobled only by virtue. Hence, Juvenal says in his eighth satire: 'Virtue is the one and only true nobility'.[119]

Commentary on Seneca's Tragedies: Extracts

PREFATORY LETTERS[120]

Letter of Nicholas de Albertinis

To his brother in religion, Nicholas Trevet, of the Order of Preachers (and dearest friend), his brother Nicholas, by divine permission bishop of Ostia and Velletri, sends greeting and affection born of sincere love.

Though the earnest endeavours of all whom we learn are striving to accomplish good please us because of the love we are duty bound to show

---

[117] *In Somn. Scip.* 1. ix. 10, ed. Willis, pp. 41–2.

[118] This meaning of zeugma, which differs from that of current usage, goes back to Isidore, *Ety.* 1. xxxvi. 3; 'zeugma is a phrase which occurs when several clauses are locked together by one word'.

[119] Juvenal, *Sat.* viii. 20.

[120] The prefatory letters and Trevet's General Prologue are tr. from *Il Commento di Nicola Trevet al Tieste di Seneca*, ed. Ezio Franceschini (Orbis Romanus XI, Milan, 1938), pp. 1–7, with the permission of Società editrice 'Vita e pensiero', Milan.

them, this is particularly true of our brethren [in religion], and most of all of those whose long-standing friendship has left an abiding impression in our memory, and whose uprightness, known to us through our own experience of it, has bound us to them with a bond of unalloyed affection: in their case we experience this joy to an even fuller degree.

In consequence, the treatise which you have written on the work of that most Christian philosopher Boethius, *On the Consolation of Philosophy*, which has reached us, and which we have read with due care and attention, has brought us to untold consolation. This is a book with which we have been familiar since youth. It never fails to please all its readers by its irregular but sweet cadences. But equally it disturbs many, not by any unpleasing, grating quality, for this is entirely wanting, but because their innate slowness in understanding holds them back. But, in our opinion, in unravelling [the problems of] this book you have set about the task so succinctly and with such lucidity that your brevity makes the reading of Boethius a pleasure for the learned, your clarity smooths the way for the unlearned, while the pleasing way in which your work is put together charms the experienced and the novice alike.

We have been so drawn by the sweet fragrance of this work that we now ask you to let us know what other obscure writings have been brought into the light of day by your studious efforts, and exhort you to research into those which seem obscure to the weaker brethren. That is why, since we know that you have now written on the *Declamations* of Seneca, we are asking you if you would be kind enough to make available to us any work of this kind, or any other fruits of your labour—and excellent fruits I firmly believe these will be—and send us copies of it. The book of tragedies from the hand of that same illustrious writer is full of such obscurities, tangled up in such deeply hidden meanings, and has interwoven into it such a jumble of mythological stories (*fabulae*), that by dint of its very obscurity it immediately puts off anyone who tries to read it. If you have the opportunity, we urge you to enable us to acquire a thorough familiarity with it, and render this book so to speak navigable and passable to all who now shun it as if it were some fearful sea. Valence, 24 April.

Trevet's Reply

To his reverend father in God and lord, worthy of every mark of sincere respect, the Lord Nicholas, by the grace of God bishop of Ostia and Velletri, Brother Nicholas Trevet [prays that] he may sit by the side of the Eternal Judge in the heavenly regions.

When the illustrious writer Boethius in his *On the Training of Students* advised that young initiates to learning be given many respites from the business of earning their living,[121] and trained in the gymnasium of the

[121] Lat. 'multiplicato Mercurii intervallo'; we take Mercury to stand for 'business, commerce' here.

poets, he prescribed Seneca before all others, and, singling out his teaching from that of the other doctrines which he distinguished, each by its proper name, he calls it 'pure teaching'.[122] By using this word he shows us that the authority of this distinguished teacher should be welcomed with open arms, and his usefulness commended to later generations. As a result of that distribution by Nature, whereby every man receives different gifts of wisdom, but all are not bestowed fully on any individual, Seneca won the leading place in moral philosophy. Adapting his teaching to the varied capacities of men's minds, he sometimes instructs the simple with plain and unadorned precepts, or again embellishes his teaching by introducing familiar examples to guide his hearers, and thus clears away the lethargy of the hypercritical, or else, by employing brief and obscure epigrammatic sayings (*sententiae*), he exercises the memory, making it work hard. Thus, he expounds his teachings to all classes, eager that they may be helped by his constant efforts, so that, to quote Plato's words of commendation, he might show that the whole world, and not just himself, benefited from his having been born.

I believe that Seneca, a mature scholar who had moved in the lofty realms of virtue, turned to writing tragedies after the manner of wise doctors, who offer their patients bitter medicines coated with honey, in order to cleanse humours and promote health without offending the palate. In this way, he might instil into tender minds ethical teachings wrapped in pleasant stories (*fabulae*), while at the same time amusing them, and might through these teachings root out vices, sow his seed, and reap a rich reward in the form of the various virtues.

But, speaking in terms of the preoccupations of the present generation, ardour for the Muses has cooled and the applause of the theatre given way to more serious business. If I may quote the words of Fulgentius in the introduction to his *Mythology*: 'now man is not bending his efforts to achieving fame in poetry, but simply to satisfying his own hunger'.[123] Consequently, the satiric wit which Philology's mother Phronesis has drawn off to adorn her daughter seems to the men of our age to bear the mark of barbarism. For the sparkling waters of the spring of the Muses have withdrawn from them back to their hidden source.

Seneca expended much effort, to good effect we believe, in writing tragedies. But these deter many from studying them by their obscurity, and elude comprehension, since they do not permit those who peruse them to see into their innermost recesses because they are wrapped in a dark cloud of mythology (*fabulae*). So, lest his efforts should be completely wasted, it pleased you, Excellency, who by constant and intense study examine the words of the wise and the mysteries therein, to bid

---

[122] *De disc. scol.* i. 5–9, ed. Weijers, pp. 95–6.
[123] *Mit.* i, prol. (ed. Helm, p. 1*; tr. Whitbread, p. 40).

me to make these [tragedies] accessible to those with little learning,[124] and profitable to all readers, by illuminating them with a commentary. So, being desirous of obeying your commands with all the powers at my disposal, as indeed it is my bounden duty to do, though I have drunk but sparingly of the springs of Helicon, I have assumed the boldness of the Muses and have joined their ranks as promptly as I could. So, working from the single manuscript available to me, I have hammered out the best explanation I could give of its various meanings (*sensūs*). With God's help this has now been completed, and I submit it for examination to the keen eye of your respected judgement. I cannot excuse every shortcoming in this work on the grounds of my ignorance and lack of expertise, yet the curtailed form of my text [of Seneca], as noted in certain passages, offers a partial defence, as does the possibility of my work becoming too prolix. For in order to avoid this [i.e. prolixity], I have not fully pursued all the hidden meanings of the myths (*fabularum integumenta*). My reverend lord, may our Lord Jesus Christ preserve you to the everlasting honour of His Church.

GENERAL PROLOGUE

St Augustine, in the sixth book of *The City of God*, tells us that Varro distinguished between three kinds of theology, which in Latin are called 'mythical', 'natural', and 'civil'.[125] Poets employ the first kind, philosophers the second, the priests and populace the third. The first relates to the theatre, the second to the natural world, the third to the city and the temple. In the first category much has been feigned which contradicts the proper status and nature of mortal men; in the second category the features of the natural world are taught in a concealed form, while the third category teaches us the various ways of worshipping the gods and the rites practised in temples. Varro would banish the first kind of theology from cities, while approving of the second and third. But Augustine is more critical of the third than the first, although he considers that both should be condemned. Therefore, he cites the authority of Seneca, who speaks against this third category in his book attacking superstitions, and in this he prefers Seneca's freedom in speaking his mind to Varro's wisdom, because Seneca had the courage to attack 'civil theology', which Varro did not dare to condemn. Thus St Augustine, comparing these two kinds of theology [i.e. 'mythical' and 'civil'], says: 'truth to tell, the temples where these rites are actually carried out are worse than the theatres where they are only feigned as happening'.[126]

Leaving aside the second and third kinds of theology and concentrating

---

[124] Reading 'insipientibus' from Franceschini's apparatus rather than 'inspicientibus'.
[125] *De civ. Dei*, VI. v–ix. Cf. Boccaccio's use of this treatment, discussed below, pp. 389–91.
[126] *De civ. Dei*, VI. x.

on the first, it should be noted that 'poetic theology' (*theologia poetica*), which operates in the theatre, has two parts, one of which may be called tragic and the other comic. According to Isidore in the eighth book of his *Etymologies*, in the chapter which deals with poets, tragic poets or tragedians are so called because in the infancy of the art the reward for those who recited was a goat, which the Greeks call *tragos*.[127] Hence Horace says: 'who competed in tragic verse with a worthless goat as prize'.[128] Subsequently, succeeding generations of tragic writers won much honour, excelling in the 'arguments' of myths (*argumenta fabularum*) invented to image the truth.[129] Likewise, Isidore in his chapter on tragic writers in book eighteen says: 'the tragedians are those who related in doleful verse events of old and the crimes of wicked kings, with the populace as their audience. Comedians are those who celebrated by words or actions the deeds of private individuals, and represented in their plays the seduction of maidens and the love-affairs of courtesans'.[130] '"Comic writers" or "comedians" are so called either from the place, because they acted their plays around the rural hamlets, which the Greeks call *comae*, or else from communal feasting, for men used to come to hear them after feasts.'[131]

The poets wrote in three modes (*modi*), either in the narrative mode, in which only the poet speaks, as in the *Georgics*; or the dramatic mode, wherein the poet nowhere speaks [sc. in his own person] but only the characters (*personae*) who have been introduced—and this mode is particularly well suited to tragic and comic writers—while the third mode is a mixture of the other two. There [i.e. in the third mode], sometimes the poet speaks in his own person, and sometimes the characters who have been introduced.[132] This is Virgil's method in the *Aeneid*. Although the book's subject matter is tragic yet it is not actually written in the tragic mode, for the poet sometimes speaks, together with introduced characters. So, Virgil in his *Aeneid*, Lucan, and Ovid in the *Metamorphoses* can be called tragic poets because their subject-matter was that of tragedy: the misfortunes of kings and great men and affairs of state. But yet this description does not exactly fit their work. However, Seneca, in the book under discussion, not only wrote about tragic subjects but also employed the tragic mode of writing. So, his book is rightly called 'the book of tragedies'. For it contains sorrowful verses on the misfortunes of great men, in which the poet never speaks in his own person, but only the characters who have been introduced.

---

[127] *Ety.* viii. vii. 5.

[128] Horace, *Ars poetica*, 220, cit. Isidore, loc. cit.

[129] Reading 'veritatis' (from Franceschini's apparatus) rather than 'varietatis'.

[130] *Ety.* xviii. xlv–xlvi.   [131] *Ety.* viii. vii. 6.

[132] This distinction between the *characteres scripturae* goes back to Servius' commentary on Virgil's Eclogues, *Comment. in Buc.*, prol.; cf. Ch. I, n. 47.

EXPOSITION OF *HERCULES FURENS*: PROLOGUE AND BEGINNING
OF COMMENTARY[133]

There are in this book ten tragedies, of which the first is *The Madness of
Hercules* (*Hercules furens*). At this point, it should be noted that comedies
and tragedies are usually preceded by an argument (*argumentum*). 'Argument', as defined here, is a story (*fabula*) which sounds like true fact, or
else it briefly sets out the rationale (*causa*) at the beginning of a book.[134]
Seneca, however, did not make use of arguments of this sort. But to make
the tragedy which follows more readily intelligible we may at this point
state by way of an argument that Hercules was the son of Alcmene, wife of
Amphitryo, and as the fable has it, the son of Jupiter. Having subjected
him to many trials, Juno ended up by ordering him to go down into the
underworld with Theseus. Besides his other wives, Hercules had married
Megaera, or Maera as she is called elsewhere,[135] and by her had several
sons. While Hercules was in the underworld, Lycus, whom he had
formerly driven into exile, captured Thebes, killed King Creon, the father
of Megaera, and his brothers, and sought to marry Megaera. When she
refused to comply, he prepared to kill her along with her sons. But
Hercules, returning from the underworld, killed Lycus and his men.
Juno, enraged at Hercules' return from the underworld, drove him mad
while he was praying after having sacrificed, and in his madness he killed
his sons and his wife. But, having regained his sanity, he was filled with
unconsolable grief for what he had done.

This [tale] is largely identical with [the material of] this tragedy. But
others say that while Hercules was absent his sons prostituted their mother.
When Hercules returned he killed them in a fit of rage, and Megaera,
enraged at this and furious with her husband, was turned into a dog. Hence,
in *Metamorphoses*, book vii, we read: 'and the cities which Maera terrified
with her newly acquired bark'. However, I believe that others explain this
incident, less convincingly, as relating to Hecuba, the wife of Priam. But
however that may be, one should note that Megaera, when it is the name of
the Fury, has a long medial syllable, but when it is the name of Hercules'
wife it shortens the medial, as the metre below shows.

From what we have said it is clear that there are four causes of this
tragedy. The cause which brought it into being (*causa efficiens*) was
Seneca. The origin of the subject-matter (*causa materialis*) is the madness

---

[133] Translated from *Nicolai Treveti expositio Herculis furentis*, ed. V. Ussani (Rome, 1959),
pp. 3–6, with the permission of Edizioni dell'Ateneo, Rome. All references to Seneca's text
are taken from *L. Annaei Senecae tragoediae*, ed. O. Zwierlein (Oxford, 1986).

[134] Cf. Hugutio of Pisa, *Magnae derivationes*, s.v. *arguo*, in Oxford, Bodleian Library, MS
Bodley 376, fo. 10ʳ; cf. in part Isidore, *Ety.* I. xliv. 5, VIII. vii. 5 ff.

[135] A confusion of three quite different mythological characters, Megera wife of Hercules,
the Fury Megaera, and Maera, who was changed into a dog according to Ovid, *Metamorphoses*, vii. 362.

of Hercules, in the course of which he killed his sons and his wife. The enforming cause (*causa formalis*) consists in the manner of writing, which is dramatic, as stated above, and in the order of its parts, which will become clear in the course of the commentary. The ultimate purpose (*causa finalis*) is the enjoyment (*delectatio*) of the audience,[136] or else, in so far as there are narrated here some actions which are praiseworthy and some which deserve censure, the book can in a certain manner be placed in the category of ethics. In that case, its end is the correction of behaviour by means of the examples set out here. That is enough by way of prologue.

Seneca's first tragedy has as its subject (*materia*) the madness of Hercules and contains five acts, of which the first contains Juno's complaint against Hercules; the second describes Lycus' pursuit of Megaera after Hercules has left her, and begins O MIGHTY [205]; the third relates the return of Hercules and begins O [RULER] OF THE GENTLE DAY [592]; the subject of the fourth is Hercules' madness, and it begins WITH AVENGING [RIGHT HAND: 895]; the fifth relates the return of Hercules to sanity and begins WHAT PLACE IS THIS? [1138]. Seneca uses the first act to do two things. First, he brings on stage Juno, making her complaint and urging on the Furies of the underworld to exact vengeance upon Hercules, and secondly the chorus who celebrate Hercules' achievements in a song addressed to the general audience,[137] at this point WITH A WHIRLWIND [162].

It should be noted that tragedies and comedies used to be recited in the theatre in the following way. The theatre was a semicircular space, in the middle of which was a small building called the 'scene' (*scena*), and within this was a platform on which the poet stood and recited his verses. Outside were the actors (*mimi*), who imitated by their gestures events recited in the verse, by adapting them to fit the character [in the play] in whose person the reciter was speaking.[138] So, while the first piece of verse in this play was being read the actor represented Juno complaining bitterly and urging on the Furies of the underworld to exact vengeance on Hercules.

EXPOSITION OF *AGAMEMNON*, ACT V [589–807][139]

The fifth act of this tragedy has as its subject the madness and prophecy of Cassandra. In respect of the first of these Seneca does two things. First, it is shown how this madness which made her utter prophecies came over Cassandra, and secondly how Agamemnon engaged in a dialogue with

[136] Cf. above, p. 325 and n. 53.
[137] 'Lat. vulgariter concinentem.' Alternatively, this could mean 'singing *en masse*'.
[138] Cf. above, pp. 325–6 and n. 57.
[139] Tr. from *Nicolai Treveti expositio Senecae Agamemnonis*, ed. P. Meloni (Università di Cagliari, Facoltà di Lettere e di Magistero III, Sassari, 1961), pp. 57–77, with the permission of Palumbo Editrice.

her, in the passage AT LAST I RETURN [782]. The first part contains seven speeches, of which the first is that of the chorus of Trojan women lamenting the ruins of Troy.

[I] This lament is written in dactylic tetrameters.[140] The chorus of Trojans, in its lament over the ruin of Troy, does two things. First it laments the fall of Troy, and secondly it shows that the death of Priam is to be lamented more than any of the other disasters [which have befallen them], in the words WHAT FIRST, [OR WHAT LAST, DO YOU PREPARE?] [649]. In respect of the first of these [i.e. the lament] the chorus is doing two things. First it commends death as an escape from their present miseries. Secondly, it laments the fall of Troy, in the words WE HAVE SEEN [612]. In respect of the first, it says WHAT A DEADLY SWEET EVIL HAS BEEN BESTOWED that is, ON MORTALS [589]. Specifying the exact nature of that evil, it says HARD that is, lasting and firm LOVE OF LIFE[141] this being the love which makes everyone strive to save his own life and avoid death, EVEN THOUGH AN ESCAPE-ROUTE FROM OUR MISERIES IS OPEN that is, by dying; and so there follows AND DEATH, WHICH GIVES US FREEDOM that is, which frees us from all our adversity, CALLS TO THE WRETCHED that is, seems to summon them to death through adversity; THAT CALM HAVEN that is, death IN ETERNAL REPOSE because the dead are removed from the turmoil and anxiety of the living. THIS [593] that is, the haven, NO PANIC MOVES that is, takes away, but all may take refuge in it; NOR THE POWERLESS GALE OF FORTUNE that is, not even the random adversity imposed by Fortune, which is here called powerless because she makes all those who give way to her powerless to live good lives;[142] OR THE FIRE, that is, the thunderbolt OF THE HOSTILE THUNDERER that is, of Jupiter, whom he calls hostile because he appears in this light to those whom he is punishing. A DEEP PEACE [596] that is, in death, FEARS NONE OF THE THINGS CITIZENS FEAR that is, he who is dead, NOR THE SEAS DRIVEN MAD BY THE HARSH NORTH-WESTERLIES that is, because of the north-westerlies, winds which blow harshly; NOT FIERCE BATTLE-LINES that is, fierce armies, the point being that he does not fear them, AND THE CLOUD OF DUST RAISED that is, caused BY BARBARIAN TROOPS OF HORSEMEN—for a great deal of dust is raised from the hooves of horses in an army; NOT FALLING WALLS does he fear, as we Trojans do, WHILE THE ENEMY'S FIRE LAYS WASTE that is, destroys, WHOLE PEOPLES WITH AN ENTIRE CITY. This is as if he were to say: 'He will not be afraid that the walls of his city will fall, or that the city and its inhabitants will be destroyed by fire started by their enemies, as happened in the case of Troy.' UNIQUE IN HIS CONTEMPT FOR THE FICKLE GODS [605] that is, the changeable gods, who send sometimes prosperity, sometimes adversity. Such is the man who scorns this present life. He will

---

[140] The chorus is, in fact, polymetric, i.e. employs a great variety of metres.

[141] The full sentence in Seneca may be translated: 'What a deadly sweet evil has been bestowed on mortals in the form of that dire love of life.'

[142] For Trevet's misunderstandings see above, p. 327.

smash his way through ALL UNVANQUISHED WAR because he cannot be vanquished.[143] For, since he does not fear death, but willingly embraces it, the victory of the opposing faction cannot harm him. Consequently he smashes through war, however powerful war may be, because in withdrawing himself from war's clutches through death, he ensures that there is no one against whom war may be waged. HE [WILL BE] THE EQUAL OF A KING AND THE GODS ABOVE [609] that is, he is on a level with the gods, who does not sadly gaze on THE FEATURES ON DISMAL that is, black ACHERON, meaning a river in the underworld, who does not gaze upon GLOOMY STYX that is, does not see the swamp in the lower world, AND HAS THE COURAGE TO PUT AN END TO LIFE that is, who has the courage to die and to go to the dwelling-place of the dead. O HOW WRETCHED IT IS NOT TO KNOW HOW TO DIE [610] that is, because by death so many miseries are avoided, as has already been said.

Then when it says WE HAVE SEEN [611], it laments the fall of Troy. At this point it should be noted that, as is related in the second book of the *Aeneid*, after ten years of war the Greeks despaired of conquering Troy by force. So they made a large wooden horse, which they filled with armed men, pretending that this was to honour Pallas, who is the goddess of war, to obtain a prosperous return voyage. So they entered the ships and pretended to be returning to Greece, but lay hidden with their whole fleet near the place which is called Tenedos. Meanwhile the Trojans came out, thinking that the Greeks had gone home, and looked at the wooden horse. A Greek called Sinon was discovered by shepherds and brought to the Trojans. He pretended that he was going to be sacrificed by the Greeks to gain a prosperous wind for the return voyage, but that he had seized an opportunity to escape and hid among the banks of marsh sedge. When he was asked why the Greeks had made the horse, he said that it was to placate Pallas, whom they had offended, and that it had been made so large deliberately so that it could not be taken into Troy. For, according to the prophecy of Calchas, if it was taken into the city, not only would Troy continue unvanquished but the Trojans would conquer Greece and make it subject to themselves. The Trojans believed all this and allowed Sinon into the city on terms of peace, and, smashing down the city gates, they brought in the horse. This done, they began to dance, and the fighting men of Troy took part in the dance. When they were all tired out, on the night following this, Sinon opened the doors in the horse, and the soldiers, coming out, devastated the city with fire and slaughter. In this way Troy, which could not be captured by force, was captured by guile.

[143] The Lat. 'indomitum bellum', meaning 'unvanquished or unconquered war', belongs to the preceding sentence and sums it up. It is one of the series of things which the man who takes refuge in death does not have to fear. But Trevet takes it with the first phrase in the next sentence, 'perrumpet omne servitium', meaning 'he will smash through all forms of slavery'. He omits to translate the 'servitium', and the end result is: 'he will smash his way through all unvanquished war'.

That is why [the chorus] says WE HAVE SEEN OUR NATIVE LAND [611] that is, Troy, which was the chief city of their country, FALLING IN RUINS ON THAT DEADLY NIGHT, WHEN YOU, DORIC FIRES that is, Greek fires, because the fires had been lit and hurled [at the buildings] by the Greeks, TOOK POSSESSION OF THE DARDANIAN ROOFS that is, the houses of Troy. SHE that is, Troy, NOT CONQUERED BY WAR, understand 'was', NOR by ARMED FORCE, AS FORMERLY SHE FELL TO THE QUIVER OF HERCULES that is, as she had been captured by Hercules by force of arms; WHICH that is, Troy, THE SON OF PELEUS AND THETIS DID NOT CONQUER that is, the real Achilles, or THE FALSE ACHILLES that is, Protesilaus, who was the friend of Achilles and fought in his armour. This is why he says DEAR TO THE ALL TOO FIERCE SON OF PELEUS that is, to Achilles son of Peleus, WHEN HE SHONE IN THE ARMS HE HAD BEEN GIVEN that is, the arms of Achilles, AND LAID LOW THE MEN OF TROY that is, the Trojans; OR WHEN that is, Troy was not vanquished, THE SON OF PELEUS HIMSELF that is, Achilles, with GRIEF that is, the grief he felt when he mourned Protesilaus who had been killed by Hector, STIRRED HIS FIERCE SPIRIT that is, became fiercer and more courageous in his attack on the Trojans. AND THE TROJAN WOMEN ON THE TOPS OF THE WALLS that is, who were on the tops of the walls, FEARED HIM SWIFT TO LEAP that is, they feared Achilles swiftly leaping to overrun the Trojans, or to assault the walls. But as for what Troy LOST THE LAST REMAINING that is, that which was the last thing left to her, HONOUR that is, the greatest honour, AMONG ALL HER MISERIES; what this honour was he specifies when he says TO BE BRAVELY CONQUERED BY FORCE. For Troy was not conquered by a display of courageous fighting, but was taken by guile, as has been said above. TROY RESISTED [623] that is, by fighting against the Greeks, FOR TWICE FIVE YEARS that is, ten, DESTINED TO PERISH BY THE FATE that is, the unhappy outcome, OF ONE NIGHT. WE HAVE SEEN THE PRETENDED GIFT that is, the horse which was alleged to be made as a gift to Pallas; a gift, I repeat, OF MASSIVE SIZE that is, of extraordinary size, AND CREDULOUSLY that is, we [i.e. the Trojans] believing the word of Sinon, DREW IN WITH OUR RIGHT HANDS that is, into the city of Troy, THE GIFT OF THE DANAI that is, of the Greeks, FATEFUL that is, made for our doom and death. MANY TIMES THE CHARGER [628-9] that is, the wooden horse, CARRYING KINGS CONCEALED IN IT that is, hidden, IN ITS CAVERNOUS SPACE, AND WAR which is hidden also in it, SHUDDERED ON THE OUTER THRESHOLD that is, of the city gate when it was being brought into the city. AND IT WAS POSSIBLE that is, it was open to us, TO TURN that is, to reverse, THE DECEPTION that is, against the Greeks, SO THAT THE PELASGIANS THEMSELVES that is, the Greeks, SHOULD FALL, TAKEN BY THEIR OWN DECEIT. OFTEN THE TARGES [633] that is, the round shields, WERE SHAKEN that is, by the movement of the horse, AND PRODUCED A SOUND that is, sounded, AND A QUIET MURMURING, because it was inside the belly of the horse, STRUCK OUR EARS that is, was heard, AND PYRRHUS INSUBORDINATE that is, not obeying THE GUILEFUL ULYSSES, ROARED that is being down in the horse with Ulysses, whom Ulysses had enjoined to keep silence. But

Pyrrhus was disobedient, roaring out of sheer anger and a desire for revenge.

THE TROJAN YOUTH [637] that is, the young men, THEIR FEARS LULLED that is, free from fear, because now that the horse had been brought into the city and the Greeks had nowhere appeared they had lost their fear, TAKES PLEASURE IN TOUCHING THE ROPES that is, those with which the horse was dragged into the city. FROM ONE SIDE that is, from one direction, ASTYANAX that is, the son of Hector, or SHE WHO WAS ABOUT TO BE BETROTHED TO that is, Polyxena, who was about to wed A HAEMONIAN PYRE that is, the tomb or ashes of the cremated Achilles, who was a ruler of Haemonia, LEAD THE TROUPES that is, by making up groups of dancers, OF A BAND OF CONTEM-PORARIES that is, those who were of an age with them; SHE namely Polyxena, A BAND OF WOMEN; HE namely Astyanax, MEN. FESTIVE MATRONS that is, festive and rejoicing, BRING TO THE DEITIES that is, to the gods, VOTIVE GIFTS. FESTIVE FATHERS that is, festive and rejoicing, APPROACH THE ALTARS: ONE EXPRESSION CAN BE SEEN ON FACES that is, IN ALL THE CITY because every-one was joyful. AND A SIGHT WE HAVE NOT SEEN EVER SINCE THE FUNERAL PYRE OF HECTOR that is, by which the body of Hector was burnt: HECUBA IS JOYFUL that is, Queen Hecuba, the mother of Hector and wife of Priam.

Then when it says WHAT NOW? [649] the chorus asks and answers a question pregnant with grief. For it asks what is the first thing they are to mourn, when there are so many things they must grieve for in such a calamitous situation. So the chorus says, O ILL-STARRED SORROW, WHAT IS THE FIRST THING, OR WHAT THE LAST, THAT YOU PREPARE TO GRIEVE OVER? ARE OUR WALLS, MADE BY THE HANDS OF DIVINE BEINGS that is, by the gods, OR THE TEMPLES BEING BURNT OVER THE HEADS OF THE GODS TO WHOM THEY ARE DEDICATED? Replying to the question the chorus says, WE HAVE NO TIME TO LAMENT THESE EVILS, but they must lament the noble king Priam: hence they say O MIGHTY FATHER, THE WOMEN OF ILIUM that is, the men [sic] of Troy, MOURN YOU. I MYSELF HAVE SEEN, I HAVE SEEN—the leader of the chorus says this, speaking in his [? gender unspecified] own person, and he[?] repeats the word as an indication of his[?] own certain knowledge[144] of the event and of his[?] grief—THE SPEAR OF PYRRHUS IN THE THROAT OF THE OLD MAN that is, Priam, SCARCE TAINTED WITH THE SMALL AMOUNT OF BLOOD, because old men have very little blood.

[II] Secondly, when Seneca says RESTRAIN [659] Cassandra is brought forth forbidding the chorus (turba) from mourning for herself and her family, as it is enough for them to mourn their own dead. So she says TROJAN WOMEN, RESTRAIN THOSE TEARS WHICH ALL TIME SEEKS [TO SHED] that is, tears whereby the ruins of Troy and the fall of Priam are mourned, AND YOURSELVES that is, you, LAMENT THE FUNERALS OF YOUR PEOPLE WITH MOURN-FUL WEEPING that is, your own funerals, LET YOUR COMPLAINTS that is, lamentations, PART COMPANY WITH MY MISFORTUNES that is, with the mis-

[144] 'Certain' because it was personal knowledge.

fortunes which have befallen me; MY TRIBULATIONS that is, miseries, DO NOT ADMIT OF that is, reject, ANY FELLOW-MOURNER. In other words, I WILL DO JUSTICE TO MY OWN ILLS that is, to mourn my own miseries.

[III] Thirdly, when Seneca says TEARS [664], the chorus is brought on to show that neither it nor even Cassandra is capable of mourning their misfortunes adequately. And in respect of this it does two things. First, it shows that it is unable to express its grief adequately. Secondly, it accuses Cassandra, who is now beginning to rave, in the words BUT WHY [693]. Concerning the first point it says IT HELPS [664] that is, it is useful, Cassandra, TO MINGLE TEARS WITH TEARS. For the person who grieves in secret, and holds his grief in, suffers more than he who bursts forth with his grief in public. Hence the chorus says SECRET CARES that is, worries, WOUND MORE SEVERELY that is, afflict, THOSE WHOSE HEART THEY SEAR. IT HELPS that is, it is useful, TO LAMENT ONE'S LOVED ONES OUT IN THE OPEN that is, in public. FOR ALTHOUGH A TOUGH AND RESOLUTE MAIDEN that is, you are, Cassandra, AND ONE WHO CAN ENDURE HARDSHIP, YET YOU WILL NOT BE ABLE TO WEEP FOR THOSE CRUEL DISASTERS but it helps us to weep. NOT THE EDONIAN, that is the Thracian BIRD; in other words the nightingale (Philomena), WHO SINGS HER NOBLE SONG ON THE BRANCH IN SPRING, SADLY SINGING OF ITYS, WARBLING HER VARYING TRILL that is, with her varying trill lamenting Itys; that is, she will [not] be able adequately to lament your destruction; NOR THE BISTONIAN BIRD that is, Thracian, namely Progne,[145] wife of Tereus, king of Thrace, who was turned into a swallow, WHO, PERCHED ON THE ROOF CHATTERING, LAMENTS THE WICKED THEFT IN THE WOODS [sic] that is, which happened in the woods, OF HER MONSTROUS HUSBAND that is, Tereus.[146]

Note. Pandion, king of Athens, had two daughters,[147] Progne and Philomena. Tereus, king of Thrace, married Progne, who, wishing to see Philomena, asked permission to go to see her sister, or else that her husband should go to their father and ask for her and bring her to her. When Tereus her husband obtained Philomena from her father, he tried to rape her. But Philomena resisted, and so Tereus cut out her tongue and, bringing her with him, gave her a dwelling in the woods, where he frequently misused her. At last, she, by weaving an account of what had happened on her loom, informed Progne. In the course of celebrating the rites of Bacchus, Progne came to the place where her sister was and brought her back home with her. Wishing to avenge herself on her husband she served up his son Itys as a meal for him. When he had eaten his son she got her sister Philomena to take the head to him. He drew out his sword and began to chase them, but the gods took pity on them and changed Tereus into a hoopoe, Progne into a swallow which dwells on

---

[145] Sic for Procne, as commonly in the Middle Ages.
[146] Tereus committed the theft by 'stealing' the honour of Procne's friend Philomela, i.e. by raping her.
[147] Cf. Ovid, Metamorphoses vi. 424–674.

roof-tops, and Philomena into the bird which takes its name from her, who is now said to mourn Itys with her warbling trill.

But, I repeat, neither of these birds WILL BE ABLE ADEQUATELY TO LAMENT YOUR HOUSE [676–7] that is, the fall of your house; in other words, of Priam and the others. EVEN IF CYGNUS, RENOWNED AMONG THE SNOWY SWANS,[148] WHO DWELLS ON DANUBE AND DON that is, on those rivers, WISHED TO SING HIS LAST that is, to lament as he is wont to do when death is nigh; in other words, [not even] he will be able adequately to lament your house. EVEN THOUGH THE HALCYONS. Note that Ceyx, son of Lucifer and king of Thrace, had a wife called Alcyone, who out of grief for her husband drowned at sea, was turned into a bird which is called the halcyon.[149] It builds its nest on the sea-shore. Ambrose has some marvellous things to tell about this bird in his *Hexameron*. For it has a voice like that of one who is mourning and is said to be lamenting the death of its mate. Hence the text says EVEN THOUGH THE HALCYONS MAKE THE NAME OF CEYX TO RE-ECHO, WHILE THE SEA-SURGE LIGHTLY SINGS ITS LAMENT. For Ceyx was the husband of Alcyone. WHEN WITH ILL-FOUNDED CONFIDENCE that is, of the sea which drowned Ceyx, AGAIN THEY BOLDLY TRUST THE CALM SEA that is, by building their nest beside the sea. And Ambrose says: 'When the sea has been stormy, after its eggs have been laid, it suddeny becomes calm and all the wind falls away.'[150] AND FEARFULLY CHERISH THEIR YOUNG WHEN THEIR NEST TOTTERS that is, when the waves smash into the birds and nest together. Although, I repeat, the halcyons utter this sound, while the sea-surge laments, that cannot adequately lament your house. NOT EVEN IF THAT TEARFUL BAND WHICH IMITATES EUNUCHS that is, men who have been castrated, WHICH, HOARSE-VOICED, PLAYING THE BOXWOOD PIPE IN HONOUR OF THEIR GREAT MOTHER, WITH HER TURRETED HEAD that is, Cybele or the Berecyntian goddess, RUSH-ING HEADLONG that is, hastening or at speed, WERE TO JOIN WITH YOU Cassandra, IN TEARING THEIR ARMS TO LAMENT PHRYGIAN ATTIS that is, Attis from Phrygia, it will not be able adequately to lament your house.

Note that Cybele or Berecyntia is said to be the wife of Saturn and mother of the gods. She represents the earth; she is depicted as being 'turreted' because of the cities and towns which have their foundations in the earth.[151] She fell in love with Attis, a Phrygian youth, and castrated him out of jealousy. Because of this her priests are castrated, and at her festival make a great din and a clashing noise, shouting so that they become hoarse. And they sound the trumpet and clash cymbals and beat tam-bourines to commemorate the story that, when Jupiter was born, Cybele hid him in the forest of Ida, lest Saturn devour him. To prevent the father

---

[148] *Sic* for Cycnus. The son of Sthenelus, Cycnus was changed into a swan. See Virgil, *Aeneid* x. 189–93; Ovid, *Metamorphoses* ii. 367–809.

[149] Cf. *Metamorphoses* xi. 410–748.

[150] Ambrose, *Hexaemeron*, v. xiii. 40 (CSEL xxxii. 172–3).

[151] 'Turreted' because statues of Cybele have a turreted crown on the head, just as statues of city goddesses, such as Roma, have.

from hearing his son's wailing, a loud noise and clashing was raised in the forest of Ida. The priests slash their arms to recall Claudia, a vestal virgin who, in disgrace for a crime she had committed, was seen to invoke the goddess with a like frenzied gesture. The goddess cleansed her of her guilt and supported her when she, unaided, dragged a ship which not even a whole crowd could pull.

O CASSANDRA, YOUR TEARS HAVE NO LIMIT [691] that is, no moderation, BECAUSE THE THINGS WHICH WE SUFFER that is, in terms of the ruin of Troy and of the royal house, HAVE SURPASSED ANY LIMIT, that is, exceed all bounds. Then, when the chorus says BUT WHY? it accuses Cassandra, who is already in a frenzy, having already received the spirit of prophecy. Hence it says, BUT WHY, Cassandra, DO YOU SNATCH THE SACRED HEADBAND FROM THE HEAD? that is, your head. A priestess's headband is a white band like a diadem from which ribands[152] hang down on either side, and these bind the headband.

[IV] In the fourth place, when Seneca says HAVE CONQUERED [695] Cassandra is brought on, admitting that her misfortunes are so great that they cannot be lamented adequately. So she says NOW OUR MISFORTUNES HAVE CONQUERED ALL MY FEARS because they are more, and greater, than any fear I have ever felt. NOW INDEED I DO NOT SEEK TO PLACATE THE GODS BY ANY PRAYER because I should be wasting my time in asking them to refrain from inflicting any further punishment, since they have done all they could [in punishing me]. Hence the following words THEY HAVE NO FURTHER WAY WHEREBY that is, in which THEY MAY HARM ME, EVEN IF THEY SHOULD WISH TO RAGE AGAINST ME. FORTUNE HERSELF HAS USED UP ALL HER POWERS that is, in harming me, and she speaks here in her own person[153] because she has neither country nor kindred. WHAT COUNTRY REMAINS? that is, to me, here or elsewhere; WHAT FATHER, WHAT SISTER HAVE I NOW? TOMBS AND ALTARS HAVE DRUNK MY BLOOD because my father was killed at the altar, and my sister at the grave of Achilles. WHAT OF THAT HAPPY THRONG, MY BROTHERS? As if she were to say, 'surely it has been slaughtered', as appears from her words. SURELY that is, certainly THE ROYAL DWELLING that is, the palace building, has been EMPTIED [sc. of its inhabitants], OF THAT WRETCHED OLD MAN that is, Priam; THOSE WHO ARE LEFT that is, the survivors who were not slaughtered, SEE IT EMPTY that is, the palace,[154] AND SEE THE OTHER DAUGHTERS-IN-LAW WIDOWED that is, made widows, SCATTERED THROUGH ALL THOSE ROOMS, WIDOWED, THAT IS, EXCEPT FOR THE LACONIAN

[152] Lat. 'vitte', technically rendered 'fillets'.
[153] Lat. 'hoc declarat in se'.
[154] Here Trevet—or his Seneca MS—is dividing up the text in a way quite different from modern editors; in any case, 'exhausta' cannot agree grammatically with 'regia'. We should take 'exhausta nempe' with the 'turba fraterni gregis' which precedes it, not with 'regia', thus translating ll. 701–3 as follows: 'What of the happy throng of brothers? Gone, all! In the empty place only sad old men are left. . . .' Tr. from the Loeb edn. by F. J. Miller, *Seneca, Tragedies*, ii (Cambridge, Mass., and London, 1968), p. 59.

WOMAN that is, the Lacedaemonian Helen. For she was not a widow, for after the death of Paris she returned to her former husband Menelaus. HECUBA, MOTHER OF SO MANY DAUGHTERS-IN-LAW (*nurum* stands for *nuruum*, an example of synaeresis),[155] OF KINGS because they had been betrothed to the sons of kings, AND THE GUIDING HANDS OF THE TROJANS, FERTILE IN PROVID-ING FUEL FOR THE [FUNERAL] FIRES that is, because many of her sons were killed, and their bodies had been burned on funeral pyres according to the customs of the ancients. EXPERIENCING NEW RULES IN THE GAME OF THE FATES [706–7] that is, the rules imposed by new events, because such an event as a noble queen being turned into a dog was hitherto unheard-of. But this is what happened to Hecuba. Hence, Cassandra says PUT ON A WILD EXPRESSION that of a dog, AND BARKED MADLY ALL ABOUT THE RUINS OF HER LIFE that is, of Troy and of her children, SURVIVING TROY, HECTOR, PRIAM, EVEN HER FORMER SELF that is, living after Troy, Hector, Priam, and herself, because after she put off her humanity she took on the nature of a dog.

[V] Fifthly, the chorus is brought on telling us how the spirit of prophecy together with her madness came upon Cassandra. So it says SUDDENLY that is, all at once, THE PHOEBAS IS SILENT [710] that is, the priest-ess of Apollo, AND PALLOR SEIZES HER CHEEKS AND A FREQUENT TREMBLING that is, frequently repeated, HER WHOLE BODY that is, possesses; HER RIBANDS STAND UPRIGHT that is, the hair of her head rises from sheer terror; hence there follows HER SOFT HAIR STANDS STIFF, HER PANTING that is, drawing fre-quent, panting breaths, HEART RAGES WITH HIDDEN MURMUR, HER EYES FALTER IN UNCERTAINTY that is, they blink in uncertainty, AND HER GAZE IS TWISTED BACK, AND GLAZES, FIXED IN A HARD LOOK that is, her eyes are. NOW TALLER THAN NORMAL that is, standing, SHE RAISES HER HEAD TOWARDS THE WINDS OF HEAVEN AND WALKS TALL, NOW SHE PREPARES TO UNLOCK HER RECALCITRANT JAWS as if to say, she gets ready to speak, and yet cannot speak. NOW THE MAENAD CAN SCARCELY HOLD IN THE WORDS WITH MOUTH STILL CLOSED that is, the priestess, IMPATIENT OF THE GOD that is, unable to endure the god.

[VI] Sixth, when Seneca says WHY [DO YOU SNATCH] ME [UP WITH THE STING-ING GOAD OF NEW] FRENZY? [720], Cassandra is brought on, mad, and in her madness she in a sense foretells the future murder of Agamemnon. So first,[156] on the grounds that, as a captive, she is unworthy to prophesy, she says WHY AM I NEWLY STIRRED that is, aroused, WITH THE STINGING GOAD OF FRENZY? That is as if she were to say: 'I grieve that this is so because it is not fitting for me, a captive. O SACRED HILLS OF PARNASSUS, WHY DO YOU SNATCH ME AWAY, BEREFT OF ALL THOUGHT? that is, my mind now fails me because of the madness that has come upon me. Mount Parnassus is a hill

---

[155] Seneca's 'regum' ('of kings') was corrupted to 'nurum' under the influence of 'nurus' ending the previous verse; the normal genitive plural is *nuruum*, which would in fact be needed for the metre if the word were right.

[156] This is the beginning of Trevet's five-part division of Cassandra's speech in ll. 720–4, which constitutes his sixth major division of Act V.

with two summits on which those who were given the spirit of prophecy used to sleep. So she says this, as if the compulsion to prophesy were displeasing to her. DEPART, O PHOEBUS that is, from me, PUT OUT THE FLAMES that is, of madness and prophecy, IMPLANTED IN MY BREAST. TO WHOSE BENEFIT that is, to help whom DO I NOW WANDER IN MY MADNESS? that is, crazed. ALREADY TROY HAS FALLEN. WHAT PURPOSE HAVE I NOW, A FALSE PROPHET? As if she were to say: 'Now that Troy has fallen it seems to me that I am going to make false prophecies, when I foretell the evil fate which is going to befall Agamemnon.'

Secondly, in her madness she makes interjections in the middle of her prophecy. So she says WHERE AM I? [726] that is, myself. THE GRACIOUS LIGHT that is, of day, FLEES AND DEEP NIGHT that is, profound night, CASTS SHADOWS ON MY CHEEKS that is, darkens and clouds over my face, AND THE ETHER that is, the heat of the ether, this being the heat which those who are prophesying inhale, LURKS IN THE HIDDEN PART OF MY LIMBS, that is, my unseen limbs; in other words, my innermost limbs, my vitals. BUT BEHOLD THE DAY BLAZES WITH A DOUBLE SUN, AND I SEE ARGOS TWICE OVER that is, a double city, RAISING UP ITS ROOFS TO HEAVEN TWICE OVER. This is said in her delirium and madness.

Thirdly, prophesying, she tells what she has seen. So she says DO I BEHOLD that is, do I see, THE WOODS OF IDA? [730] Ida is the name of a wooded mountain close to Troy. DOES THE SHEPHERD that is, Paris; for he was given the name 'shepherd' because he dwelt in the fields and woods like shepherds do, SIT AS AN ARBITER that is, a judge, A FATEFUL [ARBITER] BETWEEN POWERFUL GODDESSES? She alludes here to the fictitious story that three goddesses, Juno, Pallas, and Venus, sat by the spring in the forest on Mount Ida. Into this spring the goddess of discord threw a golden apple on which was written: 'let it be given to the one who is most beautiful'. The goddesses, competing with each other in the matter of beauty, chose Paris as judge. He judged Venus to be the winner of the apple, and she promised him Helen as a reward. O KINGS that is, Agamemnon and Menelaus, YOU MUST FEAR THAT FURTIVE BROOD that is, your wives who secretly commit adultery. THAT SCION OF THE FIELDS This may refer to Paris, whom we said above was a shepherd, or to Aegisthus, who committed adultery with Agamemnon's wife. He[157] is called 'a scion of the fields' because he took no part in military matters or in war, but was uncultured and rustic, being entirely given over to idleness and lust. So, in The Remedy for Love, we read: 'The question is asked why Aegisthus became an adulterer. The answer comes, quick as a flash, "He had time on his hands".'[158] WILL OVERTHROW THE HOUSE that is, by kidnapping

---

[157] Seneca refers here to Aegisthus, who in the myth stayed at home and did not join in the expedition to Troy. But Paris too is often depicted as unwarlike and cowardly, even as early as the *Iliad*; Trevet may be thinking of him here.

[158] *Remed. amor.* 161-2.

[Menelaus'] wife, if the prophecy is explained as relating to Paris, or by plotting to kill Agamemnon, if it relates to Aegisthus.

And, as if she is seeing exactly how Clytemnestra makes preparation to kill her husband, she says WHY IS THAT MADWOMAN [734] that is, Clytemnestra, BRANDISHING OUTSTRETCHED SPEARS that is, poised to strike, WITH A WOMAN'S HAND? WHAT MAN DOES SHE SEEK (understand 'to strike'), THAT LACONIAN WOMAN that is, Clytemnestra, called Laconian like her sister Helen, for they both came from Lacedaemonia, IN HER OUTWARD APPEAR-ANCE that is, as far as her outward appearance was concerned, BUT BEARING AMAZON STEEL IN HER RIGHT HAND? that is, the axe with which it is the custom of the Amazons to fight. And, under cover of a metaphor of a lion she adds a description of Agamemnon's death, who was first of all stabbed by Aegisthus, and then beheaded with an axe by Clytemnestra. So she says BY WHAT DIFFERENT SHAPE that is, of things seen by her. She says this because she sees in her mind the above revealed openly. But the revela-tions which follow are made in the form of the metaphor of the lion. ARE MY EYES DIVERTED? that is, the eye of her mind. THE LION OF MARMARA that is, Agamemnon, whom she compares to a lion of Marmara, because lions of Marmara are the fiercest sort, Marmara being a region of Libya, OF THE BOLD GODDESS that is, of Pallas, who is the goddess of war, to whose service Agamemnon had been dedicated because he was bellicose and warlike, THE VICTOR OVER WILD BEASTS that is, the Trojans, HAS SUFFERED BLOODY BITES UNDER AN IGNOBLE TOOTH that is, suffered cruel wounds at the hands of the ignoble Aegisthus, LIES understand 'dead', HIS NECK SORE PRESSED that is, because of the blows inflicted by Clytemnestra, who cut off his head with an axe.

Fourthly, turning to address her own people, she accuses them because they thought that she alone was safe, because Agamemnon was her lover. For after the death of Agamemnon, Clytemnestra ordered Cassandra to be killed, as will be stated later. So she says DEPARTED SPIRITS OF MY PEOPLE [742] that is, wraiths of dead Trojans, WHY DO YOU SAY THAT I, OF ALL MY PEOPLE that is, the Trojans, ALONE SURVIVE? that is, am saved. O FATHER that is, Priam, BURIED THROUGHOUT ALL TROY because everywhere in Troy are funerals that are yours, because of your sons and daughters who lie dead everywhere,[159] I FOLLOW YOU that is, because I am to be killed, just as you were killed. O BROTHER that is, Hector, the only DEFENCE OF THE PHRYGIANS that is, the Trojans, AND TERROR OF THE DANAI that is, the Greeks, I DO NOT SEE any longer, that is, in you, THE ANCIENT GLORY that is, of arms and war-fare, OR YOUR HANDS HOT FROM THE SHIPS YOU BURNT. She says this because Hector carried fire to burn the Greek ships. BUT understand 'I see' LIMBS that is, your limbs, TORN that is, pulled apart, AND YOUR STRONG SHOULDERS WOUNDED BY A SAVAGE CHAIN. O TROILUS, TOO QUICK TO ENGAGE ACHILLES

---

[159] Trevet misses the real point here: Priam is buried throughout Troy because the whole city died with him, shared in his death.

because he was too young. O DEIPHOBUS MADE A PRESENT TO THE NEW WIFE that is, you were killed as a gift to the new wife, Helen, who was the new wife of Paris, YOU PRESENT UNCERTAIN FEATURES because he was badly lacerated by wounds so that he could scarcely be recognized with any certainty from his face.[160]

Fifthly, when she ponders all this, she desires to go to the world below. So she says IT PLEASES ME [751] that is, I judge it useful for me, TO SEE THE SAVAGE DOG OF TARTARUS, AND THE REALM OF GREEDY DIS that is, Pluto, who is the god of the underworld. THIS SHIP OF DREAD PHLEGETHON that is, of the underworld stream on which sails the ship which Charon steers as he ferries over the souls who go down to the lower world, TODAY WILL CARRY ROYAL SOULS, BOTH THE VANQUISHED that is, Priam,[161] AND THE VICTORIOUS that is, Agamemnon. I PRAY YOU, SHADES that is, wraiths of the dead, I PRAY YOU ALSO, WATERS BY WHICH THE GODS OF THE UPPER WORLD[162] SWEAR that is, by which the gods of the upper world, namely the Olympian gods, are wont to swear their oaths, OPEN UP A LITTLE that is, slightly, THE FAR SIDE OF THE ROLLING[163] HEAVENS that is, the sky which is left behind us and is passing away from us, SO THAT THE THIN because of their small number,[164] CROWD OF PHRYGIANS that is, of Trojans, MAY GAZE UPON MYCENAE and so may see the death of Agamemnon. Turning towards the Trojans she says SEE, POOR SOULS, THE FATES that is, fated events, TURN BACK ON THEMSELVES for now they turn to exact retribution from our enemies. THE SISTERS THREATEN MENACINGLY that is, the three furies of the underworld who are called sisters, FILTHY CREATURES that is, defiled; THEY TOSS OUT BLOODSTAINED WORDS that is, words that exhort men to shed blood. IT PLEASES THEM that is, it seems useful to them, TO ENTER BY THE STYGIAN POOLS that is, the pools of the underworld. THEIR LEFT HAND that is, the left hand of the aforesaid sisters, CARRIES HALF-CHARRED TORCHES, AND THEIR CHEEKS GLOW HOT AND THE GARB OF THE ILL-OMENED FUNERAL that is, a dark and funeral garment, BINDS THEIR WASTED that is, lean MIDRIFF, AND THE FEARS that is, the terrors OF THE NIGHT ROAR that is, raise a tumult, AND THE BONES OF THAT VAST BODY that is, of the giant who wished to storm the heavens, LIE CORRUPTED BY LONG DECAY IN THE MUDDY SWAMP, that is, of the underworld.[165] AND BEHOLD

---

[160] Seneca's meaning is in fact the opposite to Trevet's interpretation: Deiphobus' death was a 'present from his new bride', i.e. what he got for marrying her. See Virgil, *Aen.* vi. 511–12, 523–7.

[161] Actually a reference to Cassandra herself, who will be killed with 'the victorious' one, Agamemnon.

[162] The *superi*, 'those who dwell above', the gods of the upper world. According to Homer the most binding oath they can swear is by the River Styx. See e.g. *Iliad*, xv. 37–8, *Odyssey*, v. 185–6.

[163] The *A* MSS of Seneca read 'migrantis' = 'moving', 'rolling'; modern editors adopt *E*'s 'nigrantis', meaning 'dark'.

[164] A mistake. Seneca actually means 'the shadowy (i.e. ghostly) throng of the Trojans', not 'the thin (i.e. sparse) throng'.

[165] There is a problem in Seneca's text at this point. From ll. 759 to 764 he is describing the Furies. He has been thought to be still speaking of them in l. 765, 'strepuntque nocturni metus' ('those who strike panic in the night make their noise'), but the next lines, 'et ossa vasti

THE TIRED OLD MAN that is, Tantalus, IS NOT SNATCHING AT that is, trying to quaff, THE WATERS WHICH MOCK that is, delude and deceive, HIS MOUTH. This is because he grieves at the death of Agamemnon whose ancestor he was. So there follows FORGETTING HIS THIRST, SORROWING AT THE DEATH WHICH WAS TO BE that is, the death of Agamemnon. FATHER DARDANUS that is, the ancestor of the Trojans, EXULTS because he sees the punishment inflicted on the enemy of his own race, AND CAREFULLY PLACES GRACEFUL STEPS that is, walks gracefully and cheerfully.

[VII] In the seventh place, when Seneca says HAVING NOW RANGED FAR AND WIDE [775], the chorus of Trojans is introduced, showing how Cassandra, in her frenzy, has fallen into an ecstasy, and Agamemnon has come to console her. So [the chorus] says NOW HER MADNESS, HAVING RANGED FAR AND WIDE, HAS SPENT ITSELF, AND SHE FALLS ON BENDED KNEE BEFORE THE ALTAR, LIKE A BULL NURSING A WOUND WHERE ITS NECK HAS BEEN CUT. LET US THEN LIFT HER GOD-POSSESSED[166] that is, frenzied LIMBS. AGAMEMNON, GARLANDED WITH THE LAUREL OF VICTORY, APPROACHES that is, approaches Cassandra, who is falling down as described. LIKEWISE HIS WIFE HAS MADE HER WAY TO MEET HIM that is, Agamemnon, AND COMES BACK that is, with her husband towards Cassandra, BY HIS SIDE that is WITH STEP AT ONE WITH HIS that is, at the same pace.

In the second part of this verse discourse (*carmen*) we are shown how Agamemnon addresses Cassandra. There first of all[167] Agamemnon is brought in full of joy at his return, and says AT LAST I RETURN UNHARMED [782] that is, safe and sound, TO MY ANCESTRAL LARES that is, to my ancestral gods; in other words, to my home and native land. O BELOVED LAND that is, Mycenae, GREETINGS. SO MANY that is, many BARBAROUS PEOPLES HAVE GIVEN that is, bestowed THEIR SPOILS UPON YOU that is, spoils I have won. TO YOU TROY, THAT CITY OF POWERFUL ASIA that is, which is a powerful region in Asia, Troy I say, FOR A LONG TIME PROSPEROUS, HAS SURRENDERED that is, being vanquished has submitted herself. And, turning to Cassandra, he says

corporis corrupta . . . iacent' ('and the bones of the vast body . . . lie corrupted'), have seemed to refer to one of the notable transgressors against the gods, whose fate it was to be pinned down perpetually in hell. Some editors have therefore supposed a lacuna after l. 765; Tarrant, edition, p. 316, lists the following identifications of the 'vast body': Typhoeus, the Giants, Tantalus, Geryon, Tityus, and also Priam. However, O. Zwierlein, *Kritischer Kommentar zu den Tragödien Senecas* (Wiesbaden, 1986), pp. 284–7, places the lacuna after l. 764, arguing that it concerned the grove of Lerna where the Hydra dwelt; he understands the 'nocturni metus' in l. 765 of sinister noises in the night ('unheimliche Geräusche in der Nacht'), and identifies the vast body with the Hydra, arguing that the great sinners' bodies do not moulder, nor is Dardanus (l. 774) among them, and that Tantalus (l. 768) is introduced, not as a sinner, but as the forefather of Agamemnon and his house, grieved at what will befall (l. 772) as Priam's ancestor Dardanus is pleased. So far as Trevet is concerned, although more than one giant sought to assail Olympus, Typhoeus is the heaven-stormer *par excellence*.

[166] Here Trevet again follows the *A* MSS in reading 'entheos' for *E*'s 'en deos'. Miller translates: 'to his own gods . . . Agamemnon comes'.

[167] The beginning of Trevet's nineteen-part division of the exchange between Agamemnon and Cassandra in ll. 782–807, which constitutes his seventh and final division of Act V.

WHY DOES THAT PROPHETESS that is, Cassandra, HER BODY SPRAWLING that is, with her body sprawling on the ground, AND TREMBLING, TOTTER that is, stagger, WITH NECK SWAYING TO AND FRO? no doubt because she cannot hold her head in one place. He turns and orders his attendants to look after her. So he says ATTENDANTS, LIFT HER UP, meaning Cassandra, who is lying there; RESTORE HER WITH AN ICY DRAUGHT that is, cold water, as is done when people faint because their heart stops, afflicted by grief. NOW SHE RECEIVES BACK THE LIGHT OF DAY that is, restored to her former self, HER SIGHT STILL LANGUID that is, in some way defective, because as yet she is not fully restored. Addressing her, he says to comfort her STIR YOUR SENSES that is, rise out of the lethargy which now grips you. THAT HOPED-FOR HAVEN namely Greece, that is, the haven which we hoped for in the midst of OUR TROUBLES, IS AT HAND that is, has arrived. HAPPY DAY in which one should rejoice, and not be depressed as you are. For Agamemnon assumed that it was sadness and grief which had made her swoon.

Secondly, Cassandra is introduced and makes her reply, and as if sighing out of longing for her homeland, she says TROY TOO HAD HER HAPPY DAY [791]. But now Troy is overthrown. Thirdly, Agamemnon invites her to worship the gods, saying LET US WORSHIP THE ALTARS. Fourthly, Cassandra rejects this, saying MY FATHER FELL BEFORE THE ALTAR that is, my father Priam. Fifthly, he exhorts her in particular to worship Jupiter, saying LET US TOGETHER MAKE A PRAYER TO JUPITER. Sixth, Cassandra rejects this also, saying WHAT, WORSHIP JUPITER HERCULEUS?[168] that is, shall I pray to Jupiter Herculeus? As if she were to say: 'I won't do it'. Note. Jupiter Herculeus is the name given to the image of Jupiter which has depicted on it the story of the birth of Hercules. An image of this sort was in the temple in which Priam was killed. So she refused to worship or venerate this Jupiter. In the seventh place, he accuses Cassandra because she was talking as if she were still at Troy. So he says DO YOU BELIEVE THAT YOU ARE GAZING ON ILIUM? that is, Troy. As if he were to say: 'If you believe this, you have been deceived.' In the eighth place, Cassandra replies, saying that not only does she believe that she sees Troy, but ALSO PRIAM because she sees the death of the prince and king looming, just as then [that is, in Troy] she saw that of Priam. In the ninth place, Agamemnon, wishing to bring the madwoman back to her senses, say TROY IS NOT HERE in other words, you are now in Argos and Mycenae. In the tenth place, Cassandra replies, saying WHERE HELEN IS there I THINK OF AS TROY that is, there is a disaster [here] similar to that which befell Troy. In the eleventh place, Agamemnon, consoling her, says SERVANT, DO NOT BE AFRAID OF YOUR MISTRESS that is, even though you are a servant, do not fear your mistress, namely Clytemnestra, for I will protect you. In the twelfth place, Cassandra gives Agamemnon an oblique reply, saying FREEDOM IS AT HAND. As

---

[168] Lat. 'Iovem Herculeum'; modern editions have 'Herceum Iovem'. It was at the altar of Hercean Jove that Priam was slain (cf. *Aeneid*, ii. 512 ff.).

if she were to say: 'You do well to say that I should not fear ill-treatment at
the hands of my mistress, for I shall soon be dead, and so I shall be free.'
In the thirteenth place, Agamemnon, wishing to remove the fear of death
from her, says LIVE ON, FREE FROM CARE, no doubt 'because I will protect
you, so that you won't die'. In the fourteenth place, Cassandra replies to
this, saying TO ME DEATH MEANS FREEDOM FROM CARE that is, I hope for no
other security than that which I may achieve through death. In the fifteenth place, Agamemnon removes the fear of death from her, saying
THERE IS NO DANGER that is, no danger threatens YOU that is, of death. In the
sixteenth place Cassandra warns Agamemnon of the danger he is in himself, saying BUT YOURS that is, your danger, IS GREAT that is, it threatens you.
In the seventeenth place, Agamemnon, as if despising this, says WHAT HAS A
VICTOR TO FEAR? In other words: 'one such as I am'. In the eighteenth place,
Cassandra replies, saying THAT WHICH HE DOES NOT FEAR that is, a victor can
fear that which he does not consider is to be feared. In the nineteenth
place, Agamemnon turns to his servants and orders them to guard Cassandra until her fit of madness has passed, for he thinks that everything
she has said is due to her madness. So he says SLAVES, who are to me A
TRUSTY BAND, HOLD THIS GIRL that is, Cassandra, TILL that is, until, SHE
THROWS OFF THE GOD that is, the madness conveyed through her by the god
who is prophesying, LEST HER UNCONTROLLED FRENZY DO SOME HARM that is,
commit some harmful act, UNCONTROLLED in terms of [not] being able to
control itself. Then Agamemnon, rendering his vows to the gods Jupiter
and Juno, says BUT YOU, FATHER that is, Jupiter, WHO HURL THE SAVAGE
THUNDERBOLTS, AND DRIVE that is, drive away THE CLOUDS, AND GUIDE THE CON-
STELLATIONS AND THE LANDS [OF THE EARTH], TO WHOM VICTORS that is, one of
whose number I am, BRING THE SPOILS OF TRIUMPH that is, of their victory.
AND YOU, JUNO OF ARGOS, SISTER OF THE OMNIPOTENT that is, he who excels ALL
THINGS that is, Jupiter, GLADLY WILL I WORSHIP YOU WITH VOTIVE SACRIFICE AND
THE GIFTS OF THE ARABS that is, incense, AND HUMBLE ENTRAILS [807] that is,
with the humble sacrifice of animals, in which the entrails of the animals
are drawn out and inspected. And so he calls such a sacrifice 'entrails'.

GIOVANNI DEL VIRGILIO

Commentary on Ovid's *Metamorphoses*: Extract from the Prologue[169]

'You were filled as a river with wisdom and your soul covered the earth,
and you multiplied riddles in parables and your name is spread abroad
even unto the islands' [Ecclus. 47: 16]. These words are written in the

---

[169] Tr. from Ghisalberti, 'Giovanni del Virgilio', pp. 13–19, with the permission of Leo S.
Olschki Editore.

thirty-third [*sic*] chapter of the book of Ecclesiastes [*sic*]. Four points can be noted in this passage. For, although the words are applied to something quite different from the matter at present under discussion, yet they can be marvellously well adapted to our purpose, just as if they had been spoken in praise of Ovid. But, not to waste time in idle talk, setting aside those four points which could be garnered from the aforesaid words and used to set out the praises of Ovid, I pass briefly to explain something quite different. I assert that from the aforementioned words we can extract those four causes which usually form the subject of enquiry at the beginning, or commencement, of books. The Philosopher [i.e. Aristotle] and Boethius and all the philosophers say that an essential part of knowing anything is to know the cause of that thing.[170] And elsewhere, we are said or considered to know something only when we know its causes and first principles right down to the basic elements.[171] Thus Virgil says: 'Muse, relate to me the causes....'[172] These causes, then, are four in number: the efficient cause (*causa efficiens*), the material cause (*causa materialis*), the formal cause (*causa formalis*) and the final cause (*causa finalis*)....

⟨I.⟩ So I say that the efficient cause is referred to in the words 'you were filled', as may be spoken of Ovid, who was 'filled with the river of wisdom', something which is quite obvious from all the works he wrote. This could be made clearer, if it were the appropriate moment, by comparing him to a river. But I pass over that. But it can be said that the efficient cause was twofold, that which moved and that which was moved. The moving cause was God Himself, who is the Prime Mover, who holds in His power the ordering of all mutable things. But another moving cause could be the ultimate objective (*finis*), that is, that Ovid should win the affection of the Emperor Octavian, and that his fame should be spread more widely through all the world. For, according to the Philosopher, in the field of invention the ultimate objective is the prime mover.[173] So it [i.e. the ultimate objective] is part of the efficient cause.

But the moved efficient cause was Ovid himself. He came from the city of Sulmona, and was of very noble family, for they came from equestrian stock. Sulmona was about twenty miles distant from Rome,[174] as he himself mentions elsewhere. He had another name, Publius, and I say that this was a family name. He was also Naso, as will appear in the title of this book. This author is said to have written a great many other books. First

---

[170] See esp. Aristotle, *Meta.* i. 2 (982ª); Boethius, *De cons. phil.* v. pr. i. 29 ff. (ed. Tester, pp. 386 ff.).

[171] A reference to Aristotle, *Physica*, i. 1 (184ª12–14).

[172] *Aeneid*, i. 8.

[173] Apparently a reference to Aristotle, *Physica*, ii. 3 (195ᵇ). Cf. Pietro Alighieri's use of this same idea, below, p. 477.

[174] *Sic.* Giovanni is also wrong about Ovid's name. In fact 'Publius' was the personal name, 'Ovidius' the family name.

of all he published a *Book of Epistles*, though some would have it that the first book he composed was the *Book without a Title*. But this is not true, for in the *Book without a Title* he mentions 'the epistles of Ovid', which he would not do if he had not already written it. And I say that [he published] this[175] when he had been sent to Rome to study, along with his brother, who was called Lucidius, who was two years older than Ovid. This Lucidius studied rhetoric and became a great teacher. But Ovid studied only verse composition, so much so that he could not express himself except in verse. So he says of himself: 'Whatever I tried to say turned out as verse.'[176]

His second work was the *Book without a Title*, in which he took Corinna as his subject, as can be seen from the book itself. Third, he wrote *Ovid, On the Art of Loving*, in which he taught how young men ought to court girls. This caused him to incur the enmity of Octavian, and according to some, this is why he was exiled from Rome, because he had taught unchaste [love] etc. Others say that the reason was that he had lain with the Empress, and yet others, that it was because once, as he was passing through Octavian's house, he saw Octavian committing a base and incestuous act. Others say that it was because he saw the lady Empress naked in the bath; and this was the reason, as I believe, for he himself says in his *Book of Sorrows*: 'Under orders, I saw Diana without her clothes.'[177] Ovid deliberately introduces this to indicate the cause of his exile. Because he was much loved by the people and enjoyed a very high reputation, Octavian, seeing that that was not a sufficient excuse, proceeded to accuse him of having taught young men to be unchaste.

When Ovid realized this he wished to win the goodwill of Germanicus Caesar, the nephew of Octavian, so that he might be his protector against Octavian. Therefore, the fourth book he wrote was *Ovid on the Fasti*, that is, 'concerning dignities', to do honour to Germanicus Caesar whom the people had elected to a very high-ranking position. In this work there are twelve books, according as there are twelve months in the year, because he assigned to each month its own book. But only six of these are still extant. It is said that the Church got rid of the other six because, when the Romans were discussing [the names of] the months of July and August, which at that very time were named from Julius Caesar and Augustus, Ovid inserted in the last six books of the *Fasti* many signs of Christ's coming, but made them apply to Julius Caesar and Octavian. But at any rate the book did him little good, for Octavian Caesar was not deflected by any entreaties from sending him into exile, and perhaps he would have had him killed, had it not been for the entreaties of his nephew. There-

---

[175] The antecedent seems to be the *Book of Epistles*. Giovanni seems to be saying (in this obscure sentence) that Ovid wrote this, his first book, just after he had been sent to Rome.

[176] *Tristia*, IV. x. 26.

[177] *Tristia*, II. 105. Giovanni's quotation differs radically from the accepted Ovid text.

fore, Ovid wrote his fifth book, *Ovid on the Remedy for Love*, so that he should remove the reason for his having been sent into exile. But because he saw that this was of no avail, he wrote his sixth book, *Ovid's Sorrows*, where he introduces the reason for his exile. The seventh book he composed was *Ovid, From Pontus*, the eighth book was *Ovid, Concerning the Head*, while the ninth was *Ovid's Metamorphoses*, which we have before us now. But indeed he wrote further books: *Ovid, On the Nut, On the Flea, On the Treatment of the Ears*, and other similar works, which I do not mention here, as they were of minor importance.

As regards his exile, some say that he died in exile, and Arigecus says this.[178] Others say that Octavian Caesar died two years before Ovid, and it was under these circumstances that Ovid was exiled. Others say that Octavian brought him back from exile, and when he came to Rome such a great multitude of people came to meet him because of his fame that while he was entering Rome in the midst of the people he was suffocated. So, then, it is clear what is the efficient cause of this book.

⟨II.⟩ The material cause is referred to when the text[179] says: 'and your soul covered the earth', in that it says 'the earth'. For the subject (*materia*) of this book is the treatment of change in things, for instance the metamorphosis of chaos into the four elements, and the earth into men, and so on in the case of other things, as will be apparent in the course of the book.

But it is to be understood that there are three forms of metamorphosis, natural, spiritual, and magical. Natural metamorphosis takes place in one of two ways, either by generation, when something is metamorphosed from nothing into being, or by corruption, when something from some existing state turns into nothing. Another kind of metamorphosis is spiritual, which happens in one of two ways: when someone from being sane becomes mad (that is, from being calm becomes violent), or when someone from being mad becomes sane (as when someone who is violent and stupid becomes wise and calm). Another kind of metamorphosis is magical. This is brought about by magicians who make a man seem to be an ass, without his really being so. For instance, we read in the *Life of St Antony* that a certain magician was fired with passion for a girl. He wanted her to be his wife, but was unable to have her. So, he used his magical skill to make her seem like a mare. Her parents were distraught when they saw her. At last, having heard of St Antony, they went to him and asked him if he would set free their daughter, who had been turned into a mare. St Antony replied: 'But it is you who have the eyes of horses, and that is why she seems to you to be a mare. But she really is a woman.'

---

[178] Lat. 'hoc dicit arigecus'. Reference unclear. The late Roman grammarian Agroecius or Agricius (supposing a transposition of letters) has nothing on the point, being concerned only with verbal and orthographic *differentiae*.

[179] i.e. the scriptural passage quoted at the beginning of the prologue.

Then he made a prayer over them, and sprinkled them with holy water, and the darkness fell from their eyes.[180]

Now to return to my theme, I say that Ovid treats of each sort of metamorphosis: of natural metamorphosis because he has men changed into gods, and this is possible, through the exercise of the virtues, as is clear from Boethius, book iv [of *The Consolation of Philosophy*].[181] He also treats of metamorphosis caused by magic in that Bacchus made Pentheus look like a stag, when in fact he was a man.[182] Metamorphosis, then, really is the material (*materia*) of this book.

⟨III.⟩ Third, the formal cause was referred to in the words: 'you multiplied riddles in parables'. This [formal cause] has two parts, that is, the form of the treatise (*forma tractatus*) and the form of the treatment (*forma tractandi*). The form of the treatise consists of the putting together and arrangement (*ordinatio*) of the fifteen books in this volume, and of the chapters into the aforesaid books, and of the parts within the chapters, going right down to the smallest parts which essentially introduce one idea (*sententia*) each. The manner of composition will be clear from the way the book is divided. For when an opposition becomes the basis of a comparison, as is said in the book *On Sophistical Refutations*, its terms are seen in their relative dimensions.[183] For things which are the opposite of each other, when juxtaposed, are seen to be greater or smaller. The form of the treatment, on the other hand, is the mode of proceeding, and this is twofold, that is, general and special. The general method is the quality of the style and the genre of the poem, whereas the special method is manifold because it offers definitions, is discursive and inferential, and so on in respect of its other qualities, as will appear in the course of the work.

⟨IV.⟩ The final cause is referred to when at the end of the text are added the words: 'and your name was spread abroad, even unto the islands'. This [cause] is twofold, that is, immediate and remote. The immediate objective is the identification of natural, spiritual, and magical metamorphosis, so that when the idea of metamorphosis had been established, Ovid could prove that it was possible for Julius Caesar to have been turned into a god. But the remote objective was that he himself should win everlasting fame by this and other books, and put briefly that is the aim of every poet.

Having considered these questions let us now come to the other two

[180] This story is told of St Macarius of Egypt in *Palladius de S. Macario Aegyptio* (PG xxxiv. 50); also in *De vitis patrum lib. viii: Historia Lausiaca*, chs. xix–xx (PL lxxiii. 1110B–11A. Cf. Vincent of Beauvais, *Speculum historiale*, xiv. xvii (*Speculum quadruplex*, iv. 547).

[181] Probably not *De consolatione philosophiae*, iv, met. vii. 32–5 (ed. Tester, p. 382), but iii, pr. x. 89–90 (ed. Tester, p. 280), on which see H. Chadwick, *Boethius: The Consolation of Music, Logic, Theology, and Philosophy* (Oxford, 1981), p. 211.

[182] *Metamorphoses*, iii. 708–31. Pentheus was made to look like a boar in Ovid, a lion in Euripides, *Bacchae*, and a calf in the Second Vatican Mythographer, ch. lxxxiii (*Scriptores rerum mythicarum*, ed. G. H. Bode (Celle, 1834) i. 103).

[183] Aristotle, *De soph. elen.* v (167ª7–20), xv (174ᵇ1–7), xxvi (181ª1–14), etc.

which are usually asked at the start of a book, namely, what is the title of the book, and to what part of philosophy does it pertain. It seems to me that we do not need to enquire into these questions because, once those four causes have been considered, it is immediately clear in each book what the title is and to which part of philosophy it pertains. For the title is supplied by the efficient cause, and the answer to the question 'to what part of philosophy does it pertain' is supplied by the material cause. Let us, then, state that the title of the book is as follows: *Here begins the first book of the Metamorphoses of Publius Ovidius Naso*, and in this the efficient cause and the material cause are referred to. The efficient cause is referred to in the words 'of Publius Ovidius Naso'. For Publius was his family name, while Ovid was his own. He is called Ovidius, that is, 'he who divides the egg', the egg being the world, because we rightly understand the egg to represent the world. For, just as in the egg there are four things—in the middle the marrow, that is, the yolk; above that the white; above that a thin skin or cartilege which surrounds the whole; and beyond that the hard shell—so the universe presents a similar picture. In the middle is the earth, like a yolk which is round, as will be clear later; above that is the water which should cover the whole earth, but does not do this because of the living creatures, as will be clear later; above that is the arc of heaven, which encompasses it; beyond that is the fiery ether like a hard shell, which holds everything in. And so Ovid could rightly be called 'he who divides the egg', that is, sees the whole world by reason of his wisdom. But he was called Naso because of the peculiar nature of his nose. For, just as we smell and get the scent of everything through the nose, so he wanted to catch the savour of everything in the universe. Hence the word 'knowing' (*gnarus*) comes from 'nostrils' (*nares*), and means 'wise', while 'senseless' (*ignarus*), that is, 'stupid', means, so to speak, 'without nostrils'. *Metamorphoseos* is a Greek name, and is derived from *meta*, 'concerning', and *morphoseos*, meaning 'change from one form to another'. For *hec morphosis* has the Greek genitive *huius morphosis* or *morphoseos*. Hence *metamorphoseos* is 'concerning change of form'. You will no doubt say: 'Is this not bad Latin?' No, because the Greeks have no ablative, and use the genitive instead. Another derivation is that *meta* is the same as *trans*, 'across', while *morphoseos* is 'change'. Hence the title *Here begins the first book of Metamorphosis*, that is, 'of change of form'. So the question of the title is explained.

But as to the part of philosophy to which it pertains, I say that it pertains to ethics, that is, moral philosophy, for all poets direct themselves towards behaviour.

Having considered all this, let us now come briefly to the division of the book. I say that this book is divided, after the manner of poets, into three parts, for first of all the author sets out his intention; secondly, he makes an invocation; third, he narrates ... FORMS CHANGED INTO NEW BODIES [i. 1–2]. But one really ought to say: 'bodies changed into new forms'. Yet this is wrong, for just as [those who make this objection] say that forms are not changed into bodies, equally bodies are not changed into forms. The reason is that body is in the category of substance, and form is in the category of quality. But it is impossible that the contents of categories should be transformed into each other. Hence forms cannot be changed into bodies or bodies into forms. Therefore, I say that this phrase must be interpreted in another way, by hypallage. According to Donatus, hypallage occurs when we alter one case to another, and he gives us an example: 'Give winds to the ship and commit the ship to the winds.'[184] Exactly the same thing happens here. You may perhaps say 'forms changed into new bodies and bodies changed into new forms', that is, they are to be assumed into new forms, because bodies are not changed into forms, but bodies [themselves] assume new forms. And this is possible, for, according to the Philosopher in his *Predicamenta*, substance admits of contrary qualities;[185] therefore, this is a property of substance.

PIERRE BERSUIRE

The Moral Reduction, Book XV: *Ovid Moralized*: Prologue and Extracts[186]

'They will turn away from listening to the truth and will turn to fables', says Paul, the apostle of Jesus Christ, who has planted and watered the Christian faith, in 2 Tim. 4[: 4]. I can indeed adduce this quotation to show that often one must use fables, enigmas, and poems so that some moral sense may be extracted from them, and even their very falsehood may be forced to serve the truth. For this is what Holy Scripture appears to have done in several places, where it is commonly acknowledged that it has concocted fables to demonstrate some truth. This is seen from the fable of the trees wishing to elect a king in Judg. 9[: 8]; from the thistle wishing to give his son a wife, in 4 Kgs. 14[: 9]; and from the eagle which was alleged to transport the pith of the cedar in Ezekiel [17: 3]. For Holy

---

[184] Lat. 'Trade ventos rati et trade ratem ventis.' Apparently a reference to the *Aeneid*, iii. 61 'dare classibus Austris'. Not found in the grammatical *artes* of Aelius Donatus, who does not discuss hypallage, which is actually 'a rhetorical figure by which the relations of things seem to be mutually interchanged'. The *Aeneid* commentary of Aelius Donatus is lost, but in Servius' commentary on the poem (generally supposed to have been based on the Donatus commentary), iii. 61 is indeed discussed as an example of hypallage. There is nothing about hypallage at this point in the *Aeneid* commentary of Donatus' namesake, Tiberius Claudius Donatus: *Tiberi Claudi Donati interpretationes Vergilianae*, ed. H. Georgii (Leipzig, 1905), i. 272–3.

[185] *Categoriae*, v (4ᵃ17–18).

[186] Tr. from *Petrus Berchorius, Reductorium morale, liber xv*, ed. J. Engels, pp. 1–4, 15–16, 28–30, with the permission of the Instituut voor Laat Latijn of Utrecht.

Scripture habitually uses these and similar fables and inventions so that
from them some truth may be extracted or deduced. The poets have done
exactly the same, for they originally invented fables because they have
always wished men to understand some truth by means of figments of this
kind.

If you go through the books of the poets it is quite çlear that it is hardly
ever, or even never, possible to cite a fable without its containing some
truth concerning nature or history. Hence Rabanus [Maurus], *On the
Nature of the Universe*, book xv, ch. 2 says that it is the duty of a poet to
change events which really happened, and give them another appearance
by using indirect, figurative language with a certain propriety. So in the
same passage it is said that Lucan was not a poet because he always
seemed to have composed histories rather than poems.[187]

Thus, sometimes a truth of nature underlies fables, as, for example, is
clear in the case of Vulcan, who is said to have been the son of Juno, to
have been cast down to earth from paradise and, because he fell from a
height, is feigned as having been made lame. For Juno signifies the upper
air, which truly gives birth to Vulcan, that is, the fire which we have here
on earth, and casts it down from on high through the collision of clouds.
He is said to be lame because flame always advances tortuously.

It is clear that historical truth sometimes underlies fable from the fable
of Perseus and Atlas. For Perseus is said to have killed the Gorgon and
with her head to have turned the huge giant Atlas into the mountain
which is called Atlas. This is, no doubt, because Perseus, a valiant soldier,
conquered and killed the daughter Gorgona of a king Borcus,[188] who
ruled the southern Isles which are called Gorgone, and bore off her head,
that is, her riches, kingdom, and possessions, with which he gathered an
army, so that he overcame Atlas, king of Africa, and forced him to fly to a
mountain. And so, because he henceforth disappeared, the loquacious
poets said that he had been changed into a mountain.

Therefore, because I see that Scripture uses fables to point out some
truth, either of nature or of history, it seemed appropriate for me, after my
moralization of the properties of things, and after the works of nature had
been made to relate to morals, to set my hand to moralizing the fables of
the poets,[189] so that in this way I could confirm the mysteries of behaviour
and of faith by using the very fictions of men. For a man may, if he can,
gather grapes from thorns, suck honey from a rock, take oil from the hardest stone, and build and construct the ark of the covenant from the
treasures of the Egyptians. And Ovid says that it is allowable to learn from
an enemy.[190]

---

[187] *De universo*, xv. 2 (PL cxi. 419).
[188] *Sic* for Phorcus.
[189] See our summary of the structure of the *Reductorium morale*, above, pp. 317–18.
[190] *Metamorphoses*, iv. 428.

But a great many writers have already dealt with the literal interpretation of fables, namely Fulgentius, Alexander, and Servius and a number of others. Moreover, a natural understanding is not our present purpose, for here we are discussing only the moral reduction. For it would be very difficult, indeed impossible, to give all fables a rationale according to the literal sense, as Augustine rightly concludes in *The City of God*, book three,[191] while Tully in the third book of *On the Nature of the Gods* says that first Zeno, then Cleanthes, and then Chrysippus undertook a very troublesome and quite unnecessary task in giving a rationale of invented fables.[192] So it is that in the present short treatise, which I wish to be a small part of this book of mine, I do not intend to touch on the literal sense, except very occasionally, but rather to work at the moral and allegorical exposition, following the book of Ovid which is called *Metamorphoses*, in which all the fables truly seem to be collected together as it were in the manner of a register (*tabula*).

So I shall divide this treatise into sixteen chapters; one, which will be reckoned the first, where something will be said about the forms and figures of the gods, and another fifteen in line with the fifteen books which are contained in the above-mentioned work of Ovid. But in certain places I shall add some fables which I have found elsewhere. I shall also remove and leave out those which I have judged to be unnecessary.

I trust that no one will take offence because the fables of the poets have been moralized on another occasion and, some time ago, were translated into French verse on the urging of the most illustrious lady Jeanne, formerly queen of France.[193] For indeed I had not seen that work until I had almost finished this treatise. But after my return from Avignon to Paris it so happened that Master Philip de Vitry, a very talented man and a most eager student of moral philosophy, history, and antiquities, a man well versed in all the branches of mathematical knowledge, gave me the aforesaid French book. I found there many good expositions, both allegorical and moral. So, having looked through all my own [interpretations] again, if I had not already put forward these new interpretations I assigned them to their correct place. The discerning reader will be able to judge this for himself. For generally, as often as I accept something from the aforesaid book, I make no delay in including it and setting it forth [in my own book].

So, with God's help, I shall begin with the first book of Ovid. But first of all I shall add some remarks about the forms and figures of the gods. But, because I have not been able to find in any other source a systematic

---

[191] Reference unclear; probably a free interpretation of *De civ. Dei*, III. xi.
[192] Cicero, *De natura deorum*, iii. 63.
[193] i.e. the anonymous *Ovide moralisé*, ed. C. de Boer, M. G. de Boer, and J. Th. M. van't Sant (Verhandelingen der Koninklijke Akademie van Wetenschappen te Amsterdam, Afd. letterkunde, NS XV, XXI, XXX, XXXVII, XLIII, Amsterdam, 1915–36).

series of images of the gods, in writing or painted, I have found it necessary to consult the respected master Francis Petrarch, an outstanding
poet and orator, and well versed in every kind of moral philosophy,
history, and poetry. He describes the aforesaid images in elegant verse in
one of his works.[194] I have also had to leaf through the works of Fulgentius, Alexander, and Rabanus and thus assemble from various sources the
figures and the images which the ancient writers assigned to their
fictional gods in conformity with the teachings of history or natural
history.

Very recently there has come into my hands a certain treatise in which
some images of the gods were set out with reasonable clarity, and were
even in some degree made to relate to moral expositions.[195] Having
weighed up all these sources, I have put together, as best I could, the
image of each god, and having blended all of them together I have drawn
up an allegorical or moral exposition, separated out the straw from the
wheat and gathered the wheat in my barn, to the praise and glory of the
true God who sits in the assembly of the gods but who is our God, who
before all other gods lives and reigns over all gods for ever and ever.
Amen. . . .

[MARS]

Mars is depicted as the third among the gods because the star of Mars is
third in the order of the planets. Mars was depicted as a furiously angry
man, sitting in a chariot with a helmet on his head, and carrying a whip in
his hand. A wolf was depicted in front of him, because that animal was
particularly dedicated to him by the pagans of antiquity. For he was
Mavors, that is, he who devours men (*mares*), and was called the war god
by the pagans. According to Solinus, the Neuri[196] used to make sacrifices
to him on the point of spears.[197]

For the poets made all this up on purpose to show the nature and
character of that star of Mars which is hot and dry, and therefore is said to
govern a choleric disposition. So it is through his influence that wars and
civil dissensions break out.

In allegorical terms, then, I say that we can understand this god and his
image to represent the princes of this world and tyrants, and most of all
warlike men. For they are said to sit in a chariot because they have no
stable support; indeed their situation, disposition and frame of mind all
veer about like a chariot. 1 Kgs. 25[: 29] says: 'The wicked will be whirled
about as a wagon wheel', and Ecclus. 33[: 5]: 'The heart of the wicked man

---

[194] Cf. above, p. 317.
[195] i.e. the *Fulgentius metaforalis*, ed. in part by H. Liebeschütz (Leipzig and Berlin, 1926).
[196] Bersuire's text has 'populi Neutrorum'.
[197] See *Collectanea*, xv. 1, ed. T. Mommsen (Berlin, 1895), p. 82.

is as the wheel of a wagon.' Mars is depicted as helmeted and having a terrifying countenance because in truth such men strive to appear terrifying, and take their pleasure in arms and helmets. For they exult in being the object of men's fear and in being seen in arms, and in appearing terrifying. Ecclus. 9[: 25]: 'An unjust man is a source of fear in his city.'

They are said to be armed with a whip because their whole ordained purpose appears to be to chastise others. So, the wolf is depicted going before them, by whom is designated the tyrants' rapacious and wolf-like entourage. For assuredly such worldly princes and tyrants always have by them wolves, that is, cruel and wicked officers who know how to, and wish to, snatch away the sheep, that is, to harm subjects, as a result of which they [i.e. those same officers] may themselves (in turn) engage in the activities of war. For wolves are said to be dedicated to Mars, because, assuredly, wolf-like and wicked seneschals, bailiffs, or lieutenants are held in high esteem by such cruel and unjust soldiers and princes, and [those seneschals] are devoted to them [i.e. to the unjust soldiers and princes] individually and are seen to stand before them and to be enhanced in prestige and honoured by preferment and high offices. Prov. 29[: 12]: 'If a prince gladly heeds lying words, all his officials will be wicked.'

Those are said to be the gods of war who care only about strife and war. They are also called *mavortes*, for they devour the *mares*, that is, the good and virtuous men. They are said to devour, because it is a certain fact that they usually attack males rather than females, that is, the good rather than the wicked, and those in orders rather than lay people, and consume them with their plundering and extortion. The Neuri then, that is, their wicked servants, are said to worship swords and arms to fall in with their wishes, in so far as these are said to delight in wars and disputes and in the use of arms out of affection for their masters.

Or, suppose that the chariot in which such people sit represents the noise and tumult of the vices. This chariot runs on four wheels, that is, the four evil affections or the four kinds of pride, namely, pride which has its origin in noble ancestry, in high office, in strength, and in ample wealth. Around these affections is heard the turbulence of boastfulness and pomp, and the noise of horses and attendants, as the Psalm [19: 8] says: 'Some in their chariots and some on their horses.'

Or, say that Mars signifies the sin of discord, because he sits in the chariot of the evil mind, which runs on four wheels, namely the four vices of the spirit: avarice, pride, slander, and injustice. For those are the four wheels or vices which carry Mars, that is, discord, strife, wars, and dispute. They bring that strife into being and give it strength. It is strife which is said to carry the whip, because it is through strife that others are lashed. The god is also called *Mavors* because through it males (speaking in the literal sense) are swallowed up in battles. The Neuri, that is, men who love strife and quarrels, clearly worship Mars the god of war, that is, the vice of discord, and worship, that is, love, swords to his greater glory. . . .

[DIANA]

Diana, alias the Moon, Proserpina, and Hecate, is named the seventh of the planets. So I place her seventh in the sequence and number of the mythical gods. She was depicted with the features of a lady holding a bow and arrow, chasing horned stags in the hunt. Around her dance troops of Dryads, Oreads, Naiads, and Nereids, that is, troops of the nymphs of the woods, the hills, the springs, and the seas, along with troops of horned satyrs, who were said to be the gods of the fields. The poets invented all these attributes because the moon, which is the source of [all] moisture, has it in her power to increase moisture in the woods and hills, the springs, and in the sea, and to beget the grass and the seeds in the fields and woods and waters. She also gives huntsmen light at night and so is said to be the goddess of hunting and woods and hills. So, those who dwelt in the woods and hills and springs worshipped her.

So let us say that by that goddess we can understand the glorious Virgin, who certainly is armed with the bow of pliant mercy and the arrow of prayer. By their operation the horned stag, that is, the proud devil, is overcome. So doubtless the bands of nymphs must dance around her and cluster around her with devotion, that is, the bands of holy souls and particularly of consecrated virgins and other girls. She is bound to have standing round her particularly closely, by reason of their devotion, troops of Oreads, mountain-nymphs, that is, contemplative souls; Dryads, nymphs of the woods, that is, souls devoted to the active life of labour; Naiads, nymphs of the rivers and springs, that is, souls who dwell in the rivers of the Scriptures or of devotional life; and Nereids, nymphs of the sea, that is, souls who have their dwelling in the bitter, briny element of the religious life or of penance. So, in brief, this can be said of her, S. of S. 7[: 1]: 'What will you see in the Shulamite[198] except the companies of camps?', and in the Psalm [44: 15]: 'Virgins will be led before the king in her train.' Likewise, the troops of satyrs, that is, of sinners who are in a similar way thought of as gods and mighty men in the field of this world, and who are said to be horned by reason of their pride, must dance and run hither and thither round her, begging pardon and mercy from her, and imploring help against demons and vices. And so one sings in church: 'We will run in the fragrance of your perfumes: the young maidens have loved you exceedingly' [S. of S. 1: 2–3].

Or else suppose that the satyrs, the gods of the fields, are prelates, and particularly bishops with their horns and mitres, who should, out of

[198] Here Bersuire has 'Sunamite' for 'Sulamite'.

feelings of deep affection, run to and fro around that Diana, that is, around the Blessed Virgin, serving her with devotion, and frequenting her altar with devotion, love, and the desire to serve her, repeating the words of S. of S. 1[: 3]: 'Draw me after you. We will rush to the fragrance of your perfume.'

Or suppose that Diana represents the evil woman, who is said to hold the bow and arrows because she wounds foolish men by plundering them and shoots arrows at them using temptation and lust as her weapons. So she is wont to draw companies of nymphs after her, that is, young women who are deceived by her example. She is also wont to have with her horned satyrs, that is, wanton men who are puffed up with the horns of high office. This can also be said about elderly roués[199] or even in general about the sin of wantonness. For these [i.e. the nymphs] are the women who shoot their darts and goad men on to lust, and therefore they often bring with them bands of young girls and even of men with horns, that is, prelates. Hence the words of S. of S. 1[: 2] can be addressed to wantonness: 'Your name is oil poured out, and therefore the maidens have loved you greatly.'

And if you wish, suppose that those nymphs who serve Diana, that is, young people who serve lust, are sometimes nymphs of the hills, in so far as they are of lofty ancestry; sometimes they are nymphs of the woods, in so far as they come from the ranks of the peasantry, sometimes nymphs of the rivers, in so far as they are rich and delicate, sometimes nymphs of the sea, in so far as they are penitents and religious. For, in brief, it is a true fact that today it is not possible to cite any position high or low, in the church or in the world, in which one cannot give instances of nymphs serving Diana, that is, persons obedient to wantonness. For, as is said in the psalm [18: 7]: 'For there is no one who can hide himself from His wrath.'

Or, if you wish, suppose that Diana is avarice or the desire to plunder, who incessantly shoots her arrows at that deer, that is, the timorous poor, and therefore arrogant, horned princes and stiff-necked, proud tyrants are wont to dance around her. The nymphs of the mountains, woods, rivers, and seas, that is, every sort of person, obey her. For the mountain-nymphs are those who are in mountains and towers and castles. The wood-nymphs are Cistercians and others who dwell in woods. The river-nymphs are those who dwell in towns, around which you will usually find a river flowing. The sea-nymphs are those which dwell in churches and monasteries, etc. It is scarcely possible to cite any class of person which does not serve the huntswoman Avarice. So Jeremiah [6: 13] says: 'Great and small, all are dedicated to greed. From the prophet to the priest all deal falsely.'

---

[199] Lat. 'maquerellus', Modern French *maquereau*, meaning 'pimp'.

IX

The Transformation of Critical Tradition: Dante, Petrarch, and Boccaccio

An attempt to describe in detail the debt of Dante Alighieri (1265–1321), Francis Petrarch (1304–74), and Giovanni Boccaccio (1313–75), to medieval literary theory, and the extent to which they transformed traditional doctrines, would require a book in itself.[1] The present chapter, which is of necessity highly selective, offers extracts from Dante's *Convivio* (written between 1307 and 1319), Petrarch's *Letters on Familiar Matters* (written mainly bewteen 1325 and 1366) and Boccaccio's *Genealogy of the Gentile Gods* (between 1350 and 1374). Since the attribution to Dante of the commentary-section of the *Epistle to Can Grande della Scala* is hotly disputed, and it may well not be the poet's own work, this appears in Ch. X, as do our extracts from Boccaccio's *Short Treatise in Praise of Dante* and his commentary on the *Divine Comedy*, because they very obviously fall within the category of 'assessments of the new author', Dante being regarded by many as a new *auctor* as well as the great 'new poet'.

The *Divine Comedy* itself (which was written between 1314 and 1321) is believed to have established Dante as 'one of the few poets who belong to all times and all nations',[2] but it is also very much a product of Dante's own time and place, and especially of the main intellectual movement of the day, namely scholasticism. In particular, scholastic literary theory helped to make the mould in which the *Divine Comedy* was cast—a fact which is highlighted by the long and learned series of medieval commentaries on the poem. Other medieval poems, of course, had reflected the literary interests of the academic establishment and had received their due reward in the form of glosses, Walter of Châtillon's *Alexandreis* (finished c.1182)[3] and Alan of Lille's *Anticlaudianus* (see Ch. IV) affording good examples. But there are major differences between these cases and that of the *Divine Comedy*. First, Dante's poem was not a school textbook of the usual type nor was it bounded by the confines of the trivium; it made far deeper inroads into theology than the *Anticlaudianus* had done. Then again, Dante had written not in Latin but *in vulgari*, in his native Italian. Finally, Dante commentary began with Dante himself. The *Vita nuova* ('New Life', written between 1292 and 1295), and the *Convivio* ('Banquet') are expositions of his own *canzoni*, and commentary on the *Divine Comedy* was, at the very least, fostered by Dante's *familia*: Jacopo and Pietro Alighieri produced sophisticated explanations of their illustrious father's poem, and the relevant section of the Can Grande epistle is, if not by

---

[1] In the case of Dante we already have a useful anthology, *Literary Criticism of Dante Alighieri*, tr. and ed. R. S. Haller (Lincoln, Nebr., 1973).

[2] *ODCC*, s.v. Dante Alighieri, p. 376.

[3] See *Galteri de Castellione: Alexandreis*, ed. M. L. Colker (Padova, 1978), pp. xi–xviii, xxviii–xxx, 275–514.

Dante, probably the work of a member of his circle.[4] No one worked harder at becoming an *auctor*—not just a maker of verses but an authority—than Dante, and his self-promotion was inextricably intertwined with the promotion of the Italian language.

Self-commentary, New Commentary, Vernacular Commentary. During the thirteenth century, what might be called the 'translation movement' was generating an unprecedented number of translations, into several European vernaculars, of many authoritative Latin works, and in bilingual manuscripts many different arrangements of text and gloss were assayed. The treatment of the Old French *Consolation of Philosophy* reveals some of the possibilities. Five of the twenty-two extant manuscripts of Jean de Meun's translation offer a 'parallel text' layout of the Latin original and French rendering together with extensive Latin glosses drawn from William of Conches's commentary (on which see Ch. IV).[5] The status of the Old French within this layout is difficult to gauge, but it seems to be subservient to the Latin text and gloss, an additional aid to the reader's comprehension of the original.[6] One of the stock late medieval definitions of *translatio* was, we should remember, 'the explanation of meaning (*expositio sententiae*) in another language'.[7] Manuscripts of the most popular of all the Old French translations of Boethius, the 'Anonymous Verse–Prose Version' or 'Revised Mixed Version' as it is variously called, present a very different picture.[8] The text is commonly divided into short sections, each of which is followed by a section of French commentary, often marked 'gloss', the information coming from William of Conches's commentary. Here the French is of the first importance; features of layout which had been developed in generations of scholastic manuscripts are being used in presenting a vernacular work to an audience of wealthy laymen.

In this case we are dealing with the reception of an old and long-established book, the work of an *auctor*, a 'set text' in medieval grammar-schools. Of far greater significance for the history of literary theory and criticism are the changes of attitude to vernacular works, which, while in many instances still dependent on Latin models, were beginning to demand attention of a kind which hitherto had been afforded only to the established authorities. Academic commentary became a precedent and source for 'modern' commentary (i.e. commentary on writers who were *moderni*) and even 'self-commentary': certain writers set about the business of producing

[4] On the *Vita nuova*, *Convivio*, and *Epistle to Can Grande della Scala* as self-commentary see esp. Sandkühler, *Die Frühen Dantekommentare*, pp. 50–7, 93–95; L. Jenaro-MacLennan, 'Autocomentario en Dante y comentarismo latino', *Vox Romanica*, xix (1960), 82–123; and G. R. Sarolli, 'Autoesegesi dantesca e tradizione esegetica medievale', *Convivium*, xxxiv (1966), 77–112.

[5] For discussion see A. J. Minnis, '"Glosynge is a glorious thyng": Chaucer at Work on the *Boece*', in id., *The Medieval Boethius: Studies in the Vernacular Translations of De consolatione philosophiae* (Cambridge, 1987), pp. 106–24.

[6] See N. F. Palmer, 'Latin and Vernacular in the Northern European Tradition of the *De consolatione philosophiae*', in Gibson (ed.), *Boethius*, pp. 365–6.

[7] Hugutio of Pisa, *Magnae derivationes*, s.v. *glossa*, in Oxford, Bodleian Library, MS Bodley 376, fo. 84[r]; followed by John of Genoa, *Catholicon*, s.v. *glossa* (Venice, 1483), unfol.

[8] Cf. Palmer, 'Latin and Vernacular', pp. 366–7.

commentaries on 'new' texts, texts written by their contemporaries and even by themselves.[9]

The glosses (in Italian) which Boccaccio appended to his *Teseida* (1339–41?) provide an interesting case in point.[10] This Italian epic on the life of Theseus was studiously equipped with apparatus of the kind which accompanied its Latin models in manuscript, i.e. the *scholia* on the *Thebaid* (conflated and amplified by such glossators as Arnulf of Orléans) and on the *Aeneid* (the work of Servius, 'Bernard Silvester', etc.), an apparatus designed to dispose the discerning reader in favour of the poem and underline for his benefit the superlative literary criteria in accordance with which it should be judged and esteemed. Here, techniques of exposition traditionally used in interpreting 'ancient' and Latin authoritative texts are being used to indicate and announce the literary authority of a 'modern' and vernacular work.

That statement could be applied, with even more justice, to a work which was probably one of the inspirations of Boccaccio's effort at self-commentary, the *Convivio*, a far more elaborate example since it constitutes a commentary on three of Dante's own *canzoni* and, in the first part of the work, on the methods of commentary themselves.[11] But Dante had a problem which Boccaccio did not share in the case of the *Teseida*: the poetry he was explaining seemed to describe a period of his life in which he had given way to a demeaning passion. In order that the precise historical dimensions of this problem may be illuminated, the *Convivio* must be approached by way of Dante's first major work, which was also his first attempt at self-commentary, the *Vita nuova*.[12]

The *Vita nuova*, Dante tells us at the outset, is based on a much larger book, the book of his memory;[13] he has acted as a *chiosatore* or glossator by commenting on and selecting from the words he finds there under the rubric *Incipit vita nova*. Whether this is meant to serve as the *titulus* for the whole work is unclear, as is the precise meaning of the term *vita nova*. *Novus* can mean not only 'new' but also 'first' and 'inexperienced', in which sense it could refer to Dante's early life or youth.[14] Taking the term in the sense of 'new', however, it may be taken as referring to Dante's discovery of a new possibility in his art,

[9] See esp. B. Nardi, 'Osservazioni sul medievale "accessus ad auctores" in rapporto all'*Epistola a Cangrande*', in id., *Saggi e note di critica Dantesca* (Milan and Naples, 1966), pp. 268–305; Sandkühler, *Die frühen Dantekommentare*, pp. 50–7, 70–3, 74–6, and the articles by Jenaro-MacLennan and Sarolli cit. above, n. 4.

[10] The *Teseida* glosses are printed in e.g. *Giovanni Boccaccio: Teseida*, ed. S. Battaglia (Florence, 1938), and translated into English in B. M. McCoy, *The Book of Theseus* (New York, 1974).

[11] In the following discussion we have used the edition of the *Convivio* by M. Simonelli (Bologna, 1966), and drawn on the English translation by P. H. Wicksteed (Temple Classics, 4th edn., London, 1924).

[12] We have used the edition of the *Vita nuova* in *Le Opere di Dante Alighieri*, ed. E. Moore and P. Toynbee (Oxford, 1924), pp. 205–33, and drawn on the translation by B. Reynolds (Harmondsworth, 1969).

[13] On this image of the 'book of memory' see esp. C. S. Singleton, *An Essay on the Vita nuova* (Cambridge, Mass., 1949), pp. 25–54.

[14] Cf. *Vita nuova*, tr. Reynolds, pp. 103–4.

namely, the poetry of praise.[15] This is nothing to do with Hermann the German's definition of tragedy as the art of praise—nowhere does Dante reveal any knowledge of the Averroistic *Poetics*—but rather it denotes the praise of Beatrice. An encounter with a group of ladies who asked him about the aim of his love brought Dante to the realization: '"Since there is so much joy in words which praise my lady, why have I ever written in any other manner?" And so I decided to take as the theme of my writing from then on whatever was praise of this most gracious being.'[16] This type of dramatized narration of a poet's life in the light of his poetry is very much in the tradition of the biographies (*vidas*) and prose descriptions of the origins of poems (*razos*) which had circulated along with troubadour verse (cf. above, p. 14), but of course the *Vita nuova* is on a much larger and more elaborate scale.[17] Moreover, those earlier works are third-person sketches, whereas Dante is writing about himself, here as in the later *Convivio*. In the *Convivio* he addresses the problem directly.[18] Rhetoricians forbid a man to speak of himself 'except on needful occasion', since it is impossible to speak of someone without blaming or praising him, and both self-blame and self-praise are to be avoided. Boethius and Augustine, however, spoke of themselves with good reason. In his *Consolation of Philosophy* the former sought to 'ward off the perpetual infamy of his exile, showing that it was unjust', while in his *Confessions* the latter gave 'example and instruction' by showing how his life progressed from 'bad to good, and from good to better, and from better to best'. Dante claims that he is motivated by both the fear of infamy and the wish to give instruction. He wants to dispel the impression, which the reader of his *canzoni* may have conceived, that he pursued a great passion of love. The *Convivio* will, he declares, show that not passion but virtue was his 'moving cause' (*movente cagione*, cf. the Latin term *causa movens ad scribendum*). Moreover, he purposes to explain the true meaning (*vera sentenza*) of the poems in question because no one will understand them if he does not, since 'it is hidden under figure of allegory', which explanation will give subtle instruction as well as fair delight.

This reference to allegorical interpretation indicates the basic difference between the *Vita nuova* and the *Convivio*: the latter represents a far more thorough appropriation of the principles and terminology of academic literary criticism than did the former. The main academic procedure in evidence in the earlier work is that of textual division or *divisio textus*, an aspect of the scholastic commentators' concern with *forma tractatus* or *ordinatio libri*, i.e. the

---

[15] Cf. William Anderson, *Dante the Maker* (London, 1980), pp. 136–7.

[16] *Vita nuova*, xviii (ed. Moore–Toynbee, p. 215; tr. Reynolds, p. 54).

[17] See P. Ranja, *Lo schema della Vita nuova* (Verona, 1890), and V. Crescini, 'Les razos provenzali e le prose della *Vita nuova*', *Giornale storico della letteratura italiana*, xxxii (1898), 463–5. The influence of the historiographic tradition should also be taken into account: see V. Branca, 'Poetica del rinnovamento e tradizione agiografica nella *Vita nuova*', in *Studi in onore di I. Siciliano*, i (Florence, 1966), pp. 123–48. But see also the convincing argument of J. Mazzaro, *The Figure of Dante: An Essay on the* Vita nuova (Princeton, NJ, 1981), 71–94, that Dante does not adhere faithfully to any traditional model.

[18] *Conv.* I. ii (ed. Simonelli, pp. 4–6, tr. Wicksteed, pp. 9–13).

structure and arrangement of the various parts which constituted a whole work.[19] Careful division and subdivision of a poem enables us to understand it better, Dante affirms, and the more minute the divisions the deeper the understanding will be[20] (cf. the elaborate subdivisions of the verses of Boethius and Seneca recorded in Ch. VIII). But the *Vita nuova* is far from being a *vita auctoris*—though, to be sure, it furnished abundant material for the *vitae Dantis* which later scholars habitually included in their commentaries on the *Divine Comedy*. Dante's first major work does not offer an elevated apology for poetry; it neither makes nor implies any large claim to literary authority for the *canzoni* discussed therein, either in terms of their subject-matter or their language. Its vernacular poetic is centred on the emotion of love: 'The first to write as a vernacular poet was moved to do so because he wished to make his verses intelligible to a lady who found it difficult to understand Latin.'[21] Although Dante does discuss the use of personification allegory and refers to other rhetorical devices, he makes 'no mention of allegory or of a possible different interpretation of the poems included in the work'.[22] A few years later, however, Dante moved beyond the values of the *dolce stil nuovo*, and simultaneously or in rapid succession began (and subsequently left unfinished) the *Convivio* and *On Eloquence in the Vernacular*. The former is quite clearly based on the medieval genre of the commentary on an *auctor*; indeed, Dante calls it 'quasi comento', a kind of commentary.[23] The *Convivio* begins with an Aristotelian 'extrinsic' prologue (cf. above, p. 320) about causality, in this instance the causes which inhibit man's natural desire for knowledge, and proceeds to apply an impressive amount of erudition to the matters allegedly raised by the *canzoni*, including the movements of the heavens and the earth; the angelic hierarchies; the immortality and nature of the soul; the three natures of man; the entire framework of medieval learning; the degrees of love; the ages of man; the Roman empire and imperial authority; wisdom, nobility,

[19] On these concepts see Minnis, *Authorship*, pp. 145–55, and see further the excellent description of Aquinas's idiom of *divisio textus* in A. Dondaine and L. J. Bataillon, 'Le Commentaire de S. Thomas sur les Météores', *AFP* xxxvi (1966), 110–17.

[20] See esp. *Vita nuova*, xix, where, after an elaborate division of his poem *Donne, ch'avete intelletto d'amore*, Dante declares: 'to uncover still more meaning in this *canzone* it would be necessary to divide it more minutely' (ed. Moore–Toynbee, p. 217; tr. Reynolds, pp. 58–9). Cf. the section 'The Divisions of a Poem: Two Examples' in Haller, *Literary Criticism of Dante*, pp. 83–7. *Divisio textus* is used throughout the *Convivio*: see esp. II. ii. 6 (ed. Simonelli, p. 34; tr. Wicksteed, p. 69), IV. ii. 1 (ed. Simonelli, p. 131; tr. Wicksteed, p. 232), and IV. iii. 1 (ed. Simonelli, p. 135; tr. Wicksteed, p. 238). For discussion of Dante's *divisiones* see esp. Jenaro-MacLennan, 'Autocomentario', pp. 86ff.

[21] *Vita nuova*, xxv (ed. Moore–Toynbee, p. 223, tr. Reynolds, p. 73).

[22] C. Grayson, 'Dante's Theory and Practice of Poetry', in id. (ed), *The World of Dante: Essays on Dante and his Times* (Oxford Dante Society, Oxford, 1980), p. 151. Other defences of the literal sense of the *Vita nuova* include Singleton, *Essay on the Vita nuova*, pp. 110–16, and id., 'Dante's Allegory', in R. J. Clements (ed.), *American Critical Essays on the Divine Comedy* (New York and London, 1967), p. 98. P. Mandonnet's argument, in *Dante le théologien* (Paris, 1935), that the *donna gentile* is a mere symbol who represents theology and Dante's clerical vocation was roundly criticized by E. Gilson, *Dante the Philosopher*, tr. D. Moore (London, 1948), pp. 1–81.

[23] *Convivio*, I. iii. 2 (ed. Simonelli, p. 6).

and the virtues. Love has receded before learning. Specifically, the compassionate *donna gentile* who, according to the *Vita nuova*, comforted him for a short time after Beatrice's death is now allegorized as Lady Philosophy (here Dante is, as he himself admits, influenced by the female personification created by Boethius);[24] no rival to Beatrice, but rather a means towards her now glorified self.

And here we encounter what may be described as the central dilemma of the 'modern' or 'new' commentary on vernacular love-poetry which Dante did so much to instigate: how could scholastic interpretative method, a product of a world-view wherein *amor* (the love between man and woman) was at best regarded as a limited and transitory good that had to give way to *caritas* (the superior love of God and one's neighbour), come to terms with a poetry that had human love as its main subject and professed that woman was man's joy and all his bliss?[25] Various solutions were found. Some writers took love and the lady simply as the point of departure for literature which was concerned with 'science' rather than with sex, good examples being afforded by the poem *Donna mi prega*, the *canzone d'amore* of Guido Cavalcanti (*c.*1259–1300);[26] the third *canzone* which Dante discusses in the *Convivio*, the *Contra gli erranti*, a poem about nobility in which love is explicitly abandoned; perhaps the second *canzone* analysed therein, *Amor che ne la mente*, which, in the opinion of K. Foster and P. Boyde, signifies the 'dedication of intellect and will to the Divine Wisdom';[27] and Thomas Usk's Middle English *Testament of Love* (before 1388).[28] In the commentary on Cavalcanti's poem by the fourteenth-century physician Dino del Garbo,[29] all the qualities of human love are explained, including its unpleasant and morally dangerous aspects.[30] In

---

[24] *Convivio*, II. xii. 2 (ed. Simonelli, p. 57).

[25] Here we borrow an idiom from Geoffrey Chaucer's *Nun's Priest's Tale*, in *Canterbury Tales*, VII. 3166, ed. F. N. Robinson, *The Works of Geoffrey Chaucer*, 2nd edn. (London, 1957), p. 203. In *De vulgari eloquentia*, II. ii (ed. A. Marigo (Florence, 1957), pp. 170–81), Dante describes love as one of the three most important matters (the others being safety and virtue) which ought to be treated in the ornate vernacular language. In the *Convivio*, however, the values of scholastic literary theory are uppermost in his mind; it is the implications of such theory for vernacular poetics which is our concern here.

[26] See the edn. of this text and Dino del Garbo's commentary by Bird, 'The *Canzone d'Amore* of Cavalcanti'. See further the study by Shaw, *Guido Cavalcanti's Theory of Love*.

[27] K. Foster and P. J. Boyde, *Dante's Lyric Poetry* (Oxford, 1967), ii. 173. Here the problem is, how to decide if the imagery connected with a moral personification is being used to elevate an earthly lady, or if the imagery of an earthly lady is being used to vivify a moral personification. Far more acute problems of interpretation are raised by *Voi che 'ntendendo*, on which see below, n. 45.

[28] See Minnis, *Authorship*, pp. 163–4.

[29] See the refs. above, n. 26. Dino's commentary has also been edited by G. Favati, 'La glossa latina di Dino del Garbo a "Donna me prega" del Cavalcanti', *Annuali del Scuola Normale Superiore di Pisa*, 2nd ser., xxi/1–2 (1952), 70–103.

[30] By his natural appetite, Dino declares, man is inclined towards 'venereal acts, in which there is great fury and intemperance', but 'no one should allow himself to adhere to this passion, since there is neither utility nor wisdom and virtue in it' (ed. Bird, 130, 136). Is this interpretation consonant with Cavalcanti's intention? That depends on one's own reading of *Donna mi prega*. For R. Montano, *NCE* iii. 354, for instance, it 'clearly expresses the repudiation of love by a philosopher who praises contemplation of the truth above all and

general, this is the kind of exposition which the poem demands.[31] A lady, Cavalcanti claims, had asked him to explain what love is, and this is precisely what he proceeds to do, without further reference to her: the remainder of the poem offers a condensed version of the psychological and medical doctrine which Dino was to explain at greater length.[32] Similar 'required exposition', if thus it may be called, may be found in, for example, Pietro Alighieri's commentary on the fifth canto of the *Inferno*, wherein his father had spoken of several persons 'whom love had parted from our life' (cf. our translation of this commentary below, in Ch. X).

Far more problematic is poetry in which the love of man and woman is given a value in the literal sense of the text, a value which is lost or undermined in the allegorical interpretation. An excellent example of that effect is provided by certain medieval interpretations of the story of Orpheus and Eurydice. What was for Ovid a moving tale of human grief and loss in love becomes, in the Boethius commentaries of William of Conches and Nicholas Trevet, a pertinent warning of the way in which the lower part of the soul, its concupiscible or affective element, is constantly striving to degrade the higher part, its reason or intellect (cf. above, pp. 121, 320). Something of the sort happens in Dante's allegorical interpretation of the first poem in the *Convivio*, the *Voi che 'ntendendo*, wherein the human love-object is *replaced* by an edifying personification.[33] Dante's other way out of the dilemma is, of course, recorded in the *Divine Comedy*, wherein the human love-object is *equated* with the edifying personification, as Beatrice leads the narrator through paradise, even unto the Empyrean Heaven. In this very special case, it would seem, one can be an *auctor* and be in love. (The Dante commentators, however, were inclined to make this innovation appear less daring by emphasizing that Beatrice played the role of Theology to Virgil's Philosophy). Here, it may be said, is Dante's ultimate reconciliation of the matter of vernacular poetry with the method of late medieval literary theory.

Working in a very different intellectual milieu, John Gower (c.1330–1408) coped with the same dilemma in a different but equally interesting way. In the Latin self-commentary which accompanies the Middle English *Confessio amantis*, a firm distinction is made between Gower the *auctor* of the whole work in all its ethical and philosophical ramifications, and his *personae* of the confessing lover (who speaks in the first person) and Genius, priest of Venus, who hears his confession: 'From here on the author, feigning himself to be a lover, as if in the person of those whom Love constrains, intends to write

rejects the fears and mutability of lovers', which would align Cavalcanti with del Garbo. On the other hand, Shaw, *Cavalcanti's Theory of Love*, p. 159, suggests that Dino 'has little sympathy with the importance Guido attaches to the intellectual part of love'.

[31] Because, as Anderson says, 'through drawing on the medieval language of physiology and psychology' Cavalcanti and his friends had 'transformed the tradition of love poetry and produced a new school of intellectualized and "scientific" poetry' (*Dante the Maker*, p. 109).

[32] Cf. the similar views expressed in a later, Italian commentary on *Donna mi prega* which has falsely been ascribed to Giles of Rome and seems to have been indebted to Dino's exposition, discussed by Shaw, *Cavalcanti's Theory of Love*, pp. 149–59.

[33] Cf. below, p. 382 and n. 45.

about their various passions one by one in the various sections of this book.'[34] (One may compare the similar use of *persona* theory made by Bonaventure in his Ecclesiastes commentary: see Ch. VI). Generally, the Latin commentary takes a more moralistic line than does the English text, though it must be emphasized that this self-commenting (and self-moralizing) mode is not confined to the gloss, because Gower employs it in the text as well, most notably in the sapiential *Prologus* and in the epilogue.[35] Considered as a whole, Gower's work may be seen to offer many things to many men: discerning and wise readers, guided by the self-commentary, will be very aware of its 'lore', a different kind of reader may be interested chiefly in its 'lust' or pleasure-giving qualities, while others may appreciate both its profit and delight in good measure.

In the *Confessio amantis* a Latin commentary is attached to a vernacular poem; in the *Convivio* a vernacular commentary is provided for vernacular poems, and (typically) Dante is highly articulate about why he has done this. He has, he explains, provided oaten rather than wheaten bread with which to eat the dishes (i.e. the *canzoni* themselves) served in the banquet of knowledge, for three reasons: the wish to avoid undue inversion of hierarchical order (*ordinazione*), out of 'spontaneous generosity', and from the natural love of his own language.[36]

In explaining the first of these points Dante draws on the language of hierarchical organization which we have already encountered in medieval discussions of the due order or 'subordination', to use the technical term, of the sciences (see especially our introductions to Chs. III, IV, VI, and VII). *Sapientis est ordinare*, Thomas Aquinas had declared at the beginning of his commentary on the *Nicomachean Ethics*, a work on which Dante repeatedly drew in the *Convivio*: it is the function and obligation of the wise man to 'order' in every sense of the word.[37] In his *Metaphysics* Aristotle had explained this idea by saying that a wise man gives orders but does not receive them; he must not obey a less wise man but must himself be obeyed.[38] Commenting on this passage, Aquinas explained how a 'subordinate' art or science is 'ordered' in the sense of being directed to the end of a superior art or science.[39] Similarly, Dante affirms that the inferior must serve the superior; the servant should be obedient to his lord. But if his commentary were in Latin (Latin being the superior language) it would not be the subordinate but the ruler, by reason of nobility, of virtue (*vertù*), and of beauty. Of nobility, because Latin is stable and uncorruptible whereas the vernacular is not. Of virtue, because Latin makes manifest many things conceived in the mind which the vernacular cannot. Of beauty, because the words correspond more regularly and

---

[34] *The English Works of John Gower*, ed. G. C. Macaulay (EETS, ES lxxxi–lxxxii, London, 1900–1), i. 35–6.

[35] See Minnis, '"Moral Gower" and Medieval Literary Theory', pp. 50–78.

[36] *Convivio*, i. v. 2–3 (ed. Simonelli, p. 10).

[37] *In lib. Eth.* i, lect. 1 (tr. Litzinger, i. 6).

[38] *Meta.* i. 2 (982ᵃ⁻ᵇ).

[39] *In lib. Meta.* i, lect. 2 (tr. J. P. Rowan, *St Thomas Aquinas: Commentary on the Metaphysics of Aristotle* (Chicago, 1961), i. 19).

so are more harmonious in Latin than in the vernacular. Latin follows art, whereas the vernacular follows usage. Moreover, had the present exposition been in Latin it would not have had any knowledge of, or been familiar with (the Italian term *conoscenza* denotes acquaintance as well as knowledge and recognition) the poems in question, nor would it have been obedient to them.[40] For all these reasons, then, a Latin commentary would not have been the subject of the *canzoni* but their ruler, and so it is appropriate that the *Convivio* is in the vernacular.

Having taken away with one hand, Dante now proceeds to give lavishly with the other, putting the case for the vernacular with great conviction and force. Of special interest is his use of the distinction between 'nobility of soul' and 'nobility by ancestry and rank', which is to figure so largely in the fourth treatise of the *Convivio*. The *locus classicus* of this distinction is of course Boethius' *Consolation of Philosophy*, III, pr. iii-met. iii; Nicholas Trevet's relevant commentary (in Ch. VIII) may usefully be compared with Dante's applications. In the *Convivio*, I. ix, it is argued that this Italian work was composed for those (potentially) noble-souled folk who possess only the vernacular: most of those who can read Latin have learnt it for gain and ignoble motives.

The notion of innate nobility of soul lies at the very centre of Dante's thinking in *On Eloquence in the Vernacular*, which is basically about the cultivation of Italian on the model of Latin (the beauty of which consists in its very artificiality). In the *Convivio* Latin was deemed to be the noble language because of its stability and incorruptibility; in the later treatise the vernacular is said to be the nobler in respect of its origins: it was first employed by the human race (Adam spoke Hebrew, not Latin) and it is first employed by each man, 'being natural to us'.[41] Cecil Grayson brings out the central idea very well:

... the nobility of Man and the nobility of his language lie in their natural origins, and just as natural human virtue can be fostered and can bring forth its fruits and aspire to greater perfection, so can the natural vernacular be trained and cultivated by art.[42]

Dante could be accused of having blurred, for polemical purposes, the distinction between the 'ancient' vernacular, Hebrew, and the 'modern' vernacular with which he was familiar from birth. But an answer to that charge can be elicited from *Convivio*, IV. xiv, where Dante attacks those who believe that the lapse of time is necessary to create nobility or gentility (*gentilezza*). The same 'erring ones' also believe that a churl or a churl's son may never become gentle—and here they contradict themselves by denying that it is impossible to come to the moment that begets nobility. In fact, because mankind has a common origin or root, each and every human being can cultivate the virtues and thus attain the true nobility, nobility of soul. The influence of Boethius is at once obvious and profound.

[40] *Convivio*, I. vi–vii (ed. Simonelli, pp. 12–15).

[41] *De vulg. eloq.* I. i, vi (ed. Marigo, pp. 2–9, 30–7); tr. A. G. Ferrers Howell, repr. R. Duncan (London, 1973), pp. 15–16, 22–4.

[42] C. Grayson, '*Nobilior est vulgaris*: Latin and Vernacular in Dante's Thought', in *Centenary Essays on Dante, by Members of the Oxford Dante Society* (Oxford, 1965), p. 76.

> All human kind on earth arises from the same origin . . .
> Why shout about your lineage or your forebears? If you consider
> Your beginnings and God your Author, no man is now degenerate
> Save who embracing baser things in vice forsakes his proper origin.
>
> (Boethius, *On the Consolation of Philosophy*, III, met. vi)[43]

There is, then, nothing to stop the Italian vernacular from building on its origins, which are as noble as they are natural, and attaining through careful refinement the greatness of that 'virtuous operation which is its own proper excellence', to adapt a phrase from the *Convivio*, I. x.[44] Thereby the *prezioso volgare* can achieve perfect literary nobility—and also authority, which stems from reason (whether divine or human) rather than from age. Dante does not say that in so many words, but it is obvious that he felt it. The implications for literary criticism—and for literature itself—were immense.

Innovation in Allegory. We have seen that in the *Convivio* Dante reconciled love with literary authority by claiming, in effect, that 'that was no lady—that was Dame Philosophy' (to rewrite the old joke). This claim was made possible by allegorical interpretation of a kind which might have changed utterly the meaning of a poem which had been written much earlier (between late 1293 and the spring of 1294), the *Voi che 'ntendendo*,[45] and so something must be said on Dante's famous yet by no means clear account of allegorical interpretation, with which our selection from the *Convivio* begins.

The exposition of his *canzone*, Dante declares, must be both literal and

---

[43] Tr. Tester, p. 257.

[44] *Convivio*, I. x. 8 (ed. Simonelli, p. 20; tr. Wicksteed, p. 45). On the later debate on the relative merits of the two languages see C. Grayson, *A Renaissance Controversy: Latin or Italian? An Inaugural Lecture, 6 Nov. 1959* (Oxford, 1960).

[45] For a cogent and comprehensive account of the biographical problems associated with this poem see Foster–Boyde, *Dante's Lyric Poetry*, ii. 160–2, 341–62. While they admit that there is nothing in the text 'to compel an allegorical interpretation' they conclude that there is no 'cogent reason why we should take this [i.e. the meaning as explained in the *Convivio*] as an afterthought and suppose that he did not originally write the poem with that intention'. However, we see no reason to rule out the possibility that in *Il Convivio* Dante retrospectively allegorized a poem which originally had recorded a real love-affair, this being done not as a mere 'afterthought' but as part of an attempt to elevate vernacular poetry through the appropriation (and adaptation) of scholastic literary theory. Our suggestion takes account of the moral, and moralizing, bias of the medieval commentary-tradition which Dante was drawing on in the *Convivio*. Similar effects are found in the self-exegesis of other late medieval love poets: see e.g. John Gower's self-commentary on the *Confessio amantis* (described above) and the prose preface (perhaps by the poet himself, though recently this has been disputed) to Juan Ruiz's *Libro de buen amor*, in Juan Ruiz, *The Book of True Love*, ed. A. N. Zahareas and tr. S. R. Daly (University Park, Pa., and London, 1978), pp. 23–9. The crucial point to grasp is that interpretative *distance* exists between text and gloss: their relationship is not one of semantic parity and equivalence, as most Dante scholars have assumed. The strategies of commentary are suffused with definite values which define the commentator's terms of reference, whether he is expounding an 'ancient' or a 'modern' text, someone else's work or his own. This is not, of course, to imply that Dante is trapped within the interpretative system which he has appropriated; rather, he is exploiting it with impressive awareness of its paradoxes and possibilities. Further discussion of these matters may be found in A. J. Minnis, 'Authors in Love: The Exegesis of Medieval Love Poets' (forthcoming).

allegorical, and he proceeds to consider the allegorical sense from two points of view, the 'allegory of the poets' being distinguished from the 'allegory of the theologians'. In theological texts three allegorical senses (allegorical, moral, and anagogic) may be found, but in poetry, only the one. Dante does not explain this at all well—which is hardly surprising, given the ambiguity of the term *allegoria* in late-medieval literary theory. This can designate one of three things:

(1) the secular allegory, which is essentially moral and to that extent unified and 'one', habitually extracted from classical poetry. See, for example, William of Conches's interpretation of the fable of Ulysses and Circe (above, pp. 126–30) and William of Aragon's interpretation of Orpheus in the underworld (pp. 332–6). It should be added that this type of allegory can develop different layers or levels, but these do not match the several senses of Scripture identified by theologians, as Pierre Bersuire's moralization of the *Metamorphoses* illustrates (see above, p. 324).

(2) all three allegorical or spiritual senses of Scripture, considered together as a single spiritual sense, in contrast with the literal sense on which it rests.

(3) the allegorical (i.e. the prefigural, typological, or Christocentric) senses of Scripture in particular, in contrast to both the tropological sense and the anagogic sense.

As soon as he introduces the subject of allegory, Dante instantly defines it in terms appropriate to secular allegory (cf. designation 1 above): this is the sense that hides itself under the mantle (*manto*, corresponding to the Latin *integumentum*) of fables, and is a truth hidden under a beautiful fiction. He proceeds to illustrate this with part of the fable of Orpheus, who with his lyre controlled natural things; that is to say, the wise man with the instrument of his voice makes cruel hearts tender and humble. Then he says that 'theologians and poets use this sense in different ways; but since I am concerned here with observing the ways of poets, I take the allegorical sense in the way that it is used by poets.' We are not told how the theologians actually do understand the allegorical sense; from other sources, such as those collected in Ch. VI, we know that by this they meant the prefigural, typological, or Christocentric sense (cf. denotation 3 above), and realize that Dante is shying away from the suggestion that the 'allegory of the poets'—this being the interpretative method he intends to apply to at least the first two of his *canzoni*—has anything in common with that. His profound intention in the *canzoni* was, on his own testimony, to treat of philosophy, not to prefigure Christ or His Church. Having invoked scriptural exegesis, he carries through his definitions of the other spiritual senses (the moral and the anagogical) as found in the Bible, even though he has just ruled them out of court in the present self-commentary. Dante's account would have been clearer, perhaps, if he had assimilated his allegory of Orpheus—which, after all, is a moral allegory or *moralizatio*—to his account of the moral sense of Scripture. But he has been trapped into clumsiness by the different and conflicting denotations of that tricky term *allegoria*.

What, then, of the discussion of allegory found in the commentary section of the *Epistle to Can Grande della Scala*, which many scholars still believe to be the work of Dante himself? There the *Divine Comedy* is described as '"polysemous", that is, having several meanings', and the four types of textual meaning are defined with reference to Ps. 113: 1–2 (see below, Ch. X). This is, quite clearly, an account of the 'allegory of the theologians', and the question naturally arises if we should approach Dante's masterpiece equipped with that interpretative system rather than taking it as an instance of the 'allegory of the poets'. Charles Singleton had no doubts on the matter:

> The crux of the matter, then, is this: if we take the allegory of the *Divine Comedy* to be the allegory of the poets . . . then we shall be taking it as a construction in which the literal sense ought always to be expected to yield another sense because the literal is only a fiction devised to express a second meaning. In this view the first meaning, if it does not give another, *true* meaning, has no excuse for being. Whereas, if we take the allegory of the *Divine Comedy* to be the allegory of theologians, we shall expect to find in the poem a first literal meaning presented as a meaning which is not fictive but true, because the words which give that meaning point to events which are seen as historically true. And we shall see these events themselves reflecting a second meaning because their author, who is God, can use events as men use words. *But*, we shall not demand at every moment that the event signified by the words be in its turn as a word, because this is not the case in Holy Scripture.
>
> I, for one, have no difficulty in making the choice. The allegory of the *Divine Comedy* is, for me, so clearly the 'allegory of theologians' (as the Letter to Can Grande by its example says it is) that I can only continue to wonder at the efforts made to see it as the 'allegory of poets'.[46]

But the problem may not be resolved as neatly as that. Singleton is being reductive in defining the literal sense of poetic allegory as 'only a fiction devised to express a second meaning'. Of course, such allegorical interpretation was practised in the Middle Ages—witness the standard method of interpreting the fable of Orpheus in the underworld (already discussed above), Dante's reading of Orpheus's music as wise eloquence, and indeed his treatment in the *Convivio* of *Voi che 'ntendendo*. But it is incorrect to say that for Dante and medieval writers in general *fictio* invariably meant a false, or at least different, device for the concealment of truth.[47] One may cite Arnulf of Orléans' description of Lucan as a poet and historiographer combined (see Ch. IV); Boccaccio's elaboration of the Ciceronian/Macrobian category of fiction which comprises events both 'literal' and possible (*Genealogy*, xiv, ix, translated below); the common view of the satirists as speaking the 'naked truth' (see above, pp. 116–17), which may be compared with Boccaccio's description of the comedians Terence and Plautus intending nothing other than 'the literal meaning of their lines' in their fiction;[48] and of course the insistence of the Averroistic *Poetics* that literary 'likening' should not degenerate into total fiction (see Ch. VII). Fiction, then, may be defined in its most

---

[46] Singleton, 'Dante's Allegory', pp. 95–6.
[47] This view being expressed by Grayson, 'Dante's Theory and Practice of Poetry', p. 155; cf. G. Paparelli, *Ideologia e poesia di Dante* (Florence, 1975), pp. 53–138.
[48] *Geneal. deor. gent.* xiv ix (tr. below, p. 424).

comprehensive sense as 'simply what the poet makes within him as opposed to what is created or exists outside him'.[49]

Returning to the problem of interpreting Dante's literary practice in terms of the medieval literary theory to which he contributed so considerably, it could be said that in the *Convivio* Dante is taking the line that his *canzoni* are truth-concealing 'integumental' fictions whereas in the *Divine Comedy* it is verisimilar fiction[50] which is being written: Dante did not actually visit Hell, Purgatory, and Heaven, but his imaginative account of such a journey keeps within the realm of the possible. To this extent we agree with R. H. Green's critique of Singleton's hypothesis, but in our opinion he goes too far in the opposite direction by over-emphasizing the fictivity of the *Divine Comedy*. From the list of *modi agendi* identified in the poem by the *Epistle to Can Grande* Green singles out the *modus fictivus*: 'The key word, I think, is "fictive"—and this is precisely the quality which distinguishes poetic revelation from divine.'[51] This obscures the fact that, according to many medieval theologians, fiction is found in Holy Scripture (as Ch. VI has made perfectly clear). Moreover, while there certainly was a vogue in late medieval exegesis for emphasizing the solid literal basis of Scripture—this Thomistic commonplace is echoed by Dante, and Singleton makes much of it—we should remember that not all the books of the Bible were supposed to be comprehensible in simply referential terms. The arch-literalist Nicholas of Lyre believed that the Song of Songs spoke 'in a parabolic manner' and that in Revelation St John had not always made explicit the significance of his imaginary visions, although he himself knew what they meant.[52] In the house of medieval textuality there were many mansions.

Viewed in the light of the literary theory provided in our previous sections, the claim which the Can Grande epistle makes for the significance of Dante's text must be seen as quite conservative in some respects. First and foremost, it affirms the primacy of the literal meaning in considering the subject of the *Divine Comedy*. 'If, however', it continues, 'the work is regarded from the allegorical point of view, the subject is man according as by his merits or demerits in the exercise of his free will he is deserving of reward or punishment by justice.' That sounds very much like a moral or tropological interpretation, in which Dante's characters are taken as *exempla* of what to do and what to avoid; such a reading proceeds by generalizing ethical precepts from the specifics of the literal sense rather than by subverting it. This

---

[49] Grayson, 'Dante's Theory and Practice of Poetry', p. 155.

[50] It should be noted, in considering the title *Comedy*, that 'comedy' entailed verisimilar fiction, as stated e.g. in *Ad Herenn.* I. viii. 13, and implied by Boccaccio's statement about Terence and Plautus, cit. above. For recent contributions to the debate on the relationship between truth and fiction in the *Comedy* see the lively essays by R. Hollander, 'Dante *Theologus-Poeta*', *Dante Studies*, xciv (1976), 91–136, and P. Dronke, 'The *Commedia* and Medieval Modes of Reading', in id., *Dante and Medieval Latin Traditions* (Cambridge, 1986), pp. 1–31.

[51] R. H. Green, 'Dante's "Allegory of Poets" and the Mediaeval Theory of Poetic Fiction', *Comparative Literature*, ix (1957), 122.

[52] *Bibl. glos.* iii. 1817–19, vi. 1449–50, 1457–8.

impression is confirmed by the subsequent classification of the text under ethics: 'the branch of philosophy to which this work is subject ... is that of morals or ethics'. *Ethicae supponitur*: the formula is familiar from the *accessūs ad auctores* (cf. Ch. I). In the final analysis, then, the author of the Can Grande epistle does not seem to be going very far beyond the 'allegory of the poets' as described in the *Convivio*, which type of allegory had a definite ethical intent (cf. Ch. IV).[53] That is to say, he is reducing the spiritual senses to one, namely the moral or tropological sense, perhaps under the influence of the relatively uniform and essentially moral allegory which medieval commentators were used to extracting from classical literature. (Reduction of this kind is common, it should be added, in late medieval biblical exegesis of the proselytizing kind which was produced for a relatively wide audience, good examples being the Old French *Bible moralisé*, Nicholas of Lyre's *Postilla moralis*, and the moralized Bible which constitutes book xvi of Bersuire's *Moral Reduction*.) In Dante's thought, in the Can Grande epistle, and indeed in the commentary-tradition on the *Divine Comedy*, elements from both hermeneutic traditions interweave and reciprocate.

To make the same point in a different way, the discussions of allegorical interpretation found in the *Convivio* and the Can Grande epistle seem to be exploring the common ground which medieval literary theory was defining between poetic fiction which is in some sense true and scriptural truth which can on occasion be expressed through figures, fictions, and enigmas. The slight clumsiness and rather tentative nature of Dante's account of allegory in the *Convivio* is invaluable to the historian of literary criticism because it provides an indication of the unusualness of what is happening. Dante was the great innovator who saw the possibilities with an insight that no one else had shown. The very introduction of theological allegory into a discussion of the meaning of secular poems was something new, or at least something which was done with a definite sense of occasion. And the main feature of that occasion was the aggrandisement of the vernacular. Very little of the theological exegetical system was germane to Dante's specific interpretative needs in the *Convivio*, but its invocation served his general polemical purpose very well.

What is happening in the *Divine Comedy* is, of course, far more difficult to appreciate, but the tensions are conveyed well enough by two remarks which Boccaccio made about the poem. At one point in the *Genealogy* he names Dante as one among 'many Christian poets who, under the covering of their fictions (*sub tegminibus fictionum*) have set forth the deep and holy meaning of Christianity';[54] elsewhere he declares that Dante 'stands forth rather as a Catholic and sacred theologian than a mere mythmaker'.[55] Bringing about a

---

[53] However, it should be noted that Dante affords ethics an exceptionally important position in his allegory of the various heavens and the liberal arts; there ethics is identified as the *primum mobile* which 'moulds, orders, and renders fruitful the workings of all the other sciences'. For discussion see Gilson, *Dante the Philosopher*, pp. 100 ff.

[54] *Geneal. deor. gent.* XIV. xxii; tr. C. G. Osgood, *Boccaccio on Poetry: Being the Preface and the Fourteenth and Fifteenth Books of Boccaccio's* Genealogia deorum gentilium (Indianapolis and New York, 1956), p. 99.

[55] Ibid. XV. vi (tr. Osgood, p. 113); cf. XIV. x (tr. Osgood, p. 53).

reconciliation between the fictions of the poets and the truths of the theologians was no easy task, for Dante as for his readers. Further confirmation of this is afforded by the debate, conducted over several generations of commentaries on the *Divine Comedy*, as to whether or not Dante was divinely inspired and how his text should therefore be interpreted (inspiration being necessary for spiritual sense to exist in writing, according to the theological tradition: see pp. 234, 241). The history of that debate has still to be written. It seems clear, however, that the issue of the relevance of the fourfold method of interpretation in analysing 'new' and/or secular poetry was, in the main, a matter of great interest only to Italian intellectuals. Certainly, the 'allegory of the theologians' did not occupy the commanding position throughout the cultural landscape of Western Europe which the pan-allegorists have assigned to it. If theological allegory did sporadically influence Dante's *modus componendi* in the *Divine Comedy*—and it must be recognized that he believed himself to have been specially chosen to fulfil a divine mission—this was the exception rather than the rule in late medieval literature.

Much personal credit is due to Dante, and it should be given to him. He did not, however, think and write in splendid isolation. His achievement may be considered as part and parcel of a definite cultural trend, namely, that gradual process of literary assimilation by which sacred and secular literature had, in the eyes of its readers, come together in respect of subject-matter, stylistic form, and end. The implications of Dante's establishment of 'theology' and 'poetry' as two categories which could be compared and contrasted in literary terms were worked out by later writers like Petrarch and Boccaccio, to whose contribution in this sphere we may now turn. In the Italian Trecento literary theory emerged with a degree of sophistication commensurate with that of Dante's brilliant practice in the *Divine Comedy*, and certainly stimulated by Dante's innovations.

The Classification of Poetry. In Boccaccio's *Genealogy*, xiv. vii, poetry is not classified under grammar; instead grammar, and indeed all the other liberal arts, are types of knowledge which the poet should draw on—in other words, to use the medieval term, they are 'subordinate' disciplines which serve poetry as their superior. Neither may poetry be reduced to rhetoric, for 'integumental' composition belongs to poetry alone and is the means whereby it transcends rhetoric. We are very far from the world of Hugh of Saint-Victor, who believed that the songs of the poets were the 'mere appendages of the arts' (see above, p. 122): in Boccaccio's classification the arts are the instruments of poetry, a view shared by Petrarch.[56] Indeed, Boccaccio goes so far as to term poetry a science (*scientia*) which 'has ever streamed forth from the bosom of God'. Earlier in the *Genealogy* he had shown that he understood that term in its full technical sense: the Aristotelian definition of *scientia* as being concerned with the eternal and universal is finding application in the statement

---

[56] See further Salutati's view of the *doctus poeta* who has to be prepared in the liberal arts, discussed by J. R. O'Donnell, 'Coluccio Salutati on the Poet-Teacher', *Med. Stud.* xxii (1960), 240–56, esp. pp. 252–5.

that poetry is 'a stable and fixed science founded upon things eternal, and confirmed by original principles; in all times and places this knowledge is the same, unshaken by any possible change'.[57]

In the *Genealogy*, XIV. vii, *scientia* is being used more or less synonymously with *ars* ('art'), and indeed with *facultas*, as when poetry is called 'a power (*facultas*) springing from God's bosom'.[58] However, it should be noted that in the *Genealogy*, XIV. iv, poetry as a science is contrasted with law as a mere *facultas* in the pejorative sense of a skill which is technical, limited, and variable, and (in this case) something practised for material gain.[59] Like theology and philosophy, poetry despises wealth. Like philosophy, it reveals the nature of earthly things. Like theology, it aspires to knowledge of those divine matters which transcend the nature of earthly things. In sum, as a science, the place of poetry is with theology and philosophy.

Two main strands of influence are obvious in Boccaccio's attempts to forge links between these sciences. First, there is what Dante called the 'allegory of the poets', through which the philosophical credentials of fictions were revealed (cf. our Ch. IV). Second, there was the complex of theological ideas comprising not just the standard notions concerning the senses of Scripture but, *inter alia*, the recently established theory of the 'transferred' manners of speaking which formed part of the literal sense (cf. Ch. VI). Time and time again Boccaccio compares the styles of the poets with those of the inspired authors of Scripture, greatly to the credit of the former, here incurring a debt to those schoolmen who, from the time of *Alexander's Sum of Theology* onwards, had described how the biblical *modi tractandi* include those which are affective, imaginative, figurative, and even fictional. Behind his argument that the obscurity of poetry is no good cause for condemning it (*Genealogy*, XIV. xii) lie theologians' defences of the obscurity of Holy Scripture (cf. especially Ch. V); behind his protestation that poets are not liars (*Genealogy*, XIV. xiii) lie the theologians' explanations that, even though fictions and even apparent lies are sometimes to be found in Scripture, this is no good reason for concluding that it is ever false or mendacious (cf. Ch. VI).

But such appropriation of the theological tradition must surely reach its climax in the somewhat startling proposition that theology is poetry and poetry is theology. Poetry, declares Petrarch in the first of the letters translated below, is not inimical to theology, and he uses a Dionysian argument to prove it: 'When Christ is called, now a lion, now a lamb, and again a worm, what is that if not poetic?' That is why Petrarch can 'almost say that theology is poetry written about God'. In his *Short Treatise in Praise of Dante* Boccaccio removes the 'almost' from this declaration. Not only is poetry theology but 'theology is, in addition, poetry' (see below, p. 498).

Precisely what is the nature of the relationship between poetry and theology? Petrarch says that they are similar in that both use allegorical

---

[57] *Geneal. deor. gent.* XIV. iv (tr. Osgood, p. 25). Cf. Aristotle, *Eth. Nicomach.* vi. 3–7 (1139^{b}14–1141^{b}22).

[58] On this terminology see above, p. 212 and n. 47.

[59] Tr. Osgood, pp. 21–6; cf. id., pp. 150–1 n.

discourse, although there is a considerable difference in their subject-matter, secular poetry being about 'men and the gods' and Holy Scripture being about 'God and matters divine'. Similarly, in his *Praise of Dante* Boccaccio argues that although sacred and secular writing do share a common mode of treatment (*modo del trattare*, cf. the Latin term *modus tractandi*) they can differ in subject-matter, the subject of sacred theology being divine truth whereas that of ancient poetry is pagan gods and men. They also differ in end or objective (*fine*, cf. Latin *finis*): Holy Scripture enables us to attain that glory which Christ has opened up to us, while pagan poetry moves us to virtuous action. Quite clearly, the end of poetry is not incompatible with the superior end of theology, although it is, of necessity, limited by the pagans' ignorance of Christ and their subsequent failure to understand the nature of our supreme salvation.

In the *Genealogy*, xv. viii, Boccaccio highlights certain similarities and differences between poetry and theology by using the distinction, found in Augustine's critique of Varro, between three kinds of theology: mythical or fabulous, physical, and civil or political. (Nicholas Trevet, in his commentary on Seneca's tragedies, had applied the same distinction, but with no polemical intent: see above, pp. 343–4). Augustine had found physical theology preferable to the other two kinds inasmuch as it comprised profound doctrine about nature and divinity, but he made it abundantly clear that the pagans had erred greatly in confusing things natural with things divine; this polytheism and idolatry has been utterly superseded by Christian truth. Boccaccio instead posits a sort of historical progression from the ancient theologians to their Christian successors, and declares that the old theology can sometimes be employed to good effect in the service of the new one. 'More than one orthodox poet' has clothed in fiction the sacred teachings; indeed, the poets can sometimes even be called 'sacred theologians'. Doubtless he had in mind Christian poets like Prudentius, Sedulius, Arator, and Juvencus, who are named elsewhere in the *Genealogy* in a similar context.[60] Finally, Boccaccio remarks that even sacred theologians become physical theologians when occasion demands, as when they express truth by the fable of the trees choosing a king, a reference to Judg. 9: 8–15, which scriptural passage he also uses in the *Genealogy*, xiv. ix (also translated below).

Physical theology is, in the *Genealogy*, xv. viii, identified with the doctrine of those ancient theologizing poets or myth-lovers described in Aristotle's *Metaphysics*:

... it is because of wonder that men both now and formerly began to philosophize, wondering at first about less important matters, and then progressing little by little, they raised questions about the more important ones, such as the phases of the moon and the courses of the sun and the stars and the generation of the universe. But one who raises questions and wonders seems to be ignorant. Hence the philosopher is also to some extent a lover of myth, for myths are composed of wonders. If they philosophized, then, in order to escape from ignorance, they evidently pursued their studies for the sake of knowledge and not for any utility.[61]

---

[60] See *Geneal. deor. gent.* xiv. xxii (tr. Osgood, p. 100).
[61] *Meta.* i. 2 (982ᵇ12–21), in the text of William of Moerbeke (tr. Rowan, i. 22).

In his gloss Thomas Aquinas makes clear the connection between this primal philosophy (or theology) and poetry:

> ... it is evident that the philosopher is, in a sense, a philomyth, i.e., a lover of myth, as is characteristic of the poets. Hence the first men to deal with the principles of things in a mythical way, such as Persius and certain others who were the seven sages, were called the theologizing poets.[62]

While Aquinas was interested mainly in the subsequent development of metaphysics, when the causes of things became better known and the wonder went out of speculation, Boccaccio found in Aristotle's words powerful support for his vision of poetry as a science which transcended the merely practical and utilitarian to draw its practitioners 'away into the discovery of strange wonders', 'away to the region of stars, among the divinely adorned dwellings of the gods and their heavenly splendours'.[63]

Poetry, then, for Boccaccio, as for Petrarch, was generally sacral but not sacred (although there is sacred poetry in Scripture). This distinction is a crucial one because, as Ronald Witt has argued, neither of them believed that the poet operated under direct divine influence.[64] By contrast, their older contemporary Albertino Mussato (1261–1329) claimed that poetry was a divine science because it was inspired by God—a view attacked by Giovannino of Mantua (fl. c.1315), who concluded his analysis of the relevant passages of the *Metaphysics* with the statement that since the old myth-lovers did not hand down to us a true theology they do not deserve the name of theologians.[65] To the argument that the Holy Scriptures often employed verse, Giovannino replies that even if all theology were written in verse, that would not make theology poetic: one should not simply give the name of poetry to any science that expresses itself in verse, an argument remarkably similar to one found in the Averroistic *Poetics* (see p. 291), which Giovannino may have known. It is true, he continues, that poetry and theology share the use of metaphors, but poetry uses them only to induce delight while Scripture uses them to veil divine truth. This is an explicit reiteration of the position of Thomas Aquinas (cf. p. 240). In stark contrast is the fifteenth-century Neoplatonic conception of the poet as the heir to a divinely revealed body of truth, composed under heavenly guidance, and of poetry as the supreme science. In his *On the Division and Use of the Sciences*, Gerolamo Savonarola (1452–98) set his face against such opinions, attacking those who claimed that 'since sacred Scripture and poetry both use metaphors, poetry is nothing else than theology'. 'It is one thing', he argues in the spirit of Aquinas, 'to use metaphors because of necessity and the magnitude of the subject', as in the Bible, and quite 'another to use them for pleasure and weakness of truth', as in pagan poetry.[66] Savonarola's views did

---

[62] *In Meta.* l, lect. 3, c. 55 (tr. Rowan, i. 24).

[63] *Geneal. deor. gent.* XIV. iv (tr. Osgood, pp. 24, 25).

[64] 'Coluccio Salutati and the Conception of the *Poeta theologus* in the Fourteenth Century', *Renaissance Quarterly*, xxx (1977), 538–63; cf. id., *Hercules at the Crossroads*, pp. 406–10.

[65] Witt, 'The *Poeta theologus*', pp. 540–1; Greenfield, *Humanist and Scholastic Poetics 1250–1500*, pp. 80–5, 87–9.

[66] Cit. and discussed by Hardison, *The Enduring Monument*, p. 7.

have some influence, but of course he could not turn the cultural clock back to the thirteenth century. The debate on the relationship between poetry and theology continued well into the Renaissance.

Now we may turn to consider the way in which Boccaccio lent substance to the connection between poetry and philosophy, that body of knowledge inferior only to Christian theology. In the *Genealogy*, XIV. xvii, he argues that the poets, far from being the mere 'apes' (*symias*) of the philosophers, are in fact of their 'very number', 'since they never veil with their fiction anything which is not wholly consonant with philosophy as judged by the opinions of the ancients'. But, although 'their destination is the same as that of the philosophers, they do not arrive by the same road'. The philosopher proceeds by a process of syllogizing, whereas the poet conceives his thought by contemplation (*meditando*) and, 'wholly without the help of syllogism, veils it as subtly and skilfully as he can under the outward semblance of his fiction'.[67] Here Boccaccio seems to be rejecting the common late-medieval attempt to classify poetry as the lowest part of logic, with the imaginative syllogism as its characteristic device (see Ch. VII). Savonarola attempted to restore poetry to that relatively humble position, arguing that it has its proper type of syllogism in the *exemplum*.

Poetry is 'the most faithful guardian' of philosophy, Boccaccio declares, 'protecting it as she does beneath the veil of her art',[68] and for him, as for Dante and Petrarch, Virgil is the *altissimo poeta*, the poet-philosopher *par excellence*. In the *Genealogy*, XIV. ix, x, and xiii, Boccaccio elaborates on Macrobius's assertion that Virgil successfully combined the figments of poetry with the truth of philosophy (cf. the similar orientation in 'Bernard Silvester''s *Aeneid* commentary, excerpted in Ch. IV).[69] From the work of this the 'greatest Latin poet', we are assured, 'the sap of philosophy runs pure'.[70] The *Aeneid* illustrates supremely well the Macrobian category of fiction which rests on a solid foundation of truth (the *narratio fabulosa*),[71] and Virgil's *causa recitandi* is unexceptionable, comprising as it does the desire to imitate Homer, ethical intent, and patriotic and civic zeal. Virgil cannot, then, be adjudged a liar, and the same is true for other poets.

Virgil's great limitation was, of course, that he lacked knowledge of the one true God who is known to Christians, although he did sometimes make monotheistic statements. But this ignorance is excusable, Boccaccio avers, since the poet was born in the wrong place at the wrong time. Macrobius had referred to Virgil as a man 'above error'; Boccaccio was obviously determined to depict him as a man above any error for which he could be held personally responsible. 'Surely if Virgil could have known and worshipped God in due form, nothing but that which is holy could be found in his works.'[72] Macrobius had

---

[67] Cf. Osgood's translation, p. 79.
[68] *Geneal. deor. gent.* XIV. xviii (tr. Osgood, p. 84).
[69] Cf. Macrobius, *In Somn. Scip.* I. ix. 8 (ed. Willis, p. 41; tr. Stahl, p. 126).
[70] *Geneal. deor. gent.* XIV. x (tr. below).
[71] Macrobius, *In Somn. Scip.* I. ii. 9 (ed. Willis, p. 5; tr. Stahl, p. 85).
[72] *Geneal. deor. gent.* XIV. xv (tr. Osgood, p. 75).

also described Virgil as 'schooled in all the arts',[73] which may have influenced Boccaccio's declaration, in the *Genealogy*, xiv. vii, that the poet should possess such a breadth of knowledge. Glossing Dante's address to Virgil as 'you who honour science and art',[74] Boccaccio explains that the poet honoured them

> ... by practising them well and masterfully. This is evident in his books, in which he shows the intelligent that he has understood moral and natural philosophy exceptionally well, something which pertains to science. And, in addition to that, he shows himself to have worked wonders in that which was needful for the composition of his poems, or for the parts of poems, employing in them the artifice of whatever liberal art was required by specific occasions; and this pertains not to mechanical art[75] but to speculative art, and therefore those honours (*lode*) conferred upon him by the author are well deserved.[76]

In sum, the links between poetry and philosophy seem as strong as those between poetry and theology. Poetry has been successfully upgraded within the hierarchy of knowledge.

And so Boccaccio must rethink the old etymologies. 'Poetry' is from an ancient Greek word which means 'exquisite discourse' rather than from the word which means 'feigning', and the term *fabula* denotes 'intimate conversation' (translated by Osgood as 'talking together'), an activity which is perfectly natural and which was honoured by the appearance of the risen Christ to the disciples who were talking together privately (Luke 24: 14–15). If *fabula* is to be understood in terms of fiction, this can be taken in four senses (here Boccaccio is adapting Macrobian and Ciceronian categories),[77] only one of which must be dismissed—and this is the one which has nothing to do with poetry! Above all else, what sets the poet apart is his inventive fervour (*fervor*) or mental energy (*vi mentis*), whence he is called a 'seer' (*vates*). Here Boccaccio is talking not of divine inspiration in the strict sense but rather of a god-given and unusual natural talent. The etymology of *vates*, like the others, derives from Isidore of Seville,[78] but here, as elsewhere, Boccaccio (to revert to Alan of Lille's felicitous phrase) is twisting the waxen noses of his authorities in directions which suit himself.[79] The result is a veritable transformation of critical tradition.

The Familiar Authors. In 1345 Petrarch recovered Cicero's letters to Atticus, Quintus, and Brutus.[80] On reading these 'contentious' works, he tells us, he was at once 'offended' and 'enticed'. While he took pleasure in the author's

---

[73] *In Somn. Scip.* i. vi. 44 (ed. Willis, p. 26, tr. Stahl, p. 108).   [74] *Inferno*, iv. 73.

[75] On medieval ideas of the mechanical arts see George Ovitt, 'The Status of the Mechanical Arts in Medieval Classifications of Learning', *Viator*, xiv (1983), 89–105.

[76] *Esposizioni sopra la Comedia di Dante*, iv. i. 82, ed. G. Padoan, in Boccaccio, *Opere*, vi. 190.

[77] Cicero, *De invent.* i. xix. 27. Cf. *Ad Herenn.* i. viii. 13, Macrobius, *In Somn. Scip.* i. ii. 4–21 (ed. Willis, pp. 4–8, tr. Stahl, pp. 84–7), and of course Isidore, *Ety.* i. xl. 1–7, xliv. 5.

[78] Isidore, *Ety.* viii. vii. 3, and cf. the references above, n. 77.

[79] See Ch. VIII, n. 49.

[80] See R. Pfeiffer, *History of Classical Scholarship, 1300–1850* (Oxford, 1976), pp. 9–10, who emphasizes that the evidence for Petrarch's knowledge of Cicero's *Epistolae ad familiares* is inconclusive. In any case, they were not yet called by this title, and so Petrarch could not have taken his own title thence.

style he was often annoyed by his attitudes: in adversity Cicero had been weak, and had directed many quarrels and abuses 'against famous men upon whom he had not long before lavished praise'. Hence, 'in a fit of anger', Petrarch wrote to Cicero 'as if he were a friend living in my time, with an intimacy that I consider proper because of my deep and immediate acquaintance with his thought. I thus reminded him of those things he had written that had offended me, forgetting, as it were, the gap of time.'[81] Letters to other *auctores* followed—to Seneca, Varro, Quintilian, Livy, Horace, and Virgil—all written with the same mixture of reverence, familiarity and outspokenness about their shortcomings. These writings were to form the bulk of the final book of Petrarch's *Letters on Familiar Matters*, or *Letters to his Friends* (both translations of the title having something to commend them), a collection of letters 'written in a friendly style to a number of friends'.[82] The same proximity of relationship, the same high degree of familiarity, is assumed with all the addressees, whether they be men of the present or of the past.

The innovatory nature of what Petrarch did is brought home to us by a letter to Pulice da Vicenza, which records a debate about Cicero in which Petrarch's letters to him were read aloud. An unnamed 'venerable scholar' was horrified, and refused to brook any criticism of his idol:

So taken was he with Cicero's fame and so filled with love for him that he preferred to applaud even his errors and to accept his vices together with his virtues rather than condemn anything in a man so worthy of praise. Thus, his only response to me or to others was to contrast the splendour of Cicero's name with everything being said, thereby substituting authority for reason.[83]

Respect for authority often drove out reason in the *vitae auctorum* included in the *accessūs ad auctores*, and in the later literary biographies which developed from them. However, as we have seen in Ch. VI, scriptural exegetes had coped with the challenge to literary *auctoritas* posed by recognition of the sins of such biblical *auctores* as David and Solomon. In the *Letters on Familiar Matters* Petrarch brought this kind of analysis to bear on secular *auctores*. The result, in the case of Cicero, is a depiction of a man who 'lived as a man, spoke as an orator, and wrote as a philosopher', one whose life was open to criticism but not his genius (*ingenium*) or eloquence.[84]

In addressing Cicero and other classical authors in this way, Petrarch was playing a game, as he tells us, 'with these great geniuses, impudently perhaps, but affectionately, distressedly, and, I think, truthfully. Somewhat more truthfully than I liked, indeed.'[85] Here, as in all the texts translated in this section, the traditional barriers between various kinds of writer, whether between pagan and Christian or 'ancient' and 'modern', are coming down. In his *Short Treatise in Praise of Dante* (excerpted below, in Ch. X) Boccaccio was to treat

---

[81] *Rerum familiarium libri* (hereafter *Fam.*), i. 1 (tr. Aldo S. Bernardo (Albany, NY, 1975), pp. 12–13).   [82] Ibid., p. 10.

[83] *Fam.* xxiv. 2 (tr. A. S. Bernardo (Baltimore, Md., and London, 1985), p. 315).

[84] *Fam.* xiv. 2 (tr. below).

[85] *Fam.* xxiv. 2 (tr. Morris Bishop, *Letters from Petrarch* (Bloomington, Ind., and London, 1966), p. 205).

Dante with a degree of familiarity similar to that with which Petrarch had treated Cicero, the achievement of the great 'new poet' being praised while his faults are condemned. For instance, Dante was licentious, something which may not be excused, but at least he is in good company—Boccaccio brackets him with David and Solomon.[86] The 'gap of time' has certainly been forgotten; one is reminded of Dante's own argument in the *Convivio* (cf. pp. 381–2) that time does not beget nobility, whether of soul, language, or (by implication) of literature. Thus, the authors have become 'familiar authors'—familiar to the reader and to each other. Here the foundations have been laid for Renaissance theories of authorship and literary authority.

DANTE ALIGHIERI

Il Convivio, Tract. II: *Voi che 'ntendendo* and Extracts from its Exposition[87]

You, who by intellection move the third heaven,
   hear the reasoning that is in my heart,
   for I cannot broach it to others, so strange it seems to me;
   and the heaven which pursues your power,
   noble creatures that you are,   5
   draws me into the state in which I find myself.
So it seems that talk of the life that I experience
   should properly be addressed to you:
   therefore I beg you to give it your attention.
I will tell you of the strange state of my heart,   10
   of how, within it, my sad soul weeps,
   and of how a spirit, that comes in the rays
   of your star, speaks against her.
The life of my grieving heart was, formerly,
   a gentle thought, that many times   15
   journeyed to the feet of our Lord,
   where he saw a lady in glory,
   of whom he would speak so sweetly to me
   that my soul would say: 'I too wish to go there.'
But now one appears who forces him to flee;   20
   he lords it over me with such power
   that my heart's tremor within is apparent without.

---

[86] Cf. Minnis, *Authorship*, pp. 214–15.

[87] Tr. by David Wallace from *Dante Alighieri: Il Convivio*, ed. Simonelli, pp. 29–36, 45–58, 67–9, with the permission of Casa Editrice Prof. Riccardo Patron, Bologna. Although it is generally agreed that all surviving *Convivio* MSS may be traced to a single archetype, this archetype is several removes from the autograph MS and includes many errors and lacunae. Simonelli's emendations are followed for the most part, but on occasion we have adopted those of other editors.

He forces me to look upon a lady
and says: 'He who would see salvation,
let him gaze upon the eyes of this lady, 25
but let him not shrink from anguish through sighing.'
He discovers an opponent who destroys him,
  this humble thought, who used to speak with me
  of an angel that is crowned in heaven.
The soul weeps, so much does this still grieve her, 30
and says: 'Alas, that this compassionate thought,
that brought me consolation, flees from me!'
Then she, my troubled soul, says of my eyes:
'What a moment was that when such a woman saw them!
and why, concerning her, did they not believe me? 35
I said: "In the eyes of her must surely dwell
he who destroys the likes of me!"
But it did me no good, my being aware
that suchlike should not be gazed at, since I die of it.'
'You are not dead but, O our soul, 40
  you are bewildered, you who lament so much,'
  says a gentle little spirit of love;
'for that fair lady, whose power you feel,
  has so transformed your life that you
  are scared, so cowardly have you become! 45
See how piteous and humble she is,
  wise and courteous in her greatness,
  and remember: from now on, call her your lady!
For unless you lead yourself astray, you will now see
  the beauty of miracles so marvellous 50
that you will say: "Love, true lord,
here is your handmaid; do with her what you will."'
Canzone, those who rightly understand
  your meaning will, I think, be few indeed,
  so laborious and tough do you make it. 55
So if it should, perchance, occur
  that you come before people who seem,
  in your judgement, not to understand you aright,
then I urge you, O my latest delight,
  to take heart, saying to them: 60
'Notice at least how beautiful I am!'

CHAPTER I

Now that my bread has been sufficiently prepared by my own ministra-
tions ⟨in⟩ the preceding, prefatory tractate, the time calls and requires my

ship to leave port. And so, the mainsail of reason being adjusted to the breeze of my longing, I enter the ocean hoping for a smooth passage and for a salutary and praiseworthy port at the end of my banquet. But so that this my food may prove more profitable, I wish to demonstrate (before the first course arrives) how one should eat.

I say, then, just as is set down in the first chapter,[88] that this exposition is necessarily both literal and allegorical. And so that this may be understood, it should be known that writings may be understood and ought to be expounded chiefly in four senses. The first is called literal ⟨and this is that sense which does not go beyond that enunciated by the fictitious word, as in the fables (*favole*) of poets. The next is called allegorical⟩, and this is that which hides beneath the mantle (*manto*) of such fables, and is a truth hidden beneath a beautiful falsehood: such as when Ovid says that Orpheus tamed wild beasts with his lyre and made trees and stones move towards him;[89] which shows ⟨how⟩ the wise man makes cruel hearts grow tame and humble with the instrument of his voice, and how he makes those who have no feeling (*vita*) for science and art move according to his will; and they who have no rational life at all are little better than stones. And the penultimate tractate will explain why this form of disguise was invented by the wise.[90] Truly speaking, theologians and poets use this sense in different ways; but since I am concerned here with observing the ways of poets, I take the allegorical sense in the way that it is used by poets.

The third sense is called moral; and teachers (*lettori*) must watch out for this most carefully as they go through writings, both for their own benefit and for the benefit of their ⟨pupils⟩. So, for example, one may note in the gospel that when Christ ascended the mountain to transfigure himself he took three of the twelve Apostles with him. The moral sense of this is that we should have few companions in our most secret undertakings.

The fourth sense is anagogical, that is, above the senses (*sovrasenso*), and this sense appears when one expounds the spiritual meaning of a text which, even though it may ⟨be true⟩ in the literal sense, nevertheless points through the things signified to the supernal things of eternal glory. This may be seen in that song of the prophet which says that Judea was made holy and free in the exodus of the people of Israel from Egypt [Ps. 113: 1–2].[91] And although it is manifestly clear that this is true according to the letter, that which is understood spiritually is no less true: that the

---

[88] See *Convivio*, I. i. 18, ed. Simonelli, pp. 3–4.

[89] *Metamorphoses*, xi. 1; cf. *Inferno*, iv. 140.

[90] This 'penultimo trattato' was never composed. On the subject of truths hidden beneath poetic fables, see, e.g. Boccaccio, *Geneal. deor. gent.* xiv. ix–xiii (tr. Osgood, pp. 47–69).

[91] These same verses are analysed in greater detail in the *Epistle to Can Grande della Scala*, 7 (ed. Toynbee–Hardie, pp. 173–4 (tr. below)). See also *Purgatorio*, ii. 46–8, where the same psalm is sung by souls newly-arrived at the shore of Purgatory (and so employed according to the anagogical sense given here).

soul, in her exodus from sin, is made holy and free in her power. And in demonstrating this, the literal sense must always come first as that which contains in its meaning (*sentenza*) all other meanings; and without this literal sense it would be impossible and irrational to attend to the others, especially the allegorical. Impossible, because for each thing that has an inside and an outside it is impossible to come to the inside without first coming to the outside. Hence, since in writings ⟨the literal meaning⟩ is always the outside meaning, it is impossible to come to the others, especially to the allegorical, without first coming to the literal. Furthermore: it is impossible because in each thing, natural and artificial, it is not possible to come to the form without having first prepared the matter on which the form must be imposed; as, for example, it is impossible for the form ⟨of⟩ gold to come into being if the material—that is, its substance—is not first prepared and made ready; or for the form of a coffer to come into being if the material—that is, the wood—is not first prepared and made ready. Hence, since the literal meaning is always the substance and material of the others, especially of the allegorical, it is impossible to come to knowledge of the others without knowing the literal first. Furthermore: it is impossible because it is not possible to make progress in anything, natural or artificial, if the foundation is not laid first, as it must be in house-building and in studying.[92] Hence, since demonstration is the building-up of knowledge, and the literal demonstration is the foundation of all others, especially of the allegorical, it is impossible to come to the others before coming to the literal. Furthermore: even if it were possible, it would be irrational—that is, outside rational order—and therefore one would proceed with great labour and with many errors. And so, as the Philosopher [i.e. Aristotle] says in the first book of the *Physics*, nature wishes us to proceed with due order in our acquiring of knowledge: that is, by proceeding from that which we know better to that which we know less well.[93] I say that nature wishes inasmuch as this way of acquiring knowledge is naturally innate in us. And so if the senses other than the literal are understood less (and it is manifestly apparent that they are) it would be irrational to press on and demonstrate them without first demonstrating the literal sense. For these reasons, then, I shall first discuss the literal meaning of each *canzone* and, after that, will discuss its allegory, that is, its hidden

---

[92] This association of literary study and house-building through their common need for intelligent forethought is reminiscent of a passage from Geoffrey of Vinsauf's *Poetria nova*, ll. 43–54 (ed. Faral, *Les Arts poétiques*, pp. 198–9). Cf. Chaucer, *Troilus and Criseyde*, i. 1065–9 (ed. Robinson, p. 401), and also Hugh of Saint-Victor's frequent use of the metaphor to describe proper scholarly procedure, above, pp. 74, 78–9.

[93] Aristotle is referred to as 'the Philosopher' throughout the *Convivio*, in the standard scholastic manner. In this instance, however, Dante is following Aquinas' commentary on the *Physics*: see *In Phys.*, lect. i. 6, in *Commentary on Aristotle's Physics by St Thomas Aquinas*, tr. R. J. Blackwell, R. J. Spath, and W. E. Thirlkel (London, 1963), p. 6.

truth. And occasionally, as place and time allow, I shall touch upon the other senses.

CHAPTER II

To begin, then, I say that the star of Venus had twice revolved in that circle of hers (which makes her appear in the evening or in the morning, according to season) since the passing away of that blessed Beatrice, who lives in heaven with the angels and on earth with my soul. It was then that that gentle lady, of whom I make mention at the end of the *Vita nuova*, first appeared before my eyes, accompanied by Love, and took possession of a certain place in my mind. And, just as I have ⟨recounted⟩ in the little book just mentioned, it happened (more through her gentleness than through my choosing) that I consented to be hers; for she showed herself to be moved with so much compassion at my widowed life that the spirits of my eyes made themselves her closest of friends. And having befriended her, they then so worked her within that my consent (*beneplacito*) was happy to give itself over to that image. But love is not born in a moment, nor does it grow and come to perfection immediately, but rather requires a measure of time and the nourishment of thoughts, especially when there are contrary thoughts which impede it. So before this new love might be brought to perfection there was, of necessity, many a battle between the thought which nourished it and the thought which, in opposing it, held on to the fortress of my mind on behalf of that glorious Beatrice. For the one thought was reinforced by that part ⟨of the mind⟩ concerned with things which lie continually before us, and the other from the memory of what lies behind. And the succour before me grew day by day, which the other could not, since that which ⟨was⟩ before me prevented me from turning my head behind in any way. This seemed to me so extraordinary, and also so hard to endure, that I could not tolerate it. And driven, almost, to crying out loud (and to excuse myself from favouring ⟨novelty⟩,[94] which seemed to me to me to show a deficiency of fortitude) I directed my voice to that region which gave rise to the victory of the new thought, which was most virtuous in the manner of a celestial virtue. And I began to say YOU, WHO BY INTELLECTION MOVE THE THIRD HEAVEN [1].

In order properly to take in the meaning of this *canzone*, it is first necessary to notice its various parts; its meaning will then be easy to see. And so that there may be no need to repeat these words before expounding the other *canzoni*, I say that in all subsequent tractates I intend to adhere to the order that will be followed in this one.

I say, then, that the *canzone* in question is made up of three principal parts. The first part is its first stanza (*verso*), in which certain Intelligences (whom we more often refer to as angels) are invited to listen to that which

---

[94] Simonelli emends 'veritade' to '⟨novi⟩tade'. Some earlier editors read 'varietade'.

I intend to say. These Intelligences attend to the revolution of the heaven of Venus, being the movers of that heaven. The second part comprises the three stanzas which follow the first part: this reveals that which was heard to pass within, in spirit, between differing thoughts. The third part is the fifth and last stanza: in this the author (*l'uomo*) is meant to speak to the work itself, almost as if offering it reassurance. And all three of these parts are ⟨to be considered⟩ in due order, as was stated above.

CHAPTER III

To further our present intention of more clearly discerning the literal sense of the *canzone* divided into parts above, we need to know who and how many are they who are called to listen to me, and what this third heaven is that, as I say, they cause to move. And first I shall speak of the heaven, and then I shall speak of those whom I address. And since very little may be known of the truth of such things, that little which human reason is able to see proves more pleasurable than the quantity and certainty of things that we may judge.[95] Such is the opinion of the Philosopher in his book *On Animals*.[96]

I say, then, that concerning the heavens and their location diverse opinions have been held by many people, although the truth has at last been uncovered. Aristotle, merely following the ancient crudeness of the astrologers, believed that there were only eight heavens. The most remote of these—that which should contain all the others—was supposedly the heaven where the fixed stars are, namely, the eighth sphere. Beyond this no other sphere was thought to exist. He also believed that the heaven of the sun immediately adjoined the heaven of the moon, that is, that it was the second closest to us. And this highly erroneous opinion of his may be seen, by anyone who wants to, in the second part of *Heaven and Earth*, which is in the second of the books about nature.[97] To do him justice, he does excuse himself for this in the twelfth book of the *Metaphysics*, where he freely admits having merely followed the opinion of others when obliged to speak of astrology.[98] . . .

---

[95] Simonelli suggests, op. cit., p. 35, that the meaning of this sentence depends in part on an opposition of seeing (*vedere*) to judgement (*giudicare*). Seeing is an immediate illumination that is not mediated by the senses; judgement depends on things learned through the senses.

[96] Aristotle, *De part. animalium*, i. 5 (644ᵇ32–645ᵃ1).

[97] Ps.-Aristotle, *De mundo*, ii (392ᵃ9–29).

[98] *Meta.* xii. 8 (1073ᵇ10–12). This chapter of the *Convivio* ends with reference to Ptolemy's account of the nine revolving heavens; in the following chapters their order and succession are treated, and also the Intelligences (or angels) which move the third heaven, i.e. the heaven of Venus.

CHAPTER VI

As was said above in the third chapter of this tractate, it is necessary to discuss those heavens and their movers ⟨to⟩ understand correctly the first part of the *canzone* in question; and the three preceding chapters were, accordingly, given over to such discussion. I say, then, to those that I have shown to be the movers of the heaven of Venus YOU WHO BY INTELLECTION (that is, with the intellect alone, as was said above) ⟨MOVE⟩ THE THIRD HEAVEN, HEAR THE REASONING [1–2]; and I do not say HEAR supposing that they hear sound of any kind, for they have no bodily sense, but I say HEAR meaning with that hearing that they do possess, namely, understanding through the intellect. I say HEAR THE REASONING which IS IN MY HEART [2]: that is, which is inside me, for it has not yet appeared outside. And it should be known that throughout this *canzone*, in both the literal and the allegorical sense, the HEART is taken to mean man's secret interior (*secreto dentro*) and does not refer to any specific part of the soul or body.

Having called upon them to listen to that which I wish to say, I assign two reasons as to why I must of necessity speak to them. The first is the strangeness (*novitade*) of my condition which, since it has not been experienced by the rest of mankind, would not be understood by other men as it would by those who understand the effects of their own activity. And I touch upon this reason when I say FOR I CANNOT BROACH IT TO OTHERS, SO STRANGE IT SEEMS TO ME [3]. The other reason is: when a man receives a benefit, or an injury, he must first speak of it, if he is able, with the person who gave it to him. So that if it is a benefit, he who receives it may show himself to be appreciative of the benefactor; and if it is an injury he may, with gentle words, induce its perpetrator to feel genuine compassion. And I touch upon this reason when I say AND THE HEAVEN WHICH PURSUES YOUR POWER, NOBLE CREATURES THAT YOU ARE, DRAWS ME INTO THE STATE IN WHICH I FIND MYSELF [4–6]. That is to say: it is your operation, namely, your circular motion, that has drawn me into my present state. I conclude, therefore, by saying that it is imperative that I address them as I have done; and this I express here: ⟨SO⟩ IT SEEMS THAT TALK OF THE LIFE THAT I EXPERIENCE SHOULD PROPERLY BE ADDRESSED TO YOU [7–8]. And having offered these reasons, I beg for their attention, when I say THEREFORE I BEG YOU TO GIVE IT YOUR ATTENTION [9]. But since in every kind of discourse (*sermone*) the speaker should be chiefly intent on persuading his audience—that is, on charming them with beauty (*l'abbellire*)—for that, as practised by the rhetoricians, is the beginning of all persuasions; and since the most powerful means of persuading a reader to be attentive is to promise to speak of new and momentous things, I follow my prayer for attention with this persuasion (that is, this charming with beauty): I announce my intention to them, which is to speak of new things (namely, of the conflict in my soul) and of momentous things (namely, of the power of their star). And I speak of this in the final words of this first part: I WILL TELL YOU OF THE STRANGE STATE OF MY HEART, OF HOW, WITHIN IT, MY SAD SOUL WEEPS, AND OF HOW A SPIRIT, THAT COMES IN THE RAYS OF YOUR STAR, SPEAKS AGAINST HER [10–13].

And so that these words may be fully understood, I say that this ⟨SPIRIT⟩ is nothing other than a frequent thought of commending and celebrating the beauty of this new lady; and this SOUL is nothing other than another thought, accompanied by consent, that in recoiling from this first thought commends and celebrates the memory of that glorious Beatrice. But since my mind's final decision—that is, its consent—was given in favour of this thought which was assisting memory, I call him SOUL and the other SPIRIT; just as we are accustomed to calling a city after those who defend it, and not after those who besiege it, even though both parties may be citizens. I also say that this spirit comes in the rays of the star; for it should be known that the rays of each heaven are the path along which their influence (*virtude*) descends upon things here below. And since the rays are nothing but a light (*lume*) that comes through the air from the light-source (*principio de la luce*) to the thing illuminated, and since there is no light (*luce*) except where the star is because the rest of the heaven is diaphanous, that is, transparent, I do not say that this spirit, namely, this thought, comes from their heaven as a whole, but from their star.[99]

This star, through the nobility of its movers, is of such great influence that it exerts enormous power in our souls and in other parts even though, when closest to us, it is one hundred and sixty-seven times the distance, and more, from here to the centre of the earth, which is a space of three thousand two hundred and fifty miles. And this is the literal exposition of the first part of the *canzone*.

CHAPTER VII

The words narrated above will make the literal meaning of the first part intelligible enough; so we should attend to the second part, which reveals what I was feeling of the battle within. And this part has a ⟨new⟩ division:[100] for in the first section, namely, the first stanza, I discuss the nature and origin of these conflicting thoughts (*diversitadi*) which were struggling within me; then I discuss what each of these thoughts was saying. And so I tell firstly what the party which was losing said in the stanza

---

[99] Dante follows Aquinas in distinguishing between *lux* (*luce*, the light at its source), *lumen* (*lume*, the luminosity of the diaphanous medium through which light travels), *radius* (*raggio*, the direct line of light from its source to the object it strikes), and *splendor* (*splendore*, reflected light). See the edition of the *Convivio* by G. Bunselli and G. Vandelli, introduced by M. Barbi, 2nd edn. with an appendix by A. E. Quaglio (Florence, 1964), p. 148, and cf. *Convivio*, III. xiv. 5 (ed. Simonelli, p. 117).

[100] '⟨no⟩va divisione'. Dante has already divided the *canzone* into its three principal parts; now, in discussing the second of these parts, he introduces a new or secondary division.

which is the second of this part and ⟨the third of the *canzone*; then of that
which the new thought said in the stanza which is the third of this part⟩
and the fourth of the *canzone*.

To bring out, then, the meaning of the first subdivision, it should be
known that things must be defined (*denominate*) by the highest nobility of
their form: just as man is by reason, and not by sense or by anything else
that is less noble. Consequently, when man is said to live, one must
understand by this that man uses reason, which is the particular mode of
life and action of his most noble part. And therefore whoever relinquishes
reason and uses only his sensitive part lives not as a man, but lives as a
beast; just as that most excellent Boethius says: 'he lives as an ass'.[101] I
speak advisedly, since thought is the characteristic act of reason, and
since beasts do not think, for they are devoid of reason. And I am not
speaking only of lesser beasts, but of those who have a human appearance
and the spirit of a sheep or of some other abominable beast. I say, then,
that the life of my heart—that is, my inner life—was formerly a gentle
(*soave*) thought (*soave* meaning much the same as *suaso*, that is, charming,
sweet, pleasing, and delightful). This thought often used to travel to the
feet of the lord of those to whom I am speaking, namely, to God: which is
to say that I, in thinking, was contemplating the kingdom of the blessed.
And without delay I mention the final cause (*final cagione*) of my ascending
up there through thinking when I say WHERE HE SAW A LADY IN GLORY [17].
This is to let it be known why I was certain, and am certain, thanks to her
gracious revelation, that she was in heaven. And so I, by thinking as often
as I possibly could, continued going there, almost as if in rapture.

Then, subsequently, I speak of the effect of this thought so that its
sweetness may be appreciated. So sweet was it that it made me long for
death, so that I might go where he travelled, and that I say here OF WHOM
HE WOULD SPEAK SO SWEETLY TO ME THAT MY SOUL WOULD SAY: 'I TOO WISH TO GO
THERE' [18–19]. And this is the origin (*radice*) of one of the conflicting
thoughts in me. And it should be known that the word THOUGHT and not
'soul' is used here for that which climbed up to see that blessed one
because there was a thought devoted specifically to that action. As stated
in the previous chapter, soul is taken to mean thought in general (*lo
generale pensiero*), accompanied by consent.

Afterwards, when I say BUT NOW ONE APPEARS WHO FORCES HIM TO FLEE [20],
I tell of the root of the other conflicting thought, saying that just as this
thought mentioned above used to be my life, so a second appears that
causes the first to give way. And I say TO FLEE to show that second thought
to be contrary to the first; for one contrary naturally flees from another,
and that which flees shows a deficiency of virtue (*vertù*) in fleeing. And I
say that this thought, which has just appeared, proves powerful in taking

[101] 'Asino vive'; from Boethius, *De cons. phil.* IV pr. iii. 63–4, 'Asinum vivit' (ed. Tester,
p. 334).

hold of me and in conquering all my soul; I say that he rules so powerfully that my heart—that is, my inner self—trembles, and my outer self reveals this by a certain strange facial expression.

I next show the potency of this new thought through its effect, saying that it makes me gaze upon a lady and speaks words of flattery to me: that is, to seduce me the better it reasons, before my eyes, about my intellectual affection,[102] assuring me that my affection's salvation lies in the sight of her eyes. And to make this more credible to the discerning soul, it says that a person who fears anguish through sighs should not look into the eyes of this lady. And this is a neat rhetorical procedure (*bel modo rettorico*), when a thing appears to make itself less attractive (*disabbellirsi*) without whilst making itself truly more attractive (*s'abbellisce*) within. This new thought of love could not do more to draw my mind towards consent than by discoursing in depth on the virtue of her eyes.

CHAPTER VIII

Now that it has been shown how and why love was born, and how a contradiction beset me, it is appropriate to go on and disclose the meaning of that section in which conflicting thoughts battle within me. I say that it is appropriate to speak first on the side of the soul, that is, of the long-established thought, and then ⟨of⟩ the other thought, and for this reason: because that which the speaker intends to express most weightily should always be saved until last, since what is said last remains longer in the mind of the auditor. So, given the fact that I am intent on speaking and discoursing on that which is done by the work of those beings I address, rather than on that which it undoes (*che essa disfà*), it was reasonable first to speak and discourse on the state of that part which was falling sick and then on that which was coming to birth.

Here, however, a doubt springs up which cannot be passed over without comment. Someone might say: 'Since love is the effect of these Intelligences I address, and since that which came first was love just as much as was this which follows, why does their power cause one to sicken and the other to be born? For surely it should preserve the former, for the reason that each cause loves its effect; and through loving its own effect, this angelic power should preserve that first love.'[103] To this question one may readily reply that the effect of these Intelligences is love, as was said; and since they cannot preserve this effect except in those subjects who come under the influence of their rotation, they transfer it from that region which is beyond their power to that which lies within it, that is,

---

[102] 'Intelligibile affetto', intellectual or rational affection (as opposed to sensual affection).
[103] '... e, amando quello, salva quell'altro'. Busnelli–Vandelli, p. 155, suggest that this awkward phrase might originally have been a marginal gloss that was later copied into the text.

from the soul which has departed this life to the soul which abides in it: just as human nature transfers its self-preservation in the human form from father to son, since it cannot perpetually preserve its effect in the one father. I say 'effect' inasmuch as the conjunction of soul and body is the effect of human nature; for ⟨the soul, once⟩ departed, lives on perpetually in a nature that is more than human. And so the question is solved.

But since the immortality of the soul has been touched on here, I will make a digression and speak of it; for such speaking will form a beautiful conclusion to talk of that living, blessed Beatrice, of whom I do not propose to speak further in this book. I say that of all bestial stupidities (*bestialitadi*) that which is most foolish, most vile, and most damaging[104] is to believe there to be no other life after this life; for if we leaf through all the writings both of philosophers and of other wise writers, all are found to agree in this: that there is, in us, some part which endures forever. And this seems to be the chief insistence of Aristotle in that book *On the Soul*; this seems to be the chief insistence of every Stoic; this Tully seems to insist upon, especially in that little book *On Old Age*;[105] this the apparent insistence of each poet who has spoken in accord with the faith of the pagans (*Gentili*); this the insistence of every religion, of Jews, Saracens, Tartars, and any others who live in accord with law of any kind. For if all were deceived, an impossibility (*impossibilitade*) would follow that would be horrible even to mention. Everyone is convinced that human nature is the most perfect of all natures here below. Nobody denies this, and Aristotle affirms it when he says in the twelfth book of the *Animals* that man is the most perfect of all the animals.[106] So, given the fact that many living creatures, such as brute beasts, are entirely mortal and are all without this hope (that is, of eternal life) whilst they are living; if our hope proved vain, our defect would be greater than that of any other animal, since there have already been many who have given up this life for the next. And so it would follow that the most perfect animal—that is, man— was the most imperfect (which is impossible); and that that part which is his greatest perfection—that is, his reason—was the cause of his greatest defect; which seems to be a thoroughly self-contradictory thing to say.

Furthermore: it would follow that nature had been acting against herself in fixing this hope in the human mind since, as was said, many have raced to meet bodily death in order to live in the other life; and this too is impossible.

Furthermore: we witness continual experience of our immortality in

---

[104] Most foolish ('stoltissima') because against the use of reason; most vile ('vilissima') because it reduces men to the level of beasts; most damaging ('dannosissima') because of its calamitous effects upon moral, religious and civil order.

[105] Cicero, *De senect.* 78–81.

[106] Cf. *Hist. anim.* viii. 1 (588^{a}18–24). On the compilation of Aristotle's treatises on animals used by Dante see P. Toynbee, 'Aristotle's *De Animalibus* in Dante and other medieval writers', in id., *Dante Studies and Researches* (London, 1902), pp. 247–9.

the divinations of our dreams, which could not happen if some part of us were not immortal. For if one thinks about it subtly and well, the revealer, ⟨whether corporeal⟩ or incorporeal, is bound to be immortal (and I say 'corporeal or incorporeal' because of the diverse opinions that I find on this). And that which is moved or informed by an immediate informer (*informatore*) must stand in some proportional relation to the informer; and between the mortal and the immortal there can be no proportion.

Furthermore: we are assured of it by the most true teaching of Christ, which is the way, the truth, and the light: the way, since we pass along it without hindrance towards the happiness of that immortality; the truth, because it does not admit of any error; the light, because it illumines us in the darkness of worldly ignorance. I maintain that this teaching, above all other reasonings, makes us certain of immortality, since he who sees and measures our immortality has given it to us. We cannot see this perfectly whilst our immortal and mortal parts are intermixed. But through faith we see it perfectly; and through reason we see it tinged with the shadow of obscurity (which comes about through the mixing of the mortal with the immortal). And that must be a most powerful argument for the one and the other being in us; and so I believe, so I affirm, and so am I certain of passing to another, better life after this where that glorious lady lives, of whom my soul was enamoured when it was joined in battle, as will be told in the following chapter.

CHAPTER IX

Returning to the proposed subject, I say that in the stanza which begins HE DISCOVERS AN OPPONENT WHO DESTROYS HIM [27] I intend to make plain that which my soul was speaking within me, namely, that which the long-established thought was saying against the new one. And first I briefly reveal the cause of his mournful speech, when I say HE DISCOVERS AN OPPONENT WHO DESTROYS HIM, THIS HUMBLE THOUGHT, WHO USED TO SPEAK WITH ME OF AN ANGEL THAT IS CROWNED IN HEAVEN [27-9]. This is that particular (*speziale*) thought, said above to be formerly THE LIFE OF MY GRIEVING HEART [14]. Then when I say THE SOUL WEEPS, SO MUCH DOES THIS STILL GRIEVE HER [30], I show that my soul is still on his side, and that she speaks with sadness. And I say that she utters words of lamentation, almost as if she were marvelling at the sudden transformation, saying ALAS, THAT THIS COMPASSIONATE THOUGHT, THAT BROUGHT ME CONSOLATION, FLEES FROM ME [31-2]. She may rightly say BROUGHT ME CONSOLATION since this thought, which climbed to heaven, had given her much consolation in her great bereavement. Then next, in her excuse, I say that the whole of my thought (that is, my soul, whom I refer to as TROUBLED) turns and speaks against my eyes; and this is made plain here: THEN SHE, MY TROUBLED SOUL, SAYS OF MY EYES [33]. And I tell how she speaks three things of and against them. The first is that she curses the hour in which this woman saw them. And here it should be known that although many things can enter the eye at one moment, only that which comes along a straight line into the centre of the pupil is seen truly, and ⟨that⟩ alone stamps itself on the imagination. And this is because the nerve along which the visual spirit travels runs straight to that part. And therefore one eye cannot really look at another without being seen by that other; for just as that eye which gazes receives the form ⟨on to⟩ its pupil along a straight line, so its own form travels along that same line into that eye at which it is gazing. And many times, as eyes look along this line, the bow of him against whom all arms are weak is discharged.[107] Therefore, when I say that SUCH A WOMAN SAW THEM [34] this amounts to saying that her eyes and my eyes looked on one another.

The second thing that the soul says is that she reproaches their disobedience, when she says AND WHY, CONCERNING HER, DID THEY NOT BELIEVE ME [35]. Then she proceeds to the third thing, saying that she need not reproach herself for lack of foresight, but should reproach them for disobedience; for she says ⟨that⟩ sometimes, in speaking of this lady, she had said: 'her eyes would certainly have power over me, if the path of access were open to her'; and this she is saying here I SAID: 'IN THE EYES OF HER MUST SURELY DWELL' [36]. And one may well believe that my soul knew her own disposition to be susceptible to the action (*atta a ricevere l'atto*) of this lady, and so she feared it; for the act of the ⟨agent⟩ takes effect on the duly disposed ⟨recipient⟩, as the Philosopher says in the second book of *On the Soul*. And so if wax possessed a spirit for fearing it would be more afraid of coming into the rays of the sun than a stone would be since its disposition is more powerfully affected by sun-rays.

Finally, the soul makes clear in her speech that their presumption was dangerous, when she says BUT IT DID ME NO GOOD, MY BEING AWARE THAT SUCH-LIKE SHOULD NOT BE GAZED AT, SINCE I DIE OF IT [38–9]. By SHOULD NOT there BE GAZED AT she means him whom she had already referred to as HE WHO DESTROYS THE LIKES OF ME [37]. And so she ends her words, to which the new thought replies, as will be set down in the following chapter.

CHAPTER X

The meaning of that part in which the soul speaks—that is, the long-established thought that was perishing—has been expounded. Now, in due sequence, the meaning of the part in which the new, adversarial thought speaks must be explained; and this part is all contained in the stanza which begins YOU ARE NOT DEAD [40]. To be properly understood, this part must be divided into two: for in the first part ⟨the hostile thought

[107] i.e. Love (Cupid). For dramatic examples of this phenomenon, see Boccaccio, *Filostrato*, i. 25–9, tr. N. R. Havely, *Chaucer's Boccaccio* (Cambridge, 1980), p. 27, and Chaucer, *Troilus and Criseyde*, i. 206–9, 271–307 (ed. Robinson, pp. 391, 392–3).

rebukes the soul for her cowardice; and then he ordains what this rebuked soul must do, that is, in the second⟩ part, which begins SEE HOW PITEOUS SHE IS [46].

He says, then, taking up the soul's final words: it is not true that you are dead; but the cause through which you feel yourself to be dead is a bewilderment (*smarrimento*) into which, coward-like, you have fallen on account of this lady who has appeared. And here it is to be noted that, as Boethius says in his *Consolation*, 'no sudden alteration of things occurs without some mental commotion (*discorrimento*)',[108] and this is what this thought's reproach amounts to. This thought is called a LITTLE SPIRIT OF LOVE [42] to let it be understood that my consent was bending towards him. And when he now speaks of OUR SOUL [40] (making himself familiar with her), one may understand this better and recognize his victory. Then, as was said, he ordains what this reproached soul must do in order to approach this new love, ⟨and⟩ says to her: SEE HOW PITEOUS AND HUMBLE SHE IS [46]; for against fear, with which this soul was obviously gripped, these two are an authentic remedy. And it is these two which, especially when conjoined, engender high hopes of a person, and especially pity (*pietade*), which makes every other good quality resplendent with its light. So Virgil, in speaking of Aeneas, calls him piteous (*pietoso*) by way of highest praise.[109] And pity is not what uncultured people think it to be (that is, feeling sorry for the misfortunes of others), for this is a particular effect (*effetto*) of pity which is called mercy and is an emotion. But pity is not an emotion: it is, rather, a noble disposition of mind, ready to register love, mercy, and other charitable emotions.

Then he says: just look how she is WISE AND COURTEOUS IN HER GREATNESS [47]. Here he speaks of three things which, among those things that may be attained by us, most make the person pleasing. He says WISE: now what is more beautiful in woman than wisdom? He says COURTEOUS: nothing suits a woman better than courtesy. And let poor, uncultured people not be deceived by this word too, for they believe courtesy and liberality to be the same thing. But liberality is a particular form of courtesy, not courtesy in general! Courtesy and dignity (*onestade*) are one and the same; and because, long ago, virtues and good manners used to prevail at court (just as, today, their opposites prevail) this word was taken from the courts, and 'courtesy' meant much the same as 'court usage'. If this word were taken from modern courts, especially Italian ones, it would not mean anything but 'baseness' (*turpezza*). He says IN HER GREATNESS. Temporal greatness, which is meant here, is at its best when accompanied by the

[108] See *De cons. phil.* II, pr. i. 15–17 (ed. Tester, pp. 174–7): 'But such a sudden and complete change in a man's affairs does not happen without some sort of disturbance of the mind.'

[109] See *Aeneid*, i. 544–5. Aeneas is first associated with *pietas*, his most characteristic quality, in i. 10. For discussion of this complex concept see *Aeneidos, Liber primus*, ed. R. G. Austin (Oxford, 1971), p. 33; *Eneide*, ed. Ettore Paratore (Milan, 1978–83), i. 131; also Giorgio Padoan, *Il pio Enea, l'empio Ulisse* (Ravenna, 1977).

two good qualities mentioned above because it is that ⟨light⟩ which clearly reveals the qualities of a person, good or otherwise. And how much wisdom and how much virtuous disposition pass unnoticed through the absence of this light! And how much madness and how many vices are discerned through its presence! It would be better for those poor fools of high estate who are mad, stupid, and corrupt to be of low condition, for they would not then be so infamous either in this world or in the afterlife. Truly it is of them that Solomon speaks in Ecclesiastes: 'And I have seen another most serious infirmity under the sun, namely, riches stored to the detriment of their masters' [5: 12]. Then subsequently he requires her (that is, my soul) to call the lady her mistress from now on, promising her that this will make her extremely happy once she has come to know the lady's beauties (*adornezze*); and this she says here: FOR UNLESS YOU LEAD YOURSELF ASTRAY, YOU WILL NOW SEE [49]. He does not say anything else in the remainder of this stanza. And here ends the literal meaning of all that I say in this *canzone* in speaking to those celestial Intelligences.

CHAPTER XI

Finally, in accordance with what the letter of this commentary said when it divided up the principal parts of this *canzone*, I turn round with the face of my discourse to the *canzone* itself, and I speak to it. And so that this part may be understood more fully, I say that generally it is called, in each *canzone*, a 'tornata'; for the poets (*dicitori*) who first used to employ it did so because, having sung the *canzone*, they could turn back to it again with a certain part of the song. But I have rarely composed a tornata with this intention and (so that others might grasp this) I rarely placed it within the metrical structure (*ordine*) of the *canzone* to make up the syllable-count (*numero*) which is needful for the measure (*nota*); but I composed it when there was need to say something, outside the *canzone*'s meaning, for the *canzone*'s embellishment (*adornamento*), as one will be able to see in this and in other exemplars. And therefore I say, on the present subject, that the goodness (*bontade*) and beauty of each discourse are mutually distinct and different in character: for the goodness is in the meaning, and the beauty in the embellishment (*ornamento*) of the words; and both are delightful, although goodness is the most delightful. So, given the fact that the goodness of this *canzone* was difficult to perceive because of the many persons brought forward to speak in it (which required the making of many distinctions), and given that its beauty was easy to see, it seemed to me needful for this *canzone* that people should pay more attention to its beauty than to its meaning. And this is what I am saying in this part.

But since it often happens that admonishment appears to be presumptuous, under certain conditions the rhetor (*rettorico*) speaks to others indirectly, directing his words not to him for whose benefit he speaks, but to another.[110] And this method is, in truth, adhered to here: for the words are directed to the *canzone*, and their import to men. I say, then: I believe, *canzone*, that they are rare (that is, few) who will understand you well. And I give the cause, which is twofold. First: because your speaking is LABORI-OUS [55] (I say LABORIOUS for the reason given above); then: since you make it TOUGH (I say TOUGH as regards the unfamiliarity of the meaning). Next I admonish her and say: if, by chance, you should happen to go to a place where there are people who seem to be puzzled about your meaning, do not despair, but tell them: since you cannot see my goodness, at least consider my beauty. By this I do not wish to say anything, as was stated above, other than: O men, who cannot see the meaning of this *canzone*, do not refuse her; but be mindful of her beauty, which is great in use of language (*construzione*) (which pertains to the grammarians), in the order of discourse (which pertains to the rhetoricians) and in the proportions (*numero*) of its parts (which pertains to the musicians). These things may be seen to be beautiful in her by him who looks attentively.

And this is the whole of the literal meaning of the first *canzone*, which was represented above as the first course.

CHAPTER XII

Now that the literal meaning has been adequately shown, we are to proceed to the allegorical and true exposition. And so, starting again from the beginning, I say that since my soul's first delight was ⟨lost⟩ (as is mentioned above), I remained transfixed by such sadness that no comfort could help me. After a certain time, however, my mind (which was endeavouring to heal itself) saw fit (since neither my consolation nor the consolation of others was proving effective) to resort to a method that a certain disconsolate man had employed to console himself; and I applied myself to reading that little-known book by Boethius in which, imprisoned and in exile, he had consoled himself.[111] And hearing besides that Tully had written a book in which, in treating of friendship, he had touched upon the consolation experienced by Laelius, a most excellent man, on the death of his friend Scipio,[112] I set myself to read that too. And although at first it was difficult for me to enter into their meaning, in the end I entered in as far as my knowledge of Latin (*l'arte di gramatica*), plus a little native ingenuity, would allow. (I had already seen many things through this ingenuity, almost as in dreaming, as may be seen in the *Vita*

---

[110] As Dante explains later in the *Convivio*, III. ix. 6 (ed. Simonelli, p. 102).

[111] The *De consolatione philosophiae*, referred to here as 'quello non conosciuto da molti libro di Boezio', was in fact one of the most influential and widely read books of the Middle Ages. Perhaps Dante thought that it would not be so well-known among the 'molti' who were to form the audience of the *Convivio*. Alternatively, the statement could mean that very few people can penetrate its meaning as he had done.

[112] Cicero, *De amicitia*, 10–15.

nuova.) And just as it sometimes happens that a man goes searching for silver and, without intending to, discovers gold (which a secret cause presents; not, perhaps, without divine command); so I, in seeking to console myself, found not just a remedy for my tears, but the words of authors and of science and of books. Pondering over these words, I confidently adjudged Philosophy, who was the mistress of these authors, of these sciences, and of these books, to be an exalted thing. And I imagined her formed like a noble lady, and I could not imagine her to be anything but compassionate in disposition. And, in truth, my sense gazed upon her so willingly that I could hardly turn it away. And following this imagining I began to go there where she is truly revealed, that is, to the schools of the religious orders and to the disputations of the philosophers. And within a short space of time, perhaps thirty months, I so began to feel her sweetness that love for her hunted out and destroyed every other thought. In feeling myself being lifted away from the thought of the first love towards the power of this one, I opened my mouth, as if in amazement, and gave voice to the aforesaid *canzone*, expressing my condition under the figure of other things. ⟨For⟩ no verse (*rima*) of any vernacular tongue was worthy to speak openly of the woman that I was in love with; nor were my auditors so well prepared that they could easily have understood ⟨non⟩-fictitious words;[113] nor would they have believed in the true meaning as readily as in the fictitious one, since they fully believed me to be inclined towards that first love, but did not believe in this second one. I began, then, to say YOU WHO BY INTELLECTION MOVE THE THIRD HEAVEN [1]. And because, as was said, this lady was the daughter of God, the queen of all, the most noble and beautiful Philosophy, we must consider who these movers were, and what this third heaven was. And first of the heaven, following the order established above. And here there is no need to go on dividing the text and expounding the letter; for since the fictitious word has already been turned (*volta*) from what it says to the meaning it contains, this meaning will be sufficiently obvious from the exposition given above. . . .[114]

[113] Simonelli notes, p. 58, that since the 1826 edition most editors and textual critics have added a 'non' before 'fittizie'. Busnelli–Vandelli, p. 187, support the introduction of 'non', pointing out that 'non fittizie parole' are the concern of the allegorical sense, which is true and not fictitious; 'fittizie parole' express the literal sense. Their arguments persuade us to reintroduce the 'non' which Simonelli drops from her text.

[114] In ch. xiii Dante declares that 'by heaven, I mean science, and by the heavens the sciences, because of three principal properties that the heavens share with the sciences. As we shall see in examining this word "third", they appear to agree, above all, in order and number.' Having discussed these three similarities, Dante goes on as promised to examine the term 'third'. He associates each of the seven planets with a part of the trivium or quadrivium. Here, for example is how he explains the association of Venus, the third heaven, with rhetoric, the third part of the trivium: 'And the heaven of Venus may be compared with rhetoric on account of two properties: one is the brilliance (*chiarezza*) of its aspect, which is more pleasing to look upon than that of any other star; the other is its pattern of making appearances, now in the morning and now in the evening. And these two properties are

CHAPTER XV

By the similarities argued above one may see who these movers that I speak to are: they are heaven-movers such as Boethius and Tully, who, as was said above, initiated me with the sweetness of their discourse into the love (that is, into the study) of this lady, the most noble philosophy, with the rays of their star (which is their writing about her): for in every science, writings form a star full of light which demonstrates that science. And, this being apparent, one may see the true meaning of the first stanza of the *canzone* in question by means of the fictitious and literal exposition. And by using this same exposition one may adequately understand the second stanza up to the point where it says HE FORCES ME TO LOOK UPON A LADY [23].

Here it should be known that this lady is Philosophy, who is truly a lady full of sweetness, embellished with dignity (*onestade*), wondrous in knowledge, glorious in freedom, as will be made apparent in the third tractate, which will concern itself with her nobility. And there where it says HE WHO WOULD SEEK SALVATION, LET HIM GAZE UPON THE EYES OF THIS LADY [24–5], the eyes of this lady are her demonstrations which, directed to the eyes of the intellect, enamour that soul which is free ⟨in⟩ her social situation.[115] O most sweet and ineffable looks (*sembianti*), precipitate thieves of the human mind, you who ⟨appear⟩ in the demonstration within the eyes of philosophy when she reasons with her lovers! Salvation truly abides in you and makes him who looks there blessed and free from the death of ignorance and from vice. Where it says: BUT LET HIM NOT SHRINK FROM ANGUISH THROUGH SIGHING [26], the meaning is as follows: if he does not shrink from the labour of study and the struggle of perplexities which rise up and multiply from the very first glances of this lady; and later, as her light continues to shine, they disperse, almost like morning clouds in the face of the sun; and the intellect that has become familiar with her remains free and full of certainty, just like the air which is purged and brightened by the rays of the midday sun.

The third stanza may also be understood by means of the literal exposition[116] up to where it says THE SOUL WEEPS [30]. Here one should carefully attend to a certain moral which may be noted in these words: that a man

---

contained in rhetoric: for rhetoric is the most pleasing of all the sciences, for it aims, above all, to please. And it appears in the morning when the rhetor speaks facing the auditor; it appears in the evening—that is, from behind—when it speaks from the [letter], from far away, on behalf of the rhetor.' In ch. xiv, the starry heaven is said to represent physics and metaphysics, while the *primum mobile* corresponds to ethics. On the unusually high status which Dante's allegorical scheme affords to ethics see n. 53 above.

115 'liberata ⟨d⟩e le condizioni'. Busnelli–Vandelli, p. 234, give the reading 'liberata de le con⟨tra⟩dizioni' ('free from contradictions'), which B. C. Martinelli finds more satisfactory; s.v. *condizione*, *ED* ii. 139.

116 Dante is referring us back to ch. ix.

must not, because of a greater friend, forget the favours received from a lesser one; but if it is ⟨really⟩ necessary to follow one and forget the other, the better must be followed (abandoning the other with some sincere lamentation, thereby giving cause to the one he follows to love him the more). Then where it says OF MY EYES [33], it wishes only to say that the hour in which the first of this lady's demonstrations entered the eyes of my intellect was momentous, being the most immediate cause of my enamourment. And there where the soul says THE LIKES OF ME [37], she means those souls who, endowed with ingenuity and with memory, are free from squalid and vile pleasures and from common habits. And later she says DESTROYS [37]; and later she says I DIE [39]; which appears to be contrary to that which is said above concerning the salvation wrought by this lady. And therefore it should be known that one part of the soul is speaking here, and the other part there; and these two join battle with diverse opinions, as is made clear above. So it is not surprising if there she says ⟨yes⟩ and here she ⟨says no⟩, if we observe carefully which part is descending and which part is rising.

Then in the fourth stanza, where it says A LITTLE SPIRIT OF LOVE [42], it means a thought which is born out of my studying. (For it should be known that 'love' in this allegory always means that study which is the application of a mind in love with a thing to that thing.) Then when he says YOU WILL NOW SEE THE ⟨BEAUTY⟩ OF MIRACLES SO MARVELLOUS [49–50], he is announcing that the beauties (*adornamenti*) of these miracles will be seen through her, for the beauties of miracles lie in the understanding of their causes, which she demonstrates. The Philosopher appears to uphold this at the beginning of the *Metaphysics*, saying that men begin to fall in love with this woman through seeing these beauties.[117] And this word 'miracle' will be dealt with more fully in the next treatise.[118]

All the rest of this *canzone* which then follows is sufficiently clear from the exposition made earlier. And so, at the end of this second tractate, I say and affirm that this lady with whom I fell in love after the first love was the most beautiful and most honourable daughter of the Emperor of the universe, to whom Pythagoras gave the name Philosophy. And here ends the second tractate, ⟨which is designed to expound the *canzone*⟩ that is brought to the table as the first course.

---

[117] Cf. Aristotle, *Meta.* i. 1 (981ª30–ᵇ6), where, however, there is not a word about love or beauty.

[118] See *Convivio*, III. vi. 12, III. vii. 16–17, III. xiv. 14.

FRANCIS PETRARCH

Letters on Familiar Matters, x: 4:
To his Brother Gherardo, Extract[119]

TO THE SAME CORRESPONDENT, ON THE STYLE OF THE
[CHURCH] FATHERS, AND THE RELATIONSHIP BETWEEN
THEOLOGY AND POETRY, WITH A BRIEF EXPOSITION OF
THE FIRST ECLOGUE OF HIS *BUCOLICS*[120] SENT TO
THE ADDRESSEE.

If I know your devout zeal, you will be appalled at the poem appended to
this letter as being incompatible with your religious calling and opposed
to your way of life. Do not make any hasty judgements. For what could be
more foolish than to form opinions on matters with which you are not yet
acquainted? In fact, poetry is not at all inimical to theology. Are you
surprised at this? I would almost say that theology is poetry written about
God. When Christ is called, now a lion, now a lamb, and again a worm,
what is that if not poetic?[121] You will find a thousand more instances in
Holy Scripture which it is tedious to go through in detail. For what do the
Saviour's parables in the Gospel represent if not discourse differing in
meaning from the normal meanings of the words, or to put it in one word,
'speech applied differently' (*alieniloquium*), to which we give the more
usual name of allegory?[122] But this sort of discourse is the very fabric of
poetry.

   'But the subject-matter (*subiectum*) is different.' No one denies that. In
Holy Scripture the subject is God and matters divine, while in poetry it is
man and the gods. Hence, we read in Aristotle that the poets were the first
theologians.[123] The very name indicates that this is so. For the question of
the origin of the word 'poet' has been studied, and although various
explanations are offered, the most convincing is the following. When
primitive men—primitive indeed, but eager to know the truth, and particularly to investigate the nature of the gods, for this is a natural human
trait—had begun to form a concept of some superior power which
governed the affairs of men, they considered it proper to revere that

[119] Tr. from *Francesco Petrarca, Le Familiari*, vol. ii, ed. V. Rossi (Edizione nazionale delle
opere di Francesco Petrarca XI, Florence, 1934), pp. 301–3, with the permission of G. C.
Sansoni Editore.
[120] i.e. the first of his Latin *Bucolics* (written 1346–8, revised 1364); text and translation in
Petrarch's Bucolicum carmen, ed. Thomas G. Bergin (New Haven, Conn., and London, 1974),
pp. 2–15.
[121] For the lion image, see Amos 3: 8 and Rev. 5: 5; for the lamb, Isa. 53: 7, John 1: 29, 36,
and Rev. 14; for the worm, Ps. 21: 7, cf. Isa. 41: 14, Job 25: 6. On the treatment of such images
within the Pseudo-Dionysian theory of symbolism, see above, Ch. V. And cf. Ch. X, n. 265.
[122] Cf. Isidore, *Ety.* I. xxxvii. 22. Cf. Ch. II, n. 38.
[123] Cf. Aristotle, *Meta.* i. 2 (982ᵇ), and our discussion above, pp. 389–90.

power with greater deference and more elevated worship than that shown to men. They therefore conceived the idea of having very large buildings, which they called temples; servants consecrated to the gods, whom it pleased them to call priests; and magnificent statues and gold vessels, marble tables and purple garments. Lest all this honour should have no voice, they saw fit to placate the divine with high-sounding words, and to offer sacred flattery to the gods, using a style far removed from the common and general form of speech. In addition, they introduced verse to provide an added beauty and banish tediousness. It was surely right and proper that this should be achieved by employing, not a common form of style, but one that was the result of artifice, exquisite, and new. Since the Greek word for this style is *poetes*, they called those who employed it 'poets'.[124]

You will say: 'Who on earth was the first to think up these ideas?' My dear brother, you ought to believe my word without witnesses. I have, perhaps, earned the right to be believed without witnesses, as one who reports the truth and what resembles the truth. But if you have a mind to proceed more cautiously I will provide you with witnesses very rich in testimony and inspiring the utmost confidence. The first is Marcus Varro, the greatest scholar among the Romans.[125] Next comes [Suetonius] Tranquillus, a most diligent researcher. I would not add a third, except that he is, I think, better known to you.[126] Isidore, then, mentions all this, although briefly, and on the evidence of Suetonius, in the eighth book of the *Etymologies*.[127]

But you will counter this by saying: 'I can at any rate trust a holy teacher of the Church, but your sweet song is not compatible with my ascetic way of life.' You must not think that, my dear brother. Even the venerable writers of the Old Testament employed heroic and other kinds of verse: for instance, Moses, Job, David, Solomon, and Jeremiah. It is well known that the psalms of David, which you sing day and night, are in verse, in the form in which the Hebrews read them, so that I would even venture to suggest that we might without impropriety or lack of taste call him 'the poet of the Christians'. For the actual text shows that this is so, and besides, if you are not going to believe anything I tell you today without a witness, I see that Jerome held the same view, even though he was unable to translate retaining both the metre and the sense (*sententia*) of the original, that sacred poem which speaks of 'the blessed man' [Ps. 1: 1],

[124] Cf. Isidore, *Ety.* VIII. vii. 1–2, also Servius on *Aeneid*, iii. 443, and Vincent of Beauvais, *Speculum doctrinale*, III. cx, cxi (*Speculum quadruplex*, ii. 288).

[125] Presumably a reference to Augustine's citation of Varro's threefold division of theology into fabulous, physical and civil, in *De civ. Dei*, VI. v. Cf. Boccaccio, *Geneal. deor. gent.* XV. viii (tr. below).

[126] The impeccably orthodox bishop Isidore is Petrarch's source for Varro as well as Suetonius here, Isidore being the third.

[127] Cf. Isidore, *Ety.* VIII. vii. 1–3.

that is, Christ, being born, dying, descending into Hell, ascending into Heaven, and subsequently returning [as judge]. So, he concentrated on the meaning (*sententia*). Yet even there there is a certain metrical regularity, and so we commonly call the individual, short sections of the psalms, even as they are now,[128] verses.

But that is enough of the ancient writers. It is no great trouble to demonstrate that the leading lights of the New Testament too, Ambrose, Augustine and Jerome, used verse-forms and rhythmical patterns (*rithmus*), to say nothing of Prudentius, Prosper, Sedulius, and others, not one of whose works are in prose, but all are clearly in verse.[129] So, my brother, do not recoil from something which you see pleased these men, who were so dear to Christ and so holy. Concentrate on the meaning. If it is true and wholesome, take it to yourself, irrespective of the style. The man who praises food when served in earthenware dishes, but scorns the same food when served on a golden platter, is either mad or a hypocrite. It is in the nature of a greedy man to thirst after gold, but not to be able to endure it is a characteristic of the small-minded. Certainly, the food is no better for being served up on a gold plate, but it is no worse either. Well then, poetry, just like gold, is nobler within its own species, just as lines which are drawn with the aid of a ruler are straighter than those drawn at random. Not that I think this is a reason for actively seeking out poetry. But equally, it is not a reason for rejecting it. . . .[130]

Letters on Familiar Matters, xiv: 3:
To Marcus Tullius Cicero[131]

Francis sends greetings to his dear friend Cicero.

I had spent a long time and great effort searching diligently for your letters. I found them where I least expected, and have devoured them most eagerly. I have listened to you saying many things, making many complaints, and expressing many various opinions, Marcus Tullius. Long since I realized your quality as a teacher of others. Now, at last, I see how you profited from your own teaching.

Hear now, in turn, wherever you are, what cannot now be advice, but only a lament which proceeds from the love I have for you and is poured out not without tears, by one of your spiritual descendants, who loves your name dearly. Spirit forever restless and troubled or, so that you may

---

[128] i.e. not rendered into Latin metres.
[129] Cf. Boccaccio, *Geneal. deor. gent.* XIV. xxii (tr. Osgood, p. 100).
[130] Petrarch proceeds to explain the allegorical meaning of the first of his *Bucolics*.
[131] Tr. from *Francesco Petrarca, Le Familiari*, vol. iv, ed. Umberto Bosco (Edizione nazionale delle opere di Francesco Petrarca XIII, Florence, 1942, pp. 225–31), with the permission of G. C. Sansoni Editore.

recognize your own words, 'headstrong and unfortunate old man',[132] why did you ever want to get yourself involved with so many arguments and quarrels which were destined to do you no good at all? At what stage did you abandon the retirement appropriate to a man of your age, station, and fortune? What false allure of glory caused you, an old man, to get involved in young men's wars, and, having tossed you about through every sort of vicissitude, snatched you away to a death unworthy of a philosopher?

Alas, unmindful of your brother's advice, and of all the many salutary precepts you yourself dispensed, like some traveller in the night, carrying a lamp in the darkness, you showed those who were to follow you the very path on which you yourself had such a wretched fall. I say nothing of Dionysius, nothing of your brother or your nephew, nothing even of Dolabella, if you so wish. All of these you praise to the skies at one moment and at another tear apart with sudden abuse. All this could, perhaps, have been endured. I also pass over Julius Caesar, whose well-known clemency was a refuge even for those who attacked him. I say nothing of Pompey either, with whom you appeared to be able to do anything you wished on the strength of having some sort of close bond of friendship with him. But what madness induced you to attack Antony? I believe it was love of the free republic, which you yourself admitted had already collapsed. But if your motives were pure loyalty and love of freedom, why were you on such close terms with Augustus? For what are you going to reply to your friend Brutus when he says: 'If Octavian is to your liking, you seem to me, not so much to have shunned a master altogether, but rather to have sought out a master who was better disposed towards you.'[133] Unhappy man, it only remained for you to commit this last and final error of abusing this very Brutus, whom you had praised so often, for—I won't say harming you, but not preventing those who were harming you.[134]

I grieve at your lot, my friend. Your mistakes fill me with shame and pity. Now I echo the words of that same Brutus: 'I attach no importance to those arts in which I know you have made yourself a master.'[135] For what on earth is the point of teaching others, of continually talking about the virtues in the most elaborate style, if meanwhile you do not heed your own teaching? How much better it would have been, for a philosopher above all, to have grown old in the midst of rural tranquility, as you yourself write somewhere, meditating on the life everlasting, rather than on this brief life on earth;[136] never to have held office, not to have yearned after triumphs, never to have allowed the overthrow of such as Catiline to have

---

[132] Pseudo-Cicero, *Epistula ad Octavianum*, 6 (ed. W. S. Watt, *M. Tulli Ciceronis Epistulae*, iii (Oxford, 1958), p. 216).

[133] Cicero, *Epistulae ad Brutum*, xxiv. 7 (ed. Watt, iii. 139).

[134] Cf. *Ep. Brut.* xxiii. 5 (ed. Watt, iii. 132).

[135] *Epist. ad Brut.* xxv. 5 (ed. Watt, iii. 143).

[136] *Ad Atticum*, x. viii. 8 (ed. Watt, ii/2 (Oxford, 1961), p. 61).

made you boastful? But these wishes are all in vain. Farewell for ever, my dear Cicero.

Written in the land of the living, on the right bank of the Adige, in the city of Verona in Italy beyond the Po, on 16 June, in the year 1345 after the birth of that God whom you never knew.

Letters on Familiar Matters, xiv: 4: To the Same

Francis sends greeting to his dear friend Cicero.

If the previous letter offended you—but as you yourself always say, in the words of your friend in the *Andria*: 'flattery brings you friends, but the truth unpopularity'[137]—accept this as something which may in part soothe your ruffled feelings, so that the truth may not be a source of perpetual annoyance to you. For we are made angry by just rebuke, but just praise gives us pleasure. If you will allow me to say so, my dear Cicero, you lived as a man, spoke as an orator, and wrote as a philosopher. It was your life I criticized, not your genius (*ingenium*) or your eloquence, for I admire the first, while the second strikes me dumb with wonder. Indeed, I miss no quality in your life except constancy, the desire for quiet that is necessary for a philosophical life, and a shrinking from the civil wars, once freedom had been extinguished and the republic dead and duly lamented.

Note how different my treatment of you is from the way you treated Epicurus in many places, but more particularly in your book *On Ends*,[138] for you take every opportunity to praise his life but mock his ability. I am not laughing at your expense at all: I only feel sadness when I see your life, as I have said. But I praise you for your genius and eloquence. Great founding father of Roman eloquence, not only I but all of us who deck ourselves in the flowers of the Latin tongue are grateful to you. For it is from your springs that I irrigate my meadows.[139] I freely confess that it is you who have guided me, your support which has helped me, and your shining light that has lit my path. In short, so to say, it is under your auspices that I have attained my present skill in writing, such as it is, and come to achieve my goal.

There was a second guide on the path of poetry. For the nature of things demanded that we should have one guide to blaze a trail for us in the way of unfettered prose, and another in the restricted path of metre; someone for us to admire as a speaker, and another as a singer of verse. For if both of you will excuse my saying so, neither was adequate to both tasks. This other writer was not your equal in the wide-ranging field of prose, nor were you his in the narrow confines of verse.[140] Perhaps

---

[137] *Andria*, 68.   [138] *De finibus*, esp. book ii.

[139] Cicero, *De natura deorum*, I. xliii. 120. We translate the first person plural as epistolary 'I' rather than 'we'.

[140] Cf. *Fam.* xxiv. 12, 13.

I should not have been brave enough to be the first to say so, although this was exactly how I felt. But a great writer, Annaeus Seneca of Cordova, said this before me, or else wrote down what he had heard others saying. As he himself complains, it was not the fact that he lived in a different age, but the mad frenzy of the civil wars, which deprived him of the chance of knowing you. He could have seen you, but did not. But he was loud in his praises of your works and those of that other writer. He it is who orders each of you to limit himself to his own area of eloquence, and to yield place to his colleague in other fields.

But I am tormenting you by the suspense. You are asking who that other leader was. You will know the man once you are reminded of his name. He is Publius Virgilius Maro, a citizen of Mantua, for whom you prophesied a great future. For we read that, having admired one of his youthful works, and asked who the author was, and having seen this young man, you in your old age expressed great pleasure.[141] Drawing on the inexhaustible fount of your eloquence, you paid him a compliment no less magnificent and outstanding for being mixed in with praise of yourself. For you wrote of him: 'the second hope of mighty Rome'.

This sentence, which he had heard from your own lips, gave him such pleasure, and remained so firmly fixed in his memory, that after twenty years, when you had long since been removed from human affairs, he inserted it absolutely *verbatim* in his divine poem.[142] If you had been allowed to see that work, you would have rejoiced that on the strength of his early flowering you should have prophesied so accurately the harvest that was to come. You would, moreover, have congratulated the Latin Muses on having forced an indecisive contest on the insolent Greeks, or even wrested a decisive victory from them. There are, indeed, authorities for either of these views.[143] But if I know your thinking aright from having read your books—and I believe I know it as well as if I had lived in the same house—I have no doubt that you would have made this claim [for the supremacy of Latin] in the end, and awarded Latin the prize in the realm of poetry which you had already bestowed in that of oratory, and ordered the *Iliad* to yield first place to the *Aeneid*, which indeed Propertius did not hesitate to assert right at the very beginning of Virgil's career as a poet. For, after meditating on the first beginnings of that Muse-inspired work, he quite openly declared the opinion he held of it, and the hopes it aroused, in the following verses: 'Greek and Latin writers all give way. We are witnessing the birth of something greater than the *Iliad*.'[144]

---

[141] Servius on Virgil, *Eclogue*, vi. 11.

[142] Virgil, *Aeneid*, xii. 168.

[143] Macrobius, *Saturnalia*, v. ii ff. (ed. Willis, pp. 243 ff.); Juvenal, *Sat.* xi, 180–1.

[144] Propertius, *Elegiae*, ii. xxxiv. 65–6; cf. Donatus' life of Virgil, ed. Hardie, 2nd edn., p. 12.

Enough of this second leader of Latin eloquence, 'this second hope of mighty Rome'. Now I return to you. You have heard what I think about your life and genius. Are you waiting anxiously to hear about your books, and to learn what fate has overtaken them, and how they are viewed by the world at large, or by the more learned section of it? There are indeed splendid volumes still in existence, which I cannot even enumerate, much less read from end to end. The fame of your deeds is widespread, and your reputation great and resounding on all sides. But very few study your works, whether because the times are unfavourable or because we are mentally inactive and sluggish, or else—and I am more inclined to think that this is the real reason—the cause is greed, which impels our minds in other directions. The consequence is that some of your books have been lost, perhaps irreparably, even in our own lifetime, unless I am much mistaken. That is a great source of grief to me, a great disgrace to our times, and a great loss to posterity. As if it were not shameful enough for us to neglect our own abilities, just in case our posterity should gain some profit from them, without destroying the fruits of your labour also by our cruel and intolerable neglect. It is true that the same fate I lament in the case of your books has befallen many books by excellent writers. But since at the moment it is your books I am talking about, here are the names of those the loss of which is more glaring: *On the State*, *On Domestic Affairs*, *On the Art of War*, *In Praise of Philosophy*, *On Consolation*, *On Glory*, although in the case of the last-mentioned my feeling is one of hesitant hope rather than despair founded on certain loss. But we have even lost large parts of the books that survive, so that it is just as if, having overcome oblivion and sloth in a great battle, we have to lament the loss of our leaders, not only those who have been killed but also those who are maimed or reported missing. We suffer this loss in the case of many of your other books, but most of all your books on oratory, your *Academica* and *On the Laws*, which have ended up by being so mutilated and corrupted that it might almost have been better if they had perished.

Last of all, you may wish to hear something of the present condition of the city of Rome and the Roman state, and learn what aspect your native land presents, what degree there is of mutual accord between its citizens, upon whom supreme power has devolved, in what hands and how wisely the reins of imperial power are now guided, whether Danube and Ganges, Ebro, Nile, and Don are still our borders, or whether in truth someone has arisen 'whose empire is bounded by ocean, whose fame by the stars', or who 'advances his rule beyond the Garamantes and the Indians', as that Mantuan friend of yours puts it.[145] I would hazard a guess that you will be most anxious to hear these and similar matters. This is suggested to me by your loyalty and patriotism, which was a most conspicuous trait in you, even to the point of leading to your death. But it will

[145] Virgil, *Aeneid*, vi. 794–5.

be far, far better to keep silence. For believe me, my dear Cicero, if you once hear in what a state our affairs are in, you will weep, whatever part of Heaven or Hell you inhabit.

Farewell for ever. In the land of the living, on the left bank of the Rhône in Gaul beyond the Alps, in the same year, on 19 December.

GIOVANNI BOCCACCIO

The Genealogy of the Gentile Gods: Extracts from
Books XIV and XV[146]

FROM BOOK XIV

Chapter vii: The Definition of Poetry, its Origin and Function (officium)

This poetry, which ignorant triflers cast aside, is a sort of fervid and exquisite invention, with fervid expression, in speech or writing, of that which the mind has invented.[147] It proceeds from the bosom of God,[148] and few, I find, are the souls in which this gift is born; indeed so wonderful a gift it is that true poets have always been the rarest of men.[149] This fervour of poesy is sublime in its effects: it impels the soul to a longing for utterance; it brings forth strange and unheard-of creations of the mind; it arranges these meditations in a fixed order,[150] adorns the whole composition with unusual interweaving of words and thoughts; and thus it veils truth in a fair and fitting garment of fiction.[151] Further, if in any case the invention so requires, it can arm kings, marshal them for war, launch whole fleets from their docks, nay, counterfeit sky, land, sea, adorn young maidens with flowery garlands, portray human character in its various phases, awake the idle, stimulate the dull, restrain the rash, subdue the criminal, and distinguish excellent men with their proper meed of praise: these, and many other such, are the effects of poetry. Yet if any man who has received the gift of poetic fervour shall imperfectly fulfil its function here described, he is not, in my opinion, a laudable poet. For, however deeply the poetic impulse stirs the mind to which it is granted, it very rarely accomplishes anything commendable if the instruments by which

[146] Repr. from *Boccaccio on Poetry*, tr. C. G. Osgood, pp. 39–42, 47–54, 58–69, 121–3, with the kind permission of Professor Osgood's literary executor, Mrs Jean Osgood Smyth.

[147] On the notion of poetic invention see *De inventione*, i. vii. 9, *Ad Herenn.* i. ii. 3, John of Garland's *Parisiana Poetria*, ed. T. Lawler (New Haven, Conn., and London, 1974), pp. 9–11, 19, 23, 27–31, 229–31, 238; cf. Curtius, pp. 68, 71, 77, 194, 296.

[148] Like philosophy, on which poetry feeds: cf. *Geneal. deor. gent.* xiv. v, xvii–xviii (tr. Osgood, pp. 32–6, 78–87).

[149] Cf. Petrarch, *Invectivae contra medicum*, iii, ed. Pier G. Ricci (Rome, 1950), p. 67; also Cicero, *De oratore*, i. iii. 9–11.

[150] Cf. Isidore, *Ety.* viii. vii. 3.

[151] Cf. Macrobius, *In Somn. Scip.* i. ii. 9 (ed. Willis, pp. 5–6, tr. Stahl, pp. 84–5).

its concepts are to be wrought out are wanting—I mean, for example, the precepts of grammar and rhetoric, an abundant knowledge of which is opportune.[152] I grant that many a man already writes his mother tongue admirably, and indeed has performed each of the various duties of poetry as such; yet over and above this, it is necessary to know at least the principles of the other liberal arts, both moral and natural,[153] to possess a strong and abundant vocabulary, to behold the monuments and relics of the ancients,[154] to have in one's memory the histories of the nations, and to be familiar with the geography of various lands, of seas, rivers, and mountains.

Furthermore, places of retirement, the lovely handiwork of Nature herself, are favourable to poetry, as well as peace of mind and desire for worldly glory;[155] the ardent period of life[156] also has very often been of great advantage. If these conditions fail, the power of creative genius frequently grows dull and sluggish.

Now since nothing proceeds from this poetic fervour, which sharpens and illumines the powers of the mind, except what is wrought out by art,[157] poetry is generally called an art. Indeed the word poetry has not the origin that many carelessly suppose, namely *poio*, *pois*, which is but Latin *fingo*, *fingis*; rather it is derived from a very ancient Greek word *poetes*,[158] which means in Latin exquisite discourse (*exquisita locutio*). For the first men who, thus inspired, began to employ an exquisite style of speech, such, for example, as song in an age hitherto unpolished, to render this unheard-of discourse sonorous to their hearers, let it fall in measured periods; and lest by its brevity it fail to please, or, on the other hand, become prolix and tedious, they applied to it the standard of fixed rules, and restrained it within a definite number of feet and syllables. Now the product of this studied method of speech they no longer called by the more general term poesy (*poesis*), but poem (*poema*).[159] Thus as I said above, the name of the art, as well as its artificial product, is derived from its effect.

Now though I allege that this science (*scientia*) of poetry has ever

[152] This may be contrasted with the very different view of Hugh of Saint-Victor, cit. above, p. 122.

[153] On those fables which embody moral and natural truths cf. above, pp. 118–21.

[154] As Osgood says, p. 158 n. 13, the presence in Italy of classical monuments and relics 'was of course a powerful stimulus to the first revival of humanism on that ground'.

[155] Cf. *Geneal. deor. gent.* xiv. xi, xv. xiii (tr. Osgood, pp. 54–8, 136–40).

[156] Presumably Boccaccio is thinking here of his own youthful experience of love, as well as that of Petrarch and Dante. Cf. the relevant passage in Boccaccio's *Trattatello* (tr. below, pp. 502–3), and his *Esposizioni sopra la Comedia*, i ii. 87 ff. (ed. Padoan, pp. 72 ff.).

[157] Here used in the sense of conscious skill, technique; cf. *Geneal. deor. gent.* xiv. iv, vi (tr. Osgood, pp. 25 ff., 36–9).

[158] Cf. Isidore, *Ety.* viii. vii. 2, and Hugutio of Pisa, *Magnae derivationes*, s.v. *poio*, in Oxford, Bodleian Library, MS Bodley 376, fol. 154ʳ.

[159] Cf. *Ety.* i. xxxix. 21.

streamed forth from the bosom of God[160] upon souls while even yet in their tenderest years, these enlightened cavillers will perhaps say that they cannot trust my words. To any fair-minded man the fact is valid enough from its constant recurrence. But for these dullards I must cite witnesses to it. If, then, they will read what Cicero, a philosopher rather than a poet, says in his oration delivered before the senate on behalf of Aulus Licinius Archias, perhaps they will come more easily to believe me. He says: 'And yet we have it on the highest and most learned authority, that while other arts are matters of science and formula and technique, poetry depends solely upon an inborn faculty, is evoked by a purely mental activity, and is infused with a strange supernal inspiration.'[161]

But not to protract this argument, it is now sufficiently clear to reverent men, that poetry is a practical art (*facultas*),[162] springing from God's bosom and deriving its name from its effect, and that it has to do with many high and noble matters that constantly occupy even those who deny its existence. If my opponents ask when and in what circumstances, the answer is plain: the poets would declare with their own lips under whose help and guidance they compose their inventions when, for example, they raise flights of symbolic steps to heaven,[163] or make thick-branching trees spring aloft to the very stars,[164] or go winding about mountains to their summits. Haply, to disparage this art of poetry now unrecognized by them, these men will say that it is rhetoric which the poets employ. Indeed, I will not deny it in part, for rhetoric has also its own inventions. Yet, in truth, among the disguises of fiction (*integumenta fictionum*) rhetoric has no part, for whatever is composed as under a veil, and thus exquisitely wrought, is poetry and poetry alone. . . .[165]

*Chapter ix: It is rather Useful than Damnable to compose Stories (*fabulae*)*

These fine cattle bellow still further to the effect that poets are tale-mongers, or, to use the lower and more hateful term which they sometimes employ in their resentment—liars. No doubt the ignorant will regard such an imputation as particularly objectionable. But I scorn it. The foul language of some men cannot infect the glorious name of the illustrious. Yet I grieve to see these revilers in a purple rage let themselves loose upon the innocent. If I conceded that poets deal in stories, in that they are composers of fiction, I think I hereby incur no further disgrace

---

[160] Cf. above, n. 148.

[161] Cicero, *Pro Archia poeta*, viii. 18.

[162] Cf. above, p. 388.

[163] Osgood suggests this may refer to Dante's mountain of purgatory, and perhaps the steps from circle to circle (*Purg*. xi. 40, xiii. 1, xvii. 65, etc.), or the three steps in *Purg*. ix. 76 ff., or the mystic stairway of the seventh heaven, *Par*. xxi. 8, xxii. 68.

[164] Like the trees to which Pandarus and Bitias are compared in the *Aeneid*, ix. 678–82.

[165] Thus Boccaccio affirms the superiority of poetry to rhetoric. Cf. *Geneal. deor. gent*. xiv. xii (tr. below).

than a philosopher would in drawing up a syllogism. For if I show the nature of a fable or story, its various kinds, and which kinds these 'liars' employ, I do not think the composers of fiction will appear guilty of so monstrous a crime as these gentlemen maintain. First of all, the word 'fable' (*fabula*) has an honorable origin in the verb *for*, *faris*,[166] hence 'conversation' (*confabulatio*), which means only 'talking together' (*collocutio*). This is clearly shown by Luke in his Gospel [24: 14–15], where he is speaking of the two disciples who went to the village of Emmaus after the Passion. He says: 'And they talked together of all these things which had happened. And it came to pass, that, while they communed together, and reasoned, Jesus himself drew near, and went with them.'

Hence, if it is a sin to compose stories, it is a sin to converse,[167] which only the veriest fool would admit. For nature has not granted us the power of speech unless for purposes of conversation, and the exchange of ideas.

But, they may object, nature meant this gift for a useful purpose, not for idle nonsense; and fiction is just that—idle nonsense. True enough, if the poet had intended to compose a mere tale. But I have time and time again proved that the meaning of fiction is far from superficial.[168] Wherefore, some writers have framed this definition of fiction (*fabula*): fiction is a form of discourse, which, under guise of invention, illustrates or proves an idea; and, as its superficial aspect is removed, the meaning of the author is clear.[169] If, then, sense is revealed from under the veil of fiction, the composition of fiction is not idle nonsense. Of fiction I distinguish four kinds. The first superficially lacks all appearance of truth; for example, when brutes or inanimate things converse. Aesop, an ancient Greek, grave and venerable, was past master in this form; and though it is a common and popular form both in city and country, yet Aristotle, chief of the Peripatetics, and a man of divine intellect, did not scorn to use it in his books.[170] The second kind at times superficially mingles fiction with truth, as when we tell of the daughters of Minyas at their spinning, who, when they spurned the orgies of Bacchus, were turned to bats; or the mates of the sailor Acestes, who for contriving the rape of the boy Bacchus, were turned to fish.[171] This form has been employed from the beginning by the most ancient poets, whose object it has been to clothe in fiction divine and human matters alike; they who have followed the sublimer inventions of the poets have improved upon them; while some of the comic writers have perverted them, caring more for the approval of a

---

[166] Cf. Isidore, *Ety.* i. xl. i.

[167] Here, as Osgood points out, Boccaccio alters the Vulgate Bible's term 'fabulari' to 'colloqui'.

[168] See *Geneal. deor. gent.* XIV. vii (tr. above), and XIV. viii (tr. Osgood, pp. 42–7).

[169] For the antecedents of the following discussion see the refs. in n. 77.

[170] See Aristotle, *Rhetorica*, ii. 20 (1393^{b}8–1394^{a}1).

[171] Ovid, *Metamorphoses*, iv. 31–415, iii. 582–686 (the true name is Acoetes).

licentious public than for honesty.[172] The third kind is more like history than fiction, and famous poets have employed it in a variety of ways. For however much the heroic poets seem to be writing history—as Virgil in his description of Aeneas tossed by the storm, or Homer in his account of Ulysses bound to the mast to escape the lure of the Sirens' song—yet their hidden meaning is far other than appears on the surface.[173] The better of the comic poets, Terence and Plautus, for example, have also employed this form, but they intend naught other than the literal meaning of their lines.[174] Yet by their art they portray varieties of human nature and conversation, incidentally teaching the reader and putting him on his guard. If the events they describe have not actually taken place, yet since they are common, they could have occurred, or might at some time.[175] My opponents need not be so squeamish—Christ, who is God, used this sort of fiction again and again in His parables!

The fourth kind contains no trust at all, either superficial or hidden, since it consists only of old wives' tales.[176]

Now, if my eminent opponents condemn the first kind of fiction, then they must include the account in Holy Writ describing the conference of the trees of the forest on choosing a king [Judg. 9: 8–15]. If the second, then nearly the whole sacred body of the Old Testament will be rejected, God forbid, since the writings of the Old Testament and the writings of the poets seem as it were to keep step with each other, and that too in respect to the method of their composition. For where history is lacking, neither one concerns itself with the superficial possibility, but what the poet calls fable or fiction our theologians have named figure. The truth of this may be seen by fairer judges than my opponents, if they will but weigh in a true scale the outward literary semblance of the visions of Isaiah, Ezekiel, Daniel, and other sacred writers on the one hand, with the outward literary semblance of the fiction of poets on the other.[177] If they find any real discrepancy in their methods, either of implication or exposition, I will accept their condemnation. If they condemn the third form of fiction, it is the same as condemning the form which our Saviour Jesus Christ, the Son of God, often used when He was in the flesh, though Holy Writ does not call it 'poetry', but 'parable'; some call it 'exemplum', because it is used as such.

[172] In *Geneal.* xiv. xix (tr. Osgood, p. 93), Boccaccio attacks 'certain so-called comic poets' who, with the exception of upright men like Terence and Plautus, have 'defiled the bright glory of poetry with their filthy creations'.

[173] Cf. Boccaccio's discussion of Virgil and Homer in *Gen. deor. gent.* xiv. xiii (tr. below).

[174] Cf. above, p. 384, and n. 172.

[175] Cf. the standard discussions of verisimilar fiction, e.g. *De invent.* i. xix. 27, *Ad Herenn.* i. viii. 13.

[176] Cf. Macrobius, *In Somn. Scip.* i. ii. 8 (ed. Willis, p. 5; tr. Stahl, p. 84).

[177] Cf. *Geneal. deor. gent.* xiv. iv (tr. Osgood, p. 25), where Boccaccio refers to the poems of the prophets which were written down in excellent style by poetic pens under the direct impulse of divine knowledge.

I count as naught their condemnation of the fourth form of fiction, since it proceeds from no consistent principle, nor is fortified by the reinforcement of any of the arts, nor carried logically to a conclusion. Fiction of this kind has nothing in common with the works of the poets, though I imagine these objectors think poetry differs from it in no respect.

I now ask whether they are going to call the Holy Spirit, or Christ, the very God, liars, who both in the same Godhead have uttered fictions. I hardly think so, if they are wise. I might show them, your Majesty, if there were time, that difference of names constitutes no objection where methods agree. But they may see for themselves. Fiction, which they scorn because of its mere name, has been the means, as we often read, of quelling minds aroused to a mad rage, and subduing them to their pristine gentleness. Thus, when the Roman plebs seceded from the senate, they were called back from the Sacred Mount to the city by Menenius Agrippa, a man of great influence, all by means of a story.[178] By fiction, too, the strength and spirits of great men worn out in the strain of serious crises have been restored. This appears, not by ancient instance alone, but constantly. One knows of princes who have been deeply engaged in important matters, but after the noble and happy disposal of their affairs of state, obey, as it were, the warning of nature, and revive their spent forces by calling about them such men as will renew their weary minds with diverting stories and conversation. Fiction has, in some cases, sufficed to lift the oppressive weight of adversity and furnish consolation, as appears in Lucius Apuleius; he tells how the high-born maiden Charis, while bewailing her unhappy condition as captive among thieves, was in some degree restored through hearing from an old woman the charming story of Psyche.[179] Through fiction, it is well known, the mind that is slipping into inactivity is recalled to a state of better and more vigorous fruition. Not to mention minor instances, such as my own,[180] I once heard Giacopo Sanseverino, Count of Tricarico and Chiarmonti, say that he had heard his father tell of Robert,[181] son of King Charles—himself in after time the famous King of Jerusalem and Sicily— how as a boy he was so dull that it took the utmost skill and patience of his master to teach him the mere elements of letters. When all his friends were nearly in despair of his doing anything, his master, by the most subtle skill, as it were, lured his mind with the fables of Aesop into so grand a passion for study and knowledge, that in a brief time he not only learnt the liberal arts familiar to Italy, but entered with wonderful keenness of mind into the very inner mysteries of sacred philosophy. In short, he

---

[178] i.e. the story of the dispute between the belly and the other members of the body, as in Livy, *Ab urbe condita*, II. xxxii. 8–12.

[179] Apuleius, *Metamorphoses*, iv. 28–vi. 24.

[180] See *Geneal. deor. gent.*, pref., and xv. xiii (tr. Osgood, pp. 10, 137).

[181] Son of Charles II of Anjou.

made of himself a king whose superior in learning men have not seen since Solomon.

Such then is the power of fiction that it pleases the unlearned by its external appearance, and exercises the minds of the learned with its hidden truth; and thus both are edified and delighted[182] with one and the same perusal. Then let not these disparagers raise their heads to vent their spleen in scornful words, and spew their ignorance upon poets! If they have any sense at all, let them look to their own speciousness before they try to dim the splendour of others with the cloud of their maledictions. Let them see, I pray, how pernicious are their jeers, fit to rouse the laughter only of girls. When they have made themselves clean let them purify the tales of others, mindful of Christ's commandment to the accusers of the woman taken in adultery, that he who was without sin should cast the first stone [John 8: 7].

Chapter x: It is a Fool's Notion that Poets convey no Meaning beneath the Surface of their Fictions

Some of the railers are bold enough to say, on their own authority, that only an utter fool would imagine the best poets to have hidden any meaning in their stories; rather, they have invented them just to display the great power of their eloquence, and show how easily such tales may bring the injudicious mind to take fiction for truth. O the injustice of men! O what absurd dunces! What clumsiness! While they are trying to put down others, they imagine in their ignorance that they are exalting themselves. Who but an ignoramus would dare to say that poets purposely make their inventions void and empty, trusting in the superficial appearance of their tales to show their eloquence? As who should say that truth and eloquence cannot go together. Surely they have missed Quintilian's saying; it was this great orator's opinion that real power of eloquence is inconsistent with falsehood.[183] But this matter I will postpone that I may come to the immediate subject of this chapter. Let any man, then, read the line in Virgil's *Bucolics*: 'He sung the secret seeds of Nature's frame',[184] and what follows on the same matter; or in the *Georgics*: 'That bees have portions of ethereal thought / Endued with particles of heavenly fires',[185] with the relevant lines; or in the *Aeneid*: 'Know first that heaven and earth's compacted frame, / And flowing waters, and the starry frame', etc.[186]

This is poetry from which the sap of philosophy runs pure.[187] Then is

---

[182] Cf. Horace, *Ars poetica*, 333.
[183] Perhaps a reference to Quintilian, *Institutiones*, v. xii. 17.
[184] Virgil, *Bucolics*, vi. 31–2.
[185] Virgil, *Georgics*, iv. 220–1.
[186] Virgil, *Aeneid*, vi. 724–5. These three Virgil quotations are from John Dryden's translation.
[187] Cf. Petrarch's similar views on the relationship between poetry and philosophy,

any reader so muddled as not to see clearly that Virgil was a philosopher; or mad enough to think that he, with all his deep learning, would, merely for the sake of displaying his eloquence—in which his powers were indeed extraordinary—have led the shepherd Aristaeus into his mother Clymene's presence in the depths of the earth,[188] or brought Aeneas to see his father in Hades?[189] Or can anyone believe he wrote such lines without some meaning or intention hidden beneath the superficial veil of myth?[190] Again, let any man consider our own poet Dante as he often unties with amazingly skilful demonstration the hard knots of holy theology; will such a one be so insensible as not to perceive that Dante was a great theologian as well as philosopher? And, if this is clear, what intention does he seem to have had in presenting the picture of the griffin with wings and legs, drawing the chariot on top of the austere mountain, together with the seven candlesticks, and the seven nymphs, and the rest of the triumphal procession?[191] Was it merely to show his dexterity in composing metrical narrative? To mention another instance: that most distinguished Christian gentleman, Francis Petrarch, whose life and character we have, with our own eyes, beheld so laudable in all sanctity (and by God's grace shall continue to behold for a long time), no one has saved and employed to better advantage than he his—I will not say his time but rather every crumb of it.[192] Is there anyone sane enough to suppose that he devoted all those watches of the night, all those holy seasons of meditation, all those hours and days and years—which we have a right to assume that he did, considering the force and dignity of his bucolic verse, the exquisite beauty of his style and diction—I say, would he have taken such pains merely to represent Gallus begging Tyrrhenus for his reeds,[193] or Pamphilus and Mitio in a squabble,[194] or other like pastoral nonsense? No man in his right mind will agree that these were his final object; much less, if he considers his prose treatise on the solitary life, or the one which he calls *On the Remedies for all Fortunes*, not to mention any others. Herein all that is clear and holy in the bosom of moral philosophy is presented in so majestic a style, that nothing could be uttered for the instruction of mankind more replete, more beautified, more mature, nay, more holy. I would cite also my own eclogues, of whose meaning I am, of course, fully aware; but I have decided not to, partly because I am not great enough to be associated with the most distinguished men, and partly because the discussion of one's attainments had better be left to others.

discussed by Charles Trinkaus, '*Theologia poetica* and *theologia rhetorica* in Petrarch's Invectives', in id., *The Poet as Philosopher* (New Haven, Conn., and London, 1979), pp. 95 ff.

[188] Virgil, *Georgics*, iv. 415 ff.   [189] Virgil, *Aeneid*, vi.
[190] Lat. 'sub fabuloso velamine intellectu'.
[191] *Purgatorio*, xxix. 108 ff.
[192] Here we have altered a sentence in Osgood's translation.
[193] Petrarch, *Ecl. IV*, ed. Bergin, *Petrarch's Bucolicum carmen*, pp. 48–57.
[194] Petrarch, *Ecl. VI*, ed. Bergin, pp. 74–97.

Then let the babblers stop their nonsense, and silence their pride if they can; for one can never escape the conviction that great men, nursed with the milk of the Muses, brought up in the very home of philosophy, and disciplined in sacred studies, have laid away the very deepest meaning in their poems; and not only this, but there was never a maundering old woman, sitting with others late of a winter's night at the home fireside, making up tales of Hell, the fates, ghosts, and the like— much of it pure invention—that she did not feel beneath the surface of her tale, as far as her limited mind allowed, at least some meaning—sometimes ridiculous no doubt—with which she tries to scare the little ones, or divert the young ladies, or amuse the old, or at least show the power of fortune.[195] . . .

Chapter xii: The Obscurity of Poetry is not Just Cause for Condemning it [196]

These cavillers further object that poetry is often obscure, and that poets are to blame for it, since their end is to make an incomprehensible statement appear to be wrought with exquisite artistry; regardless of the old rule of the orators, that a speech must be simple and clear.[197] Perverse notion! Who but a deceiver himself would have sunk low enough not merely to hate what he could not understand, but incriminate it, if he could? I admit that poets are at times obscure. At the same time will these accusers please answer me? Take those philosophers among whom they shamelessly intrude;[198] do they always find their close reasoning as simple and clear as they say an oration should be? If they say yes, they lie; for the works of Plato and Aristotle, to go no further, abound in difficulties so tangled and involved that from their day to the present, though searched and pondered by many a man of keen insight, they have yielded no clear nor consistent meaning. But why do I talk of philosophers? There is the utterance of Holy Writ, of which they especially like to be thought expounders;[199] though proceeding from the Holy Ghost, is it not full to overflowing with obscurities and ambiguities? It is indeed, and for all their denial, the truth will openly assert itself. Many are the witnesses, of whom let them be pleased to consult Augustine, a man of great sanctity and learning, and of such intellectual power that, without a teacher, as he says himself, he learned many arts, besides all that the philosophers teach of the ten categories.[200] Yet he did not blush to admit that he could not

---

[195] As Osgood points out, this is not quite consistent with *Geneal. deor. gent.* xiv. ix (tr. above), where he condemned 'old wives' tales' as containing no truth at all.
[196] This chapter embodies material from Petrarch's *Invectivae*, iii (ed. Ricci, pp. 68–70); cf. Trinkaus, *Poet as Philosopher*, pp. 101–2.
[197] Cf. Aristotle, *Rhet.* iii. 2 (1404ᵇ1–3); cf. Cicero, *De invent.* i. xix. 20, *Ad Herenn.* i. viii. 9.
[198] See *Geneal. deor. gent.* xiv. v (tr. Osgood, pp. 32–6).
[199] Ibid.
[200] See Augustine, *Confessiones*, iv. xvi. 28.

understand the beginning of Isaiah.[201] It seems that obscurities are not confined to poetry. Why then do they not criticize philosophers as well as poets? Why do they not say that the Holy Spirit wove obscure sayings into his works, just to give them an appearance of clever artistry? As if He were not the sublime Artificer of the Universe![202] I have no doubt they are bold enough to say such things, if they were not aware that philosophers already had their defenders, and did not remember the punishment prepared for them that blaspheme against the Holy Ghost.[203] So they pounce upon the poets because they seem defenceless, with the added reason that, where no punishment is imminent, no guilt is involved. They should have realized that when things perfectly clear seem obscure, it is the beholder's fault. To a half-blind man, even when the sun is shining its brightest, the sky looks cloudy. Some things are naturally so profound that not without difficulty can the most exceptional keenness in intellect sound their depths; like the sun's globe, by which, before they can clearly discern it, strong eyes are sometimes repelled.[204] On the other hand, some things, though naturally clear perhaps, are so veiled by the artist's skill that scarcely anyone could by mental effort derive sense from them; as the immense body of the sun when hidden in clouds cannot be exactly located by the eye of the most learned astronomer. That some of the prophetic poems are in this class, I do not deny.

Yet not by this token is it fair to condemn them; for surely it is not one of the poet's various functions to rip up and lay bare the meaning which lies hidden in his inventions. Rather where matters truly solemn and memorable are too much exposed, it is his office by every effort to protect as well as he can and remove them from the gaze of the irreverent, that they cheapen not by too common familiarity. So when he discharges this duty and does it ingeniously, the poet earns commendation, not anathema.

Wherefore I again grant that poets are at times obscure, but invariably explicable if approached by a sane mind; for these cavillers view them with owl eyes, not human. Surely no one can believe that poets invidiously veil the truth with fiction, either to deprive the reader of the hidden sense, or to appear the more clever; but rather to make truths which would otherwise cheapen by exposure the object of strong intellectual effort and various interpretation, that in ultimate discovery they shall be more precious. In a far higher degree is this the method of the Holy Spirit; nay, every right-minded man should be assured of it beyond any doubt. Besides it is established by Augustine in the *City of God*, Book Eleven, when he says: 'The obscurity of the divine word has certainly this

---

[201] Augustine, *Enarr. in ps.* cxxvi, 11, where Isa. 1: 3 is cited (CCSL xl. 1865).
[202] Cf. Wisd. 7: 21, 22.
[203] Cf. Mark 3: 29.
[204] Cf. Dante, *Paradiso*, i. 54 ff., and cf. p. 193 above.

advantage, that it causes many opinions about the truth to be started and discussed, each reader seeing some fresh meaning in it.'[205]

Elsewhere he says of Ps. 126: 'For perhaps the words are rather obscurely expressed for this reason, that they may call forth many understandings, and that men may go away the richer, because they have found that closed which might be opened in many ways, than if they could open and discover it by one interpretation.'[206]

To make further use of Augustine's testimony (which so far is adverse to these recalcitrants), to show them how I apply to the obscurities of poetry his advice on the right attitude toward the obscurities of Holy Writ, I will quote his comment on Ps. 146: 'There is nothing in it contradictory: somewhat there is which is obscure, not in order that it may be denied thee, but that it may exercise him that shall afterward receive it', etc.[207]

But enough of the testimony of holy men on this point; I will not bore my opponents by again urging them to regard the obscurities of poetry as Augustine regards the obscurities of Holy Writ. Rather I wish that they would wrinkle their brows a bit, and consider fairly and squarely, how, if this is true of sacred literature addressed to all nations, in far greater measure is it true of poetry, which is addressed to the few.

If by chance in condemning the difficulty of the text, they really mean its figures of diction and oratorical colours and the beauty which they fail to recognize in alien words, if on this account they pronounce poetry obscure—my only advice is for them to go back to the grammar-schools,[208] bow to the ferule, study, and learn what licence ancient authority granted the poets in such matters, and give particular attention to such alien terms as are permissible beyond common and homely use. But why dwell so long upon the subject? I could have urged them in a sentence to put off the old mind,[209] and put on the new and noble; then will that which now seems to them obscure look familiar and open. Let them not trust to concealing their gross confusion of mind in the precepts of the old orators; for I am sure the poets were ever mindful of such. But let them observe that oratory is quite different, in arrangement of words, from fiction, and that fiction has been consigned to the discretion of the inventor as being the legitimate work of another art than oratory. 'In poetic narrative above all, the poets maintain majesty of style and corresponding dignity.' As saith Francis Petrarch in the Third Book of his *Invectives*, contrary to my opponents' supposition, 'Such majesty and dignity are not intended to hinder those who wish to understand, but rather propose a delightful task, and are designed to enhance the reader's pleasure and support his memory. What we acquire with difficulty and keep with care is always the dearer to us'; so continues Petrarch.[210] In fine,

---

[205] *De civ. Dei*, XI. xix.   [206] *Enarr. in ps.* loc. cit.   [207] Cf. ibid. 12 (CCSL xl. 1866).
[208] In which poetry was studied; see above, pp. 37–9, 279, etc.
[209] Cf. Eph. 4: 22, Col. 3: 9.   [210] Petrarch, *Invectivae*, iii (ed. Ricci, p. 70).

if their minds are dull, let them not blame the poets but their own sloth.
Let them not keep up a silly howl against those whose lives and actions
contrast most favourably with their own. Nay, at the very outset they have
taken fright at mere appearances, and bid fair to spend themselves for
nothing. Then let them retire in good time, sooner than exhaust their
torpid minds with the onset and suffer a violent repulse.

But I repeat my advice to those who would appreciate poetry, and
unwind its difficult involutions. You must read, you must persevere, you
must sit up nights, you must inquire, and exert the utmost power of your
mind. If one way does not lead to the desired meaning, take another; if
obstacles rise, then still another; until, if your strength holds out, you will
find that clear which at first looked dark. For we are forbidden by divine
command to give that which is holy to dogs, or to cast pearls before swine
[Matt. 7: 6].

Chapter xiii: Poets are not Liars

These enemies of poetry further utter the taunt that poets are liars. This
position they try to maintain by the hackneyed objection that poets write
lies in their narratives, to wit, that a human being was turned into a
stone[211]—a statement in every aspect contrary to the truth. They urge
besides that poets lie in asserting that there are many gods, though it is
established in all certainty that there is but One—the True and Omnipotent. They add that the greatest Latin poet, Virgil, told the more or less
untrue story of Dido,[212] and allege other like instances. I fancy they think
their point is already won, and so indeed it would be, were there no one to
repel their boorish vociferations with the truth. Yet further discussion
seems hardly necessary for I supposed that I had already answered this
objection above,[213] where at sufficient length I defined a story, its kinds,
what sorts the poets employ, and wherefore.

But if the matter is to be resumed, I insist that, whatever those fellows
think, poets are not liars. I had supposed that a lie was a certain very close
counterfeit of the truth which served to destroy the true and substitute the
false. Augustine mentions eight kinds of lies,[214] of which some are, to be
sure, graver than others, yet none, if we employ them consciously, free
from sin and the mark of infamy that denotes a liar. If the enemies of
poetry will consider fairly the meaning of this definition, they will become
aware that their charge of falsehood is without force, since poetic fiction
has nothing in common with any variety of falsehood, for it is not a poet's
purpose to deceive anybody with his inventions; furthermore poetic

---

[211] Perhaps a reference to Niobe.
[212] Cf. Augustine, *Conf.* I. xiii. 22. See too Macrobius, *Sat.* v. xvii. 5; also *Anth. Pal.* xvi. 151;
Epigr. Bob. xlv; Tertullian, *De anima*, xxxiii. 9; also Ch. X, n. 216.
[213] At *Geneal. deor. gent.* XIV. ix (tr. above).
[214] Augustine, *De mendacio*, xiv. 25 (CSEL xli. 444–6).

fiction differs from a lie in that in most instances it bears not only no close resemblance to the literal truth, but no resemblance at all; on the contrary, it is quite out of harmony and agreement with the literal truth.

Yet there is one kind of fiction very like the truth, which, as I said,[215] is more like history than fiction, and which by most ancient agreement of all peoples has been free from taint of falsehood. This is so in virtue of their consent from of old that anyone who could might use it as an illustration in which the literal truth is not required, nor its opposite forbidden. And if one considers the function of the poet already described, clearly poets are not constrained by this bond to employ literal truth on the surface of their inventions; besides, if the privilege of ranging through every sort of fiction be denied them, their office[216] will altogether resolve itelf into naught.

Again: if all my preceding argument should deserve reprobation—and I hardly think it possible—yet this fact remains irrefutable, that no one can in the proper discharge of his duty incur by that act the taint of infamy. If the judge, for example, lawfully visits capital punishment upon malefactors, it is not called homicide. Neither is a soldier who wastes the enemy's fields called a robber. Though a lawyer gives his client advice not wholly just, yet if he breaks not the bounds of the law he does not deserve to be called a falsifier.[217] So also a poet, however he may sacrifice the literal truth in invention, does not incur the ignominy of a liar, since he discharges his very proper function not to deceive, but only by way of invention.

Yet if they will insist that whatever is not literally true is, however uttered, a lie, I accept it for purposes of argument; if not, I will spend no more energy in demolishing this objection of theirs. Rather I will ask them to tell me what name should be applied to those parts of the Revelation of John the Evangelist—expressed with amazing majesty of inner sense, though often at first glance quite contrary to the truth—in which he has veiled the great mysteries of God.[218] And what will they call John himself? What too will they call the other writers who have employed the same style to the same end?[219] I certainly should not dare answer for them 'lies' and 'liars', even if I might. Yet I know well they will say what I myself in part am about to say—should anyone ask me—that John and the other prophets were men of absolute truthfulness, a point already conceded.[220]

[215] Geneal. deor. gent. XIV. ix (tr. above).
[216] Cf. Isidore's definition of the officium poetae at Ety. VIII. vii. 10, reiterated by Vincent of Beauvais, Speculum doctrinale, III. cx (Speculum quadruplex, ii. 288).
[217] Cf. Boccaccio's contrast between the roles of the lawyer and poet in Geneal. deor. gent. XIV. iv (tr. Osgood, pp. 21–32).   [218] Cf. St Jerome, Epistolae, liii. 9 (CSEL liv. 463).
[219] At Geneal. deor. gent. XIV. ix (tr. above), Boccaccio mentions Isaiah, Ezekiel, and Daniel in a similar context.
[220] With this discussion cf. Henry of Ghent's analysis of apparent lies in Scripture, above, pp. 263–6; cf. pp. 209–12.

My opponents will add that their writings are not fiction but rather figures, to use the correct term, and their authors are figurative writers. O silly subterfuge! As if I were likely to believe that two things to all appearances exactly alike should gain the power of different effects by mere change or difference of name.

But not to dispute the point, I grant they are figures. Then, let me ask, does the truth which they express lie on their surface? If they wish me to think it does, what else is it but a lie thus to veil the eyes of my understanding, as they also veil the truth beneath? Well then, if these sacred writers must be called liars, though not held such, since indeed they are none, no more are poets to be considered liars who lean with their whole weight upon mere invention.

Yet without question poets do say in their works that there are many gods, when there is but one. But they should not therefore be charged with falsehood, since they neither believe nor assert it as a fact, but only as a myth or fiction, according to their wont. Who is witless enough to suppose that a man deeply versed in philosophy has no more sense than to accept polytheism? As sensible men we must easily admit that the learned have been most devoted investigators of the truth, and have gone as far as the human mind can explore; thus they know beyond any shadow of doubt that there is but one God. As for poets, their own words clearly show that they have attained to such knowledge. Read Virgil and you will find the prayer: 'If any vows, Almighty Jove, can bend Thy will',[221] an epithet which you will never see applied to another god. The multitude of other gods they looked upon not as gods, but as members or functions of the Divinity; such was Plato's opinion,[222] and we call him a theologian. But to these functions they gave a name in conformity with Deity because of their veneration for the particular function in each instance.

But I do not expect these disturbers to hold their peace here. They will cry out the louder that poets have written many lies about this one true God—whom, as I have just said, they recognize—and on that count deserve to be called liars. Of course I do not doubt that pagan poets had an imperfect sense of the true God, and so sometimes wrote of him what was not altogether true—a lie, as their accusers call it. But for all that I think they should hardly be called liars. There are two kinds of liars: first, those who knowingly and wilfully lie, whether to injure another person or not, or even to help him. These should not be called merely liars, but, more appropriately, 'wilful deceivers'. The second class are those who

---

[221] Virgil, *Aeneid*, ii. 689.
[222] Derived from the *De dogmate Platonis* ascribed to Apuleius (i. 11–12), which Boccaccio may not have known at first hand. Dante mentions the theory in *Convivio*, II. iv. 4 ff. (ed. Simonelli, p. 39). The three kinds of deity are treated at length by the undoubted Apuleius in *De deo Socratis* (of which much use was made by Augustine in *De civitate Dei*).

have told a falsehood without knowing it.[223] Among these last a further distinction is in order. For in some cases ignorance is neither to be excused nor endured. For example, the law forbids any man privately to hold a citizen prisoner. John Doe has detained Richard Roe, his debtor, and pleads exemption from fine through ignorance of the law; but since such ignorance of the law seems stupid and negligent, it can constitute no defence. Likewise a Christian who is of age should find no protection in ignorance of the articles of faith. On the other hand there are those whose ignorance is excusable, such as boys ignorant of philosophy or a mountaineer ignorant of navigation, or a man congenitally blind who does not know his letters. Such are the pagan poets who, with all their knowledge of the liberal arts, poetry, and philosophy, could not know the truth of Christianity; for that light of the eternal truth which lighteth every man that cometh into the world had not yet shone forth upon the nations. Not yet had these servants gone throughout all the earth bidding every man to the supper of the Lamb.[224] To the Israelites alone had this gift been granted of knowing the true God aright, and truly worshipping Him. But they never invited anyone to share the great feast with them, nor admitted any of the Gentiles at their doors. And if pagan poets wrote not the whole truth concerning the true God, though they thought they did, such ignorance is an acceptable excuse and they ought not to be called liars.

But my opponents will say, that whatever ignorance occasioned the lie, he who told it is none the less a liar. True; but I repeat, they who sinned in pardonable ignorance are not to be damned by the same token as the offenders whose ignorance was crass and negligent; for the law, both in its equity and its austerity, holds them excused, wherefore they incur not the brand of a lie.

If these disparagers still insist in spite of everything that poets are liars, I accuse the philosophers, Aristotle, Plato, and Socrates, of sharing their guilt. Now, I expect, these expert critics will again lift their voices to heaven and cry to the sound of harp and cithara that this objection of theirs has suffered no harm. Fools! Though one small shield be shattered, the whole front does not waver. Let them not exult, but remember how often they have now been belaboured and beaten back.

Their objection to Virgil—that no wise man would ever consent to tell the story of Dido—is utterly false. With his profound knowledge of such lore, he was well aware that Dido had really been a woman of exceptionally high character, who would rather die by her own hand than subdue the vow of chastity fixed deep in her heart to a second marriage.[225] But

---

[223] For the distinction between *mentiri* 'tell a deliberate lie' and *mendacium dicere* 'Tell an unintentional falsehood' see Nigidius Figulus in Aulus Gellius, *Noctes Attici*, XI. xi.

[224] Cf. John 1: 9, Matt. 22: 2 ff., Rev. 14: 9.

[225] Jerome praises Dido in similar terms in *Adversus Jovinianum*, i. 43 (PL xxiii. 286).

that he might attain the proper effect of his work[226] under the artifice of a poetic disguise, he composed a story in many respects like that of this historic Dido, according to the privilege of poets established by ancient custom. Possibly someone more worthy of a reply than my opponents—perhaps even thou, O Prince—may ask to what purpose this was necessary for Virgil. By way of fitting answer let me then say that his motive (*causa*) was fourfold.

First, that in the same style which he had adopted for the *Aeneid* he might follow the practice of earlier poets, particularly Homer, whom he imitated in this work. For poets are not like historians, who begin their account at some convenient beginning and describe events in the unbroken order of their occurrence to the end. Such, we observe, was Lucan's method, wherefore many think of him rather as a metrical historian than a poet.[227] But poets, by a far nobler device, begin their proposed narrative in the midst of the events,[228] or sometimes even near the end; and thus they find excuse for telling preceding events which seem to have been omitted. Thus Homer, in the *Odyssey*, begins, as it were, near the end of Ulysses' wanderings and shows him wrecked upon the Phaeacian shore, then has him tell King Alcinous everything that had happened to him hitherto since he left Troy. Virgil chose the same method in describing Aeneas as a fugitive from the shore of Troy after the city was razed. He found no place so appropriate on which to land him before he reached Italy as the coast of Africa; for at any nearer point he had been sailing continuously among his enemies the Greeks. But since the shore of Africa was at that time still the home of rude and barbarous rustics, he desired to bring his hero to somebody worthy of regard who might receive him and urge him to tell of his own fate and that of the Trojans. Such a one above all he found in Dido, who, to be sure, is supposed to have dwelt there not then, but many generations later;[229] yet Dido he presents as already living, and makes her the hostess of Aeneas; and we read how at her command he told the story of his own troubles and those of his friends.

Virgil's second purpose, concealed within the poetic veil, was to show with what passions human frailty is infested, and the strength with which a steady man subdues them.[230] Having illustrated some of these, he

---

[226] This story certainly moved St Augustine, who in *Conf.* I. xiii, 21 reports how he once wept at the death of Dido.

[227] For this controversy see above, pp. 114–16, 156.

[228] Cf. Horace, *Ars poetica*, 148, who refers to Homer.

[229] Cf. Petrarch, *Lettere senili*, iv. 5 (ed. Fracassetti, i. 252 ff.).

[230] Here Boccaccio offers a moral and allegorical explanation of the *Aeneid*; cf. Fulgentius, *Exposition of the content of Virgil according to moral philosophy*, tr. Whitbread, pp. 119–53, and the prologue to the 'Bernard Silvester' *Aeneid* commentary (tr. above, Ch. IV). The *gens Julia* was a distinguished patrician *gens* or clan at Rome, which claimed descent from Iulus (Ascanius), the son of Aeneas, and through them from Venus. To this *genus* belonged Julius Caesar, and Octavian through his adoption by Caesar.

wished particularly to demonstrate the reasons why we are carried away
into wanton behaviour by the passion of concupiscence; so he introduces
Dido, a woman of distinguished family, young, fair, rich, exemplary,
famous for her purity, ruler of her city and people, of conspicuous
wisdom and eloquence, and, lastly, a widow, and thus from former
experience in love the more easily disposed to that passion. Now all these
qualifications are likely to excite the mind of a high-born man, particularly an exile and castaway thrown destitute upon an unknown shore.
So he represents in Dido the attracting power of the passion of love,
prepared for every opportunity, and in Aeneas one who is readily
disposed in that way and at length overcome. But after showing the
enticements of lust, he points the way of return to virtue by bringing in
Mercury, messenger of the gods, to rebuke Aeneas, and call him back
from such indulgence to deeds of glory. By Mercury, Virgil means either
remorse, or the reproof of some outspoken friend, either of which rouses
us from slumber in the mire of turpitude, and calls us back into the fair
and even path to glory. Then we burst the bonds of unholy delight, and,
armed with new fortitude, we unfalteringly spurn all seductive flattery,
and tears, prayers, and such, and abandon them as naught.

Virgil's third purpose, is to extol, through his praise of Aeneas, the *gens
Julia* in honour of Octavius;[231] this he does by showing him resolutely and
scornfully setting his heel upon the wanton and impure promptings of the
flesh and the delights of women.

It is Virgil's fourth purpose to exalt the glory of the name of Rome.[232]
This he accomplishes through Dido's execrations at her death; for they
imply the wars between Carthage and Rome,[233] and prefigure the
triumphs which the Romans gained thereby—a sufficient glorification of
the city's name.

Thus it appears that Virgil is not a liar, whatever the unthinking
suppose; nor are the others liars who compose in the same manner.

FROM BOOK XV

Chapter viii: The Pagan Poets of Mythology are Theologians[234]

There are certain pietists who, in reading my words, will be moved by
holy zeal to charge me with injury to the most sacrosanct Christian
religion; for I allege that the pagan poets are theologians—a distinction
which Christians grant only to those instructed in sacred literature.
These critics I hold in high respect; and I thank them in anticipation for
such criticism, for I feel that it implies their concern for my welfare. But

---

[231] Cf. Donatus' life of Virgil, ed. Hardie, 2nd edn., p. 11.
[232] Cf. Servius on *Aeneid*, vi. 752.
[233] Cf. *Aeneid*, iv. 622-9, and the comment by Servius.
[234] On this sense of the term 'theologians' see above, pp. 389-90, 413-14.

the carelessness of their remarks shows clearly the narrow limitations of their reading. If they had read widely, they could not have overlooked that very well-known work on the *City of God*; they might have seen how, in the sixth book, Augustine cites the opinion of the learned Varro, who held that theology is threefold in its divisions—mythical, physical, and civil.[235] It is called mythical, from the Greek *mythicon*, a myth, and in this kind, as I have already said,[236] is adapted to the use of the comic stage.[237] But this form of literature is reprobate among better poets on account of its obscenity. Physical theology is, as etymology shows, natural and moral, and being commonly thought a very useful thing, it enjoys much esteem. Civil or political theology, sometimes called the theology of state worship, relates to the commonwealth, but through the foul abominations of its ancient ritual, it was repudiated by them of the true faith and the right worship of God. Now of these three, physical theology is found in the great poets since they clothe many a physical and moral truth in their inventions, including within their scope not only the deeds of great men, but matters relating to their gods. And particularly, as they first composed hymns of praise to the gods, and, as I have said, in a poetic guise presented their great powers and acts, they won the name of theologians even among the primitive pagans. Indeed Aristotle himself avers that they were the first to ponder theology;[238] and though they got their name from no knowledge or lore of the true God, yet at the advent of true theologians they could not lose it, so great was the natural force of the word derived from the theory of any divinity whatsoever. Aware, I suppose, that the title 'theologian', once fairly won, cannot be lost, the present-day theologians call themselves professors of sacred theology to distinguish themselves from theologians of mythological cast or any other. Such distinction admits no possible exception as implying an injury to the name of Christianity. Do we not speak of all mortals who have bodies and rational souls as men? Some may be Gentiles, some Israelites, some Agarenes, some Christians, and some so depraved as to deserve the name of gross beasts not men. Yet we do not wrong our Saviour by calling them men, though with His Godhead He is known to have been literally human. No more is there any harm in speaking of the old poets as theologians. Of course, if any one were to call them sacred, the veriest fool would detect the falsehood.

On the other hand there are times, as in this book, when the theology of the Ancients will be seen to exhibit what is right and honourable, though in most such cases it should be considered rather physiology or

---

[235] Cf. above, n. 125.
[236] *Geneal. deor. gent.*, pref., also xiv. vi (tr. Osgood, pp. 6, 38).
[237] *Geneal. deor. gent.*, xiv. xix (tr. Osgood, p. 93).
[238] *Meta.* i. 2 (982ᵇ12–18), cf. above, p. 389.

ethology[239] than theology, according as the myths embody the truth concerning physical nature or human. But the old theology can sometimes be employed in the service of Catholic truth, if the fashioner of the myths (*fabulae*) should choose. I have observed this in the case of more than one orthodox poet in whose investiture of fiction the sacred teachings were clothed. Nor let my pious critics be offended to hear the poets sometimes called even sacred theologians. In like manner sacred theologians turn physical when occasion demands; if in no other way, at least they prove themselves physical theologians as well as sacred when they express truth by the fable of the trees choosing a king [Judg. 9: 8–15].[240]

[239] i.e. the facts of nature, or morality.
[240] Cf. *Geneal. deor. gent.* xiv. ix (tr. above).

X
Assessing the New Author: Commentary on Dante

THE success of Dante's *Comedy* was immediate and all-pervasive: only the Bible was read or recited from with greater frequency in fourteenth-century Italy.[1] The poem's popularity brought with it, at all levels of society, a great eagerness for explanation, for clarification, and for more detail on specific episodes: a demand, in short, for commentary.[2] In this final section we shall see how the critical resources developed over several centuries of commentary on biblical and classical authors were put to work on the great text of the 'new author', Dante Alighieri.

Before concentrating upon Dante commentary proper we should note that this learned tradition represents just one aspect of the *Comedy*'s fourteenth-century reception. This greater literary history may be considered at three levels: popular writing; learned poetry; learned commentary. The *Comedy* is full of good stories: many of these were plucked from their original context and elaborated in a series of popular forms. Learned and semi-educated poets alike were eager to try out the new verse form, *terza rima*. The efforts of learned poets to develop and extend the enterprise of the *Comedy* throughout the fourteenth century form instructive parallels with the interpretative efforts of commentators: both traditions record a deepening incomprehension of the Dantean universe which becomes ever more acute as the new humanist values take hold.[3] Poets and commentators sometimes exchanged roles: Boccaccio and Petrarch wrote in *terza rima*, while Iacopo and Pietro Alighieri both resorted to verse in defence of their father. Commentators and popular writers were apt to dwell on the same Dantean episodes. Figures from the *Inferno*, such as Francesca, Farinata, Ulysses, and Ugolino, proved (then as now) irresistible; Boccaccio's account of Francesca in the *Esposizioni* as a hapless heroine tricked into marrying the wrong man is pure popular melodrama.[4] The sheer energy and volume of popular response to the *Comedy* was not something that commentators could ignore. As the century advanced learned writers became increasingly uneasy about the vernacular status of the *Comedy*. Judging the poem to be too open and accessible for its own good, they attempted to keep the illiterate at bay by 'classicizing' the text behind a high wall of Latin commentary. The fact that the *Comedy* was written in Italian and not in Latin became a source of acute embarrassment for Italian humanists.

---

[1] See G. Padoan, 'Boccaccio', in *ED* i. 649.

[2] See Sandkühler, *Die frühen Dantekommentare*, pp. 77–83.

[3] For an account of the learned poetic tradition which developed out of the *Comedy*, see Natalino Sapegno, *Storia letteraria del Trecento* (Milan and Naples, 1963), pp. 169–78; Achille Tartaro, *Forme poetiche del Trecento* (Bari, 1971), pp. 65–72.

[4] See *Esposizione sopra la Comedia di Dante*, v. i. 147–55, ed. G. Padoan, in Boccaccio, *Opere*, vi. 315–17.

The study of Dante commentary offers unique opportunities for making some sense of those elusive but interdependent terms 'medieval' and 'renaissance'. In the opinion of Giuseppe Billanovich, the differences in habits of reading and writing which divide the generation of Dante from that of Petrarch and Boccaccio are probably without parallel in Italian history.[5] Things certainly change rapidly within the Dante commentary-tradition. And yet some signs of future cultural conflict are already visible in Dante's later years. Many of the arguments that were to be mounted 'in defence of poetry' by Boccaccio and Petrarch were adumbrated by the Paduan proto-humanist Albertino Mussato (1261–1329); and some of the anxieties and aspirations of later Latin humanism were actually addressed to Dante (in Latin) by Mussato's friend and correspondent Giovanni del Virgilio.[6] Why (Giovanni asks Dante in a verse epistle) are you wasting such serious themes on the common masses? Why not write for 'nos pallentes', those of us who are pallid with study, instead of employing popular piazza idioms which we cannot but find repellent?[7] Dante, in reply, enjoys one of his cosmic jokes by composing a bucolic eclogue, thereby reviving a Latin genre that was to keep the humanists busy for many generations.[8] But he does not, of course, repent of the vernacular status of his *Comedy*.

The Beginnings of Dante Commentary. Another Latin letter, dating from the same period of Dante's life as these charming eclogues, was to assert a fundamental and far-reaching influence on the development of Dante commentary: the *Epistle to Can Grande della Scala*. Much of the scholarly and critical energy expended on this famous epistle has concentrated upon the question of authorship: did Dante write it, or not? This question has tended to displace or postpone discussion of the letter's intrinsic importance, or to pre-establish the lines along which such discussion will develop. For example, Bruno Nardi (who does not believe in Dantean authorship, excepting the first four paragraphs) finds the definition of the literal and allegorical subjects of the *Comedy* offered by this Latin epistle to be misguided and banal; Bruno Sandkühler (who sees the text as Dantean) sees the very same formulations as models of expository clarity that have never been surpassed.[9] The most recent editor of the *Epistle*, Giorgio Brugnoli, believes the question of Dantean authorship to be unresolved and, for now, unresolvable: his introduction and commentary

---

[5] 'Tra Dante e Petrarca', *Italia medioevale e umanistica*, viii (1965), 42. See also Sapegno, *Storia letteraria*, pp. 178–9.

[6] See Curtius, *European Literature and the Latin Middle Ages*, pp. 214–21, 225–7; R. Weiss, *The Renaissance Discovery of Classical Antiquity* (Oxford, 1969), pp. 16–22. For more on Giovanni del Virgilio see above, Ch. VIII.

[7] See the edition of the eclogues exchanged (two in each direction) by Enzo Cecchini in *Dante Alighieri, Opere minori* ed. P. V. Mengaldo *et al.* (Milan and Naples, 1979–84), ii. 645–89, esp. pp. 654–7 (ll. 6–24).

[8] See H. Cooper, *Pastoral. Mediaeval into Renaissance* (Ipswich, 1977), pp. 34–46.

[9] See Nardi, 'Osservazioni', pp. 268–305; Sandkühler, *Die frühen Dantekommentare*, p. 87. Nardi's arguments take the shape of a polemic waged against Francesco Mazzoni (who believes in Dantean authorship); Sandkühler takes issue with Nardi on pp. 92–5 of his study.

restricts itself to paving the way for 'new and more ample discussions'.[10]

The uncertainties which complicate such discussions stem from the manuscript tradition of the *Epistle* and from the related problem of the letter's tripartite structure. The first of these parts (paras. 1–4, accepted as genuinely Dantean by most scholars) is described as 'epistolary' since it observes the norms of the *ars dictaminis*, the art of letter-writing as practised in official correspondence. (The medieval epistle bears little resemblance to the modern personal letter and may prove misleading or exasperating when treated as a biographical source.) Our author concludes his fourth paragraph by explicitly signalling a change of generic constraints: he will put aside the formulae appropriate for letter-writers to speak 'sub lectoris officio', 'in the capacity of a commentator'. The text preserved by the oldest family of manuscripts (three fifteenth-century exemplars) ends at this point; the complete *Epistle* appears only in a second, later family of five manuscripts.[11] This second, 'doctrinal' section (paras. 5–16, assumed to be Dantean by a majority of scholars) begins and ends by quoting from Aristotle's *Metaphysics* and is chiefly concerned with the six questions traditionally asked of a work by the medieval *accessūs ad auctores*. The third and final section (paras. 17–33) offers a foretaste of exposition at the literal level as applied to the first thirty-eight lines of the *Paradiso*. Many readers doubt that this 'expository' section can be by Dante since the exposition seems somewhat pedestrian and the first-person narrator speaks impersonally of a third-person 'author'. But there is no reason why an author should not speak of his own work in the third-person voice of an expositor;[12] and we should note that the expositor feels obliged to warn us in advance that the scope of this section is limited, since it is 'but a demonstration of the form of the work' (17), i.e. simply makes explicit the poem's form. This exposition is summarily concluded in the penultimate paragraph as the author, reverting to the first person, tells us (and his patron) that he is impeded by impoverished personal circumstances. Para. 33 makes a rapid ascent through the rest of the literal level of

---

[10] *Epistole*, in *Opere minori*, ii. 519. Brugnoli offers a useful bibliographical survey of arguments for and against Dantean authorship, pp. 514–5. In his *Tragedy and Comedy from Dante to Pseudo-Dante* (Univ. of Calif. Publications in Modern Philology, cxxi, Berkeley and L.A., 1988), H. A. Kelly argues that the person responsible for the exegetical section of the *Epistle*—certainly not Dante, in his opinion—'put together his commentary . . . by drawing on Guido of Pisa's commentary (and possibly on one or other commentaries dependent on it), on one or two versions of Pietro Alighieri's commentary, and on the *Ars poetica*, at least to arrive at his treatment of literary genres' (p. 41). Kelly would place the *Epistle*'s hermeneutics between 1340 and 1373, i.e. at the *end* of the sequence of commentaries we offer on p. 442. Fresh arguments for the *Epistle*'s authenticity have been advanced by C. Paolazzi, *Dante e la* Commedia *nel Trecento. Dall'*Epistola a Cangrande *all'età di Petrarca* (Milan, 1989), pp. 3–110.

[11] See Brugnoli, ed. cit., pp. 512–13; M. P. Stocchi, 'Epistole', *ED* ii. 706. One of these five MSS contains a second, incomplete text of the *Epistle*.

[12] Sandkühler, *Die frühen Dantekommentare*, p. 91, sees such a switch to the third person as an argument for the authenticity of the *Epistle*, since many commentators speak of their work impersonally. Boccaccio was to follow this practice in glossing his own *Teseida*; John Gower did likewise in the Latin commentary he composed to accompany his Middle English *Confessio amantis*, on which see above, pp. 379–80. On the proprieties of speaking in the first person, see Dante's *Convivio*, I. ii. 2–17, ed. M. Simonelli (Bologna, 1966), pp. 4–6.

the *Paradiso* and makes a perfect end 'in God himself, who is blessed for evermore, world without end'.

In bringing us to the end of the *Paradiso*, the *Can Grande* author is closing the circle of the *Comedy*, inviting us to begin again with the *Inferno* and to continue the labour of commentary that he has set in motion. Dante's admirers were eager to accept this double invitation. Within twenty years of Dante's death in 1321 at least eight commentaries on the *Comedy* had been composed. Their interrelations are complex and their sequence uncertain; a reasonable estimate runs as follows: Iacopo Alighieri (1322), Graziolo de' Bambaglioli (1324), Anonymous Lombardus (1322–5), Jacopo delle Lana (*c.*1324–8), Guido da Pisa (1327–8), Ottimo (first version, 1329–31), *Chiose Anonime Selmi* (anonymous Selmi glosses, *c.*1337), Pietro Alighieri (first version, 1340).[13] The *Epistle* (or, at least, its doctrinal section) exerts a steady influence over this early tradition; its application of categories derived from the medieval *accessus*-tradition proves particularly influential.[14] Boccaccio was influenced by the *Epistle* both directly and indirectly: directly through his use of a Latin text of the *Epistle* and indirectly through his knowledge of earlier commentaries. It is not clear whether or not Boccaccio regarded the *Epistle* as a Dantean text,[15] but it is obvious both from his *Trattatello* ('Life of Dante') and his 1373 Dante lectures that he valued it highly, both as a biographical source and as a resource for literary theory.

The *Epistle to Can Grande* assumes great historical importance, then, as the beginning of commentary on Dante's *Comedy*. Or rather, it constitutes the beginning of post-*Comedy* criticism: for the earliest commentary on the work is offered by Dante himself as his *Comedy* unfolds. Within his *Comedy*, Dante reflects upon the relationship of his present poetic task to his own past texts,

[13] This follows the sequence proposed by Robert Hollander, 'A Checklist of Commentators on the *Commedia* (1322–1982)', *Dante Studies*, ci (1983), 181–92. Hollander notes that 'dates for early commentaries are approximate and often conjectural' (p. 182). His list, however, is now more frequently cited than that proposed by V. Cioffari, *Guido da Pisa's Expositiones et Glose super Comediam Dantis* (Albany, NY, 1974), p. xxviii. My dating of the *Ottimo*, which Hollander assigns to 1333, follows S. Bellomo, 'Primi appunti sull'*Ottimo commento* dantesco', *Giornale storico della letteratura italiana*, clvii (1980), 369–82, 533–40. In the sequence proposed by L. Jenaro-MacLennan, *The Trecento Commentaries on the Divina Commedia and the Epistle to Can Grande* (Oxford, 1974), pp. 4–6, 22–58, Guido's commentary is regarded as very early, since some portions of the Lana commentary are 'probably dependent' upon his text, and Iacopo Alighieri's *Chiose* are deemed 'dependent on Guido da Pisa'. For the Latin commentator known as Anonymous Lombardus, not featured in the sequences of Cioffari and Jenaro-MacLennan, see Sandkühler, *Die frühen Dantekommentare*, pp. 116–31. For a succinct, updated version of this work, see Sandkühler's excellent article in *Die italienische Literatur im Zeitalter Dantes und am Übergang vom Mittelalter zur Renaissance*, ed. A. Buck (GRLM, X. 1, Heidelberg, 1987), pp. 166–208. For additional information see F. Mazzoni, 'La critica dantesca nel secolo XIV', *Cultura e scuola*, xiii–xiv (1965), 285–97, and A. Vallone, *Storia della critica dantesca dal XIV al XX secolo* (Padua, 1981), i. 69–129. Vallone, p. 99, is inclined to accept Mazzoni's dating of Guido's *Expositiones* to 1343–50. The systematic computerization of some 60–80 commentaries by the Dartmouth Dante Project (directed by Hollander), plus a number of other projects currently under way in Italy, will doubtless force further consideration of these datings.

[14] See R. Hollander, *Allegory in Dante's Commedia* (Princeton, NJ, 1969), pp. 266–96; Nardi, 'Osservazioni', pp. 268–90, Sandkühler, *Die frühen Dantekommentare*, pp. 83–95, Jenaro-MacLennan, *The Trecento Commentaries*, p. 107 and *passim*.

[15] Jenaro-MacLennan, p. 5, argues against the 'traditional' view that 'Boccaccio could not have regarded the epistle as Dante's'. But see n. 295 below.

to earlier poets, ancient and modern,[16] and to the procedures of philosophy and theology. In the second canto of the *Purgatorio*, for example, Dante the pilgrim hears a company of spirits singing Ps. 113, 'In exitu Israël de Aegypto' (46) and then hears *Amor che ne la mente mi ragiona* (112), one of his own *canzoni*. This *canzone* had already been subjected to a detailed allegorical reading in *Convivio*, III; and the psalmic verse had previously been analysed in *Convivio*, II. i. 6–7, where Dante distinguishes between literal and anagogical levels of interpretation. Such analysis should not be thought of as something which comes after the fact of the poetry: indeed, it is possible to argue that it represents a precondition for the kind of poetry that Dante wished to write. As early as the *Vita nuova* Dante had objected to poetasters who cover their subject 'under the garment of a figure or rhetorical colour' but who prove incapable (when asked) of casting off that garment to reveal their 'true intention'.[17] And early in the *Paradiso* Dante the pilgrim learns something from Beatrice that Dante the author already knows: the terms of representation that will make his *Paradiso* possible. Here, as often, Dante's understanding of such terms is continuous with his understanding of Scriptural exegesis, a science which sets out to demonstrate how and why

> '... Scripture condescends
> to your intelligence, and attributes
> both hands and feet to God, whilst meaning something else.'
>
> (iv. 43–5)

The whole of Dante's career as poet and literary theorist is, then, inclusive of a process of 'auto-exegesis'.[18] The *Epistle* author, in aligning himself with this process, is attempting to keep the *Commedia* open and alive to successive acts of interpretation. At the same time he wishes to direct such interpretation along lines which extend from Dante's own theory and practice. So it is, for example, that he chooses to approach the *Comedy* through the four levels of scriptural interpretation, a system of analysis which Dante had discussed when considering how to explain the meaning of several of his own *canzoni* in the *Convivio* (see above, pp. 395–8). And in choosing to exemplify such a procedure by analysing the psalmic verse 'In exitu Israël', the *Epistle* is directing us back both to the poetry of the *Comedy* and to the theorizing of the *Convivio*.[19] More generally, the *Epistle* author evidently understands the

[16] See J. Freccero, 'Casella's Song (*Purg.* ii. 112)', *Dante Studies*, xci (1973), 73–80; R. Hollander, '*Purgatorio* ii: Cato's Rebuke and Dante's *scoglio*', in id., *Studies in Dante* (Ravenna, 1980), pp. 91–105; T. Barolini, *Dante's Poets: Textuality and Truth in the 'Comedy'* (Princeton, NJ, 1984).

[17] *Vita nuova*, xxv. 10, in *Opere minori*, i. 1, ed. D. De Robertis and G. Contini (Milan and Naples, 1984), pp. 177–8.

[18] Curtius, p. 222, speaks of the *Epistle to Can Grande* as 'self-exegesis; see also Sandkühler's discussion of Dante's 'Eigenkommentare' in *Die frühen Dantekommentare*, pp. 50–7, Jean Pepin's account of Dante's 'auto-allegoresis', s.v. 'Allegoria', *ED* i. 162, and of course L. Jenaro-MacLennan's major article 'Autocomentario'.

[19] Ps. 113 was not the most obvious choice for this demonstration: the most obvious choice was 'Jerusalem', whose four levels of meaning were established by Cassian and then (with modifications) incorporated into the *Glossa ordinaria*: see Minnis, *Authorship*, p. 34, and cf. Nicholas of Lyre's version of the example, above, pp. 266–7. Guido da Pisa, in the prologue to his *Expositiones* (tr. below), chooses the example of Minos.

delicacy of Dante's enterprise in situating the *Comedy* between the languages and procedures of the human sciences, of secular and pagan poetry, and of scriptural exegesis. He mirrors this understanding in his *Epistle*, moving deftly between these critical domains as he strives to elucidate Dante's text. This complex procedure is as evident in the final, expository part as it is in the epistolary and doctrinal sections. In paras. 21-2, for example, we move from Pseudo-Dionysius and Pseudo-Aristotle (and the commentaries of Albertus Magnus) to Jeremiah, the Psalter, Wisdom, and Ecclesiasticus before ending with Lucan's *Bellum civile*; and all of these texts are adduced to confirm (with lesser or greater authority) an identical truth.

The importance of the *Epistle to Can Grande* lies as much in its general enterprise as in its local details. Its author appreciates the *Comedy*'s ambitious willingness to keep poetry, rhetoric, theology, and philosophy within a single, unified frame; and turning to the scriptural exegetes of the early fourteenth century, he detects a kindred, unifying spirit at work.[20] Skilfully appropriating analytic techniques from such exegetes, he turns back to the *Comedy*, thereby choosing as the object of his analysis a poem whose subject is divine but whose authorship is human.[21] Such a choice is momentous in the history of literary theory and criticism: the analytic procedures generated over centuries of expounding Scripture and allegorizing ancient, pagan poems are now to be applied to the work of a living, Christian poet writing in a living language, his own vernacular. The *Epistle*'s handling of such a transitional moment is characterized by great tact and balance. These qualities are evident, for example, in the choice of *modi tractandi* which are applied to the poem: five *modi* representing the poetical and rhetorical aspects of the work are deliberately balanced against five further *modi* representing its philosophical aspects.[22] Whether or not Dante and the *Epistle*'s author are one and the same, then, their conceptions of the enterprise of the *Comedy* (and of its historical moment) are commensurate. Why begin post-*Comedy* commentary by analysing the opening lines of the *Paradiso*? Perhaps because these lines, with their dramatic juxtaposition of the fantastically fictive ('In the heaven which most receives of His light') and the bluntly factual ('fu' io', a past historic of untranslatable force), mount the most urgent and tantalizing challenge to interpretation that Dante ever threw out:

> La gloria di colui che tutto move
> per l'universo penetra, e risplende
> in una parte piú e meno altrove.
>   Nel ciel che piú de la sua luce prende
> fu' io ...
>
> (i. 1-4)

[20] See Minnis, *Authorship*, pp. 141-2.

[21] See de Lubac, *Exég. méd.* II. ii. 324. Pietro Alighieri (see below, p. 478) declares that the *causa efficiens* of the Comedy is Dante himself; Guido da Pisa, the most vigorous advocate of the poem's 'prophetic' status, appears to be hinting that Dante, as instrumental efficient cause, is working under the direction of God as primary efficient cause. Cf. below, n. 145.

[22] *Epistle*, 9. For discussion see Curtius, *European Literature*, p. 225, and cf. the scholastic treatment of the *modi tractandi* of divine science and human science, described and illustrated in Ch. VI above.

[The glory of Him who moves everything
penetrates through the universe, and glows again
in one part more, and in another less.
In the heaven that receives most of His light
I have been . . .]

Critics took up Dante's challenge to interpretation with great alacrity. Not all of them, however, were charitably disposed towards the *Comedy*. Some felt threatened or insulted by its religious and political views. Some were disturbed to find their ancestors or their cities (or even themselves) consigned to unpleasant parts of the Dantean universe; and others were alarmed to find that their greatest source of civic or artistic pride (such as the Arena Chapel at Padua) received no mention in Dante's text.[23] The most vital centre for early commentary and manuscript production of the *Comedy* was Bologna. But Dante himself had recognized (in his second eclogue to Giovanni del Virgilio) that he had made too many enemies in that city.[24] Dante's *Monarchy* was condemned to be publicly burnt at Bologna by Cardinal Bertrando dal Poggetto in 1329; the Dominican Guido Vernani wrote (probably at the Cardinal's instigation) a tract entitled *De reprobatione Monarchiae*, dedicating it (by way of reproof) to the Dante commentator Graziolo de' Bambaglioli.[25] Graziolo moved to Naples in 1334 (where he may have met the young Boccaccio): but his Dante commentary would not have found much favour at the Neapolitan court since Dante had said such unflattering things about King Robert the Wise (ruled 1309–43) and his Angevin forebears.[26] In 1335 Dominican friars at Florence were forbidden possession of Dante's poem. Vernani condemned Dante as 'vas diabuli', 'the devil's instrument'; and Cecco d'Ascoli, lecturer in medicine at the Bolognese Studio, denied Dante's ascent to heaven: Dante remained in the *Inferno*, weighed down by earthly passions.[27] Cecco was himself burnt as a heretic on 16 September 1327.

The Contribution of Guido da Pisa. Dante commentary first developed, then, in difficult, sometimes turbulent, conditions. And yet these early years were to witness the emergence of a commentator of major importance: Guido da Pisa. Guido is certainly aware of the historical delicacy of his task in celebrating the poetic and prophetic powers of Dante: towards the end of the prologue to his *Expositiones* he feels bound to point out that those *personae* whom Dante consigns to the Inferno are there not in reality, but only by way of example; and later in the same text he subjects all his findings to ecclesiastical scrutiny and correction.[28] Guido, who sees the *Comedy* both as a poetic classic and as a

[23] See L. Franzoni, 'Verona: L'aspetto urbano della città ai tempi di Dante', *ED*, v. 977.
[24] See *Egloge*, iv. 46–97, in *Opere minori*, ii. 684–9. See also Augusto Vesina *et al.*, 'Bologna', *ED* i. 660–7; P. Renucci, *Dante, Disciple et juge du monde gréco-latin* (Paris, 1954), pp. 61–6, 120–4.
[25] See F. Forti, 'Bologna. Tradizione manoscritta e commentatori', *ED* i. 666; Sandkühler, *Die frühen Dantekommentare*, pp. 77–9.
[26] See D. Wallace, *Chaucer and the Early Writings of Boccaccio* (Cambridge, 1985), pp. 31–2.
[27] See Padoan, 'Boccaccio', *ED* i. 649; Tartaro, *Forme poetiche del Trecento*, pp. 64, 72–84.
[28] See below, p. 476, and see F. Mazzoni, 'Guido da Pisa interprete di Dante e la sua fortuna presso il Boccaccio', *Studi Danteschi*, xxxv (1958), 128. Guido's obeisance to Church authority is followed by Boccaccio in his *Esposizioni*; see below, p. 512.

Christian prophecy, brings excellent qualifications to his task of commentary: long experience as a commentator and translator of classical texts is balanced against a traditional training as a professional religious. Such a balance is, essentially, similar to that of the *Epistle to Can Grande*. Guido is the first commentator to make use of the *Epistle*, and he uses it with great intelligence and discrimination.[29]

Little is known of Guido's life.[30] Born at Pisa in the second half of the thirteenth century, he became a Carmelite friar and was still active (perhaps at Florence) in the 1320s. His scholarship suggests that he knew Tuscany extremely well; he enjoyed contacts with major cities such as Naples, Rome, and (perhaps) London.[31] He explains terms from a dozen different vernaculars, including the odd word of German and Spanish.[32] The range of his erudition is enormous, taking in everything from medical, cosmographical, and astronomical treatises to eight works by Aristotle. He is familiar with texts newly in favour with or newly discovered by humanist scholars (the fourth decade of Livy as well as the first and third) and shows a marked fondness for Ovid (whose *Metamorphoses* is described as 'the pagan Bible'), Cicero, Seneca, and Valerius Maximus. Among theological and philosophical authorities Guido favours Jerome, Augustine, Boethius, Isidore of Seville, Peter Comestor, and Thomas Aquinas.[33]

Guido's earliest surviving work is an Italian prose opus known as *La Fiorita* or *Fiore d'Italia*, an encyclopaedic work of universal history which (with occasional digressions into mythology) concentrates upon biblical and Roman themes before becoming, in its second part, a prose translation of the *Aeneid*,[34] made directly from the Latin text, although the order of events is changed, incidents deemed unimportant are omitted, and detailed explanations of textual details are added. The rationale offered for such extensive translating

[29] It has even been suggested that Guido wrote the *Epistle* himself: see A. Canal, *Il mondo morale di Guido da Pisa interprete di Dante* (Bologna, 1981), pp. 68–9. For a detailed account of Guido's use of the *Epistle*, see G. Vandelli, *Bollettino della Società Dantesca Italiana*, NS viii (1901), 150–7.

[30] The bare facts are reported by F. Mazzoni, 'Guido da Pisa', *ED* iii. 325. Little can be known with certainty because, as Mazzoni reports, at least three Carmelite Guido da Pisas date from this period. For further speculations see Canal, *Il mondo morale di Guido da Pisa*, pp. 53–67; Jenaro-MacLennan, *The Trecento Commentaries*, pp. 50–7.

[31] Guido's gloss on *Inf.* xii. 120 in the *Expositiones* features a discussion of the Thames and a detailed description of the tomb of a King Henry at Westminster. His gloss on *Inf.* xxviii. 136 contains a (garbled) reference to Bertrand de Born at the court of King Edward of England (presumably mistaken for Henry II). See Canal, *Il mondo morale di Guido da Pisa*, pp. 136, 141.

[32] See Sandkühler, *Die frühen Dantekommentare*, p. 157; Canal, *Il mondo morale di Guido da Pisa*, p. 144.

[33] See Canal, *Il mondo morale di Guido da Pisa*, pp. 69–75; G. Billanovich's review of Cioffari's edition of Guido da Pisa's *Expositiones*, in *Studi medievali*, 3rd ser. xvii (1976), 261–2. Guido's use of encyclopaedic sources, such as Vincent of Beauvais and Bartholomaeus Anglicus, has been under-appreciated: see A. M. Caglio, 'Materiali enciclopedici nelle *Expositiones* di Guido da Pisa', *Italia medioevale e umanistica*, xxiv (1981), 213–56.

[34] This second part, known as *I fatti di Enea*, circulated independently and was immensely popular, especially with Italian schoolmasters. See the edition by F. Foffano (Bibliotheca Carducciana XV, Florence, 1900).

is borrowed from the opening of Dante's *Convivio*: to assist those who, for various reasons, are impeded from studying. Dante, remarkably, is treated as a great source of *auctoritas* who may enrich our appreciation of any text, whether classical or biblical: the *Comedy* is cited some fifty times in the course of the *Fiorita*.[35] This enthusiasm for Dante is carried further in Guido's *Declaratio super comediam Dantis*, a summary of Dante's *Inferno* in eight cantos of *terza rima*, each of seventy-six lines. The *Declaratio* belongs to a minor genre of poetic commentary established by writers such as Bosone da Gubbio and Iacopo Allighieri which enjoyed a short-lived vogue in the years following Dante's death.[36] Guido extends the limited capacities of this tradition, however, by adding Latin glosses to his Italian verses. This was an important step. Guido also added Latin glosses to a text of the *Inferno* in Biblioteca Medicea-Laurenziana 40. 2 and (so it now appears) to the *Purgatorio* and *Paradiso* in the same manuscript.[37] Some years later Guido collected these glosses together to form the framework of his great *Inferno* commentary, the *Expositiones et glose super comediam Dantis*.

Guido's *Expositiones et glose*, a work in Latin prose, survives complete in two manuscripts. The older of these (Chantilly, Musée Condé, MS 597 (1424), dating from the 1340s, contains fifty-five fine miniatures and provides interesting indications of Guido's development as a Dante commentator.[38] Whereas Guido's earlier commentating (in the Laurentian MS) had taken the form of interlinear and marginal glosses arranged around (and sometimes framing) a text of the *Comedy*, the Chantilly manuscript is divided into three distinct parts: a text of the *Inferno*; the *Expositiones et glose*; and the *Declaratio*. The expositions and glosses of Guido's great commentary vary considerably in length from canto to canto, but they are consistent in following a four-step procedure. Guido actually interrupts his analysis of *Inferno*, i, to draw our attention to this procedure, emphasizing the ways in which it departs from the norms of traditional commentary.[39] Guido's account of a given canto opens with a brief introduction to its narrative action, its subject-matter, and/or the moral issues raised. A paraphrase of the canto then follows, under the heading 'deductio textus de vulgari in latinum'. Next, under the heading 'expositio lictere', Guido enters into detailed discussion of the meaning (literal and allegorical) of specific verses.

[35] See Sandkühler, *Die frühen Dantekommentare*, pp. 155–6; Mazzoni, 'Guido e Boccaccio', p. 93; id. 'Guido da Pisa', *ED* iii. 326.

[36] See Sandkühler, *Die frühen Dantekommentare*, pp. 95–103; Jenaro-MacLennan, *The Trecento Commentaries*, pp. 54–7.

[37] See Canal, *Il mondo morale di Guido da Pisa*, pp. 93–129.

[38] The other is London, British Library, Add. MS 31918 (15th c.), in a direct line of descent from the Chantilly MS. Cioffari's edition of the *Expositiones* is restricted to these two MSS, although four others should have been taken into account: see Canal, *Il mondo morale di Guido da Pisa*, pp. 42–9; Billanovich, review (cit. above, n. 33), p. 257. Billanovich, pp. 254–62, offers a crushing critique of Cioffari's edition; Canal, *Il mondo morale di Guido da Pisa*, p. 8, promises an edition of the 'intero Commento guidiano'. For the miniatures in the Chantilly MS see P. Brieger, M. Meiss, and C. S. Singleton, *Illuminated Manuscripts of the Divine Comedy*, i (Princeton, 1969), pp. 52–70, 216–18. The *Declaratio super Comediam Dantis* has been reliably edited by F. Mazzoni (Florence, 1970).   [39] *Guido da Pisa's Expositiones*, ed. Cioffari, p. 9.

Finally, at the end of the 'expositio lictere', Guido lists *comparationes* and *notabilia*, comparisons (similes) and things worthy of note. This list is always introduced in the same formal way: 'In this canto the author includes three *comparationes* and six *notabilia*.'[40]

The most important formal feature of Guido's commentary is, perhaps, its effective separation of the literal from the allegorical. The Latin paraphrase of the *deductio* offers an accurate guide to the literal meaning of the Italian text, allowing the *expositio* which follows to elaborate allegorical meanings without slipping backwards into paraphrase. This procedure, which upholds the distinction between levels of exposition attempted (not always successfully) in Dante's *Convivio*, was to be taken up by Boccaccio in his *Genealogia* and was then to become the major structuring principle of Boccaccio's Dante lectures, the *Esposizioni*.

Guido's ability to work within traditional forms of exegesis and yet, through certain refinements of these forms, to generate a fresh understanding of his subject, is beautifully exemplified by the prologue to the *Expositio* (translated below). The prologue opens with an arresting image of Dante as a prophet prophesied by no less an authority than the Bible itself: the hand which writes upon Balthasar's wall 'is our own new poet Dante' ('est noster novus poeta Dantes'). But (we may pause to ask) if Dante is the hand of God, what is Guido? Just as the writing on Balthasar's wall could not be understood without Daniel's interpreting, so Dante's text awaits its true interpreter. Are we, then, to equate Guido with Daniel? In the *expositio* of *Inferno*, i, Guido (drawing on, and somewhat garbling, Macrobius) maintains that the *Comedy* is a *somnium*, a type of vision (*visio*) 'which is concealed beneath figures and made cloudy with ambiguities, and which is not to be understood or comprehended except through interpretation'.[41] Guido is to be our interpreter, our Daniel, who will first identify the clouds and then disperse them.

Guido's prologue goes on to develop two further Old Testament prophecies of Dante's *Comedy* before addressing itself to the six questions traditionally posed within the *accessus* tradition. Guido is undoubtedly following the *Epistle to Can Grande* here. But he is not content with just reproducing the *Epistle* in a mechanical fashion. He changes the order in which the questions are to be considered and follows the *Epistle*'s wording closely in just one instance. (This one moment of fidelity is itself interesting because it tells us something about the stability of the concept in question: the part of philosophy under which poetry is to be considered.)[42] The five remaining questions reveal some intelligent departures from the *Epistle*. For example, under his discussion of the book's 'moving cause' (*agens*) we find Dante considered as the author who has resurrected 'dead poetry from the darkness of the grave'. This characterization, which echoes the words spoken by Dante as he escapes from the darkness of the Inferno into the clear light of Purgatory ('but here let

---

[40] For this specific example see ibid., p. 62 (on *Inf.* iii).
[41] Ibid., p. 18, cf. Macrobius, *In Somn. Scip.* I. iii. 12. The anonymous Middle English *Cleanness*, a poem concerned with the true and false interpreting of signs, features Balthasar's feast as its final, climactic biblical scene.   [42] On this subject see Ch. I, n. 9.

dead poetry be brought back to life'), invites us to consider the *Comedy* as, *inter alia*, an allegory of poetic rebirth.[43] Under his next heading ('final cause') Guido follows the *Epistle*'s brief account but then goes on to discuss how Dante proposes to 'remove the living from their miserable condition'. This concern with how something is to be done reflects that strong interest in morals which is such a typical feature of Guido's glossing.[44] Guido then extends his discussion of 'final cause' by proposing three further objectives for the *Comedy*: to teach us to converse correctly; to bring to light again (from the darkness of oblivion) those works which help us to lead a good life; and to provide exemplary stories of good and evil men. Such formulations make it virtually impossible to separate Guido's interests in morals from his interest in poetics. And perhaps this forms part of Guido's larger polemic: that poetic regeneration and moral regeneration can hardly be prised apart.

Guido's account of the *Comedy*'s four senses or levels comes immediately after (rather than, as in the *Epistle*, immediately before) his treatment of the six questions. This account contains a brief but important meditation upon the place of poetry 'within theology', a subject that was to be taken further by Petrarch and Boccaccio (see above, Ch. IX). Guido's choice of the figure of Minos to exemplify these four senses is typically accommodating: the reader who is soon to meet Minos (a strange figure to encounter in a Christian allegory) is given some help in advance.[45] And those readers who persevere with Guido will continue to be impressed by his concern for their difficulties as they grapple with 'the new poet'. Guido is even prepared to cheer us up, as we enter the main body of his commentary, with a joke at his own expense. He explains that we see things happen in a *visio* just as they happen in real life: such as when Guido saw himself in the cathedral, being elected bishop or abbot.[46] Part of the irony here, of course, is that it was his very devotion to Dante commentary which (in the uncertain climate of the 1320s and 1330s) meant that such visions of preferment could only, for Guido, be pleasant daydreams.

In their Father's Footsteps: Iacopo and Pietro Alighieri. Dante's *Comedy* insists that members of the same family may come to very different ends: Buonconte da Montefeltro, for example, is snatched away from damnation at the last moment, whereas his father, Guido, is snatched into it.[47] Perhaps it is only appropriate, then, that the three sons who followed Dante into exile should differ so dramatically in what they have left us. Giovanni, the eldest, left

---

[43] Guido opposes the Dante of the *Inferno*, where he remains a poet, to the Dante of the *Purgatorio* and *Paradiso*, where he speaks as a theologian: see Mazzoni, 'Guido e Boccaccio', p. 62.

[44] Guido's concern with morals in this part of the prologue and in the work as a whole is often structured upon a traditional dialectic between virtues and vices: see Canal, *Il mondo morale di Guido da Pisa*, pp. 153–80.

[45] See *Inf*. v. 4–24.

[46] *Expositiones*, ed. Cioffari, p. 18.

[47] See *Purg*. v. 64–129, *Inf*. xxvii. 4–132; also *Convivio*, IV esp. chs. i, vii, x–xv (ed. Simonelli, pp. 129–31, 148–51, 158–77, where Dante argues against the assumption that a noble father will generate noble sons.

nothing.[48] Pietro, the second son, enjoyed a long and distinguished career and bequeathed to us one of the finest bodies of Dante commentary. Iacopo, the youngest, made a mess of his life and wrote commentary of inferior quality.

It seems reasonable to suppose that Iacopo and Pietro shared Dante's later years of exile, and that they were present at his death in Ravenna in 1321. A year or so later they returned to Florence to see their mother and to sort out some complex legal affairs. On 9 October Iacopo accepted minor orders and the tonsure from the Bishop of Fiesole. He later had two sons with one woman and (in 1346) a daughter with another, resisting all pressures to marry either of them. Such complex personal affairs meant that Iacopo was unable to honour financial debts incurred to Pietro. He died in the plague year of 1348, leaving his various dependants in unhappy legal and financial circumstances. While the young Iacopo had attempted to develop a career as a minor cleric, Pietro had gone to study canon law at Bologna. He moved to Verona in 1331 and pursued a public career with great success. He married in 1335 and had six or seven children, including one legitimate son and heir called Dante. He became prosperous, bought some fine properties, and died at Treviso on 21 April 1364—almost a century after the birth of his father.

Iacopo's early efforts at defending and explicating his father's work were energetic and sincere. In the spring of 1322 (just six months after Dante's death) he composed a *capitolo* in 153 lines of *terza rima*, similar in scope to Guido da Pisa's *Declaratio*. A copy was sent, with a dedicatory sonnet, to Guido da Polenta, *podestà* at Bologna.[49] In the same year Iacopo composed his Italian *Chiose* (glosses) to the *Inferno*. The prologue to this work expounds the *Comedy*'s allegory along the lines of the *Epistle to Can Grande*, but what follows shows little feeling for allegory or *fictio*: meaning is imposed upon the text from without, not discovered within, and the characters of the *Comedy* are treated like allegorical personifications representing abstract concepts. Similar tendencies dominate the *Dottrinale*, a didactic, moralizing work of encyclopaedic scope in sixty chapters of sixty verses.[50] Chs. 55–6 sketch aspects of Dante's moral teaching, and 57–9 offer rapid summaries of the contents of the three *cantiche*. The learning and procedures of Iacopo's poem are desperately old-fashioned, more reminiscent of Brunetto Latini's *Trésor* than of anything by Dante. Appropriately enough, the *Dottrinale* employs *settenari a rima baciata*, the seven-syllable couplets developed by Brunetto in his *Tesoretto* during his French exile of 1260–6.[51]

Whereas Iacopo slipped backwards into the forms and mental habits of the thirteenth century, Pietro led Dante commentary forwards into the new terrain of European humanism. His early poems show that he shared Iacopo's

---

[48] The only surviving trace of Giovanni is provided by a document from Lucca, dated 1308. For biographical details of the three brothers, see F. Mazzoni's articles on Iacopo and Pietro in *ED* i. 143–5, 147–9; also J. P. Bowden, *Pietro Alighieri's* Commentary, pp. 9–20.

[49] Dante had died at the house of Guido da Polenta at Ravenna on 13 or 14 Sept. 1321.

[50] For bibliographical guides to Iacopo's writings, see Mazzoni, 'Critica dantesca', p. 292; Mazzoni, *ED* i. 144–5; also Tartaro, *Forme poetiche*, pp. 63–6, 84–7.

[51] See Sapegno, *Storia letteraria*, p. 175; Tartaro, *Forme poetiche*, pp. 85–7; Wallace, *Chaucer and Boccaccio*, pp. 10–15.

desire to clarify and defend Dante's intentions: but (unlike Iacopo) he was prepared to wait until he was more settled and mature before attempting anything on a large scale. All Pietro's mature work was composed in Verona. He is reported to have written a Latin poem on the *Comedy* which he declaimed before a large public at a Veronese piazza.[52] But his plans for a full-scale commentary were not developed until 1337, when a war broke out between Verona and Florence; this kept him out of office until 1340. Verona was the perfect setting for such a period of enforced leisure since, with Padua (and perhaps Vicenza) it formed the heartland of the new humanism. The cathedral library at Verona was one of the most important in all Italy: Petrarch discovered the Ciceronian *Letters to Atticus* there in 1345.[53] Petrarch may have known Pietro during his student days at Bologna (1320–6); he must have met Pietro at Verona and thought highly enough of him to favour him with a metrical letter (III. vii).

Pietro, then, possessed ideal qualifications for Dante commentary: an intimate, first-hand knowledge of the full range of Dante's poetry and thought, daily contact with erudite and enthusiastic Latinists, and the native wit and independence to hold such divergent forces together. Once Pietro had committed himself to commentary he persisted with it for some twenty years, producing some three recensions of his *Commentarium*. The first of these dates from the period 1340–1, the second from 1350–5, and the third from around 1358.[54] Pietro's revisions reflect his desire to explain the bases of Dante's thought with ever greater clarity, concentrating (in humanist fashion) upon the letter of the text rather than upon extra-literary sources of inspiration. The *Comedy* is seen as the work of a 'glorious theologian, philosopher, and poet'[55] rather than (as in Guido's account) of a prophetic visionary. Pietro sees Dante, in essence, as a learned poet of classical stature; and the key term here is *poet*.

The opening of the prologue to Pietro's *Commentarium* (third recension, translated below) shows that he is fully conscious of writing within the bounds of a tradition that is, by now, well established. He accepts that some later commentator may build upon his work to produce a superior account of the *Comedy*. His own account will endeavour to improve upon what has gone before; however, his critique of earlier commentary rarely breaks out into open polemic, but remains implicit within his own distinctive procedures.

---

[52] See G. Arnaldi, 'Verona', *ED* v. 976; also Mazzoni, *ED* i. 148.

[53] See G. Billanovich, 'Tra Dante e Petrarca', *Italia medioevale e umanistica*, viii (1965), pp. 8–11, 27–9; Arnaldi in *ED* v. 976–7; Sandkühler, *Die frühen Dantekommentare*, p. 81. A thorough study of Pietro's sources is being carried out by Luigi Caricato; the first-fruits have been published as 'Il *Commentarium* all'*Inferno* di Pietro Alighieri, indagine sulle fonti', *Italia medioevale e umanistica*, xxvi (1983), 125–50.

[54] Dates follow Mazzoni, *ED* i. 148. The first recension is said to survive in a 'score' of MSS; the second survives in two MSS and is named after the most important, Florence, Bibliotheca Laurenziana, MS Ashburnham 841; the third is uniquely preserved by MS Vaticano Ottoboniano lat. 2867.

[55] 'gloriosus theologus, philosophus et poeta': see *Petri Allegherii super Dantis ipsius genitoris Comoediam Commentarium*, ed. V. Nannucci (Florence, 1845), p. 3. This phrase is applied to Dante as *causa efficiens* in the prologue to the first recension. This prologue differs markedly from that of the third recension (tr. below).

The *Epistle to Can Grande* and the structure of the *accessūs ad auctores* are by now such integral parts of the commentary-tradition that it is difficult to decide whether or not Pietro employed the *Epistle* directly.[56] Pietro, following some preliminary remarks from Macrobius and Aristotle, addresses himself to the traditional questions fairly quickly within his prologue, but he departs from traditional order by beginning with final and then effective cause.[57] The keynote of the *Commentarium* is struck, however, when Pietro moves on to discuss material cause: the emphasis here is upon literary terms such as allegory, fiction, analogues, and figures. Such an emphasis is maintained under formal cause when, in analysing Dante's *modus scribendi*, Pietro offers detailed discussion of the terms fable, history, fiction, poet, and allegory. His account of the first four questions begins and ends with some important observations on allegory that critics (then as now) often chose to ignore: that we should not seek to wring allegorical meaning from every passage; and that our habits of reading are not constant, but vary in accordance with the local demands of the text.

Having dispensed with these 'preliminary remarks', Pietro moves on to consider the book's title. This takes up over half the prologue, and sees him assuming the more expansive, encyclopaedic manner of treatment that was to characterize Boccaccio's *accessus* to the 1373 Dante lectures. Much of Boccaccio's subject-matter is foreshadowed here, too, in Pietro's discussion of the term 'comedy' and of the location of hell. And some of Boccaccio's difficulties are also foreshadowed: Pietro's discussion of comedy exposes the embarrassing fact (evident to humanists from Giovanni del Virgilio onwards) that Dante's *Comedy* is not 'lofty' enough, or is 'lofty' only in parts.[58] Pietro covers this embarrassing feature of the style of the *Comedy* with some highly selective quotation from Horace; he then moves adroitly on to discuss comic structure, an aspect of Dante's poem which fitted the facts of available theory more satisfactorily. Pietro's prologue closes with an analysis of the principal parts of the *Inferno*; the question of the part of philosophy to which the *Comedy* belongs is not raised.

The organization and style of Pietro's commentating may be judged from his analysis of *Inferno*, v (third recension, translated below). Pietro begins by dividing the canto into two sections. Each section is then considered first in its literal and then in its allegorical aspects. The first, introductory section concentrates upon the figure of Minos. Here Dante is said to be 'following Virgil to the letter'; Pietro directs us back to the appropriate Virgilian text, *Aeneid*, vi. He then elaborates the allegorical, moral, and anagogical meanings of Minos, drawing upon a remarkable range of theologians, glossators, moralists, and poets. Moving on to the second section (literal level), Pietro considers the lustful lovers who people Dante's second infernal circle. His treatment of

---

[56] See Jenaro-MacLennan, *The Trecento Commentaries*, pp. 86–104.

[57] In his first recension Pietro had addressed the question in the following order: efficient, material, formal, and final causes; then title and the part of philosophy. See *Petri Allegherii super Dant. Comoed.*, ed. Nannucci, p. 3.

[58] Pietro's account of comedy in his third recension is very different from that in his first, which leans more heavily upon the passage from Isidore of Seville employed by Boccaccio in the *accessus* to his *Esposizioni*, 23, trans. below.

Dido sees him dwelling, once again, upon 'Virgil's fiction'. Whereas earlier Christian commentators had devoted their energies to enunciating the Christian truths that lie beneath the *integumentum*, Pietro focuses upon the fictionality of Virgil's text: he speaks of Virgil speaking through the person of Dido and makes the historicity of the Virgilian account seem more provisory by citing an alternative version from Jerome. Such cautious concern with the facts of history accords well with the patient scepticism of Petrarch and John Ridevall: the Italian humanist and the English classicizing friar had both recently decided (quite independently) that Dido and Aeneas could only have met in fiction, and not in history.[59]

Pietro's modernity proves something of an obstacle to his understanding of the Paolo and Francesca episode; the spirit of the *stil nuovo*, with its concern for the 'noble heart', is evidently quite foreign to him. In Pietro's literal, or literal-minded, account, the tragedy of these celebrated lovers is put down to an excess of leisure, bad dietary habits, and a poor choice of reading-materials.[60]

Having finished his literal account of the lovers of *Inferno*, v, Pietro evidently realized that it would be tedious to return to each of them in turn at the allegorical level. And so, ingeniously, he chooses to examine the allegorical significance of Cupid, a figure that represents them all. His account of the blindness, slings, and arrows of Cupid concludes, most appropriately, with a quotation from one of the foundation texts of the European courtly-love tradition, the *De arte honeste amandi* of Andreas Capellanus.

Boccaccio as Dantean Apologist. Boccaccio's lifelong devotion to Dante expressed itself through an extraordinary range of literary roles: he was, by turns, a poetic imitator, a biographer, a transcriber and editor, a glossator, a commentator, and (finally) a lecturer, all *in honorem Dantis*. But although Boccaccio remained steadfast in his commitment to Dante, the ways in which he attempted to persuade his contemporaries of Dante's greatness shifted subtly over the decades. Early on, as a young Florentine apprentice merchant at Naples, Boccaccio simply gloried in Dante's achievement: he sought out anyone who had known Dante in person, copied down any Dantean texts he could find, and tried his hand at Dantean verse-forms. This early phase expresses itself most intensely in the *Amorosa visione*, a dream-poem in fifty cantos of *terza rima*; this features Dante as the central figure in the triumph of Wisdom, surrounded by the great authors of antiquity.[61] But the *Visione*, written several years after Boccaccio's return from Naples to Florence in 1341, is also symptomatic of a crisis in Boccaccio's development. It fails as a poem because each of its five triumphs is crowded with figures culled from classical

[59] See Smalley, *English Friars and Antiquity*, pp. 130–1, 293–4.
[60] A similar account is given by Benvenuto da Imola: see the edition of his commentary by G. F. Lacaita (Florence, 1887), i. 209; also F. Mazzoni, 'Benvenuto da Imola', *ED* i. 593–6. Speaking of Benvenuto's treatment of *Inf.* v, Mazzoni complains of the 'crude materialization of the notion of "cor gentile" ... which indicates the passing of an entire way of thinking' (p. 595).
[61] See *Amorosa visione*, iv. 7–vi. 33, ed. V. Branca in Boccaccio, *Opere*, iii. 34–40.

texts. Boccaccio is confusing vernacular poetry with Latin encyclopaedism. This tension between vernacular poetics and Latin learning, which is felt in all Boccaccio's writings on Dante, owes much to his growing involvement with Petrarch.

In Boccaccio's first *Zibaldone* or literary scrapbook, which was begun at Naples and finished at Florence, Dantean letters and eclogues are immediately followed by Petrarchan material.[62] On returning to Florence, Boccaccio frequented the Petrarchan *cenacolo*, or humanist circle, of Sennuccio del Bene even as he composed the Dantean *Visione*. Boccaccio knew himself to be the servant of two masters: he composed a biography in praise of each of them, Dante's in Italian (the *Trattatello in laude di Dante*) and Petrarch's (of course) in Latin.[63] In 1350 Boccaccio travelled to a convent at Ravenna to present Dante's daughter, Sister Beatrice, with ten gold florins on behalf of a Florentine merchant *compagnia*; and in the spring of the following year he travelled to Padua to meet Petrarch for the first time. A lesser spirit would have been crushed between two such literary giants. But Boccaccio, in these years following the great plague of 1348, was himself possessed by creative energy of giant proportions: having completed his *Decameron* he was busily amassing materials for his monumentally lengthy works of Latin encyclopaedism (whilst pursuing a successful phase of his public career). On arriving at Padua in 1351 Boccaccio was perturbed to discover that Petrarch's library contained no copy of Dante's *Comedy*. Having returned to Florence, Boccaccio sent Petrarch a copy, accompanied by a Latin metrical epistle which urged him to consider the *Comedy* seriously as a work which explored all the potentialities of the vernacular. Petrarch was moved to explain his complex (sometimes tortuous) attitude to Dante in a Latin prose letter;[64] and he was even tempted (by the example of Boccaccio's *Amorosa Visione* as well as by the *Comedy* itself) to try out *terza rima*, an experiment which lasted for over twenty years in the shape of the *Trionfi*.

Paradoxically, then, this first encounter with Petrarch persuaded Boccaccio to intensify his efforts as a Dantean apologist. The first version of the *Trattatello in laude di Dante*, composed some time between 1351 and 1355, is preserved in an autograph manuscript, where it accompanies the *Vita nuova*, the *Comedy* (with Boccaccio's own *argomenti* in *terza rima* summarizing each *cantica*), and fifteen of Dante's *canzoni*.[65] This and other manuscript evidence indicates that the *Trattatello* was not designed to be read apart from (or even in lieu of) the

---

[62] See *Lo Zibaldone Boccaccesco Mediceo Laurenziano Plut. XXIX—8*, a facsimile prefaced by Ovidio Biagi (Florence, 1915); F. Di Benedetto, 'Considerazioni sullo Zibaldone Laurenziano e restauro testuale della prima redazione del *Faunus*', *Italia medioevale e umanistica*, xiv (1971), 91–129.

[63] Interestingly, these two works were given similar Latin titles: *De vita et moribus domini Francisci Petrarcchi de Florentia*, and *De origine vita studiis et moribus viri clarissimi Dantis Aligerii Florentini, poete illustris, et de operibus compositis ab eodem, incipit feliciter* (this being the incipit which prefaces the first redaction of the *Trattatello* but was dropped for the second and third).

[64] *Fam.* xxi. 15 (tr. A. S. Bernardo (Baltimore and London, 1985), pp. 202–7).

[65] For details of this MS (Toledo, Chapter Library, MS 104. 6) and of other Dantean poems copied by Boccaccio, see *Trattatello in laude di Dante*, ed. P. G. Ricci in Boccaccio, *Opere*, iii. 848–56; Padoan, 'Boccaccio', *ED* i. 646.

Comedy: it aims (like a good introduction to a modern critical edition) to aid and encourage us in our own approaches to the text.

The *Trattatello* is a fresh and original work. Modelling itself to some extent on the Virgilian biographies of Servius and Donatus and borrowing from medieval saints' lives, it celebrates the legendary, marvellous, and mysterious powers of Dante, the poet-hero. Boccaccio's natural story-telling talents are given free rein in a whole series of charming biographical episodes: the infant Dante meets Beatrice at a party (31–4); Dante smiles at hearing some Veronese housewives speak of him as one who pops down to hell when he feels like it (which accounts for his dark complexion and curly beard, 113); Dante spends all day reading in a Sienese pharmacist's shop, oblivious to the circumambient din of an armed tournament (122); Dante conquers the Parisian theological schools in a disputation *de quodlibet*.

Such episodes would obviously appeal to a broad range of readers. The *Trattatello* does, however, concern itself with cultural questions that were of topical concern to the humanists. And the most pressing question (seen in paras. 128–74, translated below) is one that had preoccupied Dantists since the beginnings of *Comedy* commentary: the relationship of poetry to theology. Boccaccio pushes the claims for poetry further than any of his predecessors with the formulation (borrowed from Petrarch) that theology is 'a poetry of God' (154). Characteristic features of both disciplines are explored in tandem through a series of allegorizations of pagan and Christian figures. Although poetry is seen to share some of the transcendent qualities of Scripture it is far from other-worldly. In Boccaccio's account poetry plays a practical role in the establishment of civil life, and is seen as essential to its continuance (128–37, 156–8).

Some time around 1360 Boccaccio revised his *Trattatello*, making it clearer and more readily intelligible to semi-educated readers. At the same time, however, Boccaccio deliberately curbed his story-telling instincts and considered the facts of Dante's biography with a more sober eye. Many of the most charming episodes of version I were simply excised. The most significant changes in the new version, however, concern Boccaccio's reflections on poetry and its relations with theology. Boccaccio explains that by 'theology' he means not only Scripture but also scriptural exegesis.[66] His arguments for the similarities between poetry and theology in their form of treatment ('forma dell'operare') are, consequently, made more guardedly.[67] Boccaccio's defence of poetry *per se* is cut right back in version II of the *Trattatello*: it is, however, reinstated and expanded in the third and final version, completed some time before 1372.[68] Such modifications, cuts, and expansions suggest that the status of poetry and its relations with theology were still very sensitive issues in the later fourteenth century.

[66] See red. II, 95 (ed. Ricci, pp. 517–18), and cf. red. I, 141 (ed. Ricci, p. 472). Both the first and second redactions survive in autograph MSS; the third does not. Ricci's edition contains all three versions.

[67] Compare, for example, red. I, 137 (ed. Ricci, p. 47), with red. II, 91 (ed. Ricci, p. 516).

[68] For the dating of the three versions, see V. Branca, *Giovanni Boccaccio. Profilo biografico*, in Boccaccio, *Opere*, i. 108. For a comparison of the three versions see Ricci, ibid., iii. 427–35.

On 23 October 1373 Boccaccio gave the world's first *lectura Dantis* at the Florentine church of Santo Stefano di Badia. A petition for such lectures had been submitted to the Florentine civic authorities earlier that year. It was approved by a majority of 167 votes; Boccaccio was the obvious choice as lecturer. The *lecturae* were scheduled to go on for a year at the rate of one lecture per day. Unfortunately Boccaccio fell ill in January 1374, having delivered about sixty lectures (which had brought him to the beginning of *Inferno*, xvii). Florence was affected by plague between March and September 1374 and the series was discontinued. Following Boccaccio's death on 21 December 1375 the lectures were discovered in thirty-eight notebooks. It was not clear whether or not these notebooks could be called a 'book', and a legal dispute broke out over their ownership. Sadly these notebooks have not survived, and the manuscript tradition deriving from them has added fresh sources of confusion. A printed edition did not appear until 1724. The modern editor faces formidable problems in establishing a text of what is obviously a text in progress (polished in some parts, sketchy in others) and not a finished product.[69] The basic structuring principle of the *Esposizioni* is the distinction between literal and allegorical sense. The literal sense of a canto is considered first. Following a brief overview of a canto's theme or subject-matter, Boccaccio breaks the canto down into a number of constituent parts. Each of these parts is then considered in detail. This analysis is then usually followed by an allegorical exposition of the canto. At the end of the literal exposition of canto x, however, Boccaccio states that 'this canto has no allegory whatsoever' (110); and a similar claim is made for canto xi (88). The allegorical exposition of cantos xv and xvi is put off until the exposition of canto xvii; and the exposition of canto xvii was never completed.

Since Boccaccio was (by medieval standards) an old man when he assembled his *Esposizioni*, it is not surprising that he drew frequently from his own past writings, particularly from the Latin encyclopaedic works. He also borrows freely from earlier commentators, including Pietro Alighieri; he shares many of Pietro's concerns, especially his desire to record (and perhaps reconcile) the differing accounts of certain classical episodes given by various *auctores*, and also his determination to concentrate upon the letter of the Dantean text, focusing upon Dante's literary (rather than visionary, political, or religious) achievement. This aligns him against the view of Dante offered by Guido da Pisa. Boccaccio never deigns to name Guido by name, but many of his arguments suggest a hidden polemic against the Carmelite friar. Boccaccio's *Esposizioni* offer many interesting points of comparison with Guido's *Expositio*. For example, whereas Guido takes Beatrice, the beloved, to represent (allegorically) co-operative grace, Boccaccio reads the same quality in Virgil, the poet.[70] Boccaccio does, however, often sound more like Guido than Pietro, especially when he is concerning himself with allegorical meaning. His allegorical expositions often lapse into a tone of churchy moralizing.

[69] For an account of such problems, see Padoan's admirable edition of Boccaccio's *Esposizioni*, *Opere*, vi. 722–30.

[70] For this and other comparisons, see Mazzoni, 'Guido e Boccaccio', pp. 111–15.

The *Esposizioni* have proved immensely valuable to Dantists, thanks to Boccaccio's prodigious erudition and his intimate knowledge of Dante's texts: Boccaccio had copied out the entire *Comedy* many times. There is, however, something unmistakably troubled and uneven about the tone and procedure of his Dante lectures. Sometimes he follows the ways of earlier exegetes, such as when he pauses to identify a specific rhetorical figure. Sometimes he develops arcane points of learning in ways that could only interest a cultured minority; and sometimes he tells stories. From time to time he makes brave and resolute attempts at defending Dante's orthodoxy against various detractors: but such attempts often flounder, ending in confusion, self-contradiction, or misrepresentation of Dante's thought. The philosophical and religious bases of Dante's poem are quite foreign to Boccaccio: as Giorgio Padoan neatly puts it, 'Boccaccio proclaims the greatness of the "poet" Dante with great passion, but on the plane of thought he abandons him.'[71]

The first part of the *accessus* to Boccaccio's *Esposizioni* (translated below in its entirety) is structured along traditional lines. Following a studiedly modest, invocatory opening (1–5), Boccaccio runs quickly through material, formal, efficient, and final causes (6–12), deriving many of his arguments and phrasings from the *Epistle to Can Grande*. The question of the work's title detains Boccaccio (as it had detained Pietro) much longer (13–41): Boccaccio feels bound to investigate the origins and generic properties of comedy and to give some account of Dante's life. The resurgence of Boccaccio's biographical interests here is given an explicit critical justification (one which holds good for the *Trattatello*): that the quality of a poet's life (what we might term his ethos) has an important bearing upon the quality and trustworthiness of his text (28). The final question, that of the part of philosophy to which the work belongs, is (as usual) soon disposed of (42). Boccaccio then carefully acknowledges his obedience to Church authority (43) as he passes, in the second part of his *accessus*, to questions concerning his immediate subject, hell. Having stated his aims with great precision (44), he then draws upon the resources of a lifetime's learning (45–73): authorities cited range from the prophet Isaiah to the geographer Pomponius Mela.

Finally, in his last four paragraphs (74–7), Boccaccio returns to a worrying question, first broached in para. 19: why did Dante write his *Comedy* in the vernacular and not in Latin? This question, which had worried Giovanni del Virgilio and was to trouble humanists for many generations to come, finds no satisfactory answer in Boccaccio.[72] The fact that Boccaccio should feel compelled to raise it at all testifies to the powerful advances made by Latin humanism in the course of his lifetime: for most of Boccaccio's creative energies in the first half of his career (including those poured into the epical *Teseida*) had been dedicated to vernacular art. But such art had become problematic not only in and of itself (could there ever be such a thing as a

[71] 'Boccaccio', *ED* i. 649 (David Wallace's translation).

[72] For a succinct account of later Dante commentary, see C. Grayson, 'Dante and the Renaissance', in C. P. Brand *et al.*, *Italian Studies presented to E. R. Vincent* (Cambridge, 1962), pp. 57–75. For a more detailed treatment, see C. Dionisotti, 'Dante nel Quattrocento', *Atti del congresso internazionale di studi danteschi* (Florence, 1965), pp. 333–78.

vernacular Virgil?) but also in its social effects: for everyone could, to some extent, participate in it. At the heart of Petrarch's critique of Dante lies the accusation that Dante had put serious subjects into the mouths of 'ignorant oafs in taverns and market-places'.[73] And now, in 1373, Boccaccio found himself doing the same thing by giving public lectures in the vernacular on a vernacular text. Boccaccio evidently felt uneasy, because when a humanist friend wrote to him, accusing him of having prostituted the Muses by sharing their secrets with the 'volgo', he capitulated at once. In four sad sonnets Boccaccio acknowledges the folly of his *lecturae* and accepts that his sickness has been sent as a punishment from heaven.[74]

Boccaccio's *Esposizioni* of 1373 mark an awkward and fascinating moment of passage in Dante studies. And, happily, there were a number of gifted and enterprising spirits who were willing to continue where Boccaccio had left off. Benvenuto da Imola, who had sat among the audience at Boccaccio's 1373 lectures, was inspired to organize and deliver fresh *lecturae Dantis* at Bologna in 1375 and then to go on and compose a magnificent new *Comentum* [*sic*] on the *Comedy*.[75] And 1373 also saw the arrival in Florence of another curious foreigner. Geoffrey Chaucer's first encounters with the *Comedy* are recorded within *The House of Fame*, a dream-poem which measures the distance between professedly humble English 'makynge' and poetry of classical stature. It was chiefly through long study of the work of Boccaccio and Dante that Chaucer was able to move such 'makynge' into the mainstream of European vernacular poetry. Chaucer may have been profoundly grateful that the *Comedy* was written in the vernacular, in Italian and not in Latin.

DANTE ALIGHIERI(?)

Epistle to Can Grande della Scala: Extract[76]

... And so, having made an end of what I had to say in epistolary form, I will now in the capacity of commentator (*lectoris officio*) essay a few words by way of introduction to the work which is offered for your acceptance.

⟨5.⟩ As the Philosopher [i.e. Aristotle] says in the second book of the *Metaphysics*, 'as a thing is in respect of being, so is it in respect of truth';[77] the reason of which is, that the truth concerning a thing, which

---

[73] K. Foster, *Petrarch: Poet and Humanist* (Edinburgh, 1984), p. 29, translating a phrase from *Fam.* xxi. 15. 15. Foster offers a concise account of Petrarch's complex attitude to Dante, pp. 27–9, 33; see also M. Feo, 'Petrarca, Francesco', *ED* iv. 450–8.

[74] See the *Esposizioni*, ed. Padoan, in Boccaccio, *Opere*, vi, pp. xxi–xxii.

[75] See, in addition to Lacaita's fine edition, F. Mazzoni, 'Benvenuto', *ED* i. 593–6; L. M. La Favia, *Benvenuto da Imola: Dantista* (Madrid, 1977).

[76] Reprinted from *Dantis Alagherii Epistolae*, ed. Toynbee–Hardie, pp. 198–211, with the permission of Oxford University Press.

[77] *Meta.* ii. 1 (993ᵇ30–1).

consists in the truth as in its subject, is the perfect likeness of the thing as it is. Now of things which exist, some are such as to have absolute being in themselves; while others are such as to have their being dependent upon something else, by virtue of a certain relation, as being in existence at the same time, or having respect to some other thing, as in the case of correlatives, such as father and son, master and servant, double and half, the whole and part, and other similar things, in so far as they are related.[78] Inasmuch, then, as the being of such things depends upon something else, it follows that the truth of these things likewise depends upon something else; for if the half is unknown, its double cannot be known; and so of the rest.

⟨6.⟩ If any one, therefore, is desirous of offering any sort of introduction to part of a work, it behoves him to furnish some notion of the whole of which it is a part. Wherefore I, too, being desirous of offering something by way of introduction to the above-mentioned part of the whole *Comedy*, thought it incumbent on me in the first place to say something concerning the work as a whole, in order that access to the part might be the easier and the more perfect. There are six points, then, as to which inquiry must be made at the beginning of every didactic work; namely, the subject, the author, the form, the aim, the title of the book, and the branch of philosophy to which it belongs.[79] Now of these six points there are three in respect of which the part which I have had in mind to address to you differs from the whole work; namely, the subject, the form, and the title; whereas in respect of the others there is no difference, as is obvious to any one who considers the matter. Consequently, in an examination of the whole, these three points must be made the subject of a separate inquiry; which being done, the way will be sufficiently clear for the introduction to the part. Later we will examine the other three points, not only with reference to the whole work, but also with reference to the particular part which is offered to you.

⟨7.⟩ For the elucidation, therefore, of what we have to say, it must be understood that the meaning of this work is not of one kind only; rather the work may be described as 'polysemous', that is, having several meanings;[80] for the first meaning is that which is conveyed by the letter, and the next is that which is conveyed by what the letter signifies; the former of which is called literal, while the latter is called allegorical, or mystical.[81]

---

[78] Cf. the similar illustrations of relative and absolute terms in Dante's *Monarchia*, II. xi. 3 ff., ed. P. G. Ricci (Verona, 1965), pp. 262 ff., tr. P. H. Wicksteed, *A Translation of the Latin Works of Dante Alighieri* (The Temple Classics, London, 1904, repr. 1934,), pp. 263 ff.

[79] Lat. 'subiectum, agens, forma, finis, libri titulus, et genus philosophiae'. Cf. the *accessus* vocabulary discussed and illustrated in Ch. I.

[80] Probably influenced by Hugutio of Pisa, *Magnae derivationes*, s.v. *polis*, in Oxford, Bodleian Library, MS Bodley 376, fos. 154ʳ–155ʳ; cf. the quotation by P. Toynbee, 'Dante's Latin Dictionary (The *Magnae derivationes* of Uguccione da Pisa)', in id., *Dante Studies and Researches* (London, 1902), p. 106.

[81] Cf. *Monarchia*, I. iv. 2 ff. (ed. Ricci, pp. 232 ff., tr. Wicksteed, pp. 235 ff.).

And for the better illustration of this method of exposition we may apply it to the following verses: 'When Israël went out of Egypt, the house of Jacob from a people of strange language; Judah was his sanctuary, and Israel his dominion' [Ps. 113: 1–2]. For if we consider the letter alone, the thing signified to us is the going out of the children of Israël from Egypt in the time of Moses; if the allegory, our redemption through Christ is signified, if the moral sense, the conversion of the soul from the sorrow and misery of sin to a state of grace is signified; if the anagogical, the passing of the sanctified soul from the bondage of the corruption of this world to the liberty of everlasting glory is signified. And although these mystical meanings are called by various names, they may one and all in a general sense be termed allegorical, inasmuch as they are different (*diversi*) from the literal or historical; for the word 'allegory' is so called from the Greek *alleon*, which in Latin is *alienum* ('strange') or *diversum* ('different').[82]

⟨8.⟩ This being understood, it is clear that the subject, with regard to which the alternative meanings are brought into play, must be twofold. And therefore the subject of this work must be considered in the first place from the point of view of the literal meaning, and next from that of the allegorical interpretation. The subject, then, of the whole work, taken in the literal sense only, is the state of souls after death, pure and simple. For on and about that the argument of the whole work turns. If, however, the work be regarded from the allegorical point of view, the subject is man according as by his merits or demerits in the exercise of his free will he is deserving of reward or punishment by justice.

⟨9.⟩ And the form is twofold—the form of the treatise (*forma tractatus*) and the form of the treatment (*forma tractandi*). The form of the treatise is threefold, according to the threefold division. The first division is that whereby the whole work is divided into three *cantiche*; the second, whereby each *cantica* is divided into cantos; and the third, whereby each canto is divided into rhymed lines.[83] The form or manner of treatment is poetic, fictive, descriptive, digressive, and figurative; and further, it is definitive, analytical, probative, refutative, and exemplificative.[84]

⟨10⟩. The title of the book is *Here begins the Comedy of Dante Alighieri, a Florentine by birth, not by disposition*. For the understanding of which it must be noted that 'comedy' is so called from *comos*, a village, and *oda*, a song; whence comedy is as it were a 'rustic song'.[85] Now comedy is a

---

[82] Cf. Hugutio, *Magnae derivationes*, s.v. *allegoria*, MS Bodley 376, fo. 6ʳ; cf. the citations by Toynbee in *Dante Studies and Researches*, p. 106, and 'Dante's Obligations to the *Magnae derivationes* of Uguccione of Pisa', *Romania*, xxvi (1897), 543–4. Cf. also Isidore, *Ety.* 1. xxxvii. 22.

[83] Here *rithimos* refers to the rhymed lines composing the *terzine*.

[84] Cf. the two types of *modus* defined by medieval theologians, discussed in Ch. VI, above, pp. 198–200.

[85] This discussion of comedy, and the subsequent discussion of tragedy, seems to have been indebted, directly or indirectly, to Hugutio's *Magnae derivationes*. See the discussion

certain kind of poetical narration which differs from all others. It differs, then, from tragedy in its subject-matter, in that tragedy at the beginning is admirable and placid, but at the end or issue is foul and horrible. And tragedy is so called from *tragos*, a goat, and *oda*; as it were a 'goat-song', that is to say foul like a goat, as appears from the tragedies of Seneca.[86] Whereas comedy begins with sundry adverse conditions, but ends happily, as appears from the comedies of Terence. And for this reason it is the custom of some writers in their salutation[87] to say by way of greeting: 'a tragic beginning and a comic ending to you!' Tragedy and comedy differ likewise in their style of language; for that of tragedy is high-flown and sublime, while that of comedy is unstudied and lowly. And this is implied by Horace in the *Art of Poetry*, where he grants that the comedian may on occasion use the language of tragedy, and vice versa: 'Yet sometimes comedy her voice will raise, / And angry Chremes scold with swelling phrase; / And prosy periods oft our ears assail / When Telephus and Peleus tell their tragic tale.'[88] And from this it is clear that the present work is to be described as a comedy. For if we consider the subject-matter, at the beginning it is horrible and foul, as being *Hell*; but at the close it is happy, desirable, and pleasing, as being *Paradise*. As regards the style of language, the style is unstudied and lowly, as being in the vulgar tongue, in which even womenfolk hold their talk. And hence it is evident why the work is called a comedy. And there are other kinds of poetical narration, such as the pastoral poem, the elegy, the satire, and the votive song, as may also be gathered from Horace in the *Art of Poetry*;[89] but of these we need say nothing at present.

⟨11.⟩ It can now be shown in what manner the subject of the part offered to you is to be determined. For if the subject of the whole work taken in the literal sense is the state of souls after death, pure and simple, without limitation, it is evident that in this part the same state is the subject, but with a limitation, namely the state of blessed souls after death. And if the subject of the whole work from the allegorical point of view is man according as by his merits or demerits in the exercise of his free will he is deserving of reward or punishment by justice, it is evident that in this part this subject has a limitation, and that it is man according as by his merits he is deserving of reward by justice.

---

under *oda* in MS Bodley 376, fo. 140[r-v]; (cit. Toynbee, *Dante Studies and Researches*, pp. 103–4). The most thorough analysis of the genre theory in the Can Grande epistle is in H. A. Kelly's monograph (cit. above, n. 10).

[86] Cf. the definition of tragedy in Nicholas Trevet's commentary on Seneca (on which see Ch. VIII). Dante does not seem to have known Seneca at first hand: see Giorgio Brugnoli, 'Ut patet per Senecam in suis tragediis', *Rivista di cultura classica e medioevale*, v (1963), 146–63.

[87] The *salutatio* was one of the recognized five parts of a letter as defined in the *artes dictaminis*, the other four being the *exordium*, *narratio*, *petitio*, and *conclusio*. See Murphy, *Rhetoric in the Middle Ages*, pp. 221–5.

[88] *Ars poetica*, 93–6.   [89] Ibid. 75–8.

⟨12.⟩ In like manner the form of the part is determined by that of the whole work. For if the form of the treatise as a whole is threefold, in this part it is twofold only, the division being that of the *cantica* and of the cantos. The first division (into *cantiche*) cannot be applicable to the form of the part, since the *cantica* is itself a part under the first division.

⟨13.⟩ The title of the book also is clear. For the title of the whole book is 'Here begins the *Comedy*,' &c., as above; but the title of the part is 'Here begins the third *cantica* of the *Comedy* of Dante, which is called *Paradise*'.

⟨14.⟩ These three points, in which the part differs from the whole, having been examined, we may now turn our attention to the other three, in respect of which there is no difference between the part and the whole. The author, then, of the whole and of the part is the person mentioned above, who is seen to be such throughout.

⟨15.⟩ The aim (*finis*) of the whole and of the part might be manifold; as, for instance, immediate and remote. But leaving aside any minute examination of this question, it may be stated briefly that the aim of the whole and of the part is to remove those living in this life from a state of misery, and to bring them to a state of happiness.

⟨16.⟩ The branch of philosophy to which the work is subject, in the whole as in the part, is that of morals or ethics; inasmuch as the whole as well as the part was conceived, not for speculation, but with a practical object.[90] For if in certain parts or passages the treatment is after the manner of speculative philosophy, that is not for the sake of speculation, but for a practical purpose;[91] since, as the Philosopher says in the second book of the *Metaphysics*: 'practical men occasionally speculate on things in their particular and temporal relations'.[92]

⟨17.⟩ Having therefore premised these matters, we may now apply ourselves to the exposition of the literal meaning, by way of sample; as to which it must first be understood that the exposition of the letter is in effect but a demonstration of the form of the work. The part in question, then, that is, this third *cantica* which is called *Paradise*, falls by its main division into two parts, namely the prologue, and the executive part;[93] which second part begins [THE LAMP OF THE WORLD] RISES TO MORTALS THROUGH DIFFERENT PASSAGES [*Par.* i. 37].[94]

⟨18.⟩ As regards the first part, it should be noted that although in common parlance it might be termed an exordium, yet, properly speaking, it can only be termed a prologue; as the Philosopher seems to indicate in the third book of his *Rhetoric*, where he says that 'the proem in a rhetorical oration answers to the prologue in poetry, and to the prelude

---

[90] Cf. *Eth. Nicomach.* ii. 2 (1103^{b}26–31).

[91] Cf. *Monarchia*, 1. ii. 4 ff. (ed. Ricci, pp. 137 ff., tr. Wicksteed, pp. 129 ff.).

[92] *Meta.* ii. 1 (993^{b}22–3), and see above, pp. 201–2, 227–8, 246–7, 310–11.

[93] i.e. the introduction and the narrative proper.

[94] Here, and later in the *Epistle*, the writer translates Dante's lines into Latin. We have drawn on the English translation of the *Comedy* by Charles Singleton (Princeton, N.J., 1970–5).

in flute-playing'.[95] It must further be observed that this preamble, which may ordinarily be termed an exordium, is one thing in the hands of a poet, and another in those of an orator. For orators are wont to give a forecast of what they are about to say, in order to gain the attention of their hearers.[96] Now poets not only do this, but in addition they make use of some sort of invocation afterwards. And this is fitting in their case, for they have need of invocation in a large measure, inasmuch as they have to petition the superior beings for something beyond the ordinary range of human powers, something almost in the nature of a divine gift. Therefore the present prologue is divided into two parts: in the first is given a forecast of what is to follow; in the second is an invocation to Apollo; which second part begins O GOOD APOLLO, FOR THIS LAST LABOUR [*Par.* i. 13].

⟨19.⟩ With reference to the first part it must be observed that to make a good exordium three things are requisite, as Tully says in his *New Rhetoric*; that the hearer, namely, should be rendered favourably disposed, attentive, and willing to learn; and this is especially needful in the case of a subject which is out of the common, as Tully himself remarks.[97] Inasmuch, then, as the subject dealt with in the present work is out of the common, it is the aim of the first part of the exordium or prologue to bring about the above-mentioned three results with regard to this out-of-the-way subject. For the author declares that he will relate such things as he who beheld them in the first heaven was able to retain. In which statement all those three things are comprised; for the profitableness of what he is about to be told begets a favourable disposition in the hearer; its being out of the common engages his attention; and its being within the range of possibility renders him willing to learn. Its profitableness he gives to be understood when he says that he shall tell of that which above all things excites the longing of mankind, namely the joys of Paradise; its uncommon nature is indicated when he promises to treat of such exalted and sublime matters as the conditions of the celestial kingdom; its being within the range of possibility is demonstrated when he says that he will tell of those things which he was able to retain in his mind—for if he was able, so will others be also. All this is indicated in the passage where he declares that he had been in the first heaven, and that he purposes to relate concerning the celestial kingdom whatsoever he was able to store up, like a treasure, in his mind. Having thus noted the excellence and perfection of the first part of the prologue, we may now proceed to the literal exposition.

⟨20.⟩ He says, then, that THE GLORY OF THE FIRST MOVER, which is God, SHINES FORTH IN EVERY PART OF THE UNIVERSE, but in such wise that it shines IN ONE PART MORE AND IN ANOTHER LESS [*Par.* i. 1–3]. That it shines in every

[95] Cf. *Rhet.* iii. 14 (1414^{b}19–20).
[96] Ibid. (1415^{a}12–15).
[97] Cicero, *De inventione*, i. xv. 20, 21.

part both reason and authority declare.[98] Reason thus: Everything which exists has its being either from itself, or from some other thing. But it is plain that self-existence can be the attribute of one being only, namely the First or Beginning which is God, since to have being does not argue necessary self-existence, and necessary self-existence appertains to one being only, namely the First or Beginning, which is the cause of all things; therefore everything which exists, except that One itself, has its being from some other thing. If, then, we take, not any thing whatsoever, but that thing which is the most remote in the universe, it is manifest that this has its being from something; and that from which it derives either has its being from itself, or from something else. If from itself, then it is primal; if from something else, then that again must either be self-existent, or derive from something else. But in this way we should go on to infinity in the chain of effective causes, as is shown in the second book of the *Metaphysics*.[99] So we must come to a primal existence, which is God. Hence, mediately or immediately, everything that exists has its being from Him, because, inasmuch as the second cause has its effect from the first, its influence on what it acts upon is like that of a body which receives and reflects a ray; since the first cause is the more effective cause. And this is stated in the book *On Causes*, namely, that 'every primary cause has influence in a greater degree on what it acts upon than any second cause'.[100] So much with regard to being.

⟨21.⟩ With regard to essence I argue in this wise: Every essence, except the first, is caused; otherwise there would be more than one necessarily self-existent being, which is impossible. For what is caused is the effect either of nature or of intellect; and what is of nature is, consequently, caused by intellect, inasmuch as nature is the work of intelligence. Everything, then, which is caused is the effect, mediately or immediately, of some intellect. Since, then, virtue follows the essence whose virtue it is, if the essence is of intellect, the virtue is wholly and solely of the intellectual essence whose effect it is. And so, just as we had to go back to a first cause in the case of being, so now we must do so in the case of essence and of virtue. Whence it is evident that every essence and every virtue proceeds from a primal one; and that the lower intelligences have their effect as it were from a radiating body, and, after the fashion of mirrors, reflect the rays of the higher to the one below them.[101] Which matter appears to be discussed clearly enough by Dionysius in his work *On the Celestial*

---

[98] Cf. Dante's *Epist.* III (iv) (ed. Toynbee-Hardie, pp. 23–4).

[99] *Meta.* ii. 2 (994^{a}1–^{b}31).

[100] *Liber de causis*, i (ed. R. Steele as an appendix to *Opera hactenus inedita Rogeri Baconi*, xii: *Questiones supra librum de causis* (Oxford, 1935), p. 161. This work, sometimes attributed to Aristotle in the Middle Ages, is a translation by Gerard of Cremona (d. 1187) of an Arabic paraphrase of the *Elementatio theologica* of Proclus.

[101] Cf. *Convivio*, iii. xiv. 2 ff. (ed. Simonelli, pp. 116 ff.).

Hierarchy.[102] And therefore it is stated in the book *On Causes* that 'every intelligence is full of forms'.[103] Reason, then, as we have seen, demonstrates that the divine light, that is to say the divine goodness, wisdom, and virtue, shines in every part.

⟨22.⟩ Authority likewise declares the same, but with more knowledge. For the Holy Spirit says by the mouth of Jeremiah [23: 24] 'Do not I fill heaven and earth?' And in the Psalm [138: 7–9]: 'Whither shall I go from thy Spirit? and whither shall I flee from thy presence? If I ascend up into heaven, thou art there; if I descend into hell, thou art there also. If I take my wings, etc.' And Wisdom [1: 7] says: 'The Spirit of the Lord hath filled the whole world.' And Ecclus. 42[: 16]: 'His work is full of the glory of the Lord.' To which also the writings of the pagans bear witness; for Lucan says in his ninth book: 'Jupiter is whatever thou seest, wherever thou goest.'[104]

⟨23.⟩ He says well, then, when he says that the divine ray, or divine glory, PENETRATES AND SHINES THROUGH THE UNIVERSE; penetrates, as to essence; shines forth, as to being. And what he adds as to MORE AND LESS is manifestly true, since we see that one essence exists in a more excellent degree, and another in a less; as is clearly the case with regard to the heaven and the elements, the former being incorruptible, while the latter are corruptible.

⟨24.⟩ And having premised this truth, he next goes on to indicate Paradise by a circumlocution; and says that he was in that heaven which receives the glory of God, or his light, in most bountiful measure.[105] As to which it must be understood that that heaven is the highest heaven, which contains all the bodies of the universe, and is contained by none,[106] within which all bodies move (itself remaining everlastingly at rest),[107] and which receives virtue from no corporeal substance.[108] And it is called the Empyrean, which is as much as to say, the heaven glowing with fire or heat;[109] not that there is material fire or heat therein, but spiritual, which is holy love, or charity.[110]

⟨25.⟩ Now that this heaven receives more of the divine light than any other can be proved by two things. Firstly, by its containing all things, and being contained by none; secondly, by its state of everlasting rest or

[102] *De cael. hier.* iii (ed. Roques *et al.*, pp. 87–92; tr. Eriugena, PL cxxii. 1044–6).

[103] *Liber de causis*, 10 (ed. Steele, p. 170).

[104] *Bellum civile*, ix. 580, reading 'quocumque'; the preferable variant is 'quodcumque' as internal accusative with 'moveris'—every sensation within you. Jupiter is all that you perceive without (*quodcumque vides*) and within (*quodcumque moveris*).

[105] *Par.* i. 4–5: 'I have been in the heaven that most receives of His light' (trans. Singleton).

[106] Cf. *Convivio*, II. iii. 11 (ed. Simonelli, p. 37).

[107] Cf. *Convivio*, II. iii. 8 (ibid.).

[108] Cf. *Par.* xxx. 39.

[109] Cf. *Convivio*, loc. cit.

[110] Cf. *Purg.* xxvi. 63.

peace. As to the first the proof is as follows: The containing body stands in the same relation to the content in natural position as the formative does to the formable, as we are told in the fourth book of the *Physics*. [111] But in the natural position of the whole universe the first heaven is the heaven which contains all things; consequently it is related to all things as the formative to the formable, which is to be in the relation of cause to effect. And since every causative force is in the nature of a ray emanating from the first cause, which is God, [112] it is manifest that that heaven which is in the highest degree causative [113] receives most of the divine light.

⟨26.⟩ As to the second the proof is this: Everything which has motion moves because of something which it has not, and which is the terminus of its motion. The heaven of the moon, for instance, moves because of some part of itself which has not attained the station towards which it is moving; and because no part whatsoever of it has attained any terminus whatsoever (as indeed it never can), it moves to another station, and thus is always in motion, and is never at rest, which is what it desires. And what I say of the heaven of the moon applies to all the other heavens, except the first. Everything, then, which has motion is in some respect defective, and has not its whole being complete. That heaven, therefore, which is subject to no movement, in itself and in every part whatsoever of itself has whatever it is capable of having in perfect measure, so that it has no need of motion for its perfection. And since every perfection is a ray of the Primal One, inasmuch as He is perfection in the highest degree, it is manifest that the first heaven receives more than any other of the light of the Primal One, which is God. This reasoning, however, has the appearance of an argument based on the denial of the antecedent, in that it is not a direct proof (*simpliciter*) and according to syllogistic form. But if we consider its content (*materia*) it is a good proof, because it deals with a thing eternal, and assumes it to be capable of being eternally defective; so that, if God did not give that heaven motion, it is evident that He did not give it material in any respect defective. And on this supposition the argument holds good by reason of the content; and this form of argument is much the same as though we should reason: 'if he is man, he is able to laugh'; [114] for in every convertible proposition a like reasoning holds good by virtue of the content. Hence it is clear that when the author says IN THAT HEAVEN WHICH RECEIVES MORE OF THE LIGHT OF GOD [*Par.* i. 4–5], he intends by a circumlocution to indicate Paradise, or the heaven of the Empyrean.

⟨27.⟩ And in agreement with the foregoing is what the Philosopher says in the first book *On Heaven*, namely that 'a heaven has so much the more

---

[111] *Phys.* iv. 4 (211ᵇ10–12).

[112] Cf. *Convivio*, ii. vi. 9–10, iii. xiv. 3 ff. (ed. Simonelli, pp. 46–7, 116 ff.); *Purg.* xxv. 89; *Par.* vii. 74, viii. 2–3, xix. 90, xxix. 29.

[113] Cf. Dante's discussion of heavenly causation in *Monarchia*, i. ix. 1 ff. (ed. Ricci, pp. 151 ff., tr. Wicksteed, pp. 147 ff.).

[114] Cf. Aristotle, *De part. animal.* iii. 10 (673ᵃ8).

honourable material than those below it as it is the further removed from terrestrial things'.[115] In addition to which might be adduced what the Apostle says to the Ephesians of Christ: 'Who ascended up far above all heaven, that He might fill all things' [Eph. 4: 10]. This is the heaven of the delights of the Lord; of which delights it is said by Ezekiel against Lucifer: 'Thou, the seal of similitude, full of wisdom, beautiful in perfection, wast in the delights of the Paradise of God' [Ezek. 28: 12–13].

⟨28⟩. And after he has said that he was in that place of Paradise which he describes by circumlocution, he goes on to say that he saw certain things which he who descends therefrom is powerless to relate.[116] And he gives the reason, saying that THE INTELLECT PLUNGES ITSELF TO SUCH DEPTH in its very longing, which is for God, THAT THE MEMORY CANNOT FOLLOW [*Par.* i. 7–9]. For the understanding of which it must be noted that the human intellect in this life, by reason of its connaturality and affinity to the separate intellectual substance,[117] when in exaltation, reaches such a height of exaltation that after its return to itself memory fails, since it has transcended the range of human faculty. And this is conveyed to us by the Apostle where he says, addressing the Corinthians: 'I know a man (whether in the body, or out of the body, I cannot tell; God knoweth) how that he was caught up to the third heaven, and heard unspeakable words, which it is not lawful for a man to utter' [2 Cor. 12: 2–4]. Behold, after the intellect had passed beyond the bounds of human faculty in its exaltation, it could not recall what took place outside of its range. This again is conveyed to us in Matthew [17: 1–8], where we read that the three disciples fell on their faces, and record nothing thereafter, as though memory had failed them. And in Ezekiel [2: 1] it is written: 'And when I saw it, I fell upon my face.' And should these not satisfy the cavillers, let them read Richard of Saint-Victor[118] in his book *On Contemplation*;[119] let them read Bernard in his book *On Consideration*;[120] let them read Augustine[121] in his book *On the Capacity of the Soul*;[122] and they will cease from their cavilling. But if on account of the sinfulness of the speaker they should cry out against his claim to have reached such a height of exaltation, let them read Daniel [2: 3–5], where they will find that even Nebuchadnezzar by divine permission beheld certain things as a warning to sinners, and straightway

---

[115] *De caelo*, i. 2 (269^b 16–17).

[116] *Par.* i. 5–6: '[I] have seen things which whoso descends from up there has neither the knowledge nor the power to relate' (tr. Singleton).

[117] i.e. the angels. Cf. *Convivio*, II. iv. 2, III. iv. 9 ff., III. vi. 6, III. viii. 14 (ed. Simonelli, pp. 38, 83 ff., 92, 98); *Purg.* xviii. 49.

[118] Richard of St Victor is placed by Dante among the great doctors of the church in the Heaven of the Sun; *Par.* x. 131–2.   [119] *Benjamin maior*, IV. xxiii (PL cxcvi. 167 B–C).

[120] *De consideratione*, v. ii. 3, in *S. Bernardi opera*, ed. J. Leclercq, C. H. Talbot, and H. M. Rochais (Rome, 1957–77), iii. 468–9.

[121] Dante places St Augustine in the celestial rose in the Empyrean Heaven, in the company of Francis and Benedict; *Par.* xxxii. 35.

[122] *De quant. animae*, xxxiii. 76 (PL xxxii. 1076–7).

forgot them. For He 'who maketh his sun to shine on the good and on the evil, and sendeth rain on the just and on the unjust' [Matt. 5: 45], sometimes in compassion for their conversion, sometimes in wrath for their chastisement, in greater or lesser measure, according as He wills, manifests his glory to evil-doers, be they never so evil.

⟨29.⟩ He saw, then, as he says, certain things WHICH HE WHO RETURNS HAS NEITHER KNOWLEDGE NOR POWER TO RELATE [*Par.* i. 6]. Now it must be carefully noted that he says HAS NEITHER KNOWLEDGE NOR POWER—knowledge he has not, because he has forgotten; power he has not, because even if he remembers, and retains it thereafter, nevertheless speech fails him. For we perceive many things by the intellect for which language has no terms—a fact which Plato indicates plainly enough in his books by his employment of metaphors; for he perceived many things by the light of the intellect which his everyday language was inadequate to express.

⟨30.⟩ Afterwards the author says that he will relate concerning the celestial kingdom such things as he was able to retain; and he says that this is the subject of his work; the nature and extent of which things will be shown in the executive part.

⟨31.⟩ Then when he says O GOOD APOLLO, etc. [*Par.* i. 13] he makes his invocation. And this part is divided into two parts—in the first, he invokes the deity and makes a petition; in the second, he inclines Apollo to the granting of his petition by the promise of a certain recompense; which second part begins O DIVINE POWER [*Par.* i. 22 ff.]. The first part again is divided into two parts—in the first, he prays for divine aid; in the second, he adverts to the necessity for his petition, whereby he justifies it; and this part begins THUS FAR THE ONE PEAK OF PARNASSUS [HAS SUFFICED ME, *Par.* i. 16 ff.].

⟨32.⟩ This is the general meaning of the second part of the prologue. The particular meaning I shall not expound on the present occasion; for anxiety as to my domestic affairs presses so heavily upon me that I must perforce abandon this and other tasks of public utility.[123] I trust, however, that your Magnificence may afford me the opportunity to continue this useful exposition at some other time.

⟨33.⟩ With regard to the executive part of the work, which was divided after the same manner as the prologue taken as a whole, I shall say nothing either as to its divisions or its interpretation at present;[124] save only that the process of the narrative will be by ascent from heaven to heaven, and that an account will be given of the blessed spirits who are met with in each sphere; and that there true blessedness consists in the apprehension of Him who is the beginning of truth,[125] as appears from

---

[123] Cf. the similar idiom in *Monarchia*, I. i. 2–6 (ed. Ricci, pp. 133–5, tr. Wicksteed, pp. 127–8).
[124] Cf. the process of *divisio textus* which Dante has followed in the *Convivio*, discussed above, pp. 376–7.   [125] Cf. *Par.* xxviii. 106–11, xiv. 40–2.

what John [17: 3] says: 'This is life eternal, to know thee the true God', etc.; and from what Boethius says in his third book *On Consolation*: 'To behold thee is the end.'[126] Hence it is that, in order to reveal the glory of the blessedness of those spirits, many things which have great profit and delight[127] will be asked of them, as of those who behold the fullness of truth. And since, when the Beginning or First, which is God, has been reached, there is nought to be sought for beyond, inasmuch as He is Alpha and Omega, that is, the Beginning and the End, as the *Vision* of John tells us [Rev. i. 8], the work ends in God Himself, who is blessed for evermore, world without end.

GUIDO DA PISA

Commentary on Dante's *Comedy*: Prologue[128]

Commentary and gloss on the *Comedia* of Dante, made by brother Guido da Pisa, of the order of blessed Mary of Mount Carmel. To his noble lord Lucano Spinola of Genoa.

HERE BEGINS THE PROLOGUE

In Dan. 5[: 5, 25] we find it written that while Balthasar, king of Babylon, was sitting at table, there appeared before him a hand writing on the wall: 'Mane, Thechel, Phares'. That hand is our new poet Dante, who wrote, that is, composed, the most high and most penetrating *Comedy*, which is divided into three parts, of which the first is called the *Inferno*, the second the *Purgatorio*, the third the *Paradiso*. The three words written on the wall correspond to these three parts. 'Mane' corresponds to the *Inferno*, for 'Mane' is interpreted as meaning 'number', and this poet in the first part of his *Comedy* enumerates the places, punishments, and crimes of the damned. 'Thechel' corresponds to the *Purgatorio*, for 'Thechel' is interpreted as 'weighing up' or 'assessing', and in the second part of his *Comedy* he weighs up and assesses the penances of those who must undergo purgatory. 'Phares' corresponds to the *Paradiso*, for 'Phares' is interpreted as meaning 'division', and the poet in the third part of his *Comedy* divides up, that is, makes distinctions among the various orders of the blessed and the hierarchies of angels. 'Manus', then, is Dante, for

---

[126] *De cons. phil.* III met. ix. 27 (ed. Tester, p. 274).

[127] Cf. the idiom in *Convivio*, IV. 14 (ed. Simonelli, p. 139).

[128] Tr. from the text in Chantilly, Musée Condé, MS 597 (1424), as printed by Jenaro-MacLennan, *The Trecento Commentaries*, pp. 124–30, with the permission of Oxford University Press. We also consulted the text in Cioffari's edition, pp. 1–7. The translation of Guido's prologue provided by V. Cioffari and F. Mazzoni in *Dante Studies*, xc (1972), 126–37 differs from ours in some respects.

we understand a hand (*manus*) as giving (*dantem*). For *manus* is derived from *mano*, *manas* ('emanate from') and Dante is derived from *do*, *das* ('give'). For, just as a gift comes from the hand, so this most sublime work is given to us by Dante.

I must emphasize that he wrote on a wall, that is, in an open and public place, for the benefit of all, 'Mane', that is, *Inferno*, of which he enumerated the punishments and regions; 'Thechel', that is, *Purgatorio*, of which he weighed up and assessed the penances; 'Phares', that is, *Paradiso*, and showed that its position was raised above the lower regions, and distinguished in their order the states of blessedness found therein. For that excellent poet set out all things 'according to their number, weight and measurement', as is written in Wisd. 9[: 21]. He set out the *Inferno* according to numbers because he enumerates sins and their punishment; he set out the *Purgatorio* according to weight, because he weighs and assesses different kinds of penance; he set out the *Paradiso* according to measurement, because he measures the celestial regions and distinguishes the various orders of the blessed.

The vision which the prophet Ezekiel saw can surely be related to this poet and his *Comedy*. The prophet writes of this vision in the following terms: 'Behold a hand was sent to me in which was a book written within and without, and written in it were lamentations and a song and woe' [Ezek. 2: 9]. That hand is this poet. The book which comes from his hand is his most sublime work the *Comedy*, which is written within and without as it contains both literal and allegorical senses. Three things are written in that book: lamentations, a song, and woe. Woe, because that is a cry of grief and despair, relates to the *Inferno*. For 'woe' in Holy Scripture signifies 'eternal damnation', as the holy Fathers say, commenting on the text: 'Woe to that man by whom the Son of Man will be betrayed' [Matt. 26: 24], and the meaning there is: 'he will be damned eternally'. Lamentations, which are indications of a sorrow voluntarily assumed, relate to the *Purgatorio*. But song, which is the same as 'praise' and 'a song of triumph', relates to the *Paradiso*.

In truth, one can see that *Comedy* as being figured in Noah's ark, for it had three chambers. In the lowest chamber were the wild animals and reptiles; in the middle one were domestic and tame animals, while in the topmost one were the men and birds. The first chamber we can take to represent hell, in which are wild and ferocious animals, that is, men who have been condemned, and reptiles, that is, demons. The second one we can take to represent purgatory, in which are the tame animals, that is, meek souls which patiently endure their sufferings. The third one we can take to represent paradise, in which are men and birds, that is, saints and angels raised aloft in glory.

Having noted these points, let us now briefly examine six things in this *Comedy*: first of all the subject, that is, the material cause (*causa materialis*);

secondly, the form, that is, the formal cause (*causa formalis*); third, the author, that is, the activating cause (*causa agens*); fourth, the end in view, that is, the final cause (*causa finalis*); fifth, the kind of philosophy, that is, under what kind of philosophy this *Comedy* should be included or under what kind it falls; sixth and lastly, the title of the book, that is, what title should be given to this book.[129]

As regards the first question, note that the subject of this work is two-fold, the literal and the allegorical. For, if it is taken literally, I say that the subject of this work is the state of souls after death, interpreted in simple terms.[130] This state is itself divided into three parts, as the condition of souls is threefold. The first state or condition is that of these souls which have eternally been damned, and which live in the midst of their various punishments without any hope of escaping from them. That part is called the *Inferno*. The second state or condition is that of those souls which continue suffering punishment voluntarily to make reparation to God for the crimes they have committed. They suffer their punishment with hopes of ascending to glory. That part is called the *Purgatorio*. The third state or condition is that of those souls which are in blessed glory, made one with that highest and eternal God for ever more, that is, world without end. This part is called the *Paradiso*. Therefore, clearly the subject of this work is the state of souls after death, interpreted in simple terms. The whole course of this work turns upon that and relates to that.

But if the subject is taken allegorically, I say that the subject or material is man himself, according as he is liable to just reward or punishment, earning or deserving it by the free exercise of his will,[131] and how he wins renown or blame because of his merit or guilt. For the intention of the author is concerned with relating or revealing to us the punishment or glory assigned to man himself. Thus, it is clear what is the subject, or the material cause, in this work.

Concerning the second question, that is, the formal cause, note that the formal cause in this work is twofold, namely the form of the treatise (*forma tractatus*) and the form of the treatment (*forma tractandi*). The form of the treatise is threefold and follows the threefold division [i.e. the three different kinds of division] which that book admits or contains.[132] The first division is that whereby the whole work is divided into *cantiche*, and there are three of these. The second is that whereby each *cantica* is divided into cantos. For the first *cantica* is divided into thirty-four cantos; the second, into thirty-three; and the third, into the same number. So, the whole work contains one hundred cantos. The third division is that whereby each

---

[129] Cf. the 'six points' discussed in *Epist. Can Gr.* 6 (tr. above). Guido has assimilated them to the scheme of the four causes.

[130] Cf. ibid. 8 (tr. above).

[131] Cf. ibid.

[132] With this discussion of *forma tractatus* cf. ibid. 9; Guido's version is altogether more detailed and comprehensive.

canto is divided into rhymed lines (*rithimos*). The rhymed line is a grouping of verses whose ends are joined to each other and they are grouped harmoniously with similar-sounding syllables. This is one of the three sweetest [types of] sounds which give the most pleasure and soothe the mind of the hearer, and has its origin in music, which has three parts, harmony, *rithmus*, and metre, as blessed Isidore says in the third book of the *Etymologies*.[133] As far as the present work is concerned there are three kinds of rhymed verses. The first is that in which the line contains only ten syllables, while the last syllable is long and accented, as D'ABEL SU' FILLIO ET QUELLA DI NOE [*Inf.* iv. 56],[134] or again ABRAHAM PATRIARCA ET DAVID RE [*Inf.* iv. 58],[135] or ET CON RACHELE, PER CUI TANTO FE [*Inf.* iv. 60],[136] likewise in the third *cantica* OSANNA SANCTUS DEUS SABAOTH [*Par.* vii. 1].[137] For all these lines only admit ten syllables. The second kind is that in which the line has twelve syllables. Its penultimate syllable is short, as CH'ERA RONCHIOSO, STRETTO ET MALAGEVOLE [*Inf.* xxiv. 62];[138] or PARLANDO ANDAVA PER NON PARER FIEVOLE [*Inf.* xxiv. 64];[139] also A PAROLE FORMAR DISCONVENEVOLE [*Inf.* xxiv. 66].[140] The third kind is that in which the line has eleven syllables. Its penultimate syllable is long, as common usage shows, thus NEL MEZZO DEL CAMMIN DI NOSTRA VITA [*Inf.* i. 1].[141] Note also, Lucano Spinola, to whom I dedicate this commentary, that the lines of the first sort should rhyme on only one syllable or letter, that is, on the last. But the second sort should rhyme on three syllables, that is, on the penultimates and the last, and the third sort on two syllables, that is, the last two syllables, as is very clearly shown in the text. And thus the form of the treatment is clear.

The form or mode of treatment is poetic, fictional, descriptive, digressive, and transumptive, and moreover employs definitions, is divisive, makes use of proofs and disproofs, and includes exemplary stories.[142] So it is clear what the mode of treatment is.

Concerning the third question, that is, the activating cause, note that the moving cause (*agens*) or author of this book is Dante. Dante was a Florentine, of an old, noble stock, descended from those famous Romans who founded the city of Florence after the destruction of Fiesole. He was a man distinguished by his noble character and one who derived strength to a notable degree from his mastery of many branches of knowledge, and particularly the skills of poetry. For he brought back[143] dead poetry from

---

[133] *Ety.* III. xviii.
[134] 'of Abel his son, and that of Noah'.
[135] 'Abraham the patriarch and David the king'.
[136] 'And with Rachel, for whom he did so much'.
[137] 'Hosanna, holy God of Sabaoth'.
[138] 'which was rugged, narrow and difficult'.
[139] 'I talked as I went, so as not to seem exhausted'.
[140] 'ill-suited for forming words'.
[141] 'Midway in the journey of our life'.
[142] Identical with the description of the *forma sive modus tractandi* in *Epist. Can Gr.* 9.
[143] Cf. *Purg.* i. 7ff.: 'But here let dead poetry rise again . . .'.

the darkness of the grave, and in this imitated Boethius, who in his time revived dead philosophy.

Concerning the fourth question, that is, the final cause, note that the author composed this work principally to this end, though many other ends may be attributed to it. His principal intention is to remove the living from their miserable condition,[144] by [persuading them] to abandon their sins, which is why he composed the *Inferno*; to lead them back to virtue, which is why he composed the *Purgatorio*; so that in this way he may lead them to glory, and that is why he composed the *Paradiso*. Three other objectives can be attributed to this work. The first is that men may learn how to converse in a polished and well-ordered way. For no other mortal can be compared with Dante in the magnificence of his style (*lingua*). In truth he can repeat the words of the prophet: 'God has given me a skilled tongue' [Isa. 50: 4], and: 'My tongue is the pen of a scribe writing quickly' [Ps. 44: 2]. For he was the pen of the Holy Spirit, and with this pen the Holy Spirit has swiftly described for our benefit the punishments of the damned and the glory of the blessed.[145] For the Holy Spirit Himself, speaking through Dante's mouth, has openly condemned the crimes of prelates and kings and the princes of this world. His second objective is to bring to light again[146] the works of the poets which had been completely abandoned and consigned to oblivion, but in which there are many teachings useful and necessary for living a good life. For without these we cannot arrive at any real knowledge of his *Comedy*. The third objective is to condemn, by providing exemplary stories, the wicked life of evil men, and especially of prelates and princes, and, by the examples he gives, to commend on many counts the life of good and virtuous men. So, it is clear what the final cause of this work is.

Concerning the fifth question, that is, under what category of philosophy that *Comedy* falls, note that it is moral philosophy, or ethics, for the whole and the part have been made up and created not to aid speculation but for a practical end (*ad opus*). Even though in a particular section or passage the treatment is that employed by speculative philosophy, this is not principally there for the sake of the speculation, but for a practical end. For, as the Philosopher [i.e. Aristotle] says in the second book of the *Metaphysics*: 'And even now practical thinkers speculate on occasion for some specific purpose.'[147] So it is clear under what category of philosophy that most profound *Comedy* is included.

Concerning the sixth and last question, that is, the title, note that the

[144] Cf. *Epist. Can Gr.* 15.

[145] This statement is tantamount to claiming that Dante was, in some measure, divinely inspired or at least divinely assisted. Cf. the similar descriptions of biblical authors cit. by Minnis, *Authorship*, pp. 37–8, 99, and see further his account of John Gower's appropriation of aspects of such vocabulary in his *Vox clamantis*, ibid., pp. 168–77 (esp. p. 170).

[146] Literally 'renew', 'give men a fresh knowledge of'. Cf. above, n. 143.

[147] See above, n. 92.

title of this book is: *Here begins the most profound and most sublime Comedy by Dante, that most excellent poet.* Now, this *Comedy* is divided into three *cantiche*: the first is called *Inferno*, the second *Purgatorio*, the third *Paradiso.* It is called 'most profound' because it treats of the inhabitants of the underworld, and 'most sublime' because it treats of the dwellers in the heavenly places. It is called a comedy because at the beginning it inspires fear but at the end gives pleasure. To make this point more clearly and more convincingly, Lucano, I would have you know that there are four kinds of poet, each of which has its own particular art (*scientia*).

Some are called lyric poets, and they include in their works all kinds of song, and they are so called from the Greek *a potulirin*, that is, from the variety of their songs. Hence the name of the lyre, for the lyre has strings of varying lengths. David employed this sort of song in writing the Psalter. Hence Arator, a cardinal of the holy Roman Church, writing on the Acts of the Apostles, says: 'The Psalter is made up of lyric feet.'[148] Some are called satirical poets because they are replete with every sort of wit, or else from 'fullness' (*saturitas*) or abundance.[149] For they discuss many subjects at one and the same time, and are called satiric poets or satirists, from a branch of poetry (*scientia poetica*) which is called *satyra*, as a gloss on Persius says: '*Satyra* is a sumptuous table filled with every sort of produce which used to be offered to Venus in the course of a sacrifice.'[150] For this reason that second genre of poetic narrative is called *satyra* because it is full of criticism of vice and commendation of virtue. Or else, *satyra* is so called from Satyrus, a woodland god. For satyrs are creatures which have a human shape from the navel up, but below the navel they have the shape of a goat. They have two horns on their head and a curved nose. Satyrs are capricious and nimble creatures, naked and shameless and mockers of all men. That genre of poetry is nimble because it leaps quickly from vice to virtue and from virtue to vice. It is naked and shameless because it openly criticizes vices. It is given to mocking because it derides the wicked.

Some poets are called tragedians, and their art is called tragedy. Tragedy is a narrative in poetic form, which to begin with is admirable and pleasing but at the end or conclusion is stinking and inspires fear, and for this reason it gets its name from *tragos*, that is, 'a goat', and *oda*, that is, 'a song'. So, tragedy is, so to speak, 'a goat-like song', that is to say, it stinks like a goat, as is clear from Seneca's tragedies.[151] Or, as the

---

[148] Arator, *Epistola ad Vigilium*, 24 (PL lxviii. 80 A).

[149] Cf. Isidore, *Ety.* viii. vii. 8.

[150] According to F. Torraca, *Rassegna critica della letteratura italiana*, xxiii (1918), 105–7, this gloss, and much of the following discussion, is indebted to the Persius commentary of Paolo da Perugia (d. 1348). This suggestion was dismissed by Jenaro-MacLennan, *The Trecento Commentaries*, pp. 23 ff., who stresses the traditional nature of the material. Cf. the medieval literary theory of satire discussed and illustrated in Ch. IV.

[151] Cf. *Epist. Can Gr.* 10, and above, n. 86.

blessed Isidore says in the eighth book of the *Etymologies*: 'Tragedians are so called because a goat was the prize for those singing the introductory ode,[152] the Greek word for goat being *tragos*.'[153] So Horace says: 'Who vied with each other in tragic song with a worthless goat as prize.'[154]

Some poets are called comedians, and their art is comedy. Comedy is a narration in poetic form which at the beginning portrays the harsh reality of some miserable condition, but its material has a happy ending, as one can see from Terence's comedies. This book [i.e. the *Comedy*] is called a comedy because at the beginning it narrates and describes harsh circumstances, which inspire fear, for it treats of the punishments of hell. But at the end its subject is pleasant and enjoyable, for it treats of the joys of paradise.[155]

Among the lyric poets Boethius and Simonides hold the first place; among the satirists Horace and Persius; among the tragedians Homer and Virgil; and among the comedians Plautus and Terence. Dante can be called not only a comic writer because of his *Comedy* but also a lyric poet because of the wide range of his rhymed lines (*rithimos*) and their exquisitely sweet and mellifluous sound. He can also be called a satirist on account of his criticism of the vices and commendation of the virtues, and a tragedian because he relates the impressive deeds of distinguished personages. This [combination of roles] is expressed by the two verses of his epitaph, which I have written in his memory: 'Here lies the outstanding comic poet Dante, who was equally a satirist, lyricist and tragedian.' That explains the title of the book.

Now that the six questions which must be asked in any work designed to teach[156] have been explained, it must be understood that this *Comedy* contains four senses, just like the science of theology. For poetry has this in common with theology, that both sciences can be expounded in four ways. Indeed, the teachers of the past have given poetry a place within theology. For St Augustine writes in the seventh book of his *City of God* that Marcus Varro stated that there were three kinds of theology: fabulous theology, which the poets use; natural theology, which philosophers use; and civil theology, which peoples use.[157]

The first understanding or sense which the *Comedy* contains is called the historic sense; the second, the allegorical; the third, the tropological; and the fourth and last, the anagogical.[158] The first understanding is the historical. That interpretation does not extend beyond the literal meaning; as when we understand Minos [only] as being the judge and assessor of hell, who judges the souls who go down into it. The second

---

[152] Lat. 'initia canentibus', presumably referring to the *parodos* of a Greek play.
[153] Isidore, *Ety.* VIII. vii. 5.   [154] *Ars poetica*, 220.
[155] Cf. *Epist. Can Gr.* 10.   [156] Cf. *Epist. Can Gr.* 6, and above, n. 129.
[157] Actually *De civ. Dei*, VI. v. Cf. our discussion above, pp. 325, 389–90.
[158] Here the 'allegory of the theologians' (see pp. 382–5) is being applied in the interpretation of the *Comedy*.

understanding is allegorical, and by this I mean that the literal text or history signifies something by the bark and something else by the pith. According to that allegorical understanding Minos is taken as a figure of divine justice. The third understanding is tropological or moral, by which I learn how I ought to judge myself. According to that understanding, Minos is taken as a figure of human reason, which ought to rule the whole man, or else the nagging conscience, which has the job of correcting misdeeds. The fourth and last understanding is the anagogical, which must give me hope of being duly rewarded for my past actions. According to that understanding, Minos is taken as a figure of hope, and through its intercession we must expect punishment for our sins and [heavenly] glory as a reward for our virtues.

As regards the characters (*personae*) which Dante places there [i.e. in the *Inferno*], you must understand this. We must not believe that they are there in reality, but rather see them as being so many examples. For, when Dante treats of some vice, in order that we may better understand it he introduces a character who was full of that vice as an example.

Having considered all these points, let us now proceed to some sort of exposition of the text. This *Comedy*, as has been said, is divided into three *cantiche*; the first being called the *Inferno*; the second, the *Purgatorio*; and the third, the *Paradiso*. But first, let us deal with the first *cantica*, which is entitled: *Here begins the first cantica.*

PIETRO ALIGHIERI

Commentary on Dante's *Comedy*: Prologue and Exposition of the *Inferno*, chapter [*sic*] 5[159]

PROLOGUE

For a very long time men have tried with their pens to open up for the benefit of readers the meaning of the poem called the *Comedy*, written by my dearest father Dante Alighieri of Florence, which is very much enclosed and hidden beneath a protective outer covering (*integumentum*).

In my judgement they have as yet been only partly, not totally, successful in this. Following them, and not because I have any confidence in my own expertise but fired by zeal born of filial affection, I too will now try to see if, in some small degree, I can further unlock the poem's secrets by means of a commentary. I am encouraged in this by Seneca's words to Lucilius: 'It is never otiose to repeat what is not adequately expressed.'[160]

---

[159] Translated from *Il 'Commentarium' di Pietro Alighieri*, ed. R. della Vedova and M. T. Silvotti (Florence, 1978), pp. 1–18, 107–21, with the permission of Leo S. Olschki Editore.

[160] Seneca, *Epist. mor.* xxvii. 9; here Pietro read the inferior variant *dicitur* in his text of Seneca. However, there are many occasions when Pietro's reader has to cope with his mis-

Perhaps eventually another will come who, using this work of mine as a support, will 'carry the book on his shoulder', as is said in Job 31[: 36], where the *Gloss* says this by way of explanation: 'To carry a book on one's shoulder is to succeed in explaining a passage of writing.'[161] So, to help me in undertaking this work of opening up the book's secrets, may I have that key which belongs to the One who, as is written in Rev. 3[: 7], 'opens the book that has been sealed, and no one closes it, closes it and no one opens it', namely our Lord Jesus Christ; and may I likewise have the gracious help of his mother, the glorious Virgin.

Macrobius, having in mind to expound *The Dream of Scipio*, says this in a preface prior to commencing the work itself: 'I must, therefore, make a few preliminary remarks concerning this book, so that the purpose of the work of which I am speaking may become clear.'[162] I wish to follow his example, and so, before I come to the actual exposition of the poem, I have prefaced it with a foreword, and in it to some extent will touch upon the writer's intention (*mens*), that is, the ultimate cause (*summa causa*) of his work, in order to give the reader clearer knowledge of it and make him more familiar with it. For the Philosopher [i.e. Aristotle] says at the beginning of his *Physics*: 'For we think that we really know something only when we know its prime causes',[163] and in the second book he says: 'We must consider, in the matter of causes, what they are and how many. This work has been undertaken in order to gain knowledge. But we do not think that we really know anything before we learn why each thing is, and this is to learn the prime cause of all things.'[164] But the same philosopher says the following in the aforesaid second book of the *Physics*: 'The end purpose is the most powerful of all causes.'[165] So, I will begin with the final cause (*finalis causa*) of the aforesaid book, which embraces all the other causes.

For the final cause moves the efficient cause of the work, according to the requirements of that objective, while the efficient cause moves the

quotations. John Bowden, *Pietro Alighieri's Commentary*, pp. 27–8, writing about the mistakes in the first version of Pietro's commentary, complains that 'at times either he or the copyist goes astray. The errors are various: phrases and sentences are repeated or omitted; there are wrong attributions and manuscript blunders.' However, he does not appreciate that at least some of these errors are due to the fact that Pietro was taking quotations from *florilegia* and earlier commentaries, as was common practice among medieval commentators (including the most learned of them). Caricato, 'Il *Commentarium*', has demonstrated that Pietro used Gratian's *Decretum* as a *florilegium* of patristic authorities; he also notes his debt to the standard commentaries on canon law, civil law, and the Bible. The situation has been made worse by the errors in the edition of Vedova–Silvotti, on which see G. Frasso in *Aevum*, liv (1980), 381–3.

[161] Cf. *Glossa ordinaria marginalis*, Iob 31: 36 (*Bib. glos.* iii. 298), where, however, it is Holy Scripture that is being referred to. On Pietro's use of biblical exegesis see Caricato, art. cit., pp. 127, 147–50.

[162] *In somn. Scip.* i. i. 3–4 (ed. Willis, p. 2).

[163] *Phys.* i. 1 (184ᵃ12–13).

[164] Ibid. ii. 3 (194ᵇ16–20).

[165] Cf. ibid. (195ᵃ24–5). Pietro's text is particularly inaccurate here.

subject-matter and its aim is to find a suitable form in choosing that subject-matter. Thus, the objective exists in the agent's intention before all those other things which relate to that objective, and is, so to speak, the motivating cause for them. Thus, the final cause of the *Comedy* will be the objective towards which Dante aims in writing. This is, to show, from the actual results of men's actions, what men ought to do in this world or what they should avoid; and in what human goodness consists (as the Philosopher says in the first book of the *Ethics*),[166] by setting out and showing his readers the punishments which the wicked justly suffer in this world and in the next, and the rewards which the virtuous can be seen to reap in both worlds. Through seeing these, men who are virtuous in this world may be confirmed in their blessed condition, and the wicked may be separated from their wicked state. As Horace says in his *Satires*: 'Good men hate to commit crimes out of sheer love of virtue. But you will avoid crime through fear of punishment.'[167]

The efficient cause of this work is Dante, the author mentioned above. The material cause consists of the subjects just mentioned which the author sets about describing poetically by means of an allegorical fiction, treating the three kinds of life that human beings lead through the analogues and figures of hell, purgatory, and paradise. The Philosopher has this to say about these three kinds of life in the first book of the *Ethics*: 'There are three kinds of life which particularly stand out: the life of pleasure (*voluptuosa*)', and Dante will deal with this, as being a kind of hell; 'also civic life', or political and active life, and Dante will deal with this as being purgatory; 'also the contemplative life',[168] and Dante will deal with this as being paradise, in the allegorical sense.

The formal cause is twofold, the form of the treatise (*forma tractatus*) and the form of the treatment (*forma tractandi*). The form of the treatise is the combination of the parts of the volume of the aforesaid *Comedia*. But the form of the treatment is the mode of writing (*modus scribendi*) which the author intends to maintain, and this is manifold. For sometimes what he writes will have to be understood solely according to the literal sense, without any mystical understanding, as is the case with those who write fabulous stories or an historical account. For fable (*fabula*), which is so called from 'saying' (*fando*) and speaking in accordance with an invented subject, is different from history, which is defined as an account of an actual event, by means of which information can be given about past events, as Isidore says at the end of the first book of his *Etymologies*.[169] Hence, on this same subject Augustine says, in book xvi, ch. 2 of *The City*

---

[166] Cf. *Eth. Nicomach.* i. 4 (1095ᵃ18–20), i. 7 (1097ᵃ30–4), etc.
[167] Horace, *Epist.* I. xvi. 52–3.
[168] Cf. Aristotle, *Eth. Nicomach.* i. 5 (1095ᵇ17–19). Pietro is using the translation of Robert Grosseteste: *Aristoteles Latinus*, xxvi/1–3, fasc. 4 (Leiden and Brussels, 1973), p. 378.
[169] Isidore, *Ety.* I. xli. 1.

of God: 'Not all events which are recounted are to be thought of as signifying other things, but are woven into the history for the sake of those events which do have such significance. For the earth is turned over only by the ploughshare, but all the other parts of the plough are necessary so that this can be accomplished.'[170]

In the same way, this same author [i.e. Dante], in this poem of his, will describe some things through the medium of literary figures and embellishments of various sorts, used to give an attractive appearance to his work, so that serious ideas may be enlivened by light touches, in the way that other poets do. Thus, Isidore says in his *Etymologies*: 'It is a mark of poets that they transform events which really happened, and give them a quite different aspect by employing figures which refer to them indirectly, and which serve to make them more impressive, interspersing them with figments or fictions in poetic style.'[171] For fiction (*fictio*) is defined as follows: 'Fiction is the assumption that there is truth in a matter in which indubitably exists the direct opposite of the truth [i.e. falsity]'; hence 'the word "poet" (*poeta*) is derived from *poio*, *pois*, which is the same as "I invent, you invent"', according to Papias.[172] And indeed Horace, in his *Art of Poetry*, tells us that this is exactly what poets do, when he says there: 'Let those things which are invented to please be close to the truth. The poet must not demand that every fable he tells shall be believed.'[173] 'He who has mingled the useful with the pleasing wins all the applause by delighting and educating the reader simultaneously. For poets wish to edify or to delight.'[174] Likewise, the same author [i.e. Dante] writes much that is to be understood allegorically. Allegory is defined as a kind of transference of language (*alieniloquium*) to give a different meaning, as when a text says one thing and must be taken to mean something else.[175] For instance, the Apostle [i.e. St Paul], writing to the Galatians, in chapter three[176] says: 'For it is written that Abraham had two sons: the one by a bondwoman and the other by a free woman. But he who was of the bondwoman was born according to the flesh: but he of the free woman was by promise' [4: 22–3]; and this is all by way of allegory. For these two sons are the two Testaments, the Old and the New.

This allegory, seen as the genus, includes within itself as species anagogy, from which proceeds the spiritual sense, and tropology, from which proceeds the moral understanding. In the well-known words: 'The literal interpretation teaches you what happened, the allegorical teaches what you must believe, the moral what you must do, the anagogical what you must hope for.' This is what moved brother Bonaventure of

---

[170] *De civ. Dei*, XVI. ii.　　　　　　　　[171] Isidore, *Ety*. VIII. vii. 10.
[172] Papias, *Vocabularium*, s.v. *poeta* (Venice, 1491), unfol.
[173] *Ars poetica*, 388–9.　　　　　　　　[174] Ibid. 343–4.
[175] Cf. Isidore, *Ety*. I. xxxvii. 22.
[176] *Sic* for chapter four: correct in second recension (passage not in first).

Bagnoreto to say in his *Breviloquium*: 'Holy Scripture has depth, which consists in its having numerous mystical meanings. For besides its literal meaning in many places it can be interpreted in three ways, allegorically, morally, and anagogically.'[177] Likewise, Gregory in the first book of his *Moralia*, writing on this same subject, says: 'We go through some passages quickly, taking account of the historical sense alone, and we use allegory to examine some carefully by means of a figuratively based investigation. Some we go through, using only the instruments of morality expressed in allegorical terms, while we subject some passages to a more thorough investigation and—using all these means at one and the same time—we pursue our researches on three fronts. But sometimes we do not trouble to expound obvious, historical accounts lest we become obscure. Sometimes too these cannot be understood in a literal sense because, if understood only on a superficial level, they do not instruct the readers but lead them astray.'[178] I shall observe all of this completely from here on in this commentary of mine, as I shall show as my work proceeds.

Having concluded these preliminary remarks, let us now come to the title of this book, the *Comedy*, which must appear in the following form in this its first rubric: *Here begins the Comedy of Dante Alighieri and his first book in which he treats of the descent to hell.* The first question which arises concerning this is why the author called this poem of his a comedy. To understand this one should recall that in the ancient world, as Isidore says, among all the other genres of poetic song was one called comedy, when a poet sang, that is, produced his poems, and these were concerned with the deeds of private and humble individuals, written in an unassuming style. Plautus, Accius, Terence, and the other comic poets are examples. Tragedy is another genre of poetic song, when something is described in the lofty style and the subject is, for the most part, the sorrowful deeds of kings.[179] But sometimes comedy too adopts the lofty style, and so Horace, in his *Art of Poetry*, says: 'But sometimes comedy too raises its voice, and angry Chremes argues with bombastic utterance',[180] where the gloss has this to say on the above word[s] 'comedy raises': 'as Terence does in his comedy, saying "O heaven, O earth, O sea, realm of Neptune", [and] "O almighty Jupiter", etc.'[181] And with this in mind, the same Horace adds in praise of such a comic style, 'Old comedy succeeded to these forms, not without much praise.'[182] Likewise, it should be noted that, as Hugutio writes: 'Comedy begins with sad events but ends with pleasant ones, but the opposite is the case with tragedy. So, in greetings it is our custom to

---

[177] Bonaventure, *Breviloquium*, pr. 4 (tr. above, pp. 233–4; cf. also p. 267 and n. 194).
[178] Gregory, *Moralia in Iob*, 'Epist. ad Leand.' 3 (CCSL cxliii. 4).
[179] Cf. Isidore, *Ety.* viii. vii.   [180] *Ars poetica*, 93–4.
[181] Gloss on *Ars poetica*, 93: see *Scholia Horatiana quae feruntur Acronis et Porphyrionis*, ed. F. Pauly (Prague, 1858–9), ii. 461; *Pseudoacronis scholia in Horatium vetustiora*, ed. O. Keller (Leipzig, 1902–4), ii. 325. The Terence references are to *Adelphoe*, 790 and 196 respectively.
[182] *Ars poetica*, 281–2.

send our wishes for a beginning like that of a tragedy and an end like that of a comedy',[183] that is, a good, joyful beginning and likewise a good, joyful end. Therefore, with an eye to his design in writing, our author wishes and intends to write in a poetic form about the deeds of private persons in a style that is, in the main, lowly, that is, in the vernacular, his mother tongue, and also partly in a high and elevated style, when writing of heavenly things, as he does in his last book, the *Paradiso*,[184] and to begin with a sad subject (that is, the life of the underworld) and end with a joyful one (that is, things heavenly), and this he does.[185] With this in view, I believe that he finishes each book of his *Comedy* with the final words IN THE STARS as he does, so that he may end on a joyous and splendid note. So, quite rightly he called his poem a comedy.

Secondly, let us come to the other part of the said title, in which the author says that he will treat of the descent to the inferno in mystical terms. In respect of this it seems to me that two questions have to be asked. First of all, where is the actual inferno in real terms? Second, how does he say he descended into it? Because it was this author's intention to treat of the inferno in mystical terms, that is, to discuss the allegorical inferno as well as the real one, let us discuss the existence of both these forms of inferno. Despite the fact that pagan writers, particularly Platonic philosophers and the poets, have said that the real inferno was situated beneath the moon, the truth is that it is in the bowels of the earth with its demons and damned spirits. This is clearly shown by Holy Scripture. In the fourteenth[186] chapter of St Matthew, Our Lord, replying to the Jews, says: 'No sign will be given you but the sign of Jonah the prophet' [16: 4]. Just as he was in the whale's belly for three days and three nights, so the Son of Man will be in the heart of the earth for three days and three nights, that is, in the part of the inferno called Limbo. Its existence is also clearly proved by Augustine. In his book of *Retractions* he is correcting what he had said in his commentary on Genesis, chapter twelve, namely that the punishments of the inferno were to be interpreted as the images of a vision, and that the inferno was an imaginary place rather than a physical one. He says: 'As regards the infernal regions, it seems to me that I should have taught that they exist under the earth, rather than giving reasons why they are believed and said to exist under the earth, as if this were not an actual fact.'[187] It is proved by Virgil also, when he says in book vi [of the *Aeneid*]: 'Then Tartarus itself gapes sheer down and stretches to that shadowy gloom, through twice the space that one looks upward to the etherial seat of celestial Olympus.'[188] But the inferno—the inferno which

[183] See above, n. 85.
[184] In the Latin this sentence has no main verb; 'wishes' and 'intends', here translated as if they are main verbs, are in fact present participles.
[185] Cf. *Epist. Can Gr.* 10, and Guido da Pisa's prologue, tr. above, pp. 474, 475.
[186] *Sic* for sixteenth; same error in red. II (passage not in red. I).
[187] *Retractationes*, ii. xxiv (CCSL lvii. 110). [188] *Aeneid*, vi. 577-9.

exists in this world, to think in allegorical terms—is the actual situation of the wicked, which torments them: providing that one can suppose that there is [in this world] any infernal place.

One descends to the aforesaid first (that is, real and actual) hell in three ways. First of all, in reality (*veraciter*), when the evil soul leaves the body and goes down to hell to receive its due punishment for all eternity; also, in a fictitious and imaginary way, and it is in this way that our author must be said to have gone down to it;[189] also, as a result of necromancy, when someone by holding converse [with the dead] and by means of superstitious and profane sacrifices goes down to hear the [oracular] responses of the said demons. This is what Virgil describes Aeneas as doing in the aforementioned sixth book of the *Aeneid*.[190]

According to one understanding, one goes down to the aforesaid allegorical inferno in two ways: in one way by reason of virtue, and in another way by reason of vice. The descent is made by reason of virtue when, through contemplation, someone lowers himself in order to obtain knowledge of earthly things as to a kind of inferno, so that, having recognized the temporal nature and mutability of such earthly things, he may scorn them and serve his Creator. This has prompted our poets to speak concerning the acquisition of such knowledge, for example to say that a man called Hercules went down into the inferno, and Orpheus and the above-mentioned Aeneas. According to another understanding, they say that Theseus and Pirithous and some others went down to the inferno and came back from there since they were virtuous men, and were not ensnared by worldly pleasure, and that our author was among that number, with the help of Virgil, as is shown in the commentary on the following chapter.

Likewise, the descent to this inferno is made by reason of vice. For some lower themselves to the aforesaid knowledge [of earthly things] but to no good effect, for they are incapable of remaining steadfast in their good purpose[191] and of withdrawing themselves from that state [of earthly knowledge],[192] and they remain there as in a kind of inferno. This is what is said to have happened to Dirce [*sic*], wife of the Orpheus mentioned

---

[189] Here, according to R. Hollander, 'Pietro nervously attempts to assure the jittery reader that his father did not really think he had been in the Empyrean . . . but only feigns to have been there' ('Dante *Theologus-Poeta*', p. 117). See further Ch. IX, n. 50. Hollander's own view of Dante's purpose is that he 'creates a fiction which he pretends to consider not to be literally fictitious, while at the same time contriving to share the knowledge with us that it is precisely fictional' (ibid., p. 119).

[190] With this and the following account of the ways of descending into hell cf. the 'Bernard Silvester' commentary on the *Aeneid*: see Ch. IV, n. 159.

[191] i.e. the purpose of getting to know worldly things in order to scorn them and serve the Creator. Cf. above, pp. 120–1, 320, 332–6 (on the descent of Orpheus).

[192] Here something is definitely wrong with the Latin text as edited, 'et ab eius statu attrahentium': the genitive 'attrahentium' does not fit into the syntax. We translate as if the text read 'se trahentes', which seems to give the desired meaning.

above, and to Castor. The psalmist was referring to these two mystical hells implicitly and explicitly when he said: 'Let death come upon them and let them go down alive into hell' [Ps. 54: 16]. The *Gloss* at this point says: 'that is, into the abyss of worldly desire'.[193] Elsewhere the psalmist says: 'Since your mercy is great, O Lord, and you have delivered my soul from the lower pit of hell' [85: 13]. Solomon says in Proverbs [15: 24]: 'A path of life shown to the wise, that he may turn aside from the lowest pit of hell.'

Finally, let us divide this first book into its principal parts, and so that he may echo the words of Virgil in book vi—'they block it when made, and the hideous marsh with its dreary waters binds them, and Styx, encircling them with its nine coils, holds them prisoner'[194]—the author divides the book into nine parts. Or perhaps his intention is that, just as the blissful, celestial realm is divided into nine heavens and nine regions and orders of angels, so the miserable realm of the inferno may also be divided up into nine regions and orders of evil angels, so that the two opposing realms should each have the same system of government.

For in the first part, having prefaced [the work] with introductory pre-liminaries, he speaks of the first circle of the inferno, or of the book, and this first part lasts until the fifth chapter. There the second part begins in which he speaks of the punishment of the voluptuaries. This lasts until the sixth chapter. There the third part begins, in which he talks of the punishment of the gluttonous. This lasts until the seventh chapter. There the fourth part begins, in which he speaks of the punishment of the avaricious and the prodigal, and this lasts until the end of the seventh chapter, with the words WE CROSSED THE CIRCLE TO THE OUTER EDGE [vii. 100]. There the fifth part begins, in which he speaks of the marsh of Styx, in which he imagines are the souls of the hot-tempered, the slothful, the envious, and the proud, and this lasts up to the end of the ninth chapter, with the words WE ENTERED IT WITHOUT ANY STRIFE [ix. 106]. There the sixth part begins, in which he speaks of the punishment of heretics, and this lasts up to the twelfth chapter. There the seventh part begins, in which he speaks of the punishment of the violent, who are punished in three circles in different ways, and this lasts until the seventeenth chapter. There the eighth part begins, in which he begins to speak of the punishment of the fraudulent, who are punished in ten ditches,[195] and this lasts until the thirty-first chapter. There the ninth and last part begins, in which he speaks of the punishment of the treacherous, and this continues until the end of the

---

[193] *Gl. ord. interlin.*, Ps. 54: 16 (*Bib. glos.* iii. 827–8). *Pace* Caricato, art. cit., p. 50, there is no need to posit the influence of Peter Lombard's Psalter commentary at this point; it is merely incorporating the interlinear gloss 'in voraginem terrenae cupiditatis' to which we refer here.

[194] *Aeneid*, vi. 438–9, but for 'fas obstat', 'divine law forbids', Pietro in red. III reads 'facto obstant'; red. II has 'fata obstant', red. I begins the quotation at 'novies'.

[195] Lat. 'in decem bulgiis', the ten concentric *bolge* ('pouches' or 'ditches') that constitute the eighth circle of hell. Cf. *Inf.* xviii. 1 ff.

book. Having concluded these preliminary remarks let us now come to the text.

ON THE FIFTH CHAPTER OF THE *INFERNO*

THUS I DESCENDED FROM THE FIRST CIRCLE [v. 1]. In this fifth chapter the author does two things in particular. First of all, he sets out his introduction, as far as the line NOW THE DOLEFUL NOTES BEGIN [25]. There he begins to treat of souls who have been condemned for the sins of the flesh in the form of lust, and this lasts until the end of this chapter. Let us, then, proceed to explain that first, preliminary and introductory, section, in the following way.

The author first of all had spoken of the first circle in the inferno, or limbo, in which he placed for punishment the souls of infants and children and the others referred to in the previous chapter, whose punishment consisted not in a feeling of pain but rather a sense of loss, because they had not sinned by act and consent. Now, in this chapter [i.e. canto v], coming to treat of the condemned souls of those who had sinned by act and by consent, such as the licentious and others of whom he will speak presently, who suffer punishment which takes the form of a feeling of pain together with a sense of loss, he imagines that at the entrance of the second circle of hell he comes upon Minos in his role as judge of the underworld, snarling, trying and judging cases and consigning the condemned souls to their appropriate punishments, as this text says. Here he is following Virgil to the letter, for he [i.e. Virgil] depicts the fugitive Aeneas descending from the aforesaid first circle of hell (in which he too located for punishment the souls of infants and of others who had sinned albeit not by personal consent) down to the second circle of hell. There Aeneas finds this same Minos placed there to perform this same function. As Virgil says in book vi: 'Hard by these are those condemned to death by false accusation. Yet even these dwellings are not assigned without lot or judgement. Minos is the judge, and he shakes the urn. He summons a council of the silent ones and learns of their lives and the charges made against them.'[196] In terms of the allegorical outer covering (*integumentum*), Virgil and our author both use Minos as a type and figure of the human conscience, and rightly so. For no sin which involves an act can be committed without the conscience nagging [the sinner]. So Paul, in Rom. 14[: 23], says: 'Everything which does not proceed from faith', that is, everything which is done against conscience, 'is a sin. For faith is absent where there is no consciousness of any sin.' This is why the author feigns the aforesaid Minos as snarling, that is, grinding his teeth and roaring. Isaiah has something to say relevant to this in his final chapter [66: 24]: 'their worm will not die', where the *Gloss*, expounding, says: 'the worm,

---

[196] *Aeneid*, vi. 430–3.

that is, the gnawing of conscience'.[197] For, as Gregory says in the first book of the *Moralia*: 'Guilt for an act committed and a feeling of guiltlessness in the heart cannot coexist at one and the same time.'[198]

First, in saying that the aforesaid Minos examines like a judge in this entrance to hell, our author points out how in this world, conscience, by investigating our good and evil works, forces us to confess mentally what should be done or not done. Hence Origen: 'Conscience is the corrector of the spirit and the pedagogue of the soul, which is thereby separated out from evil and adheres to good';[199] and Seneca, in a letter to Lucilius, has this to say about conscience: 'It sits among us as a hallowed spirit, observing and guarding good [things] and evil [things].'[200] St John Damascene says: 'Conscience is our judge and law.'[201] Second, in feigning the said Minos as sitting in judgement, he touches on the fact that the accusation of conscience comes first,[202] because it rises as an opposition to ourselves, within ourselves, when we have sinned. So Augustine, writing to make this point to Secundus the Manichee, says: 'Think whatever you like about Augustine, my conscience alone will not accuse me in the eyes of the Lord',[203] because the witness of his conscience had gone before him. St Paul writes about this in Rom. 2[: 15]: 'who offend against the work of the law written in their hearts, as their conscience bears witness against them'. Third, he judges us by passing sentence of condemnation. So Ambrose, in a certain sermon, says this: 'conscience always convicts and judges the guilty possessor of that conscience silently and without contradiction'.[204] Juvenal speaks to the same purpose: 'This is the first punishment, that no one who is guilty is ever absolved at the bar of his own conscience (*se iudice*), even though the verdict of a praetor squared by bribery has won the day.'[205] Finally, in that he says that the aforesaid Minos (still with the same [allegorical] significance) despatches souls according as he

---

[197] Cf. *Gl. ord. marg. et interlin*, Isa. 56: 24 (*Bib. glos.* iv. 537).

[198] Apparently based on a statement in the *Moralia* in which Gregory says that 'one that is involved in great sins can never, when burthened with his own, discharge another's score; he then is shown to be clear in his own case, who could obtain for others their clearance from guilt'. *Moral. in Iob*, pr. iii. 8 (PL lxxv. 520); tr. J. H. Parker, *Morals on the Book of Job by St Gregory the Great* (Oxford, 1844–50), i. 21.

[199] Origen's commentary on St Paul's Epistle to the Romans, II. ix, as tr. by Rufinus (PG xiv. 893). [200] Seneca, *Epist. mor.* xli. 2.

[201] Cf. *Expositio fidei*, ch. xcv, l. 9 (ed. K. Kotter, *Die Schriften des Johannes von Damaskos*, ii (Patristische Texte und Studien XII, Berlin and New York, 1973), p. 222).

[202] i.e. conscience is always there in one's mind to register a protest at a wrong action. The Latin text is corrupt.

[203] Augustine, *Contra Secundinum Manichaeum* I (CSEL xxv. 905). However, as Caricato points out, Pietro almost certainly took this from Gratian's *Decretum*, which he used as a *florilegium* of patristic quotations. Cf. *Decretum*, pars II, Causa xi, qu. 3, cap. 51, ed. A. Friedberg, *Decretum Magistri Gratiani* (Corpus Iuris Canonici, I, Leipzig, 1879), col. 657.

[204] Pseudo-Ambrose, *Serm.* lii (PL xvii. 710B).

[205] Juvenal, *Sat.* XIII. 2–4.

entwines his tail around himself,[206] the author is addressing himself to the execution of the judgement of the aforesaid conscience, which takes place in the tail, that is, in the final part of our life, in which it leads evil-doers who have forgotten God to hell, to the punishment which they have earned. So Horace, in the *Satires*, says: 'Let there be a rule at hand for inflicting appropriate punishments on sins',[207] as if he were adopting conscience as such a rule. David too was thinking of this when he spoke, as a sinner gnawed by conscience: 'Turn, O Lord, and rescue my soul. Save me for thy mercy's sake. For in death there is no one who is mindful of thee, and who will confess to thee in hell?' [Ps. 6: 6]. Also relevant to this are the remarks of a gloss on the text of Revelation [9: 10], 'And they had tails like scorpions', namely: 'This must be related to the fact that everlasting death is the end of carnal desires, or to the way in which their sins draw all men towards death.'[208] Or else, when the author speaks of the tail of the aforesaid Minos in these terms, he is referring to the execution of judgement which is to come at the end of the world. As we find written in the *Decretum*: 'no one will accuse any-one else, for then, as the Apostle says, all tongues will cease, but every man will be accused only by his conscience' [1 Cor. 13: 8].[209]

Having cleared up these points, let us now come to the second part of this chapter, in which the author begins to treat of the seven principal sins of incontinence and the souls condemned in hell for indulging those sins. First of all he begins to speak here of the sin of carnal lust. He imagines that the souls of those who in this world MADE THEIR REASON SUBJECT TO THE APPETITES OF THE FLESH [*Inf.* v. 39] are punished in a fierce wind in that second circle of hell. Hence Augustine says: 'Our reason is totally engulfed by wantonness',[210] and the *Gloss* on [1] Cor. 6[: 18], 'The fornicator sins in his own body', says of such people: 'In this sin the soul is subordinated to the body.'[211] For in performing the act of fornication, the whole man is so absorbed by the flesh that his mind cannot any longer be said to be his, but the man as a whole can be called 'flesh'. This enslavement of reason happens in any form of inter-

---

[206] Cf. *Inf.* v. 4–5, 11–12. Minos wraps his tail around himself as many times as the number of the level down to which the damned soul is to be sent.

[207] Horace, *Sat.* 1. iii. 117–18.

[208] Not found in the *Glossa ordinaria* on either Rev. 9: 10 or 9: 19. Pietro appears to be using a different commentary on that biblical book: cf. below, n. 239. Neither Caricato nor we have been able to identify this source.

[209] As Caricato has pointed out, art. cit., p. 133, this is taken not from the *Decretum* itself but the standard commentary thereon as revised by Bartholomew of Brescia: *Decretum Gratiani emendatum et notationibus illustratum una cum glossis* (Venice, 1591), i. 239 (on dist. L, c. 29). By contrast, the apparently vague reference below to the enslavement of reason in extramarital intercourse is in fact a specific allusion to the *Decretum*, pars II, Causa xxxvi, qu. 1, c. 2 (ed. Friedberg, cols. 1288–89).

[210] Cf. *Serm.* lxxii (PL xxxviii. 887). Here as with other vague source-references which follow, Pietro appears to be using a *florilegium* of classical authorities.

[211] *Gl. ord. interlin.*, 1 Cor. 6: 18 (*Bib. glos.* vi. 241–2).

course except that between husband and wife, according to canon law. Our author imagines himself as finding there suffering the aforesaid punishment, among the other souls, the soul of Queen Semiramis, wife of Ninus, the former king of Babylon. On his death she was so fired with lust that she plotted to lie with her son Ninias. She decreed that everyone should be permitted to do whatever lustful act gave him pleasure and gratification, as this author [i.e. Dante] says.[212] Orosius has this to say on the matter: 'Semiramis, fired by lust, contrived that it should be lawful for her to commit fornication with anyone.'[213] As Ovid remarks: 'Jupiter decreed that whatsoever pleased him should be lawful, and the sister's marriage to a brother made everything lawful.'[214] Also [Dante depicts there] the soul of Dido who, according to Virgil's fiction, killed herself through love of Aeneas, who was deserting her and with whom she had lain, and broken the oath of chastity she had sworn over the ashes of her husband Sychaeus, who had been killed by Pygmalion, Dido's own brother. In respect of this, Virgil says in book four, speaking in the person of the said Dido: 'I was not allowed, unmarried, to pass my life free of crime like some wild animal, and thus avoid cares such as these. The vows I made to the ashes of Sychaeus have not been kept.'[215] Jerome, writing to Jovinianus, says that Dido remained chaste in her widowhood and killed herself because Iarbas, king of the Mussitani, wanted to make her his wife by force.[216] Likewise [Dante depicts there] the soul of Cleopatra, the daughter of Lagus, king of Egypt, who for a long time had fornicated with Caesar; likewise Helen, wife of King Menelaus. She abandoned him and fornicated with Paris, son of Priam. This was the reason why her husband, mentioned above [i.e. Menelaus], along with the other Greeks, besieged Troy for ten years and six months. Our author touches on this here, when he talks about SUCH A LONG TIME OF EVIL ROLLING ON BECAUSE OF HER [*Inf.* v. 64–5].

Likewise, [Dante depicts there] the shade of Achilles, son of Peleus, WHO AT THE END STRUGGLED WITH LOVE [66] as he says here in the text. At this point the author wishes to allude to the story we read about Achilles. This is that, after Hector's death by Achilles' hand, the Greeks made a truce with the Trojans so firm that the Trojans came into the Greek camp and the Greeks into Troy. Now, it happened at that time that Hecuba, the wife of Priam and mother of the said Hector, had gone outside the walls of Troy with Polyxena, her daughter, and other Trojan ladies, to perform funeral rites before the door of the said Hector's house. Achilles was so enamoured of the said Polyxena that he asked for her in marriage. The said Hecuba promised to do this if he would get the Greek army to depart from Troy. This the said

---

[212] Cf. *Inf.* v. 55–7.

[213] Orosius, *Historiae adversum paganos*, i. 4 (CSEL v. 44).

[214] Ovid, *Heroides* iv. 133–4. (Ovid has 'facit', present, and so does Pietro in red. I; corrupted to 'fecit' in red. II and red. III).

[215] *Aeneid*, iv. 550–2.

[216] Jerome, *Epist.* cxxiii, 7 (CSEL lvi. 80).

Achilles was unable to do, and he and his people with him left the said army in indignation. Nevertheless, the said Hecuba, mindful of her son Hector's death, with a view to avenging this, arranged (through negotiations conducted by her son Paris) that the aforesaid Achilles should come on a fixed day to a temple of Apollo, near Troy, to fulfil[217] the aforesaid marriage. Achilles came to the said temple, and on entering was treacherously attacked by the said Paris and many other Trojans. Achilles, fighting but unable to resist them, dragged himself to the statue of the said Apollo, where he was killed by an arrow from the said Paris. Hence Virgil, in the *Aeneid*, book vi, addressing Apollo himself in the person of Aeneas, has this to say about the affair: 'Phoebus, you who have always taken pity on the travails of Troy, who guided the weapon and hand of Paris against the son of Aeacus [i.e. Achilles] . . .'.[218]

Likewise, the author feigns himself finding there the shade of the aforesaid Paris, and of Tristan, and of the lady Francesca, daughter of the Lord Guido de Polenta, sometime lord of Ravenna, a city set by the sea on the shores of the Adriatic, where the Po, along with the tributaries which have joined it, enters that sea, as the text here says. She was the wife of Gianciotto de Malatesta of Rimini. There too was the shade of Paolo, brother of the said Gianciotto. This lady Francesca and the aforesaid Paolo, being thus related, were found together in adultery, and were killed by her aforesaid husband. At this point, so that the author may for our moral edification show us what we ought to avoid, lest we be ensnared by that lustful and wanton form of love, he introduces the shade of the said lady Francesca to relate how the said Paolo was captivated by the beauty of her person, following the promptings of his noble heart. For such love as this more readily arises in a noble breast than in a plebeian one, because of the delicacy of the food which nobles eat and the opportunities for leisure, that is, the leisure of such lovely creatures and the men who pursue them.[219] Hence, Jerome says: 'it is hard to retain one's chastity in the midst of feasting',[220] and St Bernard: 'Chastity is at risk when surrounded by rich living, even though it attacks both.'[221] Jerome also says: 'That same lust rules even when one lives by a temperate regime and wears rags.'[222] There are also the words of Ovid: 'One asks why Aegisthus became an adulterer. It is not hard to

---

[217] It is the completion of the marriage contract that is meant here, not the consummation in sexual terms.

[218] *Aeneid*, vi. 56–8; on Achilles' murder see e.g. Servius on *Aen.* vi. 57, cf. Dares, xxvii, xxx, xxxiv, who is close to Pietro.

[219] Pietro appears to be saying that noblemen are more prone to wanton love because they eat elaborate meals consisting of delicate dishes, and also because they have the leisure for loving, which the lower classes lack.

[220] Jerome, *Ep.* cxvii. 6 (CSEL lv. 420).

[221] Cf. Bernard, *De conversione ad clericos*, xxi. 37 (ed. Leclercq *et al.* iv. 113).

[222] Jerome, *Ep.* lxxix. 10 (CSEL lv. 99): 'in serico et pannis eadem libido dominatur'. For Jerome's 'serico' (silk) Pietro gives 'sicco' (dry, temperate).

see the cause. He had time on his hands',[223] and: 'if you remove leisure then Cupid's bow loses its power'.[224] Consequently, as the lady Francesca herself says, the very nature of this sort of love forced her to love the aforesaid Paolo. For, as Augustine says in *On the Instruction of the Young*, 'Nothing encourages someone to love you more than if you love him first',[225] and Seneca, in the ninth letter to Lucilius, says: 'I will show you a love-philtre without potions and herbs. Do you really want to be loved? Then love.'[226]

Likewise, the same lady Francesca tells how she and Paolo, from seeing each other, graduated to conversation which 'kindles as a fire', as is said in Ecclus. 9[: 11]. Then they proceeded to kissing, and this too was accompanied by gazing at each other and conversation. Touching came after kissing. Each of these individual acts gradually brings on the sequence of events which characterizes this wicked lust, as Cicero says in his *Topics*.[227] She adds that they were particularly led on by reading a book about the deeds of the [knights of the] Round Table, in the part where we read that Gallehault,[228] because of his love for Lancelot, caused a certain lady (whose motives were malice towards the queen or love for Gallehault), to bring Queen Guinevere to a garden where briefly and secretly the said Lancelot, her lover, kissed her. So, the shade of the said lady Francesca says finally that, just as the said Gallehault was the go-between who arranged that kiss, so the book and he who wrote it (that is, composed it) was (or were) the instigation of their kissing. So our author shows that men should avoid reading such books for the above reason. Thus, Isidore, in his *Book of Sentences*, says: 'The Christian is forbidden to read the figments of the poets and other writers, and similar books, because by the allure they offer they incite the mind too much to lust.'[229]

Having made these comments on the letter of the text, let us now come to deal with the allegory, which can be deduced in the matter contained in this chapter and earlier. It will be easy to extract this allegory if we accept this premiss, that the devil is the cause of the sin

---

[223] Ovid, *Remedia amoris*, 161.   [224] Ibid. 139.

[225] *De catechizandis rudibus*, iv. 7(2) (CCSL xlvi. 127). This passage is quoted out of context: Augustine is describing God's love for mankind which, having shown itself to us in Christ's sacrifice, encourages us to reciprocate. According to his editors, Pietro wrote not 'catechizandis' but 'cauterizandis'!

[226] Seneca, *Epist. mor.* ix. 6.

[227] Not found in Cicero's *Topics*. This misattribution arose from Pietro's misreading, or misremembering, of a passage in a civil law commentary, i.e. the gloss of Accursius on the *Digestum novum*: see Caricato, art. cit., p. 146.

[228] Not to be confused with Galahad: Gallehault was one of the characters in the Old French *Lancelot du Lac*. Lancelot confided his love for Guinevere to him, and Gallehault arranged for the two to meet; in the course of this meeting Lancelot, on Gallehault's urging, kissed the queen, and so began their illicit affair. See P. Toynbee, 'Dante and the Lancelot Romance', in id., *Dante Studies and Researches*, pp. 1–37.

[229] Isidore, *Liber sententiarum*, iii. xiii (PL lxxxiii. 185 A).

and vice of lust; that is, the impulse to lustful love is born of the devil. He is called Abadon in Hebrew, Appolion in Greek, Exterminans in Latin; by Job he is called the Leviathan [Job 41: 4], and by the poets, Cupid.

First, he is described as being blind by Virgil, who says: '[nothing conserves the strength of animals as much as] debarring love and the blinding goads of passion',[230] and Horace, in his *Satires*, says of this sort of love: 'changeable and inconstant, at the mercy of blind Fate'.[231] It is given this characteristic because it blinds us in this world in the matter of our gazing upon women, and conversely is not seeing what it is we are doing, and what is the object of our desire. Hence, in Gen. 3[: 6], where the text reads: 'The woman saw [that the tree was good to eat]', the *Gloss* says: 'it is not lawful to gaze upon that which it is not lawful to desire'.[232] Otherwise we should become blind, as Shechem, the son of Hamor, was blinded. He, having seen his mistress, fell in love with her and ravished her, as is stated in Gen. 34[: 1–3]. Likewise David, who, seeing Bathsheba washing, was fired with passion for her, and took her, and had her husband Uriah killed [2 Kgs. 11]. Likewise, Amnon, David's son, upon seeing Tamar, his beautiful sister, defiled her, as we read in 2 Kgs. [13]. Reuben committed the same crime with his father's wife, as we read in the second-last chapter of Genesis [49: 4]. This[233] moved Job to say, in the twenty-fourth chapter [24: 15]: 'The eye of the adulterer observeth darkness', and in the thirty-first chapter [31: 1]: 'I made a covenant with my eyes.' The *Gloss*, expounding this, says 'He "made a covenant, etc." lest he should incautiously gaze upon that which he would subsequently love against his will.'[234] One could add to these passages the words of Ennodius: 'Love attacks that which is mighty and makes no distinction where there is uncertainty [as to what is right and what is wrong].'[235] Note briefly also the view expressed by the author when, in describing the punishment of the souls of such lovers as these, he feigns that he is entering a place deprived of all light.

Secondly, he describes the aforesaid demon [i.e. Cupid], or rather that emotion born of the devil, in winged form. Thus, Virgil says in the first book of the *Aeneid*: 'Love obeys the orders of his dear mother, and puts on his wings.'[236] Isidore says: 'Cupid, the demon of fornication, is depicted winged because nothing is more light-minded than lovers.'[237] And this is why our author feigns that the souls of such lovers are punished in this way in a howling gale, like birds flying, named thus in a simile.[238] His purpose is

---

[230] *Georgics*, iii. 210.   [231] *Sat.* II. iii. 269.
[232] *Gl. ord. marg.*, Gen. 3: 6 (*Bib. glos.* i. 92).   [233] Presumably 'this sin', i.e. lust.
[234] *Gl. ord. marg.*, Job 31: 1 (*Bib. glos.* iii. 291).
[235] Source untraced.   [236] *Aeneid*, i. 689–90.   [237] Isidore, *Ety.* VIII. xi. 80.
[238] Literally 'named here by way of comparison', presumably referring to Dante's phrase 'And as their wings bear the starlings along in the cold season, in wide, dense flocks, so does that blast the sinful spirits . . .' (*Inf.* v. 40–2).

to allude to the condition of such people in this world under cover of allegory. For their state is one of perpetual motion and revolution, as can easily be understood. The gloss on Revelation, at the point where John is treating of soldiers who are as locusts, 'And the voice of their wings is as the voice of chariots' [Rev. 9: 9], is relevant here: 'The mention of wings refers to the speed which lovers of this sort exhibit in flitting about.'[239] Ovid says on this point: 'The lover's mind is assailed by innumerable artifices, just as a stone is pummelled about from every quarter by the sea-surge.'[240] Horace, in his *Satires*, says: 'In love there are these troubles: war, peace renewed. If someone were [to try to give an account of] these things which change just like the weather. . . .'[241] It is for this reason also that Virgil, speaking in allegorical terms, has imagined in the sixth book of the *Aeneid* that Aeneas found the souls of the said lovers being tormented in hell in a similar gale. He says this: 'Here hidden paths conceal those whom harsh love has gnawed with its cruel wasting',[242] and adds further on: 'So souls are schooled by the punishments they endure, and pay retribution for crimes committed long since. Some are hung, stretched out to the insubstantial winds.'[243]

Thirdly, he [i.e. Cupid] is described as an archer shooting arrows, as I mentioned briefly earlier, in my quotation from Ovid, because he pierces the heart of the lover with various thoughts. With an eye to this, Jerome says: 'The fiery sword is a kind of woman who shoots forth her arrows from every direction',[244] which is referred to in Prov. 7[: 23, 26]: 'Until the arrow pierces his liver', and 'and wounded many', and also in S. of S. 5 [*sic*]: 'You have wounded me, sister, with one of your eyes' [4: 9]. Hence Walter, defining this sort of love, says: 'Love is an innate passion which results from the sight of, and unrestrained dwelling upon, the beauty of a member of the other sex, the result of which is that a person wishes above all things to enjoy the other's embraces.'[245] This is why our author also feigns at this point that the said souls are tormented by the aforesaid wind, as is said in the text. That must suffice for this chapter.

---

[239] Not found in *Gl. ord.*, Rev. 9: 9. Cf. above, n. 208.

[240] *Remedia amoris*, 691–2.

[241] *Sat.* II. iii. 267–9.

[242] *Aeneid*, vi. 442.

[243] Ibid. vi. 739–41.

[244] Source untraced.

[245] Andreas Capellanus, *De arte honeste amandi*, I. i, ed. P. G. Walsh, *Andreas Capellanus on Love* (London, 1982), p. 32. Curiously, Pietro attributes this statement to Walter, the addressee of Andreas' treatise. On the reception of this work, including its popularity in Italy, see the excellent article by B. Roy, 'A la recherche des lecteurs médiévaux du *De amore* d'André le Chapelain', *University of Ottawa Quarterly*, lv/1 (1985), 45–73.

GIOVANNI BOCCACCIO

Short Treatise in Praise of Dante: Extract[246]

⟨128⟩[247] The earliest people of ancient times, although unpolished and unsophisticated, were none the less intensely desirous of knowing the truth through study, a desire which is still, as we see, natural to us all.[248] Observing the heavens to move continually to a fixed law, and observing earthly things to adhere to a certain order and to function differently at different times, these people thought that there must, by necessity, be something from which all these things proceeded and by which all other things were ordered, a superior power empowered only by itself.[249] And having diligently turned this over in their minds, they imagined that that power (which they called 'divinity' or 'deity') should be venerated with every form of worship, with every honour and with superhuman service. ⟨129⟩ And so, by way of reverencing the name of this supreme power, they devised huge and impressive houses. These they thought it appropriate to distinguish by name (as they were distinguished in form) from those houses that were generally inhabited by men; and so they called them 'temples'. And similarly, they considered there to be a need for ministers. These should be holy men, far removed from any worldly preoccupation, dedicated exclusively to divine services. Revered more than other men on account of their maturity, their age, and their way of life, these were called 'priests'. And beyond this, in representation (*rappresentamento*) of the imagined divine essence, they made, in various forms, magnificent statues. And in the service of that divine essence they made golden vessels and marble tables and purple vestments and many other appurtenances appropriate to the sacrifices that they had established. ⟨130⟩ And so that tribute to such a power should not be paid in a silent or near-muted way, it seemed to them that the power should be mollified with words heightened in both meaning and music (*parole d'alto suono*) and thereby be rendered sympathetic to their needs. And because they believed this power to surpass all else in nobility they wished to find words far removed from every plebeian or public style of speech, words worthy of being spoken before the deity in which they might offer the deity sacred blandishments (*sacrate lusinghe*). ⟨131⟩ And furthermore, in order that

---

[246] Tr. by David Wallace from the *Trattatello in laude di Dante*, red. I, ed. P. G. Ricci in Boccaccio, *Opere*, iii. 469–81 (paras. 128–74), with the permission of Arnoldo Mondadori Editore.

[247] The style and substance of paras. 128–31 is substantially indebted to Petrarch, *Fam.* x. 4 (tr. above pp. 413–15), which in its turn is indebted to Isidore, *Ety.* viii. vii. 1–3.

[248] Cf. Aristotle, *Meta.* i. 1 (980ᵃ1), etc.

[249] 'superiore potenzia de niuna altra potenziata'. Dante discusses the concept of an unmoved first mover in *Il Convivio*, iii. ii. 4; vi. 11; vii. 2 (ed. Simonelli, pp. 75, 90, 91). On each occasion he refers to the *De causis*, on which see above, n. 100.

these words should appear to have greater efficacy, they required them to be composed following the law of fixed rhythms (*certi numeri*), through which a certain sweetness might be experienced and regret and annoyance be driven away. And it was, of course, appropriate that this be done not in a popular or familiar form of speech, but in an artificial and exquisite and new one. The Greeks called this form 'poetic' (*poetes*); from this it came to pass that whatever was fashioned in this form was called 'poetry' (*poesis*); and those who fashioned it or employed such a mode of speech were called 'poets'.

⟨132⟩ This, then, was the origin of the name of poetry, and consequently of poets; and although others may assign different explanations, perhaps good ones, this one pleases me the most.[250]

⟨133⟩ This good and praiseworthy intention of the unpolished age induced many men to employ various devices to multiply the number of gods and so to win a place for themselves in the pantheon.[251] So whereas the earliest writers paid tribute to a single deity, their successors maintained that there were many of them, although they said that the one which had been adored first enjoyed, above all others, principal place. They insisted that these many deities were the sun, the moon, Saturn, Jove, and all the other seven planets, arguing for their deity by pointing to the effects of their planetary influence. And they expanded these arguments to show everything useful to men, however mundane, to be a deity: such as fire, water, earth, and suchlike. To all these, verses and tributes and sacrifices were appointed. ⟨134⟩ And then later on various people in various places began (some with one piece of ingenuity, some with another) to make themselves masters of the uneducated multitudes of their districts. They decided their primitive disputes not in accordance with written law, which they did not yet possess, but in accordance with a certain natural equity, in which some were better versed than others. Being more enlightened by nature, they endowed their lives and their habits with orderliness. They resisted whatever adverse things might come along with physical force. And they called themselves 'kings', and appeared before the people with both slaves and ornaments,[252] things unheard of among men before this time. And they commanded obedience

---

[250] Boccaccio records an alternative derivation for the name of poetry in *Genealogia deorum gentilium*, xiv. vii (tr. above, p. 421) but rejects it in favour of the derivation adopted in the *Trattatello*.

[251] 'mosse molti a diverse invenzioni nel mondo multiplicante per apparere'. Our translation of this difficult passage is indebted to Ricci's gloss (p. 884 n. 581).

[252] 'ornamenti'. Ornaments differentiate rulers from the ruled, and poets from plain speakers (see para. 153, 'ornata eloquenzia'). Boccaccio explores the complex interdependency of rulers and poets with considerable subtlety in the paragraphs which follow. For further illustration of the social functions of 'parola ornata' and 'la lingua adorna' see *Inf.* ii. 67–9, *Inf.* xviii. 91–3; Brunetto Latini, *Tesoretto*, 1610–12 (ed. and tr. J. B. Holloway (New York and London, 1981), pp. 82–3); Latini, *Rettorica*, in *La prosa del Duecento*, ed. C. Segre and M. Marti (Milan and Naples, 1959), p. 134.

and, ultimately, adoration. And provided that there was someone willing to make the attempt, all this was achieved without too much trouble: for to the commoners who observed them, such people seemed to be not men, but gods. ⟨135⟩ Such people, unwilling to trust too far in their own innate powers, began to stoke up religious sentiment and to use the resultant faith to frighten their subjects, and to secure by oaths the obedience of those that they would not have been able to constrain by force. And in addition to this they took pains to deify their fathers, their grandfathers, and their ancestors so that they might be the more feared and revered by the populace. ⟨136⟩ These things they could not accomplish satisfactorily without the collaboration of poets, who in order to amplify their own fame, to please the princes, to delight the princes' subjects, and to urge virtuous behaviour upon everyone (an appeal which would have had an opposite effect if framed in plain language) employed various and masterly fictions (little understood by dimwits today, let alone by the dimwits of that period), thereby causing to be believed that which the princes wished to be believed. Both for the new gods and for the men who imagined themselves to be descended from gods, the poets employed that same style that the first people had reserved for the true God alone, and for his praise. ⟨137⟩ From this the feats of brave men came to be compared with those of gods; and this originated the practice of singing the battles and other notable doings of men in sublime verse, mixing them in with those of the gods. Such was, and still is, the office and business of every poet. But since many people, through misunderstanding, believe poetry to be nothing more than just a fantastic form of speech (*un fabuloso parlare*), it pleases me to go briefly beyond my proposed subject-matter in order to demonstrate that poetry is theology.[253] I will then proceed to explain why poets are crowned with laurel.

⟨138⟩ If we choose to focus our minds and to scrutinize the problem rationally we shall, I believe, readily perceive that the ancient poets have, as far as human ingenuity will allow, followed in the footsteps of the Holy Spirit. As we see in Holy Scripture, the Holy Spirit revealed its most exalted secrets to future generations through many mouths, causing them to speak under a veil of many things which it intended, in due course, to reveal, unveiled, through historical actions. ⟨139⟩ And if we look closely at the works of poets, we discover that they too (being unwilling, as imitators, to appear to differ from the model they imitated)[254] described, under the cover of certain fictions, that which had happened, or which was then happening in their own time, or which they desired or expected to happen in the future. The holy and the secular writings do not, then,

---

[253] Many of the arguments in the digression which follows (138–55) are taken further in *Geneal. deor. gent.* XIV: see esp. chs. ix–x, tr. in Ch. IX.

[254] As Ricci explains, p. 885 n. 600, 'lo imitatore' here represents poetic composition, and 'lo imitato' Holy Scripture, dictated by the Holy Spirit.

have a common end (*fine*) in view: but they do share a common mode of treatment (*modo del trattare*), and it is this which most exercises my mind at present. As Gregory the Great has argued, the same praise may be given to both kinds of writing.[255] ⟨140⟩ Gregory says of Holy Scripture that which may also be said of poetry, namely, that in a single discourse (*sermone*), by narrating (*narrando*), it discloses both the text and the mystery which underlies it. And thus at a single moment it tests out the wise at the one level and reassures the ingenuous at the other; it makes public that by which little children may be nourished, and conserves in private that by which it may keep the minds of the loftiest of thinkers rapt in admiration. Thus it appears to be, if I may speak in this fashion, like a river, broad and deep, in which the little lamb may paddle, and the great elephant freely swim. But let us move on and verify these statements.

⟨141⟩ Holy Scripture—which we call 'theology'—sometimes employs the images of a story, sometimes the import of a vision, sometimes the meaning of a lament (and many other means besides) to reveal to us the high mystery of the incarnation of the divine Word; His life; the things which occurred at His death; His victorious resurrection; His admirable ascension, and all His other actions. Taught in this way, we may come to that glory (long closed off to us through the fault of the first man) which He (through dying and rising again) opened up for us. ⟨142⟩ Poets, similarly, in their works—which we call 'poetry'—sometimes employ fictions featuring various gods, sometimes transmutations of men into various forms, and sometimes gentle, graceful persuasions (*leggiadre persuasioni*) to reveal to us the causes of things, the effects of virtues and of vices and what we ought to flee from and what pursue. They do this to show how we may, by behaving virtuously, achieve that end (*fine*) which they, not knowing the true God aright, believed to be the supreme salvation. ⟨143⟩ The Holy Spirit wished to reveal in the green bush—in which Moses saw God in the semblance of a burning flame [Exod. 3: 2]—that the virginity of her who was purer than any other creature, and was to be the habitation and refuge of the Lord of nature, was not to be spoilt by the conception or birth of the Word of the Father. Through the vision, seen by Nebuchadnezzar [Dan. 2: 31–5], of a statue of many metals knocked down by a rock (which in turn became a mountain), the Spirit wished to reveal that all past ages were to be laid low by the doctrine of Christ, who

---

[255] The passage which follows (140) sees Boccaccio translating closely from Gregory the Great, *Moralia in Iob*, 'Epist. ad Leand.' iv (CCSL cxliii. 5–6). The first Italian translation of Gregory's work was undertaken by Boccaccio's childhood friend and lifelong correspondent Zanobi da Strada between 1353 and 1355, the period in which the first version of the *Trattatello* was completed: see Georg Dufner, *Die 'Moralia' Gregors des Großen in ihren italienischen Volgarizzamenti* (Padua, 1958), pp. 16–20. Dufner states that Boccaccio's translation from Gregory seems to be independent of Zanobi's inelegant rendering of the same passage (pp. 145–6). Boccaccio quotes from the Latin text of this same passage in *Esposizioni*, I. ii. 22 (ed. Padoan, p. 58). Cf. also Pietro Alighieri's use of Gregory's prefatory epistle, tr. above, p. 480.

was and is the living rock; and the Christian religion, born of this rock [1 Pet. 2: 4], was to become immovable and ever-enduring, just as we see the mountains to be. Through the lamentations of Jeremiah the Spirit wished to proclaim the future destruction of Jerusalem.[256]

⟨144⟩ In similar fashion our poets, imagining (*fingendo*) Saturn to have many children (of whom he devoured all but four) wished to make us perceive nothing else through such fiction but that Saturn stands for time, within which everything comes into being; and just as everything is produced in time, so too does time destroy all things, and reduces all things to nothing.[257] The four children not devoured by him are, firstly, Jove, that is, the element of fire; the second is Juno, spouse and sister of Jove, that is, air, the medium through which fire works its effects down here; the third is Neptune, god of the sea, that is, the element of water; and the fourth and last is Pluto, god of hell, that is, earth, which is lower than any other element.

⟨145⟩ Similarly, our poets imagine Hercules to have been transformed from a man into a god, and Lycaon into a wolf.[258] At the moral level (*moralmente*) they wish to show us that by behaving virtuously (as Hercules did) man becomes a god by participating in heaven. And by behaving viciously (as Lycaon did) man, however manlike he may appear to be, may truly be described as a beast. Everyone recognizes such bestiality in qualities which amount to defects in manhood: and so Lycaon, because of his rapaciousness and avarice (qualities which are characteristic of a wolf), is imagined as being transformed into a wolf. ⟨146⟩ Similarly, our poets imagine the beauty of the Elysian Fields, which I take to mean the sweetness of Paradise; and the darkness of Dis (*Dite*), which I take to mean the bitterness of hell. They do this so that we, attracted by the pleasure of the former and terrified by the anguish of the latter, may follow the virtues that will lead us to Elysium and flee from the vices that would hurl us down to Dis. I will refrain from expounding these things with more specific instances, since although they should be made as lucid as is fitting and feasible (and in becoming more attractive would strengthen my argument) I fear that they would drag me far further than the main subject requires or than I wish to go. ⟨147⟩ And certainly, if no more were said than that which has been said, that should enable us to understand that theology and poetry agree in their form of treatment (*forma dell operare*). But as regards subject-matter, I maintain that they are not just very different from one another, but are to some extent mutually opposed: for the subject of sacred theology is divine truth, whereas that of ancient

---

[256] The Book of Jeremiah prophesies, and then describes, the destruction of Jerusalem by Nebuchadnezzar King of Babylon in 587 BC. The prophecy is here taken to refer to the destruction of the city in AD 70.

[257] Derived from Fulgentius, *Mit.* i. 3–5 (tr. Whitbread, pp. 49–51).

[258] Cf. Ovid, *Metamorphoses*, ix. 239–72, i. 199–243. See further the account of 'transformations' trans. above, pp. 127–8.

poetry is the gods and men of the pagan world.[259] ⟨148⟩ They are mutually opposed in that theology presupposes nothing unless it be true; poetry supposes certain things to be true which are totally false and erroneous and contrary to the Christian religion. ⟨149⟩ But since certain madmen rise up against the poets, accusing them of having composed disgusting and evil fables consonant with no truth and arguing that they should exercise their abilities and offer their teachings to worldly people in a form other than that of fables, I wish to continue a little further with this current line of reasoning.

⟨150⟩ Such critics, then, should consider the visions of Daniel, those of Isaiah, those of Ezekiel, and those other Old Testament visions; traced by a divine pen, these were revealed by Him for whom there was no beginning, nor will there be an end. Let them further consider the visions of the evangelist[260] in the New Testament; these are full of wonderful truths for those who understand them. And if it be conceded that no poetic fable may be found that is, at its literal level (nella corteccia),[261] as far removed from truth or verisimilitude as these visions appear to be in many parts, let it also be conceded that poets alone have written fables that are incapable of yielding either pleasure (diletto) or profit (frutto). ⟨151⟩ I could move on without saying anything about the censure that they pass on poets for having revealed their doctrine in, or under, fables; for I recognize that through such mad censure of the poets they rashly fall into blaming that Spirit, who is nothing other than the way, life, and truth: but I do, none the less, intend to satisfy them somewhat.

⟨152⟩ It is manifestly obvious that every thing acquired with labour contains somewhat more sweetness than that which comes without effort. The simple truth, since it is readily comprehended with little exertion, delights us and passes into the memory.[262] And so to ensure that that which is acquired with labour should prove more pleasing, and should therefore be more carefully preserved, the poets concealed simple truth beneath many things which are apparently in opposition to it. And so they wrote fables, whose meaning was more covert than apparent, so that the

---

[259] Para. 147 draws upon Fam. x. 4, the Petrarchan letter utilized in paras. 128–31. Cf. above, n. 247.

[260] i.e. St John the Evangelist, here falsely identified (as was common practice in the Middle Ages) with the author of Revelation. Cf. above, p. 432.

[261] Boccaccio relies here upon his readers' familiarity with the traditional representation of the relationship of inner truth to outer form as that of a fruit or nut to its shell, chaff, or rind (corteccia); cf. Ch. VI, n. 23. The comparison is developed more explicitly in para. 153. See also Esposizioni, I. ii. 22 (ed. Padoan, p. 58), where Boccaccio speaks of the 'corteccia litterale' of the Comedy.

[262] Boccaccio's argument in the first part of this paragraph seems to owe something to Petrarch's celebrated Coronation Oration, delivered at Rome on 8 Apr. 1341. For an English translation of this Latin text, see E. H. Wilkins, 'Petrarch's Coronation Oration', PMLA lxviii (1953), 1241–50, reprinted with minor alterations in id., Studies in the Life and Works of Petrarch (Cambridge, Mass., 1953), pp. 300–13.

beauty of fables would attract those whom neither philosophical demonstrations nor persuasions could have drawn in. ⟨153⟩ What, then, are we to say about poets? Are we to maintain that they were men of no understanding (*uomini insensati*), as these present madmen (*disensati*)—speaking and not knowing what they are speaking about—judge them to have been? Certainly not. In their actions they were, rather, men of the most profound understanding (which is concealed in the fruit) and of the most excellent and highly wrought eloquence (which is apparent in the rind and the leaves). But let us return to the point where we left off.[263]

⟨154⟩ I say that theology and poetry can be spoken of almost as one and the same thing, when they share the same subject. Indeed, I will say even more: that theology is nothing other than a poetry of God.[264] And what else but poetic fiction is it to say in Scripture that Christ is now a lion, and now a lamb, and now a serpent, and now a dragon and now a rock? And Christ is described under many other names; it would take far too long to list them all.[265] What else do the words of the Saviour in the gospel amount to, if not a discourse that is at variance with its outward sense (*uno sermone da' sensi alieno*)? This manner of speaking we call, to use a more common word, 'allegory'. It is readily apparent, then, not only that poetry is theology, but that theology is, in addition, poetry. ⟨155⟩ And I shall certainly not be disturbed if my words on so great a subject merit little credence: but at least believe Aristotle, a most worthy spokesman on every great subject, who affirms that he himself found the poets were the first theologians.[266] And let this suffice for this part; and let us turn to show why the honour of the laurel crown was, among men of learning,[267] granted exclusively to the poets.

⟨156⟩ Among the many nations that dwell on the face of the earth, the Greeks, it is believed, were those to whom philosophy first opened herself and her secrets. From her treasures the Greeks carried away military doctrine, political life, and many other precious things. Through these things they became more famous and respected than any other nation. Among the other things which they drew from this treasury of philosophy was the most sacred maxim of Solon which is placed at the beginning of this little work.[268] And in order that their republic, which was then flourishing more

---

[263] See para. 146: 'I will refrain from expounding....'

[264] Cf. once again Petrarch's *Fam.* x. 4 (see above, nn. 247 and 259), tr. in Ch. IX.

[265] Such names are listed and discussed at considerable length in Isidore, *Ety.* vii. ii.1–49, and see also the Dionysian theories concerning the 'divine names', discussed and illustrated in Ch. V.

[266] Aristotle, *Meta.* i. 3 (983ᵇ), and cf. our discussion above, pp. 210 and 389–90.

[267] 'tra gli scienziati'. The *Ottimo commento*, a Florentine commentary on the *Comedy* dating from the 1330s, explains the term 'poeta' (as it occurs within the context of *Inf.* l. 73) as 'scienzato della scienzia di poesia': see Ricci, p. 886 n. 642, and F. Mazzoni, 'Ottimo commento', *ED* iv. 220–2.

[268] The opening period of the *Trattatello* is as follows: 'Solon, whose breast was reputed to be a human temple of divine wisdom, and whose most holy laws are still a clear testimony of

than any other, might walk upright and stand upright upon both feet, they ordained and implemented, in magnificent fashion, rewards for the deserving and penalties for malefactors. ⟨157⟩ But of all the rewards established by them for those who performed well, this was the highest: publicly, and with public consent, to crown with laurel the poets after the victory of their labours, and the emperors on having victoriously augmented the power of the republic; for they judged that as much glory should be given to him through whose virtue things human were preserved and augmented as to him by whom things divine were described. ⟨158⟩ And although the Greeks were the inventors of this honour, it later passed to the Latins when glory and arms gave way, throughout the world, to the Roman name. And this custom survives at Rome to this day, at least in the coronation of poets, although this happens extremely rarely.[269] But it ought not to prove too tedious to enquire why the laurel, rather than any other leaf, should be chosen for such a coronation.

⟨159⟩ There are some people who, since they know that Daphne (who was changed into a laurel) was loved by Phoebus (who was both the first author and patron of poets as well as a triumphant combatant), believe that Phoebus was moved by his love for those leaves to crown both his lyres and his triumphs with laurel.[270] And this example, they believe, was taken up by men; and so it follows that that which was first performed by Phoebus is the cause of such coronation and such leaves, bestowed on poets and emperors down to the present day. And this explanation certainly does not displease me; nor do I deny that it could have happened like that. But I am, none the less, moved by a different line of reasoning, which goes like this.[271] ⟨160⟩ The laurel, according to those

ancient justice for present-day men, was often moved to say (so some people report) that every republic, like every person, walks or stands upon two feet. With mature and weighty reasoning, he declares the right foot to be the refusal to allow any fault committed to go unpunished, and the left to be the rewarding of every good deed. He adds that if either of these said feet were taken away by vice or negligence, or if they were to function less than adequately, then the republic in question could only, without doubt, just hobble along; and if, by ill chance, it should be diseased in both feet it will almost certainly prove incapable of standing upright, or anything like upright.' Solon, born c. 638 BC, was a celebrated Athenian legislator and one of the Seven Sages of Greece. See *Convivio*, III. xi. 4 (ed. Simonelli, p. 106); *Par.* viii. 124.

[269] Petrarch's coronation in 1341 (the first such ceremony at Rome in the Middle Ages) was preceded by that of Albertino Mussato at Padua in 1315, and followed by that of Zanobi da Strada at Pisa in 1355. Boccaccio travelled to Naples in 1355 in the hope of procuring the post at the Angevin court that Zanobi had recently resigned. His mission was not successful. Like other Florentine *litterati*, Boccaccio was contemptuous of Zanobi's coronation, which was seen as a cheap imitation of the Petrarchan precedent, stage-managed for political ends. It should also be noted that Dante, in *Par.* xxv. 1–12, shortly before being examined on hope by St James, expresses his wish to return to Florence 'and to take the laurel crown at the font of my baptism'.

[270] For the story of Apollo and Daphne, see Ovid, *Metamorphoses*, i. 452–567.

[271] The arguments which follow are selected from the lengthier account given in Petrarch's Coronation Oration: see Wilkins, *Studies*, pp. 309–12.

who investigate the virtues and the nature of plants, has three most praiseworthy and noteworthy properties which stand out among its other characteristics. The first is, as we may all observe, that it never loses its greenness or its leaves. The second is that it has never been known for this tree to be struck by lightning, something which (our reading informs us) cannot be said of any other tree.[272] The third is, as we know, that it is very fragrant. The ancient inventors of this honour considered that these properties accorded well with the virtuous works of poets and of victorious emperors. ⟨161⟩ In the first place, the perpetual greenness of these leaves was said to demonstrate the fame of their works (that is, the works of those who were being crowned by them, or would be crowned in the future) which would stay alive for ever. Next, they considered the works of these men to be of such potency that neither the fire of envy, nor the thunderbolt of long-enduring time, which consumes all things, would ever be able to blast them, any more than thunder from heaven blasted this tree. And in addition to this, they said that these works of the men mentioned above would never, with the passage of time, become less pleasing and gratifying to whoever might hear or read them, but would always be acceptable and fragrant. ⟨162⟩ And so the crown of such leaves, rather than any other, was justly suited to such men, whose achievements, so far as we can tell, were in keeping with it. Not without reason, therefore, was our Dante most ardent in his desire for such an honour, or rather for such a testimony of high virtue as this is to those who make themselves worthy of being crowned with it.[273] But it is time to return to the place where we left off in entering this discussion.

⟨163⟩ Our poet was, in addition to the things said above, most haughty and disdainful of spirit,[274] so much so that he once attempted, through the agency of a friend who was moved by his entreaties, to find a means of returning to Florence, something that he desired above all other things.[275] But the friend could find no way of agreeing this with those who then held the government of the republic in their hands, except in one way, which was as follows: that Dante should, for a certain period of time, remain in

---

[272] This second property (reported, like the first and third, in Petrarch's Coronation Oration) derives from Suetonius' *Life of Tiberius*, ch. lxix: see Wilkins, *Studies*, p. 312. Boccaccio's next paragraph reproduces Petrarch's allegorical interpretation of this supposed phenomenon.

[273] See *Par.* i. 13–27, where Dante appeals to Apollo for the poetic power that will entitle him, ultimately, to crown himself with laurel. Cf. *The House of Fame*, 1091–109, where Chaucer begins by imitating Dante's appeal to Apollo but ends in self-parody.

[274] 'd'animo alto e disdegnoso molto', a description which recalls Virgil's acclamation of Dante in *Inf.* viii. 44 as 'alma sdegnosa'.

[275] This incident is recounted in a letter copied into the *Zibaldone Laurenziano*, a literary scrapbook which Boccaccio began compiling during his youthful years at Naples and completed some time after his return to Florence in 1341 (cf. above, p. 454). This letter, in which Dante addresses the friend mentioned in Boccaccio's text, survives only in Boccaccio's hand.

prison, and after that he might be offered up at some public solemnity in our principal church as a suppliant subject. He would then be at liberty, free from every sentence previously passed upon him. To Dante this procedure seemed appropriate and customary in dealing with abject and infamous men, but not with others: so, putting aside his keenest desire, he chose to remain in exile rather than to return home by such a route. ⟨164⟩ O praiseworthy scorn of a great-hearted man, how manfully you acted in holding back the ardent desire for return when offered a route that was less than worthy for a man nurtured in the lap of philosophy!

⟨165⟩ This praiseworthy scorn was matched by an accurate sense of self-worth; nor (as his contemporaries report) did he think himself to be worth less than he actually was.[276] This characteristic showed itself, to choose one memorable occasion among many, whilst he was serving with his party[277] at the head of the government of the republic. Through the mediation of Pope Boniface VIII, the Florentine faction that was then out of power called upon a brother or relative of Philip, then king of France, whose name was Charles, to straighten out the affairs of our city. All the principal members of the party to which Dante belonged met together in council to consider this proposal. They decided, amongst other things, that an embassy should be sent to the Pope, who was then in Rome. The said Pope was to be induced, through this embassy, to block the arrival of the said Charles, or to have him come by agreement with the ruling party. ⟨166⟩ And when they came to discuss who should be the leader of this delegation, all agreed that Dante was the one. To this request Dante, having paused to meditate upon it for a while,[278] said: 'If I go, who stays? If I stay, who goes?', as if he alone were of worth among them all, and all of them were made worthy through him. This remark was understood and remembered, but that which followed from it does not form part of the present subject, so I will leave it and pass on.

⟨167⟩ In addition to all this, this worthy man was most strong-minded in all his adversities. In one thing alone was he—I do not know whether I should say impatient or impassioned: that is, he was (once in exile) consumed by party affairs more than his capacity for political action warranted, and more than he was willing to have others believe. And in

---

[276] Here, as often, Boccaccio's choice of an incident to exemplify Dante's personal qualities combines contemporary reports, personal fantasy, and an impressively diligent, highly detailed reading of Dante's texts. Dante displays a clear sense of self-worth throughout the *Comedy*, and argues for the importance of such an attitude in the *Convivio*, i. xi. 18–19 (ed. Simonelli, p. 24): 'the great-spirited man always magnifies himself in his own heart, whereas the mean-spirited man, by contrast, always holds himself to be worth less than he really is'. Here Dante is following *Eth. Nicomach.* iv. 3 (1123^{b}1–2, 9–11).

[277] The 'white Guelfs': see below, n. 280.

[278] Here again, a narrative detail adds lustre to a colourful, imaginative scene, and yet still remains faithful to Dante's own literary self-realization. Cf. *Par.* xiii. 112–20, where Thomas Aquinas teaches Dante the importance of pausing to think before committing himself to any binding course of action.

order to specify the party to which he was so passionately and pertina-
ciously attached, it seems to me that I should go on writing a bit further.

⟨168⟩ I believe that it was the just wrath of God which, a long time ago,
allowed almost the whole of Tuscany and Lombardy to be split into two
parties. Where they got such names from I have no idea: but one was called,
and is still called, the 'Guelf party', and the other was called 'Ghibelline'.
And these two names were, in the ignorant minds of many people, so potent
and awe-inspiring that in order to defend the party he had chosen against
its enemy a man would think nothing of losing his possessions and even his
life, if the need arose. ⟨169⟩ And under these titles the Italian cities frequently suffered the most severe oppressions and disruptions; and our city,
which was practically the headquarters of the one faction and (following
changes among the citizens) of the other, suffered too. The ancestors of
Dante were, consequently, twice exiled as Guelfs by the Ghibellines; and it
was under the title of Guelf that Dante held the reins of the republic in
Florence.[279] But it was not, we have noted, by Ghibellines that Dante was
banished, but by Guelfs.[280] ⟨170⟩ And on realizing that he would not be able
to return, Dante so changed in his sympathies that nobody was ever a
fiercer Ghibelline and a harsher adversary of the Guelfs than he was. And
that which most shames me in serving his memory is that it is widely known
in Romagna that any half-grown woman or little child could move him to
such mad fury by speaking of political parties and condemning the Ghibellines that he would have ended up throwing stones had they not fallen
silent. And he lived with this animosity until his dying day.

⟨171⟩ I am certainly ashamed of having to blemish the fame of such a man
with any defect, but the procedural order that I have embarked upon (il
cominciato ordine) requires this, to some extent. For if I remain silent about
the things that were less than praiseworthy in him, I shall greatly undermine the credibility of the praiseworthy things that have already been discussed. And so I ask pardon from Dante himself, who is, perhaps, even as I
am writing this, looking down on me with a scornful eye from some high
region of heaven.

⟨172⟩ Amid such virtue, amid such learning as we have noted there to
have been in this magnificent poet, lust (lussuria) found most ample space;
and not just in his youthful years, but also in his maturity.[281] Although this vice

[279] Dante's ancestors were exiled from Florence in 1248 and in 1260; Dante was one of the six
Priors of Florence elected on 13 June 1300.
[280] Having achieved control of the Florentine republic, the Guelfs split into two factions.
Dante, a 'white Guelf', was sentenced to death in absentia by the 'black Guelfs' on 10 Mar. 1302.
[281] This rather curious ascription of a lustful character to Dante was, it appears, constructed
piecemeal from a somewhat literal-minded reading of certain rime and of certain incidents
from the Comedy. Perhaps such a reading, established by the early commentators on the
Comedy, suited Boccaccio at this point because, as he tells us in para. 171, the procedural order
of his treatise ('il cominciato ordine') requires that some of Dante's defects be recorded so that
his virtues might seem the more credible. For precedents in medieval theologians' discussions
of the sins of scriptural writers see above, Ch. VI, and Minnis, Authorship, pp. 103–12, and esp.

may be natural, common, and to some extent necessary, it cannot in truth be decently commended, much less excused. But who among mortals can . play the just judge in condemning it? Not I.[282] ⟨173⟩ O feeble resolve! O bestial appetite of men! What thing can women not work in us, if they wish to, since they can achieve such great things without even trying? They have charm, beauty, and natural sexual instinct[283] and many other things working continually on their behalf within the hearts of men. And that this be true, let us pass over what Jove did for Europa, or what Hercules did for Iole, or what Paris did for Helen, since as these things are poetic fictions many people of little understanding would dismiss them as fables; but let this be illustrated by things that nobody can rightly deny. ⟨174⟩ Was there more than one woman in the world when our first father, having abandoned the commandment given him by the very mouth of God, succumbed to her persuasions? Of course not. And David, even though he had many wives, only needed to see Bathsheba in order to forget, on her account, God, his kingdom, himself, and his integrity, becoming first an adulterer and then a murderer: what is one to think that he might have done, on her account, had she actually commanded anything from him? And Solomon, to whose wisdom nobody, excepting the Son of God, has ever attained: did he not abandon Him who had made him wise and, to please a woman, kneel and adore Baalim? What did Herod do?[284] What about those many others, drawn along by nothing but their pleasure? Among so many men of such calibre, then, our poet may pass, not excused but accused with his head hanging not so low as it would otherwise have done had he alone been at fault. And let this account of his more noteworthy habits suffice for the present.

Expository Lectures on Dante's *Comedy*: Prologue[285]

⟨1⟩ 'In the middle of the journey of our life',[286] etc. Our humanity, although

pp. 214–16. The antifeminist sentiments in the next two paragraphs seem to have been influenced (as Professor Ralph Hanna has suggested to us) by Walter Map's *Dissuasio Valerii ad Rufinum*. See *De nugis curialium*, dist. iv, ch. 3, ed. and tr. M. R. James, rev. C. N. L. Brooke and R. A. B. Mynors (Oxford, 1983), pp. 292ff.

[282] This is more than a rhetorical flourish: Boccaccio was the father of at least five illegitimate children.

[283] 'la vaghezza, la bellezza et il naturale appetito'. These concepts are discussed by Boccaccio in an extensive gloss to his own *Teseida*, vii. 50 (tr. McCoy, pp. 199ff.). Vaghezza and Bellezza appear as allegorical personifications within the garden surrounding the Temple of Venus.

[284] Cf. Matt. 14: 1–12. Herod had John the Baptist decapitated to please Salome, daughter of Herodias, who had charmed him by dancing on his birthday.

[285] Tr. by David Wallace from *Esposizioni sopra la Comedia di Dante, accessus*, ed. Giorgio Padoan in Boccaccio, *Opere*, vi. 1–18, with the permission of Arnoldo Mondadori Editore.

[286] Quotations from the *Comedy* follow Padoan's edition of the *Esposizioni*. The MSS of Boccaccio's commentary often give only abbreviated forms of Dante's verses; Padoan provides fuller quotations, basing his reconstruction upon exemplars of the *Comedy* copied in Boccaccio's own hand. See *Esposizioni*, ed. Padoan, pp. 725–7.

ennobled with many gifts from our Creator, is sometimes so feeble by nature that there is nothing, however minimal, that it can accomplish capably or thoroughly without divine grace. Recognizing this fact, men of worth in both ancient and modern times urge us piously and with paternal affection to petition such grace beseechingly and, with all the devotion we can muster, to beg such grace for assistance, at least at the beginnings of each of our tasks.

⟨2⟩ Everyone must come to realize this without difficulty on reading what Plato, a man of celestial ingenuity, writes on this subject at the end of the first book of his *Timaeus*, saying on his own behalf:[287] 'everybody assuredly understands it to be a custom, almost a religious obligation, to pray for divine assistance in beginning each new undertaking, whether great or small. And are not we, who are about to launch into a discourse on the nature and substance of the universe, in especial need of invoking the divine power, unless we are utterly seized by fierce frenzy and implacable madness?'

⟨3⟩ And if Plato confesses himself to have more need of divine assistance than any other man, what should I presume about myself, knowing that my intellect is sluggish, my ingenuity slight, and my memory unsteady, especially when I am taking up a burden that is much heavier than is appropriate for my shoulders? How am I to explain the artifice-laden text (*l'artificioso testo*), the host of stories, and the sublimity of meanings (*sensi*) hidden beneath the poetic veil of our Dante's *Comedy*; and how, above all, am I to explain them to men of such lofty understanding and admirable perspicacity as you, men of Florence, are universally reputed to be? Certainly, I must believe myself to be needy beyond every human need.

⟨4⟩ And so, in order that what I am bound to say may resound to the honour and glory of the most holy name of God and be of consolation and benefit to those who hear it, I intend, before going any further, to resort as humbly as I can to invoking His aid, trusting much more in His benignity than in any merit of my own. ⟨5⟩ And since we are to speak of poetic material, I will invoke such aid poetically with the Trojan Anchises, speaking those verses that Virgil writes in the second book of his *Aeneid*: 'O Jupiter omnipotent, if you may be moved by any prayers, look upon us: so much do I ask; and, if we are deserving through piety, lend us assistance, O father. . . .'[288]

⟨6⟩ And so having called upon God in His mercy to help us with His grace in the present undertaking, I think that there are three things to

---

[287] *Timaeus* 27C (Timaeus responding to Socrates), here cited in the Latin translation of Calcidius (ed. Waszink, p. 20).

[288] *Aeneid*, ii. 689–91, where the MSS have 'auxilium' ('help', 'assistance'), while some modern editors have accepted 'augurium' from a quotation in Pseudo-Probus, comm. on Virgil, *Bucolics*, vi. 31.

consider before any account of the letter of the text might be attempted. These are generally to be sought at the beginnings of each thing which pertains to doctrine:[289] the first is to show the number and character of the causes (*cause*) of this book; the second, what the title of this book might be; the third, to what part of philosophy the book in question belongs.

⟨7⟩ There are four causes of this book: material, formal, efficient, and final. The material cause is, in the work in question, twofold, as is the subject (the subject and the material being one and the same thing): for one subject is that of the literal sense and the other that of the allegorical sense, both of which appear in this book, as will become clearly apparent in the course of this exposition.[290] ⟨8⟩ Taken according to the literal sense, then, the subject is the state of souls after bodily death, understood in a simple sense;[291] for the whole course of the work in question concerns itself with that subject and with its attendant issues. Taken according to the allegorical sense, the subject is: how man, earning merit and demerit through the exercise of free will, is subject to justice for reward and punishment.

⟨9⟩ The formal cause is similarly twofold, consisting of the form of the treatise and the form of treatment.[292] The form of the treatise is divided into three in accordance with the three-fold division of the book: the first division is that according to which the entire work is divided, namely, in three *cantiche*; the second division is that according to which each of the three *cantiche* is divided into cantos; the third division is that according to which each canto is divided into rhymed units.[293] ⟨10⟩ The form or rather the mode of treatment is poetic, fictive, descriptive, digressive, and transumptive; and moreover it involves definition, division, proof, refutation, and the furnishing of examples.

⟨11⟩ The efficient cause is the author himself, Dante Alighieri, of whom we shall say more later on when we come to speak of the book's title.

[289] Boccaccio here faithfully follows the analytic procedure that formed a characteristic part of the medieval *accessus ad auctores*. However, the heading *accessus*, which Padoan gives Boccaccio's prologue, does not appear in the MSS.

[290] Numerous expressions here seem to have been appropriated from the *Epistle to Can Grande*, esp. 6 and 8 (tr. above). Padoan, p. 767, notes that the framework of the four causes and the general procedure followed here are analogous to those employed by Dionigi da Borgo San Sepolcro in the preface to his commentary on Valerius Maximus. Dionigi, who befriended the young Boccaccio at Naples in the late 1330s, had earlier taught theology at the Sorbonne. He provided Boccaccio with his first important links with Petrarch and with the proto-humanist culture of Avignon. For further details of Boccaccio's early education, see Wallace, *Chaucer and Boccaccio*, pp. 23–38. However, given the ubiquitous nature of such commentary procedures (as demonstrated by our Chs. VI and VIII), it is as unwise as it is unnecessary to posit specific precedents for Boccaccio's methods.

[291] 'semplicemente preso', a phrase equivalent to *Epist. Can Gr.* 8, 'simpliciter sumptus' ('pure and simple').

[292] 'la forma del trattato e la forma del trattare'. Cf. the discussion of the *forma tractandi* and *forma tractatus* of the *Comedy* in *Epist. Can Gr.* 9.

[293] 'rittimi'. Cf. *Epist. Can Gr.* 9, 'rithimos', and above, n. 83.

⟨12⟩ The final cause of the work in question is: to move[294] those living in this life from the state of misery to the state of happiness.

⟨13⟩ The second principal thing to be considered is what the title of the book in question might be. According to some people it is this: 'Here begins the *Comedy* of Dante Alighieri, Florentine.'[295] Another person, following the author's intention more closely, states the title to be this: 'Here begin the *cantiche* of the *Comedy* of Dante Alighieri, Florentine.' This other person, given the fact that the work is, as was said, divided into three parts, maintains the title of this first part to be: 'Here begins the first *cantica* of the *cantiche* of the *Comedy* of Dante Alighieri', wishing to show by this that the title of the complete work must be: 'Here begin the *cantiche* of the *Comedy* of Dante', etc., as was said.

⟨14⟩ But since this does not get us very far, we will leave this to the judgement of writers[296] and will pass on to consider why the writer felt compelled to entitle the work as he did. We will speak of the reasoning behind the second title, since that includes the reason for the first title, the one which is used by almost everyone.

⟨15⟩ And in arguing for this second title[297] we should, in my opinion, note how musicians found all their compositions upon certain intervals of time, long and short, and upon high and low pitch, and upon the variety of these, conjoined in appropriate and measured proportion; and this they then call 'canto'. ⟨16⟩ And poets do likewise: not just those who write in Latin, but even those who, as our author does, write in the vernacular. They fashion their verses, in accordance with the diverse qualities of various verse forms, from a fixed and determined number of feet (*piedi*) which, after a fixed and limited number of words, rhyme with one another. So in the work in question, in which all the verses consist of an equal number of syllables, we observe that the end of the third line is always consonant with the ending of the first, which ends with that consonance.[298] And so it appears that to such verses, or to works composed of

[294] 'rimuovere . . . da', following *Epist. Can Gr.* 15, 'removere . . . de'.

[295] Boccaccio here cites and rejects the title stated for the *Comedy* in *Epist. Can Gr.* 10; Padoan, p. 768 n. 17, argues from this and from subsequent details that Boccaccio did not believe in the Dantean authorship of the *Epistle*. The unidentified person referred to in the next sentence is almost certainly Pietro Alighieri (Boccaccio never mentions any Dante commentator by name in his *Esposizioni*). Pietro states the title of the book ('libri titulus') to be 'Comoedia Dantis Allegherii' (ed. Nannucci, p. 9), but in discussing the part of philosophy to which this book belongs he gives a separate title for the first part (*Inferno*): 'Incipiunt prima cantica Comoediae Dantis Allegherii, in quibus tractatur de descensu ad inferos' (p. 11). From this incipit, it seems, Boccaccio has derived the title he believes Pietro would have wished to give the entire *opus* of the *Comedy*.

[296] 'scrittori', one of several periodic reminders of the oral delivery of these lectures.

[297] i.e. for the title containing the term 'cantica', a poetic composition made up of cantos. The term 'canto' can mean both 'song' and 'poem'; cf. above, pp. 460–1, 474–5, 492–3. For further discussion of the relationship between poetry and music, see *Esposizioni*, xvi. 85–6 (ed. Padoan, p. 705).

[298] Boccaccio's discussion of *consonanza* here is indebted to the twofold definition of rhyme given in *Convivio*, iv. ii. 12 (ed. Simonelli, p. 133).

verses, it is appropriate to give the name that musicians give to their inventions, as we said before, that is, 'cantos'. Consequently, that work which is made up of many 'cantos' must be called a *cantica*, that is, a thing containing many cantos within itself.

⟨17⟩ Next, one learns from the title that this book is to be called *Comedy*. Apropos of this, it should be known that there are many and varied kinds (*maniere*) of poetic narrations, such as tragedy, satire, and comedy, pastoral (*buccolica*), elegy, lyric, and others. But I wish to consider only that which is relevant to this given title. Some people maintain that this title is ill suited to this book, arguing firstly from the meaning of the word and then from the mode of treatment (*modo del trattare*) followed by comic writers, which appears to be very different from that which the author observes in this book.

⟨18⟩ First, then, they say that the things sung in this book accord poorly with the meaning of the word, since 'comedy' means much the same as 'village song', being made up from *comos*, which in Latin means 'village', and from *odos*, which means 'song':[299] and rustic songs, as we all know, concern themselves with lowly subjects, such as the problems experienced by rustics in cultivating the earth or in maintaining their livestock, or with the crude and unsophisticated love-affairs of rustics, and with country customs. In no part of this book do the things narrated correspond with suchlike in any particular; they are concerned, rather, with persons of excellence, with the singular and noteworthy actions of vicious and virtuous men, with the effects of penitence, with the ways of angels, and with the divine essence.

⟨19⟩ Furthermore, comic style, in order to conform with its subject-matter, is humble and modest.[300] Such could not be said of the work in question, for although it may be written in the vernacular (in which even half-grown women may communicate) it is nonetheless ornate and graceful and sublime[301] (qualities which are quite foreign to the language of women). I am not saying, however, that if it were written in Latin verses, the thrust (*peso*) of the vernacular words remaining unchanged, it would

---

[299] This etymological explanation, which Boccaccio goes on to reject, is borrowed from *Epist. Can Gr.* 10.

[300] 'umile e rimesso'. See *Decameron* iv, introd. 3, where Boccaccio characterizes his own style in that work as being 'umilissimo e rimesso', a phrase which recalls *Epist. Can Gr.* 10, where the 'style of language' of the *Comedy* is described as being 'unstudied and lowly (*remissus ... et humilis*), as being in the vulgar tongue, in which even womenfolk hold their talk'. Para. 19 of Boccaccio's prologue sees him, once again, in disagreement with the *Epistle to Can Grande* even as he avails himself of its phrasings.

[301] 'ornato e leggiadro e sublime', adjectives which Boccaccio characteristically employs to evoke the rhetorical, seductive charge of (Latin) poetry: see e.g. *Trattatello*, red. I, 142 (tr. above), which speaks of the 'leggiadre persuasioni' of poets. This paragraph of the *Esposizioni* sees Boccaccio struggling to align the vernacular style of the *Comedy* with the Latin tastes of Florentine humanists, a struggle which he renews (with little more success) in his last four paragraphs here (74–7).

not be much more artful (*artificioso*) and sublime: for Latin speech is possessed of much greater art and gravity than is our mother tongue.

⟨20⟩ And another thing regarding the comic writer's art: never, within the comedy, does he bring himself forward to speak in any way. Instead, he contrives that the discourse which he thinks appropriate to the comedy's theme shall be developed by various people, whom he causes to speak together in various places, at various times, and for various reasons. However, in this book the author, having left the comedian's conventions aside, most frequently (indeed, almost always) speaks now of himself and now of some other person talking.

⟨21⟩ And similarly, it was not customary in comedies to employ comparisons or recitations from stories other than from those which appertain to the adopted theme: whereas in this book infinite comparisons are put forward and many stories are told that do not have a direct bearing on the principal intent.

⟨22⟩ Furthermore, there are things recounted in comedies that may never have chanced to happen, although they are not perhaps so far removed from the habits of men that they could never have happened at all:[302] the substantial history (*la sustanziale istoria*) presented by this book— of sinners who die in their sins being damned to eternal punishment, and of those who pass away in the grace of God being raised up to eternal glory—is, according to the Catholic faith, true and has always happened.

⟨23⟩ In addition to all this, the comedians call the separate parts of their comedies 'scenes'. This is because the comic writers recited their comedies from the place in the middle of the theatre called the *scena*. Whenever they introduced new characters to speak, actors would emerge from the *scena*, different in appearance from those who had earlier spoken and performed, and, in the guise of those who were supposed to speak, they came before the people who were watching and listening to the comedian who was narrating. Our author, however, calls the parts of his *Comedy* 'cantos'.[303]

⟨24⟩ And so, to put an end to these arguments, it appears (as was said above) that the name of 'comedy' is not suitable for this book. An author does sometimes find that one of his works has been misnamed. One cannot, however, maintain that this author had it in mind that this work should not be called a comedy, since he himself calls it *Comedy* in the

---

[302] This passage is indebted to *Geneal. deor. gent.* xiv. ix (trans. in Ch. IX), which speaks of a fictional form employed by heroic poets such as Virgil and Homer, and by 'the better of the comic poets, Terence and Plautus, for example'. Boccaccio possessed only a superficial knowledge of Plautus, but knew Terence well, having copied his comedies into what is now Florence, Biblioteca Medicea-Laurenziana, 38. 17.

[303] Cf. Isidore, *Ety.* xviii. xliii and xlix. Boccaccio offers a more detailed digression on the ancient performance of comedies later in the *Esposizioni* (i. i. 84–5). Similar accounts are given by Pietro Alighieri (ed. Nannucci, p. 9) and by Nicholas Trevet (of whose commentary on Seneca Boccaccio owned a copy) on *Hercules furens* (see above, pp. 325–6) and *Thyestes*.

twenty-first canto of this first *cantica*, saying THUS FROM BRIDGE TO BRIDGE, TALKING OF OTHER THINGS OF WHICH MY *COMEDY* IS NOT CONCERNED TO SING, etc. [*Inf.* xxi. 1–2].[304]

⟨25⟩ How, then, are we to respond to the objections that have been raised? Given that the author was a man of the most subtle intelligence (*occulatissimo uomo*), I believe that he concerned himself not with the parts that are contained in comedies, but with the whole, and that he named his book from this, speaking figuratively.[305] The whole or ensemble (*il tutto*) of a comedy, according to what one may understand from the comic poets Plautus and Terence, requires that a comedy should have a turbulent beginning, full of uproar and discord, and then the final part should end in peace and tranquillity. ⟨26⟩ The book in question conforms excellently with that ensemble: for it sets out from the pains and tribulations of hell and ends in the repose and in the peace and in the glory which the blessed enjoy in eternal life. And this needs must suffice to show that such a name may reasonably be applied to this book.

⟨27⟩ It remains to be seen who the author of this book might have been: something which is, of necessity, needful to know not only in this book but in every other book. Such knowledge prevents us from foolishly lending credence to someone who does not merit it; for as we may read: 'He who believes foolishly is believed to be foolish.'[306] ⟨28⟩ And what is more foolish than to believe the parricide on questions of humanity and compassion, the lecher on chastity, the envious on written agreement, or the heretic on the Catholic faith? Rarely does it happen that someone speaks out against his own convictions. It is, then, desirable to examine men's lives and habits and fields of study so that we may recognize how much credence should be lent to their words.

⟨29⟩ The author of the book in question was, then, as the title testifies, Dante Alighieri, a man of our city descended from noble stock. And his life was not uniform in character but, being disrupted by various shifts of circumstance, frequently diverted its course into fresh fields of study. One cannot speak adequately about his life without including some account of his studies.

⟨30⟩ From the time of his boyhood in his own homeland he was, then, chiefly dedicated to the liberal arts, and in these he made miraculous progress: for in addition to the first art[307] he was, as will shortly be

---

[304] See also *Inf.* xvi. 127–8, where Dante swears to the reader 'by the notes of this comedy', a passage discussed by Boccaccio in *Esposizioni*, xvi. 83–6 (ed. Padoan, p. 705).

[305] 'figurativamente parlando', i.e. speaking not in plain language but in the figurative language of poets.

[306] 'Qui misere credit, creditur esse miser', an expression which had become proverbial. Boccaccio probably came across it in a collection of *sententiae*: see Padoan, p. 769, n. 34; *Proverbia sent.*, ed. Walther, iv. 205, v. 292 (nos. 24277, 31241. 12).

[307] i.e. grammar, the first and most basic art taught to students of the medieval trivium (grammar, logic, rhetoric). Having mastered these skills, students might apply themselves to learning the more complex arts of the quadrivium (arithmetic, geometry, astronomy, music).

discussed, a marvellous logician and was knowledgeable in rhetoric, as his works make abundantly clear. And because it is apparent from the work in question that he was an astrologer, something which he could not have been without knowing arithmetic and geometry, I consider him to have been similarly well versed in these arts too.

⟨31⟩ And he himself tells[308] of having attended lectures in moral philosophy at Florence in his youth, and of having understood the subject wonderfully well: something which he did not choose to keep hidden in the eleventh canto of this treatise (*trattato*), where he has Virgil say DO YOU NOT REMEMBER THOSE WORDS WITH WHICH YOUR *ETHICS* EXPOUNDS [*Inf.* xi. 79–80],[309] as if wishing that it be understood by this that moral philosophy, in particular, was to him most familiar and well known.

⟨32⟩ And similarly, again at Florence, he heard lectures on (*udì*) the poetic authors, studied the historiographers, and, in addition, made the greatest of beginnings in natural philosophy, something which he wishes one to notice in the discussions undertaken in this work with ser Brunetto Latini,[310] a man who was reputed to be highly accomplished in that discipline.

⟨33⟩ But however much he applied himself to these studies, he did not escape being subjected to the greatest of pangs from that passion which we generally call 'love';[311] and he was similarly moved by a concern for public honours, something which he looked out for eagerly until the time came (things going badly for him and for those who followed his political faction) that he was obliged, through fear of worse happening, to leave Florence.

⟨34⟩ After that departure, having wandered around Italy for several years, believing himself able to find a means of returning to his homeland (only to suffer the loss of that hope), he went to Paris, and there he dedicated himself to attending lectures in natural philosophy and theology; and within a short space of time he made such progress in these subjects that on involving himself, from time to time, in certain scholastic exercises, such as lecturing, reading, and disputation (*sermonare, leggere e disputare*), he won the greatest of praise from men of discernment.

⟨35⟩ Then having returned to Italy and retired to Ravenna, he made an end of his life and labours in the manner of a Catholic Christian some time after his fifty-sixth birthday, whereupon he was buried at the church of the Friars Minor; and this without having accepted any title or doctoral degree, for he wished to take the laurel crown in his own city, as he himself testifies at the beginning of canto xxv of the *Paradiso*;[312] but death forestalled this desire, as was said.

---

[308] See *Convivio*, II. xii. 7 (ed. Simonelli, p. 57).

[309] The reference to 'your *Ethics*' is, of course, to the *Nicomachean Ethics* of Aristotle, *the Philosopher*.   [310] See *Inf.* xv. 49–120.

[311] Boccaccio considers Dante's excessive involvement in amatory and political affairs in the *Trattatello*, red. I, 170–4 (tr. above).

[312] See *Par.* xxv. 1–9, and *Trattatello*, red. I, 162 (tr. above).

⟨36⟩ His habits were serious and highly scrupulous, and were almost all laudable; but since I have already spoken of such things in a short treatise written in his praise,[313] I shall not trouble to speak further of them now. If such things are looked at with a sound mind it seems certain to me that he will be considered a very suitable and trustworthy witness in whatever material has been reported by him in his *Comedy*.

⟨37⟩ But something remains to be said about his name, and firstly about its meaning, which makes itself evident through the name itself: for each person who, with a liberal soul, gives of those things which he has received through grace from God may deservedly be called 'Dante'.[314] And he himself gave generously of such God-given gifts, something which their fruitful effect[315] does not disguise. For all those who wish to partake of it, he has put forward his singular and precious treasure in which honest pleasure and salutary profit[316] are discovered in equal measure by all those who choose to seek them with loving intelligence.

⟨38⟩ And since this seemed to him to be a most excellent gift—because of the reason given above and because he acquired it through great labour, through long vigils, and through continuous studying—he was not content to think that this name might have been bestowed upon him casually by his parents, in the way that many such names are given out every day. To show that his name was conferred on him by heavenly intent he contrives to have himself named in this book by two most excellent people.

⟨39⟩ The first of these is Beatrice, who in appearing to him in the triumphal chariot of the heavenly army at the highest point of the mountain of purgatory is intended to represent sacred theology, through which one is to believe that every divine mystery is comprehended. And among other mysteries one is to believe this one: that he was called Dante by divine intent. ⟨40⟩ In confirmation of this he has her call him Dante in that part of the thirtieth canto of the *Purgatory* in which she, in speaking, says to him DANTE, BECAUSE VIRGIL GOES AWAY [*Purg.* xxx. 55], as if wishing it to be understood that had she not recognized him to be worthy of this name she either would not have named him or would have addressed him by some other name. One might add that his name must, of course, be spelt out[317] in that place for the reason already given and, in addition, to make it

---

[313] 'in sua laude un trattatello', the phrase which provides the title for Boccaccio's *Trattatello in laude di Dante*.

[314] 'Dante' is the present participle of the verb *dare*, 'to give'. This derivation, which also appears in the *Ottimo* and Guido da Pisa commentaries, is celebrated most elaborately in *Trattatello*, red. I, 18–19 (ed. Padoan, p. 442).

[315] i.e. the *Comedy*, composed by Dante, its *causa efficiens*. Boccaccio's phrasing here was clearly influenced by *Purg.* vi. 138.

[316] Cf. Horace, *Ars poetica*, 333–4; also *Trattatello*, red. I, 150 (tr. above).

[317] 'di necessità registrarsi il nome suo'. See *Purg.* xxx. 62–3, where Dante speaks 'del nome mio, / che di necessità qui si registra' ('of my name, which of necessity is registered here', to cite Singleton's translation).

apparent that he has advanced so far in theology that, being Dante, he may prove competent in things divine without Virgil: that is, without poetry, or let us say without that rationality which governs earthly things.

⟨41⟩ The other person he contrives to have name him is Adam, our first father, to whom was granted the God-given privilege of naming all created things. And since he is believed to have named them judiciously (*degnamente*), Dante wished to show, on being named by Adam, that his own name was bestowed upon him judiciously, with the testimony of Adam himself. He does this in canto xxvi of the *Paradiso*, there where Adam says to him DANTE, I DISCERN YOUR WISH BETTER, etc. [*Par.* xxvi. 104].[318] And let what is written here suffice as far as the title is concerned.

⟨42⟩ The third principal thing that I said was to be investigated is the part of philosophy under which the book in question is to be considered. In my judgement it is to be considered under moral philosophy or ethics: for although in certain passages it is treated in the mode of speculative philosophy, this is done not for the sake of philosophical speculation *per se* but for the sake of the work,[319] which in such a passage, has demanded this mode of treatment.

⟨43⟩ Having dealt with the things mentioned above, we need to look to the particular rubric which follows, namely: 'Here begins the first canto of the *Inferno*.' But considering the variety and multiplicity of the subjects that will come under consideration in the present lecture, the slightness of my intellect, and the weakness of my memory, I intend to make it plain before going any further that if anything should be said, through carelessness or ignorance on my part, that should fail to conform with Catholic truth, then this should be regarded as unsaid, and I revoke it forthwith, and submit myself to the correction of Holy Church.[320]

⟨44⟩ Our rubric says, then: 'Here begins the first canto of the *Inferno*.' In connection with this it remains to be seen whether an inferno exists and whether there is more than one of them and in what part of the world it might be; from where one enters into it, what its form might be, what use it might serve, and whether it is called by a name other than 'inferno'.[321]

⟨45⟩ And first of all, I say that there is an inferno. This is affirmed by many scriptural authorities, and above all by Isaiah, who says: 'hell has enlarged its appetite and opened its mouth beyond measure' [v: 14]; and Virgil says in *Aeneid*, vi: 'the gateway of the infernal king';[322] and Job: 'My

---

[318] Modern editions read 'da te' ('by you') and not 'Dante'.

[319] See *Epist. Can Gr.* 16.

[320] A conventional formula. Here Boccaccio is about to pass on to arguments which involve theological issues.

[321] All these general questions concerning the inferno are addressed in *Geneal. deor. gent.* I. xiv, ed. V. Romano (Bari, 1951), i. 43–6.

[322] *Aeneid*, vi. 106.

soul will descend to the deepest hell' [17: 16]. From these authorities it is apparent that there is an inferno.

⟨46⟩ Next one asks whether there was more than one inferno: and from the sense of sacred Scripture it appears that there are three, the first of which the theologians (*santi*) call the upper inferno, the second the intermediate, and the third the lower, intending to locate the upper one in this life, full as it is of punishments, of anguish, and of sin. And speaking of this, the Psalmist says: 'The pains of death encompassed me and the perils of hell sought me out' [Ps. 114: 3]; and elsewhere he says: 'let them go down into hell alive' [Ps. 54: 16], which is to say: 'in the miseries of the present life'.

⟨47⟩ And as far as this inferno is concerned, the poets go along with the theologians in imagining it to be within the hearts of men; and, in enlarging upon this fiction, they declare there to be a doorkeeper to this inferno, and this they say is Cerberus, infernal dog, which when interpreted means 'devourer': pointing through him to the insatiability of our desires, which can never be satiated or satisfied.[323]

⟨48⟩ And the duty of this dog is not to prevent anyone from entering, but to ensure that nobody from the inferno should leave. By this they wish to suggest that where greed for riches, for public office, for pleasures, and for other worldly things enters in, it never leaves, or is drawn out only with difficulty. This they demonstrate by imagining this dog to have been dragged out of the inferno by Hercules:[324] that is, this insatiability for worldly desires to be stilled by the virtuous man and to be ejected from the heart of one so virtuous.

⟨49⟩ Next, they say that in this inferno there are Charon the boatman and the river of Acheron. And through Acheron they point to the labile and flux-like character of longed-for things and the misery of this world; and through Charon they point to time, which transports our wishes and our hopes through various intervals from one object to another: and they mean that at various times, various things that stir the appetites are carried to the heart.

⟨50⟩ They say, in addition to this, that Minos, Aeacus, and Rhadamanthus are seated in this inferno as judges and sentencers of the sins of the souls who go to that inferno. And they attribute this office to them because they were very great jurists and just men. Through them they point to the conscience of each person which, having its seat in our mind,

---

[323] Paras. 47–54 borrow from *Geneal. deor. gent.* 1. xiv, ix. xxxiii (ed. Romano, i. 43–6, ii. 475–7). Boccaccio owes much to Fulgentius, who is acknowledged by name in para. 51. For the relevant passages see *Virg. cont.*, ed. Helm, pp. 98–101 (tr. Whitbread, pp. 130–2); for Ixion and Tantalus, *Mit.* ii. 14–15 (ed. Helm, pp. 55–7; tr. Whitbread, pp. 79–80). In this and subsequent paragraphs we translate the verb *sentire* as 'to point at', thereby highlighting those moments at which Boccaccio moves us from a literal to an allegorical level of interpretation.

[324] For a fuller account of Hercules' victory over Cerberus (which formed part of the rescue of Theseus from the underworld) see *Esposizioni*, ix. i. 34–5) (ed. Padoan, p. 479).

is the foremost and most discerning judge of our actions; and because of these actions conscience afflicts and torments us with its bite.

⟨51⟩ And next they illustrate the punishments to which conscience may condemn sinners by focusing upon several tormented souls. They say that Tantalus, king of Phrygia, is there: because he presented his son as food before the gods he is forced to stand in a river with a great abundance of apples overhead and to die of hunger and thirst. They point through him to the nature of the miser, who in order not to diminish his acquisitions does not dare to draw on them and so suffers the privation of many things that he might easily enjoy. And the miserly undoubtedly correspond to Tantalus as interpreted by Fulgentius to mean 'covetous of looking': for the avaricious want nothing from their treasures beyond just gazing upon them.

⟨52⟩ Another person that they imagine to be in that place is Ixion, who according to some people was the confidant of Jove and of Juno. As such he asked Juno to lie with him; she put before him a cloud fashioned in her likeness. On lying with this cloud Ixion engendered the Centaurs; and Jove condemned him to this punishment in the inferno: that he should be bound with serpents to the spokes of a wheel that would never cease turning. By this the poets wish it to be understood that through Ixion they are pointing to those who covet power and establish some form of tyranny by force. Tyranny has only the semblance of dominion, which is what Juno represents.[325] ⟨53⟩ And as this tyranny breeds attitudes of suspicion, so are the Centaurs born: that is, the men of arms with which tyrants maintain power against the wishes of the people. And tyrants suffer this torment: that they are always threatened by revolutions; and even if they are not, they imagine themselves to be; and they are troubled by obscure anxieties. These afflictions are represented by the turning wheel and by the serpents.

⟨54⟩ In addition to this, they describe Tityus there. Because he asked Latona to comply with his indecent desires, they report him to have been condemned to the inferno by Apollo, there to have his liver perpetually pecked at by vultures, and for this liver to spring up fully grown as soon as it is consumed. Through him they are pointing to those who are thrown from a high and splendid place to a low condition. Such people are forever infested with the most gnawing thoughts, thinking only of how they may return to the place from which they have fallen. And no sooner are they released from one preoccupation than they are seized by another; and in this way they torture themselves without respite.

⟨55⟩ They also place the daughters of Danaus there and report that they are forcibly condemned to fill certain bottomless vessels with water

---

[325] Reference to Fulgentius, *Mit.* ii. 14 (ed. Helm, pp. 55–6; tr. Whitbread, p. 79), makes it clear that Juno represents true, perpetual dominion (Boccaccio's 'regno'), whereas the cloud made in her likeness represents tyranny ('tirannia') which cannot last.

because they killed their husbands; forever drawing water, they labour in vain. By this the poets wish to illustrate the foolhardiness of women, who, having defeated reason, which should be their head and guide, as is their husband, intend to bring about by their artifices that which they judge nature to have left undone, namely, to make themselves beautiful by preening and painting themselves. That which follows most often has the opposite effect, and their labour is therefore wasted. ⟨56⟩ Or they wish to point through these women to the effeminate stupidity of many people who, whilst believing themselves capable of satisfying the libidinousness of others through continuous coitus, only empty themselves without filling anyone else. But to avoid going through all the punishments written of that place, which would be many, I say only that this is what the Gentile poets[326] mean by the upper inferno.

⟨57⟩ The second inferno, as I said, they called intermediate, understanding it to be near the surface of the earth. This, in common parlance, we call 'limbo'; and the Holy Scripture sometimes calls it the 'bosom of Abraham'. And they wish this inferno to be seen as separate from the places of punishment, wishing it to be understood that the righteous of ancient times had been here, waiting for the coming of Christ. ⟨58⟩ And our author shows his understanding of this when he places here those who either did not sin or who, having acted aright, died without baptism. But this limbo is different from that of the theologians to the extent that those who were in that limbo were desiring and hoping, and their salvation came; whereas those whom the author puts here live in desire, but not in hope.[327]

⟨59⟩ They were also of the opinion that there is a lower inferno, and that this is a place of everlasting punishments apportioned to the damned. And of this the Gospel says: 'The rich man died and was buried in the inferno' [Luke 16: 22]; and the Psalmist: 'Who will praise you in hell?' [Ps. 6: 6]. And that this is so one can read in the Gospel in that part where the rich man buried in hell, seeing Lazarus above him in the lap of Abraham, beseeches him to dip his little finger into water and to flick it into his mouth, thereby refreshing him a little [Luke 16: 23–4]. And our author treats of this inferno in similar fashion from canto v onwards.

⟨60⟩ It was next asked where the entrance leading to this inferno might be, since the author gives no indication of its whereabouts on writing that which stands at the beginning of canto iii.[328] On this subject no unanimous opinion prevails among the ancients.

[326] 'i poeti gentili', a phrase which Boccaccio employs in referring to the poets of the Graeco-Roman world. See also *Esposizioni*, iv. i. 244, xii. i. 62 (ed. Padoan, pp. 231, 573), and of course the *Genealogia deorum gentilium*.

[327] 'disiderano, ma non isperano', a formulation which borrows from Virgil's words in *Inf.* iv. 42.

[328] i.e., the celebrated inscription which stands above the gate of the inferno: 'Per me si va. . . .'

⟨61⟩ Homer, who appears to be among the most ancient of poets who make mention of this, writes in book xi of his *Odyssey* of Ulysses having been sent in his ship to Oceanus by Circe in order to descend into the inferno and to learn of his future adventures from Teiresias the Theban. And he speaks of him as having come among certain peoples there, which he calls Scythians, in a place where no light from the sun ever appears, and of having found the inferno in that place.[329]

⟨62⟩ Virgil, who follows him in many things, differs from him in this, writing in the sixth book of the *Aeneid* of the entrance to the inferno being by the lake of Avernus, between Baiae and the city of Puzzuoli, saying: 'There was a deep cave, stupendous and wide-gaping, jagged and grim, by a black lake and the darkness of a forest; over this no flying creatures could with impunity wing a straight course: so noxious was the breath which came steaming from such black jaws towards the roof of the sky. And that is why the Greeks call this place Avernus', etc.[330] And he writes of Aeneas having gone down into the inferno through this cave accompanied by the Sibyl.

⟨63⟩ Statius, in the first book of his *Thebaid*, speaks of this place being on an island not far from that extreme part of Achaia, called 'Trenaron', which lies closest to the island of Crete. And he says that Tisiphone re-entered the world from the inferno at this place when Oedipus was king of Thebes. Oedipus had begged her to set discord between his sons Eteocles and Polynices. Statius writes as follows: 'journeying through the shadows and through the fields made dark by a multitude of souls she hastens to the gate of Trenaron, the threshold of no return'.[331]

⟨64⟩ And Seneca the tragedian shows himself to be in agreement with him in the tragedy of *Hercules furens*, where he speaks of the infernal dog Cerberus having been dragged out of the inferno by Hercules and Theseus through the cave of Trenarus, saying thus: 'But when he came to the borders of Trenarus, and the brightness of light struck his eyes', etc.[332]

⟨65⟩ Pomponius Mela, in the first book of his *Cosmographia*,[333] speaks of this place as being among those people who live close to its entrance on

---

[329] See *Odyssey*, xi. 1–22 (where Homer speaks of 'Cimmerians' and not of 'Scythians', a term which was used to denote any people in the far north) and 90–149. See also C. G. Hardie, 'The Crater of Avernus as a Cult-Site' in *Virgil, Aeneidos, liber sextus*, ed. with a commentary by R. G. Austin (Oxford, 1977), pp. 279–86.

[330] *Aeneid*, vi. 237–42. Note that modern editions read 'Scrupea, tuta lacu ... pinnis ... nomine Aornum' where Boccaccio has 'scrupea torva, lacu ... pennis ... nomine Avernum'. Line 242 does not appear in the best MSS; in popular etymology, 'Avernus' was connected with ἄορνος, 'birdless'.

[331] *Thebaid*, i. 94–6.

[332] *Hercules furens*, 813–14. Boccaccio was reasonably familiar with the works of Seneca and owned a copy of Trevet's commentary on the tragedies (cf. above, n. 303).

[333] See Pomponius Mela, *De chorographia*, I. xix. 103, ed. Gunnar Ranstrand (Studia Graeca et Latina Gothoburgensia XXVIII, Gothenburg, 1971), p. 21. Boccaccio consistently refers to this work, which he drew upon freely for his encyclopaedic *De montibus*, as the *Cosmographia*.

the Black Sea,[334] writing in this fashion: 'The first people to live there were the Mariandyni in a city given to them, so they say, by the Argive Hercules; it is referred to as Heraclea, which adds credibility to this legend. Close by is the Acherusian cave, which, so they say, provides a way through to the shades of the dead; and they believe that Cerberus was dragged out here' etc. Others make claims for Mongibello and [the island of] Vulcano and the like, backing them up with tales not fit for silly women.[335]

⟨66⟩ The form of this inferno, speaking of it as of a material thing, the author describes as being in the shape of a horn standing upright, its tip fixed at the centre of the earth and its mouth above coming close to the surface of the earth. Within this, a man winds himself around the hollow of the horn in the way that a man does to descend one of those spiral stair-cases that in common parlance are called 'snail-stairs'.[336] In certain areas, however, this place appears to be out of proportion with the path leading down into it, being in part cavernous and in part solid: cavernous in that he identifies places there which he calls 'circles' and within which the wretched are punished; and sometimes he describes rocks and a number of fords and rivers which could not descend, in the way he describes, through empty space.

⟨67⟩ The inferno serves divine justice in receiving the souls of sinners who have merited the wrath of God; and it torments and afflicts them according to the greater or lesser character of their sin, being to them an eternal prison.

⟨68⟩ Last of all it was asked whether it had names other than 'inferno'; that it had many of these among the poets is readily apparent. Virgil, as one reads in the sixth book of the *Aeneid*, calls it Avernus, where he says: 'Trojan son of Anchises, the descent of Avernus is easy';[337] and one calls this miserable place Avernus from *a*, which means 'without', *vernus*, which means 'gladness',[338] that is, 'place without gladness'. ⟨69⟩ And in another part of the afore-mentioned book he calls it Tartarus, here: 'then Tartarus itself gapes sheer down, twice', etc.;[339] and this name is derived from *tortura*, that is from torment,[340] which the unfortunates in this place receive. And this is, according to Virgil, the deepest part of the inferno. ⟨70⟩ He also calls it Dis in the afore-mentioned book, where he says: 'Through the empty dwellings of Dis and its hollow kingdom';[341] and it is

[334] 'mar Maggiore'. The town referred to here is Heraclea Pontica, chief city of the ancient Mariandyni (referred to by Boccaccio as 'Mariatidinei').

[335] 'con favole non assai convenienti alle feminelle'. 'Mongibello' is Mount Etna.

[336] 'chiocciole', after *chiocciola*, 'a snail': the term is still current.

[337] *Aeneid*, vi. 126.

[338] Boccaccio here switches briefly from Italian to Latin, as he etymologizes 'Averno'. He derives it from a noun *vernus*, which he must understand as meaning 'Springtime', then 'joy', 'gladness'. [339] *Aeneid*, vi. 577–8.

[340] 'tormentamento'. *Tormento* can mean both torment and torture.

[341] *Aeneid*, vi. 269.

so called from its king, who by the poets is called Dis, that is, rich and plentiful, because a very great multitude of souls are forever descending[342] to this place. ⟨71⟩ Similarly, he calls it Orcus in the book often referred to, where he writes: 'Just before the entrance, within the very jaws of Orcus';[343] and it is called Orcus, that is, dark, because it is exceedingly dark, as will become evident as the exposition goes on. In addition to this, he calls it Erebus in the aforementioned book, saying: 'We have come and sailed across the great rivers of Erebus';[344] and it is called Erebus, according to what Uguccione says, because it clings very tightly with its torments to those whom it wretchedly receives and keeps within itself.[345] ⟨72⟩ And this place is also called Baratro, as the author notes in the following remark from canto xii of this part of the *Comedy*, where he says SUCH WAS THE DESCENT OF THAT BARATRO [*Inf.* xii. 10],[346] and it is called Baratro from the shape of a vase of rushes, which is rounded, broad at the top, and narrow at the base. ⟨73⟩ This place is also called Abyss, as one reads in Revelation[347] where it says: 'The beast that will come up from the abyss will wage war against them' [Rev. 11: 7]; and in another passage: 'The key of the shaft of the abyss was given to him and he opened the shaft of the abyss' [9: 1–2]; this name means 'depth'. The said place has some more names, but let it suffice for the present to have narrated these.

⟨74⟩ Having looked into the issues spoken of above, and before moving on to discuss the organization of the lectures, it seems needful to remove a doubt which has often been raised, and raised most often by men of learning,[348] which is this; such men speak as follows: 'According to what everyone says, Dante was a most learned man; and if he was learned, how did he induce himself to compose such a work, and a work as praiseworthy as this one is, in the vernacular?' ⟨75⟩ It seems to me that one may answer such men in this fashion: Dante was certainly a most erudite man, and

---

[342] 'discendono sempre', grammatical agreement is *ad sensum. Dis, ditis* is a Latin adjective meaning 'rich', 'well-endowed'.

[343] *Aeneid*, vi. 273.

[344] *Aeneid*, vi. 671.

[345] Here Boccaccio follows Hugutio's derivation of *Erebus* from the verb *haereo*, which means 'to be closely attached, adhere, stick, cling': 'Item ab hereo li herebus bi .i. infernus quia nimis adhaereat illi qui capitur et est herebus fere tartarus seu profundissimus locus infernorum de quo dicitur quia in inferno nulla est redempcio de illo loco neminem traxit christus' (*Magnae derivationes*, s.v. *hereo*, in MS Bodley 376, fol. 88').

[346] Modern editions have 'burrato' ('deep ravine') where Boccaccio has 'baratro' ('gulf, chasm; the Abyss, Hell'). In his literal exposition of *Inf.* xii Boccaccio himself has 'burrato', glossed as 'a rocky precipice': see *Esposizioni* xii. i. 9 (ed. Padoan, p. 561). We can throw no light on why he connected 'baratro' with a vase of rushes.

[347] Revelation is discussed as a sacred text employing poetical devices in *Geneal. deor. gent.*, xiv. xiii (tr. in Ch. IX).

[348] 'litterati uomini'. Boccaccio seeks in these last four paragraphs to align his prologue with the cultural preferences of the humanists, for whom Latin and learning were virtual synonyms. The abrupt conclusion of para. 77 ('*ut supra*') suggests that these paragraphs, like various others, were added at a late, revisionary stage.

especially in matters of poetry (*in poesi*); and was desirous of fame as we all are, generally speaking. He began writing the book in question in Latin verses, like this: 'I will sing of the most distant kingdoms, bordering the watery world, that gape open widely for spirits, that assign the rewards to each man according to his merits', etc.[349]

⟨76⟩ And he had already gone on for a while when it occurred to him to change his style of writing; and the consideration that prompted him to do this was the clear recognition that liberal and philosophical studies had been wholly abandoned by princes and by noblemen and by men of excellence, who were formerly accustomed to honour poets and their works and to make them famous. And so, seeing Virgil and the others to be as good as abandoned, or to be in the hands of plebeian men and of men of low class, he surmised that a similar fate would befall his own labours, and that consequently that for which he had undertaken the work would not accrue to him.

⟨77⟩ Given this situation, it seemed imperative to him to fashion his poem in conformity, at least in its outer shell, with the intellectual capacities of contemporary noblemen. (If there be one of these nobles who should wish to see some book, and this book should happen to be in Latin, then they will have it rendered into the vernacular on the spot!) And so he came to the conclusion that if his book were in the vernacular it would be found pleasing; whereas if it were in Latin it would be disdained (*schifato*). So having laid the Latin verses aside, he wrote in vernacular verses, as we will see.

Having dispensed with this, we may proceed as indicated above.

[349] Boccaccio's source here is the *Epistola di frate Ilaro*, which he himself had copied into his first *Zibaldone* or literary scrapbook over thirty years earlier: see Biagi's facsimile. The *Epistola* was edited by G. Billanovich in 'La leggenda dantesca del Boccaccio', *Studi Danteschi*, xxviii (1949), 141–4. Billanovich argues that the *Epistola* was composed by Boccaccio himself as a rhetorical exercise.

SELECT BIBLIOGRAPHY

This Bibliography is limited to books and articles of which substantial use was made. Moreover, we have not duplicated material referred to in the Table of Abbreviations on pp. xv–xvi.

ABELARD, PETER, *Opera theologica, i: Commentaria in Epistolam Pauli ad Romanos, etc.*, ed. E. M. Buytaert, CCCM xi.
—— *Sic et Non. A Critical Edition*, fasc. i, ed. B. Boyer and R. McKeon (Chicago and London, 1976).
AHL, F. M., *Lucan: An Introduction* (Ithaca, NY, and London, 1976).
ALAN OF LILLE, *Anticlaudianus*, ed. R. Bossuat (Paris, 1955), tr. J. J. Sheridan (Toronto, 1973).
—— *Quoniam homines*, ed. P. Glorieux, *AHDLMA* xx (1953), 113–364.
ALEXANDER OF HALES, *Glossa in quattuor libros sententiarum Petri Lombardi* (Bibliotheca franciscana scholastica medii aevi XII–XV, Grottaferrata, 1951–7).
—— *Summa theologica* (Quaracchi, 1924–48).
ALLEN, J. B., 'Commentary as Criticism: The Text, Influence and Literary Theory of the "Fulgentius Metaphored" of John Ridewall', in *Acta Conventus Neo-Latini Amstelodamensis: Proceedings of the Second International Congress of Neo-Latin Studies, Amsterdam 19–24 August 1973*, ed. P. Tuynman, G. C. Kuiper, and E. Kessler (Munich, 1979).
ANDERSON, WILLIAM, *Dante the Maker* (London, 1980).
ARNULF OF ORLÉANS, *Glosule super Lucanum*, ed. B. Marti (Papers and Monographs of the American Academy in Rome, Rome, 1958).
ATKINS, J. W. H., *English Literary Criticism: The Medieval Phase* (Cambridge, 1943).
AUGUSTINE, *Confessionum libri XIII*, CCSL xxvii.
—— *Contra Faustum Manichaeum*, CSEL xxv.
—— *Contra mendacium*, CSEL xli.
—— *De Genesi ad litteram*, CSEL xxviii.
—— *De mendacio*, CSEL xli.
—— *De quantitate animae*, PL xxxii.
—— *De Trinitate*, CCSL l–lA.
—— *Enarrationes in psalmos*, CCSL xxxviii–xl.
—— *In Ioannis evangelium*, CCSL xxxvi.
—— *Retractationes*, CCSL lvii.
AVERROES, *Middle Commentary on Aristotle's Poetics*, tr. C. E. Butterworth (Princeton, 1986).
—— *Three Short Commentaries on Aristotle's Topics, Rhetoric and Poetics*, tr. C. E. Butterworth (Albany, NY, 1977). See also under HERMANN THE GERMAN
AVIANUS, *Fabulae*, ed. F. Gaide (Paris, 1980).

BARNETT, R. J., Jr., 'An Anonymous Medieval Commentary on Juvenal' (unpub. Ph.D. thesis, The University of North Carolina at Chapel Hill, 1964).
BASWELL, CHRISTOPHER, 'The Medieval Allegorization of the *Aeneid*: MS Cambridge, Peterhouse 158', *Med. Stud.* xli (1985), 181–237.

BELLOMO, SAVERIO, 'Primi appunti sull'*Ottimo commento dantesco*', *Giornale storico della letteratura italiana*, clvii (1980), 369–82, 533–40.

BERNARD OF UTRECHT, *Commentum in Theodulum*, in Huygens, *Accessus ad auctores, etc.*, 55–69.

'BERNARD SILVESTER', *The Commentary on Martianus Capella's* De nuptiis Philologiae et Mercurii *attributed to Bernardus Silvestris*, ed. H. J. Westra (Studies and Texts, lxxx, Leiden, 1986).

—— *The Commentary on the First Six Books of the* Aeneid *of Virgil commonly attributed to Bernardus Silvestris*, ed. J. W. Jones and E. F. Jones (Lincoln, Neb., and London, 1977); tr. E. G. Schreiber and T. E. Maresca (Lincoln, Neb., and London, 1979).

BERSUIRE, PIERRE, *Reductorium morale, liber xv: naar de druk van 1509; Metamorphosis Ouidiana moraliter a M. Thoma Walleys . . . explanata*, pub. J. Engels *et al.* (Instituut voor Laat Latijn, Werkmateriaal I–II, Utrecht, 1962).

—— *Reductorium morale, liber xv: Ovidius moralizatus, cap. i: De formis figurisque deorum*, ed. J. Engels *et al.* (Instituut voor Laat Latijn, Werkmateriaal III, Utrecht, 1966).

BIRD, OTTO, 'The *Canzone d'Amore* of Guido Cavalcanti according to the Commentary of Dino del Garbo', *Med. Stud.* ii (1940), 150–203, iii (1941), 117–60.

BOCCACCIO, GIOVANNI, *Esposizione sopra la Comedia di Dante*, ed. G. Padoan, in Boccaccio, *Opere*, vi.

—— *Genealogia deorum gentilium*, tr. C. G. Osgood (Indianapolis and New York, 1956).

—— *Teseida*, tr. B. M. McCoy (New York, 1974).

—— *Trattatello in laude di Dante*, ed. P. G. Ricci, in Boccaccio, *Opere*, iii. [Since going to press, a new translation of the *Trattatello* has appeared, by Vincenzo Zin Bollettino (New York and London, 1990).]

BOETHIUS, *De differentiis topicis*, PL lxiv; tr. E. Stump (Ithaca and London, 1978).

—— *The Theological Tractates, The Consolation of Philosophy*, ed. H. F. Stewart, E. K. Rand, and S. J. Tester (Cambridge, Mass., and London, 1973).

BOETHIUS, PSEUDO-, *De disciplina scholarium*, ed. O. Weijers (Leiden, 1976).

BOGGESS, W. F., 'Aristotle's *Poetics* in the Fourteenth Century', *SP* lxvii (1970), 278–94.

—— 'Hermannus Alemannus' Latin Anthology of Arabic Poetry', *JAOS* lxxxviii (1968), 657–70.

BONAVENTURE, *Opera omnia* (Quaracchi, 1882–1902).

BOWDEN, J. P., *An Analysis of Pietro Alighieri's Commentary on the Divine Comedy* (New York, 1951).

BURROW, JOHN A., *The Ages of Man: A Study in Medieval Writing and Thought* (Oxford, 1986).

CAGLIO, ANNA MARIA, 'Materiali enciclopedici nelle *Expositiones* di Guido da Pisa', *Italia medioevale e umanistica*, xxiv (1981), 213–56.

CALCIDIUS, *Timaeus, a Calcidio translatus commentarioque instructus* (Plato Latinus IV), ed. J. H. Waszink, 2nd edn. (London and Leiden, 1975).

CALLUS, D. A., 'The Date of Grosseteste's Translations and Commentaries on Pseudo-Dionysius and the *Nicomachean Ethics*', *RTAM* xiv (1947), 186–210.

—— *Robert Grosseteste: Scholar and Bishop* (Oxford, 1955).

CANAL, A., *Il mondo morale di Guido da Pisa interprete di Dante* (Bologna, 1981).

CARICATO, LUIGI, 'Il *Commentarium* all'*Inferno* di Pietro Alighieri, indagine sulle fonti', *Italia medioevale e umanistica*, xxvi (1983), 125–50.

CASSIODORUS, *Expositio psalmorum*, CCSL xcvii.

CATO (Pseudo-), *Disticha*, ed. M. Boas and H. J. Botschuyver (Amsterdam, 1952).

CHAUCER, GEOFFREY, *Works*, ed. F. N. Robinson, 2nd edn. (London, 1957).

CHENU, M.-D., *Nature, Man and Society in the Twelfth Century*, tr. J. Taylor and L. K. Little (Chicago and London, 1968).

—— *Toward Understanding St Thomas*, tr. A.-M. Landry and D. Hughes (Chicago, 1964).

CIOFFARI, V., *Guido da Pisa's Expositiones et Glose super Comediam Dantis* (Albany, NY, 1974).

Classical and Medieval Literary Criticism. See under PREMINGER, A.

COLKER, MARVIN L., 'De nobilitate animi', *Med. Stud.* (1961), 47–79.

COOKE, J. D., 'Euhemerism: A Medieval Interpretation of Classical Paganism', *Speculum*, ii (1927), 396–410.

COURCELLE, PIERRE, *La Consolation de la philosophie dans la tradition littéraire: Antécédents et postérité de Boèce* (Paris, 1967).

CRESPO, ROBERTO, 'Il prologo alla traduzione della *Consolatio philosophiae* di Jean de Meun e il commento di Guglielmo d'Aragonia', in W. den Boer *et al.* (eds.), *Romanitas et Christianitas: Studia I. H. Waszink oblata* (Amsterdam and London, 1973), pp. 55–70.

DAHAN, GILBERT, 'Notes et textes sur la poétique au moyen âge', *AHDLMA* xlvii (1980), 220–39.

DAHIYAT, I. M., *Avicenna's Commentary on the Poetics of Aristotle: A Critical Study with an Annotated Translation of the Text* (Leiden, 1974).

D'ALVERNY, M.-T., *Alain de Lille: Textes inédits, avec une introduction sur la vie et ses oeuvres* (Paris, 1965).

DANTE ALIGHIERI, *Epistolae*, ed. P. Toynbee, 2nd edn. by C. Hardie (Oxford, 1966).

—— *Il Convivio*, ed. G. Bunselli and G. Vandelli, introduced by M. Barbi, 2nd edn. with an appendix by A. E. Quaglio (Florence, 1964).

—— *Il Convivio*, ed. M. Simonelli (Bologna, 1966); tr. P. H. Wicksteed (The Temple Classics, London, 1904, repr. 1924). [Two new translations appeared after this book went to press: Christopher Ryan (Stanford French and Italian Studies, lxi, Saratoga, 1989); Richard H. Lansing (New York, 1990).]

—— *Lyric Poetry*, ed. K. Foster and P. J. Boyde (Oxford, 1967).

—— *Monarchia*, ed. P. G. Ricci (Verona, 1965); tr. P. H. Wicksteed in *A Translation of the Latin Works of Dante Alighieri* (The Temple Classics, London, 1904, repr. 1934).

—— *Opere minori*, ed. P. V. Mengaldo *et al.* (Milan and Naples, 1979–84).

—— *The Divine Comedy*, ed. and tr. Charles Singleton (Princeton, NJ., 1970–5).

—— *Vita nuova*, in *Le Opere di Dante Alighieri*, ed. E. Moore and P. Toynbee (Oxford, 1924), pp. 205–33; tr. B. Reynolds (Harmondsworth, 1969).

DEAN, R. J., 'The Life and Works of Nicholas Trevet with special reference to his Anglo-Norman Chronicle' (unpub. D.Phil. thesis, University of Oxford, 1938).

DEMATS, P., *Fabula: Trois études de mythographique antique et médiévale* (Publications romanes et françaises cxxii, Geneva, 1983).

DE RIJK, L. M., *Logica modernorum* (Assen, 1962–7).

DIONISOTTI, CARLO, 'Dante nel Quattrocento', *Atti del congresso internazionale di studi danteschi* (Florence, 1965), pp. 333–78.

DIONYSIUS, PSEUDO-, *De Caelesti hierarchia* [Erigena version], PL cxxii.

—— *Dionysiaca: Recueil donnant l'ensemble des traductions latines des ouvrages attribués au Denys l'Aréopagite*, ed. P. Chevaillier (Paris, 1937).

—— *Works*, tr. J. Parker (London, 1897–9).

DORSCH, T. S. (tr.), *Aristotle, Horace, Longinus: Classical Literary Criticism* (Harmondsworth, 1965).

DRONKE, PETER, *Fabula: Explorations into the uses of Myth in Medieval Platonism* (Mittellateinische Studien und Texte IX, Leiden, 1974).

—— *The Medieval Poet and his World* (Storia e letteratura, Studi e testi clxiv, Rome, 1984).

ECO, UMBERTO, *Il problema estetico in Tommaso d'Aquino* (Idee nuove LIII, Milan, 1970); tr. by Hugh Bredin as *The Aesthetics of Thomas Aquinas* (London, 1988).

—— *The Name of the Rose*, tr. W. Weaver (London, 1983).

EUSEBIUS, see under JEROME

EVANS, G. R., *Old Arts and New Theology: The Beginnings of Theology as an Academic Discipline* (Oxford, 1980).

—— *Alan of Lille: The Frontiers of Theology in the Later Twelfth Century* (Cambridge, 1983).

—— *The Language and Logic of the Bible: The Earlier Middle Ages* (Cambridge, 1984).

—— *The Language and Logic of the Bible: The Road to Reformation* (Cambridge, 1985).

FARAL, E., *Les Arts poétiques du XIIe et du XIIIe siècle* (Paris, 1924).

FOSTER, K., and HUMPHRIES, S. (trs.), *Aristotle's De anima in the Version of William of Moerbeke and the Commentary of St Thomas Aquinas* (London, 1951).

FRIEDMAN, J. B., *Orpheus in the Middle Ages* (Cambridge, Mass., 1970).

FULGENTIUS, *Opera*, ed. R. Helm (Leipzig, 1898).

GHISALBERTI, F., 'Giovanni del Virgilio espositore delle *Metamorfosi*', *Giornale Dantesco*, xxxiv (1933), 1–110.

—— 'Medieval Biographies of Ovid', *JWCI* ix (1946), 10–59.

GIBB, H. A. R., *Arabic Literature: An Introduction*, 2nd edn. (Oxford, 1963).

GIBSON, MARGARET T. (ed.), *Boethius: His Life, Thought and Influence* (Oxford, 1981).

GILES OF ROME, *Commentarium in primum librum Magistri sententiarum* (Cordova, 1699).

—— *De differentia rhetoricae, ethicae et politicae*, ed. G. Bruni, *New Schol.* vi (1932), 1–18.

—— *De regimine principum libri iii* (apud Antonium Bladum, Rome, 1556).

—— *Rhetorica Aristotelis cum commentariis* (Venice, 1515).

GILSON, ÉTIENNE, *Dante the Philosopher*, tr. D. Moore (London, 1948).

GRAYSON, CECIL, 'Dante's Theory and Practice of Poetry', in id. (ed.), *The World of Dante: Essays on Dante and his Times* (Oxford Dante Society, Oxford, 1980), pp. 146–65.

GREENFIELD, C. C., *Humanist and Scholastic Poetics, 1250–1500* (London and Toronto, 1981).

GREGORY THE GREAT, *Dialogi*, PL lxxvii.

—— *Moralium libri*, CCSL cxliii.

GROSSETESTE, ROBERT, see under McEVOY, JAMES, and McQUADE, J. S.

GUIDO DA PISA, *Expositiones et glose super Comediam Dantis*, ed. V. Cioffari (Albany, NY, 1974).

HÄRING, N. M., 'Thierry of Chartres and Dominicus Gundissalinus', *Med. Stud.* xxvi (1964), 281–6.

HARDISON, O. B., 'The Place of Averroes' Commentary on the *Poetics* of Aristotle in the History of Medieval Criticism', *Medieval and Renaissance Studies* IV, ed. J. Lievsay (Durham, NC., 1970), pp. 57–81.

—— 'Towards a History of Medieval Literary Criticism', *Med. et hum.* vii (1976), 1–12. See also under PREMINGER, A.

HENRY OF GHENT, *Summa in tres partes praecipuas digesta* (apud Franciscum Succium, Ferrara, 1646).

—— *Summae quaestionum ordinariarum* (in aedibus J. Badii Ascensii, Paris, 1520).

HERMANN THE GERMAN, 'Commentarium medium in Aristotelis poetriam', ed. W. F. Boggess (unpub. Ph.D. thesis, University of N. Carolina, 1965).

—— *De arte poetica cum Averrois expositione*, ed. L. Minio-Paluello (Corpus philosophorum medii aevi: Aristoteles Latinus XXXIII, 2nd edn., Brussels, 1968).

HILARY, *Tractatus super psalmos*, CSEL xxii.

HOLLANDER, ROBERT, 'Dante *Theologus-Poeta*', *Dante Studies*, xciv (1976), 91–136.

—— 'A Checklist of Commentators on the *Commedia* (1322–1982)', *Dante Studies*, ci (1983), 181–92.

HUGH OF SAINT-VICTOR, *De sacramentis*, PL clxxvi; tr. R. J. Deferrari, *Hugh of St. Victor on the Sacraments of the Christian Faith* (Mediaeval Academy of America LVIII, Cambridge, Mass., 1951).

—— *Didascalicon*, ed. C. H. Buttimer (Washington, DC, 1939); tr. J. Taylor (New York and London, 1961).

HUGH OF TRIMBERG, *Registrum multorum auctorum*, ed. K. Langosch (Berlin, 1942).

HUGUTIO OF PISA, *Magnae derivationes*, in Oxford, Bodleian Library, MS Bodley 376.

ISIDORE OF SEVILLE, *Etymologiae*, ed. W. M. Lindsay (Oxford, 1911).

IVÁNKA, ENDRE VON, 'Zur Überwindung des neuplatonischen Intellektualismus in der Deutung der Mystik: *Intelligentia* oder *Principalis Affectio*', in *Platonismus in der Philosophie des Mittelalters* (Darmstadt, 1969), pp. 147–60.

JAVELET. R., 'Thomas Gallus et Richard de Saint-Victor mystiques', *RTAM* xxix (1962), 206–33, xxx (1963), 88–121.

JEAUNEAU, E., 'Deux rédactions des gloses de Guillaume de Conches sur Priscien', *RTAM* xxvii (1960), 212–47.

—— *Lectio philosophorum: Recherches sur l'école de Chartres* (Amsterdam, 1973).

JENARO-MACLENNAN, L., 'Autocomentario en Dante y comentarismo latino', *Vox Romanica*, xix (1960), 82–123.

—— *The Trecento Commentaries on the* Divina Commedia *and the* Epistle to Can Grande (Oxford, 1974).

JEROME, *Eusebii Pamphili chronici canones*, ed. R. Helm, GCS xlvii.

—— *Praefatio in librum psalmorum iuxta Hebraicam veritatem*, PL xxviii.

—— *Tractatus sive homiliae in psalmos, series altera*, CCSL lxxviii.

JOHN OF GARLAND, *Integumenta Ovidii*, ed. F. Ghisalberti (Messina and Milan, 1933).

JOLIVET, J., *Arts du langage et théologie chez Abelard* (Études de philosophique médiévale LVII, Paris, 1969).

JOHN OF SALISBURY, *Metalogicon*, ed. C. C. J. Webb (Oxford, 1929), tr. D. D. McGarry (Berkeley and Los Angeles, 1955).

JONES, J. M., '"The Chess of Love": Translation of a Prose Commentary on *Echecs amoureux*' (unpub. Ph.D. diss., University of Nebraska, 1968).

JONES, J. W., 'Allegorical Interpretation in Servius', *Classical Journal*, lvi (1961), 218–22.

JOURDAIN, C., 'Des commentaires inédits de Guillaume de Conches et de Nicolas Triveth sur la *Consolation de la philosophie* de Boèce', *Notices et extraits des manuscrits de la Bibliothèque Impériale*, xx/2 (1862), 40–82.

KELLER, O. (ed.), *Pseudoacronis scholia in Horatium vetustiora* (Leipzig, 1902–4).

KELLY, H. A., 'Aristotle–Averroes–Alemannus on Tragedy: The Influence of the *Poetics* on the Middle Ages', *Viator*, x (1979), 161–209.

—— *Tragedy and Comedy from Dante to Pseudo-Dante* (University of California Publications in Modern Philology, cxxi, Berkeley and Los Angeles, 1988).

KENNEDY, L. A. (ed.), *Renaissance Philosophy* (The Hague and Paris, 1973).

KRISTELLER, P. O., *Renaissance Thought: The Classical, Scholastic and Humanistic Strains* (New York, 1961).

—— *Medieval Aspects of Renaissance Learning*, ed. and tr. E. P. Mahoney (Duke Monographs in Medieval and Renaissance Studies I, Durham, NC, 1974).

—— *Renaissance Thought and its Sources*, ed. M. Mooney (New York, 1979).

L'Homme devant Dieu: Mélanges offerts au père Henri de Lubac (Paris, 1963–4).

MACROBIUS, *In somnium Scipionis*, ed. J. Willis (Leipzig, 1963); tr. W. H. Stahl (New York and London, 1952).

MATTHEW OF VENDÔME, *Ars versificatoria*, tr. R. P. Parr (Milwaukee, Wis., 1981).

MAZZEO, J. A., *Medieval Cultural Tradition in Dante's Comedy* (Ithaca, NY, 1960).

MAZZONI, F., 'La critica dantesca nel secolo XIV', *Cultura e scuola*, xiii–xiv (1965), 285–97.

McEVOY, JAMES, 'Robert Grosseteste on the "Celestial Hierarchy" of Pseudo-Dionysius: An Edition and Translation of his Commentary, chapters 10–15' (unpub. M.A. thesis, The Queen's University of Belfast, 1967).

—— *The Philosophy of Robert Grosseteste* (Oxford, 1982).

McKEON, RICHARD, 'Rhetoric in the Middle Ages', in R. S. Crane (ed.), *Critics and Criticism: Ancient and Modern* (Chicago, 1952), 260–96.

McQUADE, J. S., 'Robert Grosseteste's Commentary on the "Celestial Hierarchy" of Pseudo-Dionysius the Areopagite: An Edition, Translation and Introduction to his Text and Commentary' (unpub. Ph.D. thesis, The Queen's University of Belfast, 1961).

MILLER, J. M., PROSSER, M. H., and BENSON, T. W. (eds.), *Readings in Medieval Rhetoric* (Bloomington and London, 1973).

MILLER, PAUL S., 'The Mediaeval Literary Theory of Satire and its Relevance to the Works of Gower, Langland and Chaucer' (unpub. Ph.D. thesis, The Queen's University of Belfast, 1982).

MINNIS, A. J., '"Authorial Intention" and "Literal Sense" in the Exegetical Theories of Richard FitzRalph and John Wyclif', *Proceedings of the Royal Irish Academy*, lxxv, sect. C, i (1975).

—— 'Late-medieval Discussions of *Compilatio* and the Role of the *Compilator*, *BGDSL* ci (1979), 385–421.

—— 'Langland's Ymaginatif and Late-Medieval Theories of Imagination', *Comparative Criticism*, iii (1981), 71–103.

—— 'Aspects of the Medieval French and English Traditions of the *De Consolatione Philosophiae*', in Gibson (ed.), *Boethius: His Life, Thought and Influence*, 312–61.

—— *Chaucer and Pagan Antiquity* (Cambridge, 1982).

—— 'Affection and Imagination in "The Cloud of Unknowing" and Hilton's "Scale of Perfection"', *Traditio*, xxxix (1983), 323–66.

—— '"Moral Gower" and Medieval Literary Theory', in *Gower's* Confessio amantis, ed. Minnis, 50–78.

—— (ed.), *Gower's* Confessio amantis: *Responses and Reassessments* (Cambridge, 1983).

MURPHY, J. J., *Rhetoric in the Middle Ages* (Berkeley and Los Angeles, 1974).

NARDI, B., 'Osservazioni sul medieval "accessus ad auctores" in rapporto all'*Epistola a Cangrande*', in id., *Saggi e note di critica Dantesca* (Milan and Naples, 1966), 268–305.

NICHOLAS OF LYRE, *Postilla litteralis*, in *Bibl. glos.* [see Abbreviations, p. xv above].

O'DONNELL, J. R., 'The Sources and Meaning of Bernard Silvester's Commentary on the *Aeneid*,' *Med. Stud.* xxiv (1962), 233–49.

OSGOOD, C. G., *Boccaccio on Poetry: Being the Preface and the Fourteenth and Fifteenth Books of Boccaccio's* Genealogia deorum gentilium (Indianapolis and New York, 1956).

PAETOW, L. J. (ed.), *Two Medieval Satires on the University of Paris:* La Bataille des VII Ars *of Henry d'Andeli and the* Morale Scolarium *of John of Garland* (Memoirs of the University of California IV, Berkeley, 1927).

PALMER, N. F., 'Latin and Vernacular in the Northern European Tradition of the *De consolatione philosophiae*', in Gibson (ed.), *Boethius: His Life, Work and Influence*, 362–409.

PAOLAZZI, C., *Dante e la* Commedia *nel Trecento. Dall'*Epistola a Cangrande *all'età di Petrarca* (Milan, 1989).

PARKES, M. B., 'The Influence of the Concepts of *Ordinatio* and *Compilatio* on the Development of the Book', in J. J. G. Alexander and M. T. Gibson (eds.), *Medieval Learning and Literature: Essays presented to R. W. Hunt* (Oxford, 1976), 115–41.

PAULY, F. (ed.), *Scholia Horatiana quae feruntur Acronis et Porphyronis* (Prague, 1858–9).

PETER LOMBARD, *In psalmos Davidicos commentarius*, PL cxci.

—— *Sententiae in IV libros distinctae* (Spicilegium Bonaventurianum IV–V, Grottaferrata, 1971).

PETRARCH, FRANCIS, *Bucolicum carmen*, ed. Thomas G. Bergin (New Haven, Conn., and London, 1974).

—— *Invectivae contra medicum*, ed. P. G. Ricci (Rome, 1950).

PETRARCH, FRANCIS, *Le Familiari*, vol. ii, ed. V. Rossi (Edizione nazionale delle opere di Francesco Petrarca XI, Florence, 1934).
—— *Le Familiari*, vol. iv, ed. U. Bosco (Edizione nazionale delle opere di Francesco Petrarca XIII, Florence, 1942).
—— *Lettere senile*, ed. G. Fracassetti (Florence, 1869–70).
—— *Rerum familiarium libri xvii–xxiv*, tr. A. S. Bernardo (Baltimore, Md., and London, 1985).
PIETRO ALIGHIERI, *Commentarium*, ed. R. della Vedova and M. T. Silvotti (Florence, 1978).
—— *Super Dantis ipsius genitoris Comoediam commentarium*, ed. V. Nannucci (Florence, 1845).
PINBORG, J., *Die Entwicklung der Sprachtheorie im Mittelalter* (BGPTM XLII, 1967).
PREMINGER, A., HARDISON O. B., and KERRANE K. (eds.), *Classical and Medieval Literary Criticism: Translations and Interpretations* (New York, 1974).
PRISCIAN, *Institutiones, GL* ii–iii.

QUADLBAUER, F., *Die antike Theorie des genera dicendi im lateinischen Mittelalter* (Vienna, 1962).
QUAIN, E. A., 'The Medieval *Accessus ad auctores*', *Traditio*, iii (1945), 228–42.

RALPH OF LONGCHAMPS, *In Anticlaudianum Alani commentum*, ed. J. Sulowski (Wrocław, etc., 1972).
RAVEN, D. S., *Latin Metre: An Introduction* (London, 1965).
ROBERT, BROTHER S., 'Rhetoric and Dialectic: According to the First Latin Commentary on the *Rhetoric* of Aristotle', *New Schol.* xxxi (1957), 484–98.
ROUSE, R. H., 'Florilegia and Latin Classical Authors in Twelfth- and Thirteenth-Century Orléans', *Viator*, x (1979), 131–60.
ROUSE, R. H., and ROUSE, M. A., *Preachers, Florilegia and Sermons: Studies on the Manipulus florum of Thomas of Ireland* (Studies and Texts XLVII, Toronto, 1979).
RUSSELL, D. A., and WINTERBOTTOM, M. (trs.), *Ancient Literary Criticism* (Oxford, 1979).

SANFORD, E. M., 'The Manuscripts of Lucan: Accessus and Marginalia', *Speculum*, ix (1934), 278–95.
SAPEGNO, NATALINO, *Storia letteraria del Trecento* (Milan and Naples, 1963).
SERVIUS, *In Vergilii Carmina commentarii*, ed. G. Thilo and H. Hagen (Leipzig, 1881).
—— *In Vergilii Carmina commentariorum*, Harvard edn., vol. ii (Cambridge, Mass., 1946).
SHARP, D. E., 'The *De ortu scientiarum* of Robert Kilwardby (d. 1279)', *New Schol.* viii (1934), 1–30.
SHAW, J. E., *Guido Cavalcanti's Theory of Love: The Canzone d'Amore and Other Related Problems* (Toronto, 1949).
SHIELDS, B. P. (ed.), 'A Critical Edition of Selections from Nicholas Trevet's *Commentarius literalis in Psalterium iuxta Hebreos S. Hieronymi*' (unpub. Ph.D. thesis, Rutgers University, 1970).
SINGLETON, CHARLES, *An Essay on the Vita nuova* (Cambridge, Mass., 1949).

—— 'Dante's Allegory', in R. J. Clements (ed.), *American Critical Essays on the* Divine Comedy (New York and London, 1967)., pp. 91–103.

SMALLEY, B., 'A Commentary on the Hexameron by Henry of Ghent', *RTAM* xx (1953), 61–101.

—— *English Friars and Antiquity in the Early Fourteenth Century* (Oxford, 1960).

—— 'Peter Comestor on the Gospels and his Sources', *RTAM* xlvi (1979), 84–129.

—— *Studies in Medieval Thought and Learning from Abelard to Wyclif* (London, 1981).

SOUTHERN, R. W., *Medieval Humanism and Other Studies* (Oxford, 1970).

—— *Platonism, Scholastic Method and the School of Chartres* (The Stenton Lecture 1978, Reading, 1979).

STAHL, W. H. (tr.), *Macrobius: Commentary on the Dream of Scipio* (New York and London, 1952).

STEGMÜLLER, F., *Repertorium biblicum medii aevi* (Madrid, 1949–61).

STOCK, BRIAN, *Myth and Science in the Twelfth Century: A Study of Bernard Silvester* (Princeton, NJ, 1972).

TARTARO, ACHILLE, *Forme poetiche del Trecento* (Bari, 1971).

TERBILLE, C. I., 'William of Aragon's Commentary on Boethius' *De consolatione philosophiae*' (unpub. Ph.D. thesis, University of Michigan, 1972).

TESTER, S. J., see under BOETHIUS

THOMAS AQUINAS, *Commentary on the Metaphysics of Aristotle*, trans. J. P. Rowan (Chicago, 1961).

—— *Commentary on the Nicomachean Ethics*, tr. C. I. Litzinger (Chicago, 1964).

—— *Exposition of the Posterior Analytics of Aristotle*, tr. P. Conway (Quebec, 1956).

—— *Opera omnia* (Parma, 1852–72).

—— *Summa theologiae*, i (Ia I), ed. T. Gilby (Blackfriars edn., London and New York, 1964). See also under FOSTER, K., and HUMPHRIES, S.

TOYNBEE, P., *Dante Studies and Researches* (London, 1902).

TREVET, NICHOLAS, *Commentarius in Boetii Consolationem philosophiae*, ed. E. T. Silk (unpublished).

—— *Il Commento di Nicola Trevet al Tieste di Seneca*, ed. Ezio Franceschini (Orbis Romanus XI, Milan, 1938).

—— *Expositio Herculis furentis*, ed. V. Ussani (Rome, 1959).

—— *Expositio Senecae Agamemnonis*, ed. P. Meloni (Università di Cagliari, Facoltà di Lettere e di Magistero III, Sassari, 1961).

TRINKAUS, C., *In Our Image and Likeness: Humanism and Divinity in Italian Humanist Thought* (London and Chicago, 1970), pp. 683–721.

—— '*Theologia poetica* and *theologia rhetorica* in Petrarch's Invectives', in id., *The Poet as Philosopher* (New Haven, Conn., and London, 1979), pp. 90–113.

TWYCROSS, M., 'The Representation of the Major Classical Divinities in the Works of Chaucer, Gower, Lydgate and Henryson' (unpub. B.Litt. thesis, University of Oxford, 1961).

ULLMANN, WALTER, *Medieval Foundations of Renaissance Humanism* (London, 1977).

VALLONE, A., *Storia della critica dantesca dal XIV al XX secolo* (Padua, 1981).

Vitae Vergilianae antiquae, ed. C. G. Hardie, 2nd edn. (Oxford, 1966).

WALLACE, DAVID, *Chaucer and the Early Writings of Boccaccio* (Cambridge, 1985).

WARD, J. O., 'The Date of the Commentary on Cicero's *De inventione* by Thierry of Chartres (*c.* 1095–1160?) and the Cornifician Attack on the Liberal Arts', *Viator*, iii (1972), 219–73.

WEINBERG, B., *A History of Literary Criticism in the Italian Renaissance* (Chicago, 1961).

WEISHEIPL, J. A., 'Classification of the Sciences in Medieval Thought', *Med. Stud.* xxvii (1965), 54–90.

WETHERBEE, WINTHROP, *Platonism and Poetry in the Twelfth Century: The Influence of the School of Chartres* (Princeton, NJ, 1972).

WHITBREAD, L. G., 'Conrad of Hirsau as Literary Critic', *Speculum*, xlvii (1972), 234–45.

WICKSTEED, P. H., and GARDNER, G. G., *Dante and Giovanni del Virgilio* (Westminster, 1902).

WILKINS, E. H., *Studies in the Life and Works of Petrarch* (Cambridge, Mass., 1953).

WILLIAM OF CONCHES, *Commentarius in Boetii Consolationem philosophiae*, 'second recension', in Dijon, Bibl. mun. MS 254 and London, British Library, MS Royal 15. B. III. [Actually a thirteenth-century revision: see p. 126.]

—— *Glosae in Iuvenalem*, ed. Bradford Wilson (Textes philosophiques du moyen âge XVIII, Paris, 1980).

—— *Glosae super Platonem*, ed. E. Jeauneau (Textes philosophiques du moyen âge XIII, Paris, 1965).

WIMSATT, W. K., and BROOKS, C., *Literary Criticism: a Short History* (London, 1975).

[Handwritten annotation:] Are there qual. in C3 exeg. which ⓪ are infl. by and part of exegesis of classics + pagan lit, and are more visible when viewed against that backdrop? ① So: what qual. do we see in classical + pagan comm? ② Do we see them in Calv? ⓐ Esp. Seneca; ⓑ Also biblical comm?

INDEX

Abelard, Peter: Bible commentaries 6, 65, 67–9, 89–90; on authority of patristic writings 68, 87, 90–4; on intention of Pauline epistles 70–1; *Commentary on St Paul's Epistle to the Romans* 68–9, 71, extracts 100–5; *Sic et non* (*Yes and No*) 67, Prologue 67–9, text 87–100
Abraham the patriarch 307
Abū Tammām 289n, 303
accessus (prologue) viii, 2, 12–5, 69, 115, 198, 319; texts 15–36; Dante(?) employs 441, 452; Boccaccio employs 505
Accius 480
Acron 33
Acts of the Apostles 198
Adrastus, king of the Greeks 61–2
Aegisthus, 355, 488–9
Aeschylus: *Agamemnon* 326
Aesop 37, 47–9, 119, 209, 284, 299, 425
aetiology 241, 242, 257, 261–2
affectus (disposition of the will): moved by Bible 4, 100, 200–2, 214, 216, 227, 228, 235, 236, 244, 246, 247, 249, 253; and poetry 282–3, 284; and Orpheus myth 334, 335, 379; Dante on 403
Agamemnon 346–60
Agrippa, Menenius 425
Agrippa 157
Agrippinus 97
Agroecius (Agricius) 363n
Alan of Lille 165, 171, 323n, 392; *Anticlaudianus* 124–6, 373; Ralph of Longchamps' commentary on 114, 125–6, extract 158–64; *Expositio prosae de angelis* 125; *Liber parabolarum* (*Parvum doctrinale*) 314–15
al-A'shā 300
Albert the Great (Albertus Magnus) 166, 170, 200, 444
Alcimon of Croton 49
Alexander (heretic) 91
Alexander [Neckam] 368, 369
Alexander of Hales 1, 4, 9, 69, 166; *Sum of Theology* (finished by others) 197, 200, 202–3, 209, 211, 257n, 388, extract 212–23
Alexander of Villa Dei: *Ecclesiale* 6

al-Fārābī, Abū Naṣr 279–80, 283, 292
allegory 53; in scripture 66, 71, 74, 77–81, 199–200, 204, 207, 218, 220–2, 233, 237, 241–2, 256–7, 259, 261–2; secular 120–2, 321–4; Dante and innovation in 382–8, 396–7, 489–90; Pietro Alighieri on 452, 456, 479–80, 489–90; Boccaccio on, in Dante 456; Dante on 459–60; in Dante's *Divine Comedy* 471, 475–6, 479; *see also* senses
Allen, J. B. 288
al-Mutanabbī, Abu'l-Tayyib 302 and n, 303
al-Zayyāt 303n
Ambrose, St 110n, 224, 226n, 415, 485; *Hexaemeron* 352
anagogy: in Bible 46, 168–70, 218, 220–2, 233–4, 241, 256–7, 259, 261–2; Nicholas of Lyre defines 267; Dante and 383, 396
Andreas Capellanus: *De arte honeste amandi* 453, 491n
angels 182–96
Anonymous Lombardus 442
Anselm of Laon 69, 261n
Antaeus 146
Antony, St 363
Apicius, M. Gavius 140
Apollinaris of Laodicea 91
Apuleius, Lucius 425, 433n
Aquinas, Thomas *see* Thomas Aquinas, St
Arator: *accessus* to 18–19; Conrad of Hirsau on 38; as sacred theologian 389; Guido da Pisa on 474
Archias, Aulus Licinius 422
argument (*argumentum*) 44–5; 'arguments' of myths/fables 44n, 300n, 344, 345
Aristaeus 208, 320, 332–4, 427
Aristotelian prologue, the 2–4, 197, 198–200, 314, 321
Aristotle: commentaries on 4, 13, 279–80; Abelard on enquiry in 99; on images 168, 173; influence as 'the Philosopher' 197, 200, 224, 228–9, 247, 248, 250, 277, 281, 309, 310, 328, 361, 366, 397, 399, 406, 412, 458, 462, 466, 473, 477, 478; on moral science 206–7; on first theologians (myth-lovers) 210–11, 389–90,

Aristotle (cont.)
413, 437–8, 492, 498; on becoming good 247, 249, 328–9; on tragedy 285–6; influence on Boethius 318; William of Aragon cites 319, 328, 331; on knowing 361; uses fiction 423; difficulties in 428; and lying 434; Pietro Alighieri follows 452; Concerning Heaven and Earth 310, 399, 466; Metaphysics 3, 210–11, 248–9, 380, 389, 399, 412, 441, 458, 462, 464, 473; Nicomachean Ethics 202, 223, 227, 228, 248–9, 281, 312–13, 331, 380, 462, 478, 510n; On Animals 399, 404; On Generation 246; On Sophistic Refutations 312, 364; On the Soul 308, 404, 406; Organon 279–80; Perihermenias 280, 308; Physics 3, 246, 397, 466, 477; Poetics: Averroes' commentary on 3, 277–88; text of Hermann's translation 289–307; second (lost) book 165; Politics 250, 328; Posterior Analytics 280–1, 309–10; Praedicamenta 280, 308; Prior Analytics 280, 308; Rhetoric 249n, 250, 278–9, 281, 290, 296n, 312, 462; Topics 280, 309
Aristotle, Pseudo- 444, 464n
Arnaud Amaury, Archbishop of Narbonne 125
Arnulf of Orléans 113, 115; on Lucan's Pharsalia 122, 384, extract 155-8; influence on Giovanni's Ovid commentary 321–2, 324; on Thebaid 375
art (ars) and the arts (artes): 13, 32, 37, 38, 39, 64, 69, 122–6, 130, 131, 132, 134, 200, 212–15, 248, 249, 291, 296, 297, 313, 387, 388, 391, 392, 396, 422, 509–60; extrinsic and intrinsic arts 32, 123, 130
artes dictaminis vii, 1
artes poeticae vii, 1
artes praedicandi vii, 1
Asaph 110
Ascensius, Jodocus Badius 318
Athanasius 98
Atkins, J. W. H.: English Literary Criticism, the Medieval Phase 11
Atkinson, K. 315
Atticus 392
auctor 2–3, 135–6, 198–200, 205, 207–9, 229, defined 43; Dante as 374, 377; see also authority
Augustine, St: on pagan and Christian writers 38, 59, 62; and biblical language 66, 203; errors and retractions 68, 90; Abelard on 68, 87, 90, 95–7; cites other authors 92; on Psalter 110n; and vestigia

171; on divine wisdom in scripture 203; Henry of Ghent quotes 203; and scriptural allegory 200, 242, 257, 261–2, 264; on classical theatre 325, 343; critique of Varro 389; uses verse 415; on obscurity in Isaiah 428; on lies 431; on conscience 485; on wantonness 486; Against Consentius 265; Against Faustus 97; The City of God 59, 243, 257, 264; Trevet on 316, 343; on fable 368, 478–9; on obscurity of Scripture 429–30; draws on Apuleius 433n; cites Varro on theologians 437; 475; Confessions 254, 260, 376; Enchiridion 95; Of Discipline in the Church 95; On Christian Doctrine 66, 87, 95, 204, 229, 237, 257, 271n; On the Capacity of the Soul 467; On Genesis 259; On the Gospels 95; On the Holy Trinity 59, 214; On the Instruction of the Young 489; On John 253; On Lying 209, 264; On the Master 228; On Music 244; On Predestination and Grace 264; On the Text of Genesis 90; On the Trinity 96, 213, 225; On the Usefulness of Belief 220, 222, 257, 261–2; Retractions 90, 96, 100, 481; To Consentius: Against Lying 95, 209–10, 265, 323
Augustine of Dacia 267n
Augustus Caesar see Octavian
authority (auctoritas) 68, 156, 197; God as 199; and allegorical interpretation 199; and fallibility 207–9; of Scripture 71, 235–6; 'wax nose' 323n; authority and the vernacular 374–82
Averroes (Ibn Rushd): on Aristotle's Metaphysics 3, 248, 277; Middle Commentary on Aristotle's Poetics (translated by Hermann the German) 3, 277–88, extract 289–307; Benvenuto da Imola and 287–8; anonymous question on 307–13; Dante and 376
Avianus: accessus to 16, 116; Conrad of Hirsau on 37, 49–52
Avicenna 279, 289n, 292n, 295n, 296n, 305n
Avitus 91

Baconthorpe, John 211n
Bahā'al-Dīn Zuhayr 290n
bard see vates
Bartholomaeus Anglicus: De proprietatibus rerum 317, 324
Bartholomew of Brescia 486
Bartholomew of Bruges 278, 281
Bathsheba 207–8, 490, 503
Bavius 39, 62

Beatrice: Dante and 378–9, 398, 401, 404, 455, 511
Beatrice, Sister (Dante's daughter) 454
Bede, Venerable 203, 217, 220–1, 256, 260
belief (*credulitas*) 286–7, 294–5, 306n, 311n
Benvenuto da Imola: commentary on Dante's *Divine Comedy* vii, 278, 287–8, 453n, 458; uses Hermann's translation of Averroes 278; reference to Giovanni del Virgilio 316
Bernard, St 225, 488; *Floretus Sancti Bernardi* 314; *On Consideration* 467
Bernard of Chartres 122, 135
'Bernard Silvester' 1, 113, 115–16; commentary on *Aeneid* 118, 375, 391, 435n, 482n, extract 150–4; on poetry and philosophy 122, 391
Bernard of Utrecht 12, 42n, 43n, 46n; commentary on Theodulus 37
Bersuire, Pierre, 1, 210, 314; career, 317–18; and secular allegory 321; attitude to Ovid's *Metamorphoses* 323; *Moral Reduction* 8, 318, 324, 366–72, 386; *Ovid Moralized* 8, 318–19, 321, 324, 366–72, 383, extract 366–72
Bertrando dal Poggetto, Cardinal 445
Bible (Scriptures): as literary work viii, 4, 7; as source xiii; commentaries on 3, 5–8, 68–71, 198–200; and sacred science 4; prologues to 14; Conrad of Hirsau on 57–9; symbolic value 65; as 'absolute text' 65–6; authority 68, 71, 201, 236; Hugh of Saint-Victor's exegetical theory concerning 71–86; order of books and prophecy 82–3, 101; sense and obscure meaning in 84–6, 428; Abelard on authority and errors in 89–90; Augustine on 96–8; imagery and symbolism in 172–96, 239; Nicholas of Lyre on 197; and causality in criticism 198–9; and theology as science 200–3, 212–13; affective force 100, 200–1, 214, 216, 227, 228, 235, 236, 244, 246, 247, 249, 253; signification 203–5; fallibility and sin in authors of 207–9; fiction and truth 209–12, 263–6, 424; modes 212–37; example in 236; exposition of 236–8; multiple sense in 241–3, 480; Petrarch on poetry in 414–15; *see also affectus*; fiction; individual books; senses; theology
Bible moralisé 386
Billanovich, Giuseppe 440
blame: poetry as 282–4, 289, 291–2, 305, 310n

Boccaccio, Giovanni: death vii, 456; and sacred and secular texts 4, 212; writings on Dante and Petrarch 4, 9, 321, 373, 453–8; story-telling 323; importance 373; self-commentary 375, 441n; on theology, poetry and philosophy 387–92, 455; uses *terza rima* 439, 453; influenced by Dante's *Epistle* 442; devotion to Dante 453; illegitimate children 503n; *Amorosa visione* 453–4; *Decameron* 454; *Esposizioni sopra la Comedìa di Dante* (Dante lectures): on Francesca 439; structure 448, 456–7; *accessus* to 452, 457; delivered 456; as commentary 457–8, extract 503–19; on Hercules and Cerberus 513n; *Genealogy of the Gentile Gods* 1, 210, 373; on literal meaning in Terence and Plautus 384, 385n; on Dante as theologian 386; classification of poetry and arts 387–9, 391–2, 420–2, extracts 420–38; exposition influenced by Dante's *Convivio* 448; on origin of name of poetry 493n; on fictional form 508n; on Revelation 518n; on hell 513n; *Trattatello in laude di Dante* (*Short treatise in praise of Dante*) 2, 373, 388–9, 393, 442, 454–5, 457, extract 492–503; *Teseida* 375, 441n, 457; *Zibaldoni* (scrapbooks) 454, 500n, 519n
Boethius: metres 1; on introductions 13; Conrad of Hirsau on 38, 46; on philosophy 124; on good and evil 159; on knowing 361; Trevet commentary on 316, 318; influence on Dante 378, 473; on human reason 402; as lyric poet 475; *De differentiis topicis* 92, 123; *On Music* 243; *On the Consolation of Philosophy* 46; William of Conches' commentary on 120–1, 318, 320, 328, 374, extract 126–30; William of Aragon's commentary and exposition on 315–16, 318–20, extract 328–36; Trevet's commentary on 316, 318–19, extracts 336–40; Giovanni del Virgilio on 364; Jean de Meun's translation of 374; on author's exile 376; influence on Dante 381, 407, 469; on nobility 381–2; *On the Training of Students* 337, 341; *On the Trinity* 163
Boethius, Pseudo-: *De Disciplina scholarium* 316
Boggess, W. F. 278
Bologna 445
Bonaventure, St 11, 166, 203, 206–8, 212; *Breviloquium* 197, 201, 204, 479–80, text

Bonaventure, St (*cont.*)
233–8; commentary on Ecclesiastes
197, 206–7, 212, 319, text 230–3; commentary on Peter Lombard's *Sentences*
197, 201, text 223–30; *Itinerarium mentis in Deum* 167
Boniface VIII, Pope 501
book: defined by Conrad of Hirsau 42
Borges, Jorge Luis 65: 'Averroes' Search' 288
Bosone da Gubbio 447
Brito, William 270
Bruni, Leonardo 9
Brutus 30, 33, 157, 392, 416
Buridan, Jean 281
Burley, Walter: *De vita ac moribus philosophorum* 6
Butterworth, C. E. 288

Caesar, Julius 156–7, 416
Cain 243
Calliopius 59
Callus, D. A. 166
Cassandra 346, 350–1, 353–4, 356, 357n, 358–60
Cassian 443n
Cassiodorus 110n, 272
Cassius 157
Castelvetro, Ludovico 277
catharsis 285
Cato the Censor 15, 30, 37
Cato of Utica 15
Catullus 147–8
causality in criticism 198–200
Cavalcanti, Guido 2; *Donna mi prega* (poem) 378–9
Cecco d'Ascoli 445
character, theory of 18, 23, 33, 206, 231–2, 286, 294–5, 319–20, 326, 331, 344, 379–80, 445, 476
Charles, Count of Valois, Anjou and Alençon 501
Chartres, school of 113n
Chaucer, Geoffrey: on tragedy 326; *House of Fame* 458; *Knight's Tale* 318; *Troilus and Criseyde* 397n
'Chess of Love' (anon. French poem) 2
Cicero, Marcus Tullius: Conrad of Hirsau on 38; on argument 44; on variety of words 87; influence 113, 120; on rhetoric 279; Trevet on 316; Petrarch recovers letters and addresses 392–4; Dante on 404, 409, 411; Petrarch's letters to 415–20; lost books 419; *Andria*

417; *De inventione* 123, 310n; *Dream of Scipio* 477; *Letters to Atticus* 451; *On Duties* 92; *On Ends* 417; *On Friendship* 22; *On Old Age* 404; *On the Nature of the Gods* 368; *Paradoxa* 30–1; *Rhetoric* 101, 463; *Topics* 489
Circe 127–9
circumstantiae (rhetorical circumstances) 13, 41 and nn, 55, 74 and n, 151 and n
Claudian: *Antirufinus* 160
Cleanness (anonymous English poem) 448n
Cleopatra, Queen of Egypt 158
Cloud of Unknowing, The (anon.) 167, 170
Colker, M. L. 315
collection (*collectio*) 276n
comedy: Averroes/Hermann on 284, 288; Pietro Alighieri on 452, 480–1; Dante(?) on 460–1; Guido da Pisa on 475; Boccaccio on 507–9
Comestor, Peter *see* Peter Comestor
commentator: defined 43, 229
compilatio 8n
compiler (*compilator*) 229
conditions (*statūs*) 219–20, 247
Conrad of Hirsau 37–9, 43, 60–1, 116, 119; *Dialogue on the Authors* 37–9, extract 39–64
conscience 484–5
Constantine, Emperor 54
consuetudo ('typical characteristics') 286, 294–5
Cornelia (Vestal virgin) 139n
Courcelle, Pierre 315, 318
courtesy 407
Crispinus 117, 138, 140–1, 147
Cristoforo Landino 151n
cui parti philosophiae supponitur see *pars philosophiae*
Cupid 406n, 453, 490–1
Cyprien 97–8

Dahiyat, I. M. 282
Daniel (prophet) 255, 424, 497
Dante Alighieri: Benvenuto da Imola on vii, 278, 287–8; as innovator viii, 4; on 'allegory of the poets' and 'allegory of the theologians' 1, 383–7, 396, 443; commentaries on 2, 4, 9, 14, 439–58; on Ulysses 129n; on sacred and secular literature 212; Giovanni del Virgilio and 316–17, 323; Giovanni's epitaph on 323; importance 373; self-commentary 373–82, 385, 441n, 443; and 'new' com-

mentary 377–8, 387; on vernacular and
Latin languages 377, 380–1, 386; and
innovation in allegory 382–8; Boccaccio on 386, 394, 427, 492–503, 509–11;
divine inspiration 387, 473n; condemned 445; death 450n, 510; Ghibelline sympathies 502; defects 502–3;
Amor che ne la mente mi ragiona 378, 443;
Contra gli erranti 378; *Convivio* 4–5, 373,
377; on romantic love 378–9, 382; in
vernacular 381–2; and allegory 386;
exposition of *canzoni* 394–412, 443, 448;
on gods 433n; influence on Guido 446;
on unmoved first mover 492n; on self-
worth 501n; *Divine Comedy: modi* in 5;
commentaries on 373, 442, 445; love in
379; allegory and multi-meanings in
384–6, 459–60, 471, 479–80, 505; popularity 439; written in vernacular 439–40,
457–8, 518–19; *Epistle* author's commentary on 443–4, 458–69; Guido da
Pisa's commentary on 445–9, text 469–
76; Dante's sons' commentaries on 450–
3; Pietro's commentary, extract 476–91;
Boccaccio on 453–8, extracts 503–19;
Epistle to Can Grande della Scala (dubious
attrib.) 5, 10, 373; allegory in 384–6;
commentaries on 440–1; influence on
Dante commentators 442; extract 458–
69; Guido da Pisa and 446n, 448–9;
Pietro Alighieri and 452; Boccaccio follows 457, 505; *On Eloquence in the Vernacular* 377, 381; *Monarchy* 445; *Vita
nuova* 4, 373, 375–8; author's commentary on 375–8, 409–10, 443; *Voi
che'ntendendo* 382, 384, text 394–5, exposition 395–412
Dares Phrygius 114, 116, 151
David, King (the psalmist) 70–1, 105–9,
198, 207–8, 255, 271–5, 486, 490, 503
De contemptu mundi (wrongly ascribed to
St Bernard) 314
decision, determination (*determinatio*) 212
Diana (goddess) 371–2
diction 287
didactic (*didascalicus*) mode 331
Dido, Queen of Carthage 431, 434–6, 453,
487
Didymus 91
Dino del Garbo 378–9
Dionigi da Borgo San Sepolcro 505n
Dionysius, Pseudo- vii, 1, 3; influence of
commentators on 165–8; ideas 168–73;
and Dante 444; *The Celestial Hierarchy*

125–6, 165–70; on biblical symbolism
172–3, 239–40; Gallus' Extraction of:
extracts 173–92; Grosseteste's commentary: extracts 192–6; on scriptural
forms 213, 218; on divine revelation 256,
260; Dante on essence in 464; *The
Divine Names* 167; *The Ecclesiastical Hierarchy* 167, 241; *The Mystical Theology*
166–7, 169, 170; *The Symbolic Theology*
(lost) 188
discourse writers: defined 44
discourses 291, 297–8
discovery (in tragedy) 287
disposition of the will *see affectus*
disputation (*disputatio*) 212, 232
divisio textus 4, 322, 376–7
Dominicus Gundissalinus: *On the Division
of Philosophy* 280
Domitian, Roman Emperor 61, 117–18,
139n, 142n
Donatus, Aelius 37, 366, 455
Donatus, Tiberius Claudius 366n
Dormitius 146
double efficient cause *see* twofold efficient cause
drama, classical 326
Dryden, John viii

Ecclesiastes, Book of: commentary by St
Bonaventure 197, 206–7, 212, 319,
extract 230–3; Giles of Rome cites 245;
Giovanni del Virgilio incorrectly cites
361; Dante quotes 408; *see also* Solomon
Ecclesiasticus: on explanation 239; Gio-
vanni del Virgilio quotes 360–1;
Dante(?) quotes 444, 465
Eco, Umberto: *The Name of the Rose* 165
efficient cause (*causa efficiens*) 3, 198, 228,
231–2, 245, 271, 345, 361, 365; in Dante's
Divine Comedy 444n, 452, 457, 472,
477–8, 505; *see also* twofold efficient
cause
elegy: defined 28
Empedocles 291
Ennodius 490
Epicurus 417
Epimenides 59
Epistle to Can Grande della Scala see Dante
Epistola di frate Ilaro 519n
equivocationes (alternative meanings) 154
Esau 210
Ethan 110
ethics 11, 13–14, 16, 17, 18, 19, 20, 21, 23,
24, 26, 27, 30, 33, 35, 39, 70, 115, 116, 136,

ethics (*cont.*)
155, 159, 201, 211, 226–8, 235, 248–50,
279, 281, 283, 286, 287, 296, 310n, 312,
325, 327, 342, 346, 365, 379, 385–6, 411n,
421, 422, 462, 473, 512
Eurydice *see* Orpheus and Eurydice
Eusebius: *Ecclesiastical History* 103–4
Evans, Gillian 68, 125, 205
exile 26, 27, 362–3
explanation (*explanatio*): defined 45–6
expositors: defined 43
extrinsic prologue, the 123–4, 130, 320, 377
Ezekiel (prophet) 424, 467, 470, 497
Ezra (prophet) 111, 199, 271, 275

fable (*fabula*) 16, 17, 332, 333, 336; Conrad
of Hirsau on 41, 44, 47–8, 49–51, 56;
contrast with history 113, 115, 118–20;
and lying 209–11, 431–6; Averroes/
Aristotle on 282, 299–300, 305–7; St
Paul attacks 323; Bersuire on 323,
366–9; Trevet on 324, 325, 341, 342–3;
Boccaccio on 392, 422–6, 438, 494,
497–8; Dante on 383, 384, 396; Pietro
Alighieri on 452, 478
fabulous narrative (*narratio fabulosa*) 118,
119, 152, 300n, 384, 391, 424
faith 224–6, 258
fallibility: and scriptural authority 207–9
feet (metrical): defined 43
fiction 34, 113–14, 150, 299, 305–7, 384–6,
410, 411, 450; and truth in Bible 209–12,
323, 366–7, 384, 388–9, 438, 497; Bersuire on 323–4; Boccaccio on 384, 391,
422–6, 431–6, 494, 495, 496–8, 503, 505;
Pietro Alighieri on 479; *see also* fable
fictional language (*sermo fabularis*) 286,
294–5
figurative language 205–6, 209–11, 236–7,
262, 289–90; *see also* allegory; metaphor;
symbolism
final cause, ultimate objective (*causa finalis*, cf. *finis*) viii, 23, 24, 28, 46, 54, 56,
219, 226, 230, 245, 248, 361, 402; in
Dante's *Divine Comedy* 471, 473, 477–8,
506
FitzRalph, Richard: *Sum of the Armenian
Questions* 210
Florian, Abbot 19
Florilegium angelicum 8
Florilegium Gallicum 8
form of the treatise (*forma tractatus*) 3, 198,
199, 246, 250, 273, 364, 460, 471, 478, 505;
see also twofold form

form of treatment (*forma tractandi*) 3, 198–
200, 206, 246, 250, 273, 364, 460, 471, 478,
505; *see also modus agendi*; *modus trac-
tandi*; twofold form
formal cause (*causa formalis*) 3, 198–9, 223,
245–6, 250, 273, 346, 361, 364; of Dante's
Divine Comedy 471, 478, 505
Fortunatianus 97
Foster, K. and P. J. Boyde 378
four makers (*artifices*) 158
Francesca *see* Paolo and Francesca
Francesco da Fiano 9
Friedman, J. B. 320
Fulgentius 128n, 151n, 320–2, 513n, 514;
Exposition of the Content of Virgil 435n;
Mythologiae 323, 333, 342, 368–9, 496n;
furies (mythological) 335, 345–6

Galba, Roman Emperor 150
Gallehault (knight) 489 and n
Gallus, Thomas 126, 165–70; *Extraction
of The Celestial Hierarchy* 173–91
Genesis, Book of 247, 254
Geoffrey of Vinsauf: *Poetria nova* 397n
Gerard of Cremona 280, 464n
Germanicus Caesar 362
Ghibellines 502
Gianciotto de Malatesta 488
Gilbert of Poitiers 6, 69
Giles of Rome 11; on affective force of
Bible 201, 246–7; on figurative and
broad mode 281; commentary on Aris-
totle's *Rhetoric* 281n, 311n; commentary
on Song of Songs 197, 199, 201, extract
243–7; *Donna mi prega* commentary
falsely ascribed to 379n; *On the Instruction of Princes* 201, 309n, extract 248–50
Giovanni Alighieri 449
Giovanni del Virgilio 10; Aristotelian prologue 314; commentaries on Ovid's
Metamorphoses 314, 316–17, 320n, 321–3,
extract 360–6; and secular allegory 321;
addresses Dante 440; Dante's eclogues
to 445; on Dante's *Divine Comedy* 452,
457
Giovannino of Mantua 11, 278, 390
Glossa ordinaria 69, 110n, 207, 218n, 245–7,
255, 256–7, 259–60, 261, 263, 263, 266,
271, 272, 275n, 477, 483, 484–5, 486, 490
goodness and the good 247, 249, 328–9
Gower, John 318; *Confessio amantis* 21n,
379–80, 382n, 441n; *Vox clamantis* 473n
grammar: study of 6; definitions of 12, 14,
32, 130–4; classification of 122–4;

Priscian on 130–4; barbarisms in 133; and study of poetry 279; Boccaccio on 387, 421, 509n
Gratian: *Decretum* 477n, 485, 486
Grayson, Cecil 381
Graziolo de' Bambaglioli 442, 445
Green, R. H. 385
Greenfield, C. C. 9; *Humanist and Scholastic Poetics* 10
Gregory, St 199, 224, 241, 266, 495; *Dialogues* 90, 230n; *Homily on Ezekiel* 94; *Moralia* 480, 485, 495n
Gregory of Tours 103–4
Grosseteste, Robert: on Pseudo-Dionysius 165–9; on veiled scriptural meaning 172; commentary on Pseudo-Dionysius' *The Celestial Hierarchy* 126, 171, 184n, 185nn, 188n, 191nn, extract 192–6
Guelfs 502
Guerric of Saint-Quentin 198
Guibert of Nogent 203n
Guido da Pisa: commentary on Dante 4, 9, 322, 441n, 442, 443n, 444n, 445–9, 456, 511n, text 469–76; life and career 446; Boccaccio opposes on Dante 456; epitaph on Dante 475; *Declaratio super comediam Dantis* 447; *I fatti di Enea* 446n; *La Fiorita (Fiore d'Italia)* 446–7
Guido da Polenta 450, 488
Guido delle Colonne: *Historia destructionis Troiae* 114

'habit', directive condition (*habitus*), 227, 230, 247
Hardison, O. B. 277, 288
harmony (*simphonia*) 291, 294
Haymo 103–4
Helenus 33
Heman 110
Henri d'Andeli 314; *La Bataille des VII ars* 6, 10
Henry of Ghent viii, 1, 11; on Pseudo-Dionysius 166; on theology as science 200, 202–3; on literal sense in Genesis 204n, 205; on sins of David 207–8; on lying 209, 432n; assists Tempier 211; *Sum of Ordinary Questions* 197, extracts 250–66
Henry of Settimello 332n
Hercules 345–6, 513
Hermann the German: translation of Averroes' 'Middle Commentary' on Aristotle's *Poetics* 3, 277–89, extract 289–307

hierarchies, heavenly 175, 182–6
Hilary, St 91, 97–8, 271
Hilduin 167
history (*historia*): defined 43; Hugh of Saint-Victor on biblical 66, 71, 72, 74–7, 78, 82; contrast with fable 44n, 51, 113, 118, 120, 155, 156, 327; in Scripture 110, 218, 220–2, 241, 256–7, 258, 261; in Dante's *Divine Comedy* 475–6, 478–9
Homer: Conrad of Hirsau on 38, 58, 60; Virgil follows 60, 115–16, 151, 391, 435; fiction and history in 114–15, 424, 508n; and poetry 291–2, 298; as tragic poet 475; *accessus* to 16–17; *Iliad* 16–17, 418; *Odyssey* 16–17, 435, 516
Honorius 'of Autun' 208
Horace: Conrad of Hirsau on 38, 46, 52, 54–9; Augustine cites 59; on Homer 60; as satirist 116–17, 142, 475; Arnulf on 156; Augustine on 209; Petrarch letters to 393; Pietro Alighieri cites 452, 478, 486, 490–1; *The Art of Poetry*: introduction to 32–6; and ethics 279; on comedy 461; on tragedy and poetry 475, 480; *Book of Epistles* 35; *The Book of Lyrics and Odes* 29; *Book of Discourses (Sermons)* 34; *Satires* 486, 490–1
Hosea 239
Hugh of Balma: *Viae Sion lugent* 167
Hugh of Saint Cher 198, 205
Hugh of Saint-Victor: biblical commentary 65–7; life 65; on literal and figurative language 66, 204; on poets and philosophers 122; on arts and theology 124–5, 387; on Pseudo-Dionysius 165; Henry of Ghent quotes 203; Nicholas of Lyre and 204; on senses in Bible 220–1, 242, 261; use of metaphor 397n; *Didascalicon* 37, 65–6, 271n, 325n, extracts 71–86; *Sentences* 220, 242, 247, 256
Hugh of Trimberg 38n, 41n
Hugutio of Pisa: Boccaccio cites 518; *Magnae derivationes* xiii, 374, 459n, 460n, 480–1, 518
humanism and humanists 5–11, 15, 439, 440, 457, 458
Hunt, R. W. 12–13, 123
Huygens, R. B. C. 15, 37
hypallage 366

Iacopo Alighieri 373, 439, 442, 447, 449–50; *Chiose* 450; *Dottrinale* 450
Iliad see Homer

imagery 168–70; biblical 171–96
imagination 282, 287, 289–91, 309, 406, 410
imitation (*mimesis*) 282, 290–3, 301–3, 309n
immortality 404–5
inferno (hell) 153n, 475–6, 481–3, 512–17
integument, garment (*integumentum*) 61n, 105, 113, 116, 117n, 118, 120–1, 152, 153, 154, 324, 343, 383, 385, 386–7, 391, 396, 420, 422, 453, 476, 484
intellect (*intellectus*) 215, 216, 217–20, 227, 228, 235, 243, 249, 253, 308, 309, 310, 320, 329, 331, 334, 400, 464, 467
intention, authorial (*intentio auctoris*) 2, 12, 16, 17, 18, 19, 20, 21, 22, 23, 24, 25, 26, 27, 30, 31, 32, 33, 34, 35, 46, 48, 52, 53–4, 61, 62, 69–70, 71, 99, 100, 101, 102, 105, 108, 110–11, 115, 123, 134, 151–2, 153, 155, 158, 159, 205, 227, 294, 319, 365, 473, 478, 481
intonation, musical (*thonus*) 287, 294, 296
intrinsic prologue 123, 130, 319
introductory page 42–3
investigation (*speculatio*) 216, 225
Isaiah, Book of 198, 424, 429, 457, 497
Isidore of Seville: Bernard of Utrecht and Conrad of Hirsau follow 37, 42n; Hugh of Saint-Victor quotes 72n; Peter Abelard on 94; influence 113, 120; on grammatical faults 133; on Scriptural truth 264; Trevet follows 325–6, 337; on tragedy 344; and etymology of *vates* 392; on poets 432n, 479; Boccaccio cites 452n; influence on Petrarch 492n; *Book of Sentences* 489; *Etymologiae* (*Etymologies*) 37, 337, 344, 414, 472, 475, 478–9, 498n, 508n
Italian language 377, 380–2

Jacob (biblical figure) 209
Jacopo della Lana 442
Jean de Meun: translation of Boethius 315, 320n, 374
Jeanne, Queen of France 368
Jeduthun 110
Jeremiah (prophet) 101, 109, 372, 444, 465, 496
Jerome, St: praises Juvencus 53; and pagan authors 59–60; Abelard cites 89–90, 98–9; cites Origen 91–2; letters from Augustine 98; on Paul's *Romans* 103–4; on Psalter 108, 110n, 199, 269, 271, 274–5; anon. disciple of William of Conches cites 147; on argument 226; on

Ecclesiastes 233; Nicholas of Lyre cites 269, 271, 274; uses verse 415; Pietro Alighieri cites 453, 487–8; on Dido 487; on chastity 488; *Hebraica* 204n, 271n, 274n; *On Questions Concerning the Hebrew Text* 269; *On the Best Kind of Interpretation* 60
Jerusalem: interpreted 203, 260, 267; destruction of 496
Job, Book of 91, 490
John, St, the Divine 385, 432, 469, 491, 497n
John Cassian, St 203
John Damascene, St 485
John of Garland: *Integumenta Ovidii* 322
John of Genoa: *Catholicon* xiii, 374n
John of Salisbury 122, 279
John the Saracen 167, 240n
John of Seville 280
John Scotus Erigena 125, 162–3, 167
John of Wales: *Communiloquium* 8; *Compendiloquium* 8, 14
Jonah 262
Joseph (son of Jacob) 210, 304
Joseph of Exeter: *De Bello Trojano* 114
Jourdain, C. 319
Jovinianus 487
Judges, Book of 209
judgements (*sententiae*) 215, 232
Julian, Roman Emperor 134
Juvenal: Conrad of Hirsau on 38, 58, 60; satires 116–18; anonymous commentary on (School of William of Conches) 134–50, 328; Arnulf on 156; Trevet on 316, 340; Pietro Alighieri cites 485
Juvencus 38, 53–4, 389

Kelly, H. A. 288, 441n
Kilwardby, Robert 198, 309n, 325n
knowledge, branch of *see pars philosophiae*
Koran, 304n, 306, 307n
Kristeller, P. O. 9, 316

Laeta 98
Lancelot (knight) 489
Latin language 380–1, 418, 508
Latini, Brunetto 510; *Trésor* 450
laurel, crowning with 499–500
learning, branch of *see pars philosophiae*
Life of St Antony 363
like and unlike symbols 170–2
likenesses (*similitudo*) 222
'likening' (*assimilatio*) 282–3, 289–94, 297, 384

limbo 515
literal sense (*sensus literalis*) Scriptural 203–6, 209–10, 220–3, 237–8, 242–3, 245, 258, 268–70, 480; Boccaccio on 384, 388; in Dante 385, 471, 476; Dante on 396–7; Dante(?) on 459
Livia, wife of Octavian Caesar 26–7
Livy 46, 393; *Ab urbe condita* 316
logic 6, 132; poetry as part of 279–81, 307–13, 314
Lombard, Peter *see* Peter Lombard
Lombardus, Anonymous *see* Anonymous Lombardus
Longinus 5
love: Christian 201, 246–7, 257; Dante and human 378–80, 382, 403–4, 406n, 407, 410–12, 488–9; Pietro Alighieri on 488–90
Lucan 38, 137, 151, 344, 465; *Bellum civile (Pharsalia)* 31, 114–15; Arnulf of Orléans' commentary on 122, 384, 444; extract 155–8
Lucidius Ovidius (Ovid's brother) 362
Lucilius 46, 476, 485, 489
lust 486–90
Luther, Martin 206
Lydgate, John 318
lying, lies 47, 95–6, 209–10, 222, 263, 264–6, 388, 423–5, 431–6
lyric poetry 474–5

Macarius of Egypt, St 364n
McEvoy, James 167, 171
Macrobius: and fable 113, 118–20, 300n, 392; on Virgil 150, 391; on self-knowing 153; Guido da Pisa follows 448; Pietro Alighieri follows 452, 477; *Saturnalia* 137
Maecenas 33, 35
Maevius 39, 62
Manlius Torquatus *see* Torquatus, Manlius
Map, Walter: *Dissuasio Valerii ad Rufinum* 503n
Marcus Crassus 156
Mark, St: Gospel 198
Mark Antony 157–8, 416
Mars (god and planet) 369–71
Marsh, Adam 166
Martianus Capella 46, 152n, 154; *Marriage of Philology and Mercury* 124
Massius, Bishop 94
materia (subject-matter) 2, 122, 478; in Cato 16; in Avianus 16; in Homer 17, 60;

in the *Physiologus* 17; in Theodulus 18; in Arator 19; in Sedulius 20; in Ovid 20, 21, 23, 25, 26, 27, 28, 30, 69, 363; in Priscian 31–2; in Horace 34, 55–6; Conrad of Hirsau on 46; in Aesop 48; in Sedulius 52; in Juvencus 53; in Persius 61; in Virgil 63; in St Paul 69; in Psalter 70, 108–11; of grammar 133; in Juvenal 135, 136; in Lucan 155; in Alan of Lille 158, 160; and material cause 198; in Peter Lombard 223; in Ecclesiastes 230; Giles of Rome on 248; Henry of Ghent on 251, 252, 253, 261; in Seneca 346
material cause (*causa materialis*) 198, 245, 271, 272, 361, 363, 345–6, 365; in Dante's *Divine Comedy* 450, 457, 470–1, 478, 505
Matthew, St 240, 467
Matthew of Vendôme: *Tobias* 314
Matthias of Linköping 278n
Mazzoni, Francesco 440n
Menander 46, 59
Messalina 147
metamorphosis (mythological) 363–4
metaphor 211, 239–40, 262, 468; *see also* figurative language
metre: Conrad of Hirsau defines 42–3; and diction 287; Averroes/Aristotle on art of 291, 294, 296, 299; Trevet on 336, 338–9
Miller, Paul 116, 117n, 136n
Modestus 33
modi (modes): in Dante's *Divine Comedy* 5, 388, 460, 505; and literary criticism 6; in Ovid 24; in Priscian 32; in Horace 55; *Alexander's Sum of Theology* on Biblical 212, 216–20; Bonaventure on Biblical 224–7, 235–6; Giles of Rome on 246; Henry of Ghent on 250–6; used by poets 344
modus affectivus, desiderativus et contemplativus 200
modus agendi (stylistic mode of procedure) 2, 5, 151, 198, 223, 251
modus procedendi 230n
modus scribendi (mode of writing) 478
modus tractandi (mode of procedure) 2, 69, 331; of St Paul 102; in Psalter 108, 110–11; and Scriptural authors 202–3; Boccaccio on (*modo del trattare*) 389, 495, 507; applied to Dante's *Divine Comedy* 444, 507
Montanus 147–9
moral sense *see* tropology
morals, morality 248–9; *see also* ethics

Moses 210, 254–5, 271, 273
multivocationes (plurality of names) 154
music 243–4
Mussato, Albertino 9, 313, 321, 390, 440,
  499n
mystical statements (mysticas locutiones)
  217, 221
myths 341–3, 389, 437–8

names, plurality of see multivocationes
names, Roman 26n
Nardi, Bruno 440
Neoplatonism 203
Nero, Roman Emperor 118, 135, 137, 142
  and n, 143–50, 155
'New Criticism' ('Old New Criticism')
  viii–ix
'New New Criticism' ix
Nicholas de Albertinis 340–1
Nicholas of Lyre 199, 203–4, 206, 208,
  266–70, 385; Exposition of Psalm 1: text
  274–6; Prologue to commentary on
  Psalter 198–9, 203, 206, 385, 443n, text
  271–6; Literal Postill on the Bible 197;
  General Prologue: text 266–8; Special
  Prologue: text 268–70; Postilla moralis
  386
Nicholas of Prato 324, 328
Nuzio of the Marches, ser 317

objective (finis) see final cause
Octavian, Roman Emperor (Augustus
  Caesar) 26–7, 30, 33, 63, 157, 361–3, 416
Olson, Glending 325
On Causes 464 and n, 465
ordo, ordinatio (order of arrangement) 2,
  32, 151, 198, 364
Origen 91–2, 104, 485; Peri Archon 91
Orléans (France) 6
Orosius, Paulus 487
Orpheus and Eurydice 121, 207–8, 320–1,
  332–6, 379, 383, 384, 396, 482
Ottimo commento (on Dante's Divine Comedy) 442, 498n, 511n
Ovid 1; life 22, 361–2; exile 26–7, 30, 362;
  as poet 34; Conrad of Hirsau on 38,
  56–7; Peter Abelard cites 92; fables 210;
  commentaries on 315; Bersuire on 318–
  19, 323; as tragic poet 344; on love 379,
  491; Book of Sorrows (Tristia) 26–7,
  362–3; Book without a Title (i.e. Amores)
  27–8, 362; Concerning the Head 363;
  Epistles (Heroides) 13, 15, 20–4, 70, 326,
  362; Fasti 6, 28–30, 56, 362; From Pontus

25–6, 56; Metamorphoses 10, 31, 56, 314–
  15, 496n; Giovanni del Virgilio's commentary on 314, 316–17, 319, 321–2, text
  360–6; and efficient cause 321; fables in
  323–4, 368; on justice 336; Trevet on
  344; Bersuire on 368; On the Flea 363;
  On the Nut 56, 363; On the Art of Love 24,
  25–9, 362; On the Remedy for Love 25, 337,
  355, 363; Tristia see Book of Sorrows
Ovide moralisé (Old French) 8

Padoan, Giorgio 457
Paolo and Francesca (in Dante's Divine
  Comedy) 453, 488–9
Paolo da Perugia 474n
Papias 479
parable 209–10, 222–3, 262, 424
Paris (actor) 135
Paris, University of 197–8
pars philosophiae (branch of knowledge;
  pars scientiae; cui parti philosophiae supponitur) viii, 2, 11, 13, 15, 26, 30, 31, 46,
  71, 119, 122, 124, 135–6, 159–69, 211,
  322, 365, 386, 459, 462, 471, 505, 512
Paul, St: on faith 44; justification 45; Con-
  rad of Hirsau on 59, 64; Peter Lombard
  on 69; intention of Epistles 70; Peter
  Abelard on 70–1, 94–7, 99–105; Augustine on 96–7; Epistles: to Corinthians
  101, 467; to Ephesians 467; to Galatians
  90–1, 479; to the Romans 68–9, 96, 205,
  240, 484–5; to Timothy 259–60, 323
Paulinus 99
Pegasus (lawyer) 145n
Penelope (wife of Ulysses) 20–4
Persius 38, 58, 60–1, 116, 474–5
Peter, St 163–4
Peter Comestor 319
Peter Lombard 65; Libri sententiarum 1, 69;
  Bonaventure's commentary on 200–1,
  extracts from exposition of Prologue
  223–30; Giles of Rome's commentary
  on 201–2, 247; Magna (or Maior) glosatura 69, commentary on the Psalter 31n,
  69–70, 199, 483n, extract 105–12
Peter of Poitiers 319
Petrarch, Francis: 'lives' of classical poets
  1; and sacred and secular texts 4, 212;
  Bersuire visits 317, 369; on inspiration
  321; importance 373; on theology and
  poetry 387–8, 390; and Cicero 392–3,
  451; Boccaccio praises 427, 454; uses
  terza rima 439, 454; meets Pietro Alighieri 451; scepticism 453; Boccaccio

meets 454; reads Dante's *Divine Comedy* 454; critique of Dante 458; influence on Boccaccio 492n; crowned with laurels 499n; *Africa* 317; 'Coronation Oration' 497n, 499n, 500n; *Invectives* 430; *Letters on Familiar Matters* 373, 393, 498n, extracts 413–20; *On the Remedies for all Fortunes* 427; *Trionfi* 454

Petrarch, Gherardo 413

Philip the Fair, King of France 201n

Philip de Vitry 368

Philippus Venetus 278

philosophiae, cui parti see *pars philosophiae*

philosophy: poetry and 122, 391–2; Boethius on 124; authors and 136; Dante on, as woman 378–9, 410–12; Dante's *Divine Comedy* as 512; *see also pars philosophiae*

Phoebe (of Cenchreae) 104

Physiologus: *accessus* to 17

Pico della Mirandola 9

Pierre des Prés 317

Pietro Alighieri 4, 9, 326, 373, 379; uses verse 439; career 450–1; Boccaccio follows 456, 506n; on comedy 508n; *Commentarium* (on Dante) 441n, 442, 444n, 450–2, extracts 476–91

piety 214

Pindar 60

Piso 33, 55

pity 407

planets 324, 369–72, 410n, 493

Plato 121, 319, 342, 428, 433–4, 468; *Timaeus* 504

Plautus: Conrad of Hirsau on 47; Boccaccio on 384, 385n, 424, 508n, 509; as comic poet 475, 480

plot 286–7

poem: defined 44

poesy: defined 44

poet: Conrad of Hirsau defines 43, 119; Boccaccio on 391–2, 426–7, 431–6, 497–500; not liars 431–6; Isidore on 432n, 479; Pietro Alighieri on 479

poetria (*poetrida*) 44, 55

poetry: humanist-scholastic views on 9–11, 210; relation to theology 9, 11, 124–6, 210, 387–9, 325, 413–15, 436–8, 475, 494–8; and philosophy 122, 391–2; metaphor in 240; as part of logic 279–81, 307–13, 314; as praise or blame 282–4, 289, 291–2, 304–5, 310n; Dante on theology and 387, 455; Boccaccio defines 387–92, 420–9, 455, 493–8;

Petrarch on classification of 413–15; obscurity 428–31; not lying 431–6; Guido da Pisa categorizes 474–5

Pompey (Pompeius Magnus) 156–7, 416

Pomponius Mela 457; *Cosmographia* 516

Porphyrion 33

Porphyry: *Isagoge* 13

Praepositinus 319

praise: poetry as 282–4, 285, 289, 291–2, 294, 304–5, 307, 310n

Priscian 138, 146; *Institutiones*: introduction to 31–2; William of Conches' commentary on 122–3, extract 130–4

Probus, Pseudo- 504

procedure, mode of see *modus agendi*; *modus tractandi*

Proclus: *Elementatio theologica* 464n

proem: defined 43

prologue: defined 43; extrinsic and intrinsic 123–4; 'Bernard Silvester' on purpose of 152; influence of Aristotle on 197–8, 319; in (?)Dante's *Epistle* 463; *see also accessus*

prophecy and prophets 108–9, 205

Prometheus 322

Propertius 418

prose: defined 42

prosopopoeia 28

Prosper 38, 415

Proverbs, Book of 245, 483

Prudentius 38, 389, 415

Psalm 1: Nicholas of Lyre's exposition: extract 274–6

Psalm 113: Dante analyses 396–7, 443; Dante(?) analyses 443, 460

Psalter (and Psalms) 1; Peter Lombard glosses 69–71, 199, 483n, extract 105–12; Nicholas of Lyre's commentary on 198–9, 203, 206, extract 271–6; Trevet on 316; as poetry 414; in Dante commentary 444, 465

Ptolemy: *Almagest* 332

Pulice da Vincenza 393

Pythagoras 412

Quain, E. A. 13

question, scholastic (*quaestio*): explained 212

Question on the nature of poetry, anon. 10, 280–1, text 307–13

Quintilian 393, 426

Quintus 392

Rabanus (Maurus): *On the Nature of the Universe* 367, 369

Ralph of Longchamps 114; commentary on Alan of Lille's *Anticlaudianus* 124–6, extract 158–64
Rashi (Rabbi Solomon) 199, 270, 274
Raymond, Archbishop of Toledo 280
reason: and faith 226
reciting, methods of 23
regarding (*consideratio*) 287, 294–6
Remigius of Auxerre 13
response (*responsio*) 212
Revelation, Book of 202, 385, 432, 469, 486, 491, 497n, 518
reversal (in tragedy) 287
rhetoric: decline in study of 6; Giles of Rome on 249n; and poetry 308–11, 421, 422n
rhyme 291
rhythmus: defined 42
Richard of Saint-Victor 165, *Benjamin minor* 168; *On Contemplation* 467; *On the Trinity* 224
Ridevall, John: *Fulgentius metaforalis* 8, 318, 323, 453
Robert, King of Jerusalem (Robert the Wise, King of Naples) 425, 445
Robortello 278
Rouse, R. H. & M. A. 6
Ruiz, Juan: *Libro de buen amor* 382n

Saif al-Dawlah 303
Sallust 38, 46
Salutati, Coluccio 278, 321, 387n
Sandkühler, Bruno: *Die frühen Dantekommentare* 9, 440
Sanseverino, Giacopo 425
satire, satirists 60–1, 116–19, 136–7, 474–5
Savonarola, Gerolamo 11, 278; *On the Division and Use of the Sciences* 390–1
scene (*scena*) 325–6, 346, 508
scholasticism and schoolmen 5–11, 15
Scholia of St Maximus 167
Schroth, R. 315
science 4, 5, 14, 122, 130, 200–3, 207, 212–17, 223–6, 236, 246–7, 248, 249, 250–60, 268, 281, 282, 296, 311, 313, 378, 387–8, 396, 410n, 421–2, 475
scribe (*scriptor*) 229
Scriptures *see* Bible
Secundus the Manichee 485
Sedulius: *accessus* to 19–20; Conrad of Hirsau on 51–4; as sacred theologian 389; uses verse 415; *Paschale Carmen* 12, 19n
Segni 278

Selmi glosses, anonymous 442
Semiramis, Queen of Babylon 487
Seneca the younger 156; Trevet on tragedies of 315–16, 324–8, 389, 516n; text 340–60; Petrarch letters to 393; Dante on 461; on explanation 476; on conscience 485; on love 489; *Agamemnon*: Trevet's exposition of 326–7, text 346–60; *Hercules furens*: Trevet's exposition of 325, 327, text 345–6; in inferno 516
Sennuccio del Bene 454
senses (*sensūs*; understandings, meanings) 16, 45–6, 50, 51, 83–6, 202, 203–7, 220–3, 233–5, 237–8, 241–3, 245, 252, 256–70, 324, 343, 368, 383–4, 388, 396–8, 449, 459–60, 470, 471, 475–6, 478–80
sentences 131
sententiae 55, 58, 253, 255
Servius: *Centimetrum* 43, 339; commentaries on Virgil 12–13, 19, 23n, 115, 344n
Seven Liberal Arts 161
'seven questions' 41n, 46
Sidney, Sir Philip 5
Siger of Brabant 211
signification 50, 51, 66, 67, 72–3, 84, 87, 106, 107, 110, 131, 154, 203–7, 209, 218, 220, 221, 223, 237, 238, 241, 242, 260, 261, 264, 265, 266, 267, 295, 370, 384, 396, 459, 460, 479
Simon of Tournai 165–6
Simonides 475
Singleton, Charles 384–5
Smalley, Beryl 69, 319
Socrates 291, 434
Solinus 369
Solomon, King 206–8, 231–3, 245, 271, 274, 503
Solomon, Rabbi *see* Rashi
Solon 498
solution (*solutio*) 212, 232
song 287
Song of Songs: Giles of Rome's commentary on 197, 199, 201, text 243–50; Nicholas of Lyre on 199, 385; allegory 204
soul 404–7, 471
Southern, Sir Richard 6–7
spectacle 287, 296n
speech (*sermo*) 216
Spinola, Lucano 469, 472
spiritual sense *see* allegory
Statius 38, 46, 58, 61–2; *Thebaid* 516
Strabo, Walafrid 261

Suetonius, Tranquillus: 142, 414, 500n
symbolism: in Bible 172–96, 239–40; *see also* allegory; figurative language; metaphor

Tarquinius Superbus 146–7
Tarrant, R. J. 327
Taylor, Jeremy 65
Tempier, Stephen, Bishop of Paris 211
Terence 34; Conrad of Hirsau on 46–7, 58–9; order in 151; Arnulf on 156; Boccaccio on 384, 385n, 424, 508n, 509; as comic poet 475, 480
theatre: Averroes' misunderstanding of classical 284–5, 288; Trevet on classical 325–6, 343–4, 346
Theodulus 17–18, 37–8, 46
Theodoric the Goth, King of the Romans 18, 330
Theodosius 16, 19, 50, 53
theology: supremacy of 4, 7; relation to poetry 9, 11, 124–6, 210, 325, 387–9, 413–15, 436–8, 475, 494–8; as science 200–3, 207, 215–16; Bonaventure on 228; mode of imparting 250–6; Varro divides 343; Dante on 387; Boccaccio on 388–90, 436–8, 455, 494; Petrarch on 413
theophany 162–4
Thierry of Chartres 12, 123
Thomas Aquinas, St: on poetry 10–11, 283; on Pseudo-Dionysius 166, 168; on theology as science 200; influence on Nicholas of Lyre 203–4; on Scriptural literal sense 204–5, 209; on David's sins 208; on art imitating nature 284; and poetic subdivision 377n; on theology and poetry 390; on light 401n; in Dante's *Paradiso* 501n; commentary on Aristotle's *Posterior Analytics* 280; commentary on Aristotle's *Physics* 397n; *Sum of Theology* 170, 197, 257n, 268, extract 239–43
thought (in tragedy) 286–7
Timothy 101
title (*titulus*) 2; defined 43; of Psalter 108–9, 111; in Lucan's *Pharsalia* 155; of Claudius' *Anticlaudianus* 160; of Dante's *Divine Comedy* 460–2, 473–5, 480–1, 506–7
Titus 59, 61
Tityus 333, 335–6, 514
Torquatus, Manlius 330

tragedy: defined 28; Averroes/Aristotle on 284–8, 294–8, 300, 303, 306; Isidore of Seville on 326, 344; Dante on 461; Trevet on 461n; Guido da Pisa on 474–5; Pietro Alighieri on 480
translation (*translatio*) 374
Trevet, Nicholas 1, 204n, 206n; Aristotelian prologue 314; scholarship 316; commentary on Boethius' *Consolation of Philosophy* 316, 318–20, 341, 379, 381, extract 336–40; commentaries on Seneca 315, 324–7, 389, 461n, 516n, extract 340–60; on comedy 508n
tropology (moral sense) 45–6; in Bible 71, 75, 82, 218, 220, 222, 233, 241–2, 256, 259; Dante and 383, 385–6, 396; in Dante's *Divine Comedy* 475–6
Troy: fall of 348–50, 359
truth, Scriptural 209–12, 263–6
Tucca 64
Tullus Hostilius 144
twofold efficient cause (*duplex causa efficiens*) 198, 271, 321, 361
twofold form (*duplex forma*) 198, 246, 250, 273, 361, 364, 460, 462, 471, 478, 505
twofold literal sense (*duplex sensus litteralis*) 205–6
Tyndale, William 206

Ulrich of Strasburg 166
Ulysses 20–2, 24, 59, 127–9; *see also* Homer: *Odyssey*
understandings *see* senses
Uriah the Hittite 207–8, 490
Usk, Thomas: *Testament of Love* 278
utilitas (usefulness of work) 2, 9, 16, 17, 18, 19, 21, 23, 25, 26, 28, 33, 46, 54, 70, 71, 123, 134, 152–3, 155, 158, 159, 319

Valentinian 53
Valentinus (Roman consul) 19
Valerius Maximus 505n
vanity 231
Varro, Marcus 343, 389, 393, 414, 437, 475
Varrus 64
vates (bard, seer) 43, 392
Veianus (gladiator) 35
veils 172–3
Vernani, Guido: *De reprobatione monarchiae* 445
verse: kinds of 44; *see also* poetry
Vespasian 61
Vestal virgins 139
Victorianus 123

Vigilantius 91, 99
Vigilius, Pope 18-19
Vincent of Beauvais 212n, 283; *Speculum doctrinale* 280, 414n, 432n; *Speculum historiale* 8; *Speculum maius* 14
Vincent the Donatist 204, 242, 268
Vincentius Victor 96-7
Virgil 1; as poet 34; Conrad of Hirsau on 38, 58, 62-4; Augustine cites 59; and Homer 60, 115-16, 151; on causes 361; Boccaccio idolizes 391-2, 427; Petrarch letters to 393; Cicero praises 418; hidden meaning in 424; accused of 'lying' 431, 434-6; invokes Jove 433, 504; as tragic poet 475; on blind love 490; fictional form 508n; *Aeneid* 12; and Homer 16-17; order of events 45; Statius follows 46; Conrad of Hirsau on 62-4; pleasing qualities 116; 'Bernard Silvester' commentary on 118, 482n, extract 150-4; Trevet on 316, 344, 348; and fall of Troy 348; on pity 407; Boccaccio cites 426, 435-6; Dido story 431, 434-6; Guido da Pisa translates 446; in Pietro Alighieri's commentary 452-3, 481-4; on death of Achilles 488; on love 490-1; on hell 512-13, 516-17; *Bucolics* 62, 316, 426; *Eclogues* 46; *Georgics* 62-3, 344, 426
virtue 304
vitae auctorum (or *poetae*) 2, 12-14

Waleys, Thomas 318
Walter (addressee of Andreas Capellanus) 491

Walter of Châtillon: *Alexandreis* 373
Whitbread, L. G. 37
will, disposition of *see affectus*
William of Aragon 1; commentary on Boethius' *Consolation of Philosophy* 315-16, 318-20, extract 328-36; attacks Plato 319; on Orpheus 383; *De nobilitate animi* (attrib.) 315
William of Auvergne: *De legibus* (part of his *Magisterium divinale*) 205, 218
William of Champeaux 65
William of Conches 1, 83-4n, 113, 116; and Macrobius 118-19; commentary on Boethius' *Consolation of Philosophy* 120-1, extract 126-30; Trevet follows 318-20, 328, 379, 374; on poetry and philosophy 122; commentary on Priscian's *Institutiones*: extract 130-4; on authors and philosophy 136; on grammar 279; on Orpheus myth 333n; on fable 383; on transformations 127-8
William of Conches, School of 134-50
William of Moerbeke 249n, 279, 283n, 389n
William of Nottingham 205-6
Wimsatt, W. K. & C. Brooks: *Literary Criticism, a Short History* 5
Wisdom, Book of 444, 465, 470
Witt, Ronald 390
words (*dicta*): univocal 215
World Soul 319
writing, mode of *see modus scribendi*
Wyclif, John 211

Zanobi da Strada 495n, 499n

Cal worked 1st on a secular work – Seneca.
Indeed whole tradit. of works on this
and other non-biblical books. This trad.
seems to have been distinct from bibl.
comm trad – obv. most bib. comm were Xns
~~But it clearly interacted wit.~~ Thus we
may wonder about qualities which char
it; whether those qualities appear in
Cal; and whether they infl. his comm
on the bible. There is a hist. of such
influence, so Cal wouldn't be the first

ONE WAY TO TELL WHAT TO DO WOULD BE
TO READ C'S SEN. COMM. AND SEE HOW
HE DISCUSSES TEXT. ARE THERE DIFFS?

Get Seneca!   Rem Steinmetz thoughts on Calvin...
look at Ganoczy   PMV on Romans

Printed in the United Kingdom
by Lightning Source UK Ltd.
118005UK00001B/142

9 780198 112747